NEBRASKA

Also in This Series

†*Arizona,* Malcolm L. Comeaux

†*Colorado,* Mel Griffiths and Lynnell Rubright

†*Hawaii,* Joseph R. Morgan

†*Maryland,* James E. DiLisio

†*Michigan,* Lawrence M. Sommers

†*Missouri,* Milton D. Rafferty

†*New Jersey,* Charles A. Stansfield, Jr.

†*Texas,* Terry G. Jordan with John L. Bean, Jr., and William M. Holmes

†*Wyoming,* Robert Harold Brown

Forthcoming Through 1985

Connecticut, Tom Lewis and John Harmon

South Carolina, Charles F. Kovacik and John J. Winberry

Wisconsin, Ingolf Vogeler

†Available in hardcover and paperback.

GEOGRAPHIES OF THE UNITED STATES
Ingolf Vogeler, General Editor

Nebraska: A Geography
Bradley H. Baltensperger

Nebraska is the first comprehensive examination of the patterns of Nebraska's resources, population, economy, climate, and landscape to be published in many years. Focusing especially on the people of Nebraska and the interaction between the environment and human use of the earth, Professor Baltensperger begins with a discussion of the physical environment and resources of the state and ties early patterns of development to the need to adjust settlement systems and agricultural practices to a subhumid climate.

The role of energy-intensive agriculture in the state's economy is a central aspect of the book's examination of human interaction with the environment: The impact of modern technology on Nebraska's agricultural system and on its population receives considerable attention, as do the problems associated with recent agricultural developments. Also scrutinized are the land-use conflicts generated by urban growth and by the demands of an urban society on rural Nebraska.

Bradley H. Baltensperger was born and raised in Nebraska City. He attended the University of Nebraska–Lincoln, where he received his B.A. in 1969. He was awarded his M.A. and Ph.D. degrees by Clark University in Worcester, Massachusetts. Dr. Baltensperger's research has focused on agriculture and ethnic groups on the Great Plains. He is currently associate professor of geography at Michigan Technological University.

NEBRASKA
A GEOGRAPHY

Bradley H. Baltensperger

Westview Press / Boulder and London

To my mother
and to the memory of my father
and their lives on the farm

Geographies of the United States

All rights reserved. No part of this publication may be reproduced or transmitted in any form or by any means, electronic or mechanical, including photocopy, recording, or any information storage and retrieval system, without permission in writing from the publisher.

Copyright © 1985 by Westview Press, Inc.

Published in 1985 in the United States of America by Westview Press, Inc., 5500 Central Avenue, Boulder, Colorado 80301; Frederick A. Praeger, Publisher

Library of Congress Cataloging in Publication Data
Baltensperger, Bradley H.
  Nebraska, a geography.
  (Westview geographies of the United States)
  Includes bibliographies and index.
  1. Nebraska—Description and travel. I. Title.
II. Series: Geographies of the United States.
F666.B23 1985   917.82   83-26066
ISBN 0-86531-218-4

Printed and bound in the United States of America

10 9 8 7 6 5 4 3 2 1

CONTENTS

List of Figures xi
List of Tables xvii
Preface xix

1 RESOURCES OF THE NEBRASKA ENVIRONMENT 1

   Climatic Reality 2
   The Land Endowment 9
   Water Resources 16
   Impacts of Water Use 24

2 SETTLEMENT: OCCUPANCE, UTILIZATION, AND ADAPTATION 37

   Occupants of the Great Plains 37
   Focus: Prehistoric Resources 38
   Focus: White Pressures on Indian Lands 46
   Developing a Transportation System 53
   Adapting Agriculture to the Great Plains 62
   Living with a Subhumid Environment 66

3 POPULATION: SOURCES, CHARACTERISTICS, AND TRENDS 69

   THE ORIGINS OF NEBRASKA'S POPULATION 69

   Native Americans 69
   Nebraska's Midwestern Heritage 71
   Blacks 71
   Nineteenth-Century European Immigrants 73
   Mexicans and Japanese 79

   POPULATION CHARACTERISTICS 80

   Patterns 80
   Growth 93
   Nebraskans as Midwesterners 98

4 ECONOMIC ACTIVITIES AND ECONOMIC HEALTH ... 103

Nebraska's Economic Health ... 104
Mining ... 108
Manufacturing ... 110
Transportation and Utilities ... 117
The Exchange of Goods and Services ... 125
Focus: Government in Small Counties ... 134
Future Economic Patterns ... 135

5 AGRICULTURAL PATTERNS ... 137

The Agricultural Regions of Nebraska ... 137
The Structure of Agriculture ... 141
Livestock ... 157
Crops ... 163
Forces of Change ... 173

6 INDUSTRIAL AGRICULTURE ... 177

Agriculture and Technology ... 177
Focus: Changes in Polk, Nebraska ... 181
Problems in Agriculture ... 191
Focus: Site Selection for Developing Irrigation ... 192
Technology, Energy, and Environment ... 199

7 FARMS, FIELDS, AND COMMUNITIES: THE RURAL LANDSCAPE ... 201

Nebraska Farmsteads ... 201
Farms and Farmlands ... 208
Rural Communities ... 217
How Rural Is the Rural Landscape? ... 220

8 THE COUNTRYSIDE AND THE CITY ... 221

Urbanizing the Farmer ... 222
Rural Land, Urban Uses ... 225
Focus: The Rural School Controversy ... 227
Moving to the Country ... 230
Ironies of Rural-Urban Interaction ... 238

9 URBAN NEBRASKA ... 241

Cities of the Pioneer Era: 1854–1880 ... 241
Boom and Expansion—Omaha and Lincoln: 1880–1920 ... 243
Focus: Kountze Place—An Early Omaha Suburb ... 246
Focus: The West Farnam and Cathedral Districts ... 249
Focus: Development of Omaha's Black Community ... 251
Automobiles and Decentralization: 1920–1950 ... 253
The Sprawling City: 1950–1980 ... 254
Omaha and Lincoln: Divergent Paths of Development ... 263

10 CULTURE, ENVIRONMENT, AND THE FUTURE 269

Notes.. 273
Illustration Credits 291
Selected Bibliography... 293
Metric Equivalents 299
Index 301

FIGURES

	Map of Nebraska	xxii
1.1	Annual precipitation, 1941–1970 average (map)	4
1.2	Average annual precipitation along or near 41° N	4
1.3	Monthly distributions of precipitation normals, 1941–1970	6
1.4	Annual departures from average annual precipitation in Nebraska, 1850–1979	7
1.5	Total precipitation, 1915 and 1934 (map)	8
1.6	Cattle frozen in a blizzard (photo)	9
1.7	Relief (map)	10
1.8	Topographic regions (map)	10
1.9	Dune formations in the Sandhills (map)	12
1.10	Large parallel dunes in southwestern Cherry County (photo)	13
1.11	The rough lands of the Pine Ridge (photo)	14
1.12	Rolling topography of glaciated eastern Nebraska (photo)	14
1.13	Soil parent materials (map)	15
1.14	Nebraska drainage patterns and streamflow (map)	17
1.15	Average flows on the Platte River	18
1.16	Irrigation has made the Platte Valley a productive agricultural region (photo)	19
1.17	Land irrigated from surface water (map)	20
1.18	Canoeing is one of the fastest growing forms of recreation (photo)	21
1.19	Subirrigated vegetation (map)	23
1.20	Changes in groundwater levels (map)	24
1.21	Water-level changes in the Shickley recorder wells, 1956–1981	25
1.22	Water-level changes in the Hemingford recorder well, 1969–1981	27
1.23	Water-level changes in the O'Neill recorder well, 1966–1981	27
1.24	Water-level changes in the Imperial recorder well, 1964–1981	28
1.25	Annual maximum and minimum month-end storage in Enders Reservoir, 1952–1978	28
1.26	The pattern of center-pivots surrounding Imperial (photo)	29
1.27	Proposed O'Neill Unit (map)	31
1.28	Niobrara River (photo)	32
1.29	Projected groundwater declines by 2020 using present trends (map)	34
1.30	Baseline annual water use rates by state	35
2.1	Cultural groups in Nebraska, about 1800 (map)	40
2.2	Ration day at the Pine Ridge Agency (photo)	41

FIGURES

2.3	Explorers' routes and rivers of the northern Great Plains (map)	42
2.4	Upper Missouri fur trade before 1808 (map)	43
2.5	Indian land cessions (map)	44
2.6	The rectangular survey system	47
2.7	Land claimed through use of the Pre-Emption Law, the Homestead Act, and the Timber Culture Act, 1866–1900	47
2.8	Custer County farm family, 1888 (photo)	50
2.9	A winter supply of "cowchips" for fuel (photo)	51
2.10	Farmstead surrounded by trees	52
2.11	Trails and forts (map)	53
2.12	Chimney Rock (photo)	54
2.13	Freighting train in early Nebraska City (photo)	55
2.14	The steamer *Colorado* unloading supplies (photo)	56
2.15	Railroads and the frontier, 1870 (map)	57
2.16	Railroads and the frontier, 1880 (map)	57
2.17	Railroads and the frontier, 1885 (map)	58
2.18	German-language advertisement for land (photo)	60
2.19	Russian German lands in Clay County, 1880 (map)	61
2.20	Main Street, with the railroad, Anselmo, ca. 1909 (photo)	61
2.21	Population change, 1890–1900 (map)	64
3.1	Native Americans in Nebraska, 1980 (map)	70
3.2	Black population of Nebraska, 1860–1980	72
3.3	Moses Speese family, Custer County homesteaders, 1888 (photo)	72
3.4	Foreign-born population, 1880 (map)	74
3.5	Ethnic concentrations in three counties (maps)	75
3.6	Remains of a Boyd County house built by Russian German pioneers (photo)	77
3.7	Swedish Evangelical Lutheran Salem Church, Wakefield (photo)	77
3.8	Z.C.B.J. halls are found in most Czech communities (photo)	78
3.9	Percent Spanish origin (map)	79
3.10	Ethnic concentrations (map)	81
3.11	Foreign stock, 1970 (map)	82
3.12	Population distribution, 1980 (map)	86
3.13	Rural population density, 1980 (map)	87
3.14	Brewster, one of the smallest county seats in the United States (photo)	88
3.15	Urban and rural population of Nebraska, 1860–1980	88
3.16	Population change, 1950–1970 (map)	89
3.17	Population change in Nebraska, by county, 1970–1980 (maps)	90
3.18	Population change in towns and cities, 1970–1980 (map)	92
3.19	Nebraska births and deaths	93
3.20	Average birth rate, 1978–1980 (map)	94
3.21	Median age, 1980 (map)	95
3.22	Distribution of Nebraska's population by age and sex	96
3.23	Boyd County age profiles	97
3.24	Net migration, 1970–1980 (map)	98
3.25	Projected population change, 1970–2000 (map)	99
3.26	Party affiliation (map)	100
3.27	Presidential vote, 1980 (map)	101
3.28	Country churches and ethnic groups in Nemaha County (map)	102

4.1 Per capita income (map)... 105
4.2 Poverty (map) 106
4.3 Unemployment rate, 1981 (map)... 107
4.4 Mining activity, 1978 (map) 109
4.5 Cement plant (photo).. 109
4.6 Water-powered gristmill (photo) 111
4.7 Manufacturing (map).. 113
4.8 Prepared feed plants (map) 115
4.9 Alfalfa milling is concentrated in the central Platte Valley (photo).......... 115
4.10 Electrical machinery manufacturing (map)...................................... 117
4.11 Eppley Airfield, Omaha (photo) 118
4.12 Railroad system, 1980 (map)... 120
4.13 Train loading grain at elevator in Shelby (photo) 121
4.14 Unit trains haul coal (photo)... 123
4.15 Union Pacific's Bailey Yard, North Platte (photo)..................... 124
4.16 Interior view of Burlington Northern's locomotive-repair
     facility, Alliance (photo)... 124
4.17 Electrical consumption in Nebraska.. 125
4.18 Electricity generation and transmission (map) 126
4.19 Fort Calhoun Station nuclear power plant (photo)....................... 127
4.20 Small towns offer frequently needed goods (photo)..................... 127
4.21 Food sales, 1977 (map).. 128
4.22 Clothing sales, 1977 (map).. 128
4.23 Larger towns provide a greater variety of retail goods (photo) 129
4.24 Taxable retail sales per person, 1980 (map) 130
4.25 Hotels and motels, 1977 (map)... 131
4.26 Recreation sites (map).. 131
4.27 Though small towns survive, many of their retail functions
     have closed down (photo)... 132
4.28 Number of physicians per 1,000 population, 1979 (map) 133
4.29 Licensed nursing homes, 1981 (map).. 134

5.1 Agricultural regions (map) 138
5.2 Cropland in selected counties, 1981... 139
5.3 Upland fields of corn and wheat (photo)....................................... 140
5.4 The center-pivot landscape of Holt County (photo) 141
5.5 Sandhills cattle (photo) 142
5.6 Average size of farm by county, 1978 (map).................................... 143
5.7 Change in number of farms, 1950–1978 (map).................................... 143
5.8 Average farm size and number of farms, 1860–1978 144
5.9 Distribution of farm size 145
5.10 Value of land and buildings by county, 1978 (map)....................... 146
5.11 Value of land and buildings per acre, 1978 (map) 146
5.12 Farm tenancy (map).. 149
5.13 Farm corporations, 1978 (map)... 150
5.14 Holt County land owned by P. G. Realty, 1982 (map) 152
5.15 Dundy County landscape (photo).. 152
5.16 Farms by value of sales, 1978; value of products sold by
     size of sales, 1978 154
5.17 Six fragmented farms in Otoe County (map) 155

5.18	Working cattle on a Sandhills ranch (photo)	158
5.19	A large feedlot operation (photo)	158
5.20	Cattle placed on feed, 1981 (map)	159
5.21	Hogs on farms, Dec. 1, 1981 (map)	161
5.22	Corn for grain—acreage and yield	163
5.23	Corn harvested for grain, 1981 (map)	164
5.24	Corn acreage in three counties	165
5.25	Irrigated corn (map)	166
5.26	Wheat acreage and yield	166
5.27	Wheat acres harvested, 1981 (map)	167
5.28	Wheat grown on summer fallow (map)	167
5.29	Alternate strips of wheat and summer fallow (photo)	168
5.30	Trucks delivering grain (photo)	168
5.31	Soybean acreage and yield	169
5.32	Soybean acres harvested, 1981 (map)	169
5.33	Sorghum acreage and yield	170
5.34	Sorghum acres harvested, 1981 (map)	171
5.35	Sugar beet acres harvested, 1981 (map)	172
5.36	Dry edible bean acres harvested, 1981 (map)	173
5.37	Alfalfa acres harvested, 1981 (map)	174
5.38	An alfalfa field in Cedar County (photo)	174
5.39	County agricultural land-use changes	175
5.40	A massive, modern grain elevator (photo)	176
6.1	Cultivating corn (photo)	178
6.2	Eight-row equipment (photo)	179
6.3	Small hay bales require more labor input (photo)	179
6.4	Primary nutrient consumption and irrigated acres	182
6.5	Annual installation of irrigation wells	184
6.6	Location of registered irrigation wells, 1982 (map)	186
6.7	Irrigating corn with gated pipe (photo)	187
6.8	Center-pivot irrigation (photo)	187
6.9	Center-pivot corner system (photo)	188
6.10	Center-pivot systems in 1980 (map)	189
6.11	Severe wind erosion (photo)	193
6.12	Leveling of sand hills for center-pivots (photo)	193
6.13	Large center-pivot development (photo)	194
6.14	Severe water erosion (photo)	195
6.15	Farming up and down slopes (photo)	195
6.16	Contour farming and terracing (photo)	195
6.17	Shelterbelts removed (photos)	196
6.18	Parallel terraces (photo)	197
6.19	Feedlot runoff (photo)	197
6.20	Nitrate contamination of groundwater (map)	198
7.1	Sod house in Box Butte County (photo)	202
7.2	Ornate style of the Victorian era (photo)	203
7.3	The modern ranch house (photo)	203
7.4	Housing age, 1980 (map)	204
7.5	Barn built around 1880 (photo)	205

7.6	Metal buildings dominate this farmstead (photo)	205
7.7	Corn crib (photo)	206
7.8	Vertical, glass-lined silos (photo)	207
7.9	Windmills used to be the principal source of power (photo)	207
7.10	The numerous scattered buildings of a large farmstead (photo)	209
7.11	Quarter-section landholdings (map)	210
7.12	Osage orange hedgerows (photo)	211
7.13	Farm windbreak (photo)	211
7.14	Shelterbelts in Antelope County (map)	212
7.15	Hedgerow locations, T6N, R14E, Nemaha County (maps)	213
7.16	Pivot corners with farmstead (photo)	214
7.17	In Jefferson County: a linear arrangement of houses (map)	215
7.18	Cattle guard (photo)	216
7.19	Elderberries (photo)	216
7.20	Roadside marijuana (photo)	217
7.21	St. John's Lutheran Church (photo)	218
7.22	Abandoned rural school (photo)	218
7.23	Orthogonal town plan	219
7.24	T town plan	220
8.1	The automobile eliminated isolation (photo)	223
8.2	School districts, 1949–1981	224
8.3	School reorganization (map)	225
8.4	School district reorganization in two counties (maps)	226
8.5	The Interstate 80 corridor (photo)	229
8.6	Land occupied by the Omaha Public Power District's generating station (photo)	230
8.7	Buckshot development (photo)	231
8.8	Beaver Lake (photo)	233
8.9	Leapfrog development (photo)	234
8.10	SIDs in the Omaha area (map)	234
8.11	Wooded sites (photo)	235
8.12	Suburban tract development, Springfield (photo)	236
9.1	Thirteenth and Farnam streets, Omaha (photo)	242
9.2	Bird's-eye view of Lincoln, 1880	244
9.3	Omaha today (map)	247
9.4	A typical streetcar in Lincoln, 1908	248
9.5	Ethnic neighborhoods in Omaha, 1880 (map)	250
9.6	Row housing (photo)	250
9.7	Rail lines leading away from downtown Omaha (photo)	252
9.8	Satellite view of Omaha (photo)	255
9.9	Percent population change in Douglas County, 1970–1980 (maps)	256
9.10	Black population of Douglas County, 1980 (map)	258
9.11	Racial change in Douglas County, 1970–1980 (map)	259
9.12	Omaha's new industrial sector (photo)	260
9.13	Peripheral development in Columbus (photo)	261
9.14	Downtown Omaha has become an important office center (photo)	263
9.15	Interstate highways lead to Omaha (photo)	266

TABLES

1.1	Flows required by the Blue River Basin compact	21
1.2	Effect of groundwater irrigation development on stream flows	35
2.1	Disposition of Nebraska's public domain	48
2.2	Land in farms in selected counties, 1880 and 1890	49
2.3	Estimated expenses of making a farm	52
2.4	Early irrigation	65
3.1	Birthplace of U.S.-born Nebraskans, 1980	71
3.2	Foreign-born and second-generation population of Nebraska, 1860–1980	73
3.3	Foreign stock, 1970	80
3.4	Omaha ethnic and racial groups, 1900 and 1970	82
3.5	Largest cities in 1980	92
4.1	Personal income for Nebraska and the United States, 1960–1981	104
4.2	Total employment by economic sector, 1981 average	108
4.3	Nebraska oil production, value, and wells, 1962–1980	110
4.4	Population of Cheyenne and Kimball counties	111
4.5	Manufacturing employment in Nebraska, 1981 average	114
4.6	Railroad freight in Nebraska, 1979	122
5.1	Average farm size in selected counties	144
5.2	Off-farm work	147
5.3	Selected production expenses on Nebraska farms, 1969 and 1978	148
5.4	Selected Holt County "farmers"	151
5.5	Livestock and poultry in Nebraska, 1981	157
5.6	Leading counties in livestock production, 1981	159
5.7	Cattle marketed, 1960–1982	160
5.8	Nebraska crop production, 1981	162
5.9	Leading counties in acreage of major crops, 1981	164
5.10	Leading counties in acreage of minor crops, 1981	171
5.11	Percentage of farmers raising each crop, 1940 and 1978	171
6.1	Tractors and draft animals, 1920–1959	178
6.2	Energy inputs per acre of corn production, 1945 and 1970	183
6.3	Center pivots in operation	188

8.1	Electricity, automobiles, and roads	222
8.2	Growth of selected cities and their suburbs, 1970–1980	232
8.3	Population of selected towns on the urban fringe	236
8.4	Residential development costs, Gretna, Nebraska	237
8.5	Social and environmental costs by development pattern, Gretna, Nebraska	238
9.1	Population growth in Nebraska cities, 1880–1890	245
9.2	Foreign-born population of Omaha, 1870–1980	250
9.3	Retailing in Omaha and Lincoln	262
9.4	Population change, cities and suburbs	264

PREFACE

Like the rest of the Great Plains region, Nebraska has been ill served by the generalizations and misconceptions of outsiders. The area has been viewed as the Garden of the West by some, as a worthless desert by others. Its aboriginal inhabitants valued the wealth of grasses and wildlife in what is now Nebraska, but many early outsiders considered the region merely an obstacle to be crossed. For centuries it has been mistakenly evaluated and poorly understood.

The problem persists today. Nebraska is commonly perceived as flat, treeless, and dry by travelers crossing the state. It certainly is flat in comparison to the Rockies or even the Ozarks, particularly to motorists following Interstate 80, which can numb the mind and smooth out rough terrain into gentle undulations. Because of that highway's location in the Platte Valley, travelers miss the dramatic dunes of the Sandhills, the wooded bluffs of the Missouri, the rugged pine-covered slopes of the Pine Ridge, and the deeply dissected canyons of southwestern Nebraska.

Tree cover is sparse, but hardly nonexistent—it is not true that the state tree is the telephone pole! Nebraska contains one of the largest planted forests in the world—the Bessey Division of the Nebraska National Forest near Halsey. Trees line most streams, and shelterbelts, hedgerows, and other tree plantings give the state visual diversity.

Most of the state is dry relative to the rest of the Midwest, but the climate ranges from subhumid to semiarid. Even though some years are noted for a lack of moisture, rainfall has been more than abundant in others. Nebraska's groundwater reserves dwarf those of other states and, along with surface water, are used to irrigate more than 7 million acres (2.8 million ha).

One generalization about the state is accurate—it is a farm state, even though the distribution of population might not so indicate. Fewer than 10 percent of the state's residents live on farms, while over 60 percent live in towns and cities with more than twenty-five hundred people. Omaha's metropolitan area has a population of a half million. Yet agriculture permeates the state. A disproportionate share of manufacturing activity in Nebraska is related to agriculture. Industries process farm output and produce farm inputs. Commerce in the state revolves around agriculture. When farmers prosper, retailers and wholesalers prosper. The transportation network handles large quantities of agricultural commodities. The people of the state have rural backgrounds, and many retain some ties to farming and rural communities. As a result, I have placed more emphasis on farming and the rural landscape than population statistics might suggest is warranted.

I have not attempted to compile a Nebraska encyclopedia. There are numerous sources of information about the state—statistics of population, agriculture, economy, and resources. These data are not included here. Instead, my approach is somewhat selective. I have stressed the development of the state, and I have focused on the people who settled the state and the agricultural systems they imported and modified. Throughout, I have linked processes and patterns in the state both to local resources and national trends because Nebraska is not detached from the larger political, social, economic, and technological forces affecting the nation and the world. Finally, I have emphasized the application of various concepts from the discipline of geography to patterns observed in the state—resource availability, human-environment relations, density, mobility, distance, space, and distribution, among others. Bibliographic entries indicate more information about such subjects as central-place theory, land-use theory, rural population turnaround, environmental adaptation, and the structure of agriculture. For this is not just a book about Nebraska, but a geographical study as well. I hope it provides readers not simply with facts, but with interpretations; not just with information about Nebraska, but about human use of resources. By studying the geography of Nebraska we may learn more about resources, agriculture, spatial patterns of human behavior, and human use of the earth.

This book is the product of several years of labor and of many more years of attachment to and interest in Nebraska's history and geography. My mother, who grew up five miles from the Missouri River, and my father, raised in the extreme southwestern corner of the Panhandle, gave me perspectives on the Midwest and the High Plains. C. B. McIntosh and Colbert Held first helped to shape that interest into a professional career in geography. The late Paul Riley, research associate at the Nebraska State Historical Society, guided me through the labyrinth of historical information about the state—a subject he knew in incredible detail. Martyn Bowden was a challenging, stimulating adviser who could suggest more research topics in a five-minute conversation than any one person could complete in a career. His grasp of the essence of the relations between culture and the subhumid environment provoked much of the work contained in this book.

Michigan Technological University contributed greatly to my research through a sabbatical during the 1981-1982 academic year. The Geography Department of the University of Nebraska–Lincoln provided an office and other assistance. The Michigan Tech Fund supported much of the preparation of the manuscript.

Writing a geography of Nebraska from the Upper Peninsula of Michigan was a challenge, to say the least. It could have been completed only with the assistance of a great many individuals. Foremost among them are the personnel of the reference section of the Michigan Tech library. June Hawthorne, Margaret Carlson, Dave Bezotte, Bill Rowe, and Janet Locatelli retrieved information, data, maps, references, and interlibrary loan materials. The staff of the Nebraska State Historical Society was, as usual, courteous, helpful, and efficient. Additional assistance was provided by a myriad of state and federal agencies, including the state departments of Health, Education, Economic Development, and Labor, the U.S. Soil Conservation Service, the Agricultural Stabilization and Conservation Service, and the Conservation and Survey Division of the University of Nebraska–Lincoln. Several inlaws, outlaws, and friends—John, Joyce, Jeff, and Stan—tracked down references and information when library resources and computers came up empty-handed.

Portions of the manuscript were reviewed by Ray Bentall, Paul Gessaman, Steve Kale, Al Larson, Mary Louise Quinn, Dean Rugg, Philip Vogel, Dave Wishart, and Joe Wood. Their comments, questions, and suggestions challenged my thinking on a variety of subjects and forced me to reevaluate a number of conceptions and misconceptions. Ingolf Vogeler, the series editor, and Lynne Rienner, Jeanne Remington, and Libby Barstow at Westview Press offered useful advice that considerably shortened and clarified the text. None of these individuals are, of course, responsible for any errors or misinterpretations I undoubtedly have made.

Cartographic services were provided by Steve Ryan and Debby McDowell. The base maps were prepared by the cartographic laboratory of the Geography Department of the University of Nebraska–Lincoln. I especially wish to recognize the efforts of Claire Chaput, Annette Coburn, Kriss Yokie, and Mary Cotter at Michigan Tech, who typed the manuscript and in the process learned more than they ever believed they could about a distant state.

Katie and Andy, in spite of their youth, tolerated and accepted the long hours required to complete this effort. I hope they will someday form as strong an attachment to a place as I have. Vickie Baltensperger retains that same fondness for and appreciation of Nebraska. She also provided proofreading, support, criticism, agitation, enthusiasm, and, occasionally, disgust, all while pursuing her own career and applying her own talents. Though sometimes it seemed this project would never be finished, she remained confident—that confidence was a self-fulfilling prophecy.

B.H.B.

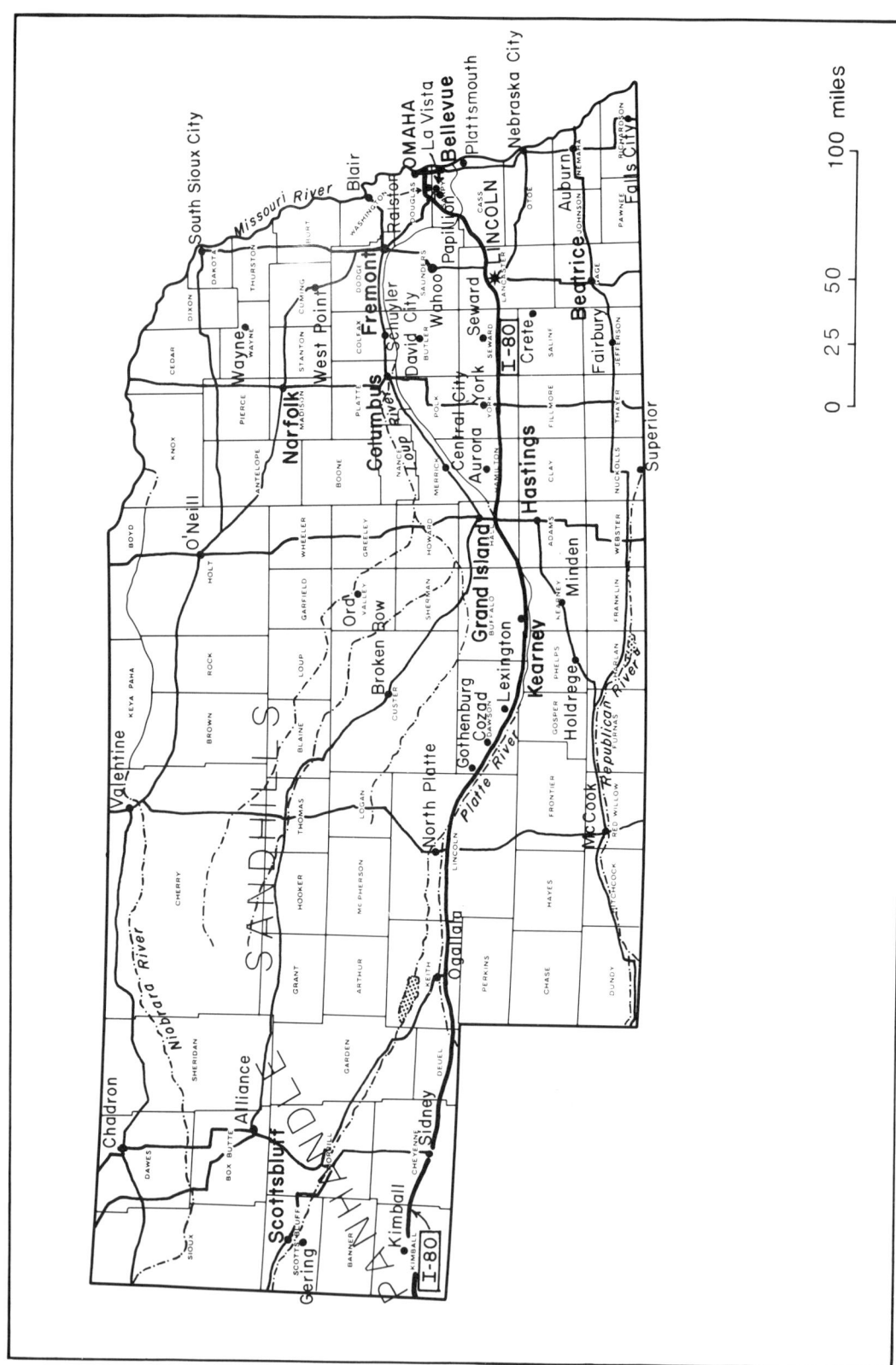

Nebraska

CHAPTER 1

RESOURCES OF THE NEBRASKA ENVIRONMENT

In a classic examination of the relations between people and environment, Ralph Hall Brown spoke of the Great Plains "as it was and as it was thought to be."[1] The Nebraska environment, central to the Great Plains region, has been perceived in sharply contrasting ways by different individuals and groups in different times. Even the early explorers of the trans-Missouri country failed to agree on the environmental realities of the area. Coronado, traveling through the plains in what is now Kansas in 1540 and 1541, was particularly impressed with the herds of bison, which he saw daily, and with rich, well-watered soil suitable for crop production. Lewis and Clark in 1804 noted a profusion of animal life on the plains, denoting a landscape along the Missouri River below the mouth of the Niobrara "most butifull." The land they reported upon contained fertile soil and a "salubrious" climate; in short it was the "Garden of the West" they had expected to find.[2]

Contrast these favorable views with the 1806 report of Lt. Zebulon Pike: "a barren soil, parched and dryed up for eight months in the year, presents neither moisture nor nutrition sufficient to nourish the timber. These vast plains of the western hemisphere may become in time as celebrated as the sandy deserts of Africa."[3] In 1823, Maj. Stephen H. Long affixed the term "Great American Desert" to his map of the region. Along with a host of other explorers and observers, he maintained that the area between the 98th meridian and the Rocky Mountains would remain the domain of nomadic hunters and be forever unsuited for cultivation.[4]

Later travelers, scientists, and promoters held similarly irreconcilable views. Those who were philosophically and politically opposed to the very idea of a desert promoted a garden image of the plains: a paradise suitable for immediate occupancy. The scenery was described as magnificent and the land as capable of producing all the crops found in the Midwest. This was a land "admirably adapted to agricultural purposes, [which will] support a large agricultural and pastoral population"[5] and "the largest unbroken tract of splendid farming land in the world."[6] Such optimists responded with acrimonious invective to the suggestion of John Wesley Powell in 1879 that successful settlement of the plains would require irrigation or ranching because traditional humid-land agriculture could not be successful in this region of insufficient rainfall.[7] In 1868 Maj. Gen. William B. Hazen had unleashed an equally bitter reaction when he described the Great Plains as worthless: "This country will not produce the fruits and cereals of the East for want of moisture, and can in no way be artificially irrigated, and will not, in our day and generation, sell for one penny an acre, except through fraud or ignorance."[8]

How could such divergent views of the same land be expressed by intelligent and observant individuals? The answers lie partly in the reality they observed. Nebraska and the plains offered nearly the entire range of conditions described by explorers, promoters, settlers, and scientists. As the early years of settlement were to confirm, rainfall was at times so low as to permit only very limited crop yields, even in the humid southeastern corner of the state. Yet in other years, bountiful yields could be secured on almost all soils. As a result, promoters and detractors alike could and did find evidence for virtually any claim they wished to make.

Some made their observations of the plains in highly favorable years; others crossed the plains in times of severe drought. Long's expedition passed through what is now Nebraska in 1820, and he described a land of shifting sand and sterility. Subsequent climatic reconstruction through the study of tree rings indicates that 1820 was a drought year of greater severity than the 1930s. The desert Long observed was as much a plains reality as the blowing soil, scanty grass cover, and withering crops of 1934.[9] The very wet year of 1915 would certainly have elicited different responses from observers. Unfortunately, the spatial and temporal variability that characterizes the climate of Nebraska and other plains states could seldom be appreciated by explorers and travelers, who saw the land for only a few days in one season of one year.[10]

The perceptions of settlers, travelers, and explorers were also colored by their backgrounds, their objectives, and their preconceptions.[11] Coronado saw the plains from a semiarid perspective and evaluated the region's suitability for the agricultural products of Spain. Pike, on the other hand, contrasted the plains with the humid lands of the eastern United States, with which he was familiar; the plains suffered by comparison.[12]

Lewis and Clark's positive reports on the region were largely conditioned by their view—shared by Thomas Jefferson—of the Louisiana Territory as a garden. Seeking a garden, they did not fail to find it. Fremont, favorably disposed toward the expansion of settlement of the West, was not inclined to find a desert; those who sought to limit expansion of settlement were gratified to discover a desert barrier to agricultural enterprise.[13]

Contemporary observers have similar problems characterizing the environment of Nebraska. The internal variations in climate, topography, soils, and water supply defy simple labels. Environmental fluctuations make a mockery of descriptions of one fixed reality. The popular images of the state held by outsiders contain some essence of reality along with substantial misconceptions. Is this a flat plain? Does it suffer from searing heat or numbing cold? Does the term *subhumid* accurately depict its principal features? The Nebraska environment—climate, land, and water—can only be understood by considering its extremes alongside its averages and by examining the internal complexity of the state.

CLIMATIC REALITY

Nebraska's climate is characterized by seasonal temperature extremes common to continental interiors, by subhumid to semiarid conditions, highly variable precipitation, and by several prominent natural hazards.

Temperature: Extremes and Averages

Areas distant from major water bodies—as is the case of Nebraska—experience substantial annual temperature variations. This important effect on climate is known as continentality. Winter temperatures are quite low; summers are exceptionally hot. The average low temperature in Nebraska in January is between 12°F (−11°C) and 5°F (−15°C), and the average daily high in July is approximately 86°F (30°C). These averages mask the overall range of temperatures, however. Lows below −22°F (−30°C) have been recorded in most locations in the state, but January temperatures above 68°F (20°C) are not unheard of. Although some summers have few days above 86°F, long periods of very hot weather are not unusual: Temperatures above 113°F (45°C) have been recorded, and daily highs above 104°F (40°C) have been maintained for as long as two weeks.[14]

Elevation is another factor that controls temperature. The state slopes imperceptibly from just over 800 ft (244 m) in the southeastern counties to elevations above 5,000 ft (1,500 m) in parts of the Panhandle. The effects of higher elevation include fewer days with extremely high temperatures and fewer days between the last frost of the spring and the first frost of fall.

Although the average date of the last spring freeze in Omaha and Lincoln is April 20, certain areas in the Panhandle are likely to have frost over a month later. Conversely, on the average the first frost of fall occurs by September 15 in parts of the northwest, but not until October 15 in the southeast. Again, there is considerable year-to-year variation. Freezing temperatures have been recorded in July in northwestern Nebraska, yet in other years the same locations may not have frost until October.[15]

The average frost-free season ranges from 120 days in the northwest to 180 days in Omaha and Lincoln. This pattern profoundly affects the distribution of some crops. Corn is especially sensitive to the length of the growing season, a trait that has been partially mitigated by the development of short-season varieties. The unpredictability of the last and first frosts is of concern not only to farmers but also to orchardists, gardeners, and nursery operators.[16]

Variability of Precipitation

Most of Nebraska's rainfall, particularly in summer, is triggered by the interaction between masses of cold arctic air and warm, moist air from the Gulf of Mexico. When either one of these air masses is dominant, precipitation is not great, but when they meet over Nebraska, the Gulf air is pushed up and over the cooler air mass, producing condensation and precipitation.

The distribution of precipitation in Nebraska is a function of distance from the Gulf of Mexico and of the barrier effect of the Rocky Mountains. Because little moisture remains in air masses coming into the plains from the west, precipitation is generally quite low near the mountains. Farther east, the barrier becomes less significant. Precipitation increases toward the dominant moisture source—the Gulf of Mexico.[17]

Average annual precipitation ranges from only 15 in. (38 cm) in Scottsbluff to more than 36 in. (91 cm) at Falls City in the extreme southeast (Figure 1.1). This tremendous difference contrasts markedly with the relative uniformity of precipitation received by stations from Des Moines, Iowa, to the East Coast (Figure 1.2). Annual precipitation along the 41st parallel ranges from 15 in. (38 cm) to 30 in. (76 cm) across the 450-mi (725-km) width of Nebraska, but varies only 10 in. (25 cm) (from 30 in. to 40 in. [102 cm]) along the remaining 1,150 mi (1,850 km) from the Missouri River to the Atlantic Ocean.

Annual precipitation fails to tell the whole story, however. To a greater extent than states to the east, Nebraska's precipitation is concentrated in the warm months of the year. Statewide, over three-fourths of total precipitation is received from April through September. Growing-season precipitation ranges from 12 in. (30 cm) in the Panhandle to over 23 in. (58 cm) in the southeast corner. By contrast, there is a dearth of moisture from November through February. June is typically the wettest month, followed by May.[18] In the eastern half of

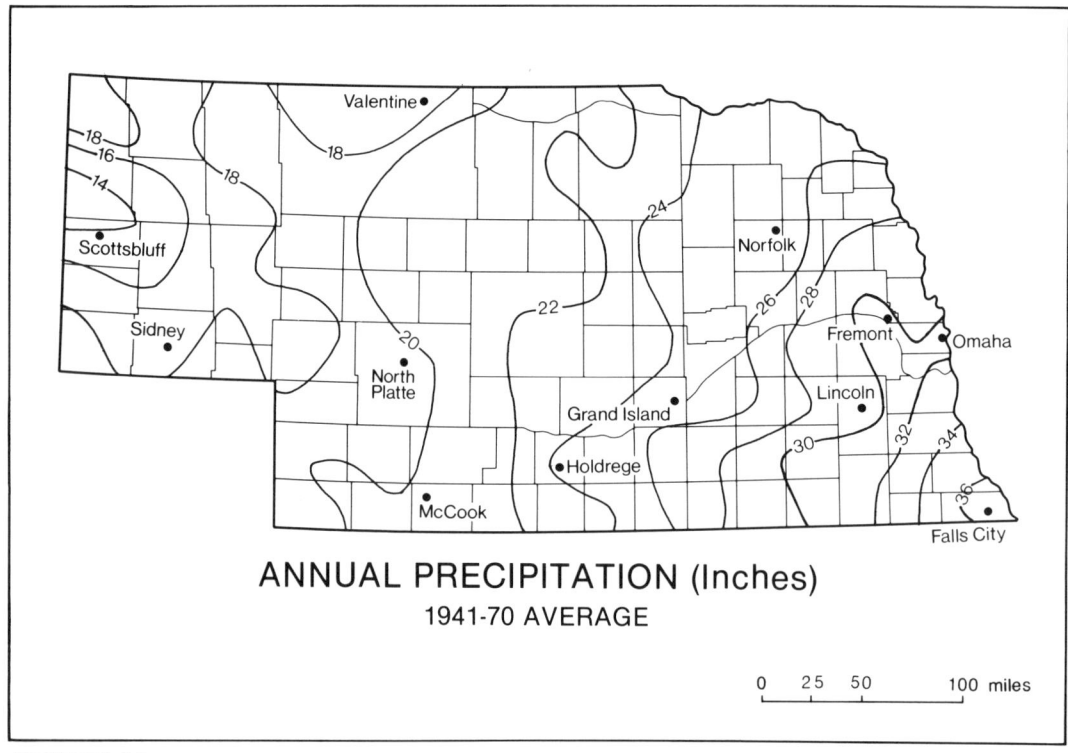

FIGURE 1.1.

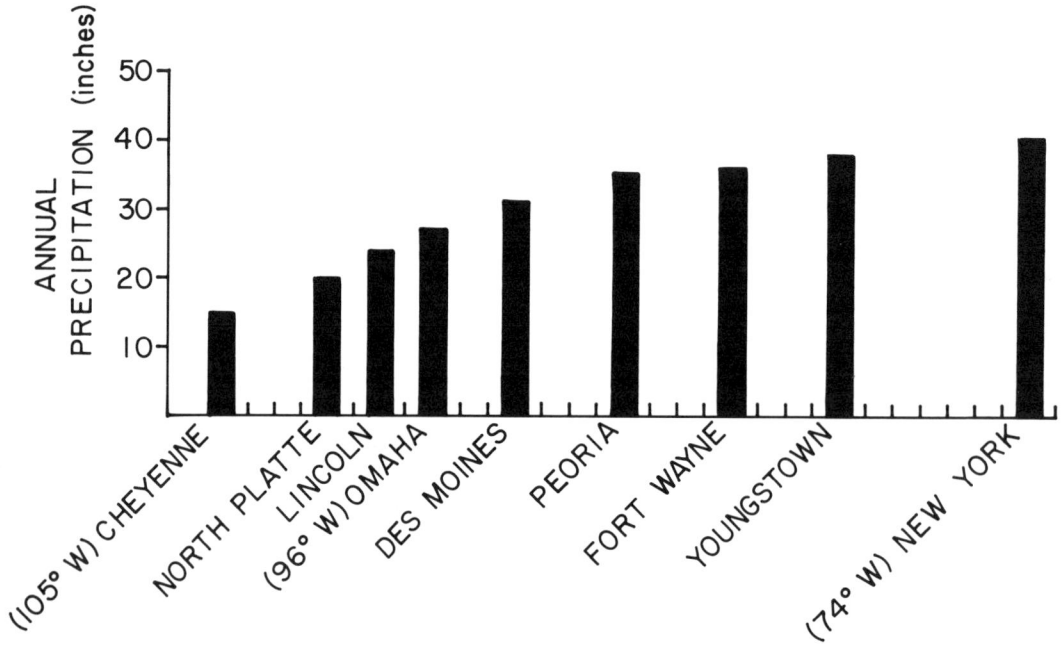

Average Annual Precipitation along or near 41° N

FIGURE 1.2.

the state July and August are also fairly wet, but farther west, precipitation falls off rapidly in late summer (Figure 1.3). Average August rainfall in Scottsbluff, for example, is less than 1 in. (2.5 cm) compared to 4 in. (10 cm) at Falls City.[19]

A most important aspect of summer rainfall is its extreme year-to-year variability. This is critical because of the dependence of crop growth upon summer moisture and because such a high percentage of annual precipitation comes in the summer. In general, the stronger the westerlies moving over the plains from the dry continental interior, the less rainfall is received. As a result, droughts have been most serious and extensive in years when the dry, continental westerlies are pronounced. In years when the westerlies are weak, cool arctic fronts and warm subtropical air masses penetrate the central plains where their conjunction triggers summer rainfall.[20]

In a state with such regional, seasonal, and year-to-year variation in rainfall, *normal* is not an especially meaningful term, but drought certainly is a normal occurrence in Nebraska. From the time precipitation records were first kept, Nebraska has experienced numerous droughts of varying magnitude, duration, and extent.[21] Local and short-term droughts were common as early in the settlement period as 1860 (Figure 1.4). The first extended drought with severe consequences occurred in the early 1890s. Precipitation amounts in 1890, 1893, and 1894 were among the lowest ever recorded in the state. Many settlers left the state forever, as crops parched and true destitution replaced hope for a rapid recovery (see Chapter 2).[22] Although the drought of the 1930s was less disruptive to life in Nebraska, climatically it was at least as severe as that of the 1890s.[23] The dry soil, unable to support normal stands of crops and grasses, began to blow. Dust storms affected millions of acres of Nebraska farmland. Average corn yields in some years fell below 5 bu. per acre (175 l per ha). Other drought years occurred in the mid-1950s, and in 1974 and 1980 precipitation was well below normal.

Many persons have speculated on the apparent regularity of drought occurrence in Nebraska, citing a twenty-year drought cycle that includes the 1890s, localized droughts in the 1910s, severe droughts of the 1930s and 1950s, and dry conditions during the 1970s. However, careful statistical study of the historical record and of the presettlement period through evaluation of tree-ring data reveals no regularity of drought cycles. The conclusion is that droughts in Nebraska have been both frequent and severe. The most accurate assessment of future drought occurrence must be that drought will occur again, but with no certainty as to when that will be.[24]

Drought may be common in Nebraska, but in many years humid conditions predominate. Contrast the pattern of precipitation in the drought year of 1934 with that of 1915, one of the wettest years on record: In 1915, nearly the entire state received more than 30 in. (76 cm) of precipitation (Figure 1.5). Twenty years later, some of the most severe floods on record occurred in 1935 in the middle of a decade of drought. In May 1982, a succession of convective storms dumped as much as 11 in. (28 cm) of rainfall on several locations. Widespread flooding and severe soil erosion occurred in much of the eastern half of the state in June as a result of thunderstorms. Farmers conditioned to prepare for drought found flooded fields; planting was delayed for a month or more.

Natural Hazards: Blizzards, Tornadoes, and Hail

Other aspects of the harsh Nebraska climate have lent themselves more readily to adjustments that mitigate potential economic and other losses. Among these are savage winter storms, tornadoes, and hail. Blizzards account for more loss of life than any other weather phenomenon in Nebraska. Blizzards during the early years of settlement were especially dangerous because rudimentary housing and transpor-

MONTHLY DISTRIBUTIONS OF PRECIPITATION NORMALS 1941–1970

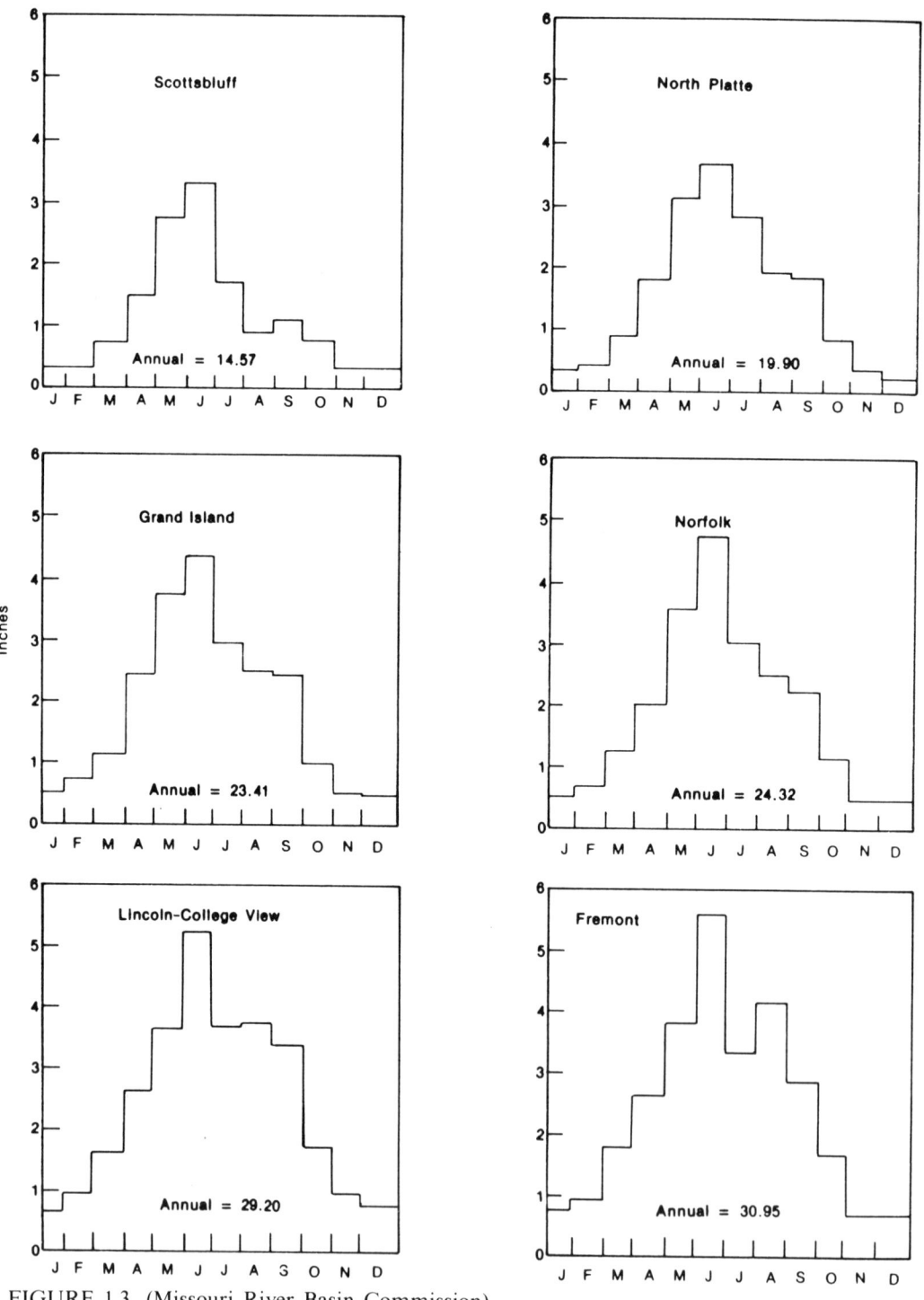

FIGURE 1.3. (Missouri River Basin Commission)

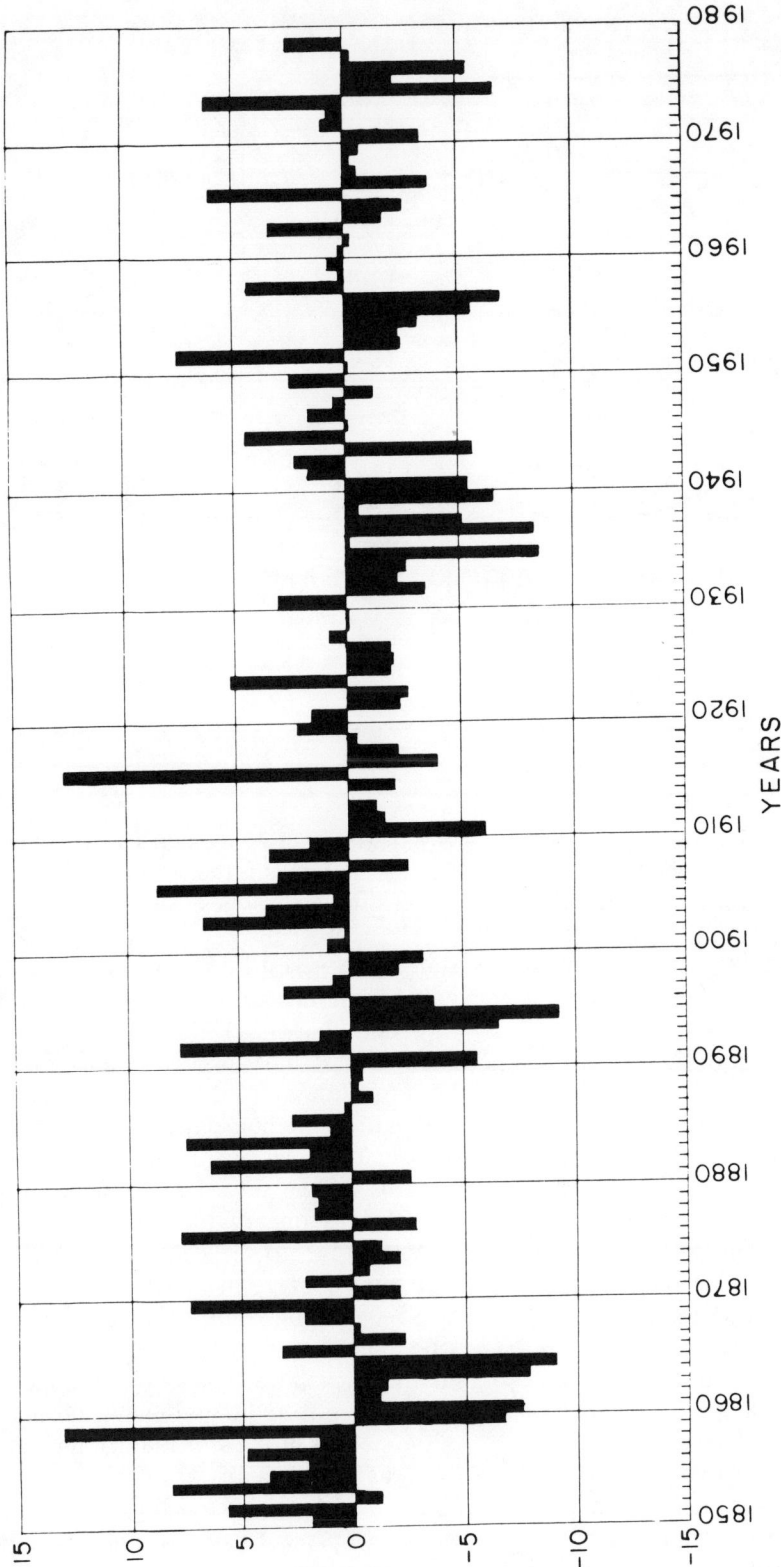

FIGURE 1.4. (UNL, Conservation and Survey Division)

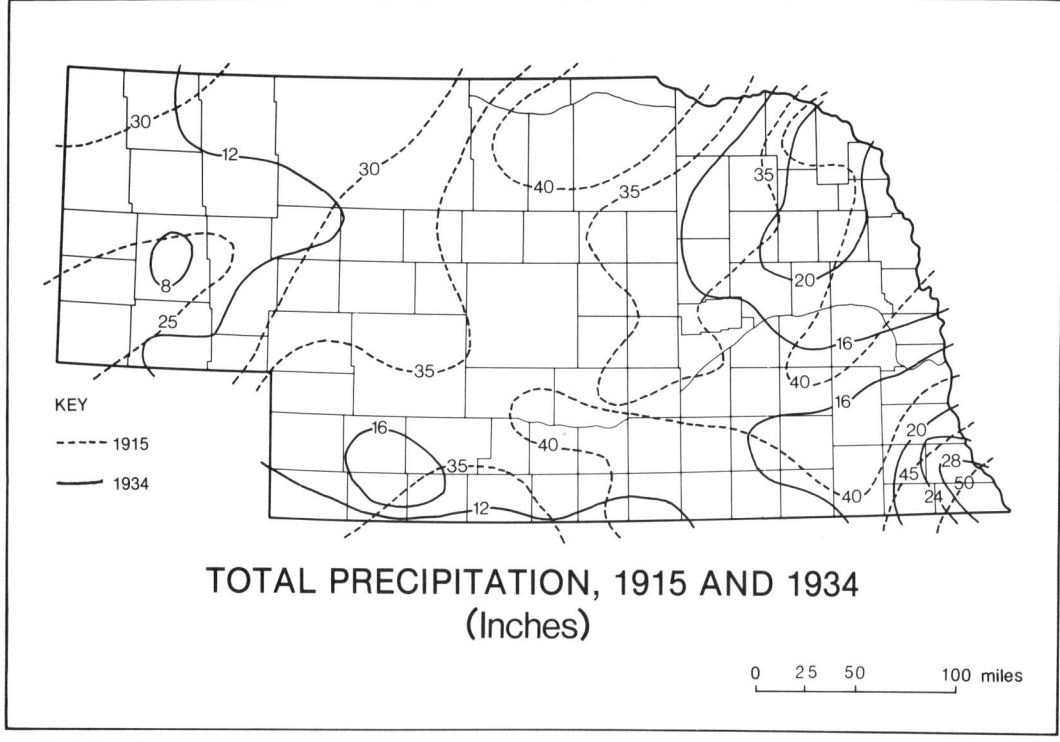

FIGURE 1.5.

tation and lack of communications systems left many settlers without adequate protection or the ability to reach safety or assistance. Most importantly, nineteenth-century residents had little or no way of knowing that life-threatening storms were imminent.

Today the ability of individuals to prepare for severe weather has improved because of well-developed warning systems and better understanding of the dangers of Nebraska storms.[25] The loss of human life has been relatively low in recent blizzards—even those that have immobilized much of the state, caused substantial economic losses (Figure 1.6), and stranded travelers.

Improved human understanding and preparation are exemplified in relation to the most locally destructive of Nebraska's weather phenomena, tornadoes—severe storms of short duration that form mostly in spring and early summer, when cold Canadian air meets moist tropical air from the Gulf of Mexico. Although Nebraska has one of the highest incidences of tornadoes in the nation, in recent years improved forecasting techniques, media warnings of severe weather phenomena, and an intense statewide interest in tornadoes have helped hold down fatalities. Comparison of two tornadoes that struck Omaha illustrates the changes that have occurred. The first, on Easter Sunday in 1913, killed 177 persons and left 7,000 homeless. The second, on May 6, 1975, swept through the southwest suburbs of the city. Even though it was recorded as one of the most devastating tornadoes ever to strike in the United States and total damage may have been as high as $500 million, only three persons were killed! This amazingly low figure must be credited to the alertness of Omaha residents, glued to radio and television reports of the storm's progress. Although the hazard of tornadoes remains as real as ever, the ability of Nebraskans to adjust to the danger tornadoes present has substantially altered their impact.[26]

FIGURE 1.6. Cattle frozen in a blizzard in the Sandhills. Driven before the wind, they wandered onto the frozen surface of a lake near Ashby, where they fell and were stranded. (NSHS)

A final natural hazard, one that primarily concerns farmers, is hail. The area east of the Rocky Mountains, including the western half of Nebraska, has a higher incidence of hail than anywhere else in the nation. The extreme southwestern part of the Panhandle experiences as many as eight days annually with hail; the season of occurrence is mainly from April through September.[27] Crop losses to hail thus are substantial in Nebraska. Wheat is particularly vulnerable: The southern Panhandle specializes in wheat production, and the season of greatest hail frequency coincides with the period when wheat has headed.

The Variability of Climatic Conditions

Average climatic conditions in Nebraska have little meaning without reference to climatic uncertainty. Total annual precipitation gives no hint of its timing, perhaps the most critical factor in its usefulness. Twenty inches (51 cm) of rain at proper intervals during the growing season are worth more to farmers than 30 in. (76 cm) derived from a few cloudbursts.

Temporal variability means unpredictability as well. Wet years may follow dry years; this complicates the efforts of farmers and others to plan for one or the other extreme. Likewise, extremes of heat and cold are frequently juxtaposed, as is typified by late winter blizzards on the heels of 77°F (25°C) warmth.

Variability is also expressed spatially in very local weather phenomena. Localized thunderstorms may dump 4 in. (10 cm) of rain on one neighborhood, causing severe soil erosion and flooding; just miles away, crops may be suffering from drought. In drier years, large areas of the state will be affected by drought, and the moist patches will be few and far between. During wetter years, moisture-deficient areas will be few and scattered. Where and when either of these conditions will prevail cannot, however, be predicted.[28]

THE LAND ENDOWMENT

Nebraska lies along the western edge of the Central Lowlands of North America and astride the Great Plains that stretch from Texas to Saskatchewan. The state's 76,483 sq mi (198,090 sq km) lie upon a

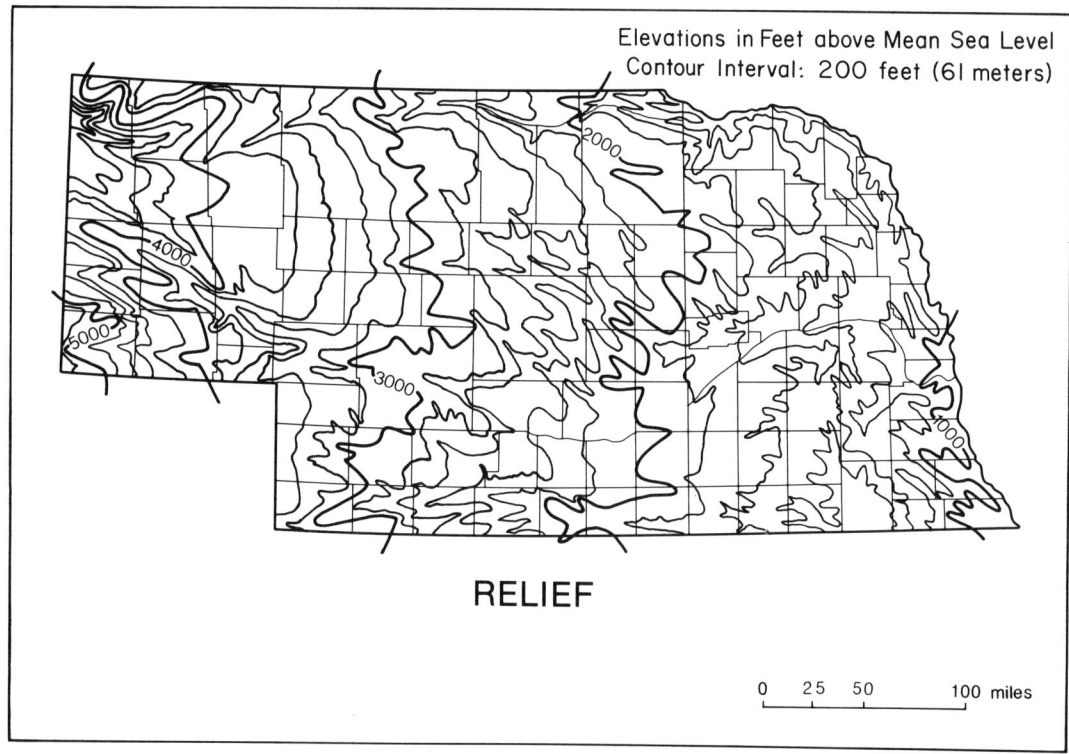

FIGURE 1.7.

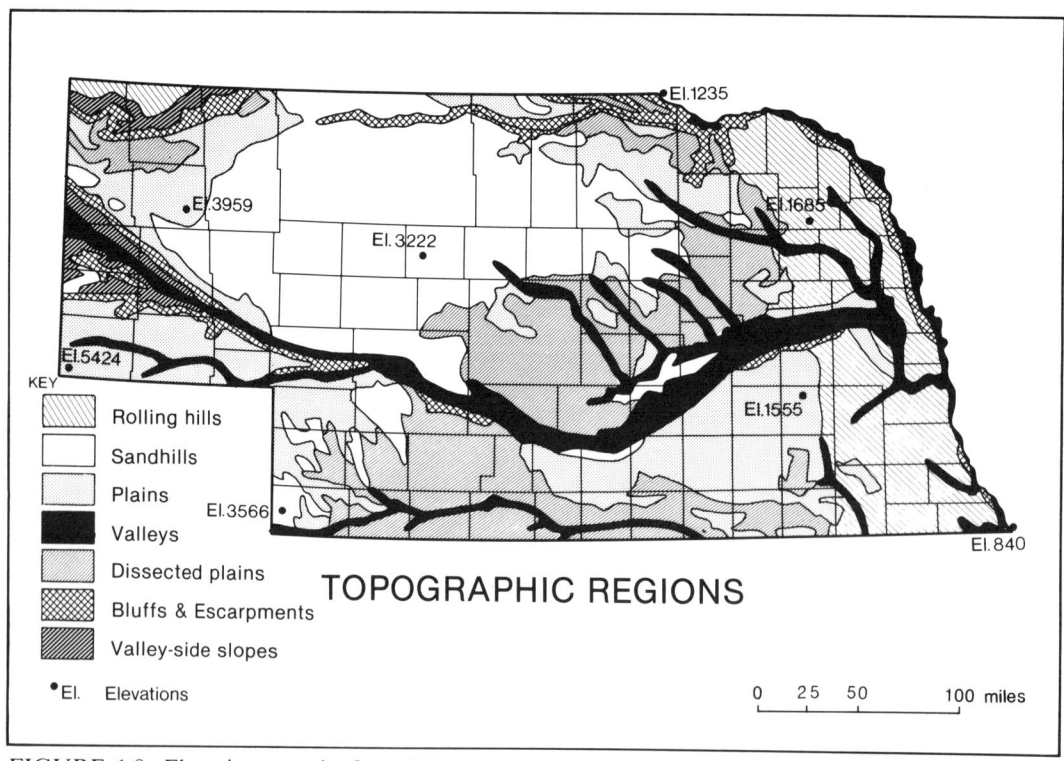

FIGURE 1.8. Elevations are in feet. (UNL, Conservation and Survey Division)

broad plain that slopes gradually from the Missouri River on the eastern border (elevation 840 ft or 256 m in Richardson County) toward the Rocky Mountains of Wyoming and Colorado (Figure 1.7), rising to the highest elevation of 5,424 ft (1,653 m) in Kimball County. Upon this plain there is considerable variation. Some of the land surface confirms outsiders' images of flatness, as along the Platte Valley or in the south-central part of the state. Yet in other areas hills, canyons, and rugged terrain dominate. Topographically, the state can be divided into valleys, plains, hills, sandhills, and bluffs and escarpments (Figure 1.8).

Topographic Regions

The most distinctive topographic region in the state is the Sandhills. This area of 20,000 sq mi (50,000 sq km) is the largest sand-dune complex in the Western Hemisphere. Dune formation probably began early in the most recent (the Wisconsin) glacial stage. Most of the sand apparently came from alluvial deposits on the floodplains of rivers flowing through the region.[29] In the western part of the Sandhills are large transverse dunes, some as high as 300 ft (90 m) and up to 10 mi (16 km) long. Farther east and south, the dunes are somewhat smaller and less linear (Figure 1.9).

Many Sandhills valleys away from major streams contain small, shallow lakes or wet meadows (Figure 1.10). Some of these lakes rise and fall with the fluctuating water table; others are not directly connected to the groundwater reservoir. A number of alkali lakes having a high concentration of salts are found in Sheridan and Garden counties. During World War I several of these formed a nationally significant source of potash.[30]

South and east of the Sandhills are extensive deposits of loess, wind-deposited silt derived from glacial outwash and from the Sandhills and transported by the prevailing north and northwest winds. The dissected-plains region is heavily mantled with loess, particularly north of the Platte River. In some areas deposits are over 100 ft (30 m) thick.[31] This region consists of a rolling to level plain, deeply incised by streams. In the southwestern counties, deep canyons alternate with nearly level uplands.

The loess plain of south-central Nebraska is nearly level, not deeply dissected, and heavily irrigated. Farther west are the high plains of the Panhandle and nearby Chase and Perkins counties. Within these plains are found two rugged areas of steep slopes and escarpments—the Wildcat Hills and the Pine Ridge—that support coniferous vegetation (Figure 1.11). Isolated buttes that punctuate the high plains give the Panhandle an appearance that is far from flat.

The four major glacial advances of the past two million years affected most of Nebraska only indirectly. The eastern quarter of the state, however, was covered with glacial ice during the first two major glacial stages, the Nebraskan and the Kansan. The landscape of the glaciated portion of the state is one of rolling hills: glacial deposits mantled with loess and modified by erosion (Figure 1.12).[32]

The floodplains of Nebraska's major and minor streams constitute the final topographic region. They range in width from more than 10 mi (16 km), along the Platte in central Nebraska, to less than 100 ft (30 m). Where these soils are fine textured and well drained they are typically highly fertile. The more coarse textured soils require greater inputs of fertilizer to render them productive. In some places alluvial soils are so wet that they are not usable for agriculture unless excessive water can be drained.[33]

Soils and the Subhumid Grassland

Nebraska soils are relatively young—mostly less than ten thousand years old. Their fertility and capacity to store and transport water are products of the parent materials from which they were formed and the vegetation that they have supported. The nature of that vegetation has been determined by the relatively dry climate marked by a strong seasonal component and high year-to-year variability.[34]

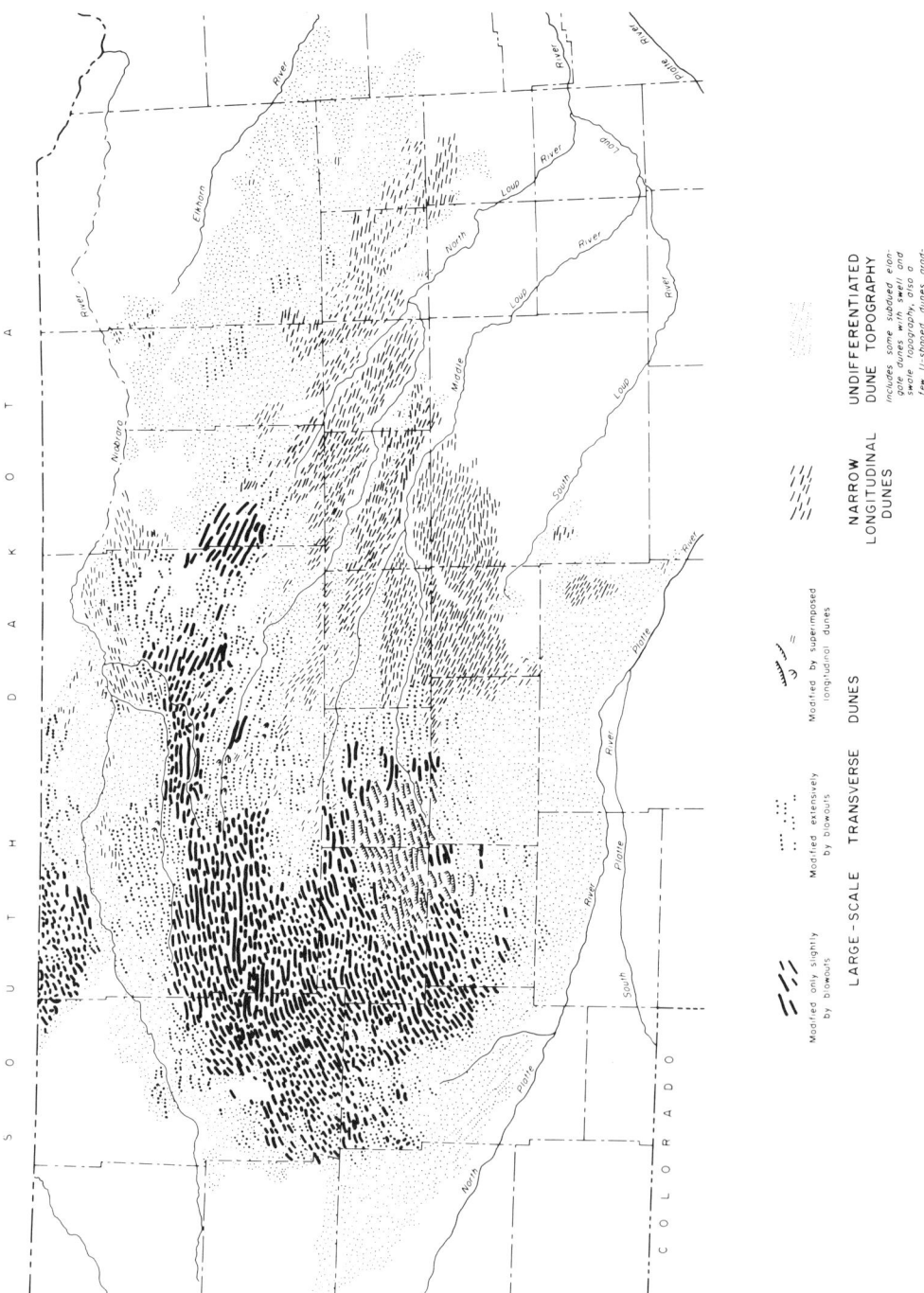

FIGURE 1.9. Dune formations in the Sandhills. Source: H.T.U. Smith. "Dune Morphology and Chronology in Central and Western Nebraska," *Journal of Geology* 73, no. 4 (1965):557–578. Adapted and reprinted by permission of the copyright holder, The University of Chicago.

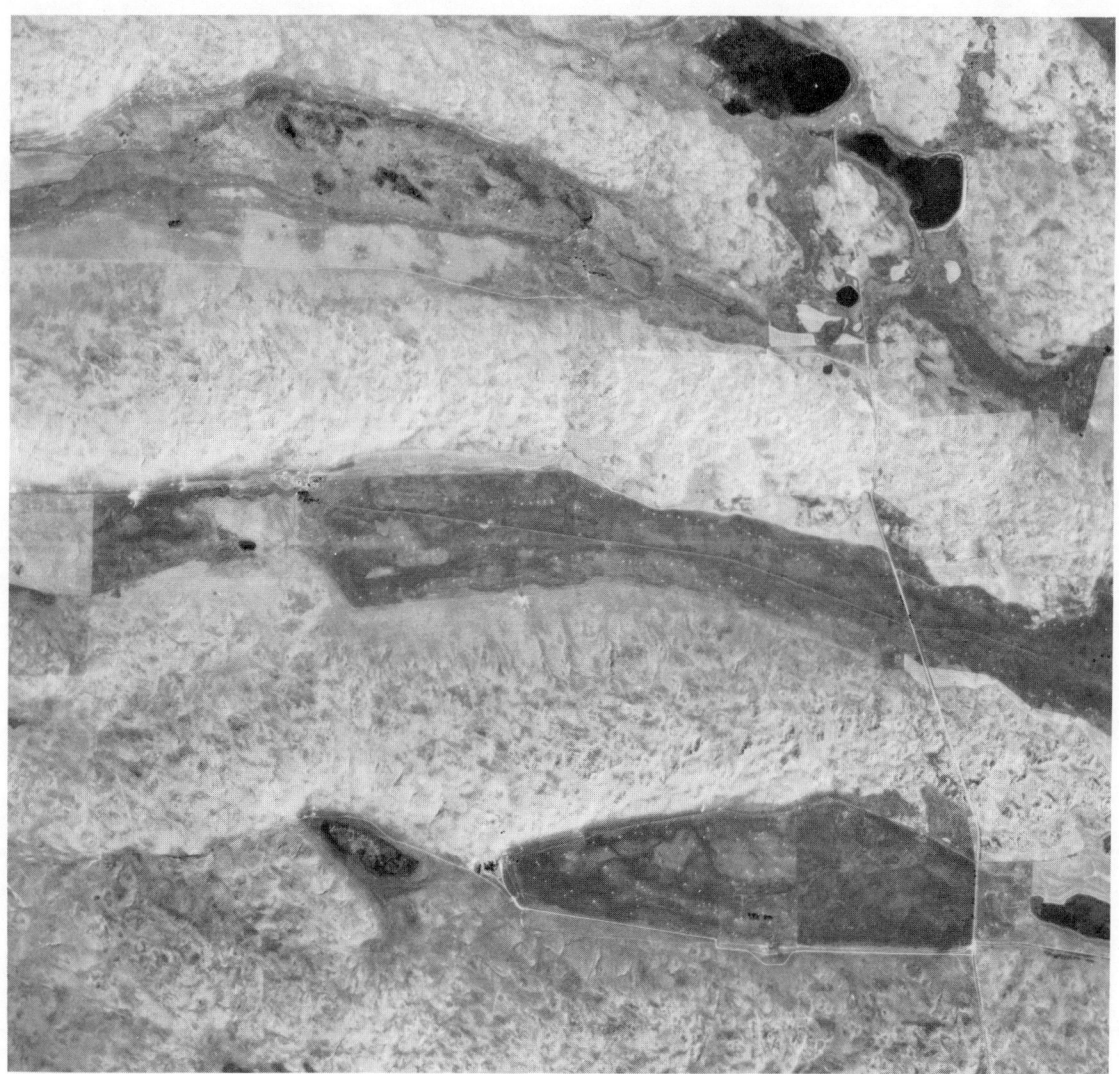
FIGURE 1.10. Large parallel dunes in southwestern Cherry County are separated by well-watered, fertile valleys used for hay production. (USDA, ASCS)

FIGURE 1.11. The rough lands of the Pine Ridge, considered one of the most scenic regions of Nebraska, support a scattered growth of conifers.

FIGURE 1.12. Rolling topography of glaciated eastern Nebraska.

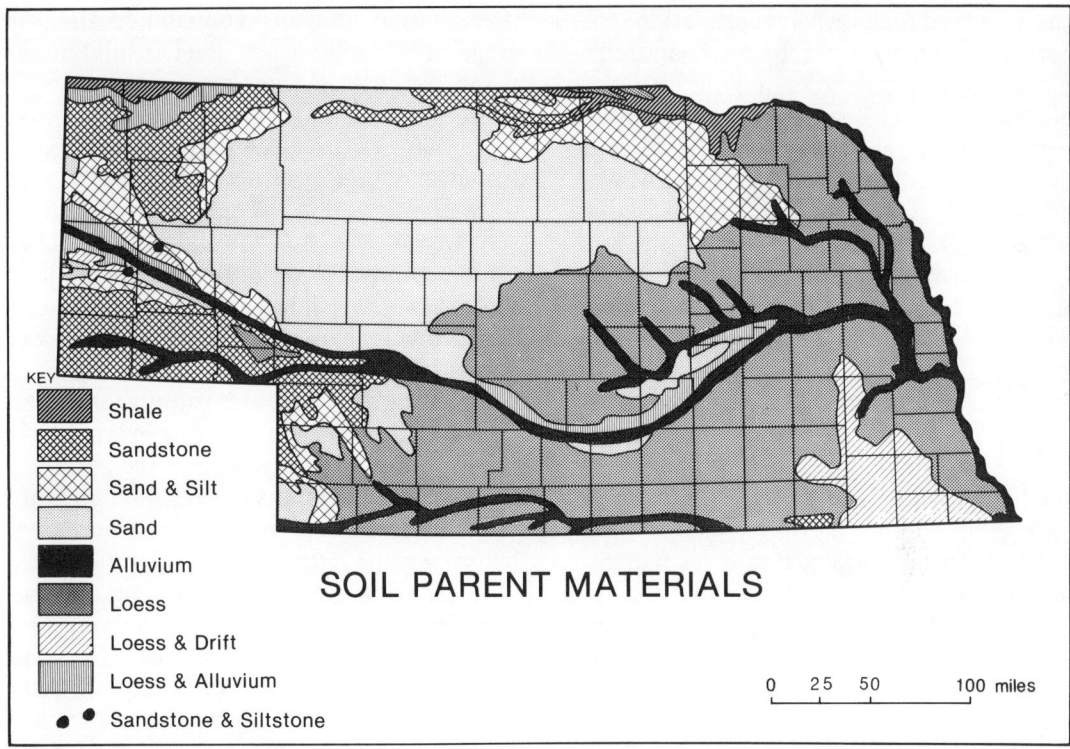

FIGURE 1.13. (UNL, Conservation and Survey Division)

The parent material of a soil (Figure 1.13) is the principal factor determining its texture, permeability, and porosity. Soils formed from sand or sandstone have a fairly coarse texture, allowing water to infiltrate rapidly, but somewhat limiting their storage capacity. In the Sandhills region these sandy soils have traditionally supported grazing and have generally been considered unsuitable for irrigation because of topography and because of their high evaporation and infiltration rates.[35] Recent innovations in irrigation, however, have opened some sandy soils to crop production where slopes are not excessive and where water is readily available.

Silty soils dominate in areas where loess is the parent material. Infiltration and evaporation are less rapid than in sandy soils, but water-holding capacity is higher; hence, loess-based soils are somewhat more suitable for irrigation. The loess region supports most of the state's crop production.

Clay soils with low permeability and very fine texture have formed on shale and on glacial till. Although crops can be grown, clay soils are poorly suited for irrigation. Alluvium is the parent material for soils on floodplains and stream terraces. Alluvial soils are mostly fertile and heavily irrigated, although some in the eastern third of the state are heavy clay soils with very poor drainage.

The "natural" vegetation of nearly all of Nebraska was prairie grass—tall grasses nearer the Missouri River and progressively shorter grasses farther west where rainfall is less. Fire is generally accepted as the most important cause of the treeless nature of the Great Plains. Extensive prairie fires, started by lightning or indigenous peoples, prevented forests from becoming established, except along the Missouri River and in the rough, broken lands of the Panhandle.[36]

The presettlement vegetation of the state

has survived only where cultivation has not taken place. Most of the Sandhills, much of the Panhandle, and the canyons of southwestern Nebraska retain their original grass cover, although grazing has altered the species composition. In eastern Nebraska, only scattered remnants of native tall-grass prairie remain.[37]

Soils formed under subhumid to semiarid conditions with grassland vegetation tend to be high in organic matter and humus, as a result of the decomposition of grasses and their root systems. Such soils retain nutrients that are likely to be leached out in more humid areas. It is this characteristic of the soil, along with upward movement of soil moisture that returns nutrients to the surface, that gives the soil its considerable fertility.[38]

Most of the soil groups found in Nebraska are Mollisols (principally Udoll and Ustoll subgroups) or Entisols. Entisols are sandy soils, whereas Mollisols form in grassland regions that have precipitation with a marked seasonal component.[39] Although fertility of Mollisols can suffer under continuous cropping, the principal soil management problem is erosion. Wind erosion is pronounced on the Ustolls of the short-grass region in the western third of the state. Soils on slopes in the eastern third of the state are especially subject to severe erosion by water.

WATER RESOURCES

Nebraska, to the casual observer, is a water-poor state. Much of the state receives inadequate precipitation for the production of many crops, the natural flow of most streams diminishes substantially during late summer, and periodic drought reduces precipitation and soil moisture well below their norms. Yet one of the paradoxes of this subhumid state is its abundant water resources.

Nearly 2 billion acre-ft (2.5 trillion cu m) of recoverable water are found beneath the surface, particularly in the central and west-central parts of the state. Additionally, precipitation annually contributes an average of 90 million acre-ft (110 billion cu m) to Nebraska's water supply. The range is from 60 to 120 million acre-ft (75 to 150 billion cu m) depending on the year. About 2 million acre-ft (2.5 billion cu m) of water flow into Nebraska from other states each year, but 8 million acre-ft (10 billion cu m) flow out of the state, meaning that about 6 million acre-ft (7.5 billion cu m) of stream flow are generated in Nebraska annually.[40]

Both the surface-water supply and the groundwater reservoir reflect a balance between inputs and outputs. For the surface-water supply, the inputs are incoming stream flow, surface runoff, and groundwater contributions; the outputs are evaporation, infiltration, diversions, and outgoing stream flow. Inputs, or recharges, for the groundwater supply are derived from infiltration of precipitation, surface water, and applied irrigation water, all of which increase the amount of water in storage. Principal outputs—in the form of evaporation and transpiration, discharge into streams, and pumping—lower the water table.

Even with such an impressive resource, however, a number of conflicts over water use have developed—conflicts tied to questions about who and what areas have, or should have, use of the state's water. Related questions concern the degree to which use of water can continue to increase, the impact of irrigation development on groundwater supplies and surface-water flows, and what should be done to protect the state's water resources.

Surface Water

The entire state lies within the Missouri River basin and is drained by the Missouri and its tributaries, most notably the Platte. Well over half the state lies within the basin of the Platte, including its largest tributaries, the Elkhorn and the Loup. Other important streams in the state are the Big and Little Blue rivers and the Republican River, all part of the Kansas River drainage system, and the Niobrara River, which rises

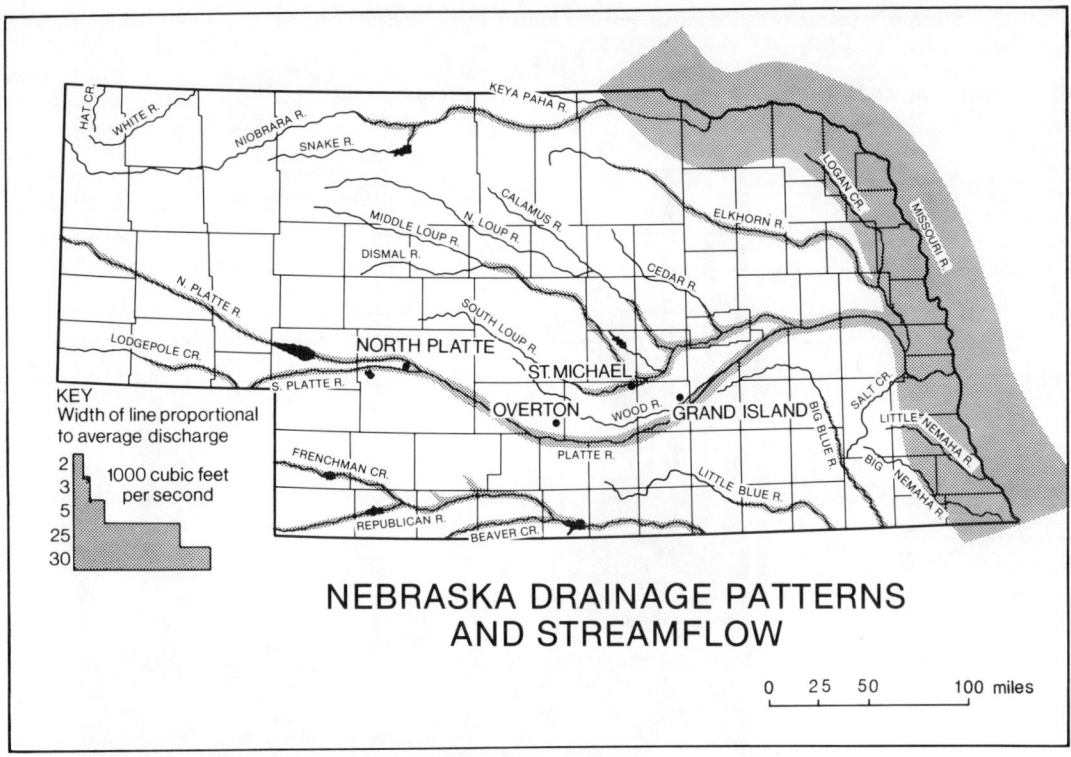

FIGURE 1.14. (UNL, Conservation and Survey Division)

in eastern Wyoming and flows across northern Nebraska (Figure 1.14).

Streams on the Great Plains commonly show considerable variability of flow, both seasonally and from year to year (Figure 1.15). On the North Platte River, which draws much of its flow from Rocky Mountain snowmelt, annual stream flow at the Wyoming state line since 1941 has varied from a low of 280,000 acre-ft (345 million cu m) to a high of 730,000 acre-ft (900 million cu m). The South Platte at Julesburg, Colorado, is even more variable, with an annual average flow of 340,000 acre-ft (420 million cu m), but a range from 60,000 to 1,366,000 acre-ft (74 million to 1.7 billion cu m).[41] Seasonal variations also affect the Platte above the mouth of the Loup. Maximum flows are recorded during June due to snowmelt in the central Rockies, followed by minimum flows in August and September.[12] However, the great range of past years has been considerably subdued by reservoirs, which hold back water during periods of excessive snowmelt and rainfall. Reservoir releases and return flows from irrigation also serve to stabilize flow.

The Loup River system and the upper Elkhorn are exceptions to a general rule of fluctuating flow. About half the total flow of the upper Elkhorn and most of the flow in the Loup River are supplied by groundwater,[43] rather than being augmented by snowmelt. Consequently, seasonal variations are not nearly so great as on many other streams. The relatively stable flow in the Loup basin contributes to greater flow stability in the lower Platte.

Rivers having the greatest variability of discharge are most subject to flooding. The 1935 flood on the Platte, for instance, produced flows as high as 37,600 cfs (cu ft per second) (3,500 cu m per second), more than the average discharge of the Missouri River! Another flood, in 1960, produced a flow of 124,000 cfs (11,500 cu m per second) on the Platte River at Louisville.[44] By contrast, the upper Loup River basin seldom

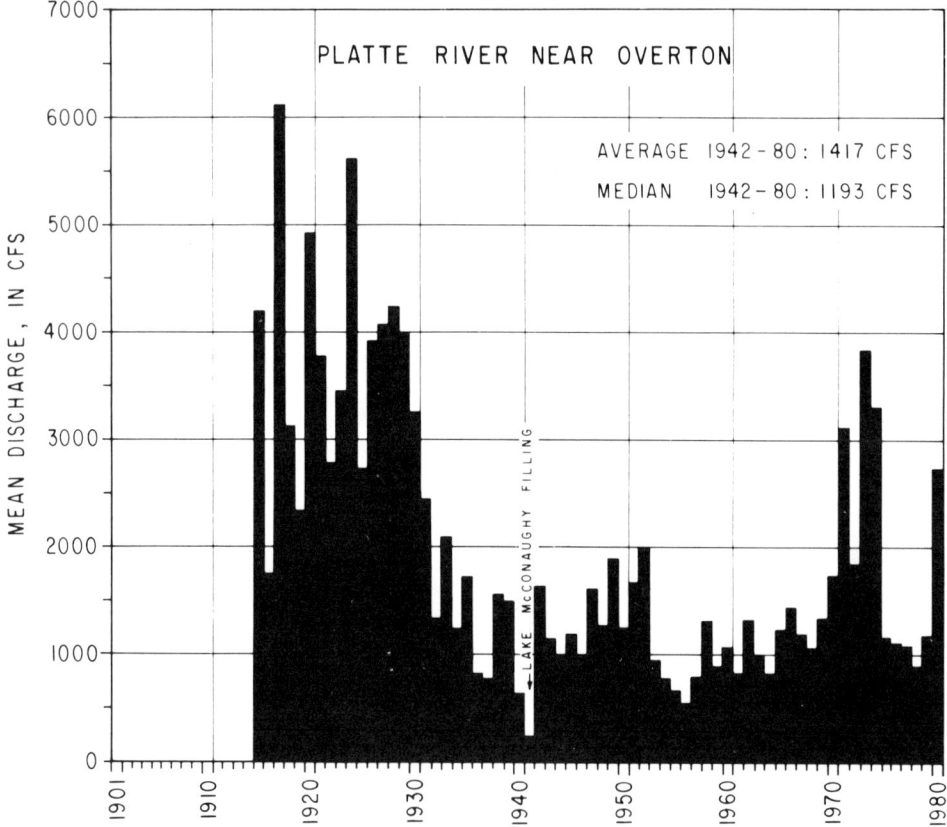

FIGURE 1.15. Average flows on the Platte River, measured in cubic feet per second (cfs), over a sixty-five-year period. (UNL, Conservation and Survey Division)

has major flood damage, as most precipitation infiltrates into the sandy soils rather than flowing overland into stream channels.

Control measures along most streams have helped reduce flood damage during the past forty years. Reservoirs, levees, and channel modification have by no means eliminated flooding, however. The Platte River basin suffers average annual flood damage of nearly twenty million dollars, mainly in the form of crop destruction.[45]

Floods are caused by several factors. On principal rivers and larger tributaries, flooding is typically a product of spring snowmelt, a period of heavy rainfall, or ice jams. Floodwaters on these rivers are usually generated over a period of days or weeks and are likely to persist. On smaller tributaries, flooding is most often caused by intense, localized rainfall, resulting in a very rapid rise of stream discharge. Such floodwaters recede much more quickly than on larger rivers.[46]

Uses of Surface Water

Nebraska surface water is put to a wide variety of consumptive and instream uses. Consumptive uses withdraw water from streams and do not directly return it. Instream uses are those that utilize water without withdrawal or diversion or that return all or most of the withdrawn water.

Irrigation in Nebraska consumed about 2.4 million acre-ft (3.2 billion cu m) of surface water in 1973 (the last year for which data are available—little change has occurred since then) (Figures 1.16 and 1.17).[47] In addition, many irrigation wells

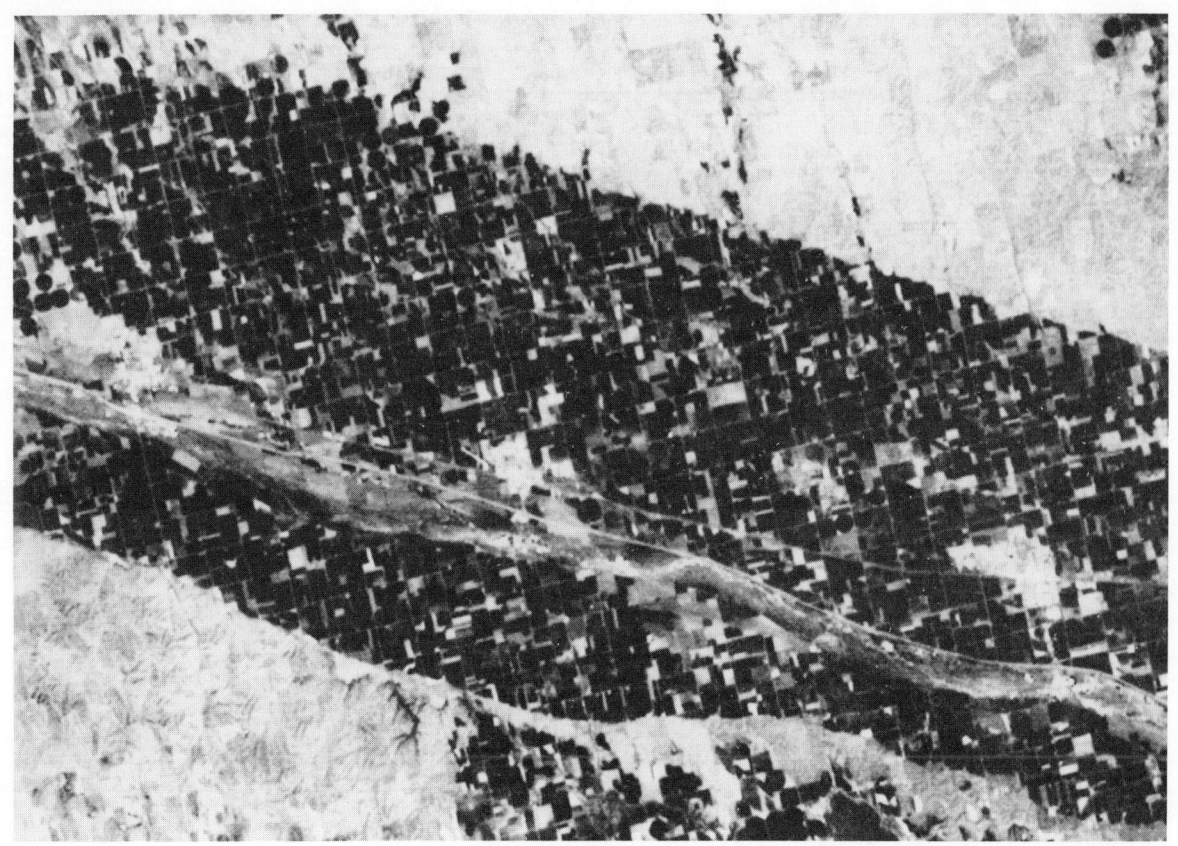

FIGURE 1.16. Irrigation has made the Platte Valley a productive agricultural region. This satellite view of Dawson County shows the contrast between the intensively irrigated lands and the grazing lands away from the floodplain. Lexington is the white area near the lower right, Cozad is near the center, and Interstate 80 is visible as the white line adjacent to the river. (Landsat photo)

depend indirectly upon surface water. Surface water applied to fields, along with infiltration from canals and laterals, has helped raise the water table in several parts of the state.

Instream uses of water in Nebraska include transportation, power generation, livestock watering, wildlife, recreation, and—on the Missouri River—navigation. Below Sioux City, Iowa, the Missouri River has been channelized to 9 ft (2.7 m) deep and 300 ft (90 m) wide. Releases from upstream reservoirs help to maintain adequate flow during the commercial navigation season of April through November. Five hydroelectric plants in Nebraska utilize instream generation facilities. A number of other hydroplants divert water from rivers, notably the Platte and Loup, for generation of electricity; they return most of the withdrawn water.[48]

Many Nebraska farmers and ranchers rely upon streams, lakes, and ponds for livestock watering. In some river basins, 50 percent of livestock water comes from surface-water supplies; most of it is impounded in farm ponds. Actual use of streams and natural lakes for livestock water probably represents about 3 to 5 percent of all livestock water supplies statewide.[49]

Of the 23,686 mi (38,134 km) of streams and canals in the state, 52 percent are considered valuable fishery resources, although reservoirs and lakes attract the larg-

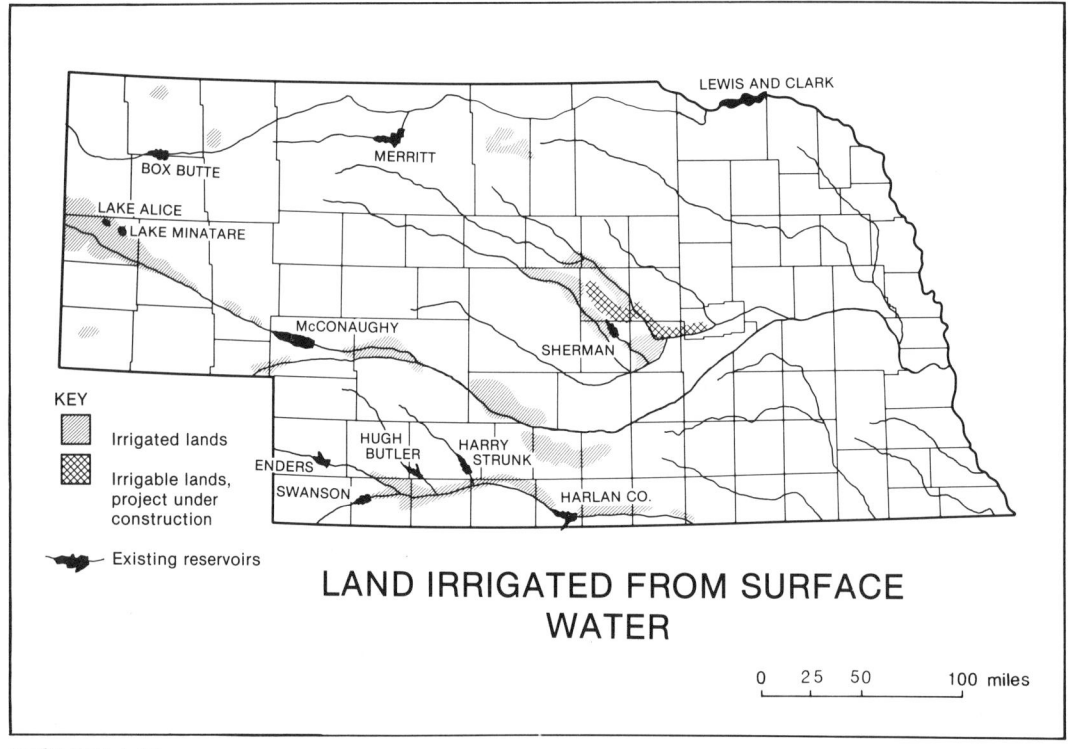

FIGURE 1.17.

est share of anglers. Waterfowl and other wildlife are also dependent on surface water. Ducks and geese use rivers and streams during migration and as winter habitat. Nongame species also are associated with flowing water. Over 200,000 sandhill cranes frequent the Platte River valley during March and April, when 80 percent of North America's sandhill-crane population migrates through the area. Whooping cranes and bald eagles utilize the larger rivers in the state.[50]

Streams and rivers provide recreation opportunities aside from hunting and fishing. Boating, rafting, canoeing, and swimming are among the more popular recreational activities. Demand for many of these is showing a rapid increase; canoeing participation, for example, rose by nearly 60 percent between 1977 and 1980 (Figure 1.18). In response, the Game and Parks Commission has established a program for leasing private land for canoe campsites along 400 mi (640 km) of streams in the state. A number of state rivers possess outstanding scenic, ecological, historical, or cultural characteristics that qualify them for possible inclusion in the National Wild and Scenic Rivers System. One stretch of the Missouri River has already been so designated.[51]

Some Nebraska stream flows are governed by compacts with other states. For example, the Blue River Basin compact between Nebraska and Kansas designates minimum flows across the state line from May through September (Table 1.1). The Nebraska Department of Water Resouces has the authority to order irrigators who pump water from the river to shut down when necessary to maintain sufficient flows into Kansas. Other impacts and decrees affect flow of the South Platte, North Platte, Republican, and Niobrara rivers.[52]

The demands on Nebraska's surface-water supply have converted many rivers in the state from natural systems into managed systems, dominated and heavily con-

FIGURE 1.18. Canoeing is one of the fastest growing forms of recreation in Nebraska. These canoeists are on the Niobrara River at Rocky Ford near Norden. (Jeffrey P. Johnston)

TABLE 1.1

FLOWS REQUIRED BY THE BLUE RIVER BASIN COMPACT

MONTH	LITTLE BLUE RIVER at Fairbury		BIG BLUE RIVER at Barneston	
	Flow level specified in compact (cfs)	Percent of time flow was exceeded 1969-78	Flow level specified in compact (cfs)	Percent of time flow was exceeded 1969-78
January	*		*	
February	*		*	
March	*		*	
April	*		*	
May	45	100.0	45	100.0
June	45	100.0	45	100.0
July	75	99.6	80	91.6
August	80	94.1	90	88.0
September	80	93.0	65	93.6
October	*		*	
November	*		*	
December	*		*	

*Flow level not specified in compact.

Source: Instream Flows Study Group Task Force, <u>Nebraska Policy Issue Study on Instream Flows</u> (Lincoln: Nebraska Natural Resources Commission, 1981).

trolled by human activity. The first irrigation ditch in Nebraska was constructed in 1859. A number of small projects were built in the late nineteenth century, particularly during the droughts of the 1890s, in the Platte and Republican valleys. The first large-scale irrigation project in the state was developed in the North Platte Valley just after the turn of the century.[53] Major dams have been built on main branches or tributaries in the basins of the Niobrara, Platte, Loup, Missouri, and Republican rivers. Flood-control and irrigation-diversion structures further modify these streams. The North Platte River, with nine dams in Wyoming—five on the river and four on tributary streams—plus Kingsley Dam near Ogallala, is one of the most highly developed streams in the United States. Its flow is affected by diversion into three major canals in Wyoming and nearly thirty smaller canals in Nebraska, along with a major diversion to the Sutherland Canal and return flows from irrigated lands.[54]

Public power and irrigation districts, the U.S. Bureau of Reclamation, the Army Corps of Engineers, and private individuals divert water from, and return flows to, Nebraska's rivers. Surface water projects completed in the 1930s and 1940s include the Tri-County Project, which delivers water from the Platte River at Lake McConaughy to 131,000 acres (52,000 ha) in Gosper, Phelps, and Kearney counties. The newest irrigation works are the Ainsworth Project in Brown County, which brings water from Merritt Reservoir on the Snake River to 35,000 acres (14,000 ha), and the Farwell Project, which diverts water from the Middle Loup into Sherman Reservoir on its way to 53,000 acres (21,000 ha) in Sherman and Howard counties.

Groundwater: The Abundant Resource

Nebraska's surface-water supply is dwarfed by the amount of water stored beneath the land surface. Groundwater supplies in the state are not only large but also widely distributed. Generally, recharge and discharge from groundwater are in equilibrium over a period of years, with a net result of fairly stable groundwater supplies. Within a given year, however, groundwater levels fluctuate in response to changing amounts of precipitation, plant growth, temperature, and irrigation demand. In most areas, recharge of aquifers occurs during the spring, with discharge taking place during the summer when water use by plants, withdrawals for irrigation, and evaporation are greatest.

Although the amount of stored groundwater is extremely large, its amount and accessibility vary across the state. The greatest supplies are found in the Sandhills, which are underlain by 700 to 800 million acre-ft (860 to 990 billion cu m) of water stored in the Ogallala formation.[55] In some parts of the Sandhills, Ogallala sediments may be as much as 800 ft (250 m) thick. Because the aquifer is quite permeable, rates of withdrawal by wells typically exceed 500 gal (1,900 l) per minute. High infiltration rates give the Sandhills one of the highest groundwater recharge rates in the Great Plains. Discharges from the aquifer in the Sandhills are primarily by evaporation and transpiration and secondarily to streams. Pumping for irrigation, though growing, remains a relatively unimportant discharge.[56]

In most of the state, large or moderate quantities of groundwater are available. In a few scattered locations, however—particularly in the rough lands bordering the North Platte River, in shale areas north of the Pine Ridge and in Boyd and Keya Paha counties and in parts of eastern Nebraska having clay soils—the principal aquifer is thin or absent. In these areas, bedrock of low permeability keeps well yields to a minimum, and impermeable soils prevent high rates of recharge through infiltration.[57]

Groundwater supplies many municipalities and farms in Nebraska. Livestock in most of the state depend on water pumped from underground supplies. In areas where the water table is near the surface, crops and grasses are supplied with water by subirrigation (Figure 1.19). Several hundred thousand acres of subirrigated land are

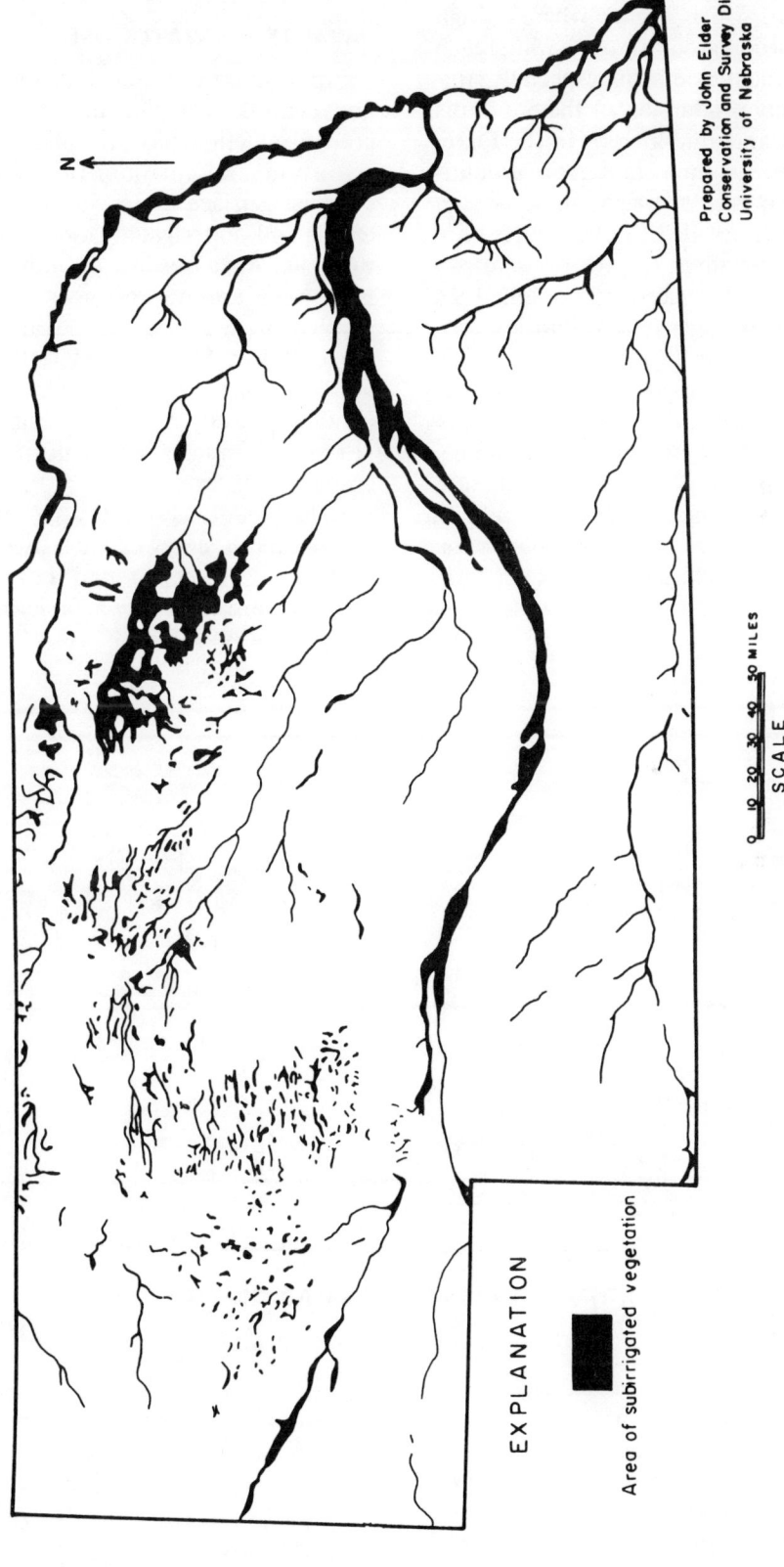

FIGURE 1.19. Subirrigated vegetation. (UNL, Conservation and Survey Division)

located in the Sandhills and near rivers. Subirrigation, which occurs where a high water table brings groundwater within reach of shallow plant roots, is especially important in hay production in the Sandhills and for corn and alfalfa crops in the Platte Valley.[58] The most important use of groundwater is, of course, for irrigation, for which over 6 million acre-ft (7 billion cu m) are withdrawn annually.

Because irrigation accounts for about 92 percent of all water use in Nebraska, Nebraskans use about twice as much water as the national average—about 4,000 gal (15,000 l) per day per Nebraskan.[59] This overwhelming commitment of the state's water resources to irrigation is not surprising, but it means that any discussion about water resources, water problems, or water policy in Nebraska centers on irrigation.[60]

IMPACTS OF WATER USE

Application of water to fields in western and central Nebraska that has enhanced crop production has also affected the distribution and availability of water resources. Surface water in reservoirs and canals and on irrigated land infiltrates into the soil. As a result, groundwater levels have risen around and near a number of reservoirs—McConaughy, Harry Strunk, Hugh Butler, Sherman, Merritt, Maloney, and Sutherland—and in the irrigated lands of the Farwell Project of Sherman and Howard counties. The greatest increase in groundwater levels is over 50 ft (15 m) on the Tri-County Project area of Gosper, Phelps, and Kearney counties. Seepage from Sutherland Reservoir and Lake Maloney has also raised the water table in much of

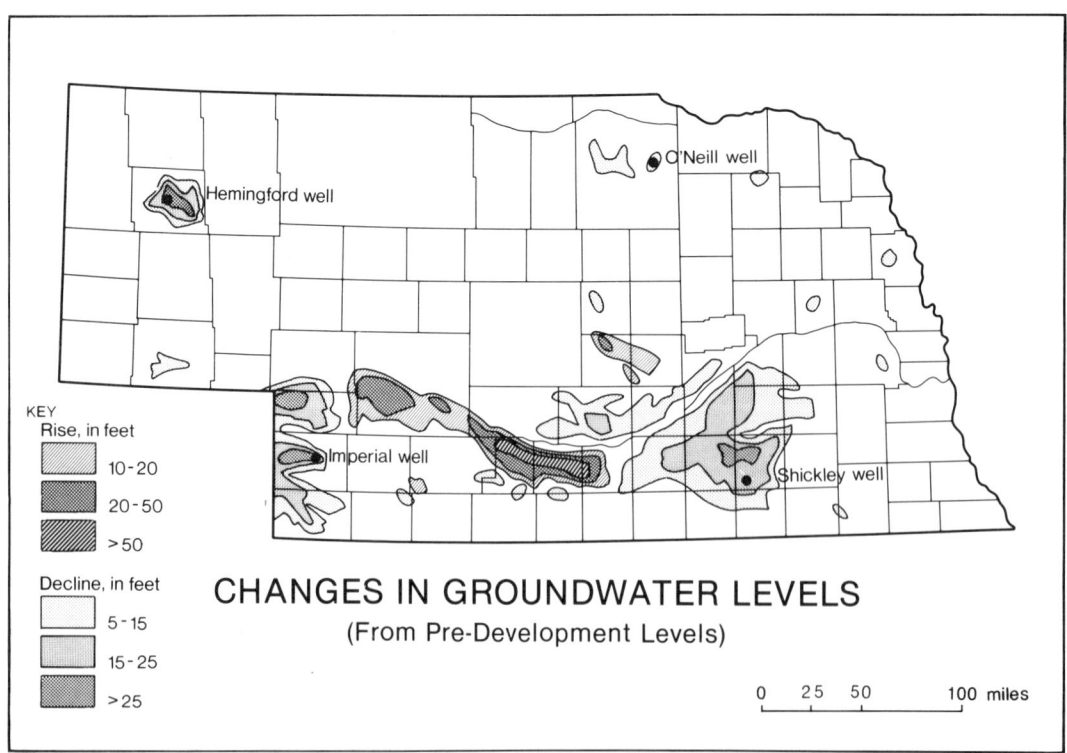

FIGURE 1.20. The four named wells all show a decline in groundwater levels. (UNL, Conservation and Survey Division)

the southern half of Lincoln County.[61] A number of farmers in these areas of augmented groundwater resources now tap the supply with wells, rather than pay the charges assessed by irrigation districts that deliver the water. One estimate suggests that as many acres may now be irrigated with groundwater from rising water tables in the Tri-County project area as are irrigated with surface water distributed by the district.[62]

Declining Groundwater Levels

In other areas, groundwater levels have declined significantly as a result of heavy withdrawals for irrigation (Figure 1.20). The largest area of declining water levels is in the Big Blue River basin, where deep-well irrigation has been practiced for thirty years. Clay, Hamilton, and Fillmore counties are especially affected (Figure 1.21). In some wells the decline is more than 50 ft (15 m) from predevelopment levels. Declines of more than 5 ft (1.5 m) have occurred on approximately 2 million acres (800,000 ha).[63]

A second area of substantial water-level decline is near Alliance, in Box Butte County, where the water table has been dropping since about 1950 (Figure 1.22). The maximum decline is more than 50 ft (15 m) just north of Alliance, but half of Box Butte County has recorded some decline from pre-1950 levels. Water levels are also measurably lower in Holt County, where intensive center-pivot irrigation development has been going on since the late 1950s (Figure 1.23). There the maximum long-term decline is about 20 ft (6 m).[64]

One of the largest areas of net long-term groundwater discharge is in the southwestern part of the state, where numerous center-pivots have been installed in the past two decades (Figure 1.24). Large areas in which the water table has declined more than 30 ft (9 m) occur in Chase and Perkins counties. Somewhat smaller declines have occurred in northern Dundy County. For most of this region, noticeable downward trends in groundwater levels began in the mid-1960s. By the mid-1970s a number of recorder wells were registering declines of 2 ft (0.6 m) per year. As of 1980, more than half of the land area in each of the three counties (over 1 million acres—400,000 ha) showed declines of 5 ft (1.5 m) or more.[65]

When the depth to groundwater increases, irrigators may have to drill deeper wells, and they most certainly face higher fuel costs for lifting water a greater distance. The decrease in groundwater supplies may reduce groundwater contributions to the surface water supply. Less water in streams puts pressure on instream uses and possibly on users of reservoirs downstream, including surface irrigators.

All these factors are present in southwestern Nebraska. Enders Reservoir in Chase County was built on Frenchman Creek by the U.S. Bureau of Reclamation in 1950 as a means of irrigating 22,000 acres (8,800 ha) below the dam. From 1954 until 1969, the reservoir was full or nearly full at the beginning of each irrigation season. After 1970, however, the water level began to fall, and in recent years it has not been adequate for all irrigation needs (Figure 1.25). In 1981 irrigators relying on Enders water had to cut their use from 18 to 6 in. per acre (110 to 37 cm per ha).[66]

The reason for the decrease in water storage in the reservoir was that flows entering the reservoir from Frenchman Creek decreased 19 percent from about 54,000 acre-ft (67 million cu m) per year from 1940 through 1967 to only 40,000 acre-ft (50 million cu m) in 1975.[67] Several causes for the low flows have been suggested, including lower than normal precipitation between 1968 and 1978 and land-use changes in the Frenchman basin that might reduce runoff. Many residents believe, however, that the most important factor has been increased consumption of groundwater. Over nine hundred center-pivot irrigation systems currently operate in Chase County alone (Figure 1.26), most of them in the Frenchman drainage system above Enders Reservoir.[68] A lowered

(text continues on page 30)

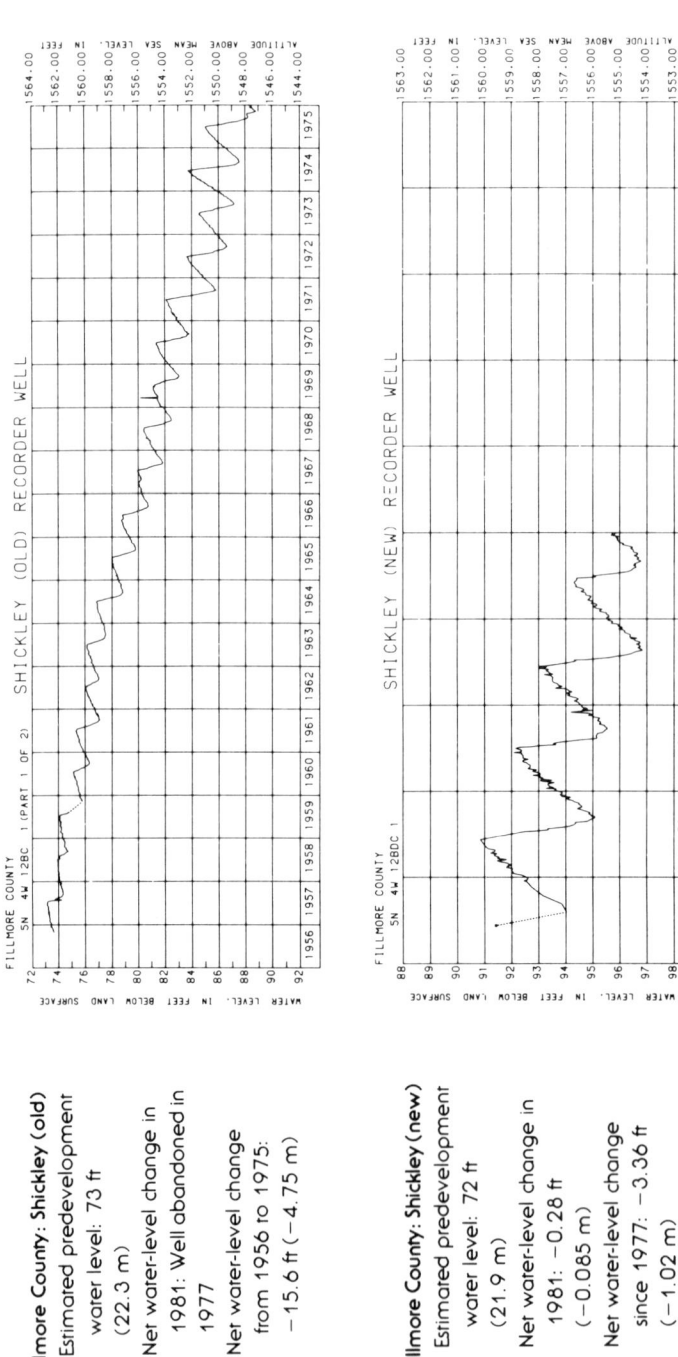

Fillmore County: Shickley (old)
Estimated predevelopment water level: 73 ft (22.3 m)
Net water-level change in 1981: Well abandoned in 1977
Net water-level change from 1956 to 1975: −15.6 ft (−4.75 m)

Fillmore County: Shickley (new)
Estimated predevelopment water level: 72 ft (21.9 m)
Net water-level change in 1981: −0.28 ft (−0.085 m)
Net water-level change since 1977: −3.36 ft (−1.02 m)

FIGURE 1.21. Water-level changes in the Shickley recorder wells (top: 1956–1975; bottom: 1977–1981). (UNL, Conservation and Survey Division)

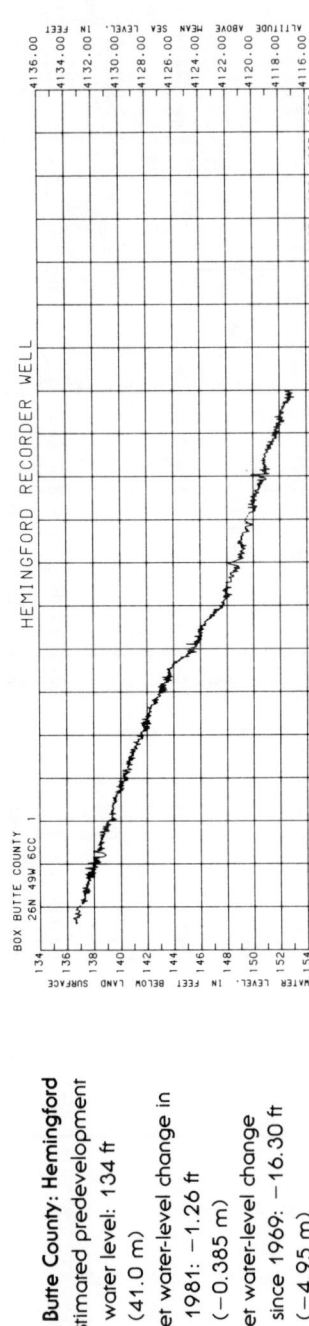

Box Butte County: Hemingford

Estimated predevelopment
water level: 134 ft
(41.0 m)

Net water-level change in
1981: −1.26 ft
(−0.385 m)

Net water-level change
since 1969: −16.30 ft
(−4.95 m)

FIGURE 1.22. Water-level changes in the Hemingford recorder well, 1969–1981. (UNL, Conservation and Survey Division)

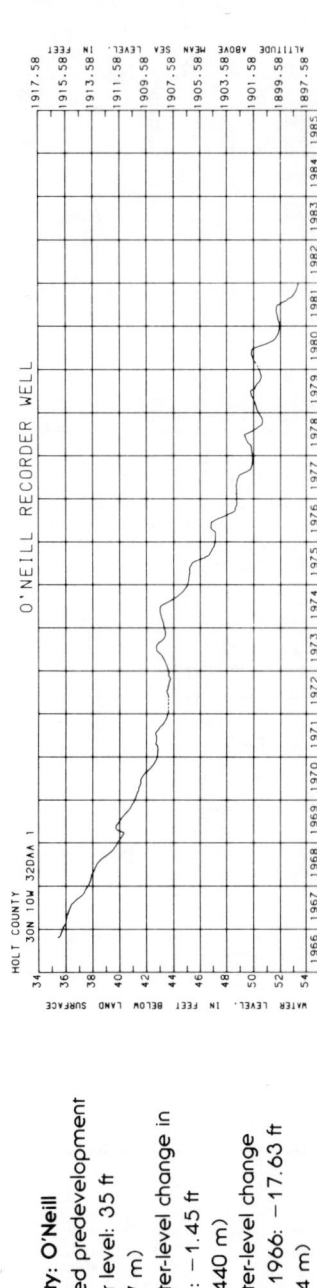

Holt County: O'Neill

Estimated predevelopment
water level: 35 ft
(10.7 m)

Net water-level change in
1981: −1.45 ft
(−0.440 m)

Net water-level change
since 1966: −17.63 ft
(−5.4 m)

FIGURE 1.23. Water-level changes in the O'Neill recorder well, 1966–1981. (UNL, Conservation and Survey Division)

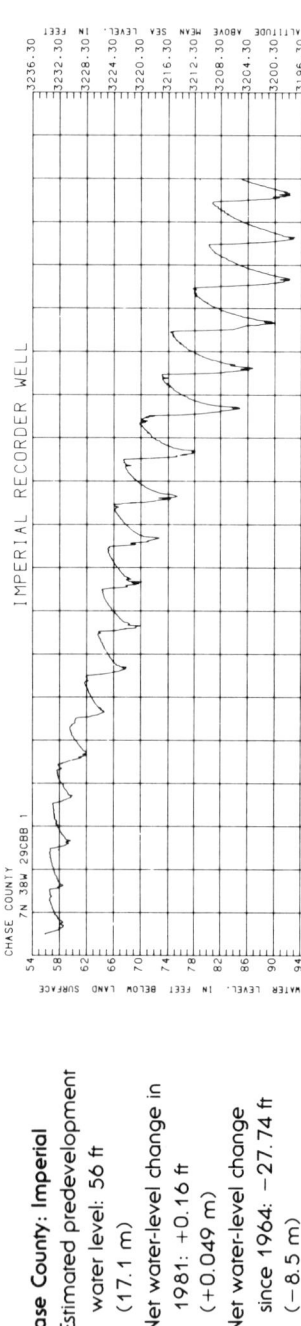

FIGURE 1.24. Water-level changes in the Imperial recorder well, 1964–1981. (UNL, Conservation and Survey Division)

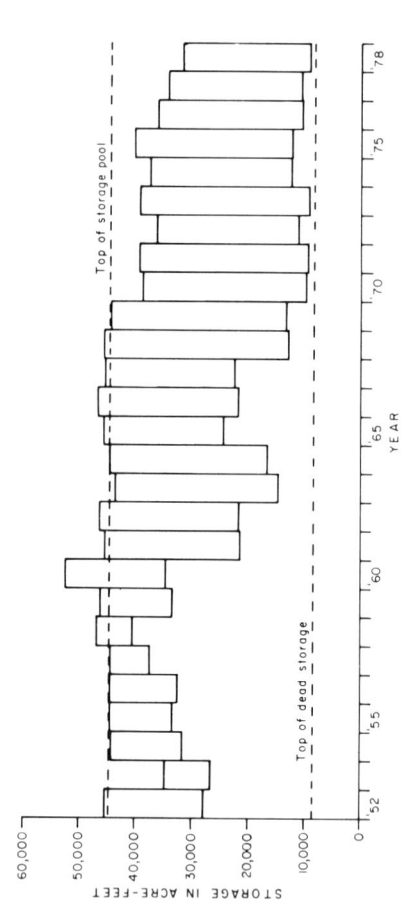

FIGURE 1.25. (*Farm, Ranch and Home Quarterly*)

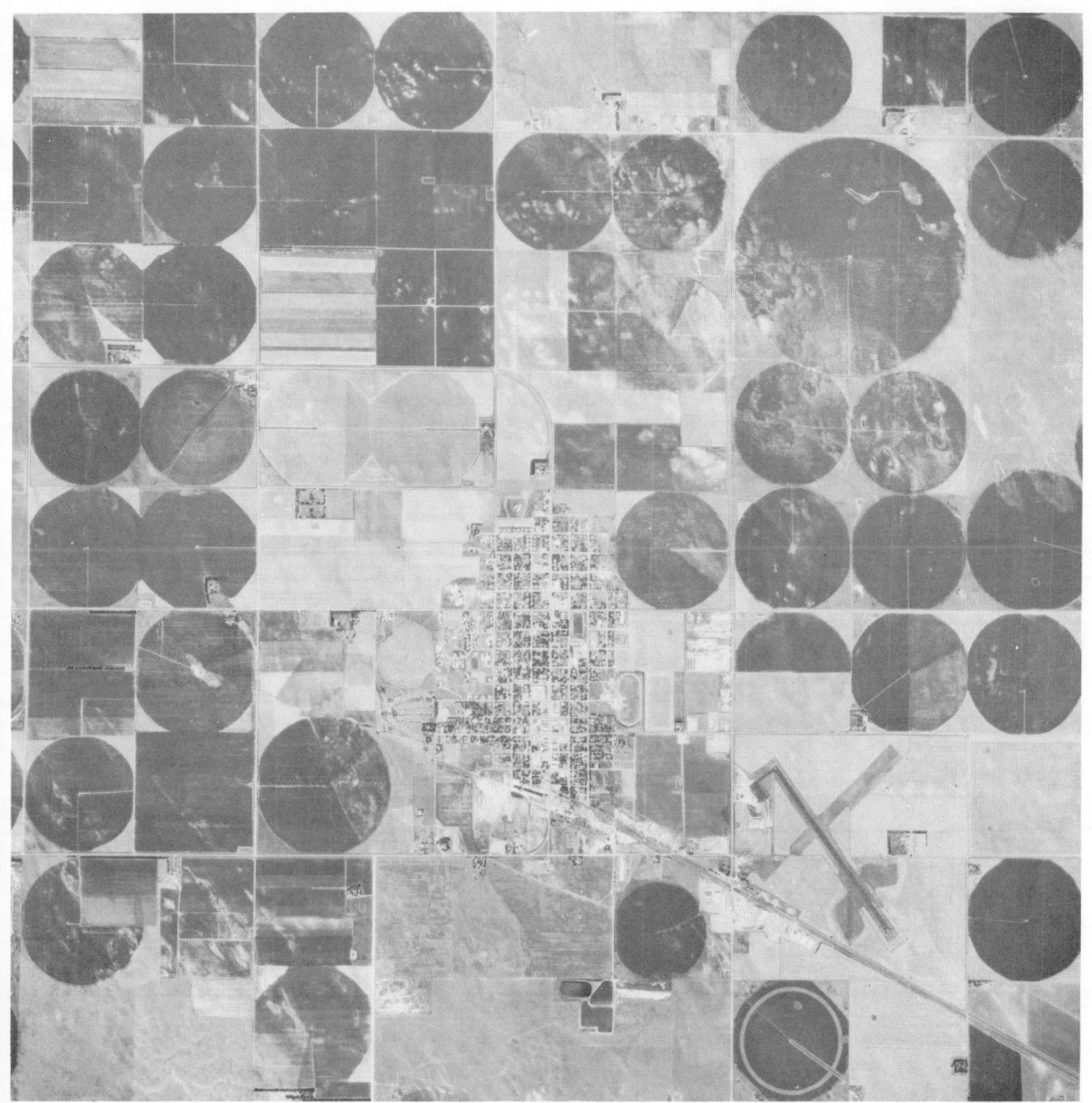

FIGURE 1.26. The pattern of center-pivots surrounding Imperial in Chase County, where groundwater levels have dropped substantially during the past decade. (USDA, ASCS)

groundwater table might well reduce the hydraulic gradient of groundwater flowing toward the Frenchman and consequently contribute to decreased stream flow and lower water levels in the reservoir. Although recent economic conditions have slowed the rate of center-pivot additions in the Frenchman basin, the Bureau of Reclamation estimates that inflow to Enders will be less than 25,000 acre-ft (31 million cu m) per year by the end of the century.[69]

Proposed Water Projects

The decrease in availability of Enders water to surface irrigators has inspired a plan by three irrigation districts to divert water from the South Platte River and deliver it to the reservoir in the Republican River basin. Project supporters have requested rights to 45,000 acre-ft (56 million cu m) of South Platte water. They point out that over 100,000 acre-ft (125 million cu m) flow from the South Platte as unused flood flows each year.

Such a viewpoint, of course, places value only on uses that require diversion, but does not consider the instream uses of water. Opponents of the plan include not only several downstream municipalities and natural resources districts that use Platte River water but also many hunters, anglers, and other persons interested in preserving wildlife habitat. Nebraska law does not currently recognize rights to water for instream uses: Water rights can only be granted for the purpose of diverting water from a stream. This is a view generally shared by irrigators and others "who place high value on the economic benefits derived from consumptive use of water, [while] those who place high value on the fish, wildlife, recreation and aesthetic considerations of streamflows"[70] feel instream uses should be given legal status.

The proposal to divert waters to the Republic basin is not the only such claim being placed on the Platte. Additional projects include a request for 125,000 acre-ft (155 million cu m) to be diverted to the Little Blue River basin and one that would bring 300,000 acre-ft (370 million cu m) into the Upper Big Blue River basin to recharge falling groundwater levels.

The prospect of large-scale transbasin diversion from the Platte River has helped to highlight the conflicts over water use in Nebraska.[71] Even more grandiose proposals call for movement of much larger amounts of water greater distances than those envisioned for the Frenchman or Big Blue areas. Several schemes for transbasin diversion involve transfer of water from the Niobrara and Loup rivers to the Platte, Republican, and Big and Little Blue basins. One would transfer Niobrara water to the Platte via five diversion dams in the Sandhills. A more extreme proposal calls for reversing the flow of the Niobrara River and diverting it south, perhaps as far as Texas, to irrigate areas where groundwater supplies have become critically short.[72] The costs for these large transfer projects are so high as to be prohibitive at the present time, but they concern many Nebraskans who fear the prospect of exporting a valuable resource.

Of more immediate interest to the Nebraskans is the possibility of water sales, particularly from the Missouri River. A recent proposal calls for the sale of water from Oahe Reservoir in South Dakota to Energy Transportation Systems Inc., a pipeline firm, for use in transporting Wyoming coal to Arkansas. This particular deal involves only 50,000 acre-ft (61 million cu m) of water per year, but some are concerned about the precedent that could be set for much larger transfers of Missouri River water. This could eventually threaten well fields and sewage-disposal systems and disrupt navigation on the river from Sioux City to St. Louis, though such depletions probably lie well in the future. In response, proposals have been introduced in Congress to require approval of similar projects by affected states.

Additional large-scale surface irrigation projects have also been proposed for Nebraska. The North Loup project, now under construction, will irrigate 53,000 acres

(21,000 ha) along and near the North Loup River. Two other proposals seek to divert up to 500,000 acre-ft (610 million cu m) of Platte River water to irrigate 125,000 acres (50,000 ha) and supplement declining water tables in Buffalo and Hall counties. This is about half the average annual flow of the river in the Grand Island area. These two projects have not yet reached the stage of a feasibility study. However, should they appear to be serious contenders for water in the river, strong opposition is likely to develop. Diversions of this scale, along with transbasin diversions to the Republican and Little Blue valleys of 170,000 acre-ft (207 milion cu m), could very likely reduce Platte flows below the level considered necessary to maintain wildlife and waterfowl habitats.

A fourth project, authorized by Congress but embroiled in controversy, is the O'Neill Unit. In many ways the debate over this proposal illustrates the principal conflicts involved in most water projects in the western half of the United States. The O'Neill Unit, for which specific plans were authorized in 1972, would feature a dam on the Niobrara south of Norden and 362 mi (583 km) of canals and laterals to deliver water to 77,000 acres (31,000 ha) of land in Holt and Keya Paha counties (Figure 1.27).

Supporters of the project point to the need to use water rather than let it run out of the state and to the economic benefits to be derived not only by irrigators but also by the local community and the state. They suggest that the project will generate $108 million of economic activity in the state annually. Proponents also point out that seepage from canals and laterals, along with application of irrigation water to fields, will help recharge groundwater supplies.[73] Total cost of the project was estimated by the Bureau of Reclamation in 1981 at $331 million, or approximately $4,000 per irrigable acre ($10,000 per ha), substantially

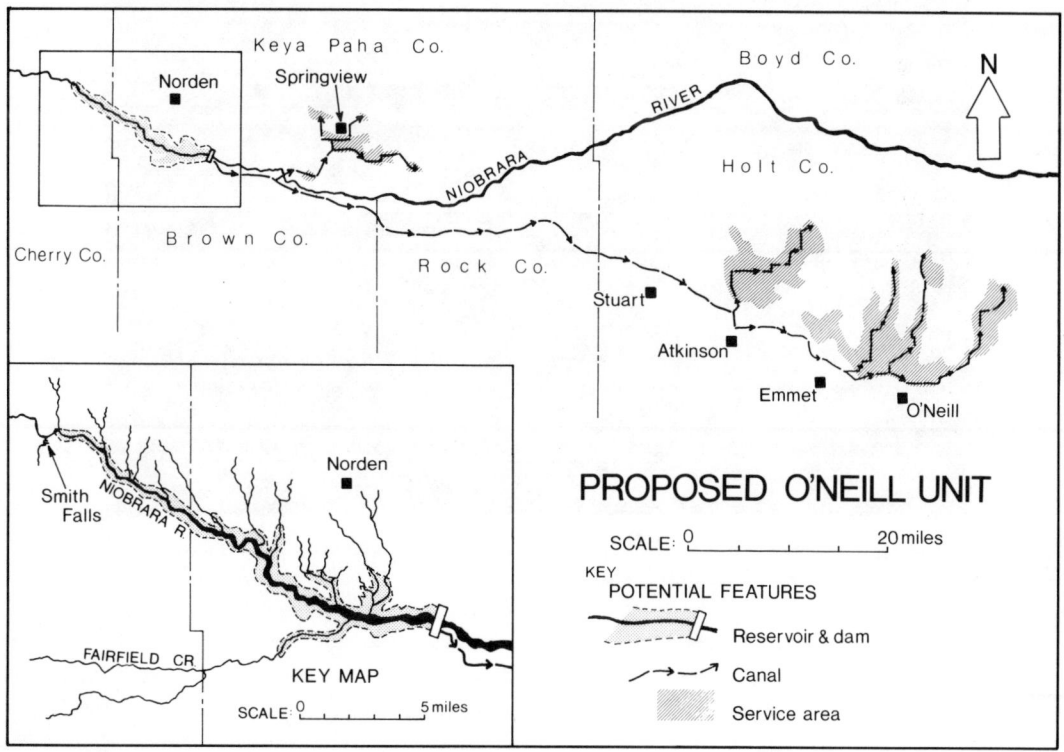

FIGURE 1.27.

FIGURE 1.28. Niobrara River, looking east. The proposed Norden Dam would inundate most of the low-lying land in this area.

higher than the cost of center-pivot irrigation. When benefits from the project, as calculated by the Bureau of Reclamation, are compared with costs, the benefit-cost ratio is computed to be 1.52:1.

Opposition has centered on the costs of the project and on the environmental impacts expected on the Niobrara River valley. Opponents have charged the Bureau of Reclamation with inflating the benefits to be derived from the project by underestimating corn production costs, overestimating yields, and assuming increased corn production would result in increased livestock feeding in the area. One analysis contends that the bureau "is assuming a technology of production and a cost of inputs more consistent with current (or even outdated) practices while assuming yield levels at least 50 percent above present averages."[74] University of Nebraska agricultural economists estimate a more accurate benefit-cost ratio of 0.27:1, using an interest rate of 3.25 percent. A more realistic rate of 10 percent would reduce the benefit-cost ratio even further.[75]

The other principal set of objections relates to the impacts on the Niobrara River and on the ecosystems of its valley (Figure 1.28). Here, debate centers on the proposed Norden Dam, a 180-ft (55-m)-high structure, which would create a 19-mi (31-km) long reservoir. About 6,300 acres (2,500 ha) would be inundated. The Niobrara is described by opponents of the project as a unique area and a biological crossroads of the nation, containing six distinct habitat types and a rich variety of plant, bird, and animal life. These environmental qualities led the Nature Conservancy, a leading land-conservation organization, to purchase a 54,000-acre (22,000-ha) ecological preserve along the river at a cost of nearly eleven million dollars in private funds. Additionally, the river has become a popular canoeing stretch, the most challenging portions of which will be inundated by the reservoir.

Other concerns have been raised about stream flows below the dam, but the criticisms that are likely to have the greatest impact are cost-related. Water projects nationwide have become increasingly difficult to justify on an economic basis, and water-project proponents face the reality of high costs, decreased support for major projects, competition from other water users, and stronger national support for preservation of natural areas.

Nebraska's Water Future

Future water availability and use have been subjects of intensive study and debate in Nebraska. Individuals and groups supporting irrigation development, stream-flow maintenance, municipal water use, habitat maintenance, environmental preservation, and other water uses have sought to influence water policy.[76]

As groundwater levels have begun to decline, the state has adopted policies aimed at controlling the quantity and quality of the resource. If the directors of a Natural Resources District believe groundwater problems require controls, they can request a hearing with the Department of Water Resources, which may establish a Groundwater Control Area. If a control area is established, the Natural Resources District may impose well-spacing restrictions, rotation of withdrawal rights, limits on withdrawals, or a one-year moratorium on new wells.[77]

Even with expected improvements in irrigation efficiency and more stringent allocation of groundwater, levels will continue to decline. Imposition of strict water-conservation measures is unlikely to prevent several irrigated areas from reverting to dryland crop production by the year 2020. Without these measures groundwater resources are projected to be exhausted on 1.5 million acres (600,000 ha) (Figure 1.29). However, Nebraska's irrigated acreage will continue to expand. Most currently irrigated areas will still have groundwater available in 2020, unlike the situation in other plains states utilizing the Ogallala aquifer (Figure 1.30).[78]

The future of the surface-water resource in the state hinges on decisions made about

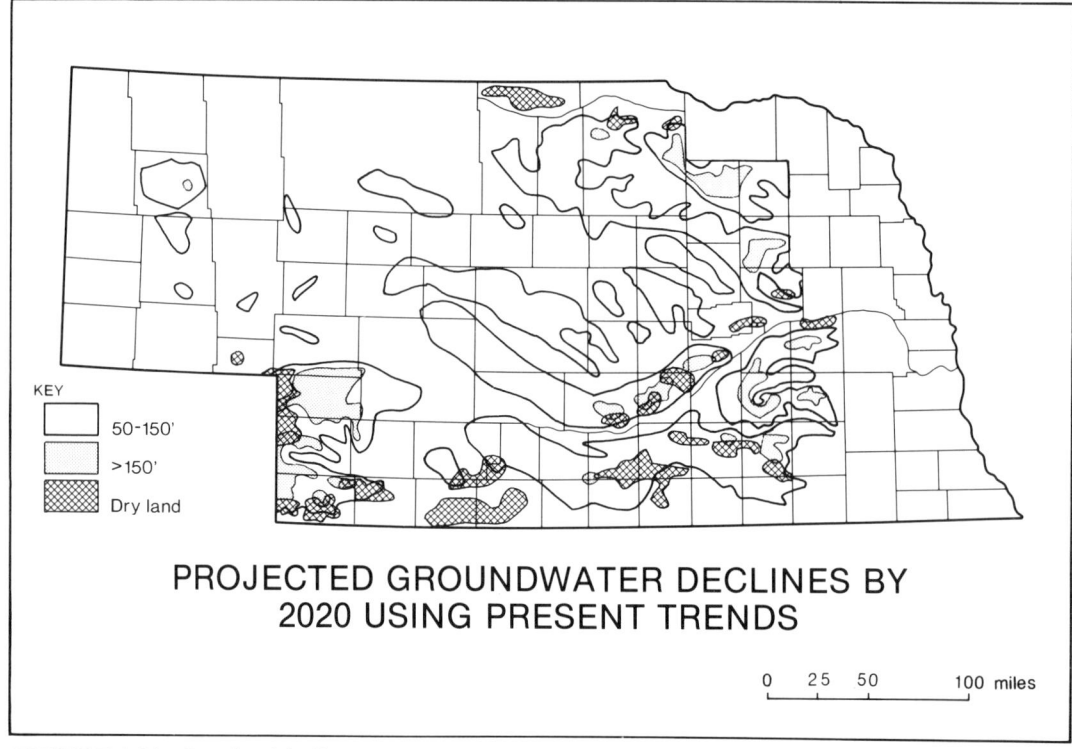

FIGURE 1.29. *Dry land* indicates areas where groundwater supplies are projected to be exhausted by 2020. (Adapted from Nebraska Natural Resources Commission)

both groundwater and surface-water use. Groundwater withdrawals will depend upon both individual and policy decisions, whereas additional surface diversions will hinge on governmental decisions and funding at the state and federal levels.

Given the probable increased use of groundwater for irrigation, it is likely that substantial reductions in average stream flows will occur, particularly in the Platte River basin (Table 1.2). Average flow in the Platte above the mouth of the Loup River is predicted to be about half its 1970 level by 2020. The number of months with no flow in the river at Grand Island is expected to increase from one per year to about four per year—in other words, zero flow one-third of the time. Many streams in the Loup River system will have similar flow reductions. The South Loup might well show zero flow as much as seven months a year, compared to the historical situation of no dry months.[79]

The impacts of surface-water irrigation projects on stream flows have also been projected. Completion of the North Loup and Cedar River projects is expected to deplete flows on those rivers, but their effect on the Loup system and on the Platte will not be severe. Development of a major project on the central Platte would reduce flows of that river by up to 25 percent of current flows at Grand Island. The combined effect of these projects, along with expected groundwater withdrawals, could reduce Platte River flow at Ashland to 55–67 percent of its 1970 condition, with groundwater development throughout the Platte basin being responsible for 80 to 90 percent of that reduction.[80] Water projects outside the state, particularly in Colorado, could also significantly affect stream flows. Possible transbasin diversions add uncertainty to the estimation of future stream flows.

The probable impacts of reduced flows

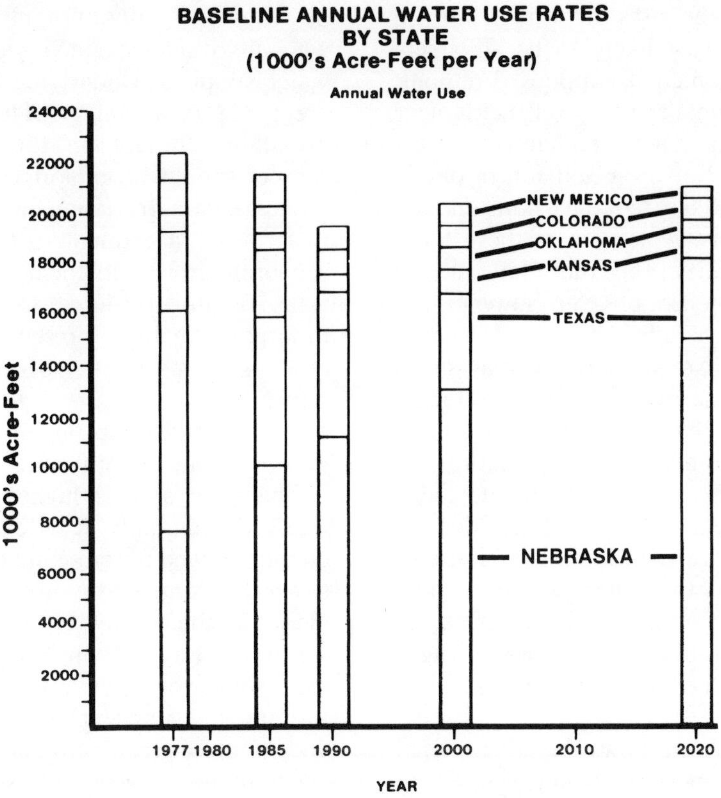

BASELINE ANNUAL WATER USE RATES BY STATE
(1000's Acre-Feet per Year)

FIGURE 1.30. (Nebraska Natural Resources Commission)

TABLE 1.2

EFFECT OF GROUNDWATER IRRIGATION DEVELOPMENT

ON STREAM FLOWS

Stream	Average Annual Flow (cubic feet per sec.)			Average Months/Yr. Without Flow		
	1970 condition	Projected Flow		1970 condition	Projected Flow	
		2020-low[a]	2020-high[a]		2020-low[a]	2020-high[a]
Elkhorn at Norfolk	499	407	353			
South Loup at St. Michael	1,252	154	69	0	1.00	6.73
Middle Loup at St. Paul	1,006	777	547	0	.57	1.83
N. Loup near St. Paul	919	738	583	0	.03	.40
Beaver Cr. at Genoa	128	88	67	0	.53	2.37
S. Platte at Julesburg	471	254	217	0	.10	.70
N. Platte at Lewellen	1,250	1,228	1,189	0	0	0
Platte near Overton	1,108	648	560	0	.20	.37
Platte near Grand Island	1,071	563	475	1.10	3.87	4.30
Platte near Ashland	5,116	3,890	3,225	0	.17	.43

[a] Low and high refer to the extent of groundwater irrigation.

Source: Missouri River Basin Commission, *Report on the Platte River Basin, Nebraska Level B Study* (Omaha: Missouri River Basin Commission, 1976). Reprinted by permission.

depend upon the uses to which surface water is put. Least likely to be adversely affected are municipal supplies. Fremont, Lincoln, and Omaha have well fields near the Platte River that are recharged in part by infiltration, but projected future developments are unlikely to reduce flows enough to cause serious depletions at these locations. Communities on the Platte above the mouth of the Loup River, however, are more likely to be affected.

A number of smaller streams may suffer flow reductions serious enough to limit their usefulness for livestock watering; others may see deterioration of subirrigation for hay production and wildlife habitat. Reductions in stream flow would also deplete populations of waterfowl and contribute to deterioration of the fishery resource. The habitats of such endangered species as the whooping crane and the bald eagle might also be threatened by major stream-flow reductions.[81]

Should instream flows be given legal standing, with permits being granted to maintain certain flow levels, some of these projections will have to be altered. Other policy alternatives include the establishment of protected flow levels, the development of a state system of protected rivers, and the imposition of restrictions on the use of groundwater upstream or along streams with significant instream values and needs.[82] Given the intensity of competition between irrigators, other consumptive users, and those who support maintenance of instream flows, the eventual nature of water resources in Nebraska is far from certain.

At opposite ends of the water-policy spectrum are those who support rapid development without controls and those who advocate sustained yield of groundwater supplies. Underlying their positions are two sets of values. The development orientation hinges on the view that resources should be exploited for short-term economic gain. Irrigation has brought wealth to farmers, investment to rural areas, and economic growth to towns, cities, and the state. To limit resource use would amount to forgoing real and present economic benefits for the possibility of unknown future returns.

Advocates of sustained-yield management of water point out that sustained discharge at a level higher than recharge rate will eventually deplete an aquifer. Reduction in well output can be accomplished either by controls on use now or by depletion of the aquifer. Groundwater mining can only delay sustained yield, but it may result in serious economic, social, and environmental impacts. Sustained-yield advocates place greater emphasis on the water needs of future generations and on noneconomic considerations such as wildlife, aesthetics, and recreation.[83]

Both positions are reflected in the debate over transbasin diversions. To irrigators relying on shrinking reservoirs or falling groundwater levels, transbasin diversion is a means of keeping flowing water within the state and of maintaining farm operations at current levels of productivity. To opponents it represents an unwillingness to accept the limited nature of resources and the need to use renewable resources at sustainable levels. As one cynical view puts it: Transbasin diversion is a way of assuring that all streams in the state will go dry at the same time.

CHAPTER 2

SETTLEMENT: OCCUPANCE, UTILIZATION, AND ADAPTATION

Physical entities such as soil, grasses, and water do not constitute resources. Nor do they determine the uses to which the environment will be put. The definition of resources and the decisions about their use are made by the cultures that occupy an area. Economy, technology, and belief systems all influence how a culture will identify resources in the physical environment.[1]

A number of different cultures have inhabited the area now encompassed by the state of Nebraska. Each has had different ways of utilizing and dealing with the physical phenomena of soil, climate, vegetation, and water. Each has modified certain aspects of the environment. Each has established a particular form of economy and pattern of settlement. This chapter examines the ways in which the white population entered the state, acquired land, established settlements, and erected transportation and economic systems that supported the growth of commercial agriculture. The development during the latter decades of the nineteenth century of an agricultural system adapted to the subhumid reality of the state will also be discussed.

OCCUPANTS OF THE GREAT PLAINS

The first inhabitants of the central Great Plains probably arrived more than ten thousand years ago. They were principally big-game hunters, dependent on now-extinct large mammals such as the mammoth and mastodon. They were almost certainly nomadic, following the movements of game animals. Archaeological sites associated with these peoples are found primarily in the western half of the state.[2]

There followed a several-thousand-year period during which rainfall was less, temperatures were higher than previously, and the plains appear to have been abandoned by humans. Presumably the large mammals migrated to more temperate regions, and the cultures that depended on them followed. About 2500 B.C. migratory hunters returned.

Not all prehistoric peoples were nomadic hunters. By A.D. 1100 several semisedentary, agricultural peoples were located in what is now Nebraska. Two of these groups, designated Upper Republican Culture and

Nebraska Culture, lived in earth-covered dwellings in villages along the bluffs of the Missouri River and on the stream terraces of the Republican and Loup rivers. Both groups were seasonal hunters who also raised corn, beans, squash, and sunflowers. They apparently took fish from the rivers, made pottery, and conducted a fairly extensive trade with other peoples. Speculation about the reasons for their abandonment of these areas around A.D. 1500 centers on drought, which may have affected crop yields and caused migration of the bison herds upon which the peoples were heavily dependent.

Nebraska's Native Cultures

During the early historic period at least three major groups inhabited present-day

---

Focus: Prehistoric Resources—A Nebraska Culture Site in Cass County

Plant materials provided a source of food, fire, and shelter. Vegetable matter may also have been used for containers and clothing, although the data are not sufficient to substantiate this assumption. The cultivation of maize is directly demonstrable, and the growing of at least beans, squash, and sunflowers at this time and place in the plains may be inferred at a high level of probability. The growing of tobacco or some similar plant is inferred on the bases that these people were horticultural and that pipes are represented in the material complex. There is direct evidence that they gathered walnuts, acorns, and wild plums. In addition, other nuts and seeds were undoubtedly gathered as food resources. Wood—oak, black walnut, green ash, plum, willow, [eastern redcedar], and cottonwood—was used in the construction of lodges and for fire. Quite probably a variety of objects were made of wood but were not preserved: bows, arrows, spoons, bowls, paddles, digging sticks, pipe stems, and hafts. Grasses were used in the construction of lodges and in fires. They were also used as lining materials in storage pits and as pads for wiping and smoothing pottery. Plant materials were undoubtedly used for the manufacture of cordage, which appears as impressions on the walls of pottery.

Animal resources were used for food, clothing, adornment, tools, and tempering for pottery. Large mammals (bison, elk, and deer), small mammals (rabbits, beaver, gophers), birds, and freshwater clams provided food. Most of the mammals were probably hunted within the wooded valley; bison may have been pursued along the grassy uplands. There is no direct evidence of fishing, although this economic activity is evidenced at similar sites in eastern Nebraska. Skins, furs, and feathers were undoubtedly used for clothing and adornment. Intensive skin working is indicated by the large numbers of scrapers, knives, and other artifacts. Mammal bones provided a source material for a variety of artifacts including hoes, awls, needles, and knapping tools. Clam shells were used as a tempering material for some pottery and may have served as small containers and spoons.

A variety of local mineral resources was utilized by the inhabitants. The fertile flood-bottom soils provided a rich medium for the cultivation of maize and other plant products, and earth was used as a construction material in building houses. The earthen cover of the lodges acted as an insulating material, keeping the house interior warm in winter and cool in summer. Clays were utilized for the manufacture of ceramic containers and pipes. Local limestones, conglomerates, and sandstones were obtained for the manufacture of grinding and abrading utensils and tools, and occasionally for pipes. Iron oxides from these local bedrocks were collected for use as pigments. Flints and cherts from local limestones and river gravels were the primary medium for the manufacture of weapon points and of chopping, cutting, and scraping tools. Glacial erratics from tills in the locality were utilized for grinding, hammering, and chopping tools. Crushed granites and sand were used as a source of tempering in the majority of the ceramics.

Some stone materials may have been obtained outside the region. Catlinite, for example, does not occur naturally [in Cass County], and certain of the colored flints and cherts do not appear to be present locally. However, the lack of obvious trade materials reinforces the picture of an intensive utilization of local ecological resources by the inhabitants of the site.

Source: David Mayer Gradwohl, *Prehistoric Villages in Eastern Nebraska,* Publications in Anthropology, no. 4 (Lincoln: Nebraska State Historical Society, 1969), pp. 111–112. Reprinted by permission of the Nebraska State Historical Society.

Nebraska. The Oneonta Culture was in the state by the early seventeenth century. These sedentary peoples cultivated crops of corn and beans, caught fish, and hunted throughout the prairies of what are now Iowa, Minnesota, Wisconsin, northeastern Kansas, and southeastern Nebraska. They were probably the forerunners of the Missourias, Otos, and Iowas who still inhabited part of southeastern Nebraska in the early nineteenth century. Members of a second sedentary culture, located near the mouth of the Loup River by 1600, were probably the early Pawnees. Like the Oneonta, they hunted, cultivated crops, made pottery, and kept dogs. Like the Pawnees, they lived in large earth lodges.

The third group, a principally nomadic culture, was located in the Sandhills on stream terraces and on the shores of lakes by 1700. Although they had some corn, they did not keep large surpluses, and they emphasized hunting. This Dismal River Culture is believed to have been the Plains Apaches, who were probably driven south by Comanches on horseback moving east out of the Rocky Mountains in the early eighteenth century.

Thus, there were nomadic hunters and village-dwelling farmer/hunters in Nebraska when early white contact with the plains cultures took place. All groups were dependent on bison, with sedentary groups raising corn and other crops. In the western half of the state where the growing season and rainfall were less favorable for corn, farming was limited or nonexistent.

Initially these groups depended upon the bison and grasses of the Great Plains and upon a climate that permitted varying degrees of success with corn growing, but the introduction of a new technology in the seventeenth and eighteenth centuries substantially changed their abilities to utilize the plains environment. That new technology was the horse, first brought to the plains by Coronado in the sixteenth century. By 1640, trading and raiding had distributed horses from the Spanish lands in New Mexico as far as present-day western Kansas. Within the next one hundred years horses had diffused as far north as the Blackfeet of what is now Alberta. The increased mobility that the horse brought to plains cultures made food acquisition much easier than before. The strength of the mounted groups increased relative to those who were still pedestrians, so that nomadic hunters benefited more than did village cultures.

Until the mid-nineteenth century the eastern half of the state was occupied by village dwellers, and the western half was populated by nomadic groups (Figure 2.1). Most numerous of the farming peoples were the Pawnees, who were settled in villages along the lower Loup, Platte, and Republican rivers. Here, on river terraces, they raised corn and other crops and produced pottery from stone and bone. Twice a year they left their settlements for extended hunting trips—a summer hunt after the corn had been cultivated and a winter hunt after the harvest. Adoption of the horse (the Pawnees had six to eight thousand horses by the early nineteenth century) allowed them to hunt more intensively, but they retained their agricultural ways.[3]

The eastern quarter of the state was the home of a number of Siouan linguistic groups: Poncas, Omahas, Otos, Missourias, and Iowas. All had probably come originally from east of the Allegheny Mountains, and most were settled in Nebraska by 1650 or 1700. The Poncas and Omahas were the more numerous and powerful groups, but all relied upon farming in combination with buffalo hunting. The decline of these eastern groups began well before white settlement of Nebraska. Gradually these peoples became heavily dependent upon white trade goods and abandoned traditional pottery and stonework in favor of metal goods supplied by traders, and their cultures were substantially modified by contact with advancing European cultures. Smallpox epidemics in the late eighteenth century, brought in by white traders and trappers, seriously reduced their numbers and strength.[4]

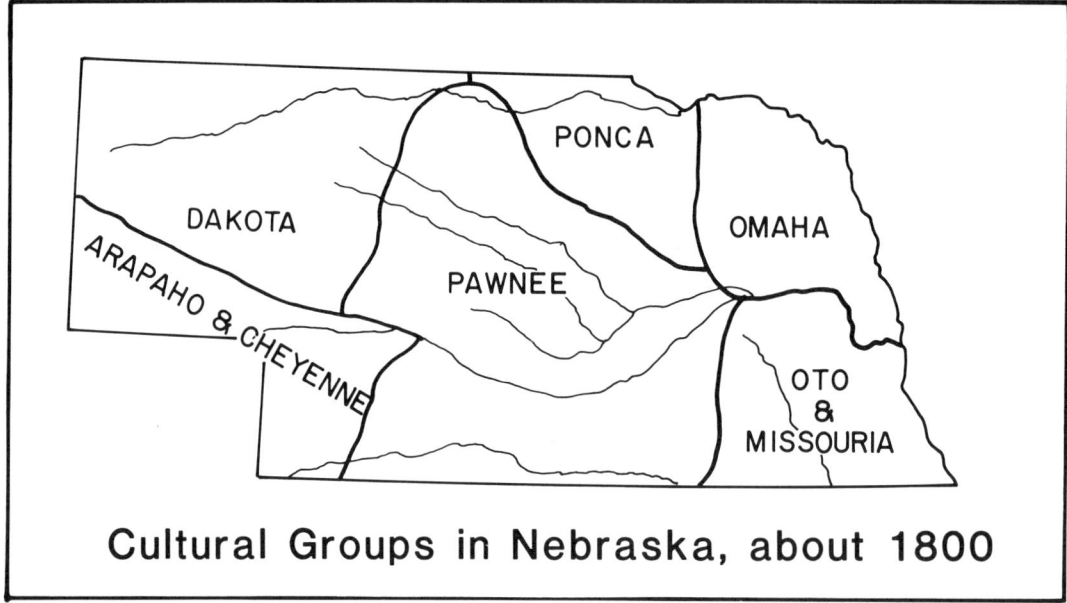

FIGURE 2.1.

The Dakotas, Cheyennes, and Arapahos of the western third of the state depended almost entirely upon the bison. They practiced little agriculture, although they gathered fruits, berries, and roots in addition to hunting. Their mobility not only made them quite powerful but also insulated them to some extent from the impact of white society, which eroded the cultures of the more sedentary groups.[5]

The Dakotas, largest of the nomadic groups, probably did not arrive in Nebraska until the early part of the nineteenth century, when they were driven out of the forests of the upper Mississippi region by Ojibwas who had guns obtained from traders. By 1800 the Dakotas were a powerful force on the central and northern plains, where they raided more sedentary groups such as the Pawnees.[6]

Dakota culture—religion, economy, social organization—was centered upon the tremendous abundance of bison. Until the middle of the nineteenth century, enormous herds grazed throughout the grasslands. The explorer John C. Fremont reported: "A traveler may start from any given point south or north of the Rocky Mountain range, and during the whole distance, his road would always be among large herds of buffalo, which would never be out of his view until he arrived within sight of the abodes of civilization."[7]

The Dakotas and other plains groups such as Cheyennes and Arapahos made thorough use of the bison: Much of the animal could be eaten; the skins provided clothing and shelter; nearly every part of the animal, including bones, horns, and hair, could be put to use. Large-scale wanton killing by plains peoples was not uncommon as long as the resource was abundant. Fire drives, stalking, or driving herds over cliffs were frequently used.[8] It seemed that only the destruction of this central resource could seriously damage Dakota culture and power.

That destruction, when it came, was incredibly swift. By 1850, buffalo were only infrequently seen along the principal migrant trails. White hunters seeking skins or sport slaughtered millions of bison, which were nearly wiped out by 1880.[9] With the near extinction of the bison came the destruction of the power of the plains Indians. Their most significant resource gone, they

FIGURE 2.2. Ration day at the Pine Ridge Agency (near the turn of the century). (NSHS)

were reduced to almost complete dependence upon government supplies (Figure 2.2).

Early Incursions by Whites

White contact with the plains did not occur until 1541, when Coronado set out to discover mineral wealth in the center of North America. For about two hundred years the Spanish, operating out of Santa Fe, were the only whites to enter the central plains. When Spanish influence waned, the French entered the region. As their interest lay principally in trade, much of their early exploration of the area now included in Nebraska had as its objective the identification of trade routes, particularly with Santa Fe. The plains were not viewed as a destination, but as a transit region.[10]

By the end of the eighteenth century, trade with Indians on the lower Missouri River was becoming important. The Spanish, back in political control, sent a number of parties up the river from St. Louis with the aim of developing trade with Indians on the plains and beyond and granted the Company of Explorers of the Upper Missouri rights to trade upstream from the Poncas. Still, the company was more interested in a route to the Pacific than in the local trade and continued to seek such a passage during its tenure in the area.[11]

U.S. interest also focused on the role of the plains as a routeway (Figure 2.3). Lewis and Clark, for all their interest in the resources of the area and in scientific and geographic observation, were first and foremost concerned with the possibilities of commerce with India and a passage to the "Western Sea." Later explorers were similarly oriented toward goals beyond Nebraska. Pike was headed for the source of the Arkansas River in 1806. Long, in 1820, crossed the state on his way to find the headwaters of the Red River. Much as it is viewed today by vacationers on their

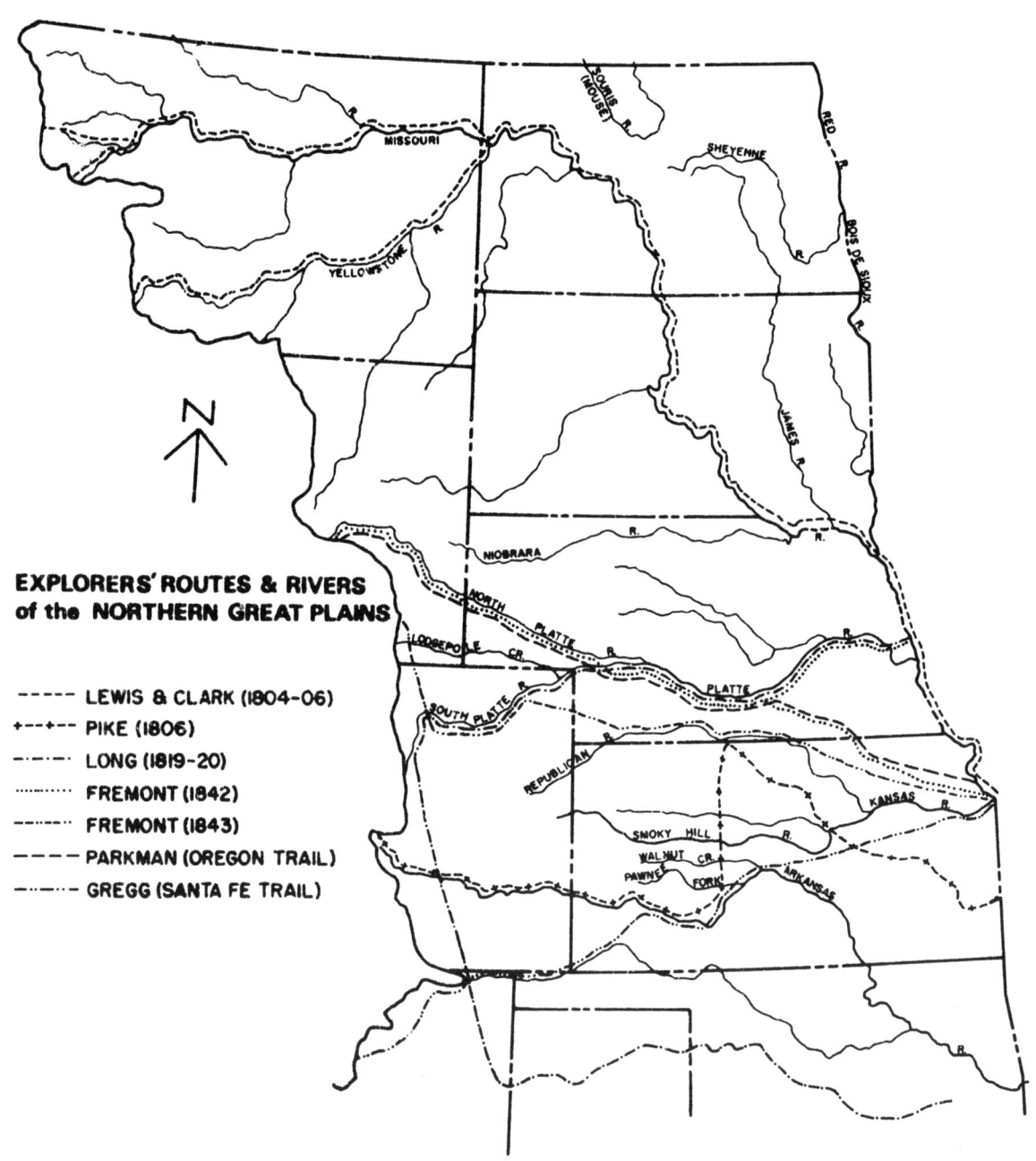

FIGURE 2.3.

way west along the Platte Valley to Colorado, California, or Yellowstone National Park, so Nebraska was seen as an obstacle or an impediment to rapid arrival at a destination.[12]

The Fur Trade

There were, however, whites who sought to utilize the resources of the region in the early nineteenth century. On Lewis and Clark's return trip down the Missouri River in 1806 they met at least eleven parties of traders heading upriver. In the early years of the fur trade, Nebraska Indians provided a substantial amount of commerce (Figure 2.4).[13] Trading posts were established along the Missouri River, particularly near the mouth of the Platte and in the Scotts Bluff area, to exchange trade goods for buffalo robes, beaver pelts, and other furs.

The first post was Fort Lisa, built in 1812 near Council Bluff by the Missouri Fur Company. This establishment was the focal point of trade with the Poncas, Omahas, and Otos. Fort Atkinson was built in the same area in 1820 to provide needed protection for the Missouri River trade.[14]

As the center of fur-trade activity moved farther west up the Missouri and the Platte, plains resources became less important and the region's role reverted to that of a highway. The Platte Valley, in particular, became steadily more important as a route to the beaver resource of the Rocky Moun-

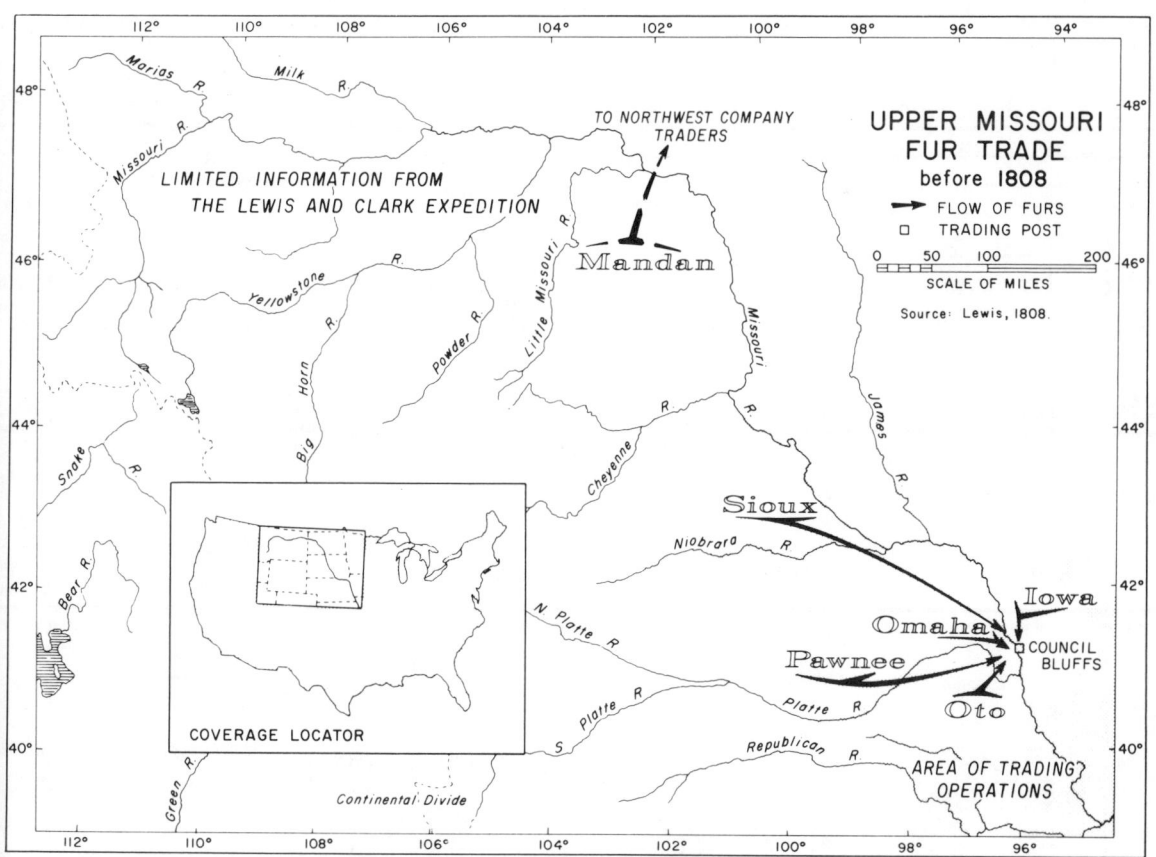

FIGURE 2.4. Source: "Images of the Northern Great Plains from the Fur Trade," by David J. Wishart in *Images of the Plains,* edited by Brian W. Blouet and Merlin P. Lawson, copyright 1975 by the University of Nebraska Press.

44 SETTLEMENT

tains. In 1825 the fur trade began operating on the rendezvous system in which trappers throughout the central and northern Rockies met each season to exchange beaver pelts for equipment and supplies. Traders, in turn, carried the pelts to St. Louis on the overland route along the Platte River, which soon thereafter became the principal road for migrants to Oregon.[15]

For Nebraska, the removal of trapping and trading activity did not mean an end to white occupance. The American Fur Company operated a post at present-day Bellevue (near Omaha) from the 1830s on. This served as a focus of settlement that eventually included Baptist and Presbyterian missions and agencies for the Omahas, Otos, Missourias, and Pawnees. Perhaps as many as fifty whites were residing at Bellevue when Nebraska Territory was created on May 30, 1854, and opened to settlement.[16]

The Farming Frontier: Acquiring the Land

Only with the arrival of large numbers of permanent settlers did whites seek to use the state's resources in more than a temporary and transitory manner. Few farmers were among the early residents at Bellevue before the territory was organized or in the community loosely associated with Fort Kearny just south of the Platte River in the central part of the state. Several ferry operators along the Missouri River at Omaha, Plattsmouth, Nebraska City, and St. Stephen made up another group of early residents. The settlement frontier had been gradually moving toward Nebraska, however. The Independence, Missouri, area was settled in the 1820s, and some settlers were located in southwestern Iowa by 1850. Approval of territorial organization in May 1854 removed one obstacle in the path of

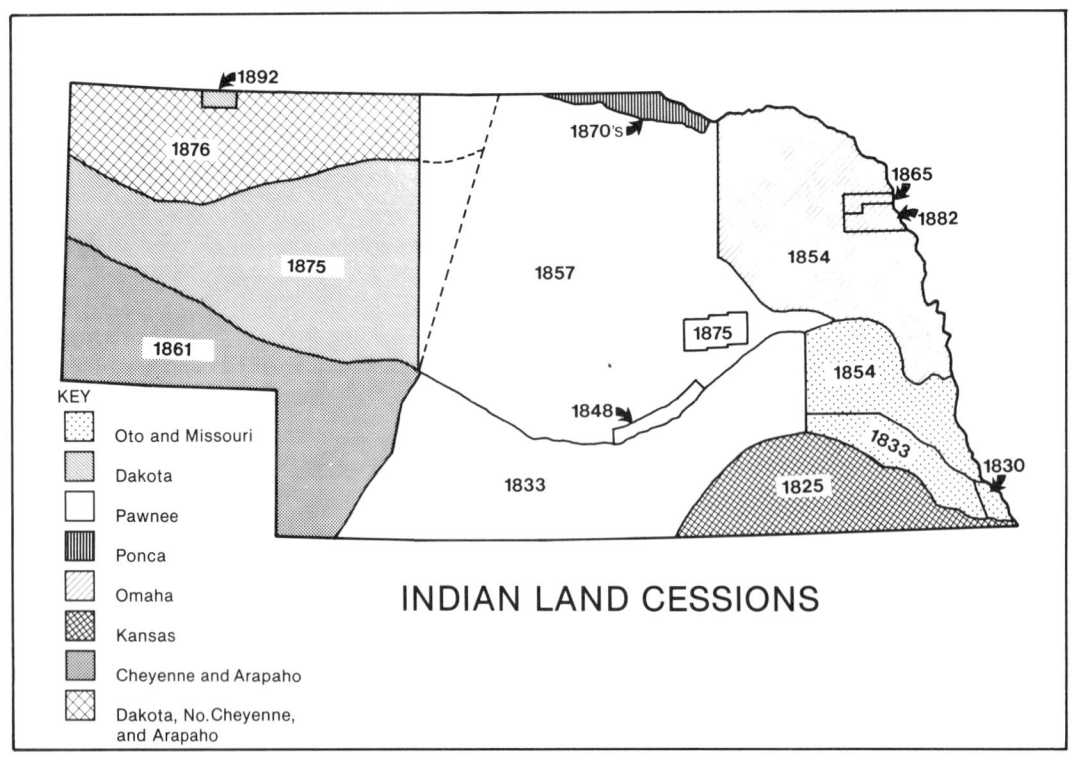

FIGURE 2.5.

permanent agricultural settlement.[17]

Before land could be acquired by settlers, however, the claims of the various Indian tribes had to be satisfied. Liquidating Indian title to lands in the eastern two-thirds of the state proved not especially difficult—most of the groups ceded their lands with little pressure. The first claims were relinquished in 1825 (Figure 2.5). By 1857, with the cession of Pawnee claims to all lands north of the Platte in exchange for a reservation in what is now Nance County, nearly the entire eastern two-thirds of the state was available for white occupance. The Poncas were removed to Indian Territory from their reserve along the Niobrara in 1877.[18]

Surveys of the land were necessary before legal title could be conveyed, however. Beginning in 1854 surveyors established the southern boundary of the state as the survey baseline. Within the next several years they also surveyed parallels, guide meridians, townships, ranges, and sections in the eastern counties (Figure 2.6), and thus formed the basic rectilinear pattern of Nebraska's lands.[19]

In the 1850s there were several means of obtaining land from the government. Under the Pre-Emption Law of 1841 settlers could claim up to 160 acres (65 ha) of land each. When the government put the land up for sale, settlers would pay $1.25 per acre ($2.09 per ha). Direct cash purchase at auction was a second possibility. A third approach was the use of military bounty land warrants, issued to veterans of the War of 1812 and the Mexican War, which were the equivalent of cash in government land transactions. Most veterans sold their warrants to land companies and other speculators, who resold them to prospective settlers or used them to select lands for later sale.[20]

After 1862, land could be acquired free under the Homestead Act, which permitted any head of a family or anyone over the age of twenty-one to select up to 160 acres (65 ha) of land. Even aliens who had declared their intention to become citizens were eligible. Title would be conferred once the homesteaders had lived on the land for five years. If settlers did not wish to wait five years, they could purchase the homesteads for $1.25 per acre and obtain title after having lived on the acres for six months. This *commutation* provision permitted many speculators and large landholders to acquire land through a second party.[21]

Later, the Timber Culture Act allowed individuals to obtain 160 acres of land if they planted 40 acres (16 ha) of trees (later reduced to 10 acres—4 ha). Many timber-culture entries were made, and final patents were issued on over 2.6 million acres (1.05 million ha), principally in the western two-thirds of the state. The amount of land actually developed as forest was minimal.[22] As one field inspector from the General Land Office wrote: "I have traveled over hundreds of miles of land in western Kansas, Nebraska, and central Dakota, nearly one-fourth of which had been taken under the 'Timber Culture Act,' without seeing an artificial grove even in incipience."[23]

Through these direct means a tremendous amount of land was conveyed to settlers and others (Figure 2.7; Table 2.1). Most Nebraska settlers did not, however, acquire free or cheap government land. Fewer than 15 million acres (6 million ha) out of a total land area of 49 million acres (20 million ha) went to settlers who utilized the Homestead or Timber Culture acts. Additional land was purchased through preemption or with land warrants. Finally, large blocks of land were sold intact. Many of these tracts were Indian lands. Others were purchased using agricultural-college scrip, a device that stemmed from a provision in the Morrill Act of 1862, which established land-grant colleges. States could elect either to receive lands within their borders to be used to support a state school or to receive scrip. Many chose scrip; they then sold it (generally to speculators) and invested the proceeds. Eventual delivery of the land to settlers, then, was through investment and land companies.[24]

Focus: White Pressures on Indian Lands

Pressure from white settlers played a considerable role in the final disposition of Indian reservation land. As settlement advanced westward, the Oto Reserve along the Blue River became more appealing to white farmers. Part of it was sold in the 1870s. In 1881 the rest of the tract was taken, and the Otos and Missourias were sent to Indian Territory.[1]

The Pawnees found their reservation (now Nance County) being gradually encircled by white farmers in the early 1870s. Settlers in need of wood for fuel and lumber stole timber from the reservation. Public officials railed against the Pawnees, who lived on good quality farm land. Furthermore, the Pawnees' agent, eager to eliminate their nomadic tradition and to encourage their conversion into full-time farmers, refused to allow them to go on their summer hunt in 1874. Faced with a loss of their resource base and hostility to their continued presence, the Pawnees chose to move to Indian Territory and the reservation was opened to white settlement.[2]

Even reservations that survived white settlement intact were not immune to pressure from white farmers. The Dawes Severalty Act of 1887 divided reservations into individual allotments for tribal members. The government held the land in trust for twenty-five years, giving Indians time to learn how to support themselves by farming. When the trust period expired, the government was to issue title to the allottee. The Burke Act of 1906 permitted title to be issued earlier to those individuals deemed competent.

Beginning in 1909 the commissioner of Indian affairs, in an effort to speed up the process, established several special commissions to determine the ability of individual Indians to manage their own affairs. The first such commission was established on the Omaha Reservation centered on Thurston County, Nebraska.

> Local whites were pressuring the Indian Office to release the reservation's rich farmland from trust status. Indeed, they were already looking forward to the termination of the trust period for the original Omaha allotments, which was due on July 10, 1909. Some whites wanted the Omaha land removed from trust status because the Omaha, along with their neighbors the Winnebago, held 240,000 of the 260,000 acres in Thurston County, Nebraska, and most of this land was in trust and could not be taxed. The Indians used the county's roads, schools, and bridges but contributed nothing to the county's revenue, and the county found it harder and harder to meet its expenses. Other whites in the area wanted the land released so that they would have an opportunity to purchase it. They realized that at least some of the Indians who received their fee patents would opt to sell their land to speculators or to the whites who were currently renting it.[3]

The special commission recommended over two-thirds of 429 adult Indians over age eighteen as competent, including many who could not read, write, or speak English and some whom they had not met. Moreover, more than one-third of those to whom title was issued stated they did not want it yet. In one day in 1910, 244 patents were issued for over 20,000 acres (8,000 ha).

Local whites took advantage of many Indians' poor understanding of credit, encouraging them to purchase equipment and horses on credit. Some were manipulated into signing documents to cover debts, and only later found they had signed away their lands. Few Indians apparently realized they owned their land free and clear and did not have to mortgage it to cover previous debts.

During 1910, more than half the land conveyed to Indians had been sold to whites. Deeds were often recorded even before the land patent had been issued. By 1912 only 2 percent of the patentees still held their land unencumbered; another 8 percent had mortgaged it; the rest had sold or lost it. "By 1936 there were only 26,625 acres of allotted land in trust and 4,000 in tribal ownership, while whites owned 108,870 acres of former reservation land. By that year three-fourths of the Omaha Indians were landless.... The policy that the government claimed was in the best interest of the Indians led to poverty and land loss on the Omaha Reservation."[4]

[1] James C. Olson, *History of Nebraska*, 2d ed. (Lincoln: University of Nebraska Press, 1966).

[2] David J. Wishart, "The Dispossession of the Pawnee," *Annals of the Association of American Geographers* 69 (1979):382–401.

[3] Janet A. McDonnell, "Land Policy on the Omaha Reservation: Competency Commissions and Forced Fee Patents," *Nebraska History* 63 (1982):401.

[4] Ibid., p. 409.

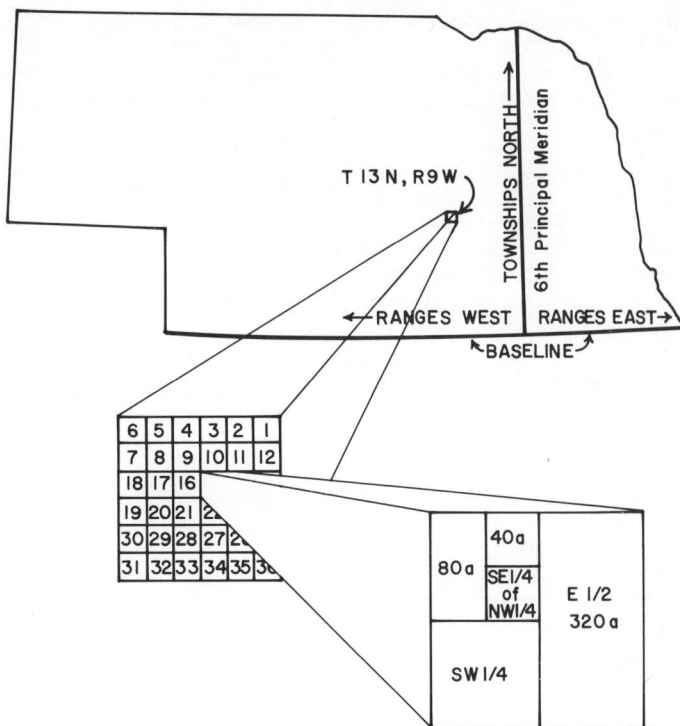

FIGURE 2.6. Surveyors divided the state into townships containing thirty-six 1-mi-square (2.59-km-square) sections. The 640 acres (259 ha) in a section (lower right) could then be further subdivided.

The Rectangular Survey System

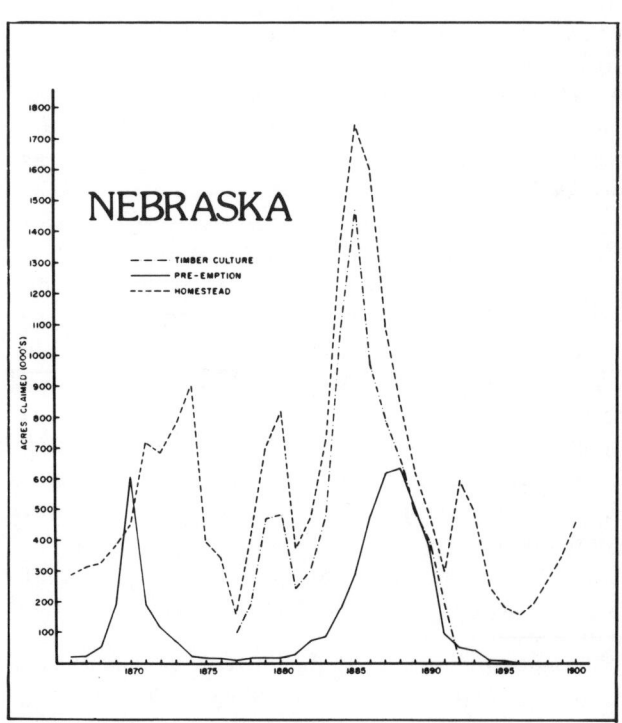

FIGURE 2.7. Land claimed through use of the Pre-Emption Law, the Homestead Act, and the Timber Culture Act, 1866–1900.

TABLE 2.1

DISPOSITION OF NEBRASKA'S PUBLIC DOMAIN (in acres)

Federal Railroad Land Grants	7,641,755.78
State Railroad Land Grants	531,103.17
Final Homestead Entries (as of 1910)	11,862,568
Final Timber Culture Entries (as of 1910)	2,546,698
Military Land Warrants	1,333,760
Agricultural College Scrip	1,123,200
Indian Lands Sold	599,018

Sources: James C. Olson, <u>History of Nebraska</u>, 2nd edition (Lincoln: University of Nebraska Press, 1966) p. 162; Homer Socolofsky, "Land Disposal in Nebraska, 1854-1906; The Homestead Story," <u>Nebraska History</u> 48(1967):237.

A final means for settlers to acquire land in the nineteenth century was from railroad companies. About one-sixth of Nebraska's land area was given to rail lines by the federal or state government to encourage rail construction. The Union Pacific (U.P.) and the Burlington and Missouri River Railroad each received 20 sections (1 section equals 1 sq mi or 2.6 square km) of land for each mile of track laid. The U.P. lands were on alternate sections stretching 20 mi (32 km) back on either side from the main line along the Platte River. Burlington lands were selected both along the railroad line and in northeastern Nebraska.[25]

In much of the state a checkerboard of landholdings developed, with odd-numbered sections held by railroads for sale and even-numbered sections open to homestead, preemption, and timber-culture entry. The rail companies were aided by restrictions on the public lands within the bounds of the railroad grants; these limited homesteads to 80 acres (32 ha) and required $2.50 per acre for preemption or homestead commutation. Much railroad land was sold directly to settlers, but a substantial share was conveyed to land companies that resold it to settlers.

Speculation abounded during that era. Some speculators were large investment companies, but many were farmers or would-be farmers seeking a profit. The commutation of 2.6 million acres (1.05 million ha) of homestead lands at $1.25 to $2.50 per acre only made sense if the individual claimants planned to sell the land or to use the title to secure a mortgage. A five-year wait, while in residence, would assure a settler of title to the land, but the individual who wanted to sell quickly needed to commute. A number of settlers undoubtedly were convinced they could make more money by obtaining cheap or free land and selling it when land values rose than by farming.[26]

Considerable criticism has been made of the Homestead and Timber Culture acts. The principal objection relates to the prevalence of fraud and speculation. Fraud was certainly common, particularly in timber-culture filings and commutations, both of which enabled some individuals to acquire very large holdings contrary to the spirit and purpose of the laws. Given the nature of the land system, speculation was almost inevitable. The public domain was not simply a means of putting land in the hands of farmers. It was also designed to help build railroads, fund agricultural colleges, and reward military veterans. Furthermore, the mobility and speculative urges of the nation's population would not have permitted any other system. Try to imagine a land system that would forbid the sale of an individual's land, even when that land was originally a gift from the federal government!

A second criticism centers on the inadequacy of 160 acres (65 ha) in a subhumid environment. Although this was undoubtedly a valid criticism farther west, during most of the nineteenth century a quarter section was plenty of land in most agricultural areas of Nebraska where few farmers, relying on their own labor, could operate more than that. In 1890 average farm size in Nebraska was only 190 acres (77 ha) (Table 2.2). Many farms were larger than this, but much of the land lay idle or was used for pasture. Farmers who failed—about half of those who filed for homesteads never obtained final title—did not do so because they did not have enough land.

A more serious problem with the system of land laws and the reason they did not fulfill the Jeffersonian ideal of making land available to all was that farming required more than just land. A farmer needed experience and capital. "Free land" did not mean a free farm. Livestock, draft animals, a minimal amount of equipment, and some cash with which to build a house and get started were essential for a pioneer family on the plains or prairies.

Farm Making

Housing was one of the first requirements of new settlers. In the eastern part of the state, local timber could be used to con-

TABLE 2.2

LAND IN FARMS IN SELECTED COUNTIES, 1880 and 1890

	Number of Farms	Average Farm Size (in acres)	Improved Acres per Farm	Percent of Farm Land Improved	Tilled Acres per Farm
1880					
Nebraska	63,387	156.89	86.84	55.4	74.30
Adams	1,505	164.25	112.75	68.6	110.52
Butler	1,471	141.46	85.86	60.7	82.25
Douglas	928	133.9	98.36	73.5	74.10
Gage	1,830	167.79	106.55	63.5	91.07
Greeley	289	195.56	36.69	18.7	34.36
Nemaha	1,373	142.27	103.12	72.5	84.94
Stanton	275	206.13	115.35	56.0	78.62
Merrick	849	153.24	86.25	56.3	69.42
Franklin	1,132	169.79	50.52	29.8	48.67
Fillmore	1,929	148.44	100.96	68.0	98.24
1890					
Nebraska	113,608	190.07	134.21	70.6	
Adams	1,764	172.34	159.47	92.5	
Butler	1,924	165.53	148.29	89.6	
Douglas	1,172	141.87	122.15	86.1	
Gage	3,002	164.01	149.77	91.3	
Greeley	733	210.55	144.57	68.7	
Nemaha	1,604	146.32	123.39	84.3	
Stanton	656	259.51	174.07	67.1	
Merrick	1,090	195.93	159.77	81.5	
Franklin	1,125	188.54	125.95	66.8	
Fillmore	2,083	159.96	145.01	90.7	
Cheyenne	1,242	213.40	84.29	39.5	
Custer	3,567	237.13	114.40	48.2	
Chase	931	209.69	88.99	42.4	
Holt	2,349	219.99	111.76	50.8	

Source: U.S. Census Office, <u>Tenth Census of the United States, 1880: Agriculture</u>; <u>Eleventh Census of the United States, 1890: Agriculture</u>.

FIGURE 2.8. Custer County farm family in their finery in front of their sod house, 1888. (NSHS)

struct log houses, or logs could be milled into boards at one of the many sawmills to make frame buildings. In central Nebraska sod houses or dugouts were often constructed and used for shelter in the 1870s and 1880s (Figure 2.8). The only costs involved lumber for a door and a few windows and poles or rafters for the roof. Though some "soddies" were plastered on the inside and used for many years, the more typical pattern was to tolerate the dampness and dirt floor only until the family could build a frame house. The conversion often occurred after settlers had become prosperous enough to afford lumber imported by rail from the Upper Midwest to the treeless plains. Residents generally utilized local resources until imported resources became available.[27]

A similar process occurred with fuel. Providing an adequate amount of wood for cooking and heating became increasingly difficult as the frontier moved away from the Missouri River. Settlers in the central part of the state utilized almost anything that would burn, including hay, corn (when the price was especially low), and dried buffalo or cattle dung (Figure 2.9).[28] Though some said this latter energy source made a particularly warm fire, few settlers persisted in its use when alternatives became available and affordable. The arrival of the railroad brought access to relatively inexpensive eastern coal.

Water was another resource problem for pioneers. Much of the state had adequate stream flow to provide for domestic and livestock-watering needs. But as settlement moved away from the watercourses and onto the uplands, water could only be obtained by hauling it great distances or by digging wells. In some areas very deep wells were a necessity. Use of a windmill made the task of lifting water great distances easier.[29]

Another costly item, though one which could be added gradually, was fencing. Adoption of a statewide herd law in 1877

FIGURE 2.9. A winter supply of "cowchips" for fuel near Hyannis. (NSHS)

meant that stock owners were required to confine their animals. This helped crop producers, but most Nebraska farmers raised both crops and livestock and therefore needed some fencing.[30] Some farmers built rail or board fences. Others resorted to ditches, sod walls, or a combination of the two, but these were probably only temporary restraints. Prior to about 1880, hedges of Osage orange were common throughout the southeastern part of Nebraska (Figure 2.10), where some counties had as much as 1,000 mi (1,609 km) of hedge in 1880. Barbed wire fences became important in the 1880s and 1890s because they were easy to construct and were less expensive than most other forms of fencing. Again, local resources gradually gave way to imported materials.[31]

Most farmers required some machinery, although one to two hundred dollars would probably buy an adequate supply during most of the nineteenth century. Additional funds were often required for breaking sod. More importantly, farmers needed financial reserves, particularly in the first few years when little sod had been broken and production was small.[32] One early estimate of the capital required is summarized in Table 2.3.

Add to these expenses the dependence of farmers on weather and crop prices, both notoriously unpredictable, and one can get a fairly good idea of the difficulties associated with pioneer farming. Many farmers mortgaged land to purchase supplies, machinery, and livestock, thereby facilitating the conversion of land into farms but increasing the financial risks of any crop failure. As one scholar has remarked, "The surprising thing is not that many pioneers failed to establish going commercial farms in the 1870s and 1880s, or fell heavily into debt, but the remarkable thing is that so many of them succeeded."[33]

Success for most farmers meant the ability to sell their products. Farmers sold some of their production locally and supplied many of their own needs (including vegetables, fruits, meat, and repairs), but much had to be purchased. Food, clothing, and equipment required cash from the sale of grain and livestock. The hoped-for luxuries—a carpet, curtains, a piano—called for additional cash. If they were to acquire such items, pioneers could not be subsistence farmers for long. They had to be commercial operators. Survival and success as commercial farmers necessitated a means of getting products to market.

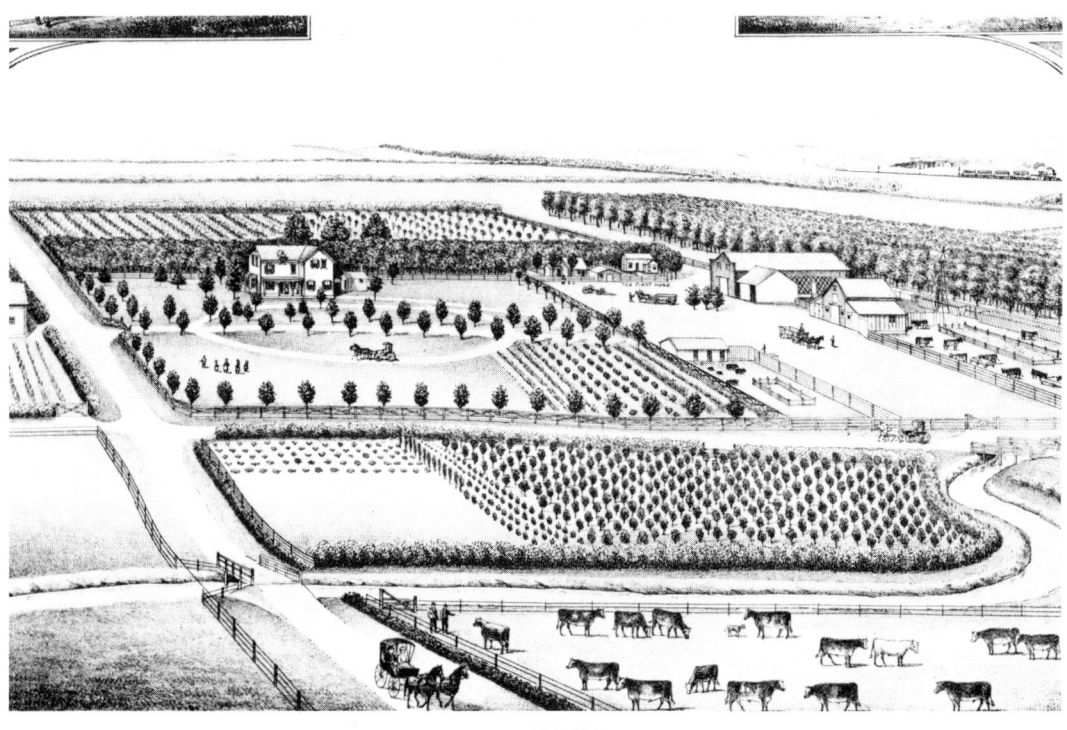

FIGURE 2.10. This drawing from the 1885 *Atlas of Nebraska* shows that one of the first acts of many early settlers was to plant trees. This Saunders County farmstead is surrounded by windbreaks, orchards, and ornamental trees. Hedgerows in the background served as fences. (NSHS)

TABLE 2.3

ESTIMATED EXPENSES OF MAKING A FARM

House	$250.00
Breaking 40 acres	120.00
500 Walnut Fencing Posts	25.00
500 Holes for Posts	5.00
Lumber for Fence	125.00
Nails	6.37
	$531.37

Source: Homer Socolofsky, "Land Disposal in Nebraska, 1854-1906; The Homestead Story," <u>Nebraska History</u> 48(1967):229, citing <u>Nebraska Farmer</u>, June 1861.

DEVELOPING A TRANSPORTATION SYSTEM

Emigrant Trails West

In the 1840s, migrants to western settlement frontiers began traversing the state. The route across present-day Nebraska almost invariably followed the Platte Valley, especially west of Fort Kearny. Because this corridor was the focus of traffic, variations in the route of migrant trails in the eastern half of the state were tied to the points of origin on the Missouri River. Although the Platte Valley route was used by trappers in the 1820s and 1830s, the first migrant use of the Oregon Trail occurred in 1841. In 1843 at least one thousand people followed this route, and the numbers increased annually thereafter. Most Oregon-bound migrants began near Independence, Missouri, traveled west along the Kansas River, north and west along the Little Blue, and then overland to the Platte (Figure 2.11). A few traveled farther up the Missouri by boat and crossed the river into Nebraska at various locations.

Mormons headed for Utah started at Florence, on the northern edge of present-day Omaha. In the mid-1850s some Mormons embarked at Nebraska City or nearby Wyoming. The Mormons generally stayed on the north side of the Platte, while those bound for Oregon and for California followed the south bank of the river (Figure 2.12).[34]

With the discovery of gold in California, traffic along the Platte increased dramatically. In 1850, probably fifty-five thousand persons were on the trail. The number dropped somewhat in subsequent years, but remained significant until rail connections were made with the West Coast. Such massive migration required a certain degree of protection. In Nebraska, Fort Kearny was established near present-day Nebraska City,

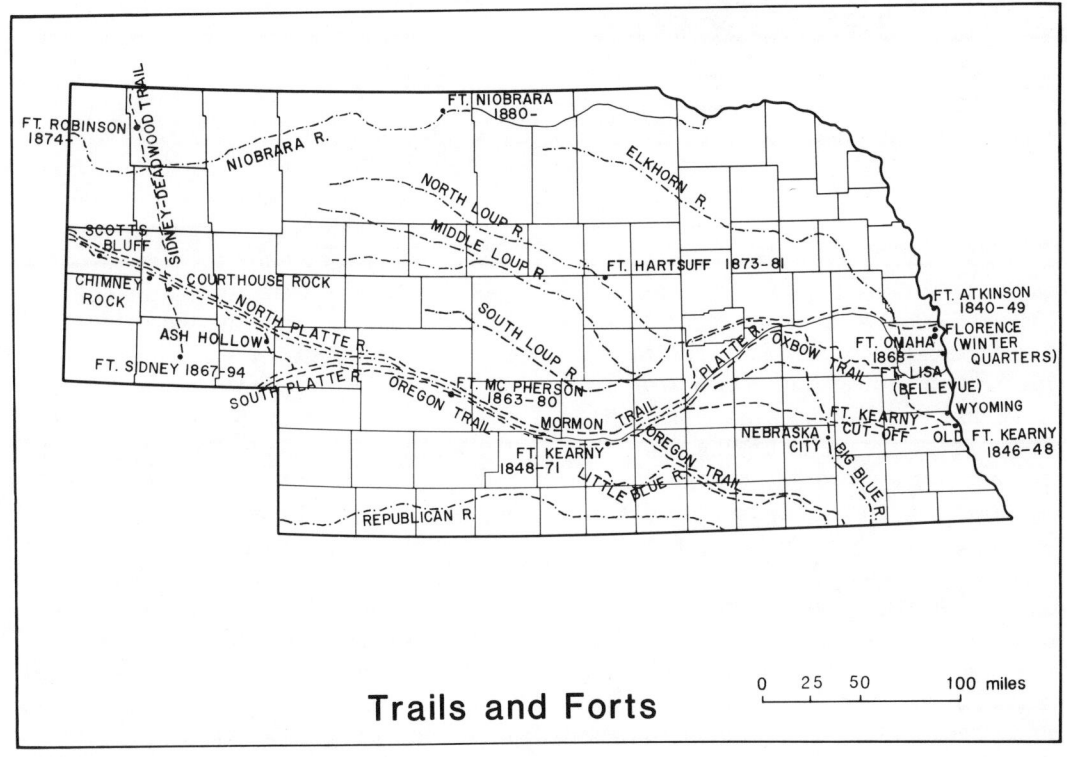

FIGURE 2.11.

FIGURE 2.12. Chimney Rock was one of the first dramatic landmarks encountered by migrants on their westward trek along the Oregon Trail.

then in 1848 moved 200 mi (320 km) west when the mass of migrants failed to use the Nebraska City route.[35] Later Fort Sidney was built to protect railroad construction crews, and Fort Robinson was established along one of the trails leading from the railroad to the Black Hills gold fields.[36] Few forts were primarily concerned with providing protection for the agricultural frontier. Fort Hartsuff in the Loup Valley and Fort Niobrara near Valentine may have reassured settlers, but actual military activity connected with these posts was very limited. In most of Nebraska the agricultural frontier was never very close to areas of Indian-white hostilities. Only around the several scattered reservations were white settlers in proximity to Indian lands.

Moving Freight Across the Plains

The Colorado mining boom, which began in 1859, was the focus of much transportation activity. Freight of all kinds was carried by wagon along the Platte River route during the late 1850s and early 1860s. Food and military supplies were the principal items shipped overland, although more exotic cargoes such as cats and frozen oysters were occasionally hauled to Denver.[37]

Nearly one hundred different firms were involved in early freighting out of Omaha and Nebraska City, but most traffic was associated with a few very large companies, most notably the partnership of Russell, Majors, and Waddell. In 1857 they selected Nebraska City as the eastern terminal for their line, which had contracts to supply the army in Utah and to carry military supplies to army posts in the mountains and plains. They spent approximately $300,000 to develop their operation at Nebraska City and in the process made it the second-largest city in the state (Figure 2.13). The freighters followed the Oxbow trail and later used the Nebraska City–Fort Kearny Cutoff.[38]

Freighting businesses were important to the development of territorial Nebraska in several ways. Not only did they attract a labor force and spur urban growth, but they also stimulated agricultural development. The food requirements of the military and the miners in Colorado provided a ready market for farm products. In a period when the nearest railroads were hundreds of miles east of Nebraska and when steamboat traffic on the Missouri River was the principal connection to eastern markets, the freight lines and their contracts gave Nebraska's aspiring commercial farmers an outlet.

Mail was another important cargo. Mail service to Salt Lake City from Independence was initiated in 1850. Service along the Platte Valley route was somewhat sporadic—minimal during the winter and un-

FIGURE 2.13. Freighting train in early Nebraska City. (NSHS)

predictable most other times. Another mail line, established in 1860, linked Omaha to Denver. The most dramatic mail system was the Pony Express, which operated for little more than a year in 1860 and 1861. Again, the route was from Independence along the Oregon Trail and the Platte Valley. Though a losing venture from the start, the Pony Express demonstrated the possibility of year-round travel along the Platte Valley—the route that was soon selected for the first transcontinental railroad. The Pony Express discontinued operations when it was superseded by the transcontinental telegraph line from Omaha to California in the fall of 1861.[39]

Arrival of the Rails

When the controversy over the location of the transcontinental railroad was settled by the Civil War, and when the economic disruption of the war had passed, construction of the first rail line west of the Missouri River began. In 1865 only 40 mi (64 km) of the line were built, but in 1866 tracks were laid to North Platte. Statehood came to Nebraska on March 1, 1867, and in that year the entire state was spanned by rail, and Cheyenne, Wyoming, was the winter terminus.[40]

Rail construction acted as a considerable spur to town development in Nebraska. Towns where the track ended boomed temporarily with the invasion of workers and their pay. Fremont, North Platte, and Sidney were particularly affected. Omaha, however, was the big winner in both the short and long term. The eastern gate of "the natural highway across the continent"[41]— the Platte Valley—was the city from which construction of the railroad was directed. Rails, ties, and supplies were shipped into Omaha by steamboat until 1867, when rail lines connected Council Bluffs to the midwestern railnet (Figure 2.14). In Omaha these materials were assembled and shipped west on the railroad to the construction sites. The city's prosperity and growth seemed assured.

Although the Union Pacific line was built to cross the plains, not primarily to serve Nebraska, it greatly stimulated settlement of the state and made possible the westward extension of the frontier. Prior to the arrival of rails, settlement in the state was concentrated within about 50 mi (80 km) of

FIGURE 2.14. The steamer *Colorado* unloading supplies for the Union Pacific Railroad at Omaha, 1865. (NSHS)

the Missouri River (Figure 2.15). The high cost of transportation by wagon made more distant locations very unattractive.

Following completion of the Union Pacific, a number of railroads were constructed in Nebraska. The Burlington and Missouri River Railroad laid tracks from Plattsmouth to Lincoln in 1870. Three years later that line stretched to central Nebraska. Other companies laced the eastern quarter of the state with rails before financial crisis ended construction activity for several years. The area of the state that was well served with rails by 1873 was settled rapidly during the 1870s (Figure 2.16).

The second rail boom began in 1879. When it was over twelve years later, nearly the entire state was served by railroads. The settlement frontier moved west with the rails, and counties with the best rail connections grew most rapidly (Figure 2.17). What had begun as one "finger" stretching along the Platte River developed in twenty years into a dense network serving a large population. In the course of two decades Nebraska was transformed from a transit region to a transportation origin and destination.

The Role of Railroads in Settlement

Through their land grants railroads had a stake in the occupance of the state by agricultural settlers. Those settlers could be counted on to purchase land and to produce commodities that would be transported to market by rail. In order for these ends to be achieved, the rail companies had to "sell" the state. Their merchandising included land, agricultural development, and urban growth.

In spite of the activities of explorers, surveyors, and trappers, most Americans had little knowledge of the trans-Missouri country in the middle of the nineteenth century. Some historians maintain that at that time most Americans accepted Long's label of the "Great American Desert" for the Great Plains region. This belief, it is claimed, retarded settlement of the trans-Missouri West until improved information became available. Although this may have been true among the well-educated economic elite of New England, among the general populace—the "average" farmer most likely to relocate in the West—the

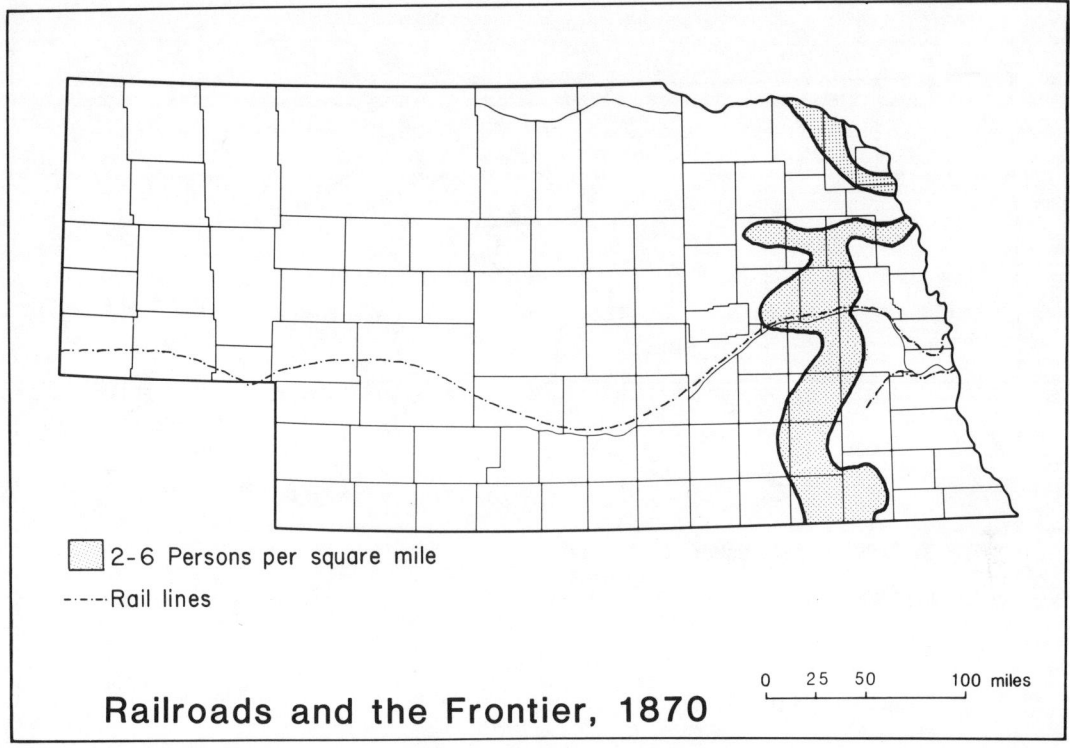

FIGURE 2.15. The shaded area represents the frontier zone. Higher population density and more settled conditions prevailed east of the frontier. Farther west, white settlement was extremely sparse.

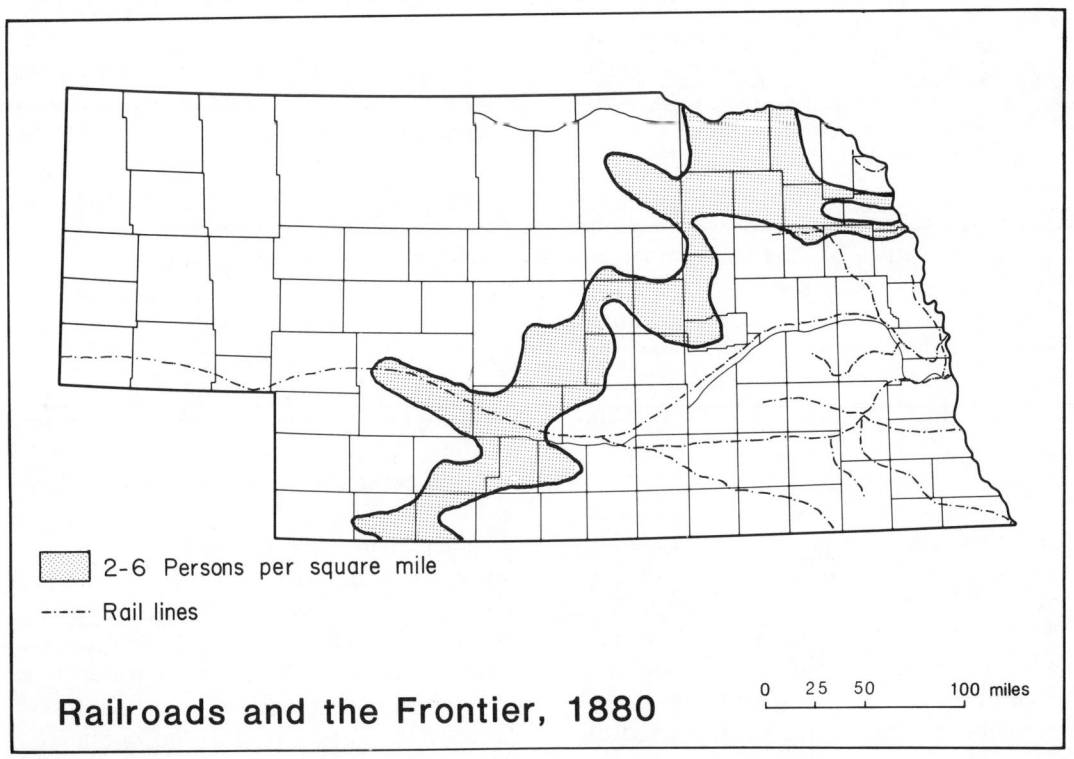

FIGURE 2.16.

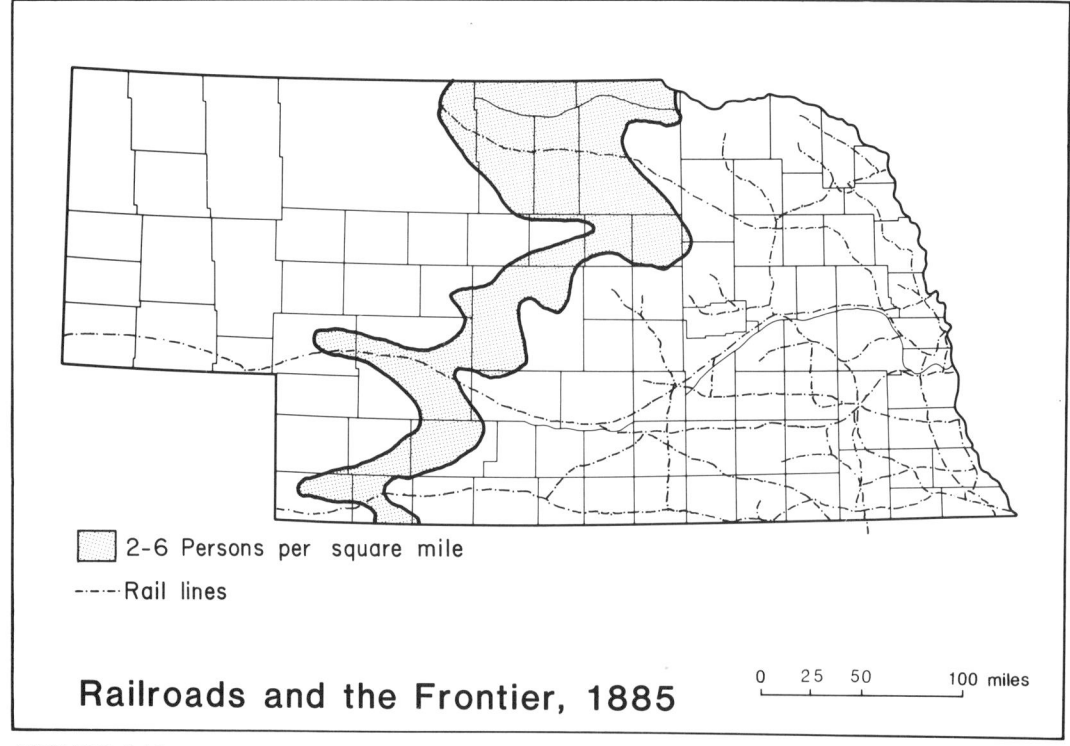

FIGURE 2.17.

desert image was little known and of minimal influence. The plains were a vague, poorly understood land for most white Americans on the eve of settlement.[42]

Promoters (called "boomers") filled the void. Some publicity was circulated by land companies, town companies, and state and local governments, but the most important sources of information about the central Great Plains were the railroad companies. During the last third of the nineteenth century the Burlington, the Union Pacific, and other lines circulated millions of pamphlets in the Midwest, the East, and Europe.[43]

The image of Nebraska portrayed in the "boomer" literature was one of abundance, prosperity, and similarity or superiority to the rest of the Midwest. The soil was labeled fertile and virtually inexhaustible. One publicist insisted that "mud in the usual sense in other States, is almost wholly unknown in Nebraska."[44] Promoters emphasized the temperate climate, similar to Illinois and Pennsylvania. Winters were said to be pleasant, mild, and short. Rainfall data presented the state as comparable to the Midwest, particularly in growing-season precipitation. Seldom did promoters suggest that rainfall amounts varied significantly from east to west. Many promotional pamphlets, particularly those oriented toward European immigrants, said nothing at all about precipitation, leaving the impression that there was adequate moisture for all crops of humid midlatitude regions.[45]

This deception was repeated in discussions of crop yields. Many publications claimed corn would produce an average of 40 to 75 bu per acre (3,500 to 6,500 l per ha) and that wheat would return between 20 and 30 bu (1,750 to 2,600 l), impressive figures compared to statewide averages in the Midwest that seldom exceeded 40 bu for corn or 15 bu (1,300 l) for wheat. The prospective migrant could only conclude that yields would at least equal those found in Illinois, Iowa, or Ohio.[46]

Promoters recognized that they would be selling land and encouraging settlement in much of the state, not just in the eastern quarter. Boomers emphasized the internal homogeneity of Nebraska in soils, climate, and crop production. The state was "one unbroken stretch of arable land,"[47] reported one writer. Some early pamphleteers suggested that the western half of Nebraska would be oriented toward grazing, with agriculture confined to the eastern part of the state—a view strikingly similar to that espoused by John Wesley Powell.[48] But by the mid-1870s very few promoters indicated such a regionalization—the frontier of settlement was moving too close to that earlier "agricultural limit" and those western lands would soon be for sale.[49]

The disappearance of a western limit to agriculture was easily explained by promoters. By the 1880s a commonly utilized theory in the promotional literature was that "rain follows the plow." This idea, which had been circulating for several decades, flowered during the boom of the 1880s. Samuel Aughey, a professor at the University of Nebraska, published statistics showing that rainfall was increasing and claimed this resulted from the breaking of the sod. Aughey viewed unbroken sod, trampled for generations by millions of buffalo, as virtually impervious to water, which therefore ran off and flowed out of the state. By plowing, farmers could increase infiltration and make more moisture available for evaporation, which would increase precipitation.[50] Thus the drier portions of Nebraska were not condemned to eternal aridity but could be salvaged, indeed were being salvaged by an army of settlers. Not only would Corn Belt farmers settle Nebraska, they would bring the Corn Belt with them. Irrigation would not be necessary, nor would settlers have to change their farming practices. The land would change for them, not the other way around.

With time, promotional imagery became increasingly inaccurate in two ways. As the theory of increasing rainfall was incorporated into pamphlets, intrastate homogeneity was emphasized, and the earlier distinction between a pastoral western Nebraska and an agricultural eastern section was abruptly dropped. Second, these highly inaccurate views became strongest during the mid-1880s when farmers were settling the upper Republican Valley and much of the Panhandle. The idea that Corn Belt agriculture could be practiced in central Nebraska in the 1870s was flawed, at best. But the belief that this same system could be transferred in unmodified form to western Nebraska in the 1880s was pure deception.[51]

Both the Burlington and the Union Pacific encouraged colonization, particularly by Europeans. In addition to the pamphlets published in German, Swedish, French, Czech, and other languages (Figure 2.18), the companies sent immigration agents into the field. These agents helped organize colonies, arranged passage to the United States, and coordinated travel to Nebraska. The companies frequently sold large blocks of land to colonies (Figure 2.19), helping to establish the pattern of ethnic clusters that dominates much of eastern and central Nebraska today.[52]

Town Building in Nebraska

Farmers who intended to engage in commercial agriculture required connections with the rest of the nation. Towns and cities provided those links, serving as provisioning centers for farmers and as collection points for farm products.

The earliest towns in the territory hoped to be more than just rural service centers, however. Before the coming of the railroad, town speculation was rampant. Budding settlements vied with "paper towns," which existed only in the minds of their owners and promoters.[53] The towns platted in the 1850s sought means of assuring their survival and success. Countless towns hoped to acquire the state university or the state capitol and often made space for these institutions on their plats. If neither of

FIGURE 2.18. German-language advertisement for land owned by the Burlington and Missouri Railroad. (NSHS)

these could be secured, even the penitentiary or insane asylum was an acceptable alternative. Few places were likely to garner one of these plums, however, so most contented themselves with seeking the county seat.

Disputes over county seats were the wars of frontier Nebraska. Fraudulent elections to select a county seat might be followed by theft of the county records, showdowns, court battles, and more thefts of records. In some counties the seat eventually ended up in the largest town, but in many counties a compromise location was eventually chosen.[54] Sometimes the site was not a town at all, but the geographical center of the county. Clay Center, for example, was born in the conflict among Harvard, Sutton, and the towns of southern Clay County. In fact, most of the county seats in south-central Nebraska were selected largely on the basis of their centrality and accessibility to the population they served.

During the territorial period only a few towns grew to any significant size. They survived the transition into the railroad era by virtue of their economic strength, whereas many smaller places withered and died when bypassed by the rails. After 1870, most new towns were located along existing or planned railroad routes. East of Grand Island, rural population density became great enough to warrant a fairly dense network of rails. Farther west, however, rural population was more scattered, and no rail network developed. Instead, several through routes were supplemented by widely spaced dead-end feeder lines, a pattern most pronounced in and near the Sandhills.

Town development became heavily dependent on rail connections, as a town without a rail line was not a town for long. The interconnection among towns, railroads, and farms was well understood: "Farmers expected that trade-center towns would be created, merchants expected that there would be a surrounding population to support the trade, and railroads did their part by replicating in the West that system of town-country settlement familiar to Americans."[55]

The rail companies understood these relationships, as well, and platted and developed towns in order to promote and control business along their routes (Figure 2.20). They generally located towns at 7- to-10-mi (11-to-16-km) intervals to efficiently serve rural residents and discourage effective competition from independent town ventures. In two enduring acts that remain on the landscape today, the Burlington and the St. Joseph and Grand Island Railroad (the St. Joe) named their towns alphabetically. The Burlington platted Crete, Dorchester, Exeter, Fairmont, Grafton, Har-

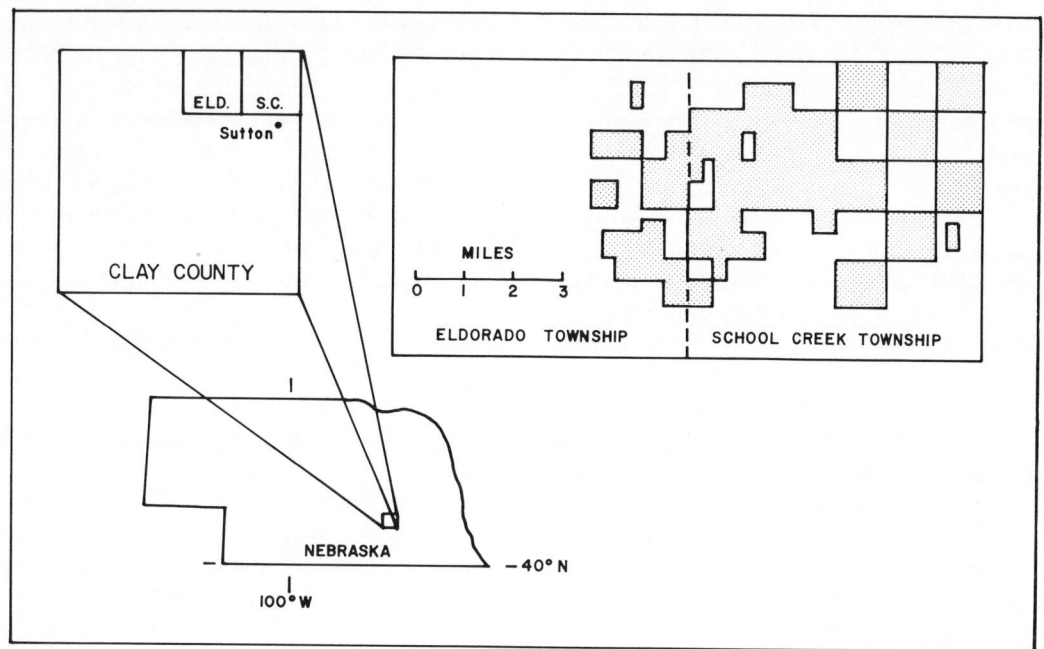

FIGURE 2.19. Russian German lands in Clay County, 1880, are indicated by shaded areas. (Association of American Geographers)

FIGURE 2.20. Main Street, with the railroad at the far end, Anselmo, ca. 1909. (NSHS)

vard, Inland, Juniata, Kenesaw, and Lowell. The St. Joe had Alexandria, Belvidere, Carleton, Davenport, Edgar, Fairfield, and Glenville. Rail companies also recruited merchants to establish businesses in their towns, helping to assure that farmers would patronize the railroad and the railroad town.[56]

Most towns influenced only a limited rural area, but a few places attracted more substantial investment and development. Omaha, because of its accessibility both to the agricultural productivity of the plains and to eastern markets, grew rapidly once rail connections were in place. The meatpacking industry was particularly prominent in the nineteenth-century growth of the city. A number of large packers located in Omaha in the 1880s and 1890s, assuring continued expansion of the city's population. Lincoln and a number of smaller cities—Grand Island, Hastings, Beatrice—also boomed in the 1880s (see Chapter 9).

The Impact of Rails

By the late 1880s, Nebraska's economic infrastructure was in place. Railroads crisscrossed the state, linking towns with cities and cities with larger cities. Railroad lines tied Nebraska's economy and settlements to the national economy, brought in the luxuries and necessities provided by the rest of the country, and hauled away the products of Nebraska's fields and farmsteads. In short, the railroads were the spur to all activity. Wrote an early booster, "We have but to touch our Western prairies and hills with the iron wand and cities spring up: towns cluster along the streams and highways, and the broad plains blossom with wheat, corn and barley."[57]

The "iron wand" and integration into the national economy had important implications for resource use in Nebraska. No longer were resources local in nature. Sod for houses, Osage orange hedge for fences, and buffalo chips and twisted hay for heat had no role in the new Nebraska. Resources became "delocalized."[58] Dependence now was placed upon imported building materials, farm supplies, and energy resources. Production of crops and livestock became oriented less toward feeding a family and more toward earning cash with which to buy farm and household necessities.

Delocalization can be viewed as either bane or blessing. In many ways farmers were more comfortable. Sod houses, though warm in winter, could not compete with the appeal of frame houses with roofs that did not drip for three days after a thunderstorm. Shoveling coal into a furnace was highly preferred to carting buffalo chips in from the "west 40." Commercial agriculture permitted the purchase of many items that were out of reach when cash flow was minimal.

On the other hand, delocalization meant increased dependence on human forces beyond the control of individuals or neighborhoods. The decisions that mattered were now made far beyond the borders of Nebraska and affected the price of farm commodities, the cost of purchased inputs, and the expense of transportation to and from the Nebraska farm.

Most nineteenth-century farmers were fully aware of the two-sided nature of the railroad coin and of the dangers inherent in dependence on rail service. Unless a town was served by two railroads, it was highly vulnerable to the pricing policies of one company. Great distances to market and the lack of rail competition in most of the state meant substantially higher transportation rates for plains farmers than for farmers east of the Missouri River. Delocalization and the commercialization of agriculture made prosperity as much a matter of distance and distant economic decisions as of hard work, competent management, and good weather.

ADAPTING AGRICULTURE TO THE GREAT PLAINS

Although crop prices and freight rates were of critical importance, farmers still had to contend with a physical environment and had to produce crops and livestock from the land even if explorers, scientists, and boomers could not agree on its true nature. Their survival and prosperity hinged upon accurate evaluation of the capabilities of the environment and informed understanding of the true nature of soil and climate.

Because the early settlers came to the Great Plains from humid environments with humid-land institutions and agricultural systems unsuited to a subhumid environment, a number of technological and institutional innovations were essential before this dry, level, treeless region could be successfully occupied. Among these were barbed wire, windmills, and agricultural practices.[59]

The Corn Belt farmers who settled eastern and central Nebraska expected a Corn Belt, and they proceeded to establish one.[60] As settlement pushed onto the drier high plains, the limitations of the climate for the successful implementation of midwestern agriculture became more pronounced. That recognition of those limitations would occur seems, in retrospect, inevitable, but the strength of the image of the garden was sufficient to delay accurate understanding and adjustment of the agricultural system for some time.[61]

Grasshoppers, Drought, and Emigration

Conditions in the early 1870s impressed the semiarid character of the plains upon settlers in central and southwestern Nebraska. The combination of drought and grasshoppers, which struck the state especially hard in 1874, destroyed crops in many frontier communities. Farmers were destitute, and suffering was acute in some areas. Frontier settlers appealed to state officials for assistance, asking for food, clothing, and seed for the next year's crop. The U.S. Army distributed clothing and food to many settlers in southwestern Nebraska. Congress appropriated funds to buy seed, and private charities donated supplies, but the aid was far from adequate. Some pioneers left the state for their old homes farther east.[62]

Out of this disaster came a dramatic reordering of agricultural emphasis. Corn, the preferred crop of newly settled regions, was supplemented with wheat. This more diversified system better enabled farmers to survive natural disaster. In south-central Nebraska the system that emerged from the early 1870s involved corn with some wheat on the bottomlands and wheat, better adapted to dry conditions, on the uplands.[63]

The renewed settlement boom of the late 1870s and early 1880s destroyed that adapted system. Newly arrived settlers, heavily influenced by promotional misinformation and the belief that rainfall was or would be increasing, sought to grow corn on land that received less than 20 in. (50 cm) of rainfall each year. According to a correspondent to the *Nebraska State Journal* from Haigler, in the extreme southwest corner of the state, "The breaking plows are fast solving the question of rainfall, which has been the question involved in the success of this 'cattle country.'"[64] The huge numbers of these boomer-influenced settlers overwhelmed the adapted earlier settlers in central Nebraska, and the ratio of corn to wheat acreage skyrocketed. Farther west the newcomers moved into previously unoccupied country and concentrated on corn production.[65]

In Red Willow County in 1880, for example, only 20 percent of the residents had been there for more than two years. Corn became virtually the only crop in bottomland precincts. One bottomland precinct in Webster County reported no wheat whatsoever in 1890. On the uplands the corn-to-wheat ratio ranged from 2:1 to 12:1.[66]

Happily for the settlers, the early 1880s were favorable years for corn. Rainfall was generally satisfactory, and the specialization in corn paid off; this confirmed in the minds of many settlers the idea that rainfall was increasing. When dry periods struck in the late 1880s the reaction of farmers was not necessarily to adjust and diversify immediately. Rather they often sought to ignore the problem or to find short-term solutions.

Drought in the 1890s

One response to drought was to seek the services of rainmakers. Some recognized these practitioners as charlatans, but among farmers in the driest counties the demand for moisture was so great that they were willing to pay several thousand dollars, should rain fall subsequent to rainmaking activities, without questioning whether or not there was a cause-and-effect relationship.[67]

In spite of rainmaking activities, the drought deepened. Drought was widespread in 1890, 1893, and 1894 and scattered in 1895. As in 1874, the frontier counties were hardest hit because farmers were not sufficiently established to have developed adequate reserves. The extent of privation was considerable. The state government appropriated several hundred thousand dollars for seed, feed, and supplies, but nothing could make up for the unusually low rainfall. North Platte received barely 11 in. (28 cm) of rain in 1894, and Culbertson had only 6.81 in. (17.3 cm). The idea of increasing rainfall was defeated.[68]

Thousands of western farmers made the only adjustment possible—they left. In the counties west of the 100th meridian there were six thousand fewer farms in 1900 than there had been in 1890. Banner County shrank from 2,400 people in 1890 to 1,100 at the turn of the century; Perkins County declined from 4,400 to 1,700 (Figure 2.21).

Adaptation to Drought

Those who remained in western Nebraska set about the task of redesigning an agricultural system more in accord with climatic realities. The 1890 drought spurred the development of several irrigation projects in the North Platte and the upper Republican valleys. By 1894, the possibility

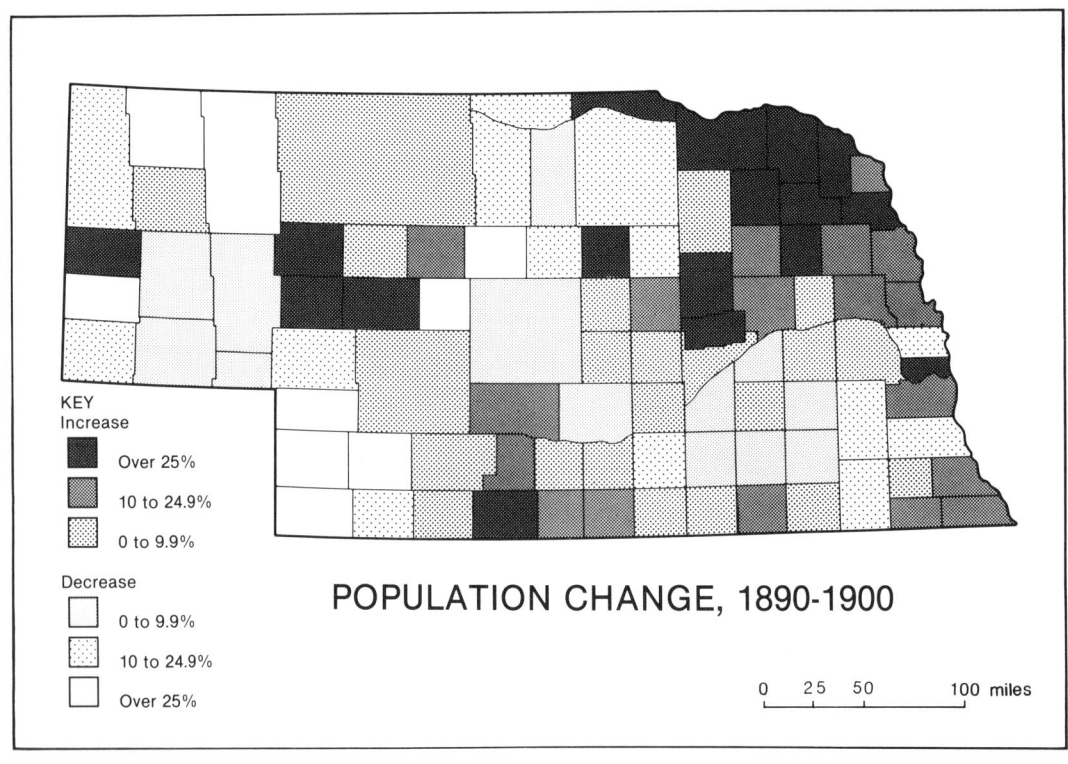

FIGURE 2.21.

TABLE 2.4

EARLY IRRIGATION

County	Number of Irrigators		Acres Irrigated	
	1889	1899	1889	1899
Buffalo		20		1,393
Cheyenne	36	162	3,154	21,288
Dawes	12	105	267	4,027
Dawson		333		20,097
Deuel	4	101	125	11,794
Dundy	4	63	41	4,552
Holt		21		2,218
Keith	6	73	295	12,646
Kimball	11	21	441	4,225
Lincoln	37	200	3,049	22,508
Platte		46		1,488
Red Willow	3	31	72	1,542
Scotts Bluff	70	291	2,753	29,244
Sioux	23	50	1,316	1,433
all others	8	415	231	10,083
Total	214	1,932	11,744	148,538

Sources: U.S. Census Office, Eleventh Census of the United States, 1890: Agriculture; Twelfth Census of the United States, 1900: Agriculture.

of irrigation was being discussed in central Nebraska, but actual irrigation development was much slower than in the driest area (Table 2.4).[69]

Farmers without irrigable land experimented with broomcorn, kafir corn, Jerusalem corn, sorghum, sugar beets, alfalfa, and other crops, in the hope of finding something more drought tolerant. Wheat acreage increased. The farther west the farm, the more intent was the farmer on finding alternative crops.[70]

New tillage practices were also tried. Listing—planting in deep furrows between ridges of soil—was advocated as a way of supplying more soil moisture to corn. Subsoiling and deep plowing had their advocates. By the early years of the twentieth century many of the practices of scientific dry farming were being utilized, such as frequent cultivation, summer fallow, and surface and stubble mulching. Through experimentation, the farmers of western and central Nebraska developed agricultural practices better suited to low rainfall.[71]

Livestock and Ranching

A further adjustment, one particularly distasteful to the boomers of the 1880s, was to emphasize grazing—a tacit recognition of moisture deficiency on the plains relative to the Midwest.[72] Many farmers found this a necessary change during the 1890s. Some expanded their cattle herds, while others converted their operations entirely to extensive livestock ranching.

A grazing economy was an established tradition by the 1890s. The first large-scale grazing of cattle probably occurred in western Nebraska in the late 1850s or early 1860s, as bison became scarce. During the 1870s Texas cattle drives were often made as far as Nebraska railroad terminals. In 1870, 40,000 to 50,000 cattle were trailed to Schuyler and shipped east on the Union Pacific. Plattsmouth was also a railhead, but dense settlement in southeastern Nebraska precluded its use after a year or two. When settlers pressed into the Blue River Valley, Kearney became the principal shipping point. Ogallala became the northern terminus of the trail by 1873. Over 100,000 cattle were shipped out of Ogallala annually until the middle 1880s.[73]

While the trail drives were going on, large cattle operations were being developed in western Nebraska—primarily in the southern Panhandle, in southwestern Nebraska, and in Custer County. Capital poured into the plains from eastern and European investors seeking huge profits. The boom could not last, however, and the open-range cattle industry collapsed in the mid-1880s for several reasons. Disastrous blizzards killed thousands of head of cattle. Economic collapse resulted from overspeculation, and some of the largest ranches folded. The range became unduly overcrowded as more and more investors sought profits from a limited grassland resource. Finally, the wave of agricultural settlement moved inexorably westward.[74] By the middle 1880s, only the Sandhills had not been entered by pioneer farmers.

In the Sandhills, ranchers seemed to have found a refuge from the "nesters" (farmers). Many small ranches grew and were joined by larger outfits such as the Spade ranch of Sheridan and Cherry counties. Ranchers first grazed their cattle on public land that remained open to settlement. When farmers sought to occupy this public domain they encountered harassment and intimidation by ranchers. A number of ranchers fenced off large portions of the public land, still theoretically open to homesteading. Several ranchers had over 100,000 acres (40,000 ha) fenced, although they owned far less. The most notorious case was that of the Spade ranch, which controlled 500,000 acres (200,000 ha). Not until after the turn of the century did that ranch remove its illegal fences. Much of its land was soon claimed by homesteaders utilizing the provisions of the Kinkaid Act.[75]

This 1904 act was yet another attempt to devise a land system consistent with the subhumid conditions of the Great Plains. The "Kinkaiders" were permitted to file for up to 640 acres (260 ha) in a thirty-seven-county area of western Nebraska. Within a decade millions of acres were claimed, and the population of the Sandhills grew. Unfortunately, the Kinkaid provisions were too little, too late. More than 640 acres were required for even a modest ranch in the Sandhills. Many of the Kinkaiders, unable to thrive on such small ranching operations, plowed the land in futile attempts to produce crops.

Although Kinkaiders did not settle everywhere in the Sandhills, they were of enormous influence in several counties. However, out-migration began soon after 1910; by 1930 most Kinkaiders had either become ranchers through the purchase of additional land or had left the area, their lands passing into the hands of established ranchers.[76] That the Sandhills were clearly not agricultural land seemed to be the lesson of the Kinkaiders. One Kinkaider wrote: "Truck growing as well as general farming has proved a delusion and snare. Our garden has been blown nigh unto death by blighting winds, scourged by hail and pinched by drought."[77] Finally, it seemed, the ranchers had a region permanently free of farmers—a conclusion not disputed again until the 1970s, when irrigation began to invade the Sandhills.

LIVING WITH A SUBHUMID ENVIRONMENT

As Nebraska's settlers pressed westward, they encountered an environment not especially well suited to the mixed crop and livestock agriculture of the Corn Belt. The substantial adjustments that had to be made could only occur when farmers learned what was possible and what was difficult in a subhumid region. Acknowledgment of the true subhumid nature of much of the state was a necessary first condition for the adoption of drought-resistant crop varieties, dry farming, and summer fallow and for increased emphasis on grazing. These changes allowed farmers to deal with the drought hazard.

The impact of drought decreased through time as farmers developed adaptive strategies and as society developed institutions for preventing human disaster when crops failed. During the early droughts—in the 1870s and 1890s—crop failure meant destitution, deprivation, and population loss in the hardest-hit areas. There was little outside assistance other than hastily collected charitable contributions that might help farmers stay on their land. Many abandoned their farms and did not return.[78]

A growing perception of the region as the "Breadbasket of the World" made drought-relief programs more palatable to the nation in later years.[79] During the nineteenth century Nebraska was somewhat peripheral to national agricultural output. As farmers mechanized and expanded their production per acre and per worker, their commercial orientation and the rail access to markets made Nebraska one of the most important agricultural states. As farmers became more closely tied to national economic forces, independence decreased. This new world hinged on interdependence.

The present-day distribution of Nebraska's population is a product of nineteenth-century settlement processes, the uses made of natural resources, and the pattern of the transportation system. The characteristics of the population are in part reflections of their origins and cultural backgrounds. It is to these "roots" that we now turn.

CHAPTER 3

POPULATION: SOURCES, CHARACTERISTICS, AND TRENDS

Both continuity and change characterize Nebraska's population. The principal ethnic groups today—Germans, Swedes, Czechs, blacks—had arrived in large numbers by 1890. The religious and political affiliations of contemporary Nebraskans bear a striking resemblance to nineteenth-century patterns, but population distribution has changed dramatically in a century. The nineteenth-century concentration of people in rural areas has been seriously eroded. Some counties and towns have grown substantially, but others are smaller than they were in 1890. In the nineteenth century the state was growing due to net inmigration. During most of the twentieth century it has grown in spite of net outmigration.

Who are the Nebraskans? The answer necessarily encompasses their range of geographical and cultural origins, location and distribution, patterns of population change, political and religious preferences, occupations, and employment.

THE ORIGINS OF NEBRASKA'S POPULATION

Most Nebraskans today are white, English speaking, and native born. By and large they are descendants of midwesterners and easterners who came to the state in internal migration streams, there to be joined by Europeans who emigrated to the United States in the late nineteenth and early twentieth centuries. Other Nebraskans are Native Americans, blacks, Asians, and Spanish-speaking people. In most cases, the present distribution of population-origin groups is not strikingly different from the pattern of one hundred years ago.

NATIVE AMERICANS

Few of the Native American cultures present in Nebraska at the time of early white settlement remain in the state. Most sedentary groups were removed to Indian Territory (now Oklahoma) following their cession of lands to the U.S. government in the middle of the nineteenth century. Only the Omahas retained a reservation in Thurston County, Nebraska. The nomads of the High Plains were relocated either in Indian Territory or in western South Dakota after their efforts to defend their lands and treaty rights were curbed by the military might of the federal government.

The Indian population of Nebraska today (approximately 9,000) includes, in addition to remnants of groups that were in the state in the early nineteenth century, groups relocated to Nebraska approximately one hundred years ago. The Santee reservation in Knox County was established for Sioux from Minnesota, and the Winnebago reservation in Thurston County houses descendants of a culture that was removed from Wisconsin. Approximately one-third of the population of Thurston County (2,406 out of 7,186) and 4 percent of Knox County's 11,457 people are Indians.[1]

Nebraska's reservations exhibit many of the problems that afflict the reservation system throughout the nation. Unemployment is high (Thurston County's unemployment rate is among the highest in the state) because of a dearth of job opportunities. Efforts to convert Indians into farmers in the late nineteenth century were largely unsuccessful, due in large part to the Dawes Severalty Act described in Chapter 2. Touted as a means of encouraging agriculture among Indians, it actually prompted many to obtain titles that were conveyed to speculators and eventually to white farmers.[2] Lacking land resources, reservation populations were thrust into poverty and unemployment.

The proximity of Nebraska's reservations to moderate-sized cities has helped hold unemployment and poverty rates below those in more sparsely settled states. Efforts to attract industry to reservations have met with modest success.

Other major concentrations of Indians in the state are found in Lincoln and Omaha, where they represent 0.5 percent of the population (Figure 3.1). These urban clusters are somewhat recent phenomena, paralleling a nationwide trend of rural-to-urban migration of Native Americans.[3] As recently as 1960 only 484 Indians lived in Omaha and Lincoln. By 1980 over 3,000 lived in the two metropolitan areas. Scotts Bluff County had 455; Sheridan County's

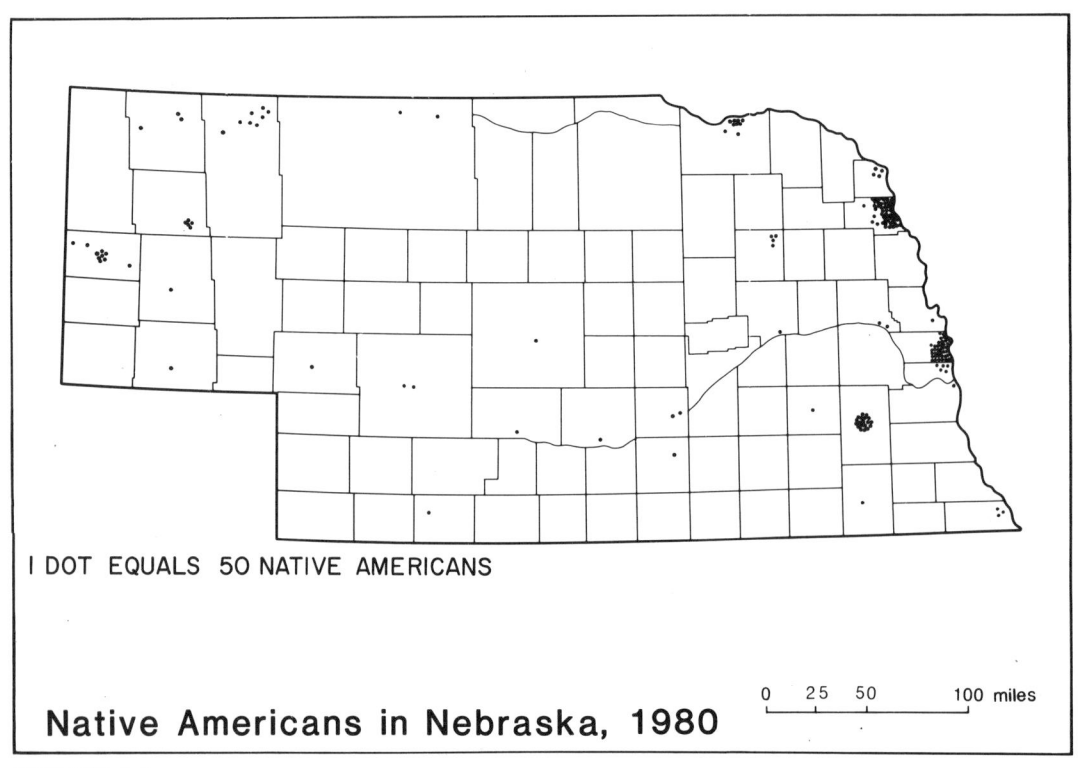

FIGURE 3.1.

392 American Indians constituted over 5 percent of the population.

NEBRASKA'S MIDWESTERN HERITAGE

American-born whites with midwestern or northeastern backgrounds were the largest group in Nebraska during the settlement period. During the 1850s the greatest number of settlers came from Iowa, Illinois, Ohio, Indiana, New York, and Pennsylvania. By 1870, over two-thirds of Nebraska's U.S.-born residents from outside the state had been born in these six states, a pattern that held in subsequent years.[4]

Many settlers with eastern birthplaces were actually midwesterners, as well. Most migrants to nineteenth-century frontiers did not move directly from their place of birth, but from some intermediate location. Therefore, even those settlers with eastern birthplaces often entered the state with midwestern backgrounds and experience.

The role of the South in providing settlers to Nebraska was relatively minor. In 1860, only 1,319 persons were recorded as having been born in the South (not including border states) out of 22,260 persons born outside Nebraska. This was fewer than the contribution of Missouri alone.[5]

As a consequence of these migration patterns, early agriculture was midwestern, as were patterns of settlement, land division, and urban form. The language of Nebraskans is basically midwestern; so are their religious preferences, social activities and organizations, and political inclinations. To a great extent these midwestern forms are variants of patterns established in the New England and Middle Atlantic cultural hearths.[6] The ties of Nebraska to the Midwest are still apparent in recent migration patterns. In 1980, the North Central census region, roughly the Midwest, was the birthplace of 59 percent of all Nebraskans born in the United States outside Nebraska (Table 3.1).

BLACKS

Nebraska's location relative to the principal migration streams of nineteenth-century settlement meant that the number of blacks in the population was quite small prior to 1880, although a few slaves and free blacks were reported in the 1860 census. The first sizable migration of blacks to Nebraska coincided with the dramatic movement of the "Exodusters" from south to north in 1879 (Figure 3.2). In that year as many as fifteen thousand blacks may have entered Kansas, with somewhat fewer turning toward Nebraska. Most of these

TABLE 3.1

BIRTHPLACE OF U.S.-BORN NEBRASKANS, 1980

	Number	Percent of Native Born Population
Born in Nebraska	1,015,594	71.9
Northeast	28,573	1.9
North Central	252,762	16.5
South	69,300	4.5
West	79,286	5.2
Total	1,445,515	

Source: U.S. Bureau of the Census, Census of Population: 1970, Vol. 1, Characteristics of the Population (Washington: U.S. Government Printing Office, 1973).

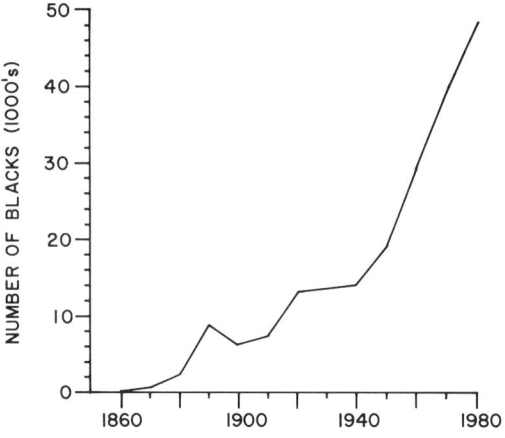

Black Population of Nebraska
FIGURE 3.2.

early arrivals, destitute and looking for work, settled in Omaha or Lincoln. Eventually, however, most Nebraska counties recorded a few black residents.[7]

By 1890, the black population of the state had reached its widest distribution. Blacks were present in seventy-eight of Nebraska's ninety-three counties. The greatest number were in Lincoln and Omaha, but six other counties reported over 100 black residents. Cherry County, in the heart of the Sandhills, had a black population of 170. Nearly 400 blacks were in Dawes County, site of Fort Robinson.

Many of these black pioneers were farmers (Figure 3.3). Some claimed homesteads under provisions of the Kinkaid Act. During the twentieth century the black population gradually abandoned farms and small towns and moved to larger cities. By 1910 only four counties contained more than one hundred blacks: In that year they constituted more than 1 percent of the population in Dawes, Douglas, Lancaster, and Wheeler counties.[8]

Nebraska's black population is heavily urbanized today. In 1980, only 1,281 of the state's 48,389 blacks lived outside the Lincoln or Omaha metropolitan areas. Nearly 40,000 blacks resided in Douglas County. Sarpy and Lancaster counties each reported approximately 3,500 blacks; Adams and Hall counties contained over 100 blacks.[9]

As in most U.S. cities, Nebraska's urban blacks are spatially concentrated (see Chapter 9). In Omaha the majority of the black population is in North Omaha, with some recent expansion into the northwest sector of the city. A smaller concentration is found in South Omaha, south of the Union Stockyards. In Lincoln, most blacks live in the area immediately east of the downtown campus of the University of Nebraska.

FIGURE 3.3. Moses Speese family, Custer County homesteaders, 1888. (NSHS)

NINETEENTH-CENTURY EUROPEAN IMMIGRANTS

Beginning in the 1830s large numbers of immigrants entered the United States. The earliest groups to migrate in sizable numbers were Irish, English, and Germans. Immigration slowed considerably during the Civil War, but revived in the 1870s and reached immense proportions in the 1880s.[10] It was principally during these two decades that Nebraska's European migrants entered the state, although some Europeans continued to arrive during the 1890s and the early part of the twentieth century (Table 3.2).

Although many immigrants settled in Omaha or Lincoln, large numbers of most ethnic groups selected agricultural lands across the state. The colony-based settlement system (see Chapter 2) was the single most important reason for the intensive clustering of individual ethnic groups in spatially distinct units. Many of these colonies were located directly on the frontier. The Germans who settled Madison County were in the vanguard of settlement, as were Germans in Hall County and Irish in O'Neill. By 1880 the populations of some counties were overwhelmingly composed of foreign-born farmers; English-speaking peoples were often a distinct minority (Figure 3.4). Some townships were inhabited almost entirely by one or another ethnic group (Figure 3.5).[11] Once the initial colonies were established, Old World friendship, kinship, and community ties often assured the continued concentration of ethnic groups.[12]

English-Speaking Immigrants

One of the larger groups of settlers included immigrants from England, Wales, and Ireland. The English were found in nearly every county in the state. Because

TABLE 3.2

FOREIGN-BORN AND SECOND-GENERATION POPULATION

OF NEBRASKA, 1860-1980

	Foreign-Born	% of Total Population	Native-Born of Foreign or Mixed Parentage	% of Total Population
1860	6,351	22.0	b	---
1870	30,748	25.0	19,369	15.7
1880	97,414	21.5	99,602	22.0
1890	202,542	19.0	250,420	23.6
1900	177,347	16.6	325,885	30.5
1910	176,662	14.8	362,353	30.4
1920	150,665	11.5	372,503	28.7
1930	119,199	8.4	364,507	26.5
1940	82,101	6.2	b	---
1950	57,273[a]	4.3	b	---
1960	40,238	2.9	217,921	15.4
1970	28,796	1.9	175,556	11.8
1980	31,001	2.0	b	---

[a]Whites only.

[b]Not reported.

Source: Compiled from U.S. Censuses of Population.

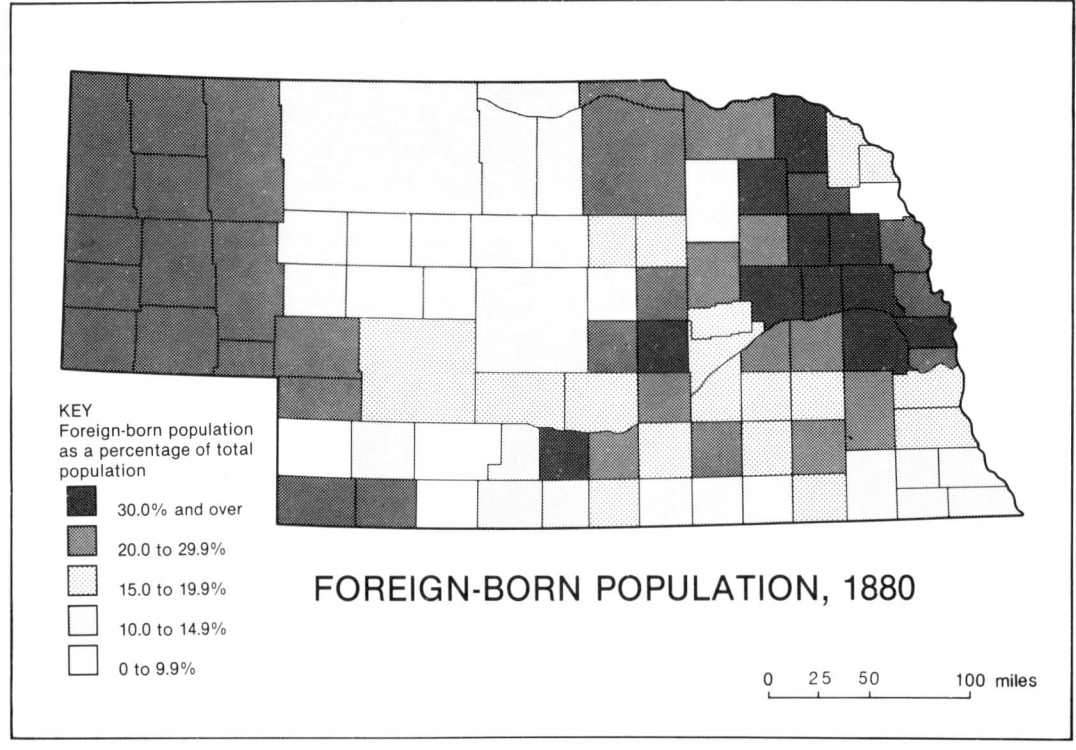

FIGURE 3.4.

they were not readily distinguishable from native-born inhabitants in either language or religion, they settled in a dispersed pattern and were easily assimilated into their larger communities. Today English and Welsh settlements are difficult to recognize.[13]

The efforts of the Irish Catholic Colonization Society and "General" John O'Neill to settle Irish on U.S. farms produced several Irish communities. The best known of these is O'Neill, in Holt County, where the first settlers arrived in the spring of 1874. Because of the colony's remote location, considerable discontent was expressed by the settlers. O'Neill was criticized for having lured individuals without the necessary pioneering skills onto the plains. Even though many of the original Irish colonists left O'Neill soon after arrival, there were nearly four hundred Irish-born residents in and near five Holt County towns in 1880.[14]

In 1877, O'Neill located twenty-five families in Greeley County at the townsite of O'Connor, named after the bishop of Nebraska. In 1970 nearly 2 percent of the country's population was still Irish stock—either born in Ireland or with one or both parents born in Ireland. Irish concentrations are also still present in Boone County and in Omaha, where 40 percent of the state's Irish stock was located in 1970.[15]

German Settlement

Germans were the largest immigrant group in Nebraska. In 1900 German Americans (immigrants and their children) made up more than 14 percent of the state's population. Even as late as 1930 over 12 percent of the state's residents were German stock, making Nebraska one of the "most German" states in the nation.[16] Most Nebraskans born in Switzerland, Alsace, and Russia, and many of those coming from Austria, were also German-speaking.

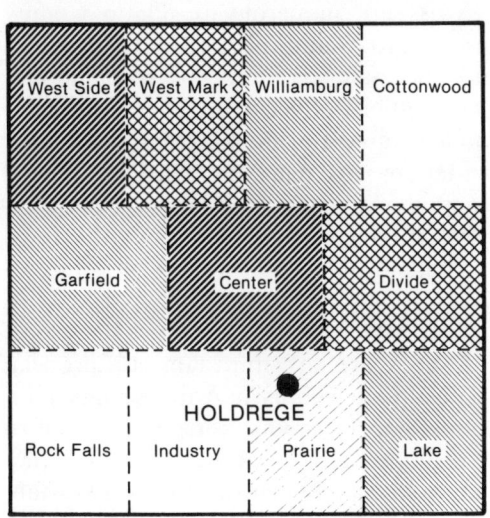
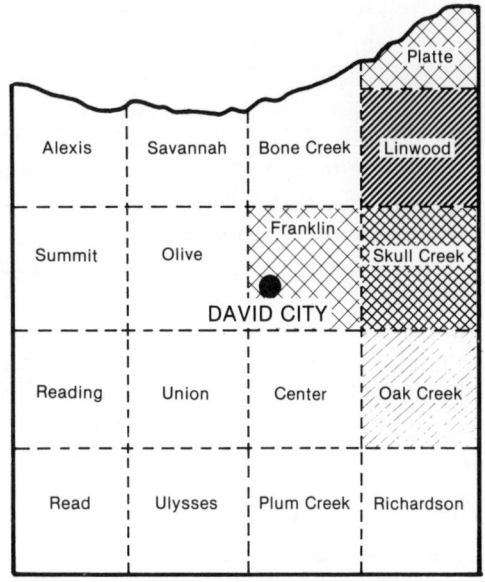
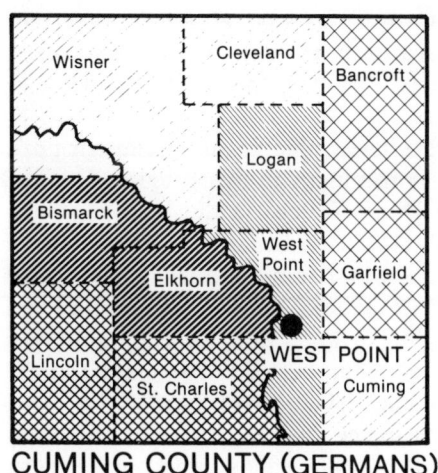

ETHNIC CONCENTRATIONS IN THREE COUNTIES

FIGURE 3.5. Sources: John R. Kleinschmidt, "The Political Behavior of the Bohemian and Swedish Ethnic Groups in Nebraska, 1884–1900" (M.A. thesis, University of Nebraska, 1968); and Frederick C. Luebke, *Immigrants and Politics: The Germans of Nebraska, 1880–1900,* copyright 1969 by the University of Nebraska Press.

The earliest German settlements were made in Otoe County and Hall County, on the western edge of the frontier. After the Civil War, German settlers, many arriving from Wisconsin, concentrated in the northeastern part of the state. Pierce County in 1870, soon after initial settlement, was over 90 percent German. Cedar, Wayne, Madison, Stanton, Cuming, Platte, and Dodge counties also developed impressive concentrations of Germans.[17]

More than any other group except the English, the German population was widely diffused across the state. In a number of counties German stock still is more than 10 percent of total population. Only in the Sandhills and parts of the Panhandle have Germans not been a sizable minority.

Other Germanic Language Groups

Many German-speaking settlers actually arrived from Russia. These Russian Germans (or German Russians) were descendants of people who had migrated from Germany to the Volga region of Russia in the eighteenth century and to South Russia and Bessarabia early in the nineteenth century. In Russia they lived in exclusively German neighborhoods, retained use of the German language, and had considerable political autonomy. Culturally, they remained Germans. In the 1870s, faced with growing pressures of Russification and the strain of a growing population on a limited land base, many Russian Germans began to migrate. Some went to South America or Canada, but the majority moved to the central and northern Great Plains.[18]

Because their communities in Russia had been organized along religious lines, most of the Nebraska colonies contained but one denomination. Catholic Russian Germans were not common in Nebraska, but Mennonites settled in Jefferson County near Jansen and in York County at Henderson. Evangelical Russian Germans dominated settlements in Clay, Adams, and Scotts Bluff counties, as well as in Lincoln.[19] The Russian Germans, the fourth-largest European ethnic group in the state, are clustered in their areas of early settlement (Figure 3.6). In Clay, Hitchcock, Scotts Bluff, and Morrill counties, Russian German stock constituted over 5 percent of the population in 1970.[20]

Swiss are numerous in Platte County and are also found in Pawnee, Richardson, and Sheridan counties. The most famous Swiss settler in Sheridan County was Jules Sandoz, subject of the biography *Old Jules* written by his daughter Mari. A related group, the Dutch, is found in large numbers only in Lancaster County near the town of Holland.[21]

Scandinavians

Swedes are the third-largest European nationality in Nebraska. Although less ubiquitous than Germans, persons of Swedish descent are found in all but a few counties. The greatest concentrations were established in the 1870s and 1880s, particularly in Burt, Phelps, and Polk counties. Swedes have generally been assimilated rather easily into U.S. society, although a certain amount of ethnic pride and consciousness has become evident in recent years (Figure 3.7).[22]

The other sizable Scandinavian group is Danes, prominent in Washington County, where Dana College is the only four-year Danish college in the United States. Other important settlements are in Howard County. Smaller Danish communities are found in Nuckolls and Kearney counties. The largest number of Danes can be found in Omaha.[23] The small number of Norwegians in the state (about three thousand in 1970) is spread across the northeastern part of Nebraska, with the greatest numbers in Madison and Boone counties.

Eastern Europeans

Unlike other states, where Slavic immigrants generally chose urban locations, in Nebraska Czechs settled both in rural and urban areas. About 30 percent of Nebraska's Czechs reside in Omaha. In 1970 immigrant and second-generation Czechs constituted over 7 percent of total county

FIGURE 3.6. Remains of a Boyd County house built of chalk by Russian German pioneers. (NSHS)

population in Butler, Colfax, Saline, Saunders, and Valley counties.[24] Vaclav Vodicka, a Czech who served as a land agent for the Burlington Railroad in the 1870s and 1880s, directed many Czech immigrants to the counties where they are concentrated today. Lesser clusters were also established in portions of Knox, Fillmore, Cass, Boyd, Box Butte, and Dodge counties.[25]

Czech community life often centered around the church. The policy of the Catholic church was to provide for "national" churches with services in the native language of the parishioners wherever possible. Eventually there were about fifty "Czech" parishes in the state. Although the language is seldom used in services today, many of these churches retain a strong identification with Czech tradition.[26]

Czech Protestants were invariably Moravian Brethren, organized as Presbyterians; a few parishes remain in the state. Because religion was seen by some Czechs as representing the Hapsburg empire, many joined no church. This tendency was more pronounced among immigrants from Bohemia; those from Moravia were more likely

FIGURE 3.7. Swedish Evangelical Lutheran Salem Church, Wakefield. (NSHS)

FIGURE 3.8. Z.C.B.J. halls are found in most Czech communities. This one is in rural Saline County.

to retain their adherence to Catholicism. Fillmore and Saline county Czechs were less likely to attend church, compared to those in Colfax, Butler, and Saunders counties.[27]

Nebraska Czechs are known for their fraternal organizations (Figure 3.8). The best-known social organization of Czech Americans was the Sokol, dedicated to physical fitness. Numerous Sokol chapters were organized in Czech communities, where they sponsored gymnastics meets, educational programs, Czech language classes, and social activities.[28] Their impact is evident in the success of the gymnasts trained at the South Omaha Sokol, several of whom have led the University of Nebraska–Lincoln to a string of national gymnastics championships in recent years.

Poles were more likely to settle in Omaha, locating in several neighborhoods of South Omaha, particularly Sheelytown. But they were also numerous in several rural counties in the central part of the state. The first Polish settlement was made in the late 1860s just west of Columbus, near the village of Tarnov.[29] Other Polish settlements were made in Howard, Sherman, and Valley counties, as well as in Nance County, where Polish stock was 7 percent of total population in 1970.

Other eastern Europeans who have settled in Nebraska have been principally urban. In 1970 there were over thirteen hundred Lithuanians and nearly fourteen hundred Yugoslavs in Omaha. A smaller number of Latvians have congregated in Lincoln.[30]

Other European Immigrants

Italians, especially from southern Italy and Sicily, settled in Omaha, which reported fifty-five hundred persons of first- or second-generation Italian background in 1970. In the early years of the twentieth century, Italian settlement focused on Little Italy immediately south of the downtown Omaha warehouse district. Subsequently, Italians have become more dispersed through the city, with a strong foothold being maintained in the original neighborhood, including the "Italian" church, St. Francis Cabrini. Italians were among Omaha's first fruit and vegetable vendors and are strongly identified with the restaurant business.[31]

Many early Jewish settlers were merchants—either itinerant peddlers or store owners in various small towns and cities. The largest number of Jews, however, located in Omaha. In the 1880s Omaha's Jewish population increased with the influx of eastern and southern Europeans to the United States.[32] These newer immigrants, mostly orthodox Jews fleeing from persecution in Russia, Lithuania, Hungary, and Romania, clustered on the southern edge of downtown Omaha between 9th and 13th streets. Eventually, most Jews in Omaha became involved in business activity, and many became prominent in the civic life of the city. Most recent estimates put Omaha's Jewish population at sixty-five hundred.[33]

There was at least one attempt to locate east European Jewish refugees in an agricultural colony in Nebraska, an activity commonly undertaken by established German Jewish organizations endeavoring to settle incoming Russian Jews. The Nebraska colony, in Cherry County, contained fifteen immigrant families who homesteaded land available under the Kinkaid Act about 1910. Once title was acquired, all these families left the region.[34]

MEXICANS AND JAPANESE

The population of Spanish background in the state is primarily of Mexican origin. Their earliest settlement was related to the disruption caused by the Mexican Revolution, along with the opportunities available for labor on the railroads, in the meatpacking industry, and in the sugar-beet fields of the Panhandle.[35]

Nebraska's twenty-eight thousand persons of Spanish origin have concentrated in the western part of the state. In 1980 large numbers were found in Scottsbluff, North Platte, Kearney, and Grand Island, as well as in Omaha and Lincoln in the eastern part of the state (Figure 3.9). In fact, nearly all towns in the Platte Valley

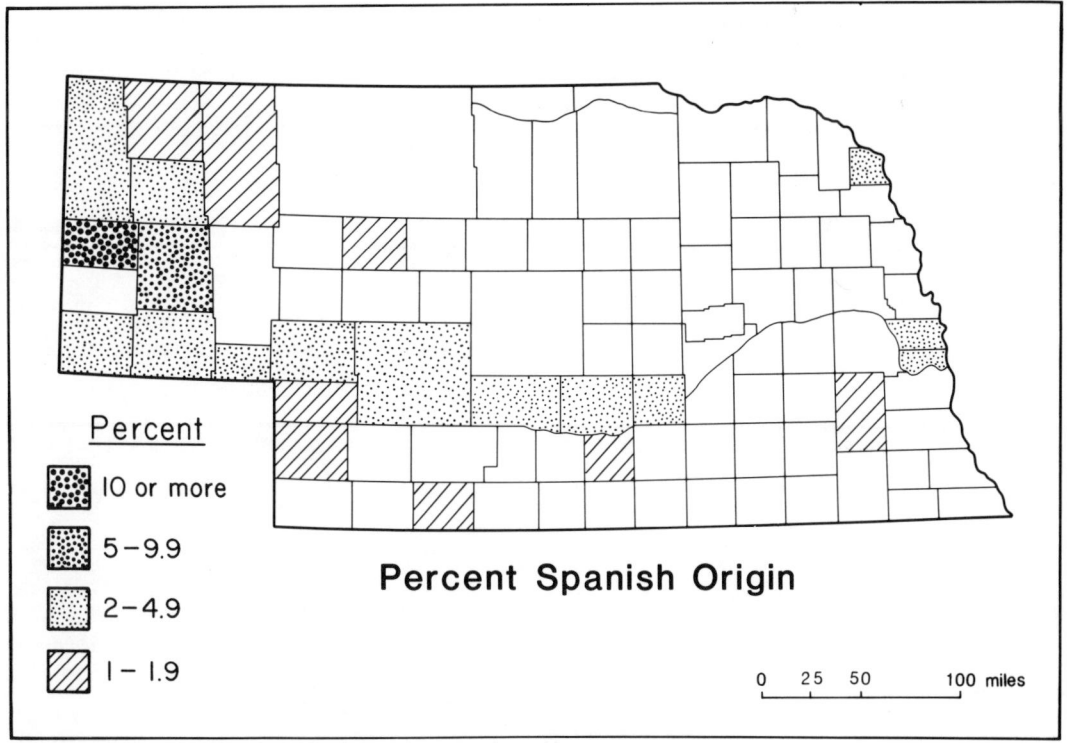

FIGURE 3.9. Based on *1980 Census of Population.*

have a sizable Mexican American minority; they are found in limited numbers in almost every county in the state.

Mexican Americans in Nebraska have retained much of their culture. Most important is use of the Spanish language, although this has declined in recent decades. Cultural cohesiveness and awareness, as a result, are more pronounced among Mexican Americans than among most other ethnic groups that participated in the settlement of the state.

Japanese immigrants also entered Nebraska around the turn of the century and provided labor for railroads and the sugar beet industry. After this initial activity many became farmers in the Platte Valley.

Today some remain in that area, but a large number also live in Omaha.[36]

POPULATION CHARACTERISTICS

PATTERNS

The Distribution of Foreign Stock

Most nationalities that were prominent in early settlement remain numerous today (Table 3.3). In 1970, four counties—all in the eastern third of the state—reported

TABLE 3.3

FOREIGN STOCK, 1970

Country of Origin	Number of Foreign Born or Native Born of Foreign or Mixed Parentage
United Kingdom	11,083
Ireland	4,846
Norway	3,183
Sweden	17,099
Denmark	13,202
Netherlands	1,754
Switzerland	2,054
France	1,296
Germany	62,726
Poland	8,333
Czechoslovakia	19,551
Austria	3,612
Hungary	1,060
Yugoslavia	1,599
U.S.S.R.	14,160
Lithuania	1,428
Greece	859
Italy	6,414
Other Europe	3,823
Western Asia	771
China	543
Japan	1,106
Other Asia	1,428
Canada	8,247
Mexico	5,552
Cuba	608
Other America	1,017
All other	726
Not reported	6,272
Total	204,352

Source: U.S. Bureau of the Census, Census of Population: 1970, Vol. 1, Characteristics of the Population (Washington: U.S. Government Printing Office, 1973).

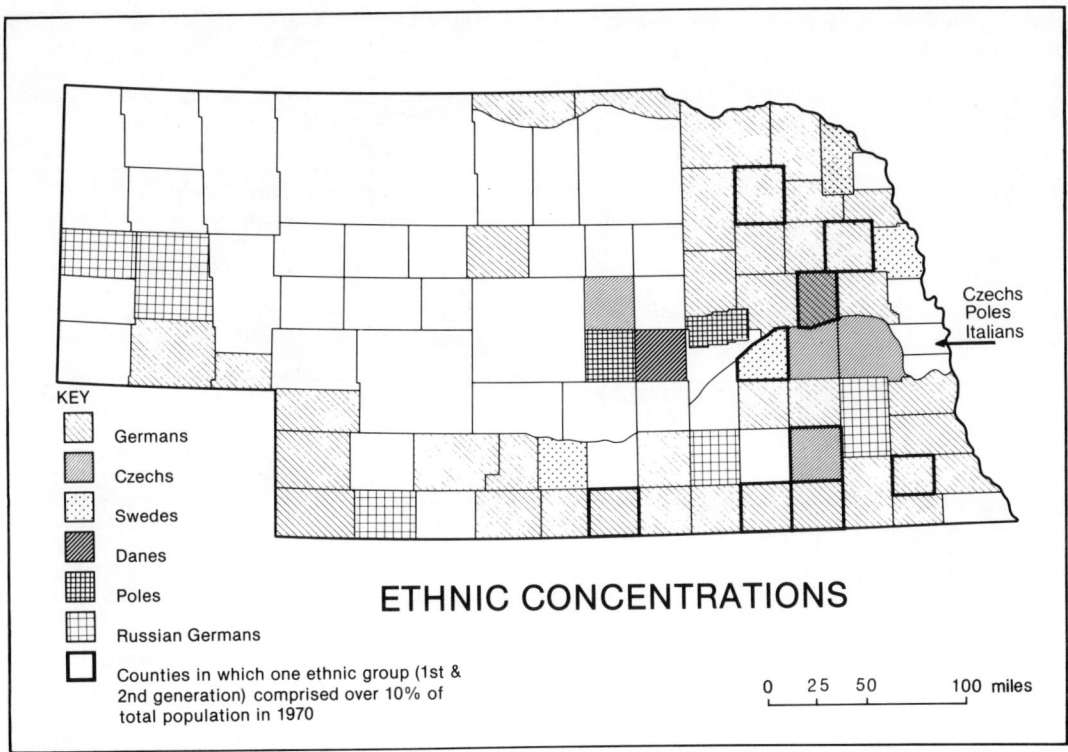

FIGURE 3.10.

more than 20 percent of their populations as foreign stock (Figure 3.10). The greatest concentration was in Colfax, with 24.7 percent of the population either foreign-born or children of at least one foreign-born parent. Of the twenty-two counties with 15 to 20 percent foreign stock, only Scotts Bluff and Morrill, with their preponderance of Mexican Americans and Russian Germans, were in the western half of the state. The "least ethnic" area of the state has always been the Sandhills.

The distribution of Nebraska's foreign element is a product of the time of arrival of each ethnic group, the background of that group, and the role of various agencies in colonization.[37] Those who came in the greatest numbers, English and German immigrants, settled in nearly every county in the state (Figure 3.11). Germans were somewhat concentrated in the northeastern counties, but had limited presence in the western half of the state.

Land agents and the railroads played important roles in the relatively segregated settlement of Czechs, Poles, Swedes, and Danes. The earlier arrivals usually settled in the eastern portion of the state, whereas those groups that came in the 1880s were typically found farther west, where land was still available. Czechs, many of whom arrived in the 1870s, are located farther east than the Poles, who settled somewhat later. Timing was not the only factor in spatial distribution: groups that came after 1890, particularly if they already had an urban orientation, concentrated in Omaha and Lincoln (Table 3.4). Italians, Jews, and smaller groups from eastern Europe are overwhelmingly urban. Mexicans concentrated in the Platte Valley where the greatest opportunities for field labor and railroad employment have traditionally been found.

Immigrants have been remarkably persistent in the areas they initially settled. Many rural immigrant groups were more

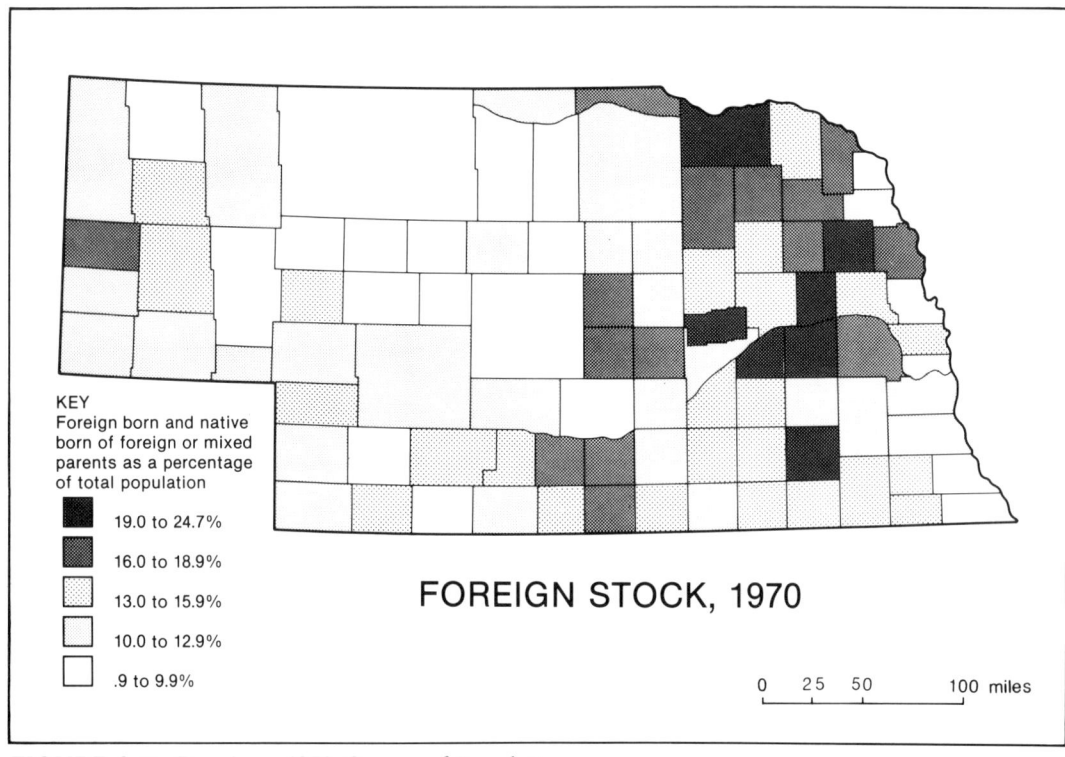

FIGURE 3.11. Based on *1970 Census of Population.*

TABLE 3.4

OMAHA ETHNIC AND RACIAL GROUPS, 1900 and 1970

	1900[a]	1970
Total Population	128,556	347,328
Blacks	3,443	34,431
Indians	7	1,131
Chinese	0	186
Japanese	96	329
Filipinos	NA	140
Foreign Stock[b]	70,277	54,026
Austria	1,287	1,299
Canada	1,154	2,236
Czechoslovakia	6,184	5,411
Denmark	4,643	3,331
England, Scotland, and Wales	4,623	2,236
Germany	14,206	9,103
Hungary	443	588
Ireland	9,145	1,894
Italy	718	4,842
Lithuania	NA	1,125
Mexico	NA	1,629
Norway	556	827
Poland	1,743	4,382
Russia/USSR	1,717	2,727
Sweden	7,623	3,383
Yugoslavia	NA	1,120

[a] Includes South Omaha

[b] Foreign born or native born of foreign or mixed percentage

Source: U.S. Censuses of Population, 1900; 1970

likely to remain in one area than were the more mobile U.S.-born settlers. When individuals did move out of an ethnic community, they frequently relocated in a similar ethnic cluster elsewhere, and they were likely to be succeeded by persons of similar ethnic background. The phenomenon of chain migration, whereby migrants selected locations near people they already knew from the Old Country, was important in maintaining the ethnic character of individual neighborhoods.

The Modern Ethnic Landscape

Several factors have led to a decreasing impact of ethnicity upon the appearance and behavior of communities. Most important has been the decline of native languages. Immigrants often learned only the bare essentials of English, but their children frequently embraced English and spoke their native tongue only when necessary. This trend accelerated during and after World War I and the drive for Americanization. After this time it was rare to find schools where instruction was given in languages other than English.[38]

Restrictions on the use of foreign languages hastened the adoption of English, particularly in German communities. The State Council of Defense, formed by the legislature in 1917, along with county councils monitored the loyalty of the state's residents. Especially repugnant to these bodies were the forty or so German-language newspapers and the use of German in public: "The use of the German language in the teaching of children of grade school years, and the use of that language in a very large number of the churches of the state [have] been a potent preventative means against the Americanization of the people who [come] under such influence."[39]

The legislature passed laws prohibiting the teaching of any school subject in a language other than English, requiring that all public meetings be conducted in English, and requiring that copies of all materials published in a foreign language be filed with the State Council of Defense. Although the prohibition on instruction in a foreign language was struck down by the U.S. Supreme Court in *Meyer v. Nebraska* in 1923, anti-German sentiment induced many Germans to downplay their heritage. Immigrants changed the spelling and/or pronunciation of their names. Germantown and Berlin were renamed Garland and Otoe, respectively, in an effort to minimize German visibility on the landscape.[40]

The relative isolation of an ethnic group has been another important factor in the assimilation process. Large ethnic groups that settled apart from native-born Americans and other ethnic peoples were more likely to retain their cultures. During the nineteenth century it was often possible for individuals to have little or no contact with mainstream U.S. culture for long periods of time. Greater mobility and mass communication decreased this isolation, making U.S. culture accessible to ethnic groups and eroding ethnic identity and distinctive cultural traits. Intermarriage of the second and third generations with native-born Americans or other ethnic groups is a third factor that has led to greater cultural homogeneity.

In general, the most easily assimilated groups in Nebraska have been English, Scandinavians, and Germans. Later arrivals such as Czechs and Poles have been less likely to ignore their cultural heritage. Russian Germans and Jews maintain a considerable amount of ethnic identity; Mexican Americans and blacks have also remained distinctive in the outward manifestations of their cultural backgrounds.

The diverse origins of Nebraska's population are apparent in the landscape. The place-names of the state, for example, are a product of groups that have been here for centuries and those who settled more recently. The name of the state is an Oto term. Many of the state's rivers carry Indian names or English translations of native terms. Indian words or names of the various tribes were often used in naming towns and counties (Otoe, Pawnee, Sioux, Cheyenne, Arapahoe, Dakota City, Nehawka, Ponca). The French, traders and trappers in the early nineteenth century, supplied the names Bellevue and Papillion. The latter was applied both to the town and the stream, which is generally pronounced close to the French, *Pah-pee-oh,* and spelled almost phonetically: *Papio.*

Because most place-names were applied by early settlers and surveyors, generally of midwestern or New England background, the place-name landscape is dominated by the names of military heroes, presidents, governors, and other prominent individuals. When European ethnic groups settled, few major features remained to be named. Germans contributed Bismarck township and Friedensau. The Irish influence is evident in O'Neill and O'Connor. Danes have Dannebrog and Dannevirke. Swedes have Stromsburg, Swedehome, Swedeburg, and Malmo; Czechs named Prague, Bruno (Brno), and Plasi (originally Plzen); and Poles named Posen and Warsaw.

The association of many of Nebraska's ethnic groups with a "national" church is one of the clearest landscape reminders of the ethnic background of an area. Mennonite churches dominate Henderson, a Russian German community. Lutheran congregations are in Swedish, Danish, and many German neighborhoods. Czech Catholic churches remain common in the principal counties of Czech settlement, as well as Omaha, where at least three churches have mainly Czech parishioners. St. Wenceslaus, the patron saint of Czechs, is the preferred name of Czech congregations. St. Stanislaus is the "Polish church" in Omaha, which also contians St. Francis Cabrini, the Italian parish. In many smaller cities two Catholic parishes continue to operate, one a "national" church—German, Polish, or Czech—the other less identified with a single ethnic group.

Omaha's ethnic diversity is evidenced by Our Lady of Guadalupe Catholic Church, four synagogues, a Romanian Orthodox church, a Greek Orthodox church, two Serbian Orthodox churches, a Ukrainian Catholic church, a Latvian Evangelical Lutheran church, four African Methodist Episcopal churches, and the Bohemian Brethren Presbyterian church. Many of these congregations are associated with well-defined ethnic neighborhoods. Ethnic parishes may include parochial schools, which often dwarf the public schools in size and influence.

Other than the obvious features, such as churches and business signs that reveal the ethnic background of the owner, landscape evidence of ethnic-group settlement is slim. The economic pursuits of rural ethnic peoples usually were modified after settlement in an effort to fit in with the dominant economic system of the area and make a profit. Thus, German farmers accustomed to growing rye and barley would not do so for long in a region where little or no market existed for the product. German immigrants accustomed to growing wheat would not stand out as unusual in a wheat-growing section of the state

Some cultural traits did persist. For instance, in the nineteenth century Russian Germans often grew rye on small plots in order to make rye bread.[41] The gardens of ethnic Nebraskans generally reflected their heritage. In fact, the greatest retention of cultural traits other than religion is probably found in food ways. Cafes and restaurants in Czech communities continue to serve duck, dumplings, and kolaches; Italian restaurants emphasize Italian specialties; and Mexican neighborhoods are served by Mexican restaurants. Such persistence is found not only in commercial establishments, which sometimes cater to recent surges of popular interest in diverse cuisine, but in family and neighborhood gatherings as well.

Some ethnic groups are associated with particular forms of music and organizations. Mexican Americans' use of Spanish-language music and the prevalence of polka bands in Czech communities come immediately to mind. A number of Mexican folk-dance groups perform in the state, and several branches of the Sokol remain active.

In the past two decades a resurgence of interest in cultural heritage, often demonstrated at ethnic festivals across the state, has occurred. Some festivals are short-lived local affairs; others, such as Wilber's Czech festival, have been going on for many years and attract thousands of visitors. Such celebrations are often awash in sentimentalization of heritage: "Perhaps there [are] people in the community who wished that their ancestors had had the good taste to wear Bavarian clothes and frilly dirndls and dance colorful dances, but the point is that they didn't; instead they baked, butchered, and made soap."[42] But most festivals are concrete manifestations of the lure that ethnicity has in the late twentieth century.[43]

Density and Distribution of the Population

Historically, eastern Nebraska has contained the state's largest towns and cities, the greatest concentration of smaller places, and the densest rural population. Over 50 percent of all Nebraskans reside within 50 mi (80 km) of the state's eastern border (Figure 3.12). Only one-fourth of the population lives west of Grand Island. The western half of the state (approximately west of Lexington and Broken Bow) contains only about 15 percent of the state's people.

This distribution is a product of both agricultural patterns and urban development. In the humid eastern third of the state, rural densities are high. Farther west, where rainfall diminishes, densities decline. The sparsest rural population is in the Sandhills region, where nearly all towns are smaller than 1,000, and rural population densities may fall below 1 person per sq mi (.4 per sq km) (Figure 3.13). The extreme case is Arthur County, with 513 people in 1980. Of these, 124 live in the county seat (and only town) of Arthur, leaving only 389 people in the 704 sq mi (1,823 sq km) that comprise the county.

Small farm numbers generally mean towns and cities are few and small, as well (Figure 3.14). In the eastern counties, numerous towns provide farm supplies, services, and shopping for a dense rural population. But in most western counties, the smaller number of farms cannot support as many centers.

Although Nebraska has been a rural state during most of its history, 43 percent of its population is now located in the counties of Douglas (location of Omaha), Sarpy (suburban Omaha), and Lancaster (Lincoln). This state, with a dominantly rural image, is actually very urban. Furthermore, many medium-sized cities are also located in the eastern third of the state—Grand Island, Hastings, Fremont, Norfolk, Columbus, and Beatrice.

The nonmetropolitan population of the eastern third of the state is rather evenly distributed, but farther west the densest populations are found in the Platte Valley. Here are located the largest cities of western Nebraska (Kearney, North Platte, and Scottsbluff), numerous smaller towns and cities, and dense rural settlements utilizing good soil and irrigation water. The continuing role of the Platte Valley as a transportation corridor (both the interstate highway and the railroads follow the river) has attracted jobs and population growth. Away from the valley, population densities are much lower.

Nearly everywhere in western Nebraska, river valleys support higher densities than do uplands. Surface-irrigation projects are associated with smaller farm sizes in the Republican Valley and along the Middle Loup. Population densities are also higher along the highways and railroads paralleling Lodgepole Creek, the upper Elkhorn, Beaver Creek in southwestern Nebraska, and the North Loup River. The only area of western Nebraska with dense populations away from rivers is the northern Panhandle, where Alliance and the towns in Dawes and northern Sheridan counties are associated with transportation corridors.

Urban/Rural Trends

Nebraska's population has been moving steadily toward urban areas. Only 23.7 percent of the population lived in towns and cities larger than twenty-five hundred at the turn of the century, but by 1980 that

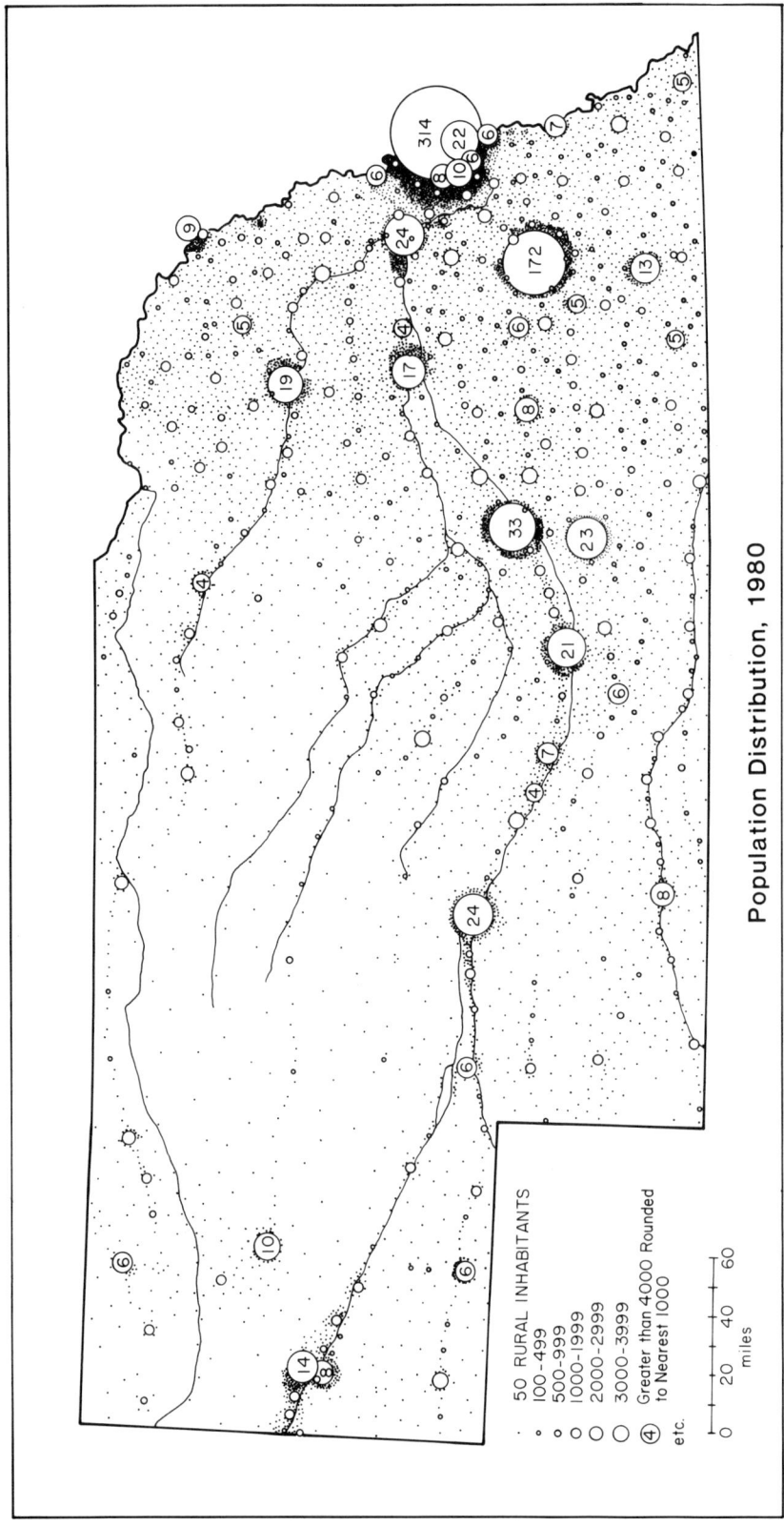

FIGURE 3.12. Population Distribution, 1980

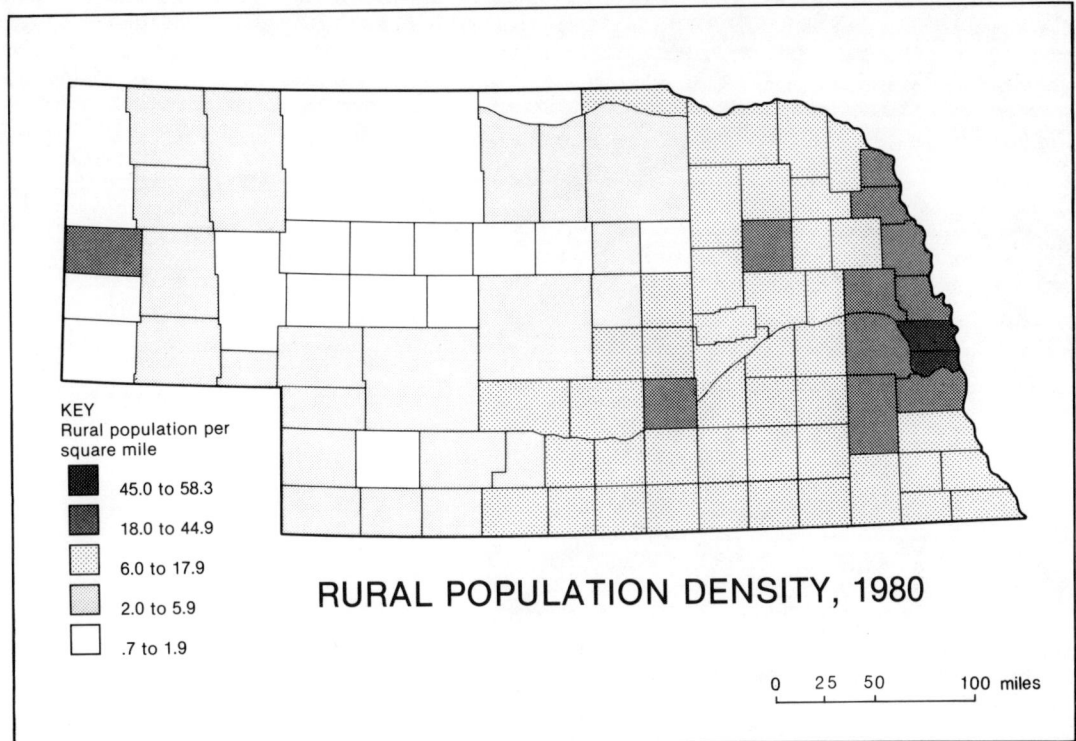

FIGURE 3.13.

figure had grown to 62.9 percent (Figure 3.15).

Between World War II and 1970, most growth was concentrated in the metropolitan areas and in a few other cities, such as Fremont, Norfolk, and Grand Island. Most rural counties lost population as the labor needs of agriculture declined with increasing mechanization. The greatest population declines were found in counties farthest from urban growth centers (Figure 3.16).

Since 1970, several dramatic changes have occurred in population trends (Figure 3.17). Although most of the large cities (between 10,000 and 40,000) have continued to grow, Omaha's growth has ceased. Between 1970 and 1980 the city's population declined 10 percent, mirroring a decline in large-city populations nationwide (Table 3.5). This decrease reversed a century of continual growth. The decline was not simply the movement of city dwellers to the suburbs. During the 1970s the Omaha metropolitan area grew by only 6 percent (compared to 22 percent growth during the 1960s); this reflecting less inmigration from rural areas.

Suburban growth did not cease, however. Sarpy County, almost wholly suburban, grew 30 percent in the 1970s to become the third most populous county in the state. Additional suburban growth occurred around Lincoln and South Sioux City (in Dakota County) and in the western half of Douglas County, where several precincts more than doubled their populations during the decade.[44]

A more striking trend was the reversal of population decreases in small towns and counties.[45] Although only twenty-one non-metropolitan counties grew during the 1960s, thirty-four gained population in the 1970s. Many of the rapidly growing counties contained larger cities, but some were rural. In a few cases, counties that had lost pop-

FIGURE 3.14. Brewster, population forty-six, is one of the smallest county seats in the United States. It provides government services to a very sparse rural population. Note the narrow band of irrigated agricultural land along the North Loup River. (USDA, ASCS)

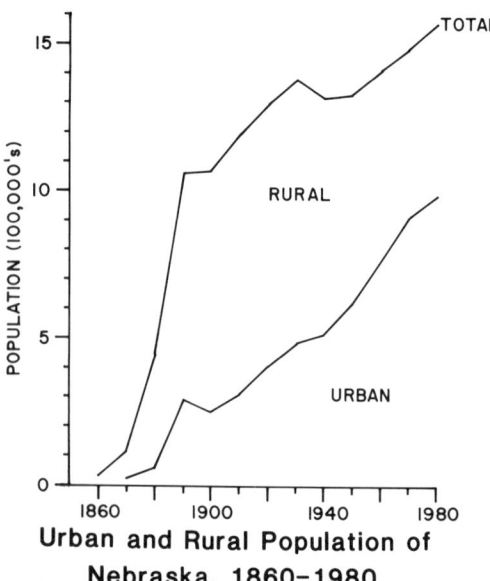

Urban and Rural Population of Nebraska, 1860-1980

FIGURE 3.15.

ulation every decade since the 1920s began to grow. The population of Stanton County, just east of Norfolk, had decreased steadily from its peak level of 7,809 in 1930 to only 5,758 people in 1970. During the 1970s Stanton County grew by 12.5 percent. Perkins County, which had declined from 5,834 to 3,423 between 1930 and 1970, grew by 5.2 percent during the 1970s.

Many smaller cities recorded similar population turnarounds (Figure 3.18). Only a few towns in the one thousand to fifty thousand range lost population during the 1970s. Most that did were located away from the Platte River/Interstate 80 corridor—for instance, near the Kansas border. By contrast, nearly all towns and cities along the interstate highway grew.

A number of factors seem to have been

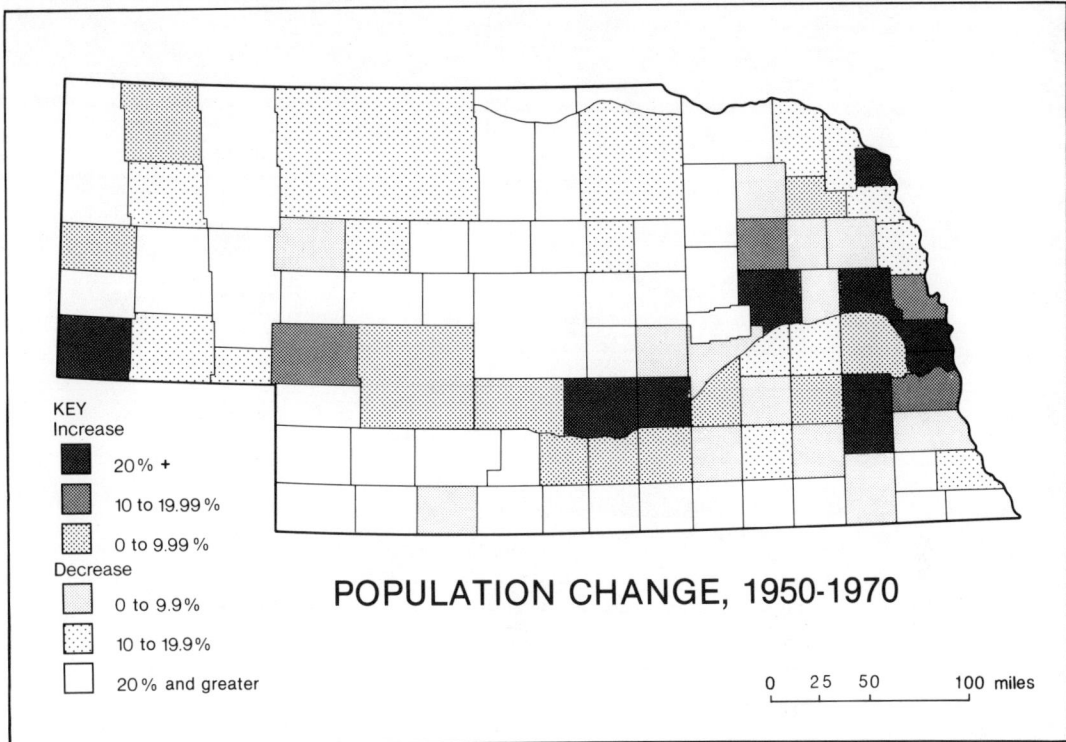

FIGURE 3.16.

responsible for the dramatic nationwide reversal of rural population loss. After World War II, improved transportation facilities and advances in communications decreased rural isolation. The diffusion of services, such as electricity, made rural areas more desirable residential locations (see Chapter 8).[46] Improved transportation and communications also made rural areas more appealing to employers. Manufacturing activity in rural areas grew rapidly during the 1960s and 1970s and was facilitated by relatively low energy costs. This, coupled with a growing preference for the quality of rural life, encouraged migration to smaller places in the nation.[47]

In Nebraska, new employment opportunities in manufacturing were concentrated in counties along the Platte Valley transportation corridor. Outside the Panhandle and Douglas County, every county through which the interstate highway runs grew during the 1970s. Other growing counties included those with cities of more than ten thousand people—places most likely to attract new jobs (see Chapter 4).

Chase, Holt, Perkins, and Rock counties, although away from the major transportation corridor and lacking large towns, grew rapidly during the 1970s. In each case, the introduction and expansion of center-pivot irrigation resulted in agricultural intensification: Land previously used for grazing or extensive wheat production was converted to corn. The increased flow of income into these counties appears to have reversed rural population decline.

Despite these trends, during the 1970s the Great Plains region lagged behind the rest of the country in the revival of nonmetropolitan growth and many Nebraska counties continued to lose population. This was most pronounced away from the transportation corridor in counties containing no large city. The southern tier of counties along the Kansas border and a number of

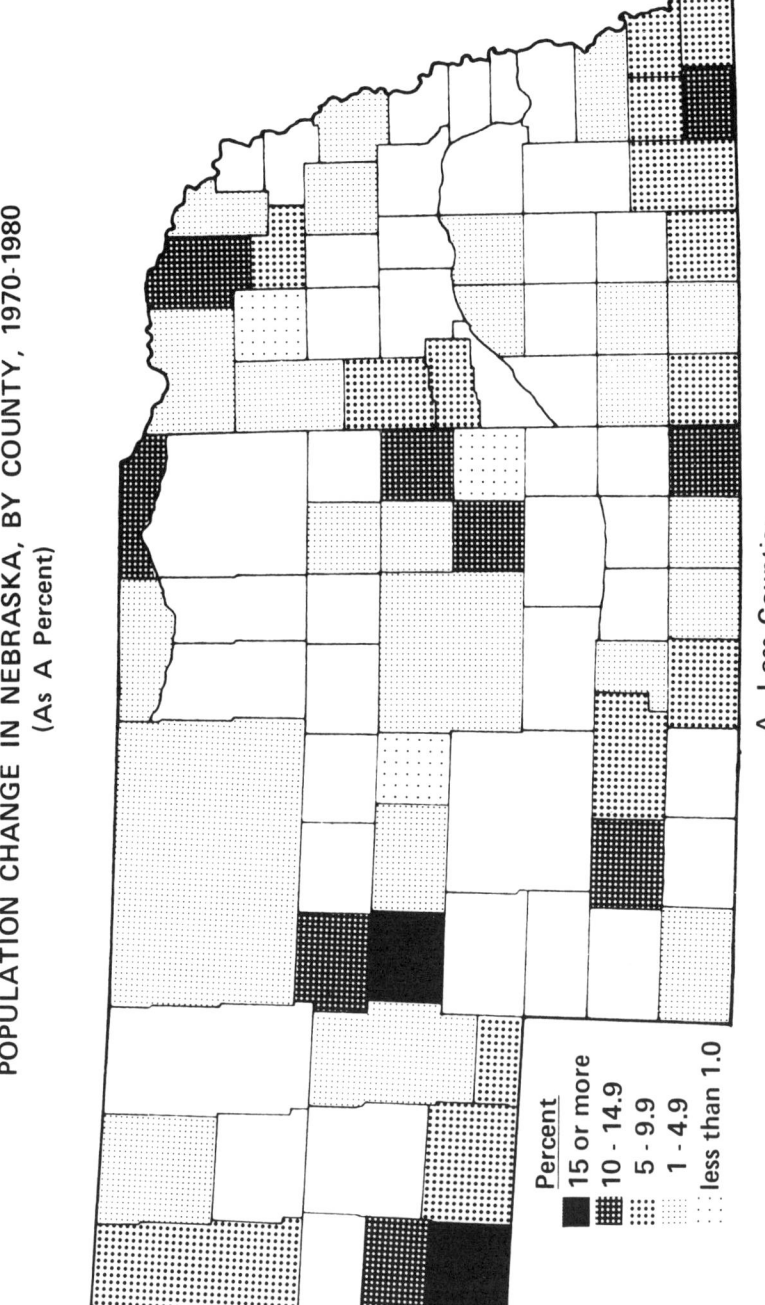

FIGURE 3.17

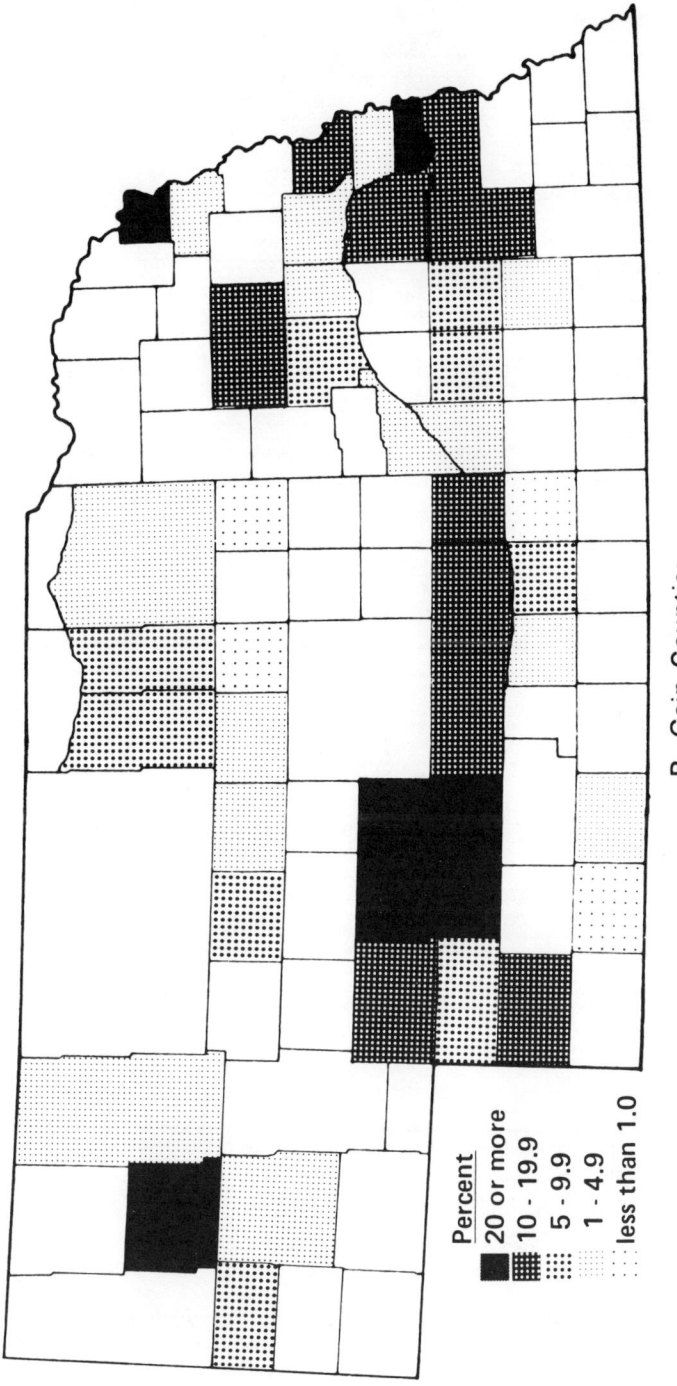

FIGURE 3.17 (continued) (UNO)

B. Gain Counties

TABLE 3.5

LARGEST CITIES IN 1980

	1980 Pop.	1970 Pop.	% Change 1970-1980
1 Omaha	313,939	347,328	− 9.5
2 Lincoln	171,932	149,518	+15.0
3 Grand Island	33,180	31,269	+ 6.1
4 North Platte	24,509	19,447	+25.9
5 Fremont	23,979	22,962	+ 4.4
6 Hastings	23,045	23,580	− 2.3
7 Bellevue	21,813	19,449	+12.2
8 Kearney	21,158	19,181	+10.3
9 Norfolk	19,449	16,607	+17.1
10 Columbus	17,328	15,471	+12.0
11 Scottsbluff	14,156	14,507	− 2.4
12 Beatrice	12,891	12,389	+ 4.1
13 Alliance	9,920	6,862	+44.6
14 La Vista	9,588	4,807	+99.5
15 South Sioux City	9,339	7,920	+17.9

Source: U.S. Bureau of the Census, <u>1980 Census of Population, Volume 1, Characteristics of the Population, Chapter B, General Population Characteristics</u> (Washington: U.S. Government Printing Office, 1982).

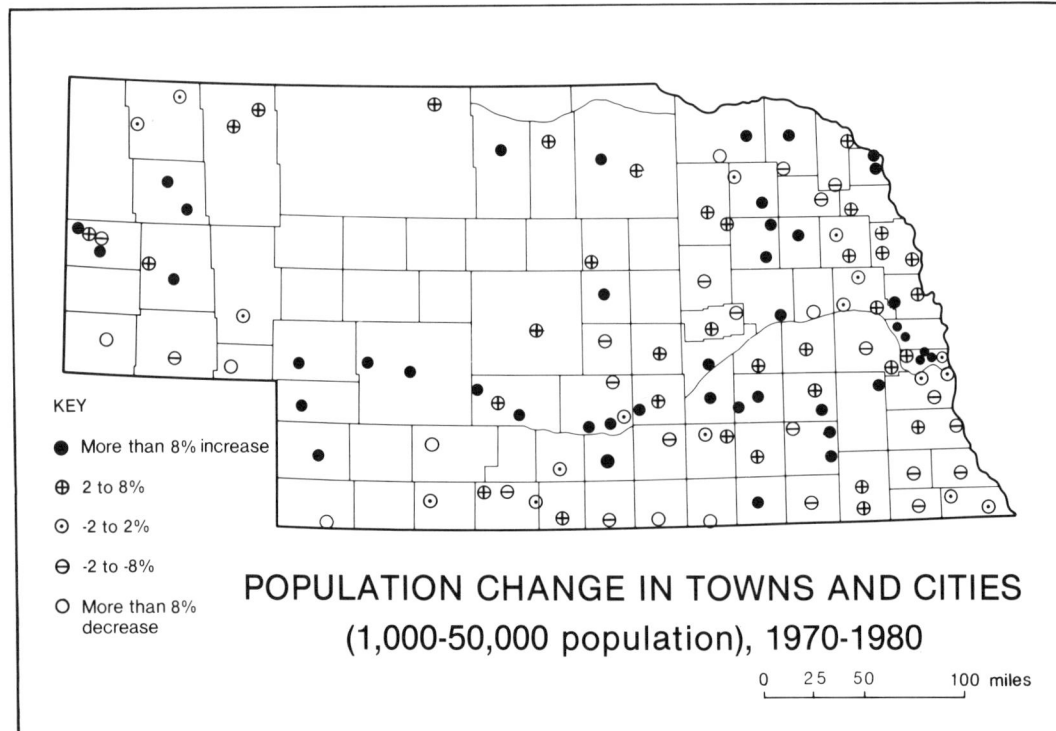

FIGURE 3.18.

counties in the central part of the state were among the biggest "losers" (see Figure 3.17).[48] In many of these counties, population decline has occurred in nearly every decade since 1890. Greeley County, for example, near the center of the state, had 8,685 people in 1920. After five decades of consecutive decline it had only 4,336 in 1970. This fell to 3,462 in 1980, about 40 percent of its 1920 population. Hayes County, with a population of 3,603 in 1930, recorded 1,530 in 1970 and only 1,356 in 1980, a fifty-year decline of 62 percent.

GROWTH

Nebraska's population (1.57 million in 1980) has been growing slowly, but fairly steadily, since 1900. Only between 1930 and 1940 did the state's population decline.

Natural Change: Births and Deaths

The population changes registered in the state, as well as within counties and towns, are actually a product of two sets of forces: natural change and migration. Statewide growth in Nebraska has traditionally relied more heavily on natural increase—the difference between birth and death rates—than on net inmigration. In most years until the 1970s, the surplus of births over deaths more than counterbalanced net outmigration and permitted the state to grow. This was most noticeable in the baby-boom years from about 1947 until 1962, when birthrates were high (Figure 3.19). In 1961, the peak year, 34,544 children were born in the state—about 20,000 more than the number of deaths.[49]

Along with the rest of the country, Nebraska birth and fertility rates plummeted in the mid-1960s. In the 1950s the number of children per family had been quite high. The fertility rate (number of births divided by the number of women between the ages of fifteen and forty-four) was 130/1,000. By 1973 that rate had dropped to 71/1,000. Even with a greater number of women

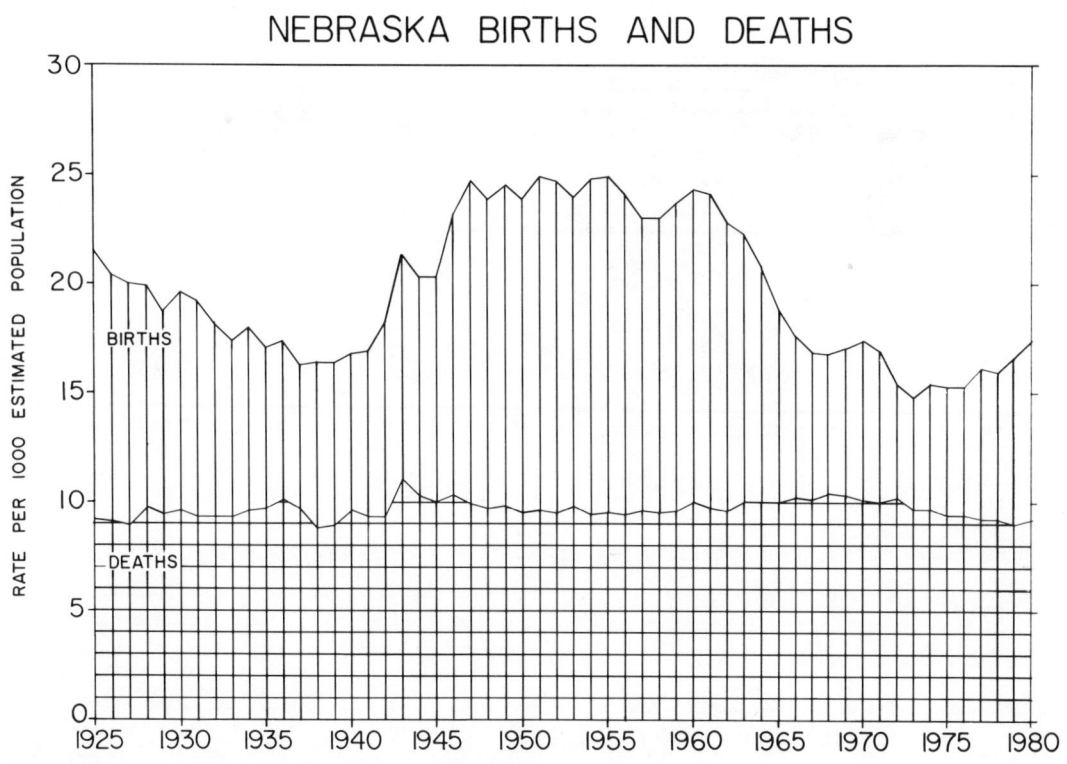

FIGURE 3.19. (Nebraska Department of Health)

entering childbearing years than ever before, the number of births in that year declined to under 23,000. Both fertility rate and number of births have increased somewhat since that time, to 77.4/1,000 and 27,335 in 1980. The birthrate of 17.4/1,000 in 1980 (nearly the same as the national figure) was about the same level as ten years earlier and was well below the 24.9 recorded in the 1950s. Because the number of deaths and the death rate have held fairly steady for the past thirty years, fluctuations in the birthrate have dramatically affected natural growth, which reached a low of under 8,000 in 1973 and has since risen to about 12,000 per year.[50]

The birthrate by county ranged from 10.9 to 23.4 per 1,000 in the late 1970s (Figure 3.20).[51] Some of the differences are attributable to the small population of many counties, which permits the birth of just a few children to alter the rate noticeably. Birthrates below the state average are more common in the southern half of the state, whereas higher rates are found in the Sandhills and the Panhandle. The lowest rates are along the southern border, an area with a higher proportion of the elderly than the state as a whole. A number of counties there have recorded more deaths than births in recent years, a situation of natural population decrease that has been fairly uncommon in rural areas.[52]

Death rates also vary within the state, and again, age of the population is a major factor in the pattern. The highest rates are found in the southern two tiers of counties with the greatest share of elderly in the population, while the lowest has been in Sarpy County (3.4 deaths per 1,000 population), as a result of a low median age and few persons over sixty-five. However, Nebraska has one of the lowest death rates in the country when adjusted for age of the population. The south-central portion of the state in particular has a very low

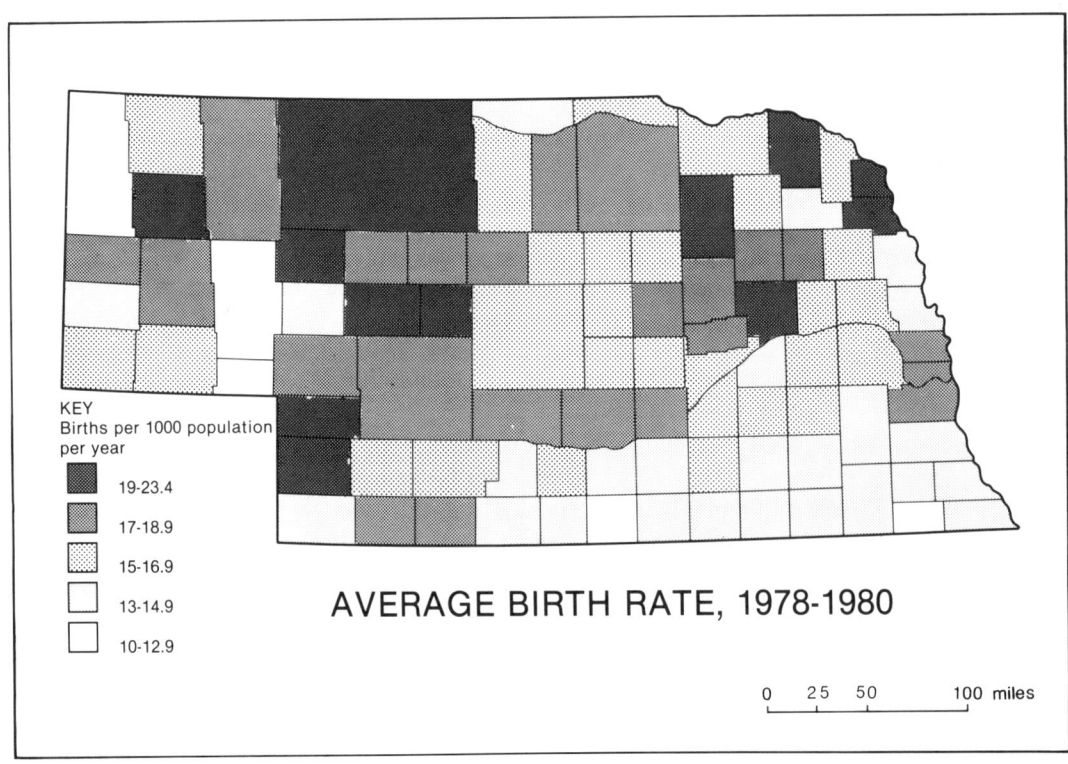

FIGURE 3.20. (Nebraska Department of Health)

age-adjusted death rate, although the factors behind this are not well understood.[53]

Age Structure

Clearly, the age structure of the population is an important key to understanding the rates of deaths and births. One of the simplest measures of the age of a population is median age (Figure 3.21). Nebraska's 1980 median age was 29.7, meaning that half of the population was younger and half was older than this. The lowest value was 25.3 in Sarpy County. Both Douglas and Lancaster counties were near the state median, but most rural counties had older populations. In six counties the median age was over 40, with a high of 45 in Pawnee County. The pattern of median age is closely associated with whether or not a given county has been growing. The highest median age in all the counties that gained population in the 1970s was 35.7. Of the counties that grew more than 10 percent during that decade, none had a median age above 32.3 On the other hand, counties with median ages above 40 lost population most rapidly.[54]

Generally, counties with high median ages had over 20 percent of their populations over the age of sixty-five. Such counties have the greatest outmigration, particularly of young adults looking for jobs in nearby or distant cities. The trend is especially pronounced in many small towns and villages. Because farmers have traditionally retired in nearby towns, median ages of some small places are above fifty. In some towns over one-third of the population is over age sixty-five.[55]

Examination of Nebraska's age pyramid reveals the changes that have taken place in the population (Figure 3.22). After a low birth rate in the 1930s came the baby boom of the late 1940s and 1950s, which produced the largest age group in Nebraska history. In 1960, these young children represented

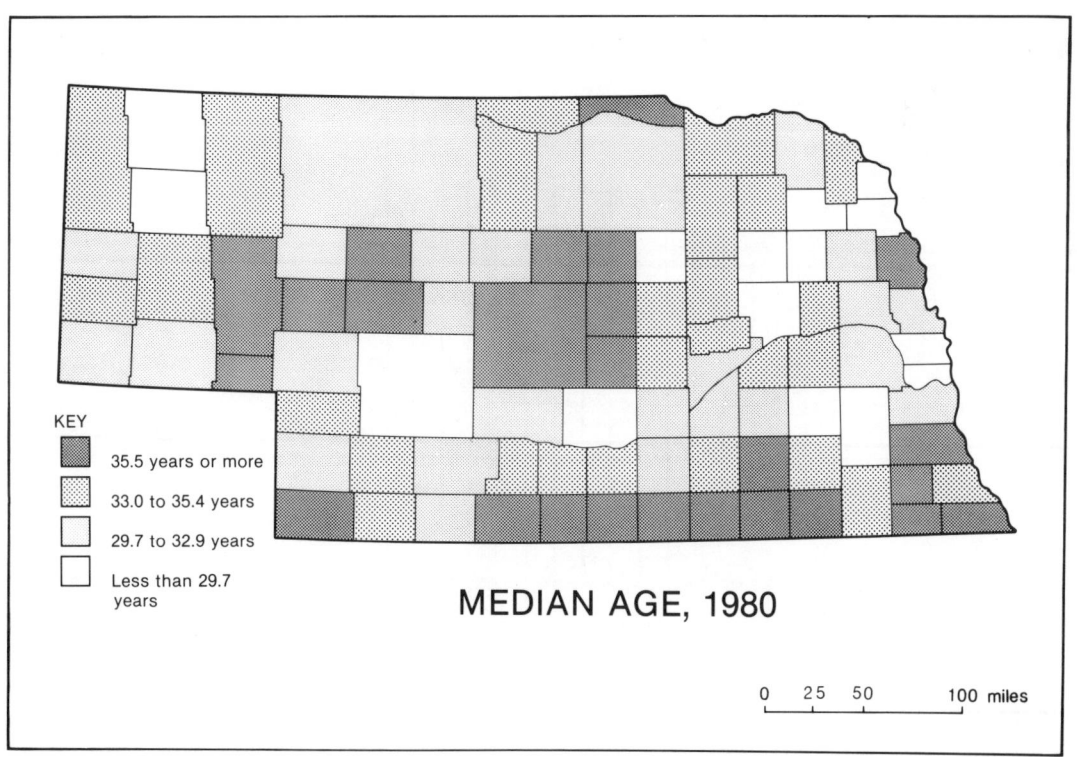

FIGURE 3.21. Based on *1980 Census of Population.*

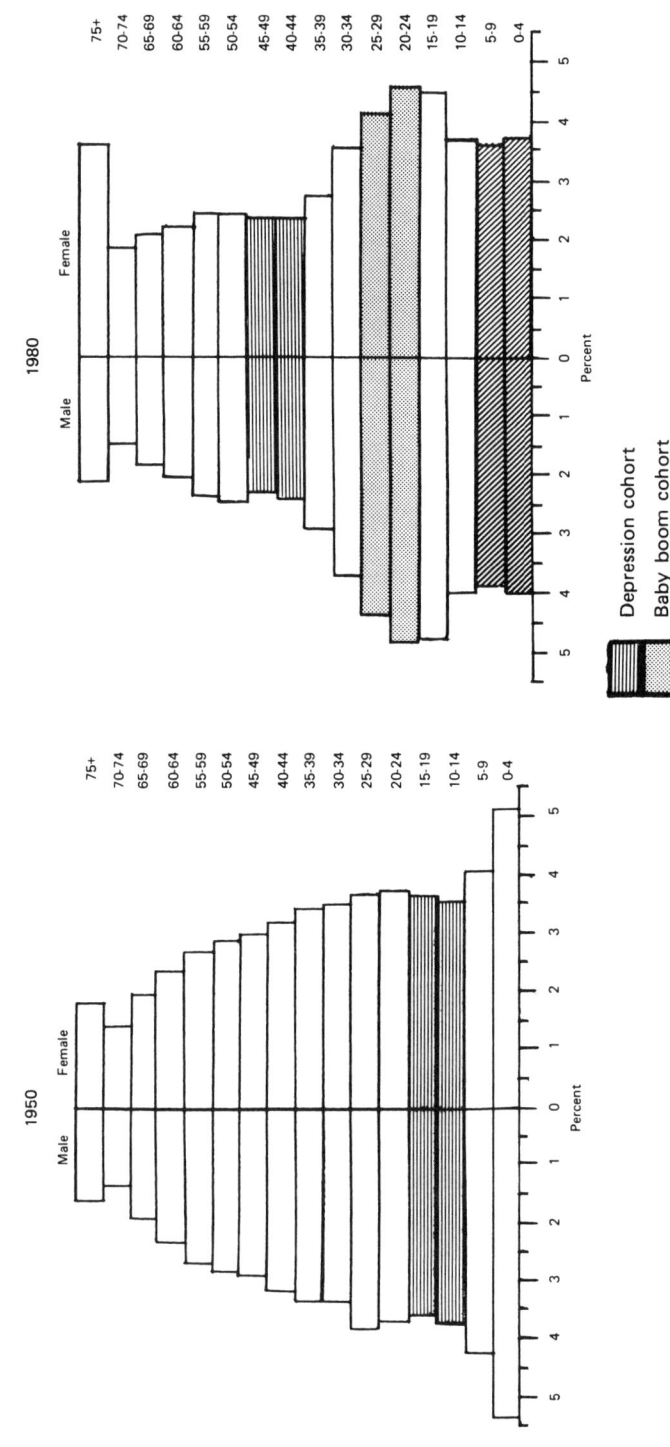

FIGURE 3.22. (UNL, Bureau of Business Research)

over 11 percent of the state's population. Today, as young adults, they remain the largest age group, accounting for nearly 10 percent of the population. Since the baby-boom era, the size of each successive age cohort has declined. As the number of children has decreased, the older age brackets have increased their share of total population.[56]

Nebraska's age profile closely resembles that of the United States as a whole. The pyramids of some counties like Douglas and Lancaster are similar to the state's, but those of many rural counties clearly show a large number of elderly and a high median age.

Where job opportunities are limited, particularly in counties far from the larger towns and cities into which industry has been moving in recent years, the population of young adults is quite small. For instance, a large proportion of young adults have left Boyd County (on the South Dakota border) to find employment. That this is a product of postwar trends can be confirmed by comparing the 1930 and the 1980 profile (Figure 3.23). Fifty years ago, outmigration after high school was not especially dramatic. Today, few young adults remain in the county. Boyd County has been losing population steadily for fifty years and at the same time has been growing older.[57] Because "aging" counties have so few young adults, the number of births has continued to decline. The near future will likely bring smaller school enrollments, closed schools, and greater difficulty in providing educational services in those schools that manage to survive.

Migration

Outmigration is nothing new for Nebraska. From the close of the settlement period to the 1970s the state has experienced a net loss of population through migration quite regularly, estimated as 175,000 in the 1930s; 135,000 in the 1940s; 117,000 in the 1950s; and 73,000 in the 1960s.[58] Although Nebraska lost more migrants than it gained, some individual counties had net inmigration. These were generally counties with a city larger than ten thousand people. Smaller counties contributed migrants to fuel that urban growth.[59]

During the 1970s migration trends changed dramatically. Between 1970 and 1980 net outmigration was less than thirteen thousand. Furthermore, although only

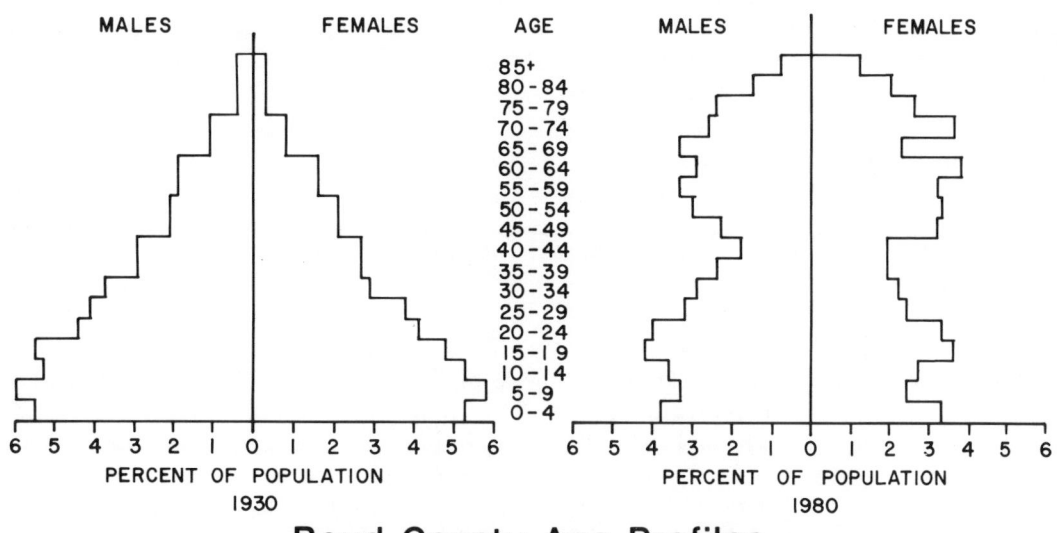

Boyd County Age Profiles

FIGURE 3.23.

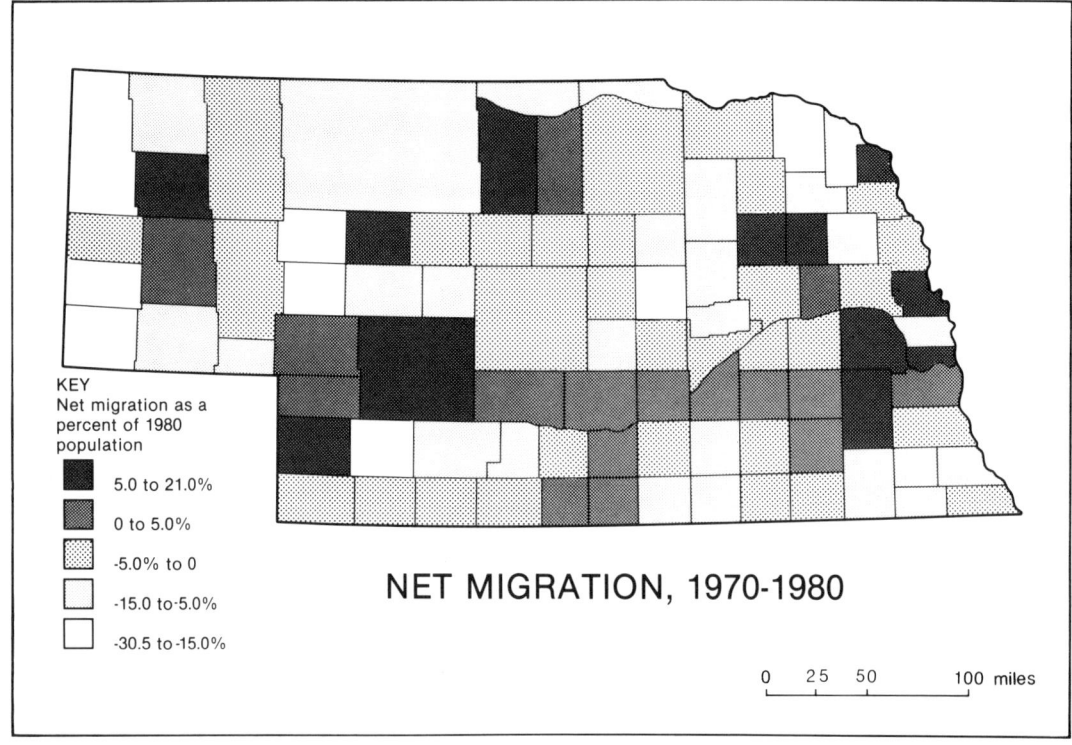

FIGURE 3.24.

six counties recorded net inmigration during the 1960s, twenty-eight did so during the 1970s, and all but thirteen had less outmigration than previously. Counties with net inmigration were found all across the state, including urban and rural areas, both west and east, and even in a number of southern border counties where population declines have been so severe in recent decades (Figure 3.24).[60]

If the nationwide trend of net urban-to-rural migration continues, many Nebraska counties may find population growth occurring in the future (Figure 3.25). The degree to which such projections are realized will depend on continuance of the forces that led to the "rural renaissance" of the 1970s. Some see in the rural turnaround a fundamental shift in U.S. population distribution that will continue through the 1980s and beyond. Others suggest that rural growth was simply a one-time quirk of the 1970s and that the forces

that produced growth—cheap energy, irrigation development, and dispersal of manufacturing—have weakened.[61] Clemente and Krannich argue that "the 1980s may well be characterized by a second turnaround, with a resumption of migration flows out of rural areas toward metropolitan and urban areas."[62]

NEBRASKANS AS MIDWESTERNERS

Patterns of age structure, migration, and natural change fail to give a sense of the character of Nebraska's population. What are Nebraskans really *like?* How do they differ from people in other parts of the country? How do they differ regionally across the state?

It is tempting to characterize Nebraskans with many of the descriptions applied by John Fraser Hart to midwesterners as a whole—to say that they place great value on materialism, functionalism, and tech-

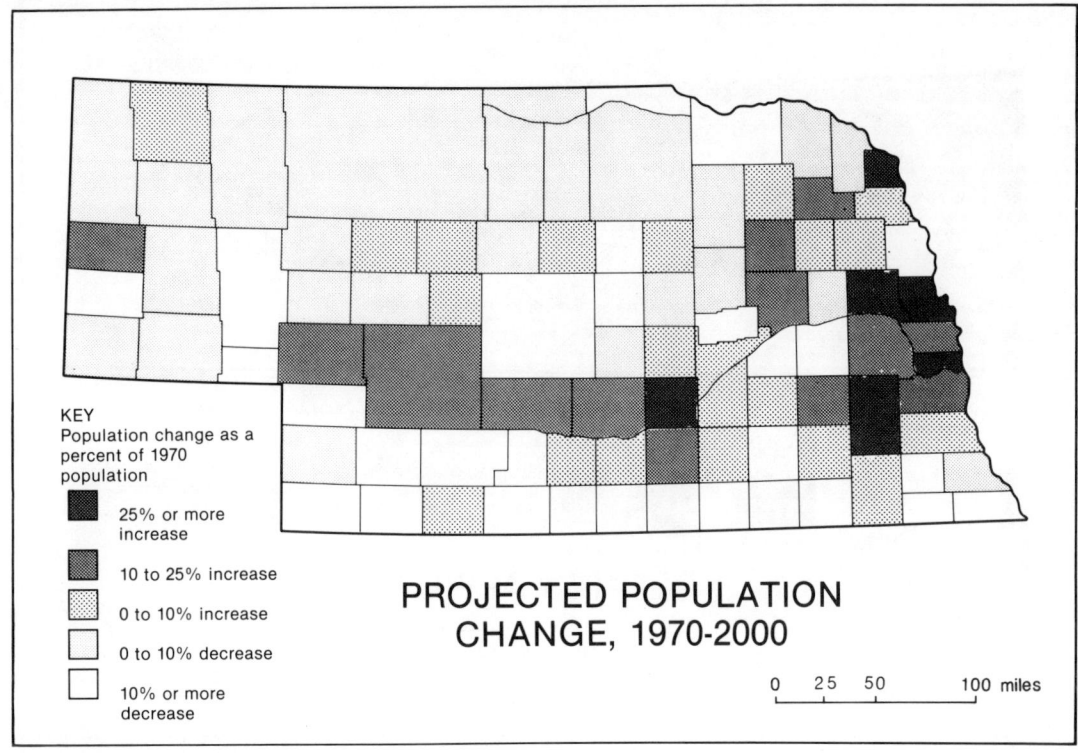

FIGURE 3.25. (UNL, Bureau of Business Research)

nology.[63] Hart described the midwesterner as a conspicuous consumer, particularly of the latest fashion, the most powerful boat, and housing in the best neighborhoods. To the midwestern (and presumably the Nebraskan) mind, the purpose of any activity, and especially that of government, should be problem oriented and practical, with the end result being a clear-cut solution. This is manifested in education, said Hart, where applied subjects such as agriculture and engineering are emphasized over those that stress less-measurable quantities. "What good is it (to me)?" is a question and an attitude frequently expressed. Finally, a trust in technology, and in the latest and biggest machines, is common, as is a distrust of outsiders, of government, and of all sorts of nonconformity.[64]

Many attributes of Nebraskans are more properly those of rural populations. In general, rural residents are more likely to be products of a work ethic, making less use of leisure time and participating less in recreational activities than their urban counterparts. Rural dwellers are also more individualistic regarding economic matters, more isolationist in their outlook toward foreign policy, and more oriented toward local control in government.[65]

However, the state's residents are a diverse lot in many ways and are not so easily pigeonholed. The residents of the Panhandle are substantially different from Omahans. Sandhills ranchers are not the same as Corn Belt farmers. These differences are evident in several aspects of Nebraska culture, including politics and religion.

Political Affiliation

Nebraska is clearly identified in the popular mind as rock-ribbed, conservative Republican territory. Yet its two most famous political figures are a populist Democrat, William Jennings Bryan, and a progressive,

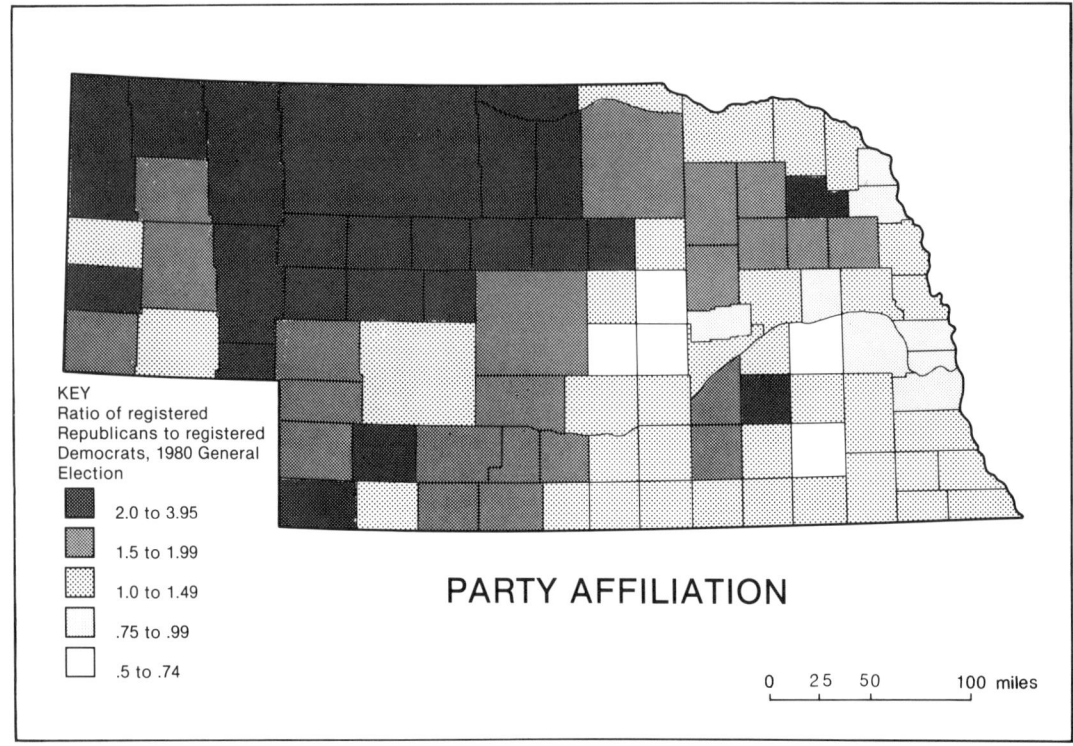

FIGURE 3.26. (Nebraska Legislative Council)

independent Republican, George Norris. The latter was allied with the New Deal and was endorsed for reelection by Franklin Roosevelt. The generally conservative outlook of Nebraska politics has been punctuated by occasional streaks of radicalism—from the Populists of the 1890s and the Farm Holiday movement of the 1930s to the activist postures and strikes of several farm organizations in the past two decades.

In presidential elections, Nebraska leans to the Republican party and conservatism, having voted for a Democrat only once in the last forty years (in 1964). Conservatism is also expressed in a distrust of professional politicians and of centralized governmental functions.[66] Most Nebraskans, particularly in rural areas, would prefer that decisions be made locally—preferably at the county level rather than in Lincoln, and certainly not in Washington.

Republicans are strongest in rural counties of the western half of the state (Figure 3.26). In some Sandhills counties the ratio of registered Republicans to Democrats was nearly 4:1 in 1980. The principal exceptions to Republican dominance in the west are counties with larger cities. Scotts Bluff and Lincoln counties have nearly as many Democrats as Republicans, as does Cheyenne County. Here, blue-collar workers and greater nonagricultural employment dilute the Republican leanings of rural residents.

Farther east the proportion of Democrats increases. About a dozen counties recorded more Democrats than Republicans in 1980, even after a period of Democratic slippage. As might be expected, Democrats were dominant in the metropolitan Omaha area with its large number of blue-collar and ethnic voters who traditionally favor that party. On the other hand, Lancaster County gave the Republicans a slight edge. Proportionately, the greatest Democratic strength lay in several rural counties in central and east-central Nebraska. Sherman, Greeley, Butler, and Saline counties have nearly twice as many Democrats as

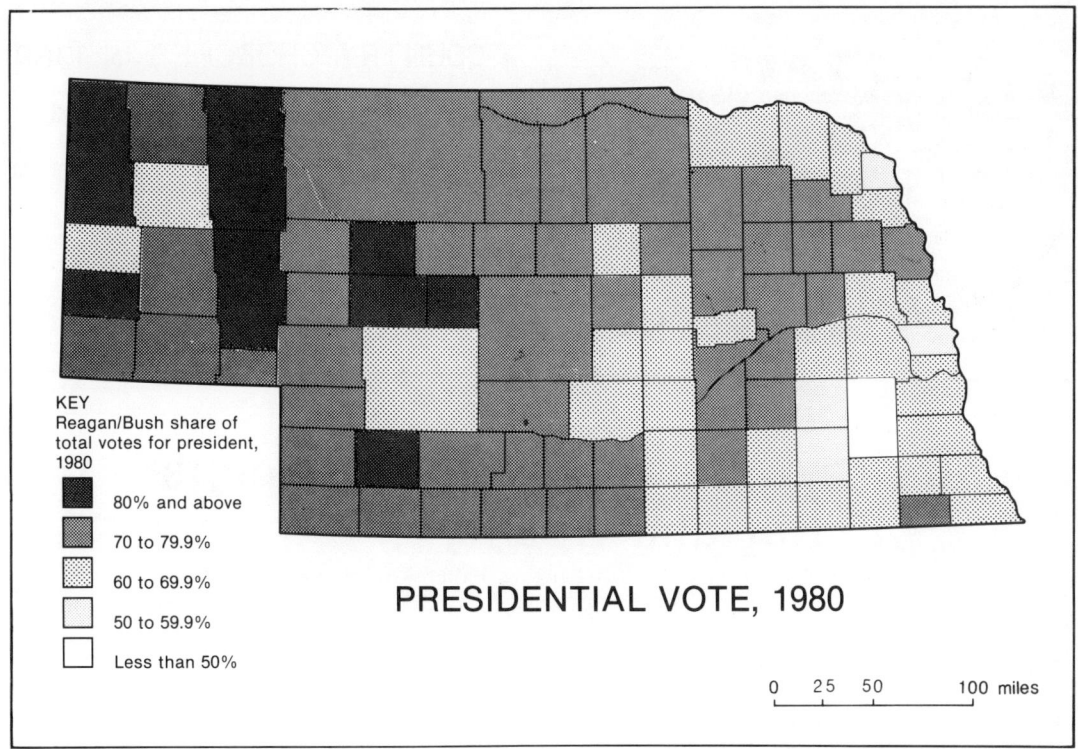

FIGURE 3.27. (Nebraska Legislative Council)

Republicans. Czechs and Poles, predominantly Catholic, are the largest groups in those counties. Concentrations of Germans and Scandinavians tend to lean toward the Republicans.[67]

There are, of course, differences between party registration and voting behavior. Republican candidates for president seldom fail to win large majorities in Nebraska. In 1980, for example, Reagan and Bush carried all but Lancaster County. The share of votes cast for the Republican ticket went as high as 89 percent in Banner County and was well over 75 percent in most of the Sandhills and the Panhandle (Figure 3.27). The lowest majorities were generally in the ethnic counties with greater Democratic strength.

Republican though the state is in registration and presidential voting, Nebraskans exhibit a substantial independent streak in gubernatorial elections. During the past twenty-five years, only two Republicans have been elected governor—they held office for a total of eight years. Democrats, albeit somewhat conservative by national standards, have also been elected to the U.S. Senate. Straight party-line voting is not a strong tradition in Nebraska.

Religion

The large, mainstream Protestant bodies that predominate in the Midwest are strong in Nebraska as well. The most numerous Protestant denominations in Nebraska are Methodists, Presbyterians, and Lutherans. Both Methodists and Presbyterians are widely distributed, whereas Lutherans are more numerous in the eastern half of the state, particularly in counties with a sizable German or Scandinavian element. Denominations that have their national strength concentrated in the South—Church of Christ, Baptist, and Assembly of God—are relatively less numerous in Nebraska.[68]

The largest denomination in the state is Roman Catholicism. Roman Catholic churches are found in the larger towns and

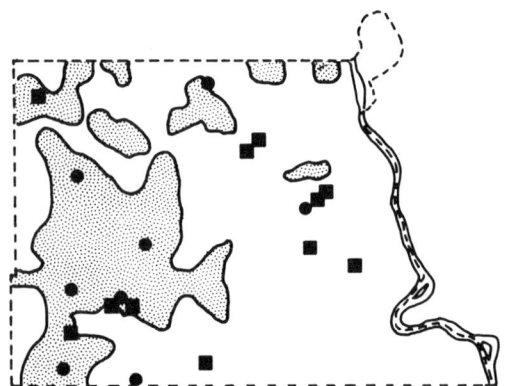

Country Churches and Ethnic Groups in Nemaha County

FIGURE 3.28. Source: Robert Stoddard, "Changing Patterns of Some Rural Churches," *Rocky Mountain Social Science Journal* 7, no. 1 (1970):61–68. Modified and reprinted by permission.

cities and in rural ethnic communities. Rural congregations are common in counties with large numbers of Czechs, Germans, and Poles. Catholic churches are relatively few in the western half of the state, except in the larger towns.[69]

The other denomination with many rural churches is Lutheranism. Both Catholic and Lutheran churches, along with Congregational, Methodist, and Presbyterian congregations, were commonly found outside small towns in the late nineteenth century. Because transportation was difficult, parishes were located in rural areas to serve the largest number of faithful without requiring a long journey to church. In general, Catholic and Lutheran parishes were organized by ethnic groups; Methodists, Presbyterians, and others were not so associated. As transportation improved and as rural population densities began to fall, many rural churches found they did not have large enough congregations to survive. Churches closed, and former parishioners were not terribly inconvenienced by a 10- or 15-mi (16- or 24-km) drive to the nearest town with a congregation of their faith.[70]

Consolidation and relocation of churches was much more common among the nonethnic denominations than among Lutherans and Catholics (Figure 3.28). Rural churches of these denominations, presumably because of their ethnic identification, remain an important component of the religious landscape of contemporary Nebraska. It is rare, however, to find operating congregations of Methodists, Presbyterians, Baptists, or Congregationalists in the countryside, even though they may thrive in small towns.[71]

That Nebraskans should resemble the Midwest in so many ways is not especially surprising. Political and religious preferences of the state's people reflect their heritage—the American Midwest, along with northwestern and central Europe. Nebraskans resemble the Midwest in innumerable other ways, including language patterns, crime rates, housing traditions, educational attainment, and attitudes toward education.[72] Furthermore, most Nebraskans think of themselves as midwesterners.[73] Nebraska's economy, particularly the importance of agriculture and the growing role of manufacturing, is midwestern as well.

CHAPTER 4

ECONOMIC ACTIVITIES AND ECONOMIC HEALTH

Like that of the rest of the Midwest, Nebraska's economic health is heavily dependent on agriculture, but much of that dependence is indirect. Less than 5 percent of the population (about 10 percent of the labor force) is engaged in farming, but many more depend for their livelihoods on providing agricultural goods and services, processing agricultural products, producing agricultural equipment, transporting farm goods, and selling farm supplies.[1]

Irrigation equipment from Nebraska is sold around the world. Implements produced in Nebraska supply farmers throughout the United States. Many firms in the state are dependent on the overall health of agriculture in Nebraska and elsewhere. Small towns and cities rely on retail purchases by farmers of food, clothing, health and legal services, and farm equipment and services. When farm income is up, these activities prosper; when farm income drops, the level of retail activity slows and businesses close.

Such economic fluctuations might be expected to moderate as the state's economy diversifies. Small towns in particular, tied to the retail needs of a steadily decreasing number of farm families, have sought to attract manufacturing plants in the hope of stabilizing their economies and reducing outmigration. But in some counties farm earnings still account for more than 60 percent of total income.

The distribution of natural resources, particularly those critical for agriculture—soil, water, climatic factors—has influenced the pattern of farming activities and of economic activities that service the agricultural sector. Yet physical features are not the sole determinants of economic location. Transportation and communication links to the nation and the world tie Nebraska's resources to consumers and permit national trends in industrialization, technology, consumer demand, residential preference, marketing, and life-style to permeate the state. Government policies and activities at the local, state, and national level have directed Nebraska's economic development. Furthermore, the people of Nebraska and the qualities they possess as a labor force, as consumers, and as entrepreneurs have enabled certain activities to prosper, while others have faltered.

For some activities, certain of these factors are relatively unimportant and others stand out. Public policy had some effect on the development of the center-pivot irrigation industry in the state, for example, but both Nebraska's resource endowment and historical accident were much more crucial. On the other hand, the development of the central Platte Valley as an important manufacturing region owes much to the decision to locate the interstate highway along that route and to the superb rail links that area enjoys. The mix of these factors—

environment, population, location, government policy, and historical accident—is responsible for the patterns of economic health in the state.

NEBRASKA'S ECONOMIC HEALTH

In most years per capita income in Nebraska is lower than the national average. Exceptions to this generalization occur in years of high farm prices. In 1973, for example, farm income was 85 percent higher than in 1972, and Nebraska's total income topped $8 billion, over $5,000 per person (Table 4.1). Generally, Nebraskans receive an average of 90 to 100 percent of national per capita income. A national trend toward increased income for farmers is evident in Nebraska. In 1978 U.S. farmers earned 91 percent of the income of nonfarm residents, compared to only 37 percent in 1940.[2]

Wealth and Poverty

It is more difficult to estimate average income at the county level. Actual income figures provide only a rough estimate of the true economic fortunes of a county, particularly where farm income represents a sizable proportion of total income. Farm income is dependent on the amount of farm products sold and the price obtained for those products, as well as production expenses. Because prices for many agricultural commodities range widely from year

TABLE 4.1

PERSONAL INCOME FOR NEBRASKA AND THE UNITED STATES

1960-1981

Year	Nebraska Income (millions of $)	U.S. Income (billions of $)
1960	2,846	402.3
1961	2,913	417.8
1962	3,159	443.6
1963	3,265	466.2
1964	3,364	499.2
1965	3,761	540.7
1966	4,040	588.2
1967	4,238	630.0
1968	4,528	690.6
1969	5,248	754.7
1970	5,578	811.1
1971	5,974	868.4
1972	6,785	951.4
1973	8,104	1,065.2
1974	8,278	1,168.6
1975	9,310	1,265.0
1976	9,618	1,391.2
1977	10,489	1,538.0
1978	11,832	1,721.8
1979	13,672	1,943.8
1980	14,300	2,160.2
1981	16,234	2,404.1

Source: University of Nebraska-Lincoln, Bureau of Business Research

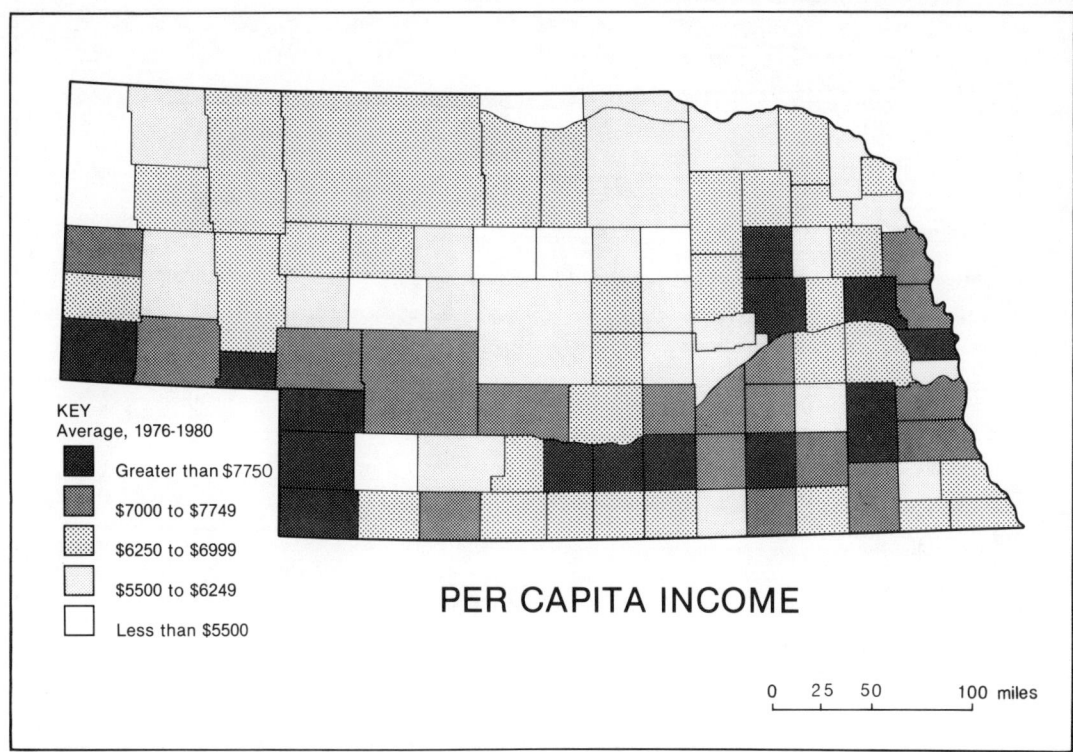

FIGURE 4.1. (Nebraska Department of Economic Development)

to year, farm income can fluctuate dramatically.[3] The validity of median income as a measure of economic health depends on what is included as income and the relative importance of farm and nonfarm income. Different means of estimating farm income can produce substantially different results, so data must be used with caution.[4]

The statewide per capita income from 1976 to 1980 averaged $7,261. Omaha and Lincoln have higher than average incomes, as do the more populous counties of the Platte Valley and counties with large cities (Figure 4.1). Rural counties tend to have income levels somewhat below the state average, particularly in the northeastern part of the state and in the Sandhills. Some rural counties, however, consistently have fairly high incomes, especially in the more heavily irrigated areas of southwestern and south-central Nebraska.[5]

These patterns are reflected in the distribution of families below the poverty level (Figure 4.2). The 1980 census found 8.0 percent of Nebraska families below the poverty line ($7,412 for a family of four), somewhat lower than the national average (9.6 percent). High poverty levels were concentrated in rural counties. Several counties—Greeley, Boyd, Logan, Blaine, and Thurston—had over 20 percent of their population below the poverty line. Most were dependent on agriculture and experienced population loss during the 1970s. The lowest incidence of poverty was found in and near larger cities and in the prosperous central Platte Valley. Twenty-three counties recorded poverty levels below the state average. Nearly all of them contained a city of more than five thousand people and most gained population during the 1970s. In only a few of the counties with low poverty levels was agriculture the major source of income and employment.[6]

Economic health, by either measure, is associated with urbanization and economic

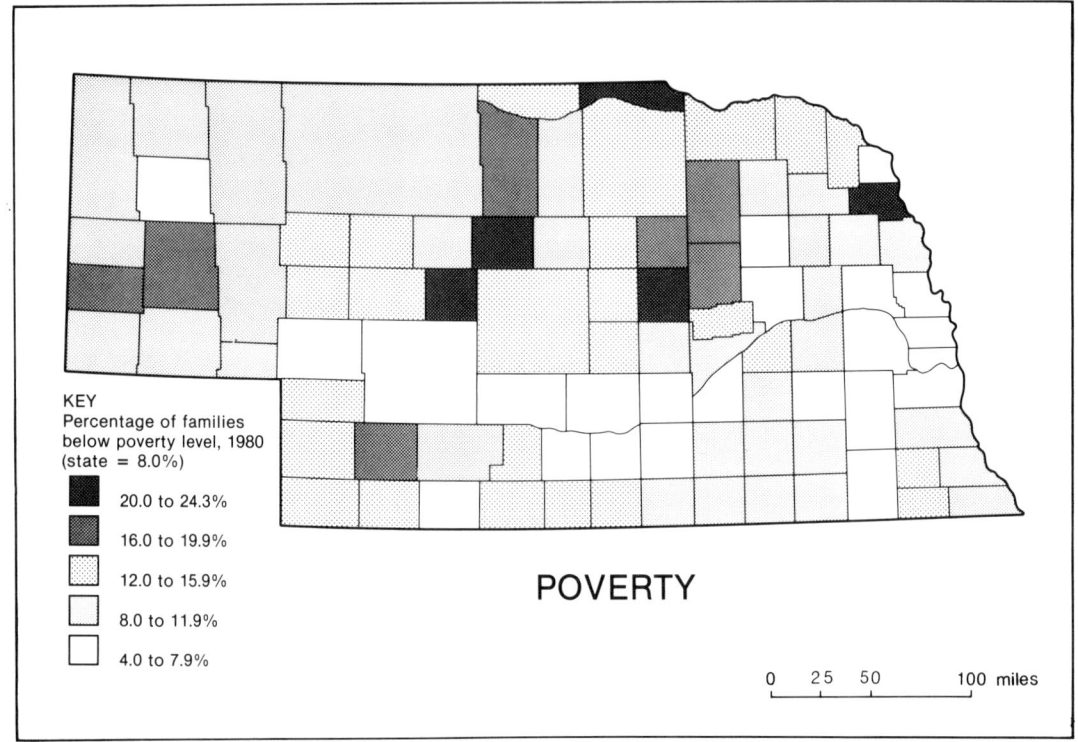

FIGURE 4.2. (UNL, Bureau of Business Research)

diversity. The Omaha and Lincoln metropolitan areas are particularly strong, but the Interstate 80–Platte River corridor counties have impressively low poverty rates and high per capita income. Here the economy rests upon a mix of irrigated agriculture, retail trade, and manufacturing. Transportation links to east and west have spurred growth of the area's population and economy.

Several poverty pockets do not show up in this county-level analysis. Subcounty areas with sizable minority populations have higher poverty rates and lower incomes than the county averages. The incidence of poverty among blacks in the state was 25.3 percent, roughly the national average. Because most blacks live in Douglas and Lancaster counties, their lower incomes and higher poverty levels are obscured by the larger, more affluent white populations. Native Americans also have lower incomes, as can be seen in the relatively high incidence of poverty in Thurston and Knox counties.[7]

The Labor Force

The income of the state and of individual counties reflects the proportion of the population that is in the labor force and the wages and salaries received by workers. About 57 percent of the state's people are employed or seeking employment, slightly lower than the national average. The difference is partly attributable to Nebraska's higher median age. Counties with a high proportion of persons over sixty-five years of age generally have lower labor-force participation rates than those with more people in the eighteen to sixty-five age group. Many of the latter counties contain a larger city and offer more employment opportunities than do rural areas.[8]

In these urban counties employment opportunities for women are greatest. Consequently, the highest rates of participation in the labor force by women are found in Omaha and Lincoln and in counties with cities of more than five thousand people. Rural counties, especially those far from employment opportunities, are more likely to have female participation rates below 30 percent.[9]

Unemployment rates are consistently lower in Nebraska than in the nation as a whole. Because there are fewer manufacturing jobs than in the rest of the country, the number of Nebraskans laid off during economic downturns is relatively small. Rural counties seldom experience high unemployment (Figure 4.3). Most counties have unemployment rates below 3 percent, even when the statewide rate may be over 4 percent and the national average 10 percent.

Highest unemployment rates occur in Omaha, with its concentration of manufacturing, and in counties bordering the Missouri River. Here are a number of small cities—Falls City, Nebraska City, Plattsmouth, Blair—that traditionally were important centers of employment. Bypassed by the interstate highway system and the stimulus it provides to economic development, these places gradually lost manufacturing employment at the same time that their roles as trade centers declined. The highest unemployment rate is in Thurston County, where large numbers of landless Omaha and Winnebago Indians have had difficulty obtaining needed education and job skills. Box Butte and Lincoln counties, both dependent on the rail industry, show great fluctuations in unemployment rates.

Wages in Nebraska are somewhat lower than the national average, even for workers in the same employment category. In 1974, for example, Nebraska manufacturing employees received hourly wages 8 percent lower than the national average. One of the attractions of Nebraska to industry has been

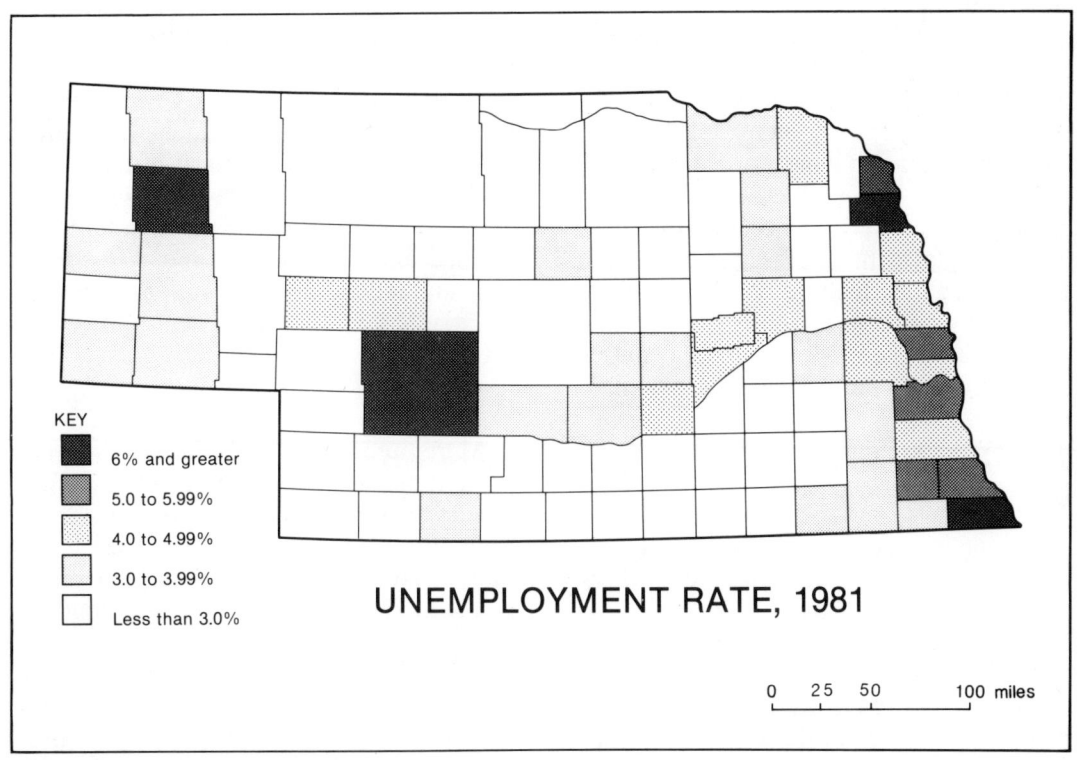

FIGURE 4.3. Based on material from Nebraska Department of Labor.

TABLE 4.2

TOTAL EMPLOYMENT BY ECONOMIC SECTOR, 1981 AVERAGE

Agriculture		73,346
Manufacturing		94,947
Durable Goods	48,465	
Non-Durable Goods	46,482	
Mining		1,682
Construction		26,337
Transportation		30,348
Communication and Utilities		16,724
Trade		162,547
Wholesale	48,053	
Retail	114,494	
Finance, Insurance and Real Estate		41,179
Services, except Domestic		120,867
Government		130,473
Total		698,450

Source: Nebraska Department of Labor.

the lower wages paid in the state. Thus, many industries that have located in Nebraska have high labor needs, particularly for relatively unskilled labor. The lower rate of unionization in the state also attracts labor-intensive industries.[10]

As agricultural employment has declined, employment in manufacturing, trade, services, and governmental sectors of the economy has gradually increased. Each of these categories had more workers than did agriculture by 1981 (Table 4.2). These four categories are likely to account for most future employment increases in the state. Even though agriculture is the primary source of income in two-thirds of Nebraska's counties, the more populous counties are most reliant on services and manufacturing.[11]

MINING

Mining is relatively unimportant in Nebraska. Fewer than two thousand workers were employed in extractive industries in 1981. Historically most important have been Nebraska's sand, gravel, and limestone operations. Over two thousand sand and gravel pits have been utilized during the twentieth century; about two hundred are currently active in supplying state construction needs (Figure 4.4). They are concentrated along major rivers, particularly in the more densely populated areas where sand and gravel use is heaviest. The largest operations are in counties adjacent to Nebraska's metropolitan areas. Clay is produced by a few firms for brick production. Limestone mines are concentrated in Cass County, near Louisville and Weeping Water, where nine quarries produced 69 percent of the state's limestone in 1975 (Figure 4.5). Nebraska's limestone production is in the form of crushed and broken rock and is used for concrete and other construction purposes, for roadbases, and in agricultural applications.[12]

Oil and Gas

More important to Nebraska in total value is the oil and gas industry. The first oil discoveries in the state were made in Richardson County in 1939, but significant finds in the early 1950s made Cheyenne and Kimball counties the largest producers. Additional fields were opened in Red Willow and Hitchcock counties in the early 1960s. State production peaked at nearly 25 million barrels in 1962. By 1969, production had fallen to half the 1962 level,

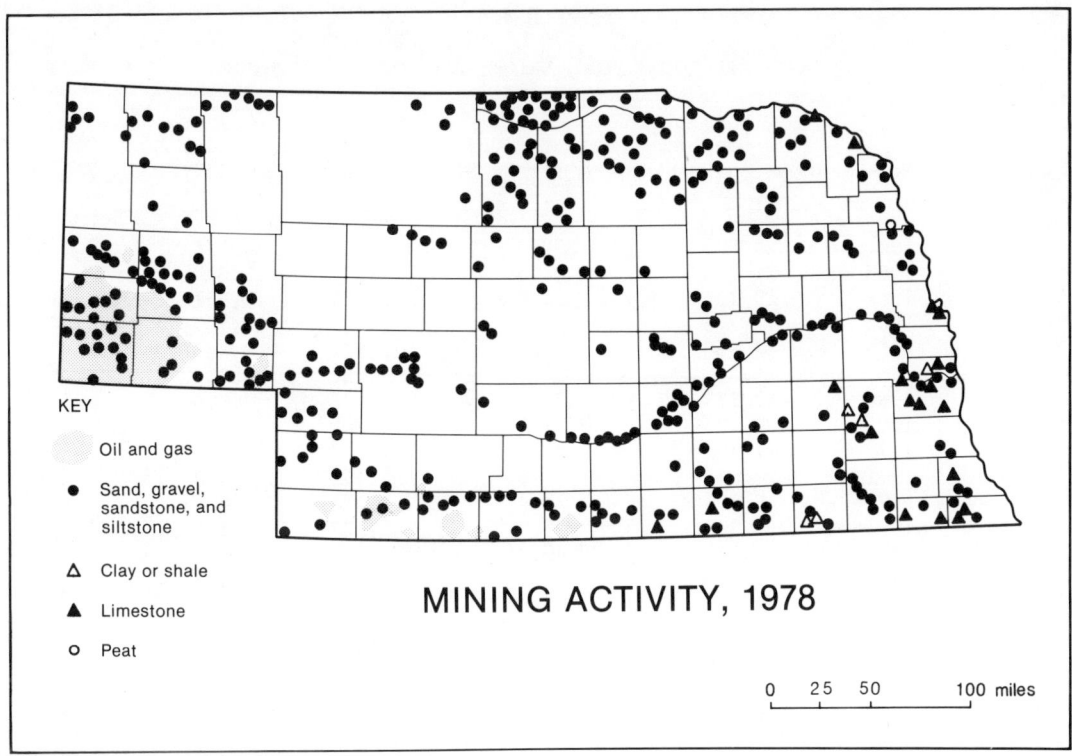

FIGURE 4.4. (UNL, Conservation and Survey Division)

FIGURE 4.5. Cement plant in Louisville. Mining operations are visible in the upper left corner of the photo. (Ash Grove Cement Co.)

TABLE 4.3

NEBRASKA OIL PRODUCTION, VALUE, AND WELLS, 1962-1980

Year	Oil Production (000s barrels)	Estimated Value (millions $)	Producing Wells	Barrels/Well
1962	24,885	$70.4	1,763	14,115
1963	21,846	61.8	1,732	12,613
1964	19,114	51.6	1,711	11,171
1965	17,216	45.8	1,611	10,687
1966	13,850	37.7	1,511	9,166
1967	13,373	36.8	1,430	9,352
1968	13,183	36.8	1,403	9,396
1969	12,106	36.1	1,305	9.277
1970	11,451	35.4	1,244	9,206
1971	10,062	34.0	1,191	8,448
1972	8,705	29.4	1,114	7,814
1973	7,240	28.0	1,107	6,540
1974	6,611	45.2	1,127	5,866
1975	6,120	55.1	1,190	5,143
1976	6,182	55.6	1,291	4,789
1977	5,968	62.4	1,382	4,318
1978	5,862	66.8	1,469	3,990
1979	6,068	102.0	1,551	3,912
1980	6,240	NA	1,693	3,686

Source: University of Nebraska, Bureau of Business Research.

and it was halved again by 1977. The rising price of oil, however, resulted in 1979 production valued over $102 million, the highest ever in the state (Table 4.3).[13] In 1980, the major producing counties were Red Willow, Cheyenne, Kimball, Hitchcock, and Banner.

Although the economic and social impacts of oil have been substantial in the McCook area, Kimball and Sidney underwent transformations commonly associated with a boom and bust economy. Kimball County's population nearly doubled in the 1950s, and Cheyenne County grew by several thousand (Table 4.4). As production dropped during the 1960s, the population declined almost as abruptly as it had risen. Businesses that had thrived and expanded during the boom faced falling sales. Governmental services such as schools had expanded to meet the needs of a burgeoning populace. Now there were fewer persons to serve, but considerable costs still had to be met from a shrunken tax base. Oil is still an important component of the economy of these two counties, but the disruptive effects of the oil boom have passed, and the oil industry is better integrated into both communities.

MANUFACTURING

Early Manufacturing Activity

Early manufacturing in Nebraska relied on local resources and local energy. Gristmills and sawmills were scattered throughout the settled portions of the state. Because they relied on flowing water for an energy source, most mills were small (Figure 4.6). The high cost of transporting either raw materials or finished products by wagon insured that most of them served only local needs.[14]

Improved transportation led to major changes in the structure and pattern of

TABLE 4.4

POPULATION OF CHEYENNE AND KIMBALL COUNTIES

Year	Cheyenne County	Sidney	Kimball County	Kimball
1940	9,505	3,388	3,913	1,725
1950	12,081	4,912	4,283	2,048
1960	14,822	8,004	7,975	4,384
1970	10,778	6,403	6,009	3,680
1980	10,057	6,010	4,882	3,120

Source: U.S. Censuses of Population.

manufacturing in Nebraska after the Civil War. Within two decades rail lines provided nearly every community with manufactured goods and construction materials from the East, as well as access to eastern markets for agricultural products. Three principal trends affected manufacturing during the last third of the century—increasing nationwide specialization, intrastate concentration, and growing dependence of Nebraska manufacturing on agricultural products.

Specialization in that period was a function of lowered transportation costs nationwide, which made it easier and cheaper for Nebraskans to buy their lumber from Wisconsin and Michigan than to mill it locally. This was also true of manufactured items from eastern industrial cities. Locally oriented industries such as sawmills declined in importance, even as the population of the state skyrocketed.

Industry became more concentrated in Omaha, the hub of rail activity and the most populous city in Nebraska. More than half the state's manufacturing activity in 1890 was found in Omaha. Some industries—such as the manufacture of bricks, soap, beer, and clothing—were oriented to local and regional needs, but far more important was the food-processing industry, particularly meat packing.[15] Omaha's su-

FIGURE 4.6. Water-powered gristmill in Neligh, now preserved by the Nebraska State Historical Society.

perior rail connections to the population centers of the East and Midwest made it a prime location for the conversion of agricultural raw materials into foodstuffs for the nation. Well into the twentieth century Omaha's manufacturing was almost synonymous with meat packing. Nebraska and Iowa beef and pork were collected in one of the world's largest stockyards and butchered in nearby packing plants by a semiskilled and unskilled labor force drawn heavily from eastern and central Europe.

Decentralization of Industry

Since World War II, regional specialization has continued to be fairly important, but manufacturing has become more dispersed within the state and less tied to agriculture. In 1958, 52 percent of all manufacturing activity in the state took place in Omaha. In 1977 the Omaha metropolitan area, excluding Council Bluffs, provided thirty-one thousand manufacturing jobs, only 35 percent of the state total, and a value added by manufacturing of $1.1 billion, 39 percent of the state total.[16] Manufacturing growth was recorded in Lincoln, as well as in smaller cities such as Norfolk, Grand Island, Columbus, and Scottsbluff. Even small centers, such as Broken Bow, Henderson, Lexington, and Ogallala, attracted substantial industrial investment.

Such dispersion is characteristic not only of Nebraska but of much of the South, the Midwest, and elsewhere on the Great Plains. Nonmetropolitan manufacturing growth has become significant for several reasons.[17] Probably most important has been improved transportation, particularly the interstate highway system. Nebraska communities along Interstate 80 have greatly benefited from their access to raw materials and markets. Other highways have been improved as well, so that manufacturing has become a significant force even in cities like Norfolk, which is 60 mi (96 km) from the nearest interstate highway (Interstate 29 near Sioux City, Iowa). Not surprisingly, manufacturing plants in nonmetropolitan Nebraska rely more upon trucks than trains for the shipment of their products.

A second factor in nonmetropolitan manufacturing is labor cost, skills, and productivity. Wages are somewhat lower in smaller cities than in Omaha and Lincoln. This reflects the level of industrial skills found in most rural areas, the lower rate of union activity outside larger cities, and a pool of underemployed persons—those without full-time employment or working at jobs below their level of skill. A large number of farm men and women seek off-farm employment in order to supplement low or variable farm incomes with wages. The historically low rate of female participation in the labor force in rural areas has resulted in a labor supply that has been attractive to manufacturing firms. The growing role of industry in rural Nebraska has enabled more women to join the wage labor force.

The productivity of rural workers is critical in many industries' decisions to locate in nonmetropolitan communities. Employers believe that a rural work ethic results in employees who deliver maximum effort for their pay and that rural absenteeism and turnover rates are lower.[18] Because of these labor-related advantages, most firms selecting small-town and -city locations for manufacturing are labor-intensive, rather than capital-intensive operations (food processing is an exception to this generalization).

A final factor in nonmetropolitan industrialization is the emergence of more positive attitudes toward small towns and cities. Small towns are increasingly viewed as appealing places to live. This improved image and the availability of inexpensive amenities, such as lower housing costs, low crime rates, and fresh air, have encouraged population growth in much of rural Nebraska.[19]

The pattern of industrial activity within cities has also become more dispersed. Many of the factors in nonmetropolitan manufacturing growth are also responsible for the suburbanization of industry. As U.S. industry has shifted from rail to highway transportation, central-city locations have become less desirable. In the rail era, manufacturing necessarily clustered near rail terminals, but highways do not produce such aggregations. Consequently, manufacturing activities in Nebraska have shifted to suburban locations more accessible to major highways. Land in the suburbs is generally less expensive, so manufacturing facilities usually have more space and less congestion. The increased use of electricity in manufacturing operations (which reduces the need for proximity to power plants and coal supplies) has also encouraged peripheral growth of industry. This suburban pattern, particularly of light manufacturing, is found not only in Omaha, but in cities such as Columbus, Norfolk, Grand Island, and Lexington and in smaller towns.

Manufacturing Patterns

Nebraska still has not become a major manufacturing state, but employment in that sector has been growing. Fewer than 50,000 persons were employed in manufacturing in 1947, but by 1979 that figure surpassed 100,000. Despite nonmetropolitan dispersal, manufacturing is concentrated in the eastern third of the state (Figure 4.7). The metropolitan areas of Omaha and Lincoln account for the largest share of manufacturing employment, with several smaller centers having considerable importance—notably Columbus, Norfolk, Grand Island, and Dakota County. In five counties—Colfax, Dakota, Platte, Saline, and Stanton—over one-third of the nonagricultural work force is in manufacturing. In the western two-thirds of the state, manufacturing is concentrated in the Platte Valley, with its agricultural productivity and superior transportation facilities. West of Norfolk and Columbus, there is relatively little manufacturing away from Interstate 80 and the Platte.

The tie between agriculture and industry in Nebraska is clear in the continuing importance of food processing, which accounts for almost 30 percent of all manufacturing employment (Table 4.5). Food processing

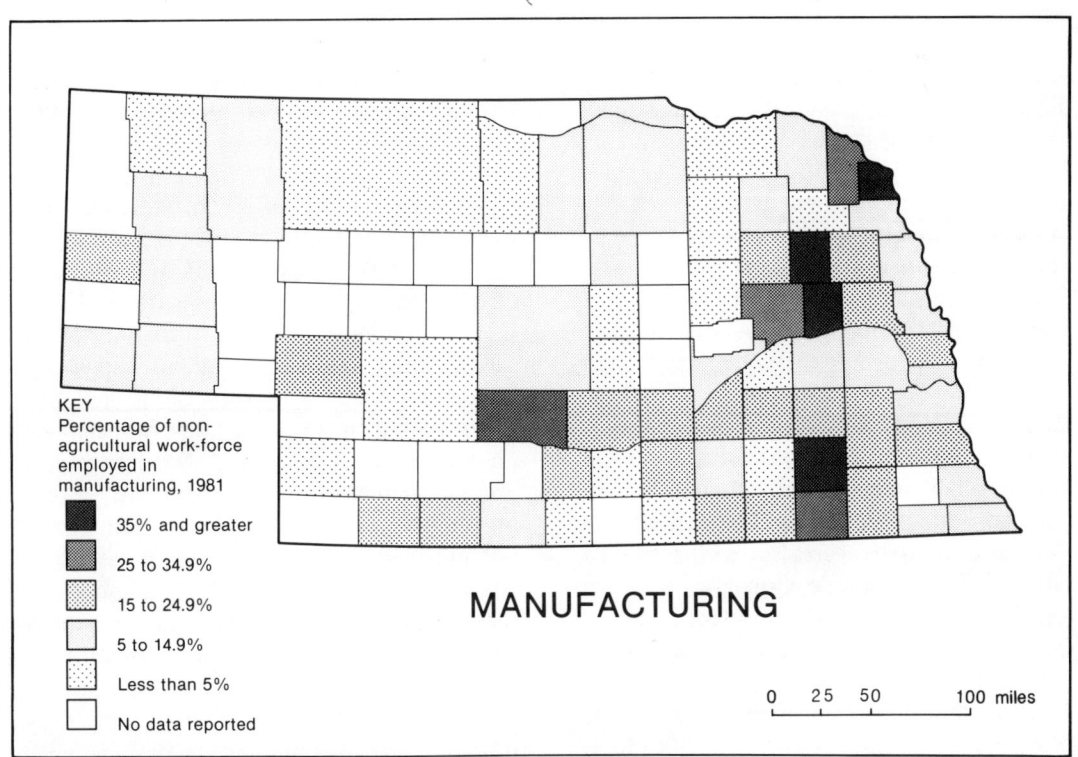

FIGURE 4.7. (Nebraska Department of Economic Development)

TABLE 4.5

MANUFACTURING EMPLOYMENT IN NEBRASKA, 1981 AVERAGE

Durable Goods (48,465)		
Lumber and Wood Products		1,907
Stone, Clay, Glass and Concrete		2,758
Furniture and Fixtures		1,579
Primary Metals		1,800
Fabricated Metals		6,792
Machinery (excluding electrical)		13,157
Farm Machinery and Equipment	7,519	
Electrical and Electronic Machinery		9,513
Transport Equipment		5,164
Other Durable Goods		5,795
Non-Durable Goods (46,482)		
Food and Kindred Products		27,057
Meat	14,783	
Dairy	1,635	
Grain Milling	4,397	
Other Food Products	6,242	
Textile Products and Apparel		2,306
Printing and Publishing		8,080
Chemicals and Allied Products		2,697
Other Non-Durable Goods		6,342
Total		94,947

Source: Nebraska Department of Economic Development.

has not grown as fast as many other industries during the past three decades, however. In 1954, 50 percent of manufacturing employment was in food-related areas.[20] The greatest employment in this sector is in meat and poultry processing, dairy products, and grain mill products, particularly livestock feed and pet food. Prepared-feed plants have the most diffuse distribution (Figure 4.8). Typically they have fewer than fifty employees and are as likely to be located in small towns as in larger cities. The heaviest concentration is in the central Platte Valley (Figure 4.9). A number of plants producing bakery products, flour, pet food, and breakfast cereals are clustered in Omaha. These include Conagra, Kellogg, and ITT Continental Baking Co. Lincoln, Grand Island, Hastings, and Crete are other important centers.[21]

Meat- and poultry-processing firms employ over half the workers in the food industry. Iowa Beef Processors of Dakota City has a labor force of more than twenty-five hundred. Other major meat processors include Hormel in Fremont, Monfort in Grand Island, and American Stores in Lincoln. Meat and poultry operations are found in most of the larger towns and cities of eastern Nebraska and the Platte Valley.[22]

The influence of agriculture is also evident in the state's chemical industry. Nebraska produces 4 percent of the nation's nitrogen fertilizer and has several pesticide plants. Like food processing, fertilizer plants are widely scattered across the state to best serve local agricultural needs. Other important chemical products in the state include drugs and soaps. Most of the pharmaceutical firms specialize in veterinary supplies and are concentrated in or near Omaha and Lincoln.[23]

Fabricated metals is one of the more important growth industries in Nebraska.

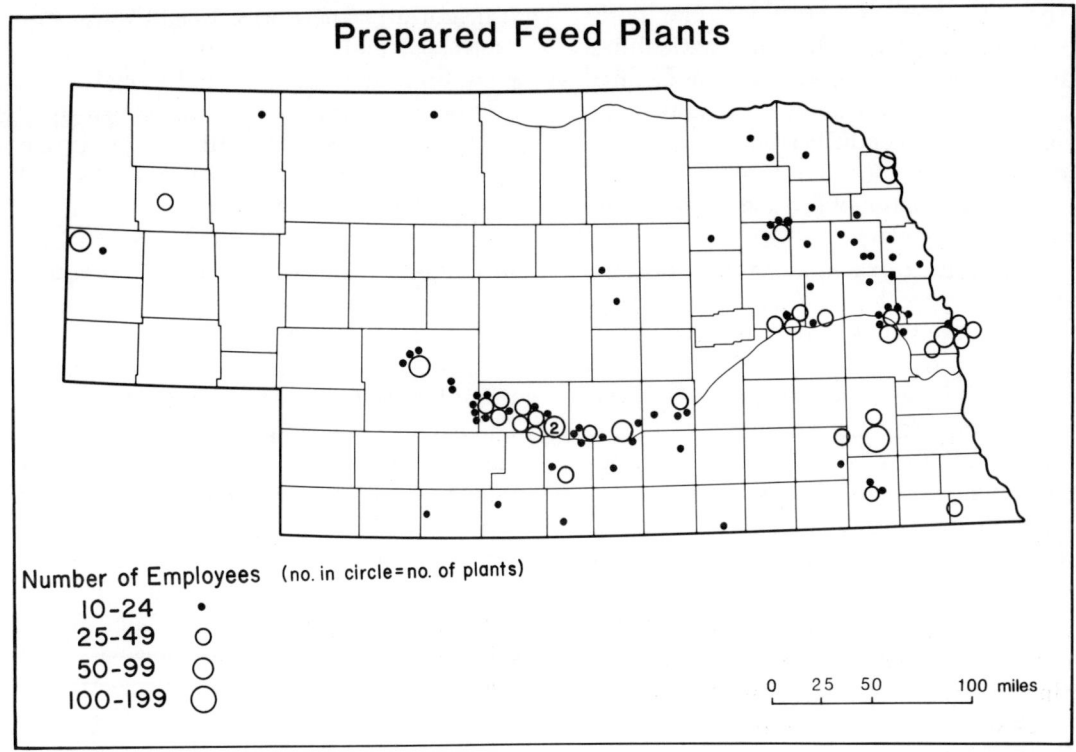

FIGURE 4.8. (Nebraska Department of Economic Development)

FIGURE 4.9. Alfalfa milling is concentrated in the central Platte Valley, in proximity to alfalfa production and large cattle-feeding operations.

Nearly half the seven thousand workers are employed in Omaha or Lincoln. Other important centers include Columbus, Grand Island, Kearney, and Hastings. The industry is also oriented to the state's agricultural sector. Among the products manufactured are grain bins, irrigation pipe, tanks, and culverts. Other products include mechanic's tools (including Vise-Grips, manufactured in DeWitt), automobile seat frames, and hydraulic cylinders.[24]

Nonelectrical machinery production has also undergone substantial growth. More than half the plants and employees in this category produce farm and garden machinery. Over seventy-five hundred workers manufacture irrigation equipment, hay- and grain-harvesting equipment, livestock equipment, and tillage and fertilizer application equipment. Nebraska is the nation's foremost manufacturer of center-pivot irrigation systems. Valmont Industries in Valley is the country's largest producer, but other nationally prominent firms include Reinke Manufacturing in Deshler, Lockwood Corporation in Gering, and Lindsay Manufacturing in Lindsay. All have sizable sales throughout the United States and worldwide. Sperry–New Holland produces a range of farm machinery from plants in Lexington, Columbus, and Grand Island, and Behlen in Columbus manufactures metal buildings and grain-drying systems.[25]

Farm machinery and equipment plants are located in rural areas and smaller cities, rather than in Omaha and Lincoln. This reflects an orientation toward the market for their products, as well as the numerous factors that have resulted in rural industrial development. An additional factor relates to the innovation process.

Center-pivot irrigation manufacturing illustrates this facet of industrial location. Most of the pivot manufacturing operations began on a small scale as a result of the particular inventiveness of one individual who turned an idea into a product—first in a tool shed, eventually in a large plant. A map of the location of such plants would be little more than a map of tinkerers and inventors. Rather than a company choosing a location best situated with regard to transportation networks, freight rates, raw materials, and markets, these companies grew up around creative individuals.

Nonfarm equipment manufacturing, by contrast, is clustered in the major urban centers with their large labor forces and potential markets. Among the large manufacturers of machinery are Sperry Vickers in Omaha, Outboard Marine Corporation in Lincoln, and Control Data, with operations in both cities.

Electrical machinery and equipment manufacturing is also concentrated in Omaha and Lincoln (Figure 4.10). Half the state's employment in this category is in Omaha, with Western Electric being the largest single employer. Other nationally known firms include Square D in Lincoln, Dale Electronics in Columbus and Norfolk, and TRW Corporation in Ogallala. Nearly all manufacturing in this category is of communications equipment and electronics components.[26]

Other important manufacturing categories include transportation equipment, instruments, rubber and plastics products, and printing and publishing. Transportation-equipment manufacturers employ over five thousand workers in the state. Products include motorcycles (Kawasaki in Lincoln), truck trailers, shock absorbers (Monroe in Cozad), railroad freight cars, and auto mufflers. Lincoln is especially important in the manufacture of transportation equipment, accounting for nearly 40 percent of employment in this category.[27]

Medical and dental instruments are produced by a number of firms, the most prominent of which is Becton Dickinson, with plants in Columbus, Holdrege, Broken Bow, and Santee. Other products are meters and other measuring instruments, optical instruments, and scientific and engineering instruments. Other important centers are Omaha, Lincoln, Norfolk, and Nebraska City.[28]

Rubber and plastics products produced

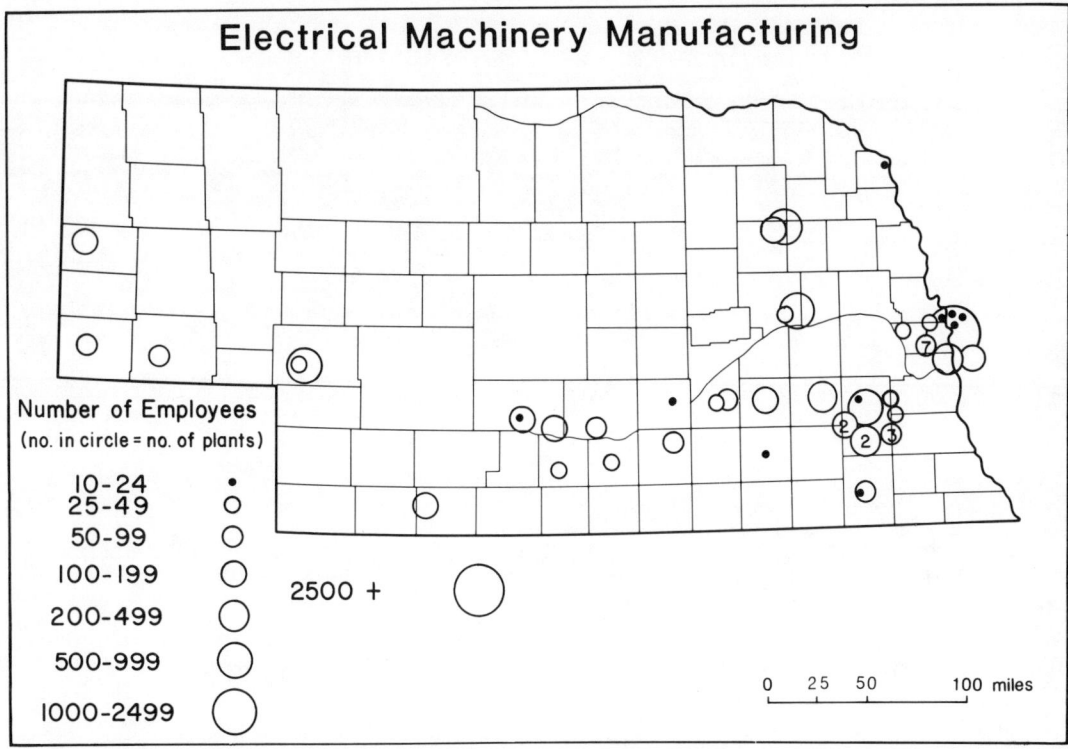

FIGURE 4.10. (Nebraska Department of Economic Development)

in the state include fiberglass items, plastic pipe and tubing, belts, and hoses. The industry is concentrated in Omaha and Lincoln, site of Goodyear Tire and Rubber, the largest plant in this category.

By contrast, publishing is one of the least concentrated industries in the state. There are about 150 weekly and daily newspapers in Nebraska. Most cities of ten thousand and several smaller towns support daily papers. Some daily newspapers circulate in just one or two counties, indicating only local impact. This is the case of the dailies in Alliance, Holdrege, Kearney, York, Columbus, Fremont, Beatrice, Nebraska City, and Falls City. Other newspapers reach a more regional audience. The *Scotts Bluff Star-Herald* dominates the southern Panhandle; the *North Platte Telegraph* circulates in the central Platte Valley and western Sandhills. Southwestern Nebraska is oriented toward the *McCook Daily Gazette*. The *Grand Island Independent* and the *Hastings Daily Tribune* dominate central and south-central Nebraska, respectively. The *Norfolk Daily News* is preeminent in northeastern Nebraska, and the *Lincoln Journal* and *Star* circulate widely in the southwestern part of the state. The *Omaha World Herald* is the only statewide paper in Nebraska. It reaches at least 25 percent of the households in over half of Nebraska's counties and has a wide circulation in western Iowa, as well.[29]

TRANSPORTATION AND UTILITIES

Both the agricultural and manufacturing components of Nebraska's economy rely on the state's transportation and utilities distribution systems. The movement of raw materials to manufacturers and of inputs to farms takes place over a complex network of roads, rails, and water. This system also enables agricultural products and manu-

FIGURE 4.11. Eppley Airfield, Omaha. Note the city's role as a transportation hub: Interstate 29 east of the river in Iowa leads to downtown Omaha; rail lines converge on the city in the lower right corner of the photo. Omaha is also an important port for goods shipped on the Missouri River. (USDA, ASCS)

factured items to reach markets in the rest of the nation and the world. Both agriculture and industry depend upon a reliable supply of energy delivered through transmission lines and pipelines and by truck and train. Transportation, communication, and energy link the components of Nebraska's economy and fuel the state's economic health.

Air traffic is of less importance in Nebraska than rail and truck traffic. Commercial airlines serve more than a dozen Nebraska communities and commuter airlines reach a number of other cities, but more than three-fourths of the state's air traffic is into or out of Omaha (Figure 4.11). Omaha and Lincoln are the only airports with more than one major carrier. Most smaller towns have either private or municipal air fields which serve light planes for personal use or agricultural spraying. Air cargo traffic is also concentrated in Omaha.

Water Transportation

River transportation was once a dominant force in Nebraska. Many early settlers entered the state on Missouri River steamboats operating out of St. Louis. Most manufactured goods shipped to the area during the territorial period came by water. Today, commercial water transportation is relatively unimportant. Most of the downstream traffic on the Missouri River channel below Sioux City consists of farm products, particularly wheat, corn, and sorghum. Upstream traffic is much lighter, meaning many barges must travel empty. Most important of the products shipped upstream are fertilizer, cement, salt, flour, and petroleum products. When speed is not essential, water transportation is a highly advantageous and relatively inexpensive way to transport bulk cargoes. The principal Nebraska ports are Omaha and Nebraska City.[30]

The Rail Network

Railroads, which crisscrossed the state by the 1880s, retain an important place in the transportation network of the state. Nebraska's railnet consists of four principal carriers: Union Pacific, Burlington Northern, Chicago and Northwestern, and Missouri Pacific. The Burlington and the Union Pacific together account for more than 90 percent of the total ton-mileage in the state. Nearly every county has some rail service, and few communities of one thousand people are without rail connections. This density is attributable to the rapid development of the rail systems in the late nineteenth century, when competing railroad companies sought to connect farm communities with markets. Many firms overbuilt, probably anticipating greater rural populations than resulted. Population density decreased during the twentieth century, resulting in three times as much rail mileage per person as nationally and a network density quite similar to the national average in spite of a relatively sparse population.

Reflecting the historical orientation toward eastern markets, the railnet is aligned in an east-west fashion. The greatest concentration is in the southeastern part of the state. The Sandhills, on the other hand, have comparatively little rail service. The density of Nebraska's railnet has been decreasing gradually (Figure 4.12). Rail companies have sought to abandon little-used track in order to keep costs down, but small communities on lines proposed for abandonment have reacted strongly to the idea of reducing their links to outside markets. Rail abandonment has been especially pronounced in the northeastern counties. Grain elevators and small towns would seem to be most vulnerable to abandonment, although some studies suggest that the impact has not been as great as anticipated.[31]

In most abandonment cases, rail traffic is already quite low. Shippers have increasingly focused on fewer, high-volume terminals. Elevators with unit-train capability, for instance, have substantial economic advantages over small elevators on light-density branch lines. The implications of abandonment for small communities may include loss of jobs and tax revenue, increased transportation costs for feed, fertilizer, and

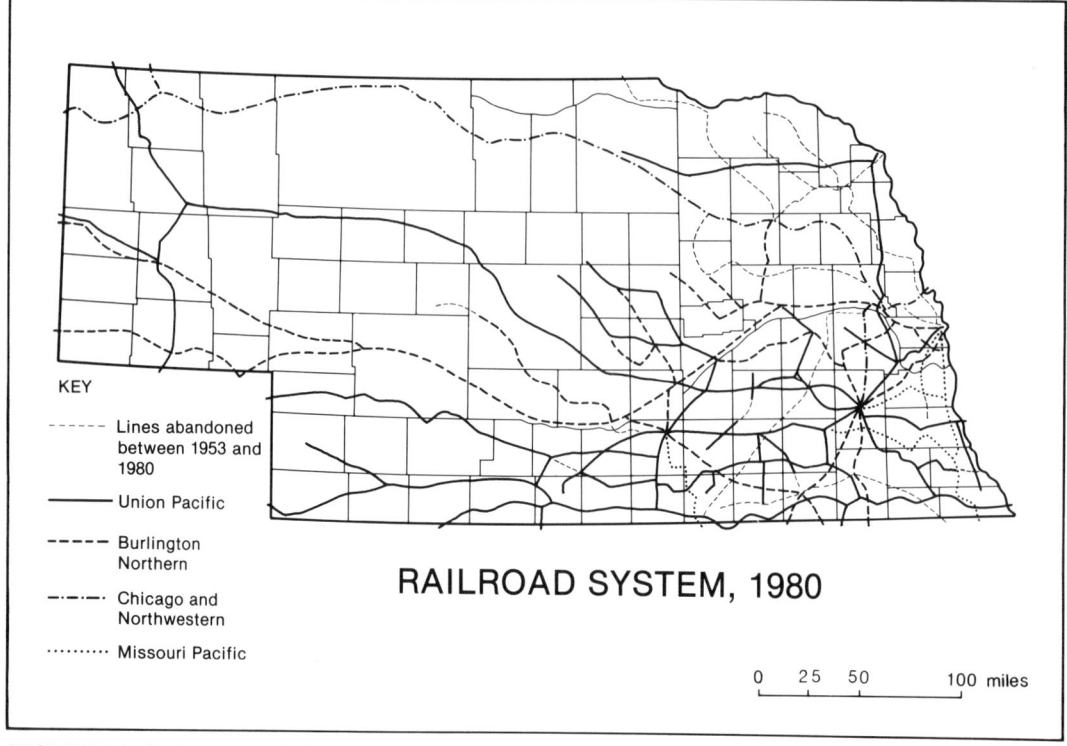

FIGURE 4.12. Based on information from Nebraska Public Service Commission.

lumber, and decreased attractiveness for industry.[32]

The commodities carried by rail include both Nebraska products and imported goods. The most important locally generated commodities are grains (Figure 4.13), although meat, fertilizer, sand, and rock are also transported (Table 4.6). Coal from Wyoming and Montana is the principal import.[33] Both the Union Pacific and Burlington Northern run a number of unit coal trains through the state to eastern destinations (Figure 4.14).

Railroads are more energy efficient and less expensive than trucks for medium to long hauls of bulk commodities of low value. This is seen in the dominance of mineral and agricultural products in Nebraska's rail tonnage relative to manufactured items. The importance of haul length to railroads is illustrated in the fact that 70 percent of the tonnage and 80 percent of the ton miles of freight carried over Nebraska railroads pass through the state, rather than originating or terminating in it.[34]

Railroads provide substantial employment in many parts of the state. Large repair facilities and switching and classification yards are found in Lincoln and North Platte (Figure 4.15). Other cities with economies heavily reliant on the railroad include Omaha, location of the headquarters of the Union Pacific Railroad, and Alliance.

Western coal has been especially significant for Alliance, which has boomed since 1970. When the Burlington Northern began construction of its multimillion-dollar complex of shops in the early 1970s (Figure 4.16), Alliance was a relatively quiet farm and ranch center of 6,862 people. The annual railroad payroll of $50 million has attracted considerable population growth (by 1980 the city had grown to 9,869) and a number of side effects common in boom

FIGURE 4.13. Train loading grain at elevator in Shelby. (Union Pacific Railroad)

TABLE 4.6

RAILROAD FREIGHT IN NEBRASKA, 1979

	Terminating in Nebraska (Tons)	Originating in Nebraska (Tons)
Farm Products	1,521,541	14,642,019
Coal	4,571,670	2,050
Nonmetallic Minerals, Except Fuels	1,607,133	1,433,471
Food and Kindred Products	992,881	2,710,298
Lumber and Wood Products, Except Furniture	277,401	14,355
Furniture and Fixtures	13,989	15,073
Pulp, Paper and Allied Products	335,556	5,745
Printed Matter	466	3,106
Chemicals and Allied Products	1,238,075	617,819
Petroleum and Coal Products	235,085	40,229
Rubber and Miscellaneous	12,249	6,102
Stone, Clay and Glass Products	437,047	312,918
Primary Metal Products	551,814	143,215
Fabr. Metal Products, Except Ordn. Mach., and Transp.	45,305	36,262
Machinery Except Electrical	21,001	43,334
Electrical Machinery, Equipment and Supplies	14,435	3,353
Transportation Equipment	87,409	24,150
Waste and Scrap Materials	327,169	287,793
Other	199,600	156,244
Total Car Load Traffic	12,489,826	20,497,536

Source: Nebraska Public Service Commission, Annual Report, 1979-1980.

town situations. Housing costs have skyrocketed, wages have risen to keep pace with railroad wages, and pressure on public services has increased. Electricity use has grown substantially and electric rates have risen, as well. Sewer lines are inadequate for probable future needs, and school enrollments have pressed the capacity of the system's physical plant. Crime has also increased, producing changes in the ways residents evaluate the quality of life in their city.

Nevertheless, retail sales in the entire region have risen, and the influx of people has given more support to local social institutions. More high school graduates now stay in the local area, rather than leaving for college or jobs elsewhere. This, plus the movement of young workers into the community, has led to a decrease in the median age of the population. Unlike the boom-and-bust cycle encountered in nearby Antioch during the potash boom of World War I, the impact of the railroad on this community is likely to last for many years.[35]

The Highway System

Most people and goods in the state utilize the highways, which link communities throughout the state in a network roughly as dense as that of the rest of the nation. The number of miles of road per person is higher than the national average and

FIGURE 4.14. Unit trains haul coal from Wyoming mines to distant power plants. (Burlington Northern Railroad)

gasoline taxes are among the highest in the country, but congestion on Nebraska's roads is somewhat lower.[36]

By far the most important routeway is Interstate 80, which runs through Omaha and Lincoln, along the Platte Valley in central Nebraska, and into Colorado and Wyoming. Daily traffic on the interstate averages as high as fourteen thousand vehicles between Omaha and Lincoln and is only slightly lower west of Lincoln. Other major federal highways, mostly two lanes, complete the system. The greatest road density is in the eastern third of the state where population density is highest. The most heavily used routes include U.S. 30 from Omaha to Columbus, U.S. 275 from Norfolk to Omaha, and U.S. 73-75 and 77 running south from Omaha and Lincoln, respectively.[37]

Trucks carry a variety of agricultural products and manufactured goods in Nebraska. Most small-town industrialization taking place during the past twenty years has been heavily dependent on the highway network, rather than on railroads. Overall, commercial vehicles account for roughly one-third of total highway traffic.

For most state residents the automobile is not only the primary form of passenger transportation, it is the only form available. Although passenger travel by rail is possible on the route from Omaha to Denver, for most communities departure times are not conducive to either short- or long-distance travel.

Buses travel a number of routes in the state, but they are used primarily for longer-distance trips. As in the rest of the United States, the availability of intercity bus service has been decreasing, leaving residents of many rural areas and small towns with no alternative to the automobile. The impact of these developments has been most pronounced among the rural elderly.

Urban transportation systems are found

FIGURE 4.15. Union Pacific's Bailey Yard in North Platte is one of the largest and most modern classification yards in the country. (Union Pacific Railroad)

FIGURE 4.16. Interior view of Burlington Northern's locomotive-repair facility in Alliance. (Burlington Northern Railroad and Harr, Hedrich-Blessing)

in Omaha and Lincoln and have experienced increased ridership in the past decade. Some smaller communities have limited public transportation service, either in the form of door-to-door buses or taxi companies. Many small-city cab companies have ceased operation altogether; bus systems have struggled for public acceptance with only limited success.

The Electrical Power System

Electricity in Nebraska is generated, transmitted, and distributed solely by publicly owned utilities. Two organizations, the Nebraska Public Power District and the Omaha Public Power District, generate over 90 percent of the state's electricity. As in the rest of the nation, electricity consumption has grown substantially during the past two decades, although the rate of increase has slowed somewhat since the mid-1970s. The burgeoning demand for electricity to power irrigation and other agriculture-related activities, as well as for the growing industrial sector in the state, has required expansion of the state's generating capacity (Figure 4.17). Generating plants are still oriented primarily toward coal, but nuclear power now provides approximately one-fourth of the electricity in the state. Several small hydroelectric facilities supplement coal and nuclear plants (Figure 4.18).

Generating capacity in the state is concentrated in just a few facilities—nuclear plants at Ft. Calhoun and Brownville (Figure 4.19), along with coal-burning generators near Nebraska City, Omaha, Sutherland, and Lincoln. The most important locational factors are the concentration of electricity consumption in the eastern third of the state and the abundance of water required as a coolant, supplied mainly by the Missouri and Platte rivers.

THE EXCHANGE OF GOODS AND SERVICES

In predominantly agricultural regions, trade and services provide a large share of

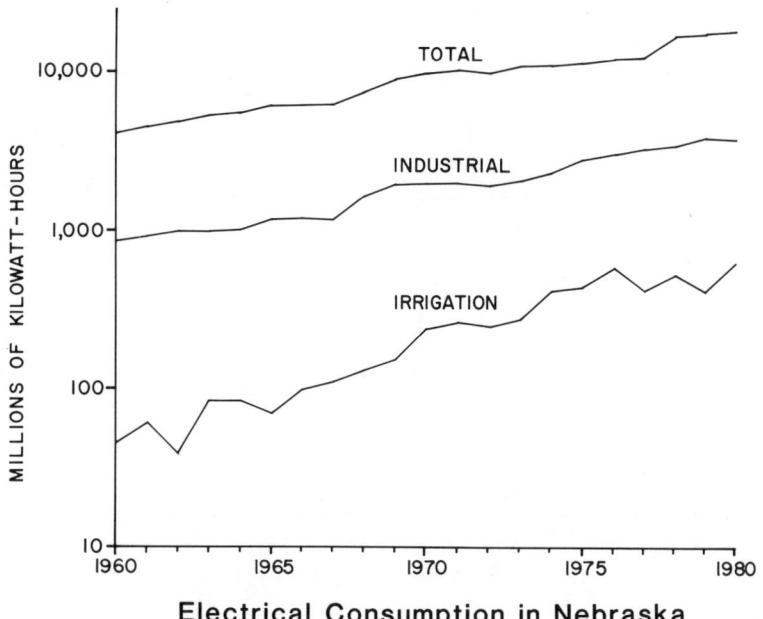

Electrical Consumption in Nebraska

FIGURE 4.17. Note the logarithmic scale on the *y* axis. Use of electricity for irrigation rose much faster than total consumption. Industrial use rose somewhat faster than the total. (UNL, Bureau of Business Research)

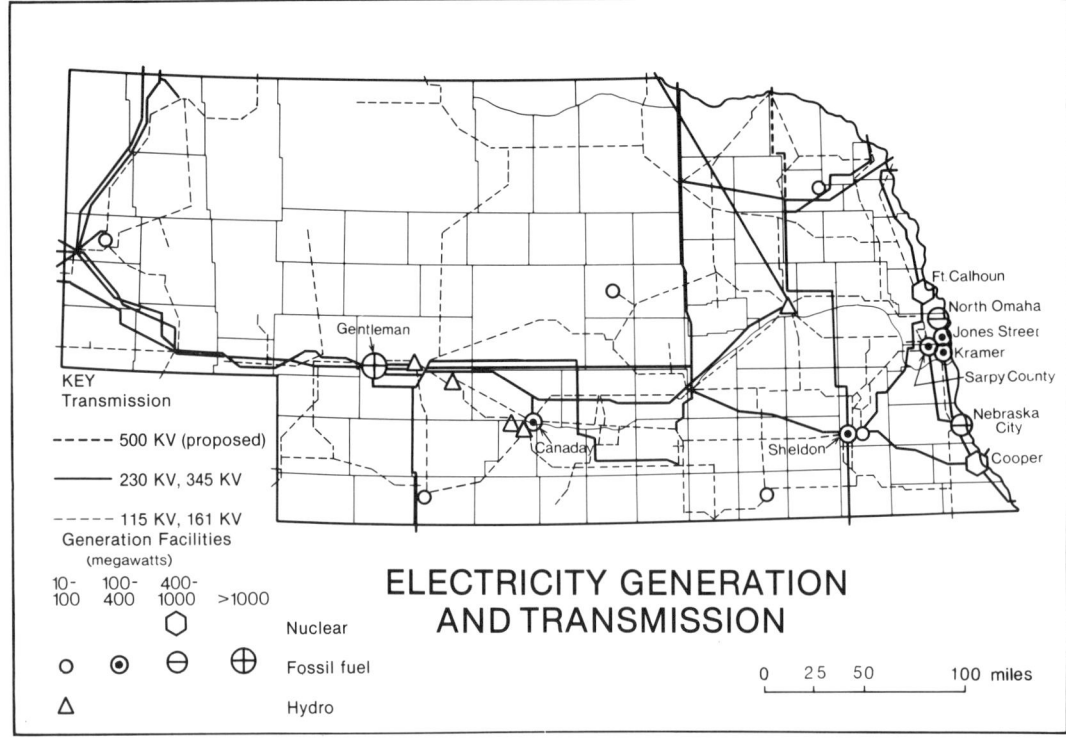

FIGURE 4.18. (Nebraska Public Power District)

nonagricultural employment, whereas areas with more diversified economies are not so heavily dependent on these activities. In Nebraska, counties with a major manufacturing component have a smaller share of their labor forces involved in retailing or services than do counties where agriculture dominates. Some counties, however, have such small populations that they are unable to support more than a minimal number of retail establishments or personal and professional services. Counties with a large share of employment in this sector are generally those in which one or two towns with two to ten thousand people provide goods and services to the rural populace.

Wholesale activity in Nebraska is dominated by Omaha. Douglas County has nearly 50 percent of the state's wholesale activity, but only 25 percent of total population. Omaha is the center of warehousing in the state, as well as the principal location for wholesaling of agricultural products, construction materials, machinery, equipment, and many other goods. Other wholesaling centers include Lincoln, Norfolk, Grand Island, and Scottsbluff, but their level of activity is considerably smaller than that of Omaha.[38]

Omaha's dominance is not nearly so noticeable in retail trade—it accounts for only 32 percent of state retail sales. This is because the delivery of goods to the consumer is more closely associated with the distribution of population. There are substantial variations in the importance of retailing in individual counties and towns, however.

Low-order goods—items offered by stores that can survive with only a small number of customers—are found in the smallest communities in the state.[39] Gas stations, taverns, and grocery stores are generally found even in towns with only fifty or one hundred people (Figure 4.20). Because such establishments are patronized frequently,

FIGURE 4.19. The Fort Calhoun Station, one of two nuclear power plants in Nebraska. (Omaha Public Power District)

FIGURE 4.20. Small towns offer frequently needed goods such as gasoline and food, but do not have sufficient populations to support businesses with higher thresholds.

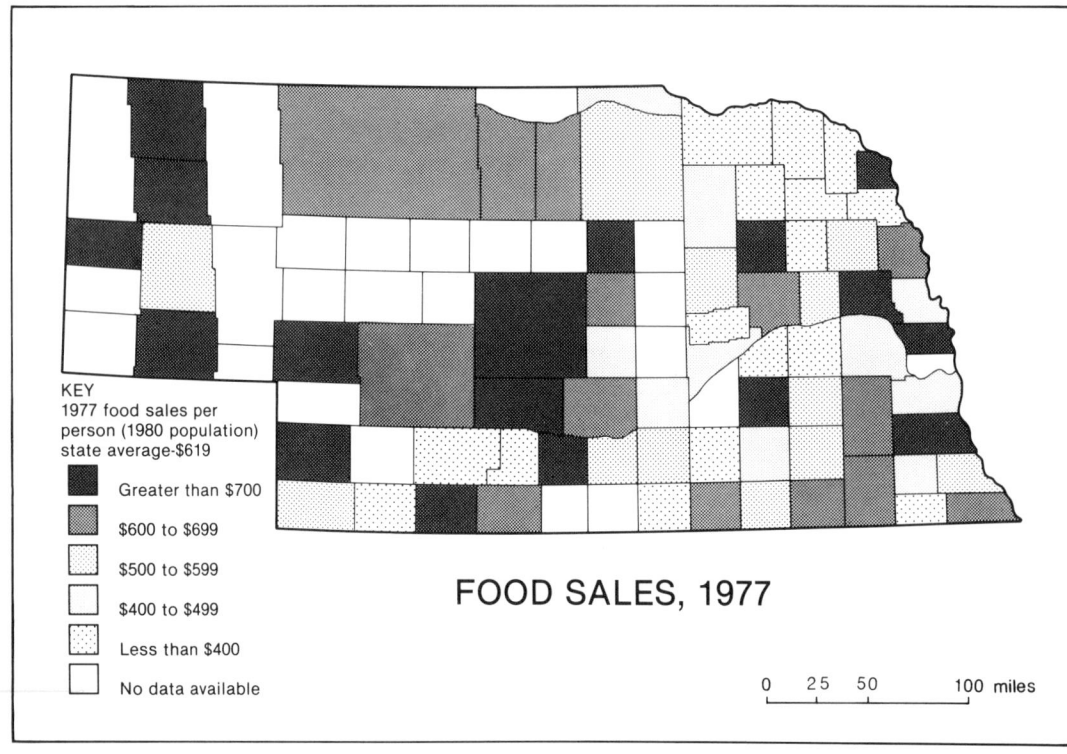

FIGURE 4.21. Based on *1977 Census of Retail Trade.*

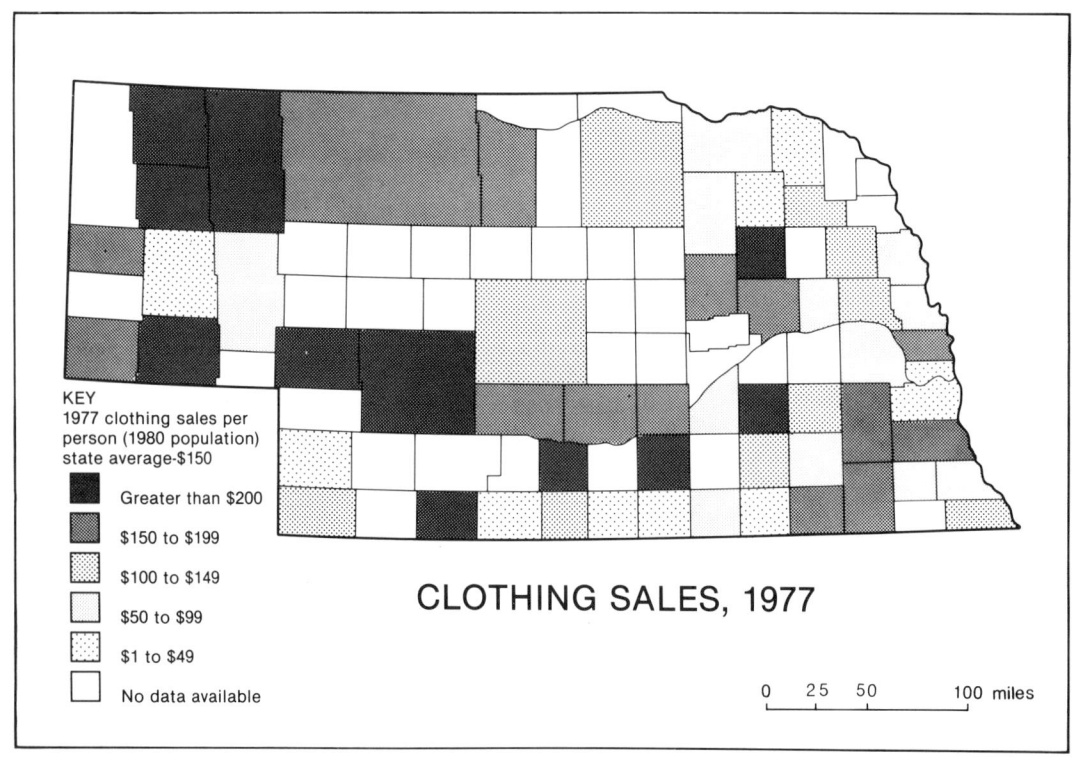

FIGURE 4.22. Based on *1977 Census of Retail Trade.*

most customers prefer not to drive great distances to reach them. Hence, they are widely distributed throughout the state. The pattern of food sales (Figure 4.21) shows that volume of food sales is roughly proportional to county population. Food sales in individual towns may not be so closely tied to town population because small-town grocers are patronized by both town and rural residents.

Striking differences exist among counties in the relative importance of food sales in the entire retail-trade picture. Geographically isolated counties and those with no large towns are likely to show a very great share of retail trade transacted in food sales. More-populous counties, however, are less reliant on food sales because higher-order goods make up a greater share of retail sales.

High-order goods are those that require a greater population (referred to as the threshold population) to bring a retail establishment into business and to keep it operating at a profit. These tend to be less frequently purchased items such as furniture, clothing, and automobiles. Only in larger places are there enough potential customers to support stores offering higher-order goods. The pattern of clothing sales illustrates the importance of larger populations (Figure 4.22). Small places have few or no clothing stores, and residents may have to travel great distances to shop for clothing (Figure 4.23).

Some places serve a much larger trade area than might be predicted from their populations. These regional retail centers not only provide lower-order goods to the local populace, but also offer higher-order goods both to the local area and to a regional market that may stretch over several hundred miles. Omaha's retail attractions, for example, may draw customers from several hours away. Likewise, Lincoln, Grand Island, North Platte, Norfolk, and Scottsbluff are major regional retail centers. Other important retailing cities include Fremont, Kearney, and Hastings (Figure 4.24). Sioux City (Iowa), Cheyenne (Wyoming), and Denver (Colorado) also attract customers from Nebraska.

Only in the largest centers, Omaha and Lincoln, are very high order goods and services provided. Such enterprises as continental restaurants, certain medical specialists, dinner theaters, symphonies, and professional sports have very high threshold populations. They are concentrated in the state's two metropolitan areas.

Establishments that depend on the tourist trade respond less to local population numbers than to numbers of travelers passing through the area. Hotels and motels

FIGURE 4.23. Larger towns, like David City, provide a greater variety of retail goods and services.

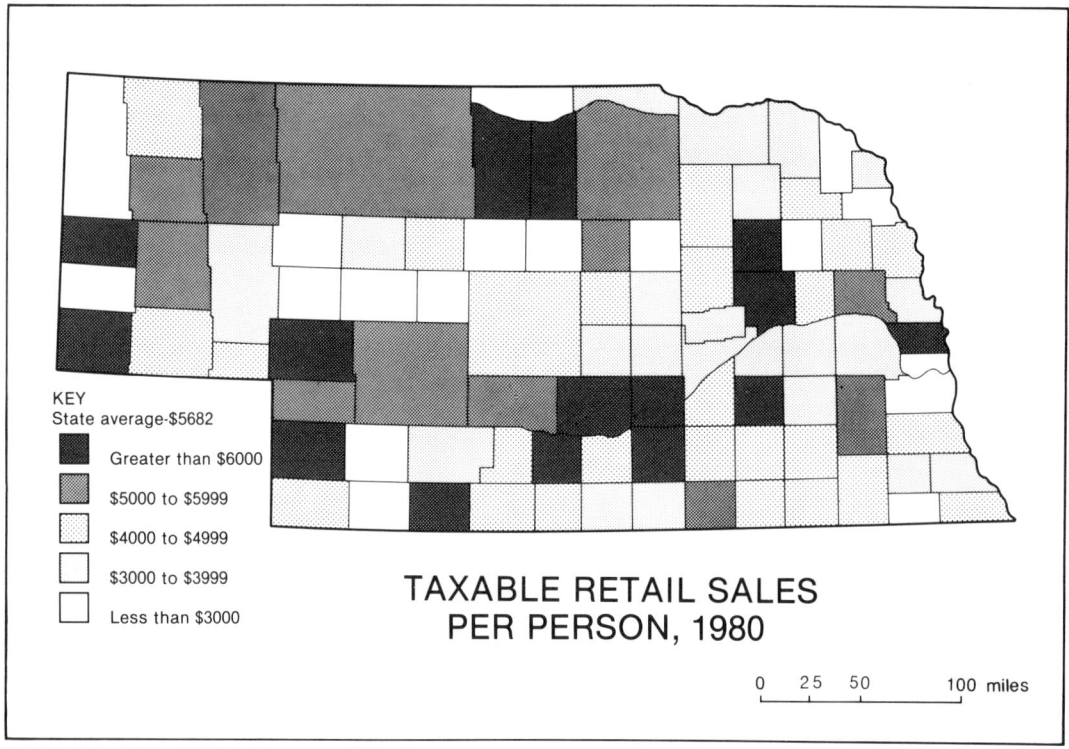

FIGURE 4.24. (UNL, Bureau of Business Research)

cluster along the principal tourist routes through the state, particularly Interstate 80 (Figure 4.25). In larger cities, lodging receipts are more dependent on conventions and business travelers. Though most tourist travel in Nebraska is oriented toward destinations outside the state, summer visitors bring substantial revenue into Nebraska through the purchase of goods and services (gasoline, motel rooms, and so forth) along the travel route and in visits to Nebraska tourist attractions. Among the more popular sites are Fort Robinson State Park near Crawford, Scotts Bluff National Monument, the state capitol, Boys Town, and Pioneer Village in Minden. Other state parks, recreation areas, and wayside areas dot the state (Figure 4.26). Camping, hunting, fishing, and boating are also popular.

The Declining Position of Small Towns

The role played by villages and small towns in the economic landscape of Nebraska has been radically altered during the past half century. In the settlement period, small towns provided a range of lower-level goods and services to the rural areas of the state. After 1920, though town populations often remained stable, their service role dwindled as farm consolidation reduced rural populations. Fewer farmers in the countryside meant fewer customers in stores, fewer clients for attorneys and doctors, and fewer supporters of local social institutions. Simultaneously, greater mobility meant small-town merchants had to compete with businesses in larger towns. As Hawley and Mazie have indicated, "the interest and activities of the farm community [spread] over a much wider area at the expense of the old local associations and the patronage of local stores."[40] Small-town enterprises could offer neither the selection found in larger places nor competitive prices. Higher prices and smaller selection led to fewer customers, which further impaired the stores' ability to compete.[41]

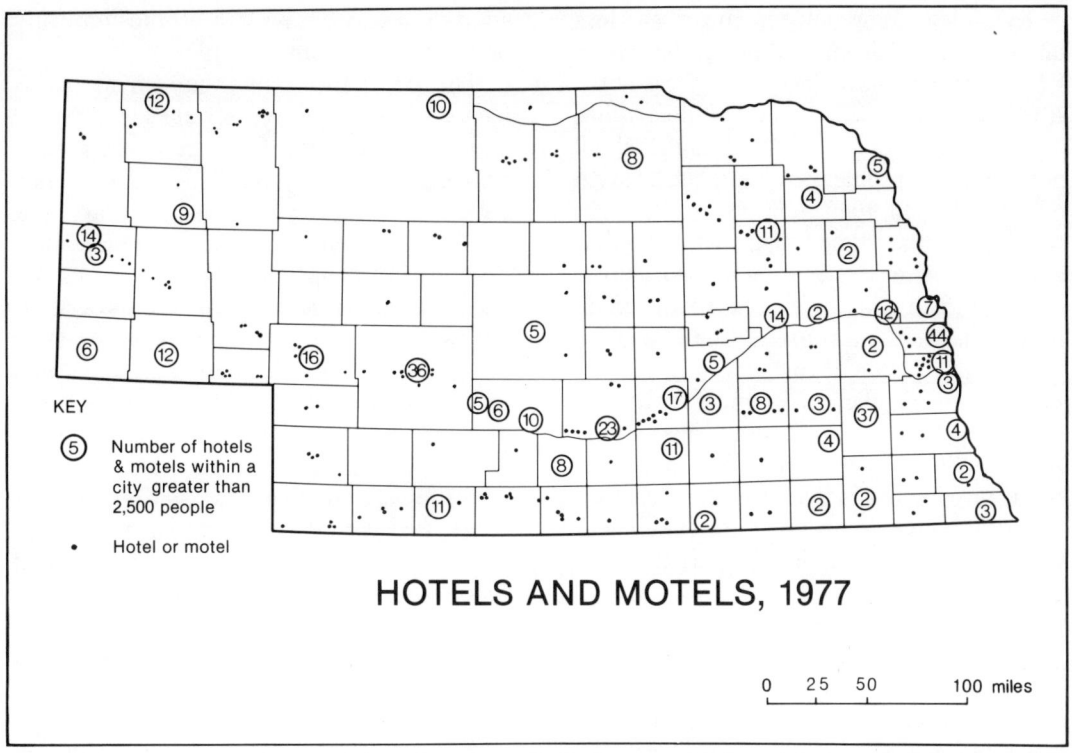

FIGURE 4.25. Generalized locations based on *1977 Census of Selected Service Industries.*

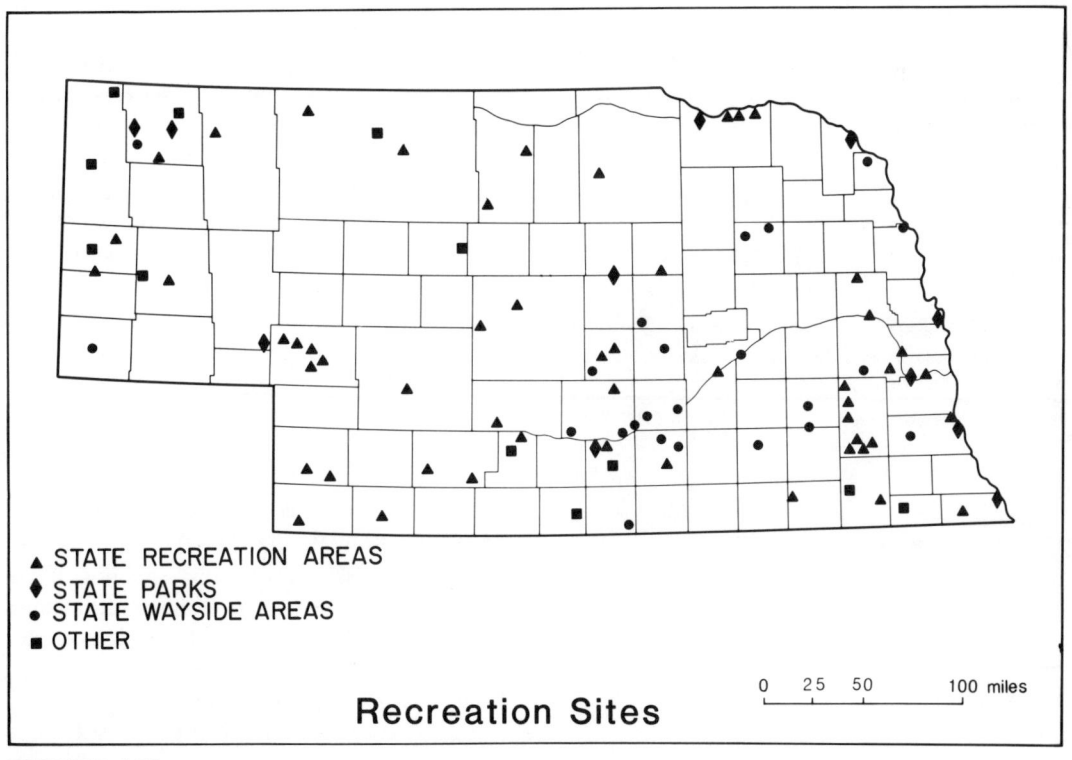

FIGURE 4.26.

For villages, competition meant the loss of the cafe, the drugstore, or the hardware store. In the smallest places even the grocery store, the gas station, and the post office closed. The loss of the local high school posed further problems. The consolidation of several area high schools (or the absorption of one village district by another) and the use of buses that consolidation often entailed took away one of the main reasons farmers patronized small towns.[42]

Although larger towns generally did not suffer as much, the speed and low cost of traveling to more distant larger places took some business away. The effect has been pronounced in towns that lie in the "shadow" of larger centers.[43] An excellent example of this process of "functional usurpation" is Plattsmouth, only 20 mi (32 km) south of Omaha. Though its population is over six thousand, Plattsmouth lacks many of the retail functions usually found in a town that size. There is no department store and a limited selection of clothing. Most residents of the city and the surrounding rural area travel to Bellevue or Omaha, with their greater selection and lower prices, to buy shoes, home furnishings, apparel, and medical care. They stay in Plattsmouth for banking services, pharmaceuticals, hardware, gasoline, and groceries—lower-order goods and services with thresholds typically below two thousand people.

The populations of many small towns have risen in recent years, but such a change belies the economic fortunes of their business centers. Many hamlets, for example, have grown in the past twenty years, but most have seen decreases in retail, processing, and congregational—organized social—functions. A study of Nebraska hamlets with fewer than 150 persons in 1980 found an overall decrease between 1963 and 1980 of 42.7 percent in the number of retail business establishments. Nearly half the gas stations and general or grocery stores closed during that period (Figure 4.27). Processing functions such as grain elevators also decreased. Congregational functions declined by 23 percent, led by schools and churches. Not all economic functions suffered, however. Fertilizer and other chemical plants increased by nearly 200 percent in hamlets.[44]

The only type of hamlet that experienced an increase in numbers was the "dormitory" hamlet. Many commuters to nearby larger towns and cities prefer to live in these smallest of settlements. Twenty years ago most dormitory hamlets were clustered near Omaha and Lincoln. As rural industrialization has proceeded, more and more hamlets have come within commuting range of manufacturing employment. Additionally, hamlet residence appeals to many "footloose" workers such as truckers and sales personnel who have fewer locational constraints than workers based at one site.[45]

Of all the changes that have occurred in small-town activity, probably none has produced as much concern as the declining availability of professional services, particularly medical care. As rural populations have fallen, and as medicine has become more specialized, doctors have moved to larger towns. Many communities now have too few doctors for the population (the state average is 1.44 doctors per 1,000 population), or have none at all (Figure 4.28). Likewise, the trip to a hospital may involve a long drive for many Nebraskans.[46]

FIGURE 4.27. Though small towns survive, many of their retail functions have closed down. (USDA, SCS)

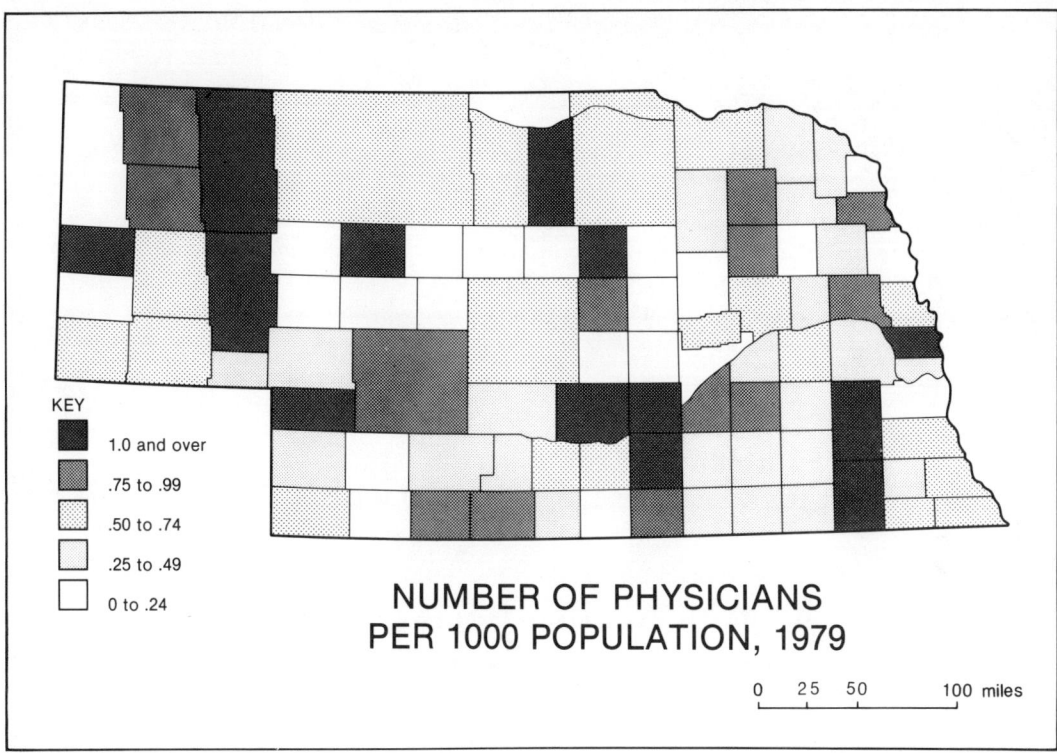

FIGURE 4.28. (Nebraska Department of Health)

Faced with this shortage of health care, smaller places have undertaken strenuous efforts to attract medical expertise. Some towns have established committees to search for doctors interested in practicing in small towns or have constructed clinics in the hope that doctors will be attracted by a ready-made practice. Yet the concentration of medical care has continued apace. The only health-related activities that have remained well distributed throughout the state are nursing homes (Figure 4.29). These facilities have a smaller threshold population, because of limited needs for equipment and professional staff, and can be profitably operated even in small towns. The contrast between the diffuse pattern of nursing homes and the much more concentrated pattern of hospitals and doctors illustrates the differences in populations needed to support each activity.

The emerging pattern of retail and service activities is one of increasing concentration in larger centers. As a consequence of changes in technology, economies of scale in retailing, transportation, and rural population density, larger centers have experienced population growth and expansion of their retail and service functions. Smaller places have stabilized their populations, even as tertiary activities (goods and services) have continued to depart.

Governmental Functions in Nebraska's Economy

The operations of governments—federal, state and local—have significant impact on the economy of Nebraska. Statewide, about 130,000 persons are employed by government, representing over 20 percent of total state nonagricultural employment. Omaha and Lincoln together account for over half the federal employees in the state. Sarpy County, home of Offutt Air Force Base, ranks third. Unlike the state and local governments, federal employment in Ne-

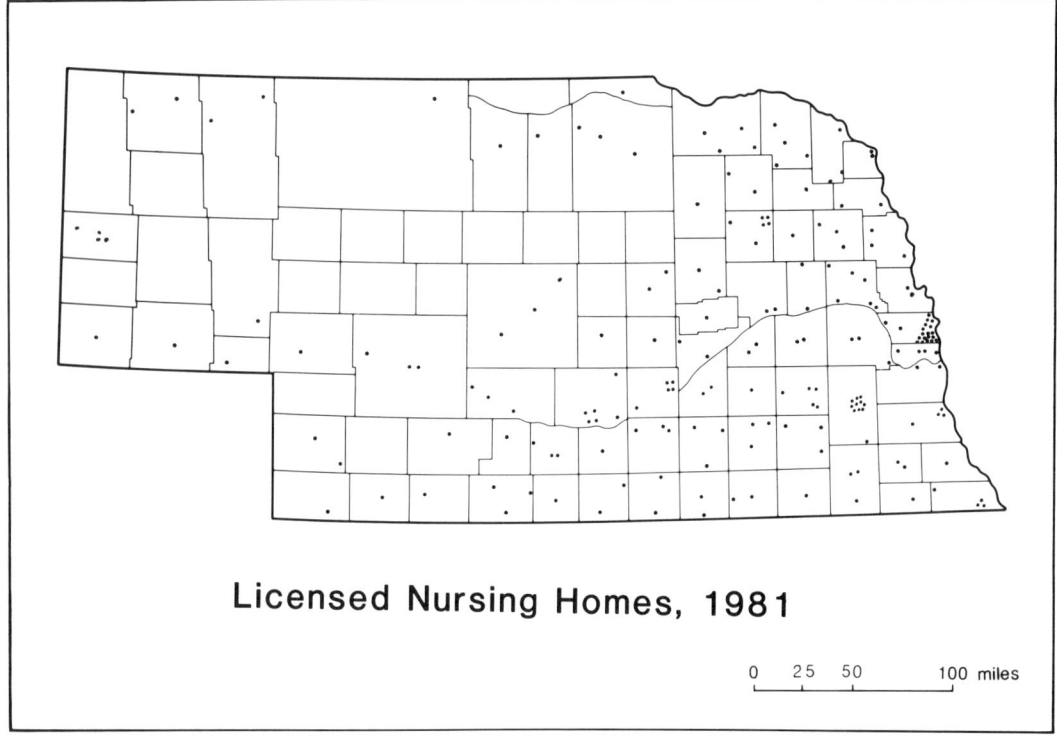

FIGURE 4.29. (Nebraska Department of Health)

braska has changed little over the past thirty years.

Employment by the state of Nebraska is concentrated in Lancaster County. Nearly 50 percent of state government workers are in the state capital of Lincoln, which contains the headquarters of most state agencies and the main campus of the University of Nebraska. Other counties with a sizable share of state-government employment include those with a state college—Buffalo, Wayne, Dawes, and Nemaha. Most counties with a city over ten thousand also have a large number of state employees. Between 1974 and 1981, employment by state agencies grew by about 19 percent—from 27,000 to 32,000.

Over half the employees of government in Nebraska are attached to counties and municipalities. In 1981, local-government employees numbered nearly 82,000, which was 22 percent higher than seven years earlier. Counties with few people must still maintain school systems and provide road maintenance and other essential government services (the student-teacher ratio in many small high schools is necessarily lower than that in larger systems). Even a minimal labor force of elected officials places strain

Focus: Government in Small Counties

Small political units often have difficulty supporting the services usually associated with counties. Arthur County has its own county clerk, attorney, sheriff, treasurer, and school superintendent, as well as three county commissioners. In 1980 the county had about fifty local government employees, representing nearly 10 percent of the total county population. The comparable figure for the state as a whole was about 4.3 percent. This kind of "inefficiency" in government is the price sparsely populated areas must pay for retaining a high degree of local control.

upon a limited tax base. That pressure is all the greater because local governments in Nebraska receive very little revenue from the state government, instead being funded primarily by the local populace.

FUTURE ECONOMIC PATTERNS

The patterns of economic health and activity that develop during the next several decades will be products of changes in several factors. Among these are the distribution of resources and their exploitation, governmental policies, transportation and communications technology, national trends in population distribution, and decisions by several million individuals.

The importance of manufacturing in the state will hinge on the national trend of industrial deconcentration toward rural areas and on the cost of transportation. If rural communities continue to be perceived as attractive environments and continue to be accessible due to low-cost transportation, Nebraska's manufacturing sector should continue to grow. However, energy costs play a major role in this equation. If the price of fuel should skyrocket, industrial concerns may decide that the labor and amenity advantages of rural Nebraska are outweighed by the disadvantage of locations peripheral to the nation's consuming public. Furthermore, manufacturing has been claiming an ever smaller share of national employment, whereas jobs in the service sector have been growing.

The future role of tertiary activities in Nebraska is likewise linked to transportation costs, but rural population density and the impact of communications are also important. Continued concentration of retailing seems likely unless transportation costs climb steeply. This may be mitigated somewhat if farm numbers stabilize and if small-city populations continue to hold their own, but with inexpensive transportation consumers will continue to bypass hamlets and towns for the variety and price advantages of larger centers.

The service sector may not be similarly affected. Assuming that the reverse migration of the 1970s continues, rural areas will increasingly be populated by former city and town dwellers with urban expectations for services. Some observers predict that refinements in communications technology will reduce economies of scale in the service sector, permitting small service providers to prosper. Moreover, communication links may give rural areas access to services such as specialized medical diagnosis or library collections, which are currently not available without a long journey.[47]

Future economic health and population growth are dependent on several social and technological variables. Above all, the economic health of the state depends upon the health of agriculture. Many manufacturing activities are closely tied to agriculture; much retail activity is agriculture oriented and provides consumer items and agricultural inputs to farm residents; the transportation system carries agricultural supplies and products.

CHAPTER 5

AGRICULTURAL PATTERNS

Agriculture is the most important source of income in Nebraska. Though there are only sixty-six thousand farms in a state with 1.57 million people, agriculture pervades the entire state. Many Nebraskans also have farm roots so the state remains rural in both background and outlook. But Nebraska's agricultural economy and rural areas have changed profoundly. This and following chapters examine the nature and patterns of agriculture in the state, with particular attention to the dramatic forces that have altered farming and the rural way of life during the past several decades.

THE AGRICULTURAL REGIONS OF NEBRASKA

Regionalization is a simplification process designed to reduce the confusing complexity of reality into a discrete number of homogeneous compartments by ignoring subtle differences among places and highlighting major contrasts. Nebraska is an agricultural transition zone between the midwestern Corn Belt to the east and the ranching and extensive wheat-growing areas to the west (Figures 5.1 and 5.2).

The eastern quarter of the state resembles the Corn Belt and is, agriculturally, an extension of western Iowa. Corn Belt agriculture is characterized by a mix of nonirrigated crops, particularly corn and soybeans, with varying amounts of wheat, oats, alfalfa, sorghum, and pasture. Principal livestock include hogs and beef cattle—cow-calf operations as well as feeder cattle. Generally, both livestock and cropping activities are found on each farm, with livestock providing the major means of marketing crops. Farms are somewhat smaller in the Corn Belt section then elsewhere in Nebraska and resemble the image most Americans have of the family farm—a mix of crops, livestock, and barns set in a rolling landscape. Three subregions can be identified. In the northeastern part of the state (subregion I_a), nearly all farm receipts come from livestock. Numerous large cattle-feeding and hog operations consume the crops produced, with little grain left over for the cash market. Corn is the dominant crop in every county in the northeast, with soybeans an important second crop. South of the Platte River (subregion I_b) the Nebraska Corn Belt is characterized by greater acreage devoted to soybeans and by less intensive livestock production. Sorghum and wheat are also important crops. Nowhere is irrigation the dominant form of crop production. A little farther west (subregion I_c), corn gives way to sorghum and wheat, with some soybeans. Both cattle and hogs are raised, as in southeastern Nebraska. In diversity of crops and livestock, this is the Corn Belt, but without the corn!

The central irrigated region extends along the Platte River from North Platte to Schuyler and includes the relatively level lands of counties south of the river. This is cash grain country, with corn by far the dom-

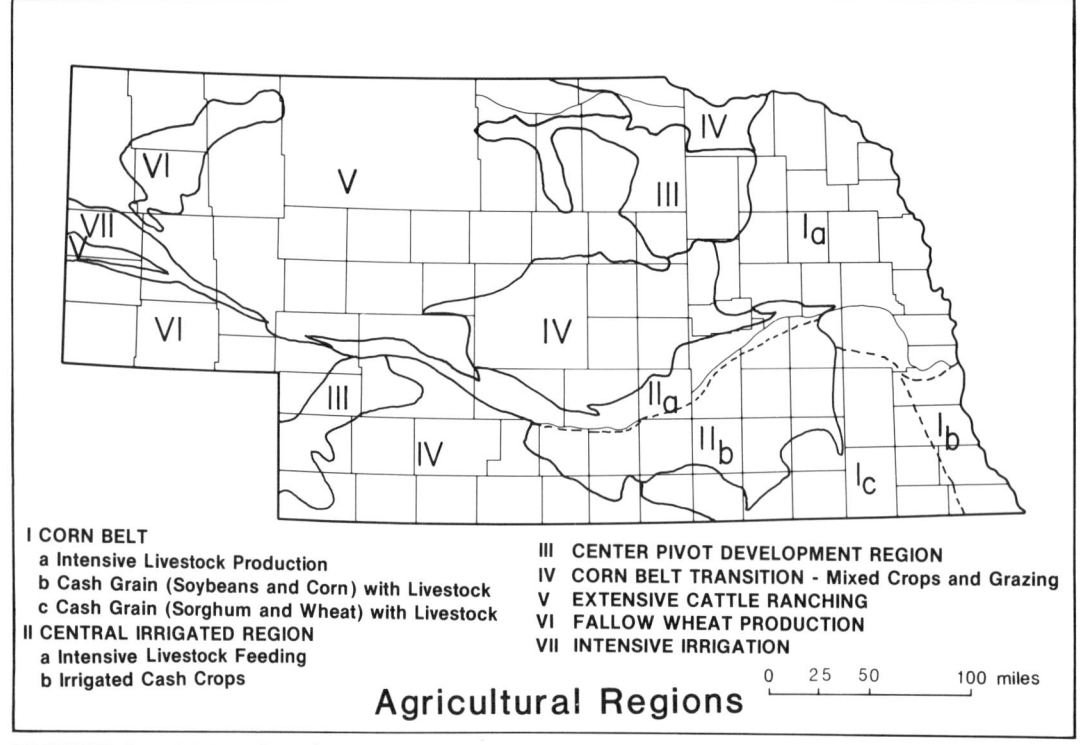

FIGURE 5.1. (University of Nebraska Press)

inant crop. In some counties over 80 percent of the cropland is in corn. Sorghum and wheat occupy most of the nonirrigated land. Livestock are important only along the Platte, where extensive cattle-feeding operations are found (subregion II_a).

Farms in this area are somewhat larger than in the Corn Belt, averaging between 350 and 700 acres (140–280 ha). Farm output is prodigious. Six counties in this region each sell over $100 million worth of agricultural products annually—the greatest such concentration in the state. Dawson County sales are nearly $200 million. Seven counties in the region produce over 15 million bu (530 million l) of corn each year. Farms in this region are quite prosperous. Value of land and buildings per farm is among the highest in the state, and more farms report annual sales over $20,000 than in most other areas.

In the central and southwestern parts of the state is a transitional region (region IV) between the Corn Belt to the east and extensive ranching and wheat production to the west. This is mostly nonirrigated land with inadequate rainfall for corn production. In the southwestern portion of this discontinuous region, wheat fields on tablelands are punctuated by deep, pastured canyons (Figure 5.3). Irrigation is used along the Republican River. The central transition subregion and an area in Knox and Boyd counties are characterized by corn and alfalfa interspersed with grazing lands. Several small areas with surface irrigation and scattered center-pivots are found here. Much land formerly planted to corn and small grains without irrigation has been converted to pasture in the past forty years. Crop acreage has declined steadily, and livestock numbers have increased.

The transition from Corn Belt to more extensive crop and livestock production has not been easy. Farm numbers have dropped

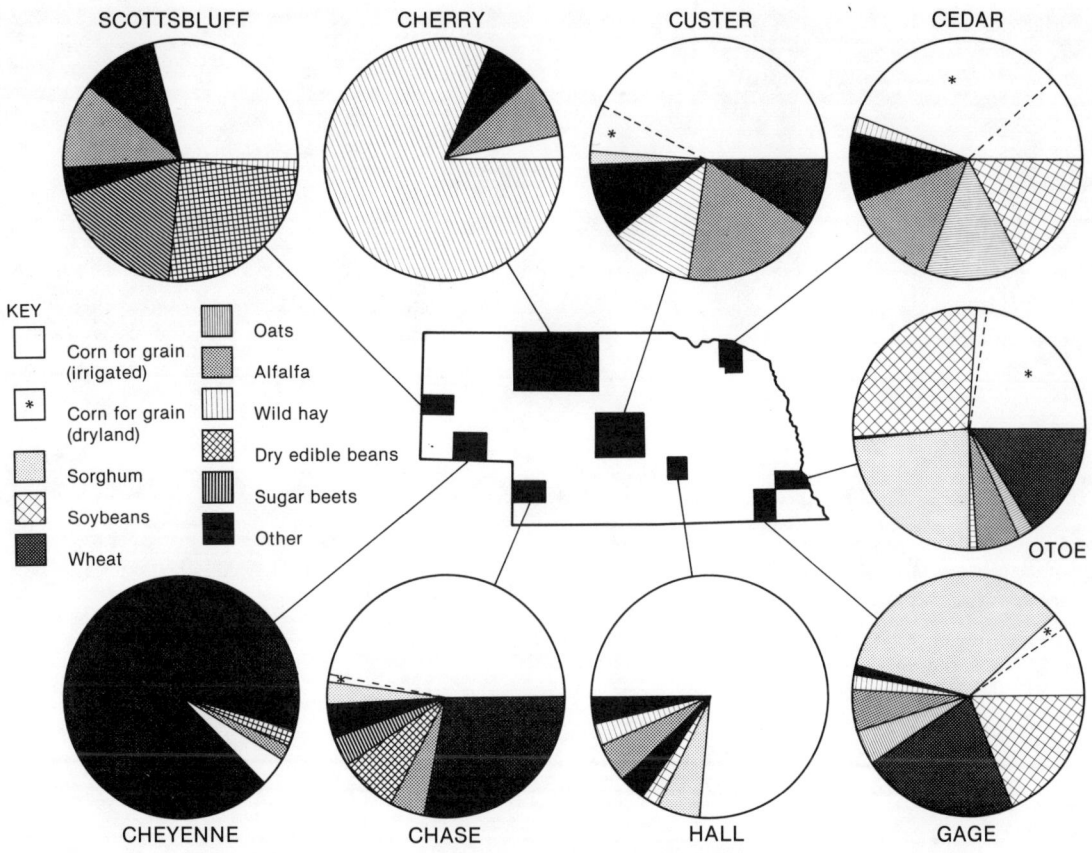

CROPLAND IN SELECTED COUNTIES, 1981

FIGURE 5.2. (NCLRS)

more rapidly here than elsewhere in the state.[1] Abandoned farm buildings dot the countryside and the average value of land and buildings per farm lags behind other counties.

Two areas of the state stand out because of the very rapid growth of center-pivot irrigation (region III). The northeast edge of the Sandhills has seen extensive pivot development for corn production since about 1960. Holt County, in 1981, was third in the state in corn acreage and production (Figure 5.4). Antelope County was first in acres, seventh in bushels produced. Prior to pivot development, Holt County produced corn on limited dryland acreage. Antelope County had substantial corn acreage, nearly all unirrigated.

The southwestern pivot region developed rapidly in the early to mid-1970s. As in the northern area, pivots here have been established on sandy soils. The dramatic shift from cattle ranching to irrigated corn production is one of the most fascinating phenomena of Nebraska's agricultural geography. It has played a major role in reversing several decades of decreasing corn acreage in the state. The Corn Belt region of Nebraska, as a consequence, is no longer the most important source of corn in the state. Not all grazing land in these two areas has been converted to cropland, and some dryland small grains are still produced, mainly in the southwest. But irrigated corn and continuing pivot development are the principal features of this emerging region.

Large-scale cattle ranching is practiced

FIGURE 5.3. Upland fields of corn and wheat are separated by deep, pastured canyons in Frontier County. (USDA, ASCS)

in the Sandhills and the counties of the northern Panhandle (region V) (Figure 5.5). Some scattered center-pivots have been installed by ranchers for the production of alfalfa and other forage crops, but the overwhelming land use is grassland. Wild hay is also harvested to supplement livestock feed.[2]

Extensive wheat production is found in the southern Panhandle and parts of the northern Panhandle (region VI). Almost all the wheat here is produced on summer fallow. Less-productive land is used for pasturing cattle. Livestock sales provide a not insignificant share of income, even in counties with the greatest wheat acreage.

In most of this region, crops other than wheat account for less than 10 percent of cropland. An exception is Perkins County, where pivot-irrigated corn competes for land with dryland wheat.

The North Platte Valley contains the greatest concentration of intensive irrigation (region VII). Major crops are dry edible beans, sugar beets, and corn, along with some potatoes and alfalfa. Cattle and sheep feeding are also important. Farms are much smaller than in surrounding wheat and cattle-ranching counties—427 acres (173 ha) in Scotts Bluff County.

THE STRUCTURE OF AGRICULTURE

The agricultural activities of Nebraskans exhibit considerable diversity. As pointed

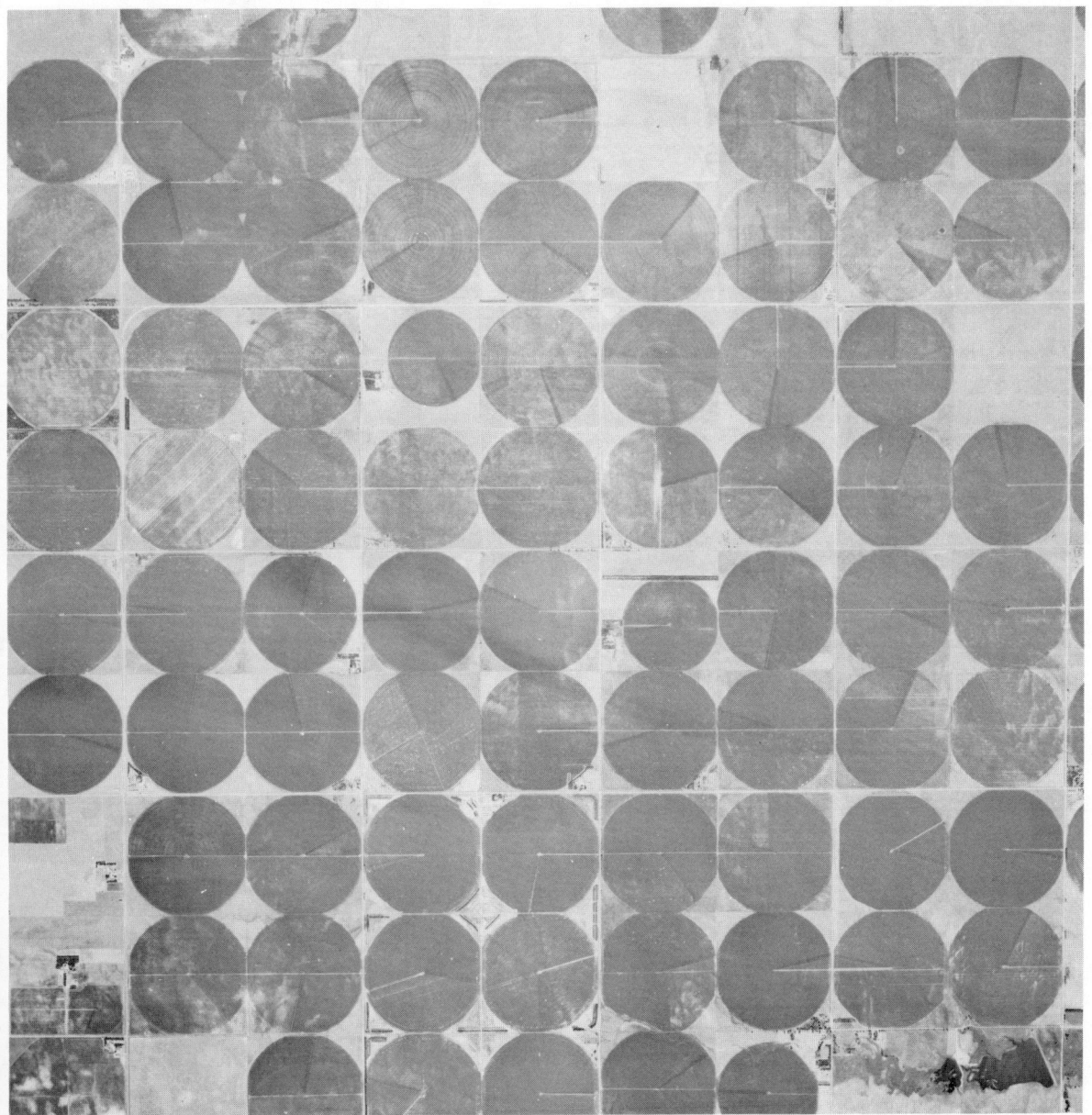

FIGURE 5.4. The center-pivot landscape of Holt County north of Atkinson. (USDA, ASCS)

FIGURE 5.5. Sandhills cattle congregate near windmill. Most land in the Sandhills is still used for grazing, in spite of recent irrigation development in some areas.

out in the earlier discussions on settlement, Nebraska contains elements of two agricultural traditions: a Midwestern mixed-farming region that is part of the Corn Belt and a plains agriculture emphasizing ranching and wheat production in a subhumid environment. A third, rapidly developing system is that of irrigated farming, which combines a set of desert-land techniques with the humid-land crop of corn.

Farm Size and Number

The transition from the Corn Belt to the agriculture of the plains is especially evident in the number and size of farms. The smallest farms are in the eastern counties, whereas in the west, particularly in the Sandhills, much larger operations predominate (Figure 5.6). In Cherry County, for example, the average "farm" contains over 5,000 acres (2,000 ha). Only such large operations can succeed where extensive grazing is the rule. Where crop production utilizes most of the land, farm size is generally much smaller, but scale is closely related to the principal crop produced. Because the labor required for wheat production is substantially less than for corn, farms in the major wheat-growing areas tend to be larger than those found in corn-producing counties.

The mechanization process (including the introduction of larger and more sophisticated equipment) has not only made farm expansion possible, but has made growth a requisite of economic survival. With a fixed amount of agricultural land (little has so far been lost to residential development), such expansion is accomplished by consolidation of farms, resulting in a decreasing number (Figure 5.7). In 1935, there were approximately 134,000 farms in the state; today the number is half that. In the intervening half century, the smaller (usually marginal) farms have been squeezed out of business (Figure 5.8; Table 5.1). The only size category smaller than 500 acres (200 ha) that increased its share of total farm numbers between 1964 and 1978 was that of farms under 100 acres (40 ha). Perhaps as a result of so-called hobby farming, this category increased from 13.5 percent to 19.7 percent of Nebraska farms during the fourteen-year period (Figure 5.9).[3]

The principal economic stresses of agriculture are often compounded for small farmers. As the costs of production inputs have risen relative to prices received by farmers, profit margins have shrunk. Increased output appears to be the best—perhaps the only—way to maintain income levels. Expansion cannot occur without laborsaving agricultural technologies, how-

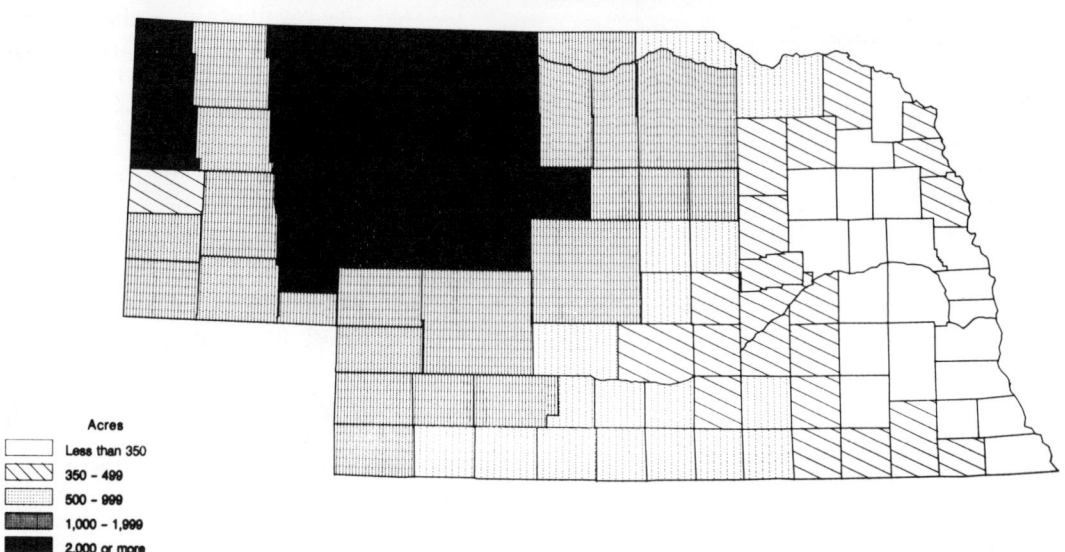

FIGURE 5.6. Taken from *1978 Census of Agriculture*.

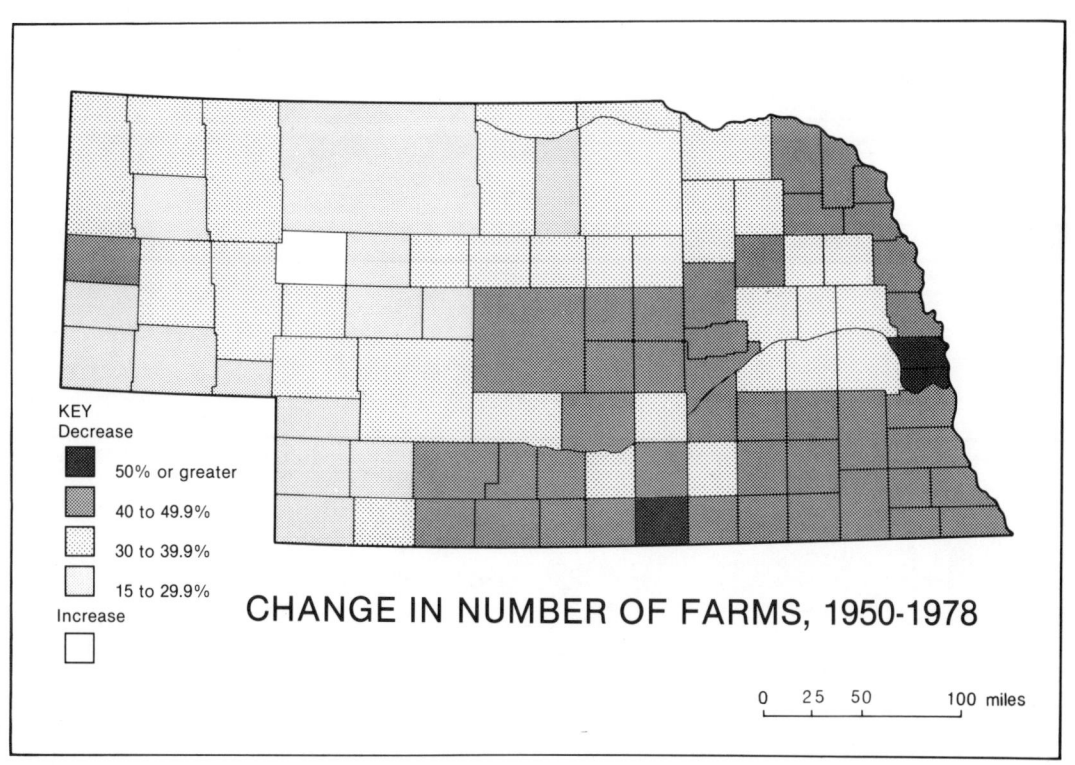

FIGURE 5.7. Based on censuses of agriculture.

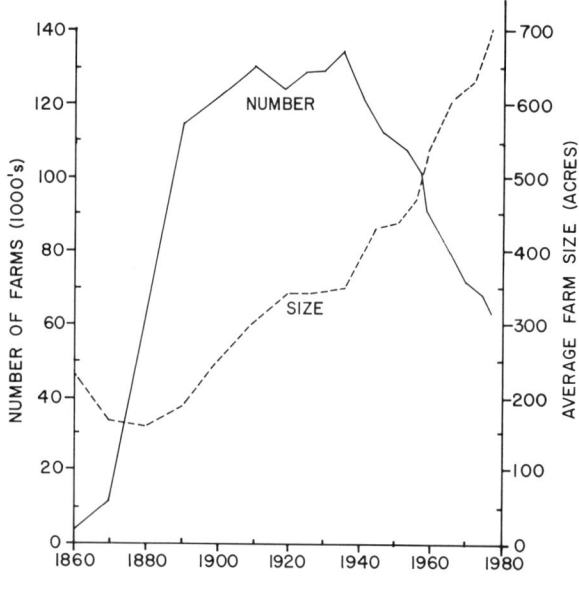

Average Farm Size and Number of Farms, 1860–1978

FIGURE 5.8.

ever. In order for farmers to be able to handle more land, larger machinery must be utilized; one result of this is that efficient use of large machinery necessitates farm expansion.

A principal advantage of larger farms is their ability to spread the cost of machinery over more land. A forty-thousand-dollar tractor costs the same whether it is operated 500 or 1,500 hours per year, on 400 or 1,200 acres (160 or 480 ha). Thus, capital investment and farm expansion fuel each other. The limit to increasing returns to scale probably is reached when the labor required to farm an additional acre exceeds the amount of additional time and effort farmers are willing to commit to the operation. At some point increased farm size produces even greater increases in the complexity of the operation, so that quality of management begins to suffer. There is no clear evidence that larger farms produce

TABLE 5.1

AVERAGE FARM SIZE IN SELECTED COUNTIES
(in acres)

	Franklin	Frontier	Holt	Cheyenne
1910	236	416	524	540
1920	246	434	590	601
1930	248	447	560	579
1935	249	434	581	559
1940	291	529	619	645
1945	327	588	719	735
1950	341	664	759	759
1954	397	698	791	833
1959	425	509	911	894
1964	482	576	1,050	967
1969	518	1,020	1,059	998
1974	587	1,038	1,145	1,023
1978	620	1,034	1,068	1,064

Source: U.S. Censuses of Agriculture.

higher crop yields or greater returns on investment than smaller farms, but they do produce more income.[4]

The number of farms in Nebraska decreased by about 2,000 per year between 1950 and 1964. In the late 1960s that rate fell to about 1,500 per year; it was under 1,000 per year in the early 1970s. Farm numbers dropped by only about 400 per year between 1974 and 1978. It is unclear, however, why the slowdown in farm consolidation occurred and whether this was a temporary aberration or represented some fundamental shift in pressures on farm size. It may simply reflect the increase in the number of very small farms.

Land Values

In 1981 the average value of an acre of Nebraska farmland was over $658, more than ten times the value recorded in 1950. The average value of land per farm was $500,000 in 1981, compared to only $25,000 in 1950.[5] These figures mask considerable intrastate variation in land value. Average value of land and buildings per farm recorded in the 1978 Census of Agriculture ranged from $163,000 in Boyd County to over $1 million in Grant County (Figure 5.10). Most Sandhills counties have average farm values over $400,000. Farm values in counties where crop production dominates generally fall between $200,000 and $400,000.

Farm value per acre shows considerably more variation. The least-expensive land is in the Sandhills, where grazing land was valued under two hundred dollars per acre in 1981 (five hundred dollars per ha). Highest land values are in the eastern third of the state; this situation reflects the enhanced value of lands on the outskirts of expanding urban areas, higher annual precipitation, and the greater intensity of agriculture. Irrigated crop land is the most valuable statewide, selling for over two thousand dollars per acre (five thousand dollars per ha) in many areas. (Figure 5.11).[6]

The current earning potential of farm-

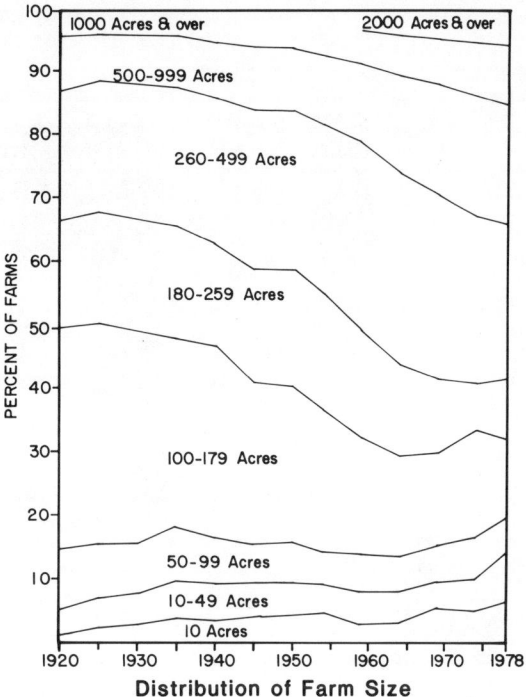

FIGURE 5.9.

land seldom justifies the high land costs and interest rates. Often the production costs for a crop, excluding the cost of land, can barely be met by the value of the harvest. Under such circumstances high land values can only be based on an expectation of future increases in farm earnings or of continuing increases in land prices.

Expensive land is one of the most serious obstacles encountered by young farmers seeking to develop viable operations. Older farmers with little debt can survive periods with little or no return on investment, but beginning farmers face formidable costs for land purchase and debt service.

Nevertheless, land values are expected to continue to rise. Farmers seeking to enlarge their operations place considerable pressure on the land market—the principle motivating factor behind half of all farmland purchases. Another 25 percent of farm purchases are made as an investment or hedge against inflation. Tax benefits to per-

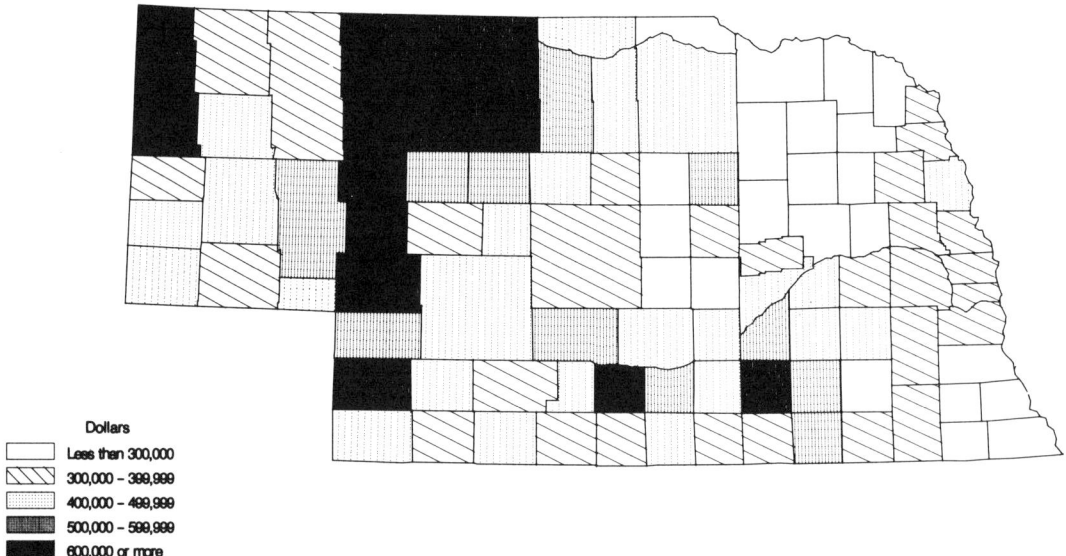

FIGURE 5.10. Taken from *1978 Census of Agriculture.*

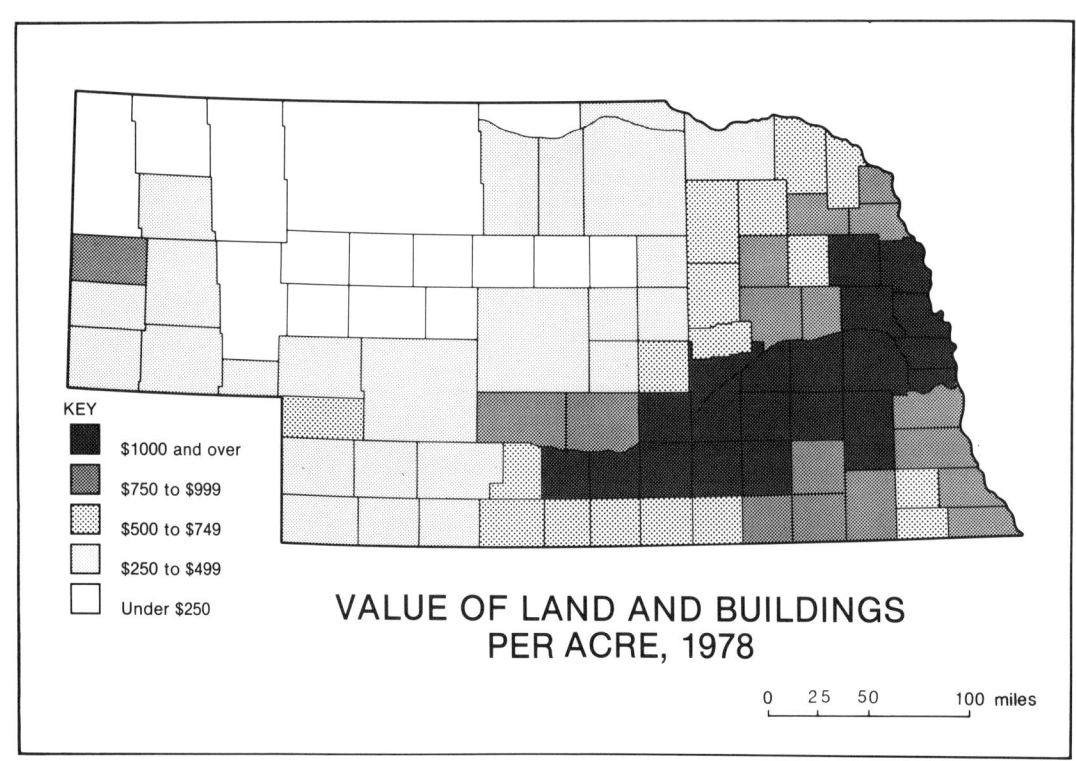

FIGURE 5.11. Based on *1978 Census of Agriculture.*

sons in high tax brackets make land an attractive investment and make it possible for investment-oriented buyers to pay three or four times as much for land as those who seek to make a living farming that land. In some areas the demand for homesites has helped to push land values upward. In others, land purchased for irrigation development has contributed to escalating land prices. Another factor is that because most land sales take place as a result of retirement or estate settlement, little land is generally for sale within the "commuting range" of a given farmer. This slow turnover pushes prices up.[7]

Farmland ownership remains attractive to nonfarmers considering the long-term appreciation of their investment. Those who farm expensive land will often have problems with adequate cash flow in the short run unless they have some other source of income available.

Off-Farm Income

Increasingly, farmers rely on nonfarm income to "carry" their costs of farming. Nonfarm income can be produced either by working spouses or by outside employment of farmers, which implies part-time farming. The number of Nebraska farm men and women with off-farm employment has increased dramatically in the past several decades.[8] In many instances off-farm employment provides the primary income to families and simultaneously makes continued ownership and operation of the farm possible (Table 5.2).

Dual employment (income from both farm and nonfarm sources) has become more common, in part because of the increased availability of manufacturing employment in many smaller towns and cities. Some farmers supplement their farm income with custom work. Custom haying,

TABLE 5.2

OFF-FARM WORK

	Percent of Farm Operators Reporting Days of Work Off-Farm, 1978			
	0 Days	1-99 Days	100-199 Days	200 or more Days
All Farmers	59.1	16.4	5.7	18.8
Full Owners	54.8	11.4	5.7	28.0
Part Owners	69.3	18.0	4.1	8.6
Tenants	49.2	22.8	8.2	19.7
Farm Size 10-49a.	29.7	11.2	7.9	51.1
Farm Size 140-179a.	50.2	15.9	9.6	24.5
Farm Size 260-499a.	65.8	19.2	4.9	10.1
Farm Size 1000-1999a.	73.5	17.2	3.6	5.6
Farming is Principal Occupation	72.6	19.5	4.2	3.7
Sales under $20,000	66.2	19.9	7.5	6.4
Farm Sales over $2,500				
Full Owners	59.3	12.1	5.7	23.0
Part Owners	70.0	18.1	4.1	7.8
Tenants	51.3	23.2	8.2	17.3

Source: U.S. Bureau of the Census, 1978 Census of Agriculture (Washington: Government Printing Office, 1981).

fertilizer application, or combining helps pay for expensive equipment and may produce additional income.[9]

Dual employment is often connected to part-time farming, which should not be confused with "gentleman farming" of 10-acre (4-ha) surburban plots. True part-time farmers seek to continue operation of a farm by supplementing farm income with funds from other sources. Advances in agricultural technology have allowed farmers to handle farm activities in less time than previously. The structure of the farm operation can also be altered to allow the off-farm job to complement the farming activities: Labor-intensive endeavors such as dairying might be replaced by grazing or small-grain production, for example. Off-farm employment is especially important on small farms, where farm income is more likely to be inadequate and excess labor is more common. In many cases, off-farm work is sought only seasonally. Prior to the improved off-farm employment opportunities in recent years, small farmers were often unable to survive. Now dual employment "may well provide the staying power for many farm families to remain on the farm."[10]

The High Cost of Farming

High land prices and the rising costs of production inputs have produced a tremendous demand for capital. Mortgages to finance land purchases have been common in the state since it was opened to white settlement, but non–real estate farm debt is now roughly equal to real estate farm debt.[11] Farmers routinely borrow funds to purchase production inputs such as seed, fertilizer, pesticides, and machinery (Table 5.3). Beef feedlot operators require capital to purchase feeder stock. Irrigators borrow money to install new irrigation systems.

A typical farmer may well have an investment in equipment alone of several hundred thousand dollars. In 1980 it was not unusual to find new tractors selling for $30,000 to $70,000. A self-propelled combine costs another $70,000. Add another $8,000 each for a plow and a disk, $7,000 for a grain drill, and $12,000 for an eightrow corn planter, and the farmer has a tremendous financial commitment.[12] Including 10 to 15 percent annual inflation on most farm equipment gives some sense of the capital intensity of modern agriculture. Center-pivot equipment adds even more.

Center-pivots are expensive. As of 1975, the average cost of installing a center-pivot, not including well drilling, land leveling, or the cost of the land, was about $60,000. This investment provided water to 133 acres (53 ha) at an average cost of $450 per acre ($1,100 per ha), often much more than the purchase price of the land. Interest, taxes, and insurance are extra. The annual cost of production inputs is substantial, too. Estimated annual cost to own and operate a center-pivot in 1975 was over $35,000. At these levels, 125 bu of corn per acre (10,900 l per ha) results in a break-even

TABLE 5.3

SELECTED PRODUCTION EXPENSES ON NEBRASKA FARMS, 1969 and 1978

	1969	1978
Seeds, Bulbs, Plants, and Trees	$30,412,000	$111,325,000
Commercial Fertilizer	74,977,000	267,572,000
Other Agricultural Chemicals	20,923,000	88,366,000
Petroleum Products	77,025,000	223,341,000

Source: U.S. Census of Agriculture, 1978

price of $2.12 per bu ($0.06 per l). The risks to the farmer are substantial, considering that the first $2.12 of each bushel of corn are already committed to pay for producing the crop.[13]

Land Ownership and Farm Operation

In part because of the costs and the difficulty of acquiring farm real estate, farm operators are not necessarily landowners. In Nebraska 40 percent of all farms are owner operated. Another one-third are operated by farmers who own some land and rent additional land. The remaining fourth are run by tenants who own no land of their own.

In Nebraska, tenancy has been one means of dealing with the high cost of farm land. It has made possible the entry of young farmers who do not ordinarily have sufficient capital or borrowing ability to "jump" into farming all at once. With time, they may acquire the necessary funds to purchase land and thereby become either part or full owners.[14]

The present tenancy rate is substantially lower than in the past. In some counties the 1940 tenancy rate was 60 percent, compared to present levels below 20 percent. What happened in the intervening period reflected to some extent the purchase of land by former tenants. A more important factor, however, has been that hard-pressed tenants moved out of farming, and their operations were taken over by farm owners seeking to expand.[15]

The lowest tenancy rates are found in counties with the highest average farm values. Sandhills tenancy rates are generally below 20 percent (Figure 5.12). Rates elsewhere are somewhat higher, with most counties in the principle grain-producing regions recording 20 to 27 percent tenancy. The highest rate is 35 percent in Scotts

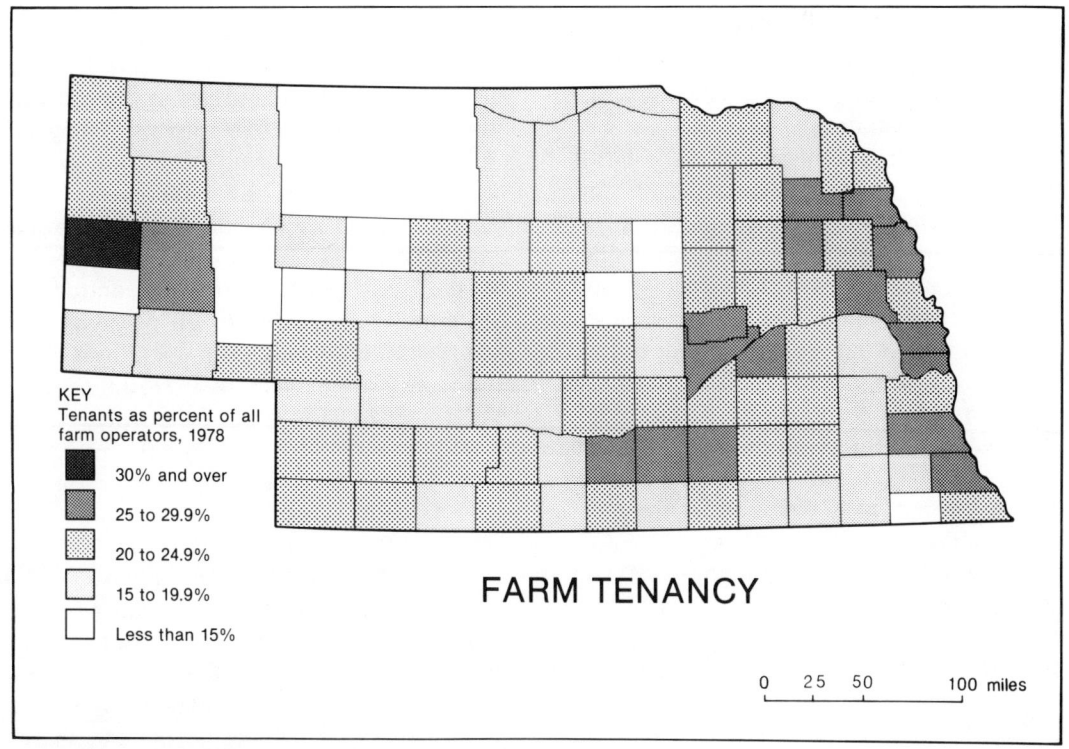

FIGURE 5.12. Based on *1978 Census of Agriculture.*

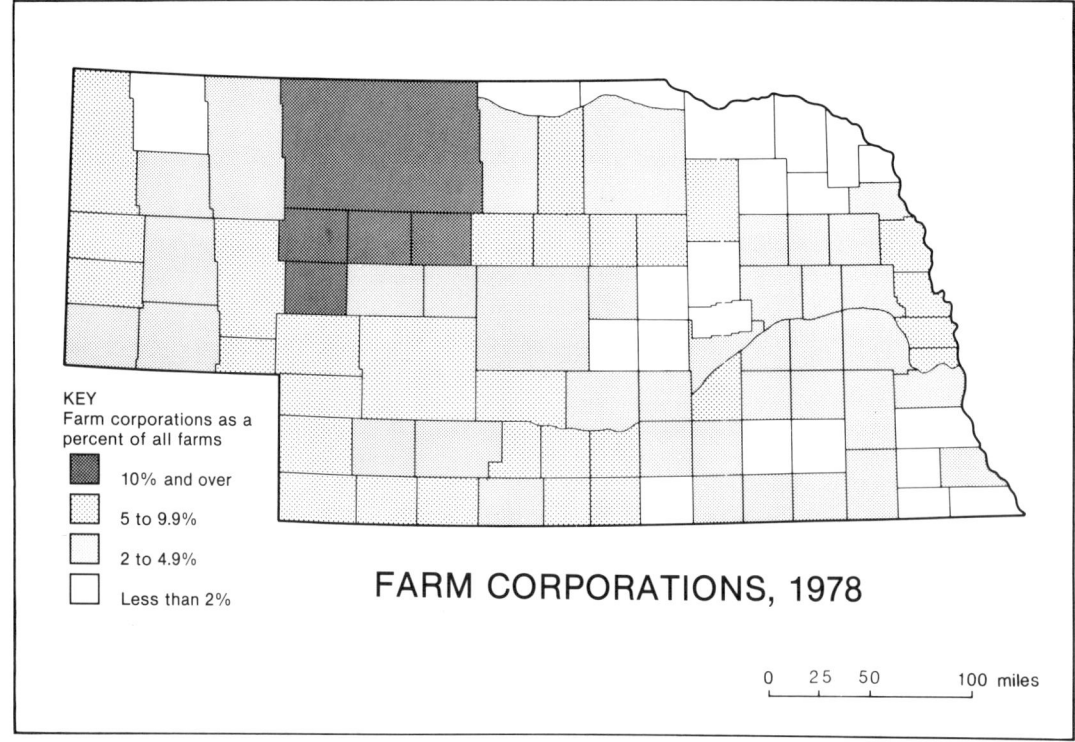

FIGURE 5.13. Based on *1978 Census of Agriculture.*

Bluff County. Many owner-operators have expanded by becoming part owners, that is, by renting additional land.

A small, but growing, number of farms are operated by farm managers. In this system, farm owners are another step removed from actual farm operations. Under simple tenancy, the owner and the tenant generally make many management decisions jointly—what crops to plant, how much and what type of fertilizer to apply, and number of animals to be grazed—although the degree of control that the owner chooses to exercise varies considerably. Owners in this situation are most likely active or retired farmers.

Under the farm-management system, a farm manager is hired by the owner to find a tenant, plan the operation of the land, arrange for the marketing of grain and livestock, and prepare financial reports. The owner generally has no direct involvement with the farming operation and is more likely to be a bank, insurance company, or investor, although nonresident heirs and retired farmers also make use of managers.

Most Nebraska farms are owned by one or more individuals, but an increasing number are owned by corporations or limited partnerships. The majority of these in Nebraska are family corporations, contrary to the popular image of an oil company executive directing field-crop operations from Houston headquarters. In 1978, 3.6 percent of Nebraska farms were incorporated. Over 6 million acres (2.4 million ha)—13.3 percent of Nebraska's farm land—were owned or leased by corporations. Because Nebraska's farm corporations are heavily concentrated in the Sandhills (Figure 5.13), their average size is approximately 2,562 acres (1,037 ha), nearly four times the average farm size in the state. Of the 2,399 farm corporations in the state in 1976, over 80 percent reported no out-of-state shareholders with more than 10 percent of their stock. Most were corporations formed specifically to operate an existing farm with control vested in a family.[16]

For a family, incorporation simplifies transfer of ownership and estate settlement. Inheritance taxes can be minimized through transfer of stock by gift. Equalizing an estate is much simpler when each heir is given stock rather than land. In the former case the farm remains one unit. In the latter situation several heirs are each left with parcels that may not be large enough to assure an adequate living, so one heir often goes into debt to buy out the others. Incorporation also aids in providing for retirement of the farm owner and making credit available to the farm operation. One of the drawbacks of incorporation is a considerable increase in paperwork.[17]

Although most farm corporations are family arrangements, nonfamily corporate farming is common in some areas (Table 5.4; Figure 5.14). Prudential Insurance Company owns over 10,000 acres (4,000 ha) in Lincoln County and 3,760 acres (1,500 ha) near Bassett, where it raises corn under center-pivot irrigation. Prudential also acquired nearly 20,000 acres (8,000 ha) in northern Holt county from National Farms, a Kansas City company. Colorado cattle feeder William Foxley purchased 14,000 acres (5,600 ha) in Wheeler County, where his corporation installed forty-seven center pivots at an estimated cost of $2.8 million in 1981 and constructed a feedlot capable of holding up to ninety thousand cattle.

Dundy County has attracted irrigation investment from several companies. Cornhusker Farms operated forty-nine pivots in 1975 and employed a full-time manager in Imperial. At least two corporations with Dundy County land utilized the services of a land and investment company that arranged for the acquisition by investors of about 7,000 acres (2,800 ha) of undeveloped range land in the county (Figure 5.15).[18]

Investor-oriented corporate farms differ significantly in their mode of operation from the family-farm corporation. Nonfamily corporations generally depend upon managers to oversee their investments. Unlike the traditional farm-management system in which the manager arranges for a tenant, the custom farm manager employed by corporate farms utilizes hired labor to operate machinery owned by the manager.

TABLE 5.4

SELECTED HOLT COUNTY "FARMERS"

Community Housing, Inc.
Downtown Realty Co.
Eagle Creek Land Co.
JBL Enterprises, Inc.
Lincoln Ag-Products Co.
Midwest Grain Co.
Midwest Irrigation Co.
National Alfalfa Dehydrating and Milling Co.
Olson Bros. Manufacturing Co.
P. G. Realty, Inc.
Phoenix Investment Co.
Sun Valley Acres, Inc.
Triangle Curry Co.
Triangle Land Co.
The Weller Foundation, Inc.

Source: Holt County Plat Map, 1982.

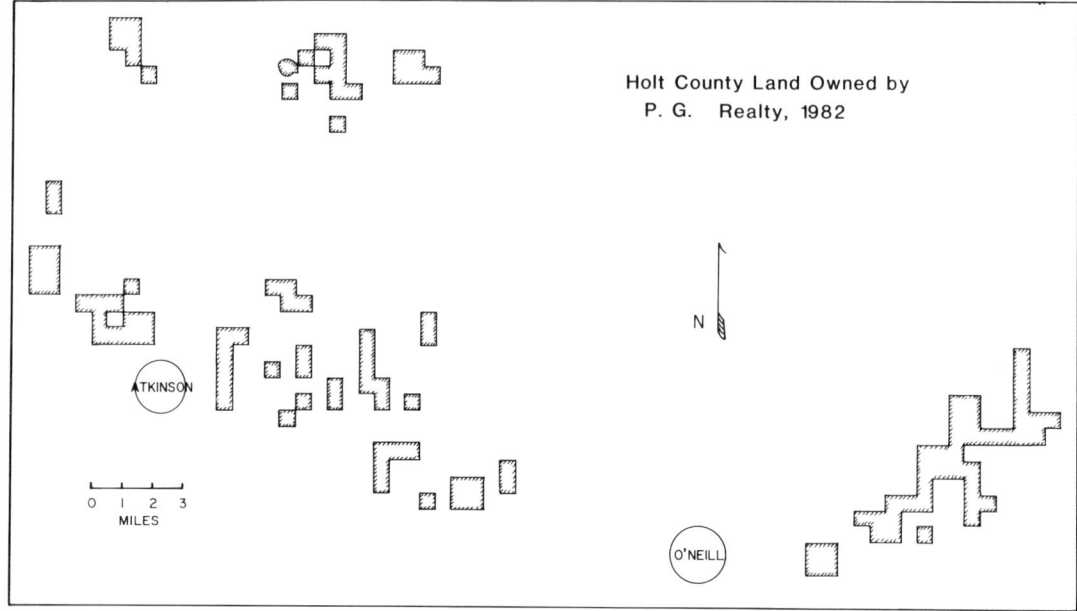

FIGURE 5.14. Based on 1982 plat map of Holt County.

FIGURE 5.15. Dundy County landscape. Signs indicate the locations of investor-owned land managed by a Colorado firm. (Center for Rural Affairs)

Investors have been attracted by the prospect of profits from developing inexpensive grassland for center-pivot irrigation.

Concern over investor-oriented corporate farming led Nebraska voters in 1982 to approve an initiative that would prevent further acquisition of farmland by nonfamily corporations. Family-owned corporations were defined in the initiative as those in which a majority of the voting stock is held by a family and at least one family member either lives on the farm or is engaged in the day-to-day labor and management of the farm.

Concern over such activity is not due to the nature of corporate structure, which is successfully, wisely, and prudently used by thousands of farmers in the state. Nor is it necessarily related to the large scale of operations of most investment-oriented corporations. Rather, concern is expressed about the nature of nonresident investment and the investor's overriding interest in the appreciation of land values, rather than in short-term cash flow or long-term ecological stability.

Sandhills developments have been criticized because plowing of grasslands threatens to produce substantial wind erosion. The U.S. Soil Conservation Service rates soil capability on a scale from one to eight. The last four classes are considered to be nonarable—unsuited to crops. Over half of the pivots established in 1975 on nonarable soils in Dundy County, where the principal limitation is wind erosion potential,[19] were owned by outside investors. The investment orientation of such operations is believed by many observers to be related to less interest in careful stewardship of the land resource.

Another factor prompting concern over the corporate "invasion" of agriculture is the tax and capital acquisition advantages that large corporations possess relative to smaller, "family-farm" operations. These advantages give large corporations an ability to pay substantially more for land and still turn a profit.

A third factor is the investor's role in the local community. When land is owned by local residents, whether farmers or not, the principal economic and community benefits accrue to the local area. Businesses in nearby towns furnish the farmer with clothing, hardware, food, and utilities. The farmer contributes to the strength of local institutions, such as schools, civic organizations, and religious institutions. The outside investor takes most of the profits outside the area, purchasing locally only those inputs directly related to the farm operation, including fuel and perhaps, but not necessarily, seed, fertilizer, and machinery. Local institutions receive taxes, but few other benefits. Many secondary economic impacts of agriculture are thereby exported; this results in a decline in the economic and social health of the rural community.[20]

Although owner-operators are interested in profit, their commitment to a local area and to agriculture is long term. The time horizon of outside investors is necessarily shorter. If water supplies should decrease significantly, investors might be inclined to abandon an irrigation operation or to seek to get as much as possible of the diminishing water supply. Left behind would be traditional owner-operators with a non-mobile land supply interspersed with the erosion-scarred lands of investors.

Farm Types

Family farm is a term that encompasses a range of farm types and eludes easy definition.[21] Rodefeld has suggested that categorizing farms simply on the basis of ownership is not especially meaningful. He proposes a functional classification system based on two variables: level of land ownership by the farm manager and level of labor provision by the farm manager. Rodefeld's four classes are family-type farm, tenant-type farm, larger-than-family–type farm, and industrial-type farm.[22]

The operator of the family-type farm owns most of the land and equipment and provides most of the labor. On the tenant-type farm, the farmer supplies the labor and often owns the equipment, but does not own most of the land resources. Both differ from the larger-than-family–type farms and industrial-type farms in their source of labor. The manager of the larger-than-family farm owns the land resources, but most labor is hired. The industrial farm likewise relies on hired labor, but land and often nonland resources are owned by someone other than the farm manager.[23]

Nineteenth-century land policies encouraged the family-type farm through the availability of abundant cheap or free land. High risk and low rates of return on investment made farm ownership unattractive to most nonfarmers.[24] During the late twentieth century, however, family farms have declined both as a proportion of all farms and in their share of farm production. Agricultural output and wealth have become increasingly concentrated in large farms.

In 1978 Nebraska's 10,324 largest farms (15.7 percent of all farms in the state) accounted for 66.2 percent of total agricultural products sold (Figure 5.16). The largest 10 percent of farms sold 44.8 percent of agricultural products in 1964; by 1974

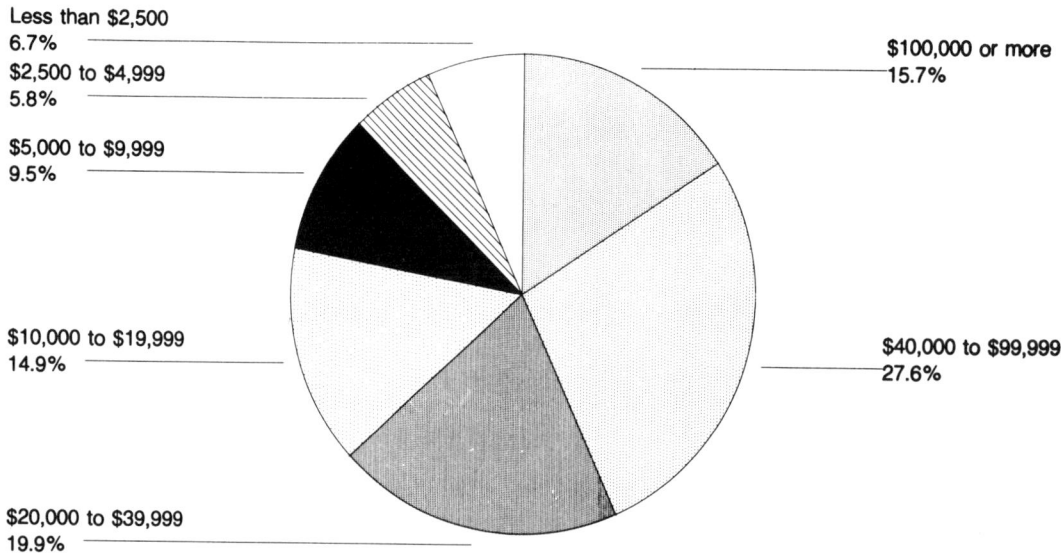

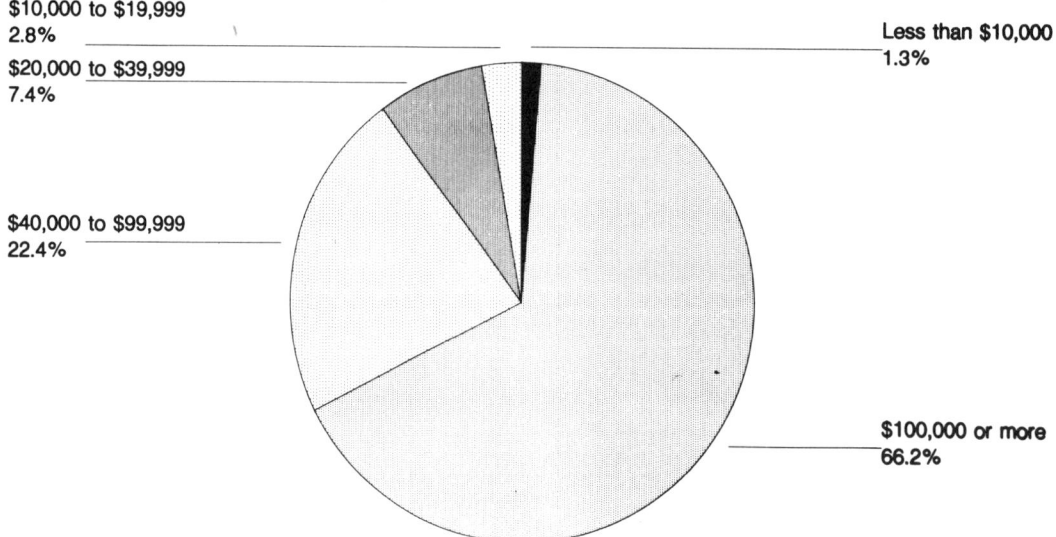

FIGURE 5.16. Based on *1978 Census of Agriculture.*

that figure was up to 52.8 percent and in 1978 reached 56.2 percent. (The increase in number of very small farms during the same period must be taken into account in considering these numbers.)

Even when smaller farms are eliminated from consideration, the growing concentration of Nebraska farm production is clearly evident. Many factors are responsible for the relative decline in family farms, including the difficulty small operators have in acquiring capital, the tax advantages of larger operations, the competition from nonfarmers who bid up land prices, and the increasing cost of livestock and machinery.[25]

Family-type farms, which may appear doomed from the viewpoint of economics, offer certain social advantages, however. Family-type farms are related to greater involvement in local organizations, social and political activities, and community activities in general. Large farm size has generally negative effects on the economic viability of small towns.[26]

Changes in farm type may be accompanied by changes in composition of the labor force, education levels, residential stability, age structure, voting levels, community participation, and the number, sizes and types of local businesses.[27] The evidence indicates that larger-than-family and industrial-type farms produce "social consequences that reduce the quality of life in rural communities."[28]

In Nebraska the industrial-type farm is not a serious problem, although the margins of the Sandhills have felt some effects. Nevertheless, some would suggest that the concentration of agricultural production in the hands of a small number of industrial farms, as is characteristic of California, is an ominous portent for Nebraska's agricultural future.

Many observers predict that agricultural concentration will accelerate. The changes they envision in land tenure in much of the Great Plains include more absentee ownership, an increase in the role of paid farm managers, and continuing pressures to expand.[29] One agricultural economist has warned, "the direction would suggest some movement toward a 'landed' aristocracy," even though total agricultural productivity may well suffer as a result.[30]

Fragmented Farms

When farmers seek to enlarge existing operations, the decision of where to acquire additional land depends primarily on the availability of land for rent or sale. It is common for farmers to be forced to purchase or rent land that is not contiguous with their existing operations. Although the typical farm of a century ago and even in the 1940s consisted of a single block of land, the "average" Nebraska farm of today is made up of several spatially distinct parcels, often separated by many miles (Figure 5.17).[31]

Fragmented farms in much of the world result from the division of large holdings

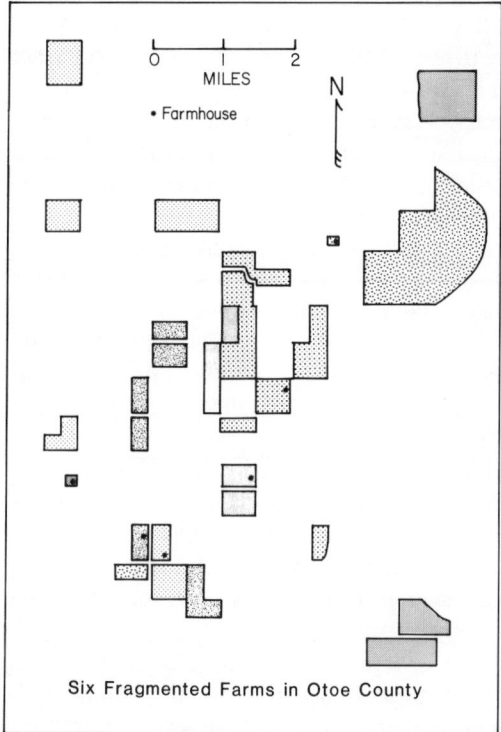

FIGURE 5.17. Each pattern represents a different farm.

into smaller parcels through inheritance. The numerous small, scattered fields make the operation inefficient and resistant to mechanization. In Nebraska, fragmentation is an adjustment to a tight land market that enlarges farms and aids in the economic survival of farmers.

Numerous problems are caused by noncontiguous tracts. Costs to farmers in money and time are increased. Fuel is used traveling from one holding to another; more wear and tear on machinery and tires increases replacement costs. Some farmers may spend the equivalent of three to four days each year traveling between holdings. Prices are substantially higher for machinery designed to be transported. Possibly as much as 12 percent of the cost of some types of equipment can be directly traced to the mechanisms for folding an implement to road width. As the size of equipment increases, as in the recent adoption of twelve-row corn planters, such costs become more significant.[32]

Even when large equipment is prepared for travel on roads, it seldom conforms to a 10- or 12-ft-wide (3- or 3.7-m-wide) lane. This often causes long detours to avoid narrow bridges. The mix of slow-moving farm machinery and faster automobiles and trucks on the road contributes to accidents. The likelihood of farm accidents is five times as high on the road as it is in the field, and the chances of such an accident being fatal are eight times as great.[33]

Locating livestock away from the home farm increases travel time and costs and makes effective oversight of animals more difficult. Rustling is a greater threat when livestock are not nearby. This has become more of a problem as decreasing population densities in rural areas have made less effective the informal watchdog system, under which farmers watched out for one another's interests.[34]

In general, farm management becomes more difficult when farms are fragmented. Farmers are likely to have less information about livestock health or soil moisture at distant locations. Repairs are more difficult and time consuming. Theft and vandalism are more of a problem, particularly at the expanding edge of a city or suburb, yet to move tractors and other machinery requires so much time that many farmers leave their equipment in distant fields until the operations are complete.[35]

"Sidewalk" and "Suitcase" Farmers

When large numbers of noncontiguous tracts constitute a farm operation, little advantage exists for farmers to live on one of those tracts, rather than in a nearby small town or city. Farmers who relocate are often referred to as sidewalk farmers. Each working day they commute to fields, yet they have the advantages of small-town living such as paved streets, municipal water and sewer service, and proximity to social institutions and retail services.[36] This arrangement is found throughout Nebraska, but is probably more common in the western third of the state, particularly in winter-wheat areas where management needs are lower and labor requirements are concentrated in a few periods of the growing season.

These conditions are also conducive to "suitcase farming"—commuting longer distances. Suitcase farmers, particularly numerous in Kansas and eastern Colorado, have been a part of the agricultural landscape of the Great Plains for most of the twentieth century. Most of Nebraska's suitcase farmers live either in eastern or central Nebraska or in Colorado and operate farms in the southern Panhandle or the southwestern counties. Most raise only wheat and travel to their farms in early fall to prepare the ground and plant, returning in July for the harvest. The rest of the year the "farmers" are found in other, often nonagricultural, occupations.[37]

Costs of production are probably somewhat less for suitcase farmers than for residents, but returns are also lower in most instances. Why, then, has suitcase farming survived? As noted in Chapter 1, year-to-year variations in precipitation characterize the subhumid Great Plains. Economic pressures on farmers in bad years are considerable. Land prices, which fluctuate with the vagaries of the weather, dip especially low during a series of consecutive dry years. Most suitcase farmers appear to have bought their farmland in years of low yields and prices, when resident farmers were most likely to sell out. When moister conditions returned, suitcase farmers converted grassland to wheat. In other words, "absentee ownership was a speculative reaction to wide fluctuations in land values."[38]

LIVESTOCK

Although outsiders may think of Nebraska as a homogeneous land of corn and cattle, the state exhibits considerable agricultural diversity. Agricultural production ranges from wheat to pinto beans and from hogs to poultry (Table 5.5). Nevertheless, there is some accuracy to the outsiders' perception. Almost everywhere you go you will find some corn and cattle.

These two principal products of Nebraska farms are, of course, inextricably linked. Farmers raise cattle to eat corn and then grow corn to feed to cattle. Although most farms in the state report both livestock and cropland, the sale of livestock is the source about two-thirds of total farm income. In some counties, particularly in the Sandhills and in the northeastern part of the state, livestock sales contribute over 90 percent of total income. In only a few counties in the wheat belt and the deep-well irrigation areas do livestock sales provide less than 60 percent of total farm income.[39]

Beef Production

The availability of plenty of pasture lands and feed grains makes beef production a logical choice for Nebraska farmers. Nebraska's geographic position, including good-quality transportation links to major centers of food consumption in the Midwest and West, also favors production of beef to satisfy national needs. The development of irrigation in the past several decades has led to a great increase in the amount

TABLE 5.5

LIVESTOCK AND POULTRY IN NEBRASKA, 1981

		Quantity
Hogs and Pigs. Dec. 1, 1981		4,100,000
Hogs Marketed, 1981		6,073,000
All Chickens, Dec. 1, 1981		4,150,000
Chickens Marketed, 1981		1,650,000
Eggs Produced, 1981		802,000,000
All Cattle and Calves, Jan. 1, 1982		7,250,000
Cattle Placed on Feed During 1981	4,350,000	
Beef Cows, Jan. 1, 1982	2,148,000	
Calves Born, 1981	1,970,000	
Milk Cows, Jan. 1, 1982	122,000	
Cattle Marketed, 1981		3,877,000
Milk Produced		1,400,000 lbs.
All Sheep and Lambs, Jan. 1, 1982		225,000
Sheep and Lambs Marketed, 1981		176,000
Wool Produced		1,728,000 lbs.

Source: Nebraska Agricultural Statistics, Annual Report, 1980-1981 (Lincoln: Nebraska Crop and Livestock Reporting Service, 1982).

FIGURE 5.18. Working cattle on a Sandhills ranch. (Sandhills Cattle Association)

of grain available. To the extent that cattle in the state are fattened on Nebraska corn, transportation costs for feed are held down.

Most cattle in the state are raised on pasture until being marketed as feeder cattle. About half the calves come from ranches in the western half of the state (Figure 5.18). They are then fattened for market in feedlots. These operations range from the small farmer-feeder with just a few animals to large commercial feedlots with over one thousand head. The latter market over 60 percent of the cattle for slaughter in the state (Figure 5.19).[40] The major feedlots are concentrated in the central Platte Valley from Cozad to Grand Island, in the northeast (particularly Cuming County), and near Omaha. Cattle feeding is uncommon in the Sandhills (Figure 5.20; Table 5.6).

Traditionally, most farmers maintained a small herd of cows and placed their calves on feed—an effective way of converting grain into an easily marketable commodity. Recent trends have been away from smaller lots toward specialized feeding operations.

FIGURE 5.19. A large feedlot operation, showing cattle on mounds that provide good drainage. At the far end of the operation is a lagoon for waste. Horizontal (or trench) silos at the left of the picture store feed. (UNL, Cooperative Extension Service)

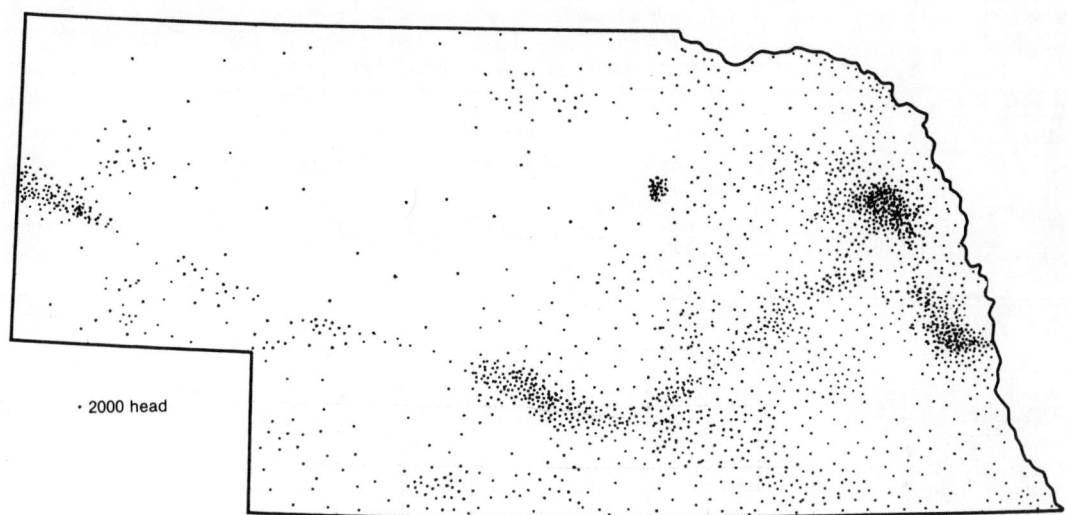

CATTLE PLACED ON FEED, 1981

FIGURE 5.20. (University of Nebraska Press, NCLRS)

TABLE 5.6

LEADING COUNTIES IN LIVESTOCK PRODUCTION, 1981

	All Cattle		Cattle Placed on Feed		Hog Inventory (Dec., 1981)	
1.	Cherry	400,000	Cuming	425,000	Cuming	221,000
2.	Custer	240,000	Dawson	264,300	Knox	160,000
3.	Dawson	240,000	Scotts Bluff	207,000	Cedar	155,000
4.	Cuming	232,000	Saunders	154,200	Clay	155,000
5.	Holt	215,000	Hall	132,200	Platte	128,000
6.	Lincoln	180,000	Sarpy	113,000	Gage	112,000
7.	Sheridan	175,000	Adams	198,300	Holt	96,000
8.	Scotts Bluff	160,000	Stanton	98,000	Dodge	94,000
9.	Knox	148,000	Polk	96,500	Antelope	92,000
10.	Buffalo	120,000	Cass	92,000	Dawson	92,000
11.	Wheeler	120,000				

Source: Nebraska Agricultural Statistics, Annual Report, 1980-1981 (Lincoln: Nebraska Crop and Livestock Reporting Service, 1982).

TABLE 5.7

CATTLE MARKETED, 1960-1982

Year	Total Cattle Marketings -000 Head-	Year	Total Cattle Marketings -000 Head-
1960	2,251	1972	4,288
1961	2,291	1973	3,909
1962	2,396	1974	4,144
1963	2,546	1975	4,014
1964	2,820	1976	4,195
1965	2,910	1977	4,201
1966	3,286	1978	4,427
1967	3,418	1979	4,262
1968	3,621	1980	3,977
1969	3,498	1981	4,277
1970	3,550	1982	4,897
1971	3,560		

Source: Nebraska Crop and Livestock Reporting Service.

Owners of these larger lots generally purchase their feeder cattle and often produce the feed as well.

Large feedlots are highly mechanized. Corn is mixed automatically with protein supplements, minerals, and medications. Augers deliver the grain to feed bunks with push-button precision. Because capital investment is substantial, feeder cattle must be cycled in and fat cattle shipped out on a year-round basis. The profit to be made depends on the relative prices for feeders and fat cattle. Fluctuating market prices make cattle feeding a risky business, one in which fortunes are made and farms are lost.

Cattle feeding showed particularly rapid growth beginning in the 1960s. The number of fed cattle marketed rose from about 2.5 million to almost 5 million—highest in the nation (Table 5.7). The number of calves produced in the state could not keep up with this expansion, however, and about half the cattle placed on feed had to be imported from other states.[41]

Dairying

Dairying has never been one of the dominant agricultural activities in Nebraska, but milk and dairy products contribute 4 percent of all farm income. Dairying has declined gradually from a peak of 800,000 cows in the early 1930s to fewer than 130,000 currently. The capital expenses required to meet sanitary standards led thousands of farmers with a few head to eliminate their dairy operations. Those who remain in dairying have become more specialized in order to survive. Output has shifted from butter, cream, and cheese to whole milk, which accounts for 90 percent of Nebraska's dairy products.[42]

Hog Farms and Factories

Nebraska ranked fifth in the United States in 1981 in total number of hogs, when about four million were reported on the state's farms. Pork production, traditionally associated with the midwestern Corn Belt, is found primarily in northeastern Nebraska (Figure 5.21).

The introduction of controlled-climate buildings and automated feeding and manure-handling systems brought pigs in from the muddy lot and concentrated them in "confinement" operations on concrete slabs. Medications to prevent disease permitted high-density operations. The effect was a

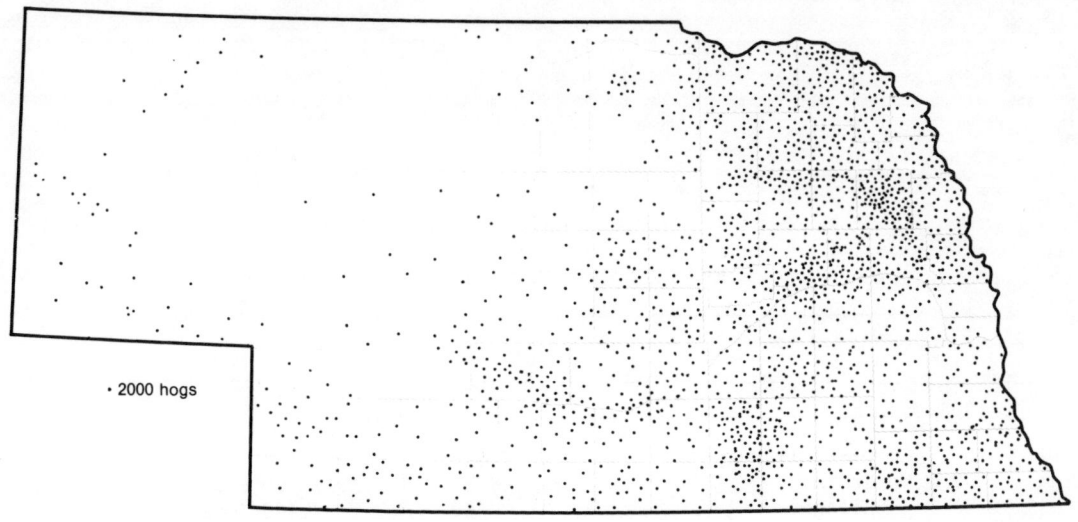

HOGS ON FARMS, DEC. 1, 1981

FIGURE 5.21. (University of Nebraska Press, NCLRS)

dramatic reduction in labor needs, along with improved weight gain and year-round operation.

Confinement hog production requires considerable capital investment. Beginning in the late 1960s, farmer cooperatives were organized to produce feeder pigs in confinement. This was a means by which individual farmers could combine their resources to take advantage of new technologies. About the same time, nonfarmer investors in high tax brackets saw the attractions of hog factories (substantial tax breaks accompany investment in equipment and specialized buildings). By 1981, 24 percent of the feeder pigs in Nebraska were produced by about 120 hog factories, which used hired labor and were owned by groups of farmers, nonfarm investors, or both. Only 32 percent of the state's farmers now raise any hogs, compared to 67 percent just thirty years ago. Pork production in Nebraska is shifting dramatically from the diversified small- and medium-sized farm to factories with names like Oink, Inc.; Pig Palace, Inc.; or the less flashy Nebraska Feeder Pigs, Inc. Essentially these are nonfarm enterprises.[43]

Other Livestock and Poultry

For the past several years, Nebraska farmers have reported about 200,000 sheep and lambs—sixteenth in the nation. In total number of sheep on feed, however, the state ranks fifth. The greatest concentration of sheep is in Scotts Bluff County. As with other livestock, the number of small flocks that farmers maintain for supplemental farm income has decreased in recent years, with a strong trend toward intensive management of larger flocks. This has not been sufficient to reverse the decline in sheep numbers, which were over 1 million as recently as the late 1940s.[44]

Concentration has been most evident in poultry production. In 1940 chickens were raised by over 80 percent of all Nebraska farmers. Farmers used eggs for their households and sold some to local groceries. Today only 9,000 of Nebraska's 66,000 farms (14 percent) raise chickens. About 6,000 of these farms report fewer than 100 chickens, but 34 farms have over 10,000 chickens each. Those 34 producers report 2.4 million chickens, 75 percent of all the chickens in the state.[45]

TABLE 5.8

NEBRASKA CROP PRODUCTION, 1981

Crop	Acres Harvested (x 1000)	Production (x 1000)
Corn -- All Purposes	7,460	---
Grain	6,980	802,700 Bu.
Silage	465	7,440 Tons
Forage	15	---
All Wheat	2,950	106,200 Bu.
Oats	395	15,405 Bu.
Barley	23	897 Bu.
Rye	38	798 Bu.
Sorghum -- All Purposes	2,210	---
Grain	2,060	164,800 Bu.
Silage	90	945 Tons
Forage	60	---
Soybeans for Beans	2,120	82,680 Bu.
Beans, Dry Edible	220.0	3,850 Cwt.
Great Northern	---	2,118 Cwt.
Pinto	---	1,700 Cwt.
Red Kidney	---	32 Cwt.
All Hay Harvested	3,700	7,165 Tons
Alfalfa Hay	1,650	5,115 Tons
All Other Hay[a]	2,050	2,050 Tons
Alfalfa Seed	25.0	1,750 Lbs.
Popcorn, Shelled	88.0	308,000 Lbs.
Potatoes, All	9.0	2,472 Cwt.
Summer	1.1	220 Cwt.
Fall	7.9	2,252 Cwt.
Sugar Beets	78.3	1,887 Tons
Millet	33.0	64,350 Lbs.
Total Acres Crops[b]	19,291	---

[a] Includes Wild Hay.

[b] Harvested acreages for winter wheat, rye, and all hay are used in computing total plant acreage.

Source: *Nebraska Agricultural Statistics, Annual Report, 1980-1981* (Lincoln: Nebraska Crops and Livestock Reporting Service, 1982).

Egg factories are concentrated in the eastern fourth of the state—both Colfax and Butler counties contain about 300,000 chickens and Dixon County contains the state's largest operation. Most broilers are raised in small flocks; broiler production is fairly widely distributed.[46]

CROPS

The Central Role of Corn

By far the most important crop in the state is corn. Nebraska annually raises about 7 million acres (2.8 million ha) of corn—about 14 percent of all the land in the state. It is the third-largest corn-producing state in the nation, surpassed only by Iowa and Illinois. Nearly 1 billion bushels (35 billion liters) of corn are harvested as grain each year (Table 5.8).

For over one hundred years corn has been the principal crop of Nebraska. Most Nebraska settlers were, after all, from the Corn Belt and grew the crop with which they were most familiar and which was most suitable as feed for livestock. By the early 1930s, over 10 million acres (4 million ha) of corn were planted. Corn acreage showed a gradual decline until the mid-1960s, when increasing use of irrigation bolstered corn acreage in drier portions of the state (Figure 5.22).

Today, the eastern Corn Belt counties are not the largest corn producers in the state. Corn is concentrated in the irrigated central Platte Valley, the irrigated areas of Hamilton and York counties, and the northeast portion of the state (Figure 5.23; Table 5.9). Only in the heart of the Sandhills and in the Panhandle is corn relatively unimportant. There, the lack of sufficient moisture precludes dryland corn, and a short freeze-free season limits irrigated corn production.

The introduction of center-pivot irrigation has made corn production possible in several areas that had been marginal for the crop. Considerable irrigation development has occurred in Holt County, which raised 137,000 acres (55,000 ha) of corn in 1973, but in 1981 reported 222,000 acres (90,000 ha) (Figure 5.24). In southwestern Nebraska, substantial corn acreage is now under irrigation in Chase, Perkins, and Dundy counties.

As corn production has moved westward in Nebraska, corn acreage in the dryland Corn Belt counties of southeastern Nebraska has dropped sharply. Limited groundwater supplies have kept irrigation development to a minimum. Soybeans,

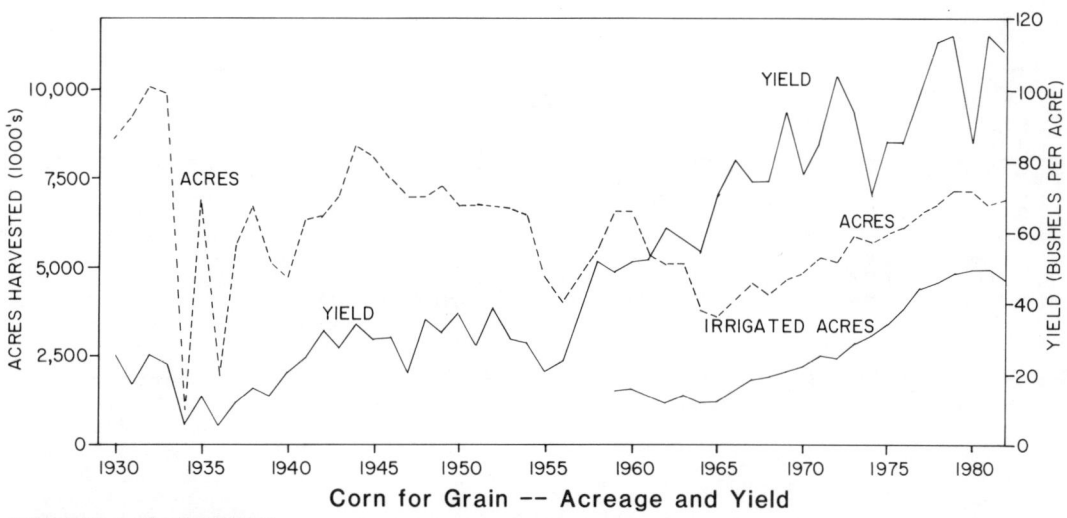

FIGURE 5.22. (NCLRS)

Corn for Grain -- Acreage and Yield

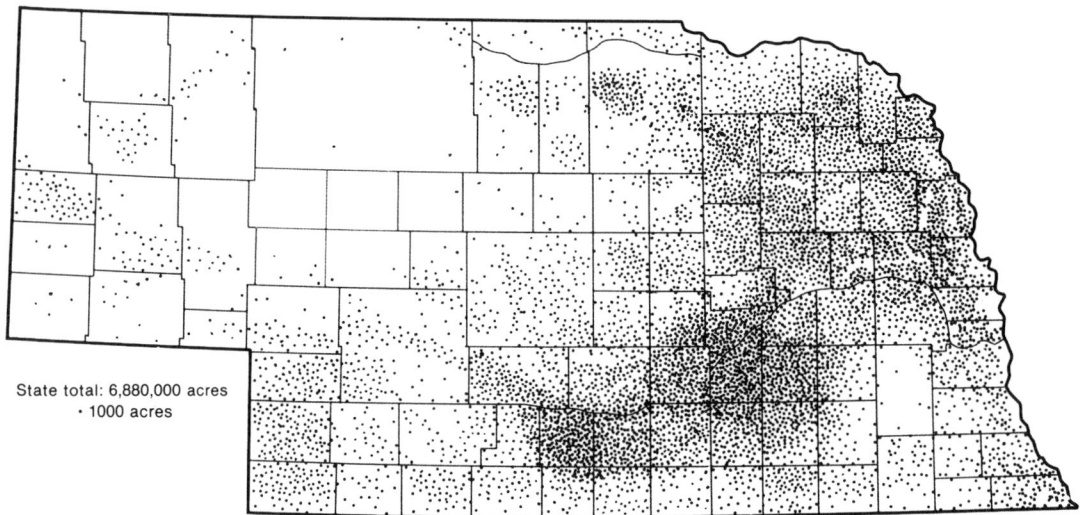

CORN HARVESTED FOR GRAIN, 1981

FIGURE 5.23. (University of Nebraska Press, NCLRS)

TABLE 5.9

LEADING COUNTIES IN ACREAGE OF MAJOR CROPS, 1981

	Corn for Grain		Soybeans		Sorghum for Grain		Winter Wheat		Alfalfa	
1.	Antelope	225,600	Saunders	130,400	Lancaster	137,400	Cheyenne	248,400	Dawson	71,000
2.	Hamilton	213,400	Cass	103,800	Gage	126,300	Kimball	196,000	Custer	65,900
3.	Holt	210,100	Burt	99,900	Seward	100,100	Perkins	180,100	Knox	57,700
4.	Phelps	196,900	Richardson	93,700	Butler	81,200	Box Butte	115,100	Lincoln	55,200
5.	Hall	186,700	Dodge	87,800	Polk	76,400	Deuel	94,100	Dawes	51,600
6.	Dawson	182,200	Platte	86,900	Fillmore	76,000	Banner	86,400	Cuming	46,400
7.	York	176,400	Cuming	83,200	York	74,500	Lancaster	84,600	Buffalo	46,300
8.	Custer	175,300	Otoe	76,900	Clay	72,100	Gage	83,800	Sheridan	45,000
9.	Buffalo	174,800	Madison	75,100	Saline	71,300	Hitchcock	80,500	Holt	43,700
10.	Platte	172,300	Gage	72,100	Nuckolls	66,100	Red Willow	79,500	Cedar	42,400
					Otoe	66,100	Furnas	79,500		

Source: Nebraska Agricultural Statistics, Annual Report, 1980-1981 (Lincoln: Nebraska Crop and Livestock Reporting Service, 1982).

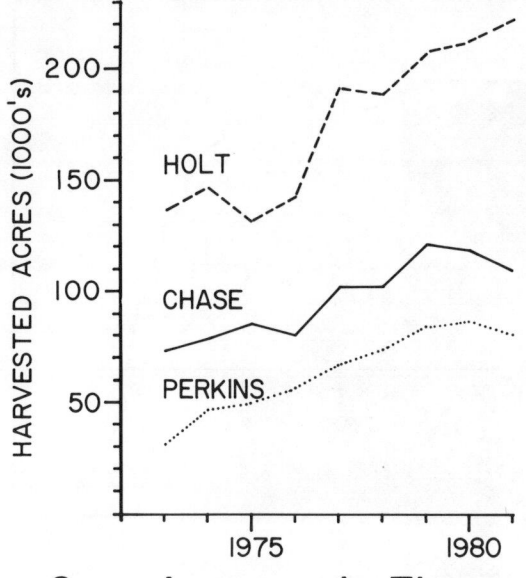

Corn Acreage in Three Counties

FIGURE 5.24. (NCLRS)

wheat, and sorghum, crops not generally irrigated, have supplanted corn as the leading crop.

The role of irrigation can hardly be overestimated. By 1981, nearly three-fourths of Nebraska's corn acreage was irrigated. Dryland corn was grown on 2 million acres (600,000 ha), but because of lower yields on unirrigated land, only one bushel in six was produced on dryland. In moist years dryland corn yields can be substantial. The statewide average was 87.6 bu per acre (3,087 l per ha) on dryland in 1979, and one county recorded 109 bu (3,841 l). The next year, however, the state dryland average fell to 48.2 bu (1,698 l), with the highest county yield being only 69 bu per acre (2,431 l per ha). Other recent years have seen even lower averages—27 bu per acre or 951 l per ha in the drought year of 1974, for example. In severe drought periods, such as the mid-1930s, virtually no crop is harvested. This yield fluctuation is clearly undesirable. Where adequate groundwater or surface water is available and the expense of irrigating can be justified by the increase in yields, irrigation has taken hold (Figure 5.25).[47]

Irrigated corn is not independent of weather conditions. Hot weather, accompanied by strong winds, can reduce corn yields, but not as much as on unirrigated fields. In 1979, the statewide irrigated corn yield was 128 bu per acre (4,510 l per ha) about 50 percent greater than for unirrigated corn. In 1980, the irrigated corn yield fell to 101 bu (3,559 l), but that was more than double the dryland yield.[48] The use of fertilizers, chemicals for weed and insect control, and improved strains of seed have all contributed to rising corn yields.[49]

Wheat Production

Wheat has generally been the second most important crop in Nebraska (Figure 5.26). The state, the sixth-largest winter-wheat producer in the nation, lies at the northern end of the great winter-wheat belt stretching from Texas through Kansas and Colorado. Winter wheat is planted in the fall, occasionally is used as pasture during fall and spring, and is generally harvested in early July.[50] Nebraska's wheat acreage is concentrated in the southern Panhandle and in southwestern Nebraska. Other important areas include the Box Butte tablelands of the northern Panhandle and the counties along the Kansas border (Figure 5.27).

Very little of Nebraska's wheat is irrigated, but much of it is grown on summer fallow, a system designed to store soil moisture and nutrients during one growing season for use in the next. A typical pattern is for fields to be disked after harvest to turn the stubble into the soil. Fields are tilled periodically to keep down weeds and to reduce the rate of soil moisture evaporation. The following fall wheat is planted. The result is a substantial increase in yields in the drier parts of the state.[51] Summer fallow is standard practice in the Panhandle and southwestern Nebraska, but in southeastern Nebraska less than 20 percent of the wheat is grown on summer fallow (Figures 5.28 and 5.29).

Much wheat is harvested by custom

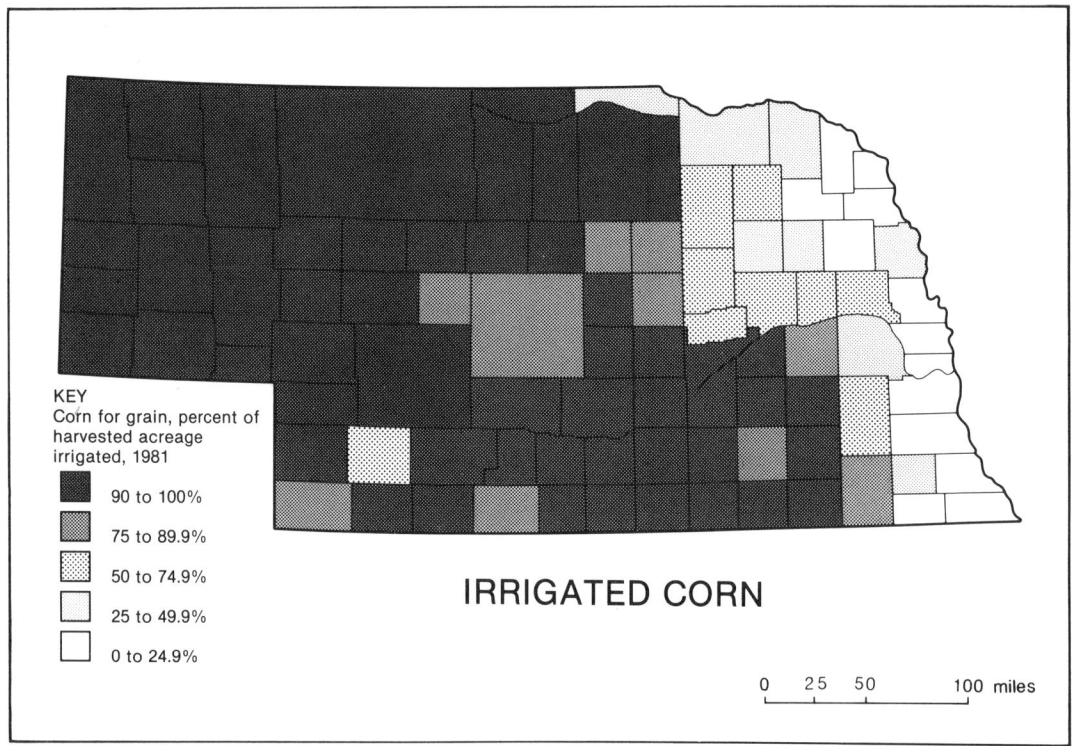

FIGURE 5.25. (NCLRS)

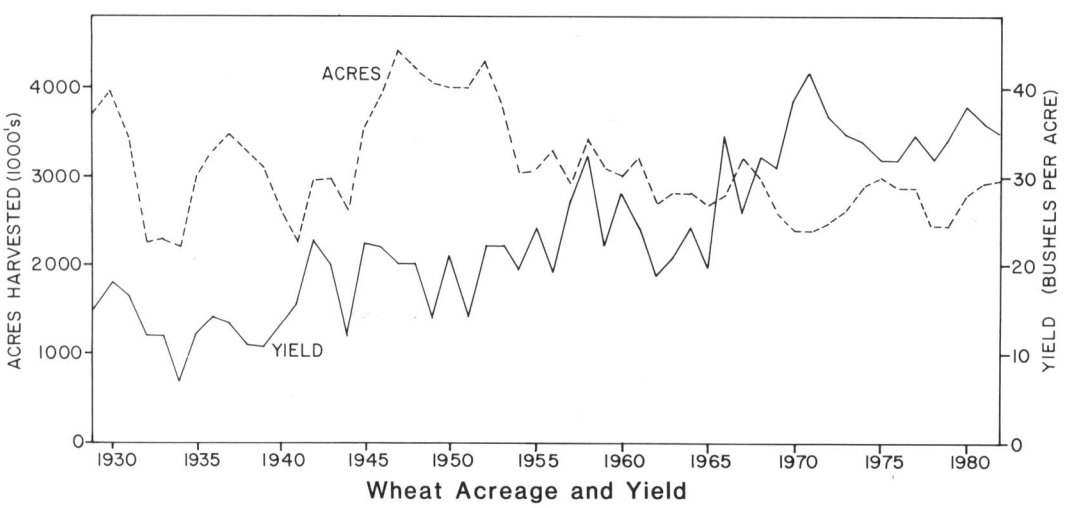

FIGURE 5.26. (NCLRS)

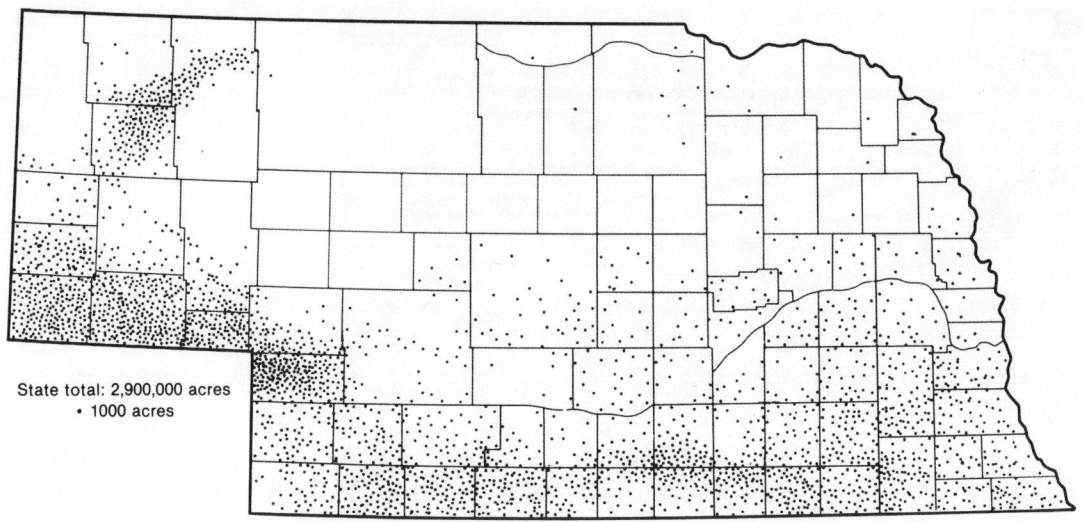

State total: 2,900,000 acres
• 1000 acres
WHEAT ACRES HARVESTED, 1981

FIGURE 5.27. (University of Nebraska Press, NCLRS)

KEY
Percent of harvested wheat acreage grown on summer fallow, 1981
80 to 100%
60 to 79.9%
40 to 59.9%
20 to 39.9%
0 to 19.9%
No wheat acreage
WHEAT GROWN ON SUMMER FALLOW
0 25 50 100 miles

FIGURE 5.28. (NCLRS)

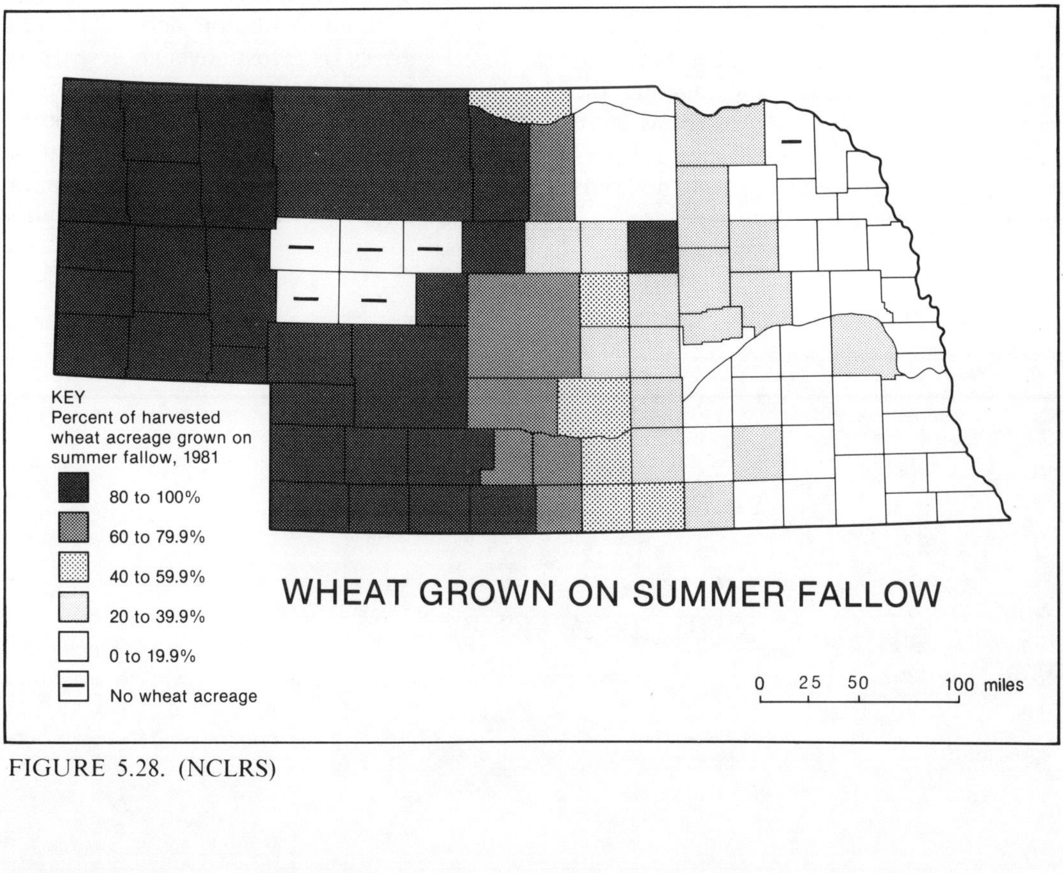

FIGURE 5.29. Alternate strips of wheat and summer fallow help hold down wind erosion on this Scotts Bluff County field. (USDA, SCS)

operators. Teams of workers with several combines and trucks follow the wheat harvest northward during the harvest season, beginning in Texas in May and ending in the fall in Saskatchewan and Alberta. The typical harvest crew will not travel the entire distance, but may participate for only several hundred miles.[52] Farmers contract with a harvest crew in order to complete the harvest in as short a time as possible (Figure 5.30). This helps minimize grain losses from severe storms or fallen grain and holds down machinery costs.

Other Major Crops

Soybean production has increased dramatically in recent years. Increasing world demand for soybean oil and meal has pushed Nebraska soybean acreage from minor crop status to about 2 million acres (800,000 ha) (Figure 5.31). Most soybean acreage is found in the northeast and in counties bordering the Missouri River in the southeast (Figure 5.32). Less than 20 percent of soybean acreage is irrigated—mostly south of the Platte River on the western margins

FIGURE 5.30. Trucks delivering grain to elevators during wheat harvest. (UNL, Cooperative Extension Service)

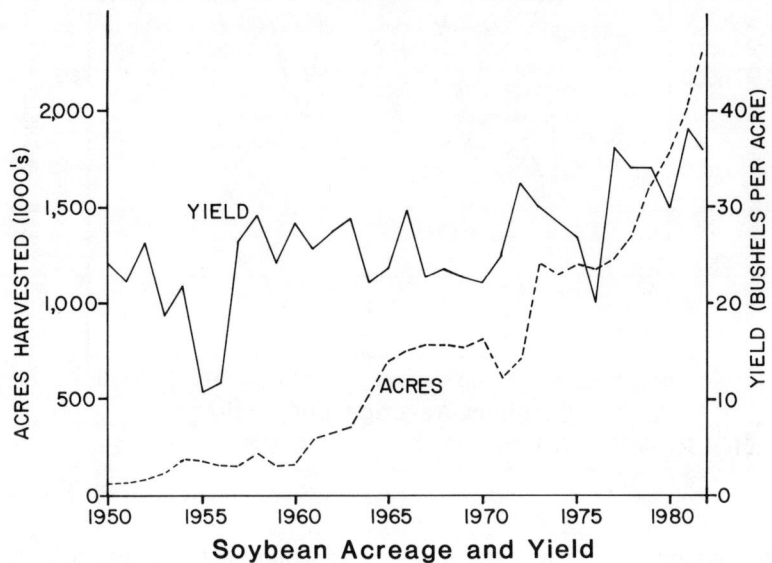

FIGURE 5.31. (NCLRS)

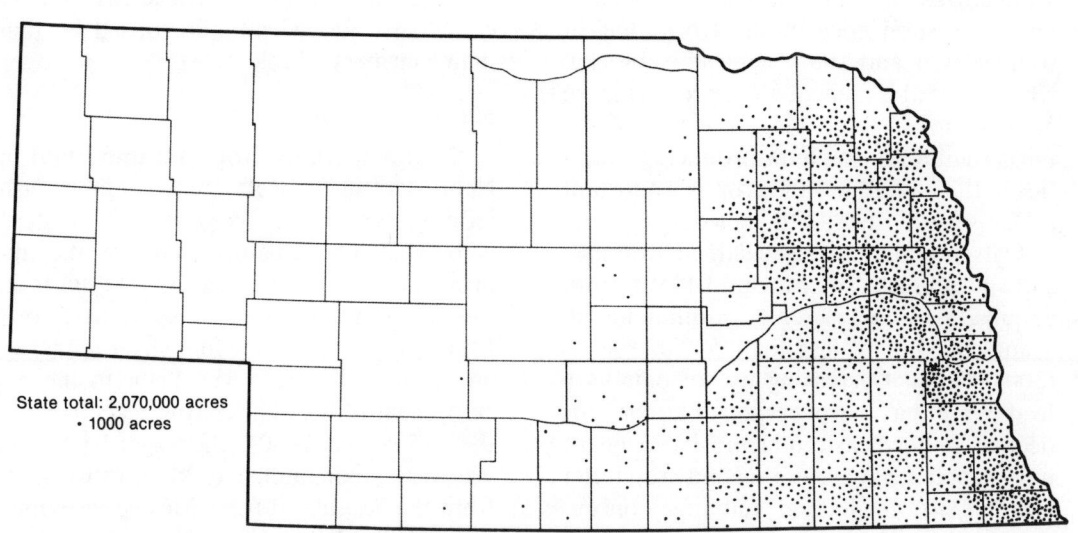

SOYBEAN ACRES HARVESTED, 1981

FIGURE 5.32. (University of Nebraska Press, NCLRS)

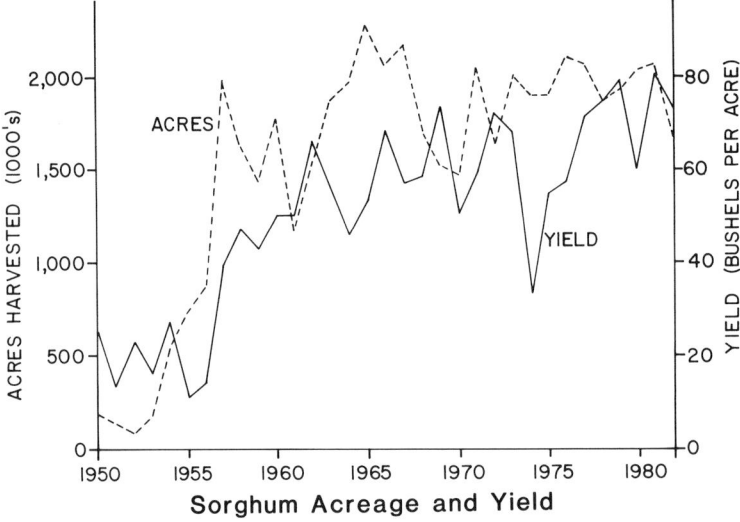
FIGURE 5.33. (NCLRS)

of the soybean region, where acreage has increased markedly during the past decade.

Sorghum acreage—third largest in the United States—has also increased during the past thirty years (Figure 5.33). Sorghum is more drought and heat tolerant than corn and is grown almost entirely on dryland. Sorghum has become especially important on the western edge of the Corn Belt in southeastern and south central Nebraska, where rainfall is inadequate for corn (Figure 5.34). Lancaster and Gage are two of the most significant sorghum-producing counties in the nation, but the crop is important as far west as the 100th meridian.

Oats production has declined dramatically in Nebraska since the mid-1950s, from about 2.5 million acres (1 million ha) to a current level of less than 500,000 acres (200,000 ha). Decreasing use of oats as a feed grain has been responsible for this decline. In northeastern Nebraska soybeans have supplanted oats as a second crop (after corn). Oats production remains concentrated in the same northeastern counties, but is found in nearly every county. (Table 5.10).

Other small grains have shown similar acreage declines. Barley, raised by a third of all farmers in 1940, was harvested by only 662 farmers in 1978. Total acreage is less than 30,000 acres (12,000 ha). Rye was raised by only 255 farmers. Increasingly, in part because of the nature and cost of machinery, Nebraska farmers specialize in only two or three crops, in contrast to the more diversified systems of forty years ago. Corn is the only crop grown by more than 40 percent of all farmers, whereas in 1940 corn, oats, and wheat were raised by that many farmers (Table 5.11).

Specialty Crops

Several specialty crops are important in Nebraska. Sugar beets are a valuable cash crop grown under irrigation in western Nebraska. The greatest share of the approximately 80,000 acres (32,000 ha) is in the North Platte Valley, especially Scotts Bluff County, where the four sugar refineries are located (Figure 5.35). Prior to the development of beet-harvesting machinery in the 1950s and 1960s, the sugar-beet crop was very labor intensive. Migrant workers, from the South and from Mexico, provided most of that labor. Hand hoeing was eliminated with the introduction of herbicides in the 1960s.

Nebraska is the nation's number one producer of Great Northern beans and is a major producer of pinto and kidney beans. Most of the dry edible beans are produced

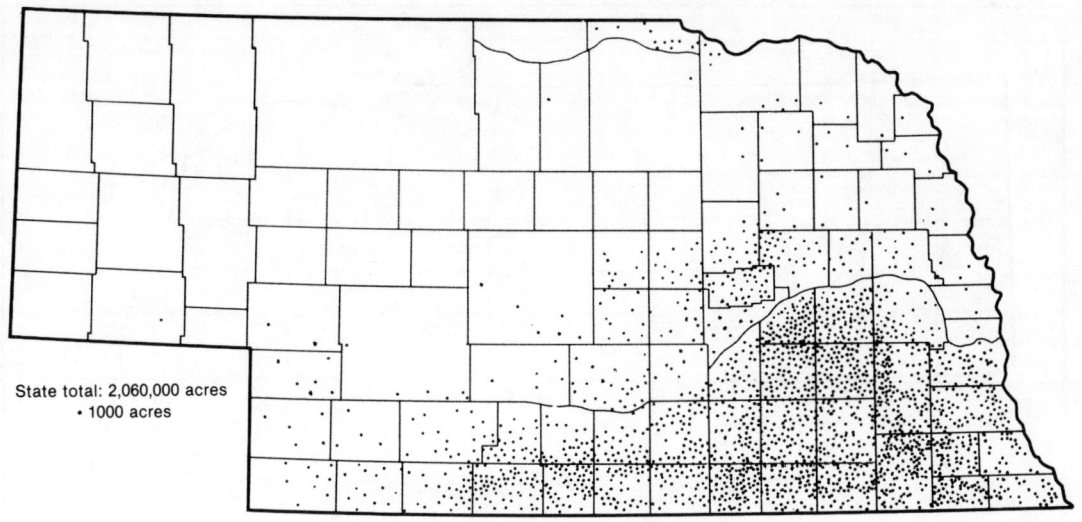

SORGHUM ACRES HARVESTED, 1981

FIGURE 5.34. (University of Nebraska Press, NCLRS)

TABLE 5.10

LEADING COUNTIES IN ACREAGE OF MINOR CROPS, 1981

	Oats		Sugar Beets		Wild Hay		Dry Edible Beans	
1.	Cedar	43,300	Scotts Bluff	33,530	Cherry	339,600	Scotts Bluff	46,000
2.	Knox	35,000	Box Butte	13,940	Holt	229,600	Box Butte	39,000
3.	Dixon	25,400	Morrill	9,970	Sheridan	87,500	Morrill	34,000
4.	Thurston	18,200	Chase	8,470	Rock	84,700	Chase	17,100
5.	Gage	17,600	Keith	3,760	Lincoln	83,600	Perkins	16,300

Source: Nebraska Agricultural Statistics, Annual Report, 1980-1981 (Lincoln: Nebraska Crop and Livestock Reporting Service, 1982).

TABLE 5.11

PERCENTAGE OF FARMERS RAISING EACH CROP, 1940 and 1978

	1940	1978
Corn for Grain	73.7	60.1
Corn, cut for silage	11.7	13.1
Oats	44.7	16.0
Wheat	46.3	33.5
Soybeans	1.1	25.5
Sorghum, for grain	17.6	27.9
Barley	34.8	1.0
Rye	13.2	0.4

Source: Calculated from U.S. Censuses of Agriculture.

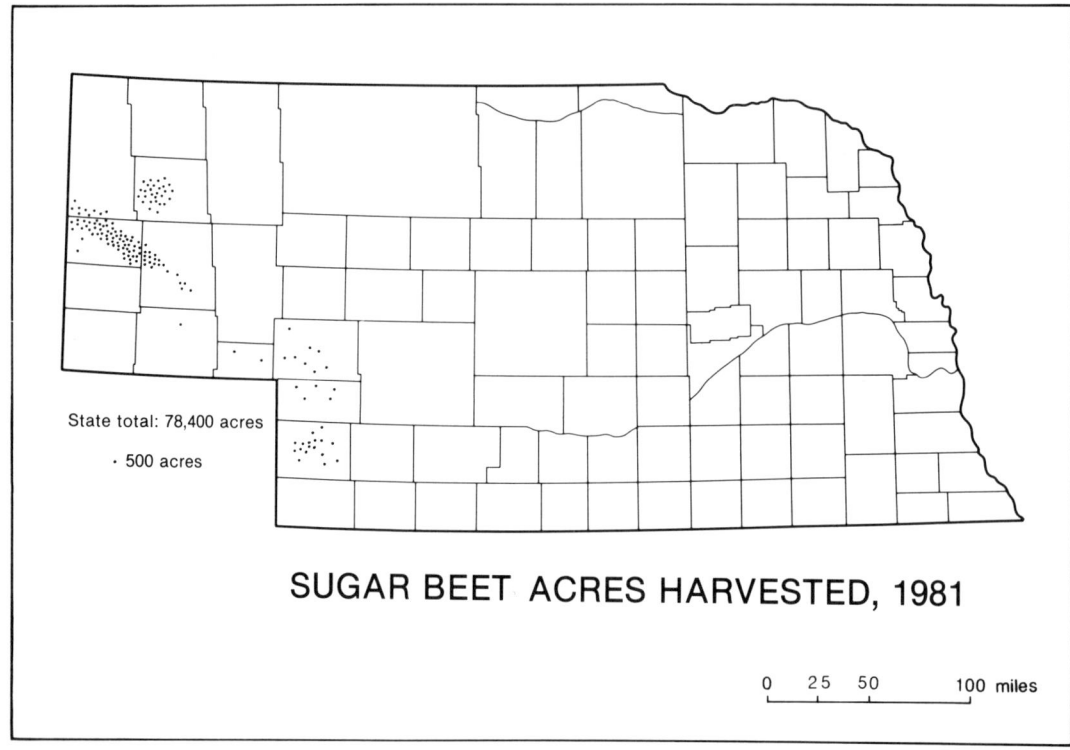

FIGURE 5.35. (NCLRS)

in the North Platte Valley and Box Butte County (Figure 5.36). Center-pivot irrigation has opened formerly dryland areas to edible bean production. Consequently, Scotts Bluff County's acreage has remained fairly constant, but its share of total acreage has fallen from about 50 percent to 25 percent of the state's production in the last decade.

Center-pivot irrigation has also played a major role in potato production. Most potato acreage is found in the Panhandle, where fall potatoes are produced under irrigation. Center-pivot irrigation is particularly suitable for the 70 percent of the crop used for processed potatoes, mainly potato chips.[53] The regularity with which sprinklers deliver water to the crop assures the uniform potatoes needed for chipping.

Commercial fruit and vegetable production occurs on a limited scale in Nebraska. Onions, melons, tomatoes, cucumbers, and sweet corn are the more important vegetable crops. Apples are the major fruit crop, raised on 560 acres (220 ha), mostly near the Missouri River. Other fruit crops in the extreme eastern part of the state include cherries, peaches, plums, and grapes. In recent years, Nebraska has led the nation in the production of popcorn, with over 300 million lb (136 million kg) harvested.

Forage Crops

Nebraska's forage crops—hay and silage—provide about 80 percent of the feed for the state's cattle. Nearly half the state's land surface is in grasses, either as native rangeland, particularly in the Sandhills, or as pasture seeded to introduced perennial grasses. Wild hay is harvested from nearly 2 million acres (800,000 ha) annually. Most of that is in the Sandhills.

The most important hay crop in the state is alfalfa, which is harvested from over 1.5 million acres (600,000 ha) annually; about one-fourth of it irrigated. The growth of

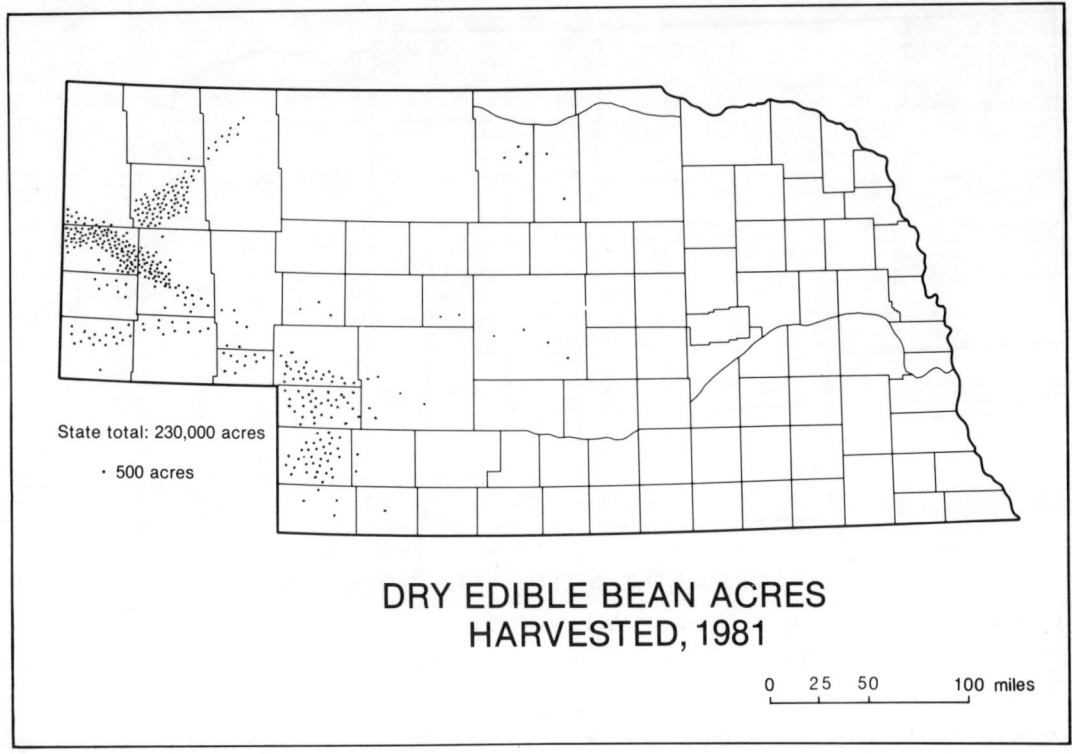

FIGURE 5.36. (NCLRS)

the feeder cattle industry in recent years has led to the concentration of alfalfa production in areas with the most cattle on feed—northeastern Nebraska and the central Platte Valley (Figures 5.37 and 5.38). Dawson County, largest producer in the state, typically reports 75,000 acres (30,000 ha) with total production of over 300,000 tn (272,000 t) per year.

Most alfalfa is fed directly to livestock, but about 25 percent of it is dehydrated. This reduces the volume of the crop, making it more transportable, while preserving its nutritional value. Most dehydration plants are found along the Platte, especially in Dawson County, near the greatest concentration of alfalfa fields. Dehydrated alfalfa is generally utilized by commercial-feed manufacturers and by large cattle feeders.

Silage is produced from about 0.5 million acres (200,000 ha) of corn and sorghum each year. When these crops are properly stored, their feed value can be preserved for long periods. The use of silage in cattle feeding and dairy operations helps to explain the distribution of corn-silage production in the northeastern counties and the central Platte Valley. Although some dryland corn is harvested for silage during drought years, most silage corn is irrigated and is grown explicitly for silage production. Sorghum silage is produced in the same areas as grain sorghum—principally the southern third of the state.[54]

FORCES OF CHANGE

The Corn Belt and the fallow-wheat region have both shrunk somewhat in Nebraska as alternative systems of crop and livestock production have been introduced. In fact, the wheat region was not easily identifiable until the 1940s (Figure 5.39). The sorghum subregion of the Corn Belt is an even more recent development. Most

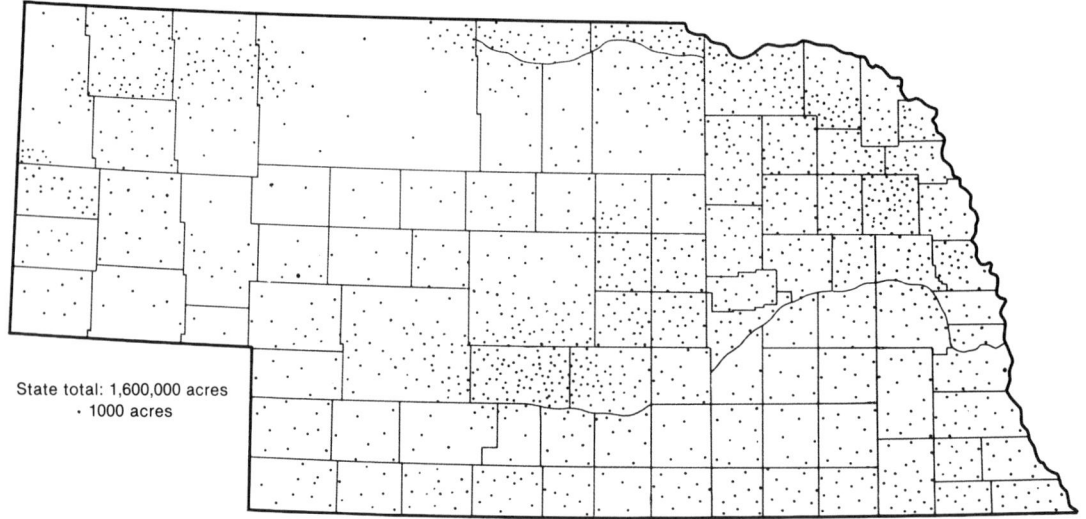

ALFALFA ACRES HARVESTED, 1981

FIGURE 5.37. (University of Nebraska Press, NCLRS)

important in the changing map of Nebraska agricultural regions has been the introduction of well irrigation—initially in the Platte Valley and the Blue River basin, more recently in the Sandhills.

Nebraska's agriculture has changed markedly during the past several decades. Technological innovations have altered the way farmers work, what work they do, and how many farmers there are. Economic forces have altered farm size and ownership, the mix of crops and livestock, and the regional patterns of various kinds of agricultural activities. Government policies increasingly shape agricultural enterprises.

During the 1970s, U.S. agriculture underwent a massive transformation (Figure 5.40). Farm exports increased dramatically, and concern over national balance-of-payments difficulties thrust farm exports into the

FIGURE 5.38. An alfalfa field in Cedar County.

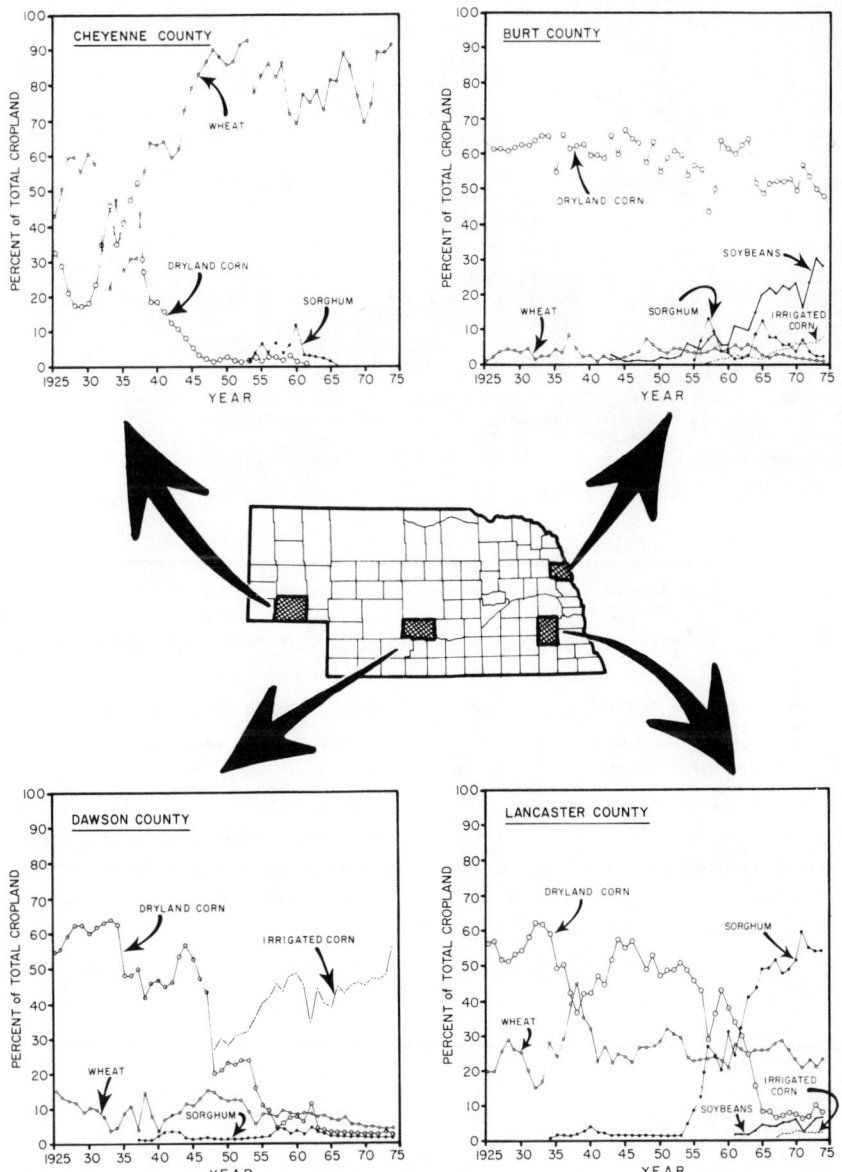

FIGURE 5.39. County agricultural land-use changes. (UNL, Nebraska Water Resources Center)

FIGURE 5.40. A massive, modern grain elevator, representing the export orientation of Nebraska agriculture in the 1970s and 1980s, towers over an elevator representing the grain-storage capacity of an earlier era. (UNL, Cooperative Extension Service)

center of trade and foreign-policy considerations. Concern with environmental quality focused on the use of agricultural chemicals. The "energy crisis" forced agriculture to confront questions of energy use and efficiency. As more and more individuals and groups expressed interest in agriculture, farm policy became food policy.[55]

Food and agriculture policies are "being increasingly influenced by events off the farm, outside agriculture, and even outside the U.S."[56] The myriad of influences on agriculture is only one of the factors compromising the traditional independence of the farmer. Dependence on off-farm income, rising farm indebtedness, and the growing importance of contract farming have tied farmers to forces outside agriculture and limited their range of management decisions. Many have, in effect, ceased to be independent entrepreneurs and have instead become production workers in the energy- and capital-intensive world of modern industrial agriculture.[57]

CHAPTER 6

INDUSTRIAL AGRICULTURE

The transformation from small-scale, labor-intensive farming to large-scale, capital- and machine-intensive agriculture has been going on for over a century. Mechanization that occurred in U.S. agriculture in the middle of the nineteenth century changed the ways farmers raised crops and livestock. Some of the drudgery of farm labor was relieved by the mechanical reaper that replaced the scythe, the development of horse-drawn machinery on which the farmer could ride, and similar innovations.

Yet, even by 1920, the majority of farmers were "still largely self-sufficient with respect to what they and their livestock consumed, and horses and mules were the chief source of power."[1] Farmers continued to use simple tools, provided their own seed, and depended on human and animal labor and locally produced energy (Figure 6.1). In fifty years there had been little change in technology or yields.

AGRICULTURE AND TECHNOLOGY

Innovations since 1920 have changed not only the nature of agriculture but also the nature of rural society. The replacement of horses with tractors, the increasing use of fossil fuels to power machinery and to produce commercial fertilizers and pesticides, the development of hybrid seeds, and the dramatic increase in the role of irrigation have all had major impacts on Nebraska's agriculture, on the structure of the state's farm economy, and on rural life.

Twentieth-Century Mechanization

The introduction of tractors to Nebraska farms began before World War I, but widespread acceptance was not immediate. The economically and climatically favorable years of the late 1910s were terminated abruptly with agricultural depression in the 1920s. Few farmers had adequate capital for a major purchase such as a tractor; furthermore, most farm implements had not yet been adapted for use with tractors. Drought and depression in the 1930s further postponed tractor adoption (Table 6.1). As late as 1940 there were still 500,000 horses and mules on Nebraska farms, about half the maximum number of 1 million reported in the late 1910s and still about 4 horses per farm.[2]

During the 1940s, a period of high farm profits that coincided with widespread availability of machinery, tractors almost completely supplanted horses.[3] Apart from the obvious reduction in the backbreaking labor associated with using draft animals, the principal reason tractors were adopted was improved labor efficiency. Difficulties in obtaining an adequate labor supply, particularly for seasonal work, had always plagued farmers.[4] Mechanization was also

FIGURE 6.1. Cultivating corn in Burt County, ca. 1905. (NSHS)

related to the increasing size of farms.[5]

Often the acquisition cost of the machinery was so great that it could only be justified if used on a larger farm. Mechanization fueled expansion just as expansion made mechanization more necessary. During the past twenty years increasing scale and additional mechanization have proceeded hand in hand. Whereas the farmer of 1950 might have used a small tractor to pull a two-row corn planter, larger farm size in the 1980s often justifies the use of eight- or twelve-row equipment (Figure 6.2).

"Square" hay balers (Figure 6.3), which move slowly and require substantial labor input, have been replaced by larger, faster machines that need only one operator. Most corn is harvested by picker-shellers, whereas it used to be shelled mostly by custom operators and a shelling crew.

Finally, farmers, like most Americans, are fascinated by machines. Not infrequently farmers acquire machinery even though the cost cannot be justified by the size of the farmer's operation. Social acceptability, keeping up with the latest trends,

TABLE 6.1

TRACTORS AND DRAFT ANIMALS, 1920-1959

	Horses and Mules	Tractors	Percent of Farms Reporting Tractors
1920	1,061,243	11,100	8.3
1925	982,330	18,765	13.9
1930	853,269	40,729	29.3
1935	725,465	NA	NA
1940	510,468	70,761	53.4
1945	439,472	96,203	72.9
1950	216,759	127,154	81.7
1954	99,760	163,296	88.8
1959	68,281	180,087	90.5

Source: U.S. Censuses of Agriculture.

FIGURE 6.2. Eight-row equipment speeds planting.

having another tool to tinker with, and similar noneconomic factors affect farmers just as they do other Americans.

Prior to twentieth-century mechanization, most farm inputs came from the farm itself. What little had to be purchased consisted of hardware and a few implements. Tractors required gas and oil, and eventually new implements had to be acquired. As the size of equipment has grown, the cost of machinery has increased even more rapidly. A nineteen-foot disk, for example, costs about twice as much as a thirteen-foot disk, and a 120-horsepower tractor generally sells for 2½ to 3 times as much as one with 60 horsepower.[6]

The desire of farmers to increase farm size in order to make most efficient use of machinery and time helps push land prices upward. The closed circle is that "as farmers invest in bigger machinery, they are willing to pay more and more for the land they need to put it to use. With more land for collateral, farmers buy more machinery and then need yet more land."[7]

As the number of purchased farm inputs has increased, the farmer's interdependence with the nonfarm sector has grown. Farmers like to view themselves as independent entrepreneurs, free to make their own decisions, but their input costs are now affected by energy policies in the United States and the Middle East, by interest rates that fluctuate with national economic indicators, by environmental laws designed in Lincoln and Washington, D.C., and by other factors over which they exert minimal influence. Increased production costs require increases in productivity per farm and per acre. This is often possible only if additional purchased inputs—fertilizer, hybrid seed, pesticides—are utilized. Con-

FIGURE 6.3. Small hay bales require more labor input than recent innovations in haying equipment.

trol slips farther away from the farmer as inputs become global, rather than local.

With rising machinery cost per farm, farmers must make the fullest possible use of their investments. One consequence is greater specialization of operations. Few farmers can justify the cost of specialized machinery to be used on just a few acres. More efficient use of that equipment can be made on several hundred acres. Similarly, livestock operations have become more specialized.[8]

Elimination of many sidelines that characterized Nebraska farms a generation ago is not solely due to mechanization and its costs. Both government policies and changing values of farm families have also been important factors. Many farmers with a few cows were pushed out of dairying in the 1950s and 1960s, because the expensive equipment required to meet the higher health standards could only be justified by farmers with large dairy herds.[9] The percentage of farms raising milk cows declined from 85.8 in 1940 to 8.8 in 1978, according to the U.S. censuses of agriculture.

Furthermore, many of the small-scale, commercially oriented activities found on farms thirty years ago did not yield much return for the labor expended on them. As more farmers have taken off-farm employment and as more farm women have entered the wage labor force, less time is available for low-return enterprises like a small flock of laying hens (see Chapter 5). Farm families are smaller, and children are more likely to be involved in school and recreational activities of their own than was the case in 1950. Labor-intensive, low-return farm products do not mesh well with a 1980s life-style.

Farm mechanization, whether cause or effect of expanding farm size, is tied directly to declining farm population, which in turn has had a dramatic impact on the rural community. As small farmers are bought out by large farmers and as retiring farmers sell, the farm population decreases. In communities that depend for their survival on purchases by farm families, depopulation of the countryside leads to small-town decline. Specialized retail stores close down in smaller towns, leaving behind only those that offer items of basic consumption, and professional services become increasingly scarce in towns under several thousand (see Chapter 4).

Noncommercial activities have suffered as well. As the number of parishioners dwindles, churches either close or consolidate with those in nearby towns. Numerous smaller school systems are no longer able to support a high school. Finally, the political base of rural areas has been steadily eroded. Small towns and villages increasingly function primarily as retirement communities and as suppliers of feed, fertilizer, and fuel.

Energy Requirements of Agriculture

The mechanization of agriculture in Nebraska and the United States was made possible not simply by the development of the internal combustion engine but also by the consumption of inanimate energy used to power tractors and other machinery. Without fossil fuels, industrialized agriculture could not have developed. If this power source were seriously disrupted, modern agriculture would cease to function.

The use of energy in agriculture involves much more than filling tractor tanks. Overall, U.S. agriculture probably consumes more energy than any other industry in the country. Calculations made by David Pimentel of Cornell University indicated that in 1970 about 800,000 kilocalories of energy were used as fuel to farm each acre of corn in the United States. But other uses consumed even more energy. The greatest energy expenditure was for nitrogen fertilizer— 940,000 kilocalories, more than was used for fuel, fertilizer, and all other uses combined in 1945.[10]

Corn never yielded a statewide average of more than 50 bu per acre (3,850 l per ha) before the mid-1950s. Then, as the application of inorganic fertilizers began to rise (Figure 6.4), yields rose as well. By the early 1970s, annual averages had topped

Focus: Changes in Polk, Nebraska

Mr. and Mrs. Halstead Robison from Hood River, Oregon, stopped in the *Progress* office last Friday for a short but pleasant visit. Her maiden name is Ellouise Mills and she retains a fondness for Polk.

"Does Polk still have band concerts?" She was remembering the Wednesday night summer crowds and walking the four blocks of Main Street with other girls and the feigned casualness with which they would contrive meetings with boys. We told her band concerts were no longer played.

Fifty, sixty years ago small rural towns took pride in their bands. Polk had a good one and received many invitations to play concerts. Veterinarian Dr. R. L. Peterson was director. . . .

"It's a different world," we told Ellouise. And we have thought much about the changes that have occurred in the past half century. Do we detect a decline in the richness of rural life, or is it only that we are growing older and cantankerous? We continue to be critical of agribusiness or industrial-ag because in it we see a deemphasis of human values with increasing reliance on the machine.

Skills are lost in rural towns as farms become bigger and customers fewer. Julius Peterson, operator and owner of the Polk Mill, knew how to mill flour (white, rye, graham, whole wheat), chicken feed, bran, breakfast food, corn meal, and other products we have forgotten since reading a *Progress* ad we found in a 1920s issue. No one walking the street of Polk today has those skills.

Today no one can haul wheat to Polk and have it ground into flour. Today no one can bring in cream and eggs, sell those products to a produce station, and then spend the money shopping the stores. As a clerk in the Pure Food Grocery we recall farm wives trading butter for groceries. Some took pride in their product, displaying its butter-mold shape which usually included a decorated peak. Some farm butter was popular with customers, some was not.

At first change came gradually as farm mechanization took hold. No farmer regretted the substitution of machines for hand labor. A now retired farmer told of scooping ear corn, picked that afternoon, into the crib. After coming in from the field with a wagonload, he had to do chores and couldn't get to the scooping until after supper. Sometimes he scooped by lantern light. Elevators took over that chore and mechanical pickers eliminated hand picking.

As we watch the absorption of smaller farms into larger spreads we also witness, with alarm, the decline in number of businesses on Main St. This development is explained to us as "progress." When we ask: "Progress towards what?" no one has a ready, reasonable answer except, perhaps, to suggest that illusive and elusive target, "success."

We walk the four blocks of Main St. and remember how it was in the 1920s. Then it seemed permanent. Now we understand how transient it is.

Source: Norris Alfred, reprinted with permission from the *Polk Progress,* Polk, Nebraska.

---

100 bu per acre (7,700 l per ha), and yields above 150 bu per acre (11,600 l per ha) were not uncommon. By 1980, total fertilizer use in Nebraska was over 2 million tn (907,000 t), over half of that in the form of nitrogen. Approximately 96 percent of the corn acreage in the state was fertilized with commercial nitrogen, at an average rate of about 150 lb per acre (168 kg per ha). Most grain sorghum and 60 percent of the wheat crop also receive nitrogen. Rising prices for fertilizer due to higher petroleum prices during the 1970s did not result in any significant reduction in fertilizer use by Nebraska farmers. The amount of nitrogen applied to corn leveled off, but it increased for wheat. Total state consumption of ammonia in 1980 was double that of 1969 and 50 percent higher than in 1973.[11]

Pesticides are extensively used on farms to control weeds and insects. These products, relying upon fossil fuels as raw materials, are highly energy intensive, and their use has been increasing rapidly. The most widespread use of chemicals is to control weed growth in crops and, to some extent, in pastures. While only 2.2 million acres

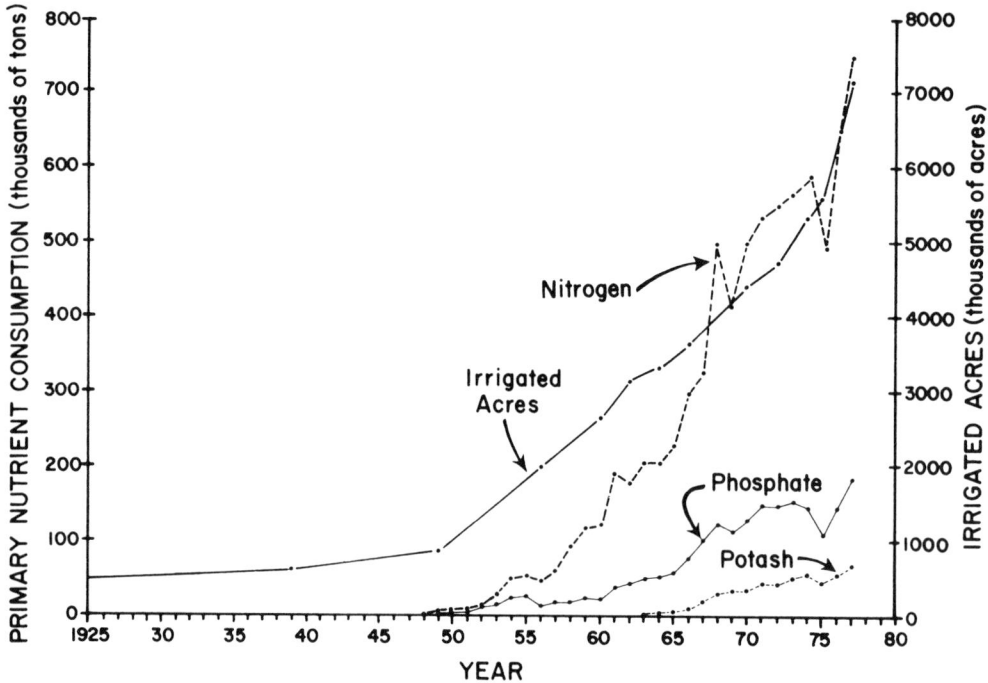

FIGURE 6.4. Primary nutrient consumption and irrigated acres in Nebraska. (UNL, Nebraska Water Resources Center)

(880,000 ha) of Nebraska cropland were treated for weed control in 1964, by 1978 that figure was over 7 million acres (2.8 million ha). Five million acres (2 million ha) were treated for insects and diseases in 1978, compared to only 1.6 million acres (640,000 ha) in 1964. As more land has been converted to minimum tillage, which relies upon herbicides rather than cultivation for weed control, chemical use and therefore energy use has increased on Nebraska farms. Chemicals are also applied for the control of insects on livestock and poultry.[12]

Use of fossil fuels and petroleum-based products on Nebraska farms has reduced labor requirements and increased yields per acre, while increasing total farm expenses. As a result, farms are often said to have become more efficient. As former Secretary of Agriculture Clifford Hardin pointed out, "Using a modern feeding system for broilers, one man can take care of 60,000 to 75,000 chickens. One man in a modern feedlot can now take care of 5,000 head of cattle. One man, with a mechanized system, can operate a dairy enterprise of 50 to 60 milk cows."[13] He might have added that one farmer, using modern equipment and chemicals, can harvest over 1,000 acres (400 ha) of corn or wheat.

The inaccuracy of this view, which pictures the farmer feeding fifty people compared to only ten a few decades ago, is that farmers have a lot of help. Machinery manufactured around the country, gasoline and diesel fuel produced in the Middle East and refined in Louisiana, and chemical fertilizer manufactured in Nebraska and elsewhere help farmers raise crops and feed livestock. Some analysts suggest there are as many as two workers in support industries for each farmer. Transportation and marketing of these farm needs require additional labor. Farmers are not alone in feeding those 75,000 chickens or 5,000 cattle.[14]

In efficiency of energy use, Nebraska's

farms, like those elsewhere in the nation, have not fared well. As energy applied per acre has increased, yields have increased, but not as rapidly. Pimentel found that total energy input per acre of corn in the United States rose from 925,500 kilocalories in 1945 to 2,896,800 in 1970, and corn yield rose from 34 to 81 bu per acre (2,960 to 7,053 l per ha). In terms of the ratio of energy output to energy input, corn production efficiency dropped from 3.7:1 in 1945 to 2.8:1 in 1970 (Table 6.2).

Large farm size appears to be inversely related to energy efficiency in agricultural operations. Buttel and Larson have indicated that larger farms use more energy per acre of corn, per acre of wheat, per dollar of crop production, per bushel of corn produced, and per bushel of wheat raised.[15] Large farms are more efficient in their use of labor, due to their increased level of capital-intensive mechanization. Large farms are also more profitable, but this should not be confused with efficiency.[16] Energy inputs into crop production have continued to increase because the additional production achieved more than equals the costs of those products.

Alternatives such as reduced use of commercial fertilizers and pesticides, accompanied by increased application of manure and use of crop rotation to maintain fertility, have received little attention from most Nebraska farmers. However, research has shown that feedlot manure can produce yields roughly comparable to those achieved with commercial ammonium nitrate fertilizer, while significantly reducing operating costs and energy intensiveness. Yields on "organic" farms appear to suffer in comparison with conventional farms in wet years, so net crop returns are slightly lower; but in drier years yields are similar and returns are slightly higher. Research at the

TABLE 6.2

ENERGY INPUTS PER ACRE OF CORN PRODUCTION, 1945 and 1970

Input	Units	1945 Amount	1945 Energy Equivalent (10^3 kilocalories)	1970 Amount	1970 Energy Equivalent (10^3 kilocalories)	Ratio 1970/1945
Labor	hours	23	12.5	9	4.9	0.39
Machinery	Kcal x 10^3	180	180.0	420	420.0	2.33
Gasoline	gallons	15	543.4	22	797.0	1.47
Nitrogen	pounds	7	58.8	112	940.8	16.00
Phosphorus	pounds	7	10.6	31	47.1	4.44
Potassium	pounds	5	5.2	60	68.0	13.08
Seeds	bushels	0.17	34.0	0.33	63.0	1.85
Irrigation	Kcal x 10^3	19	19.0	34	34.0	1.79
Insecticides	pounds	0	0	1	11.0	∞
Herbicides	pounds	0	0	1	11.0	∞
Drying	Kcal x 10^3	10	10.0	120	120.0	12.00
Electricity	Kcal x 10^3	32	32.0	310	310.0	9.69
Transportation	Kcal x 10^3	20	20.0	70	70.0	3.50
Total Input		--	925.5	--	2,896.8	3.13
Corn Yield	bushels	34	3,427.2	81	8,164.8	2.38
Output/input ratio		--	3.70	--	2.82	--

Source: David Pimentel, et.al., "Food Production and the Energy Crisis," Science 182 (November 2, 1973):444-45. Reprinted by permission of David Pimentel and Science. Copyright 1973 by the American Association for the Advancement of Science.

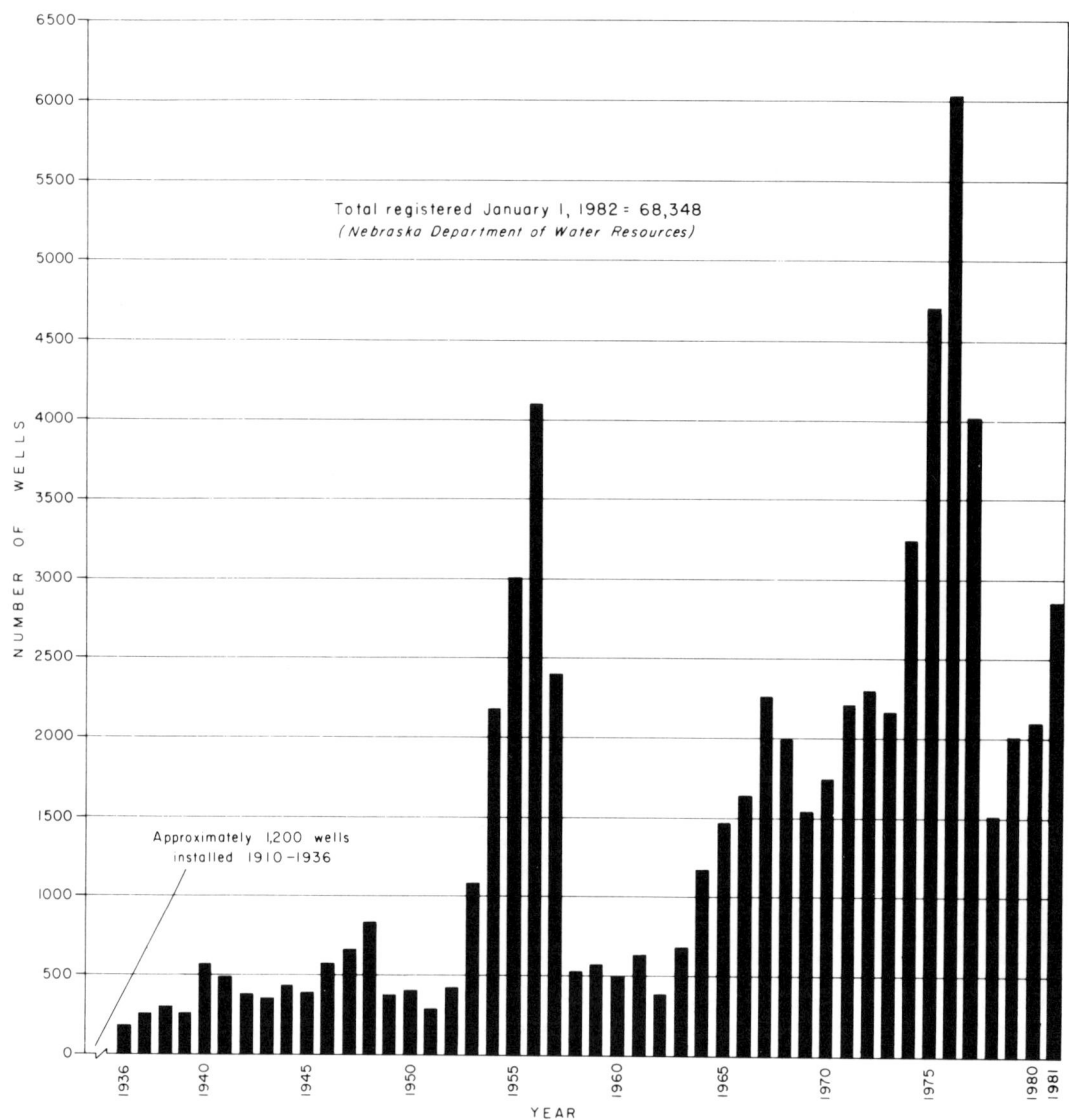

Annual installation of irrigation wells in Nebraska through 1981 (estimated from historical surveys and irrigation well registration data)

FIGURE 6.5. (UNL, Conservation and Survey Division)

University of Nebraska indicates that irrigated corn is as responsive to manure as to commercial inorganic fertilizer.[17]

Genetic Selection

One of the most important agricultural innovations of the twentieth century has been the development of improved seed varieties. Hybrid corn, widely adopted in Nebraska during the 1940s, is produced by seed companies within the state and throughout the Midwest. It can be planted closer together, is more responsive to fertilizer, can be more easily cultivated, and gives substantially higher yields than the seed saved from the previous year's crop—the system used before World War II.

In "improved" varieties, plant energy is diverted in one of several directions—rapid growth, stronger stalks, higher yields, or some other factor. Selective breeding cannot solve all problems. "We are fooling ourselves when we expect a plant to resist disease, discourage predators and competitors, withstand unfavorable climatic and nutritional conditions, grow rapidly, reproduce abundantly, and still yield a bountiful harvest that is tasty, nutritious, and beautiful."[18] Traditional seed varieties were able to adapt to plant diseases and pests, but modern hybrids cannot. They can only be replaced by new varieties that are resistant to specific diseases. As larger and larger areas are planted to relatively few strains, the uniformity produced by modern genetic selection exposes a great proportion of the U.S. corn crop to possible widespread devastation.

In 1970, southern corn blight caused perhaps a 15 percent decrease in U.S. corn production. Nebraska farmers were spared most of the effects of the blight, which was concentrated in the southeastern states. Nevertheless, increasing uniformity of seed varieties makes it impossible to prevent similar occurrences in the future.[19] Farmers take a certain amount of risk in the "improvement" of their crops; the return has thus far been well worth that risk.

Irrigation

Undoubtedly the most dramatic impact of technology on Nebraska's agriculture in the past two decades has been the rapid growth of irrigation. Irrigated acreage in the state rose from 4 million acres (1.6 million ha) in 1970 to 7.2 million acres (2.9 million ha) in 1980, an increase much more rapid than in the two states with more irrigated land than Nebraska—Texas and California. Some estimate irrigated acreage could double within twenty years and that eventually 40 percent of the state (20 million acres—8 million ha) could be irrigated. Surface irrigation is still concentrated along the Platte and Republican rivers, with additional lands along the Middle Loup River.

Severe drought in the 1930s led to a boom in irrigation. After leveling off in the moist 1940s, well drilling accelerated in the dry early 1950s and peaked at over four thousand wells added in 1956 (Figure 6.5). Most of this development took place in the central Platte Valley and the counties east and south of the river. This is the area that is most heavily irrigated today (Figure 6.6). Hamilton and Merrick counties, for example, have over half their total land area under irrigation.

Center-Pivot Technology

Prior to about 1960, irrigation was confined to level or very gently sloping land. Water was delivered to fields by canal or pump and distributed by ditch or pipe (Figure 6.7). Water flowed down crop rows or reached crops by flooding of the entire field. The development of center-pivot systems changed all that. Although other forms of sprinkler irrigation have been employed in Nebraska, the amount of labor required has limited their appeal. The center-pivot, on the other hand, needs little labor and has the advantage of being usable on lands with topography unsuited to gravity irrigation (Figure 6.8).

The center-pivot was invented by Frank

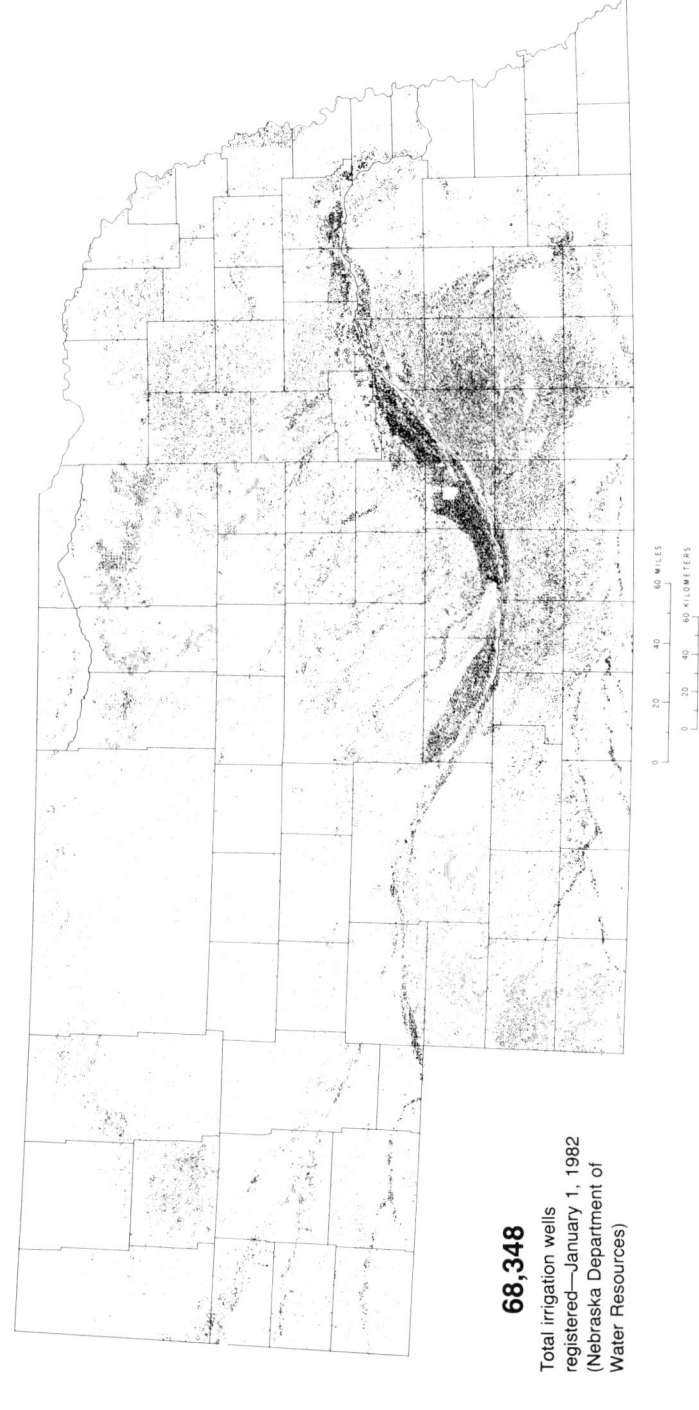

FIGURE 6.6. (UNL, Conservation and Survey Division) Location of registered irrigation wells as of January 1, 1982

FIGURE 6.7. Irrigating corn with gated pipe in Adams County. (USDA, SCS)

FIGURE 6.8. Center-pivot irrigation can be used on rolling terrain unsuited to gravity delivery of water.

Zybach, a Colorado wheat farmer, in 1949. It was first produced commercially in 1952 and is now manufactured on a large scale by approximately twenty companies, many located in Nebraska. The center-pivot is really a pipeline suspended above ground and fitted with sprinkler nozzles. Fixed at one end, the pipe, typically 0.25 mi (0.4 km) long, rotates about the field on wheels. The irrigated circle has an area of about 133 acres (53 ha), which can be covered during a time span ranging from one day to one week.

The irrigated circle leaves 27 acres (11 ha) of unirrigated land in the corners of quarter sections. Recent developments may eventually eliminate pivot corners. Corner systems, which trail behind the outer end of the main pivot, irrigate nearly all the land in the quarter section (Figure 6.9). When the corner of the field is reached, the corner system swings out in an arc that may bring as much as 150 acres (61 ha) in a quarter section under the sprinklers. This is accomplished at considerable expense, limiting widespread adoption of corner systems to date.

The center-pivot fits well into the confines of the quarter section, but it is less compatible with fences, trees, windmills, and houses. They can be removed to allow unrestricted cycling of the irrigation system. Where this is not possible, an alternative is to irrigate only a portion of the

FIGURE 6.9. Center-pivot corner system. (Nicholson, Kovac, Huntley & Welsh)

circle. A number of pivots are used on arcs of only 330 degrees or so. When the pivot reaches a certain point, it reverses, sparing farmsteads and trees.

Whereas gravity systems concentrate water near one end of a field and provide inadequate moisture for the other end, center-pivots achieve a uniform distribution of water. This is particularly significant on sandy soils, which often absorb moisture so rapidly that they cannot be irrigated by gravity. The center-pivot has turned many formerly unirrigable lands into irrigated lands.[20]

Once the technology became available, center-pivots were adopted very rapidly (Table 6.3). By the end of 1981, nearly 3 million acres (1.2 million ha) of Nebraska land were irrigated by center-pivots, more than in any other state in the nation. The most intensive development has occurred in the north-central counties, mostly on sandy soils (Figure 6.10). In some portions of Holt County one can drive 15 mi (24 km) and see continuous center-pivots on both sides of the road. Holt County alone had 1,883 pivots in operation in 1981.[21]

A second area, with similar soils, is the southwestern corner of the state. Like the north-central area, many of these center-pivots have been installed on land that had never been used for crops. Native grassland on sandhills was plowed up and planted to corn. Some wheat fields were converted to irrigated corn. Other concentrations of center-pivots are found in regions previously irrigated, either by surface systems as in the Tri-County area or by wells as in Hamilton, York, and Fillmore counties.

Clearly, irrigation increases the average

TABLE 6.3

CENTER PIVOTS IN OPERATION

1972	2,735	1977	15,014
1973	3,901	1978	17,254
1974	6,269	1979	18,553
1975	8,949	1980	20,133
1976	12,574	1981	21,793

Source: University of Nebraska-Lincoln, Conservation and Survey Division.

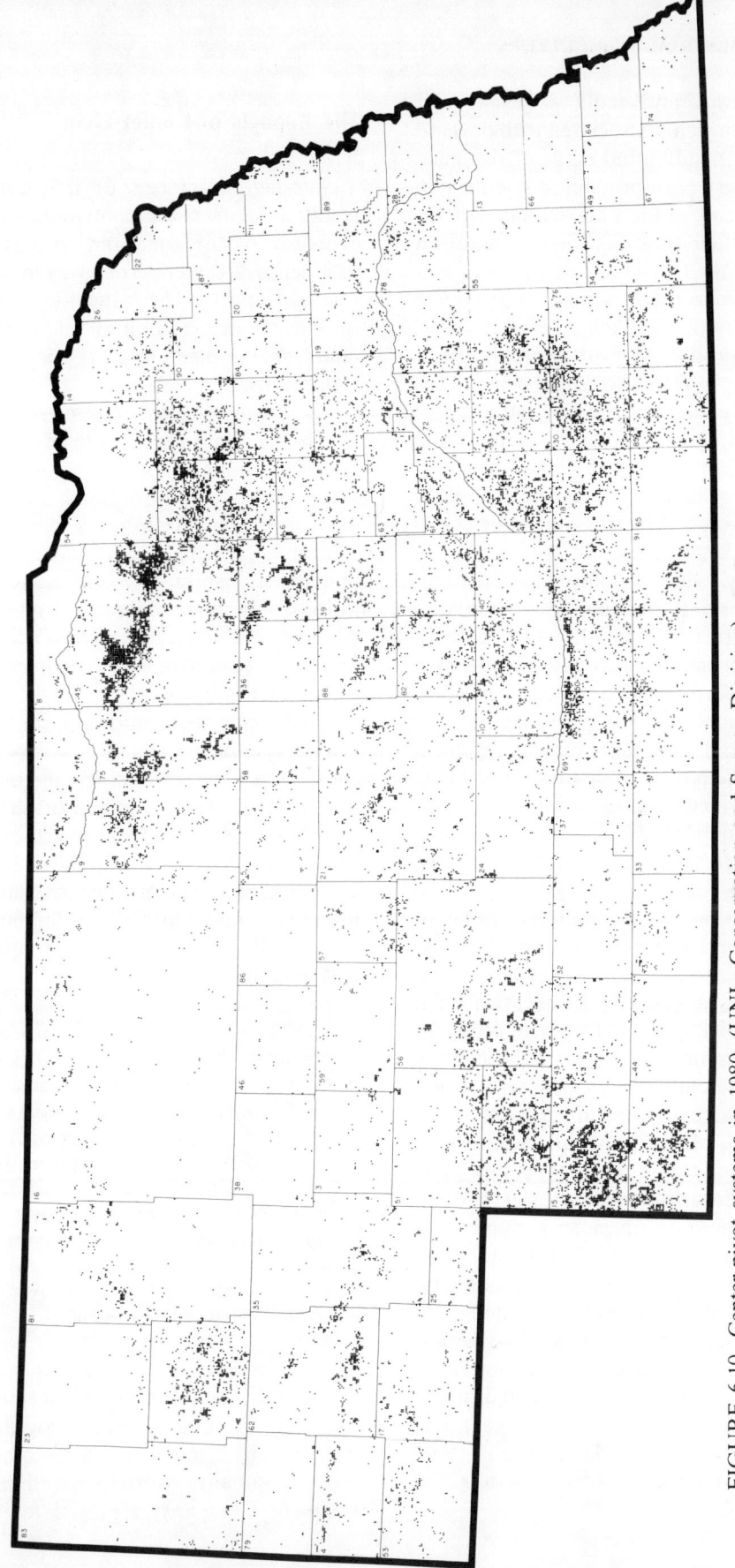

FIGURE 6.10. Center-pivot systems in 1980. (UNL, Conservation and Survey Division)

yield of crops and reduces year-to-year variability in yields associated with dryland agriculture in subhumid areas of the state. In the largest corn-producing counties in the central part of the state, irrigated yields are two to four times as high as those on unirrigated land. About 70 percent of Nebraska's corn acreage is now irrigated.[22]

No less important than the role of irrigation in productivity are its implications for land use. In Holt and neighboring counties, land previously grazed by cattle is now producing 130 bu of corn per acre (11,300 l per ha). Land prices in most "new" irrigated areas have risen sharply. The shift from livestock to crops has been very significant to local communities.[23]

Ranching, with low output per acre, requires few inputs. When that same land is used for irrigated corn, however, a score of economic activities are affected. To produce corn, farmers require seed, fertilizer, pesticides, larger tractors, implements, grain elevators, and bins, all provided by local dealers. Foremost among these merchants are well drillers and distributors of irrigation equipment. Grain must be transported to local elevators for storage or shipment by rail.

As land values rise and the value of irrigation and other farm equipment investment increases, the local tax base grows. Increased economic activity in town often means a growing population with needs for expanded community services, including schools, churches, physicians, and retail activities. Much of the investment in irrigation is cycled through the community a number of times and affects the state economy through increased sales and income tax revenue. Because a number of major manufacturers of irrigation equipment are located in the state, each purchase of a center-pivot, a well, or gated pipe bolsters the health of Nebraska businesses. The value of increased production as a result of irrigation was estimated to be $500 per acre in 1970 (the most recent data available).[24] This translates into a total impact on Nebraska's economy of over $3.5 billion.

The Impacts of Center-Pivot Irrigation

Although all forms of irrigation have resulted in dramatic contributions to the economy of the state and to agricultural productivity, center-pivot irrigation has had special impacts. These include changes in the nature of agricultural investment and land ownership and impacts upon the physical environment.

As already discussed, center-pivots are expensive. Their capital-intensive nature is one of their attractions to investors. A 1976 study showed that one-fourth to one-third of all center-pivots in a six-county region centering on Holt County were owned by nonfarmers, absentee individuals, corporations, and other nonlocal multiple owners. At that time, one corporation owned 127 pivots in Holt County, 13 percent of all pivots in the county.[25]

Center-pivots are appealing to both developers and investors. Developers purchase land, drill wells, shape the land, and put pivots in place. High-tax-bracket investors purchase the land and irrigation equipment from the developer. The operation works like this: The investor purchases land for $725 per acre ($1,790 per ha) plus $375 per acre ($925 per ha) for the equipment and gets an

> investment credit and accelerated depreciation on the $375 per acre of irrigation equipment. . . . The 10% investment credit immediately reduces his taxes by $37.50 per acre. Capital cost recovery provisions allow him to depreciate the equipment over five years. . . . Because interest is deductible, the 50% income tax bracket taxpayer recovers half of each dollar spent on interest through tax savings. . . . The tax code rewards conversion of rangeland to center-pivot irrigated cropland, typically by as much as $115 per acre.[26]

Complicated financial arrangements are involved in some center-pivot developments. In the mid-1970s a Colorado real estate company, Western Land and Investment Company, arranged for the acquisition of thousands of acres of Dundy County rangeland by wealthy investors seeking to shelter some of their nonfarm income from taxes.[27] Western Agriculture Land Corporation, an affiliated company,

> was the first purchaser of a 1,360 acre Dundy County ranch in April, 1975. One day later the ranch was sold to the Allard Company [which owned 20 operating Dundy County pivots in 1975]. Yet another [affiliated company], Medicine Bow Land and Cattle Company, was the first purchaser of a 1,110 acre Dundy ranch in December, 1974, which less than three months later was sold to Dolson Outdoor Advertising.[28]

A subsidiary, Western Agri-Management, offered investors farm-management services and hired individuals to conduct the actual farming activities on a partial sharecropper basis, in which about three-fourths of the income from the farm is paid to the landlord—including the farm-management company and the actual investor.[29]

PROBLEMS IN AGRICULTURE

The productivity of Nebraska's agriculture depends upon the continuous availability of resources—good soils, abundant water, a good-quality environment. Yet several problems confront agriculture. For many irrigators it is the steady lowering of water tables that threatens to reduce yields and, in some areas, to bring an end to irrigation (see Chapter 1). Other farmers must contend with soil erosion. Increasingly, agricultural pollution threatens the quality of rural water and air.

Soil Erosion and Conservation

From the time agriculture was first practiced in the state, erosion has occurred. Problems have been particularly evident during major droughts, when dry soils and reduced soil cover permit widespread wind erosion. Erosion by water has been most severe in periods when farmers have expanded their cultivated area by farming more erosion-prone soils.

In spite of concerted efforts to control soil erosion over the past fifty years, wind and water continue to take their toll. Erosion by water is concentrated in the eastern third of Nebraska, where rolling hills and clay or silt soils dominate and where rainfall is often intense. The U.S. Soil Conservation Service estimates an annual rate of soil loss of 20 tn per acre (45 t per ha) per year in Douglas County, 27 tn (61 t per ha) per year in Washington County, and 36 tn (81 t per ha) in Burt County 5 tn per acre (11 t per ha) is considered an acceptable loss. Because 1 in. (2.54 cm) of soil over an acre weighs about 150 tn (336 t per ha), 36 tn per year amounts to nearly 1 in. of soil lost every four years. The statewide average is approximately 8 tn per acre (18 t per ha) per year on Nebraska's 18 million acres (7.3 million ha) of cropland. Some severely affected areas have probably lost about half their topsoil in the past one hundred years.[30]

About 17 million acres (7 million ha) of the state are susceptible to wind erosion. This land is confined to the drier half of the state and includes about 60 percent of the Sandhills, where even minimal disruption of the grass cover is likely to produce blowouts, which may broaden and destroy nearby vegetation.[31] Blowouts often form around telephone poles or windmills or along cattle trails (Figure 6.11).

Center-pivot irrigation in the Sandhills has been responsible for increased wind erosion. Many Sandhills pivots have been placed on land that has been shaped—the steeper hills leveled off to permit the pivot and implements to move through the field (Figure 6.12). This brings poorer soils to the surface, often fostering erosion. In some Sandhills developments, center-pivot irrigation areas appear not as green circles on a brown background, but as circles of beige, indistinguishable from the surrounding landscape (Figure 6.13). Wind erosion has also been a problem on fallow land in the southwestern and Panhandle wheat region. Because the land lies without vegetation

Focus: Site Selection for Developing Irrigation in the Sandhills

Throughout most of the Nebraska Sandhills, the saturated thickness of the underlying Ogallala aquifer is sufficient to provide ample water of high quality for irrigation. If water for the crop is the only consideration, there are few problems. Depending on the extensiveness and intensity of development, normal draw-down during the irrigation season may affect shallow domestic or livestock wells and wet meadows.

Irrigation can supplement crop water needs but, due to limitations in irrigation system design, many pivots may not be able to supply enough water during hot weather stress periods in July or August. Since sands and loamy sands do not have a large moisture-holding capacity, the crop can suffer moisture stress even when the system is operating at full capacity. This can seriously limit yields.

Irrigation management on sandy soils is critical to reduce the risk of low yields. Excess water, especially in May and June, can leach nitrate-N from the root zone. Underwatering can cause moisture stress and severe yield reductions. Periodic inspection of fields and soil probing to 2 or 3 feet [.6 or .9 m] is essential to determine irrigation effectiveness.

Sandy soils can be grouped into four basic types: 1) dry valleys, 2) intermittently wet valleys, 3) rolling sands, and 4) choppy sands.

The dry valleys are level areas between dunes, and usually have soils with more organic matter, more silt and clay, and a higher water-holding capacity. They are the best sites for development and include the Anselmo, Dunday, and Thurman soil series.

The wet, or intermittently wet valleys, include the Cass, Car Els, Elsmere, Lawlet, Loup, Ord, Orvina, and Wann soil series. The main limitation to developing these soils is their high water table. Water may stand on them or the water may only be 1 or 2 feet [.3 or .6 m] below the surface. These soils can be good sites if they are drained and the water table is kept at least 3 feet [.9 m] below the surface at all times. However, establishing drainage is usually expensive and many sites in low areas cannot be drained without pumping away the drainage water.

The rolling sands are primarily Valentine sand. These soils are suitable for development if the topography is not too broken. The SCS [Soil Conservation Service] limits development of sandy soils to slopes less than 6.5 percent if row crops are grown. If close-grown crops, such as wheat, alfalfa, barley, oats, or grass are planted, slopes can be up to 9.5 percent. The rolling sands are less fertile, more dense, and have lower water-holding capacity than soils in inter-dunal valleys. Consequently, their production potential is 15 to 20 percent less than the valley sands.

The choppy sands are too steep and broken to logically consider development with present technology. If part of a pivot covers a choppy sand area it can be managed, but the risk of wind erosion is great. The choppy sands are more subject to wind erosion than the rolling sands due to a higher proportion of coarser sands. Current guidelines suggest leaving these areas in native range.

A major problem with moving soil, or "nob knocking," on pivot sites to even terrain is tht the cuts usually leave the dense, infertile sub-soil as the new surface. The high soil density and low water-holding capacity of these cut areas make them substantially less productive than other areas, even when fertilized adequately.

Source: Gary W. Hergert, "Irrigation in the Sandhills: Site Selection for Developing Irrigation." NebGuide G82-608 (Lincoln: University of Nebraska–Lincoln, Cooperative Extension Service, 1982). Reprinted with permission.

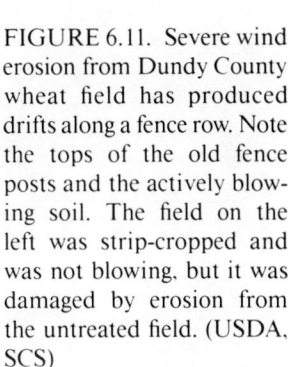

FIGURE 6.11. Severe wind erosion from Dundy County wheat field has produced drifts along a fence row. Note the tops of the old fence posts and the actively blowing soil. The field on the left was strip-cropped and was not blowing, but it was damaged by erosion from the untreated field. (USDA, SCS)

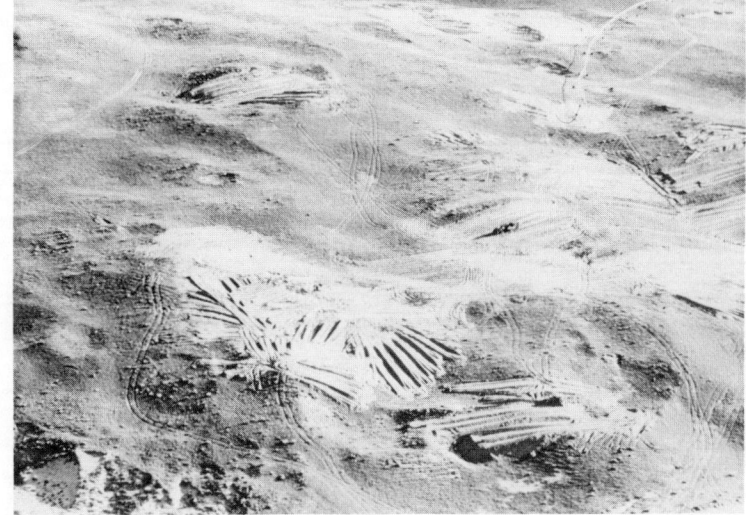

FIGURE 6.12. Leveling of sand hills for center-pivots in Wheeler County. Leveling removes protective grass cover, brings less fertile subsoil to the surface, and promotes wind erosion in many circumstances. (Nebraska Game and Parks Commission)

for much of the year, soil is susceptible to blowing unless conservation measures are undertaken.

Soil conservation practices are widespread on Nebraska farms, although they are not universal. Water erosion can generally be held in check through a combination of terraces and waterways designed to slow runoff (Figure 6.14). Farming on the contour, rather up and down hills, also cuts soil losses (Figures 6.15 and 6.16). More recently farmers have been leaving crop residue on the surface of the soil. The residue holds more water and slows the rate of runoff. These minimum-tillage systems generally involve the use of special implements, but in combination with contour farming and terracing, such practices can cut soil losses on even fairly steep slopes to as low as 3 tn per acre (6.7 t per ha) per year. Because weeds are controlled with herbicides rather than cultivation, however, operating costs may be somewhat higher.[32]

FIGURE 6.13. Large center-pivot development in Wheeler County in 1980. The light-colored areas indicate wind erosion of fragile sandy soils. (USDA, ASCS)

FIGURE 6.14. Severe water erosion on overgrazed pasture in Buffalo County. (USDA, SCS)

FIGURE 6.15. Farming up and down slopes contributes to water erosion. (Terry L. Cartwright)

FIGURE 6.16. Contour farming and terracing reduce water erosion. (UNL, Cooperative Extension Service)

Wind erosion can be minimized with reduced tillage, strip-cropping (where fallow fields and wheat lie side by side in long strips running perpendicular to the prevailing wind direction), and shelterbelts. Strip-cropping is widely practiced in western Nebraska. Shelterbelts consist of multiple rows of trees designed to reduce wind speed on fields, thereby cutting wind erosion and at the same time helping to retain soil and crop moisture. They were planted in many areas under a federal program beginning in the 1930s.

Total adoption of soil conservation practices has not occurred for a variety of reasons. Even with government cost-sharing assistance, many farmers find that the benefits of soil conservation are spread over too long a period to offset the initial costs. One popular technique has been the construction of terraces fitted to the contour of the land, but uneven terrace spacing can disrupt field operations. The alternative—parallel terraces, often accompanied by subsurface drainage and land shaping—is considerably more expensive.

Technological innovations have put other pressures on sound conservation practices. Many shelterbelts have been removed in the state in order to make way for center-pivots (Figure 6.17). In some cases terraces have been removed to accommodate large equipment and center-pivots.[33]

Farmers are frequently exhorted to produce more food for the world. High crop prices during the early 1970s gave additional impetus to farmers to plant "fencerow to fencerow." This brought more marginal land into production.[34] Erodible lands in the Missouri River bluffs were cleared of trees, terraced, and planted to corn (Figure 6.18). Former rangelands were converted to wheat, increasing the potential for erosion. Future pressures to increase output may be translated into expansion of irrigation, increasing the potential for wind erosion on sandy soils.

Agriculture and Pollution

Pollution associated with both livestock and crop production has received growing attention in the state. Concentrations of

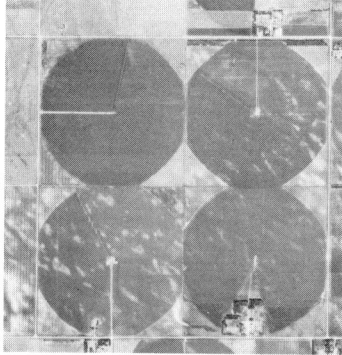

FIGURE 6.17. Shelterbelts removed to accommodate center-pivot irrigation in Holt County. Left photo, 1967; above, 1974. (USDA, ASCS)

FIGURE 6.18. Parallel terraces help reduce erosion on steep slopes in some situations, but may foster more erosion in others. Until a few years ago, this Otoe County field was covered with trees. Clearing and terracing has converted the hillside to cropland.

cattle or hogs in relatively small areas produce special environmental problems. Most attention has been given to runoff of animal wastes and possible contamination of streams and groundwater supplies. Holding ponds and basins to retain animal wastes are required for all livestock operations where runoff is likely to result in discharge into water supplies (Figure 6.19).[35]

In large-scale confinement of livestock the concentration of manure, density of animals, and limited movement of air has resulted in severe odor problems. Although farmers are required to use "reasonable techniques" to minimize odor, neighbors often object to such operations. Rural residents are accustomed to the smell of livestock and animal wastes as an integral part of rural life, but air quality in the vicinity of some livestock units has been so intolerable that several private nuisance suits have been filed in Nebraska, mostly by long-time residents concerned about the quality of their immediate environment.[36]

Both livestock and crop production have contributed to high nitrate levels in some groundwater supplies. Nitrate concentrations are health hazards, particularly for infants. When nitrates are ingested they are converted to nitrites, which inhibit the ability of the blood to carry oxygen. Some animals, particularly hogs, are also ad-

FIGURE 6.19. Feedlot runoff. State regulations mandate control of livestock waste. (USDA, SCS)

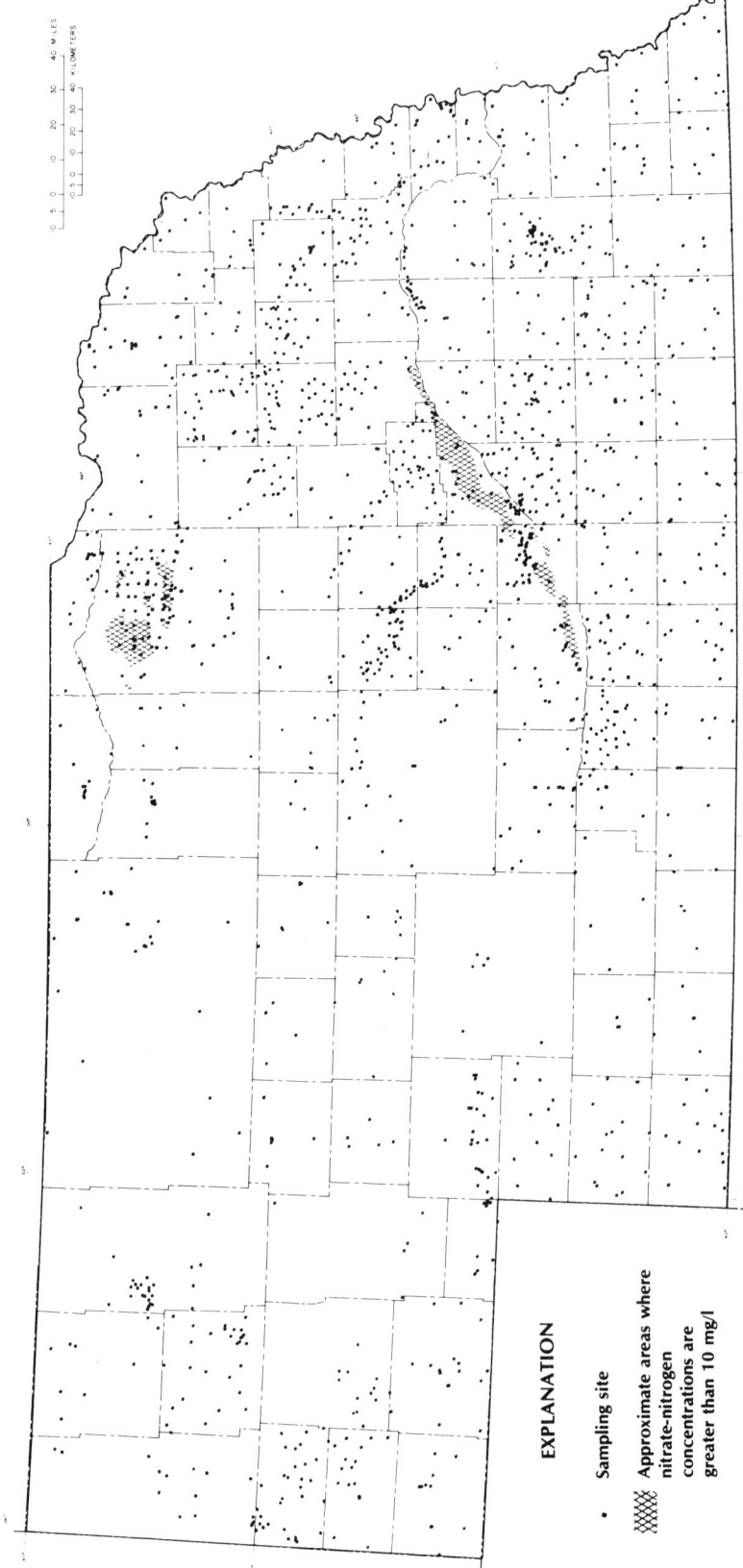

FIGURE 6.20. Nitrate contamination of groundwater. (UNL, Conservation and Survey Division)

versely affected by high nitrate concentrations. The acceptable level of nitrates for drinking water is 10 parts per million.

Nitrate contamination has been identified and studied in several areas of Nebraska (Figure 6.20). Potential sources of contamination include precipitation, natural soil nitrogen, and livestock feedlots in certain locales. Studies of Holt County and the central Platte Valley, however, reveal that by far the most important source of contamination is commercial fertilizer. Where heavy amounts of fertilizer are applied to highly permeable irrigated soils, as much as 50 percent of the nitrogen may infiltrate to the groundwater supply.[37]

Nitrates in surface water likewise appear to be mostly due to commercial fertilizer. Concentrations are highest in those areas of the state with the greatest corn acreage. Cattle density shows some relationship to nitrate levels in streams, as well.[38]

TECHNOLOGY, ENERGY, AND ENVIRONMENT

Farming in Nebraska has always been a risky proposition. Farmers in the late twentieth century have adopted a range of risk-reducing technologies—irrigation, pesticides, commercial fertilizer, hybrid seeds, and grain dryers—that have increased production costs and that require fossil fuels.

The resultant farm expansion, energy use, technological advances, and specialization have combined to put inordinate pressure on the physical environment and the renewable resources that sustain agriculture. There is some evidence that increasing farm size and the rise of investor-owned corporate farms are associated with less concern with soil erosion.[39] Increasing specialization has aggravated pest problems and has led to decreased use of crop rotation. Manure, once a valuable resource, is seldom applied to fields but instead accumulates in feedlots, where it leaches into the soil and, in some cases, contaminates groundwater.[40]

Risk in Agriculture

Widespread adoption of energy-intensive agricultural technologies has reduced but not eliminated the environmental risks of farming. Irrigation will not prevent crop losses from drought, nor will insecticides prevent all insect damage, but the net effect of technological agriculture has been to improve the likelihood of good crop yields and to increase overall farm productivity.

However, risks of different sorts have become more significant: environmental damage, economic failure, supply cutoffs, and damage to the national, and even the world, food system. The risk of environmental damage is the harm to the sustainability of agricultural ecosystems—notably soil and water—caused by the spread of crop monoculture, agricultural pollution, soil erosion, damage to soil structure and fertility, and depletion of groundwater supplies. These may not be serious threats in Nebraska in the short run, but they could eventually become so.

Economic failure is a direct consequence of the increasingly capital-intensive nature of agriculture. As the level of investment rises, the risks to the individual farmer of crop failure also increase. Losses due to weather prior to World War II were in many ways less serious than today. "With living and production expenses high, a full or partial crop failure—or low prices—can be disastrous."[41]

Food production has become one component in a food-provision system that includes oil and natural gas, implement manufacturing and distribution, the chemical industry, transportation, steel and aluminum, and food processing. Control, decision making, and agricultural resources have become delocalized.[42] Control of agricultural production is a national concern. Decisions affecting agriculture are made in legislatures, Congress, board rooms, supermarkets, and foreign countries. Resources used in agriculture include not just soil, water, and climate, but oil, fertilizer, steel, plastic, and pesticides. Farmers receive higher yields and greater income as a result, but they have surrendered control and face very real possibilities of supply disruption.[43]

The risk of damage to the overall food system lies in growing regional specialization of agriculture and increasing world dependence upon the North American Great Plains for food. Much of the United States and many parts of the world have delocalized their food supply, preferring to depend on places like Nebraska and its specialized, highly productive agriculture.

Drought in the 1890s and 1930s produced outmigration and destitution, although substantial federal assistance lessened the impact of the latter drought.[44] Since the 1930s, the Great Plains have become central to the world food system. Climatic disaster there will now be felt worldwide. If anything is certain about Great Plains climate, it is that severe drought will occur in the future.

Nebraska's Agricultural Future

The future of agriculture in Nebraska depends on how farmers, public officials, and policies deal with several issues. Heavy use of nonrenewable energy supplies ties agriculture to oil. Irrigated agriculture is especially vulnerable to energy costs, but fertilizer, fuel, and pesticide use place all farmers in potentially difficult positions.[45] Problems of soil erosion, depletion of fertility, water pollution, solid waste, and groundwater supply must be dealt with. Finally, society must examine the issue of farm size and ownership. Technology, tax policy, agricultural research, and other factors favor farm expansion. But there may be social values to be gained from smaller farms and large numbers of farmers.[46]

Traditionally, agriculture was associated with financial independence and minimal interdependence with other sectors of the economy. Farmers engaged in subsistence and semisubsistence activities and espoused an agrarian outlook—farming was a way of life. During the twentieth century farming has become a way of making money, with emphasis on purchased inputs, sales of commodities, capital investment, and specialization.

Some traditional farmers still seek to avoid heavy debt in order to remain secure in land ownership. Some pursue diversified operations and produce items for home consumption.[47] But "progressive agriculture"—emphasizing profits, productivity, size, and high risk—is becoming more dominant. Fossil fuels, energy-intensive technology, and nonlocal inputs have become critical components of agriculture and are increasingly evident in the rural landscape of Nebraska.

CHAPTER 7

FARMS, FIELDS, AND COMMUNITIES: THE RURAL LANDSCAPE

Nebraska's outward appearance—its landscape—is dominated by human activity. Evidence of the "natural environment" is minimal. Economic pursuits, religious preferences, social forces, and technology have transformed a physical landscape of landforms, vegetation, soils, and water into a cultural landscape of farms and crops, towns, roads, and power lines.

Cultural landscapes reveal much about the people who were instrumental in their formation. Thus, many landscape elements are relics—products of an earlier era. But relic features are inevitably mixed with those formed by contemporary processes. Nebraska's landscapes contain and express both past and present cultures and their impact on the physical environment.

Perhaps most important of the cultural forces that have shaped the landscape is agricultural technology. As the tools, techniques, and energy sources used in agricultural production have changed, so have the buildings, fields, crops, and vegetation that dominate the rural scene. Nebraska's landscape represents an interface between the latest available technology and the technology of an earlier era.

Another aspect of rural patterns is rectangularity. Roads, land ownership, field patterns, and even buildings in much of Nebraska are oriented toward the cardinal directions, a product of the search for order and regularity during the Enlightenment. Although technology, changing tastes and preferences, and transportation planning have modified the rectangular nature of the landscape, more of that influence remains than has been destroyed.

Finally, the Nebraska landscape is reflective of the trends of national culture. Standardization of tastes, improvements in mobility and communication, and the development of economic interdependence among regions and economic sectors are dominant influences on the twentieth-century Nebraska landscape. The patterns found in the state cannot be examined in isolation from regional and national trends.

NEBRASKA FARMSTEADS

Farmsteads are the center of farm operation. A typical farmstead includes a house, a garage, a partially utilized barn, several buildings—either small frame structures or new large metal buildings—for livestock, one or more sheds or enclosed buildings for machinery storage, a shop, an abandoned hen house, a half dozen grain bins, and perhaps an outhouse left from the days prior to indoor plumbing. These buildings and associated gardens and livestock pens may be spread over several acres.

Housing

Many houses built during the settlement period made use of native building materials—stone for foundations and brick for construction—where suitable raw materials were close at hand. Log houses were built by early settlers in most areas before the railroad era, but where timber was scarce, sod houses were built (Figure 7.1). Some are still standing.

Houses constructed after the initial few years of settlement resembled national trends in style and materials. The first major boom in house construction came in the 1880s. Because many of those structures remain in use, one of the dominant architectural styles in modern Nebraska is Victorian. Built for a large family, the Victorian house featured two stories, a sizable porch, a fenced yard, and any number of shade trees, mostly oaks, elms, and maples (Figure 7.2). This stereotypical form was more common in the eastern half of the state than farther west, as areas settled later achieved prosperity after the ornate styles of the Victorian era had fallen into disfavor.

In western Nebraska the smaller houses of the early twentieth century predominate. Some were two-story houses of simple design; one-story bungalows were also common, particularly in the Panhandle and in the Sandhills.

Since 1950, the so-called ranch house has dominated rural house construction in Nebraska. Occasionally it is even found on ranches! When an older farm house is abandoned, it is replaced by modern, one-level housing (Figure 7.3). The farm family, increasingly urban in life-style and values, now has a family room, a master bedroom, 2 baths, and perhaps even a "country kitchen"! Only in rapidly growing counties are more than 40 percent of the houses of postwar vintage. Even there, new houses are concentrated in towns and cities. Counties with the greatest outmigration and population loss have the largest stock of prewar housing (Figure 7.4).

Farm houses generally give an air of permanence to Nebraska farmsteads, not surprising in that many farm houses have been occupied for several generations by the same family. In some instances, however, a mobile home serves as the farm house. This may suggest the difficulty some farmers have in acquiring affordable traditional housing, or it may be an indication

FIGURE 7.1. Sod house in Box Butte County. A number of sod houses still stand in Nebraska. (NSHS)

FIGURE 7.2. The ornate style of the Victorian era still dominates in many rural areas and small towns of Nebraska.

FIGURE 7.3. The modern ranch house (right) on a southeastern Nebraska farm has replaced the two-story nineteenth-century farmhouse in the left background.

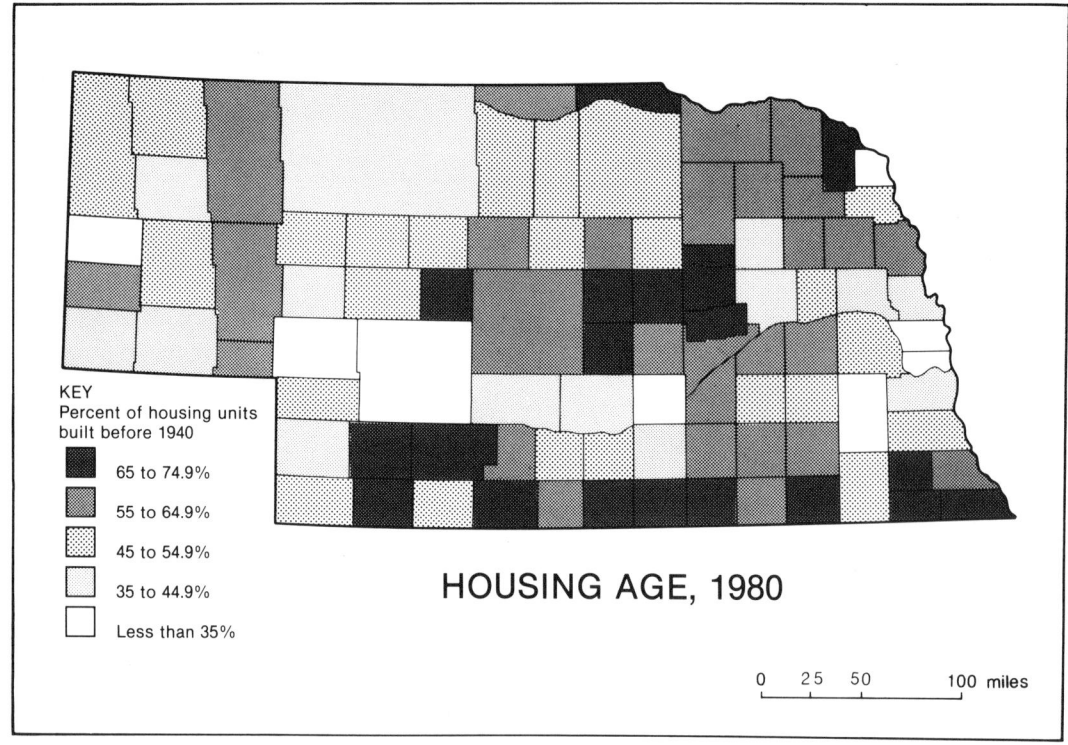

FIGURE 7.4. Based on *1980 Census of Housing.*

that the farmer is not likely to remain on the land. When ranches in the sand hills of northwestern Dundy County were converted to irrigated crop production by investors in the mid-1970s, tenant farmers, mostly from Colorado, were brought in. Because housing was scarce, many of the tenants brought mobile homes with them. Presumably, if their contracts are not renewed or if investors pull out, tenants at least have dwellings to take away from Dundy County.

Barns and Pseudobarns

The nineteenth-century frame barn remains a common structure on many Nebraska farms, particularly in the eastern two-thirds of the state. Although there are many barn styles, a common one is a three-story structure. The lower level was used for livestock; the upper level was a hay loft (Figure 7.5). The main level typically included one or more rooms for grain storage, as well as an area for storing implements or making repairs. Such a structure was well suited to a diversified farming operation, but was less common in the ranching and wheat farming areas of the state.

The general-purpose barn has considerably less utility on the modern specialized farm. The hay loft has been made obsolete by changes in feeding methods and hay technology. Grain storage needs dwarf the capacity of barn granaries, and the size and number of implements far exceed the space available in barns. The lower level is not easily adapted to automated feeding systems and is too small. Many barns have been partially adapted to current operations, are left unused, or have been destroyed. Their functions have been transferred to single-story structures.

Steel or aluminum buildings, available in turquoise or orange, now dot the landscape (Figure 7.6). Some are especially adapted to housing livestock, such as hogfarrowing operations. Others are used for equipment storage. The other principal functions of the traditional barn, grain and hay storage, are missing. Equipment to produce large hay bales permits effective outdoor storage, and many farmers who still use small bales stack them outdoors, sometimes covered with plastic to keep out moisture. Grain is usually stored in metal bins found on nearly every modern farm.

Outbuildings

Farmers have always had additional outbuildings for specialized purposes. Many are relics, now abandoned but suggesting former patterns of farm operations. Hen houses either have been razed or are used for miscellaneous storage. Only a few of the small hog houses that used to be scat-

FIGURE 7.5. This barn, built around 1880, had a top-floor hay loft, granaries and tool storage on the main floor, and livestock quarters on the ground floor. Hay could be thrown out the window or down an interior chute to the animals.

FIGURE 7.6. Metal buildings serving specialized functions dominate this farmstead. Note the older, traditional barn to the right of the center of the photo.

FIGURE 7.7. Corn crib still in use in Butler County.

tered about large pens or small pastures still exist.

Prior to widespread adoption of the picker-sheller for harvesting corn, most farmers stored ear corn in cribs. The more permanent of these structures were made of wood, with sufficient space between the boards to allow air to flow freely through the stored crop and dry it. These buildings were often attached to a larger building housing machinery, a shop, or small-grain storage in overhead bins. In some instances, a built-in elevator delivered grain from an underground pit to the bins. Less substantial corn cribs consisted of wire or snow fence affixed to poles in a cylindrical shape and topped with a metal roof (Figure 7.7). They were filled via a portable elevator, many of which came into widespread use in the 1950s. Cribbed corn was shelled after it had dried sufficiently and was either sold or fed to livestock.

Picker-shellers and grain dryers have made corn cribs somewhat obsolete. Probably 80 percent of the state's corn crop is now stored as shelled grain in metal bins. Newer models include slatted floors that allow air to be forced upward through the grain by large fans. The drying process must ordinarily be commenced immediately after the grain is placed in the bin to prevent dangerous buildup of heat and humidity. Grain drying is now one of the major consumers of electricity on Nebraska farms.

The cribs that stored Nebraska's corn now stand empty or are used for machinery storage, an important function given the cost of new buildings and the cost of replacing rusting equipment. Some still store ear corn, however, particularly in the northeastern and central parts of the state. This is a reasonable alternative to grain drying if older corn pickers can be kept operable, but it is becoming increasingly difficult to find spare parts and custom shellers.

As the amount of corn and sorghum silage has increased, silos have been constructed to store chopped green crops, particularly corn. Horizontal (pit or trench) silos are cheaper to construct, but vertical silos have proved popular because they are easily adapted to automated feeding (Figure 7.8). Most obtrusive are the blue metal silos that preserve green crops in nearly fresh condition. In spite of their cost—as much as $100,000 or more—they have been adopted virtually everywhere in the state, in contrast to the traditional masonry silo, which was confined mostly to the northeastern counties. Plastic-bag silos, a modern wrinkle, are essentially giant Baggies and can be found lying about a few Nebraska farms. Their chief advantage is low initial cost.

At one time nearly every farm had a cellar and a windmill. Root crops and canned fruits and vegetables from the orchard and garden were stored in the cellar. Few remain in use today, as farmers' food is supplied by supermarkets. Windmills, used for pumping water and, during the

FIGURE 7.8. Vertical, glass-lined silos are commonly a component of automated feed-mixing systems.

1920s and 1930s, for generating electricity, were equally widespread. The extension of electrical lines into rural areas from the 1920s through the 1950s eliminated dependence upon an unreliable energy supply. It is a very rare windmill that still supplies water for the farmhouse, although many remain on the landscape as relics (Figure 7.9). In ranching areas, where population and power-line densities are very low, numerous windmills provide water to cattle in remote areas. They are especially common in the Sandhills, where the cost of providing electricity to every well would be prohibitive.

Farmyards—Form and Function

There is more to the farmyard than buildings. Farmsteads contain the materials of farming, often in seeming disarray. The popular vision of the immaculate, neatly trimmed farmyard, with a place for everything and everything in its place, is rarely found in the real world. Farmers are seldom so short of work that they devote themselves to tidying and straightening the farmyard. The items needed frequently in the farm operation—scrap metal, lumber, wire, fence posts, tires—are found in piles alongside barns and other farm buildings. Outdoor storage, which would likely result in deterioration of wood and metal in more humid climates, places these low-value items where they are most accessible.

Farmers are handy at making things work. Although proper repairs are essential, the press of time often dictates haphazard repairs using materials at hand. A prime example is the multifunctional nature of wire, which is more versatile than glue,

FIGURE 7.9. Windmills like this one used to be the principal source of power on Nebraska farms. The distribution of operational windmills now is restricted to ranching areas. (Terry L. Cartwright)

screwdrivers, or Vise-Grips. Many a battery, combine, pickup, and tool has been patched temporarily (or even semipermanently) with wire. Piles of tangled fencing or baling wire characterize the farm scene across the state. In the absence of wire, fences have been repaired with twine, bed springs, logs, or other available, but unconventional, materials. The farmyard generally exhibits less formal beauty than functional disarray.

Regional Patterns of Farmsteads

The nature of the farmstead is a product of the nature of agricultural operations in a region. This is because "the successful production of each kind of crop and each kind of livestock requires its own more or less distinctive structure or structures, and the farm operation which produces a given combination of crops and livestock requires a distinctive ensemble of such structures."[1] The principal differences among farmsteads in Nebraska are related to the crops and livestock produced on the farm and the relative importance of each.

The largest farmsteads are found where operations are most diversified. In Nebraska this includes the corn and livestock regions of the eastern third of the state (see Chapter 5). Until forty years ago the diversified farmsteads described at the beginning of this section were found in most of the state except in the Panhandle and Sandhills.

More recently, farm specialization has made these sprawling farmsteads outdated. The cash-grain farms in the Panhandle and the central part of the state often include only the farm house, a machine shed with a shop, and a gaggle of grain bins. Livestock farms may contain extensive feedlots, several silos, and an automated feed-mixing plant. In the Sandhills, ranch headquarters are often small. Few buildings are needed to house a limited array of equipment, machinery, and supplies, although increased corn production on many ranches is changing this picture somewhat. Facilities for temporarily holding livestock complete the picture.

The rapid expansion of pivot-irrigated corn production in areas formerly devoted to ranching or dryland mixed farming has produced farmsteads that are virtually new. Here metal buildings, grain bins, and metal silos far outnumber traditional frame barns and outbuildings. Ranch-style housing and mobile homes are more common than nineteenth-century varieties. The newness of many farmsteads has allowed farmers to more carefully plan farmstead layout for efficient operations.

Because of the increasing size and decreasing number of farms in Nebraska, more farmsteads are unused than are in full operation (Figure 7.10). Abandoned farmsteads may include a house, barn, and other outbuildings, or no structures at all. Partial abandonment may take the form of housing rented to nonfarmers or the use of old buildings to store implements or bags of fertilizer, seed, or feed. New grain bins may be constructed alongside deteriorating corn cribs and chicken coops. Where no buildings remain, the former farmstead is often marked by a number of large trees that the owner has not bothered to remove.

Abandoned farmsteads give some evidence of the former density and size of farms, as well as the typical distance between neighbors in an era when most Nebraskans lived on farms. In some parts of the state there are distinctive patterns to farm abandonment. In the central and south-central transitional region, few farms in the valleys have been abandoned, but farmsteads on the uplands stand unused.[2] Farm operations have literally gone "downhill" to be closer to towns, paved roads, schools, and other amenities and necessities.

FARMS AND FARMLANDS

Farm abandonment does not mean land abandonment. The amount of land in farms has remained virtually unchanged for de-

FIGURE 7.10. The numerous scattered buildings of a large farmstead are now simply impediments to tractors and equipment. (UNL, Cooperative Extension Service)

cades. Although some land may revert from cropland to pasture or vice versa, it seldom stands unused for long.

In spite of farm expansion, the landscape has retained its basic rectangular pattern, a legacy of the survey system imposed upon it in the nineteenth century (Figure 7.11). Nearly all roads, except in the Sandhills, follow section lines. Only a few new road rights-of-way have been secured since the nineteenth century, so cardinal directions continue to dominate the land. Even in expanding suburbs, new highways typically follow the old section-line county roads.

Landholdings are similarly constrained by the survey system. The basic units of the "40" and the quarter section are clearly visible, even in areas where average farm size is 500 acres (200 ha). Fences, tree rows, hedges, and other farm borders are tenacious landscape features. An expanding farm does not necessarily obliterate evidence of the small farm era.

Trees on a Grassland

Trees are especially valued in this grassland state, which was once known as the Tree Planter State because of the efforts of J. Sterling Morton that led to the establishment of Arbor Day. That spring ritual finds thousands of school children across the state planting some traditional or exotic species of tree to beautify school grounds or public parks. Yet trees, for all their beauty and shade, also get in the way, particularly when they stand in the middle of productive fields. Trees are ritually planted and unceremoniously removed.

Early settlers found some trees in Nebraska. Along the Missouri River, its bluffs, and its tributaries were forests of oak, maple, hickory, ash, hackberry, elm, and

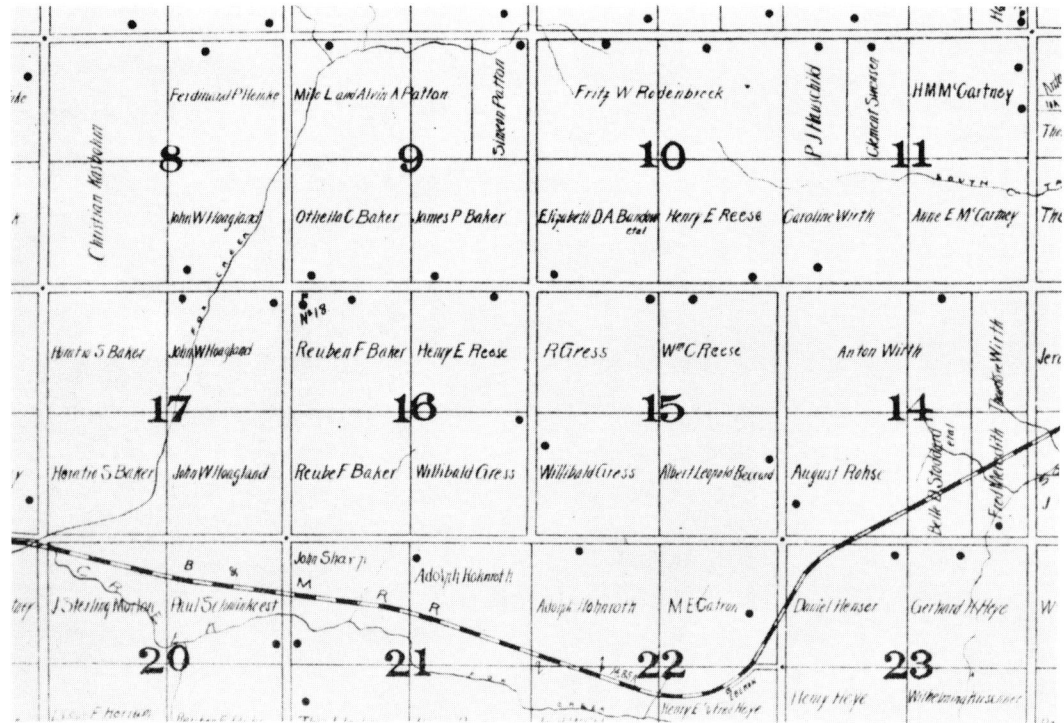

FIGURE 7.11. Quarter-section landholdings dominated most of the state during the settlement era and well into the twentieth century. In this map showing 1912 farm ownership in central Otoe County, each numbered square is a section. Even though farm consolidation has changed most of the farm boundaries, the rectangularity of most fields remains intact. (NSHS)

other species. Away from the Missouri, however, trees were confined to the immediate margins of streams. Only in the Pine Ridge area of the northwest and in the rougher lands along the North Platte River were there trees away from stream banks. Even much of the Platte, now lined with trees, probably supported only a few cottonwoods and willows.

The thousands of miles of Osage orange trees that were planted as hedges no longer serve that function. Even so, they are still one of the most striking features of the rural landscape in southeastern Nebraska, where they enclose fields and border county roads (Figure 7.12).[3]

Two organized tree-planting efforts occurred in the twentieth century. University of Nebraska botanist Charles Bessey was convinced that some species of trees could grow in the Sandhills. After ten years of experimentation, large-scale plantings were begun in 1902 in what is now the Bessey Division of the Nebraska National Forest, located between the Dismal and Middle Loup rivers in Thomas and Blaine counties.[4] A nursery was established and eventually trees were planted on 30,000 acres (12,000 ha). A 1965 fire, started by lightning, destroyed over a third of the forested area, much of which has since been replanted. Most of the trees in the Niobrara Division, southwest of Valentine, were also transplanted from nurseries.

In the 1930s, in response to severe wind erosion on the plains, the federal government instituted the Great Plains Shelterbelt Program. Several hundred million trees and shrubs were planted in an effort to conserve soil and water. Many of these bands of five to seven rows of trees remain in northeastern and central Nebraska, where they

FARMS, FIELDS, AND COMMUNITIES 211

FIGURE 7.12. Osage orange hedgerows still border many fields in southeastern Nebraska.

FIGURE 7.13. This farm windbreak in Sheridan County includes both deciduous and evergreen trees on the north side of the farmstead. (USDA, SCS)

are typically found along the north and/or west sides of protected property (Figures 7.13 and 7.14).

The removal of trees from Nebraska farms has been going on even as additional trees have been planted. Shelterbelt and hedgerow mileage has decreased because high land values and the cost-price squeeze on farmers make the trees seem expensive luxuries. The typical hedgerow occupies about 3 acres per mi (0.75 ha per km). Shelterbelts consume as much as five times that acreage—land that may be viewed as nonproductive, at least in the short run.[5] Erosion prevention, valued by most farmers, may be seen as expendable or may be accomplished through other means such as reduced tillage. In an effort to boost production, farmers have helped return much of Nebraska to the treeless condition that early settlers worked so hard to overcome.

Center-pivot irrigation has put particular pressure on shelterbelts, because of their width and their location in areas of major pivot development.[6] Hedges have not been so affected because irrigation is unimportant in most hedge areas and because they typically are found only on section and quarter-section lines and do not interfere with pivot operations (Figure 7.15). Many

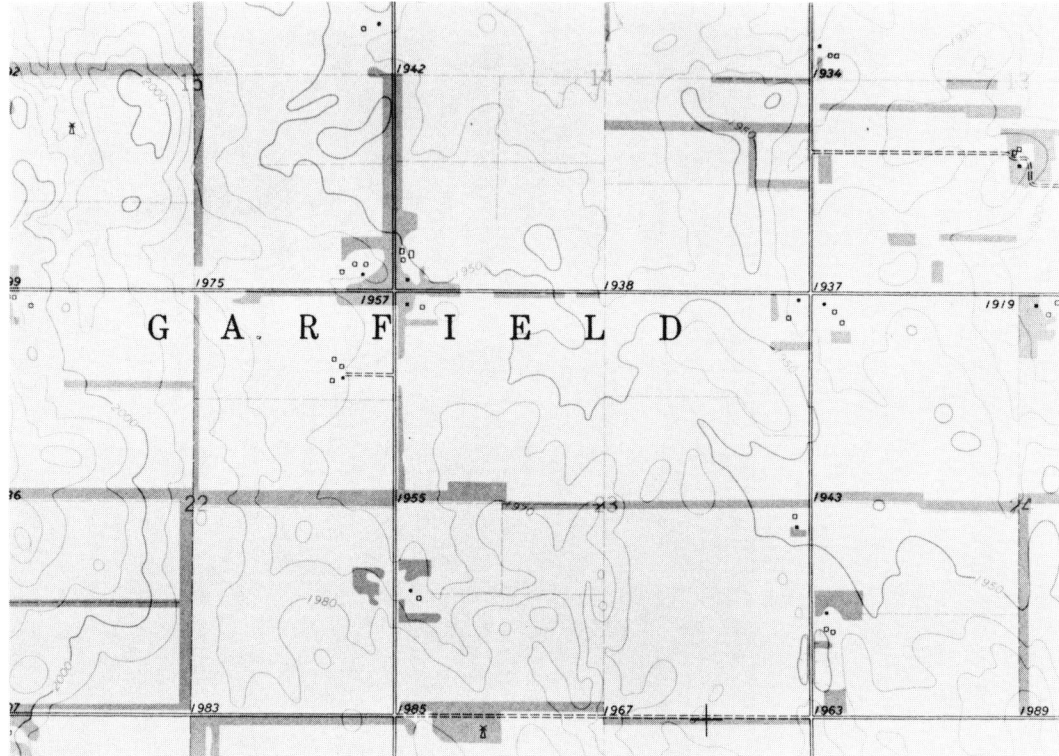

FIGURE 7.14. Shelterbelts in an Antelope County township are represented by shaded areas.

farmers continue to see substantial benefits in shelterbelts and hedgerows for erosion control, moisture retention, wildlife habitat, enhanced crop yields, and esthetic qualities. Removal is further slowed by the costs involved as well as by the tenacity of the Osage orange, which does its best to frustrate bulldozers and herbicides.

Field Patterns

The rectangularity of landholdings, hedges, and shelterbelts does not fully determine the pattern of fields in Nebraska. One of the most important factors is terrain. In rolling and hilly parts of the state, many fields are shaped to conform with the land, bending around hills and along winding streams and gullies. In the table and canyon country of the Loup Valley and the southwest, fields are fitted onto the level upland and are bounded by the sides of canyons that pierce the tablelands.

Fields in much of the state are terraced to reduce runoff, interrupted by grassed waterways to reduce runoff speed, and punctuated by small dams and farm ponds. Newer parallel terrace systems, compatible with larger machinery, are spaced at multiples of equipment width and often include expensive underground drainage that slows runoff rates, but does not take up valuable cropland. Many wheat farmers in the Panhandle have aligned their fields perpendicular to the prevailing wind direction. Stripcropping, with alternating fields of wheat and fallow, reduces wind speed over the fallow field, resulting in less erosion and greater moisture retention for the following year's crop.

Since irrigation was first introduced in the state, canals and laterals have snaked across the lands bordering the Platte and Republican rivers in the western part of the state. The shape of fields, however, was

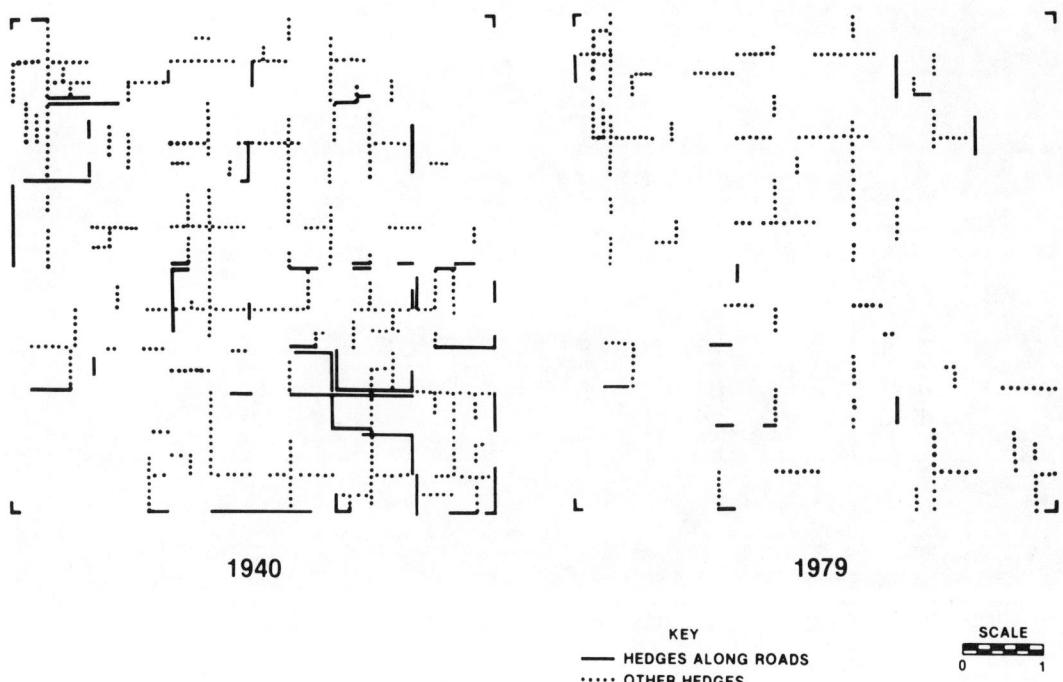

FIGURE 7.15. Hedges, particularly those along roads, have been removed during the past forty years.

little affected. The development of deep-well irrigation placed pumps and long lines of gated aluminum pipe upon the land to distribute water to fields. Some land had to be leveled, but field shape continued to conform to the rectangular survey.

Center-pivot irrigation has literally changed the shape of the farming operation. Fields are no longer rectangular or sinuous, but circular. In some areas such as Holt County, contiguous circles cover hundreds of square miles, like so many rows of canned beans on a grocery shelf. Only the corners of quarter sections are not irrigated. Some corners are occupied by farmsteads or by farm equipment and grain bins (Figure 7.16). Others are used as dumps for uprooted shelterbelts or may contain the remnants of shelterbelts out of reach of the pivots. Some corners have been planted to trees. In Holt County, some corners contain factories for hogs that consume corn from adjacent circles. Other options include planting wheat, sorghum, or some other predominantly dryland crop. A few corners are pastured, although the amount of fencing needed, relative to the area enclosed, is considerable. Others are planted to dryland corn, obscuring the circular nature of fields during humid years.[7]

On ranch land in Wheeler County that was converted to irrigation by Foxley and Co. of Denver, the constraints of the rectangular-survey system and the associated pattern of roads were not a factor in pivot location. Pivots were placed on the land in a nested fashion, reducing the 27 unirrigated acres (11 ha) to less than 15 (6 ha).

FIGURE 7.16. Pivot corners with farmstead and windbreaks. (USDA, SCS)

This is not possible in most areas of the state, however, and has seldom been used, even in Sandhills developments.

One might expect the ethnic background of many Nebraskans to have influenced the shape of farm fields. Many European migrants came from communities where farm houses were located in villages, with fields scattered about the countryside or stretching away from the village. Although several colonies in Nebraska attempted to create a village pattern, the nature of land division and the constraints of the survey system generally resulted in abandonment of such efforts within a few years. A group of Mennonites near Jansen in Jefferson County created a quasi-village settlement system, however. Their 160-acre (65-ha) farms were 0.25 mi wide and 1 mi long (0.4 by 1.6 km). A succession of these "long-lot" farms along one stretch of road known as "Russian Lane" created a dense pattern of settlement with as many as thirty-seven farm houses along a 4.5-mi (2.8-km) section of road (Figure 7.17). By the early 1950s the long-lot arrangement of farms had nearly disappeared, but there were still twenty-four houses.[8] By the early 1980s only about twelve houses remained.

Fencing the Land

Fencing needs today are substantially different from those in the settlement period. Growing specialization means not all farmers keep livestock. Cattle or hogs are more likely confined in feedlots, rather than in pastures, reducing the fencing requirement. The old dictum that a fence must be "horse high, bull strong, and pig tight" no longer applies. Horses are few, artificial insemination keeps bulls from cows, and pigs stay on concrete.

In cash-grain areas most fences have been removed because they are unnecessary and

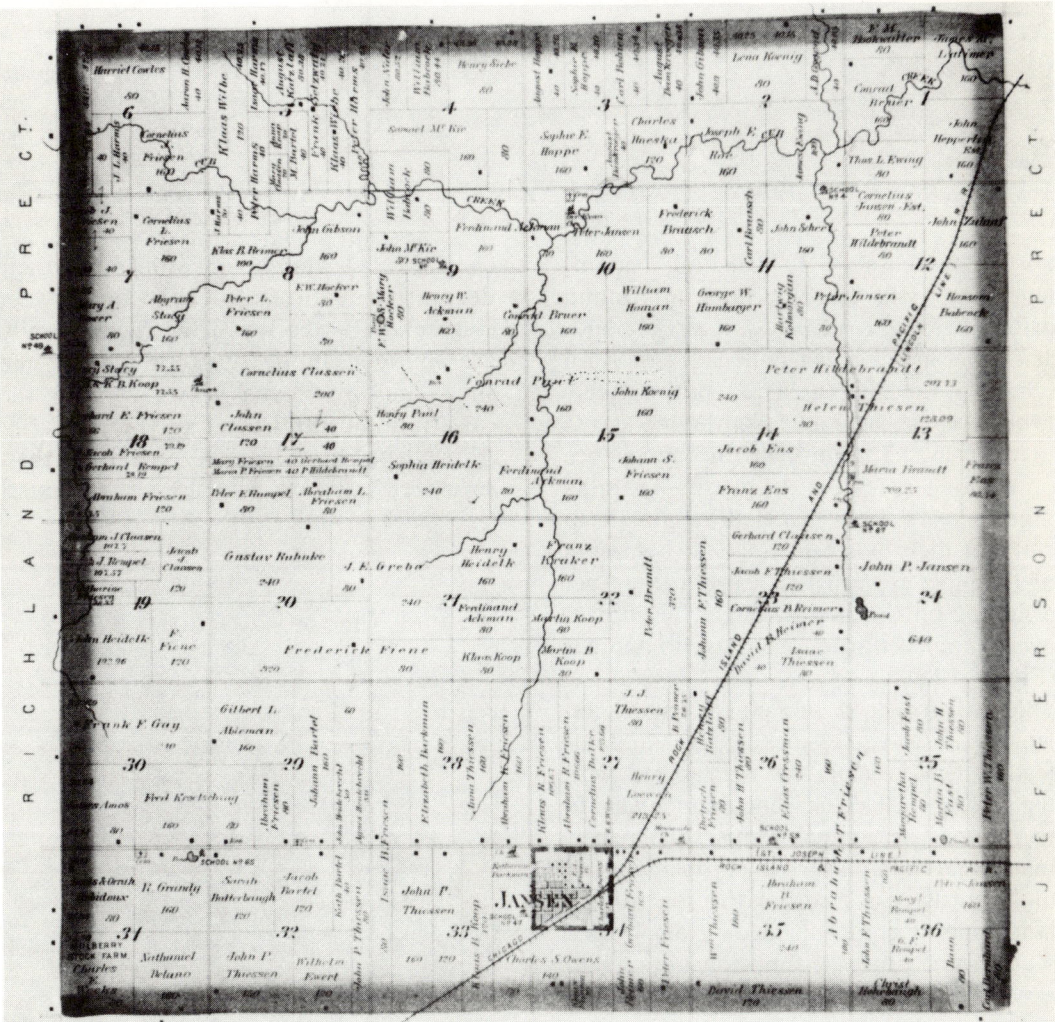

FIGURE 7.17. Mennonites in Jefferson County favored a linear arrangement of houses and long, narrow farm holdings, as shown on this 1885 plat map. Note the succession of farms north and south of the road that runs along the north side of Jansen. Some of those farms were 80 acres (32 ha), but were .125 (.2 km) wide by 1 mi (1.6 km) long. Similar patterns appear along some of the north-south roads. These long holdings are still somewhat visible on land ownership maps. (NSHS)

FIGURE 7.18. Cattle guard allows vehicles to cross, but keeps cattle where they belong.

obstruct machinery. In ranching regions, fences are still essential and are found primarily along roads and property boundaries. Because fencing both sides of rural roads in ranching areas is prohibitively expensive, ranchers allow cattle free access to roadways. To eliminate the annoyance of opening gates, cattle guards—parallel pipes or bars set over a shallow pit—keep cattle in their assigned range. The spacing of the pipes is such that cattle cannot get a footing on the guards, but vehicles pass over unimpeded from one range to another (Figure 7.18).

Many farms now rely on electric fences, which are movable, inexpensive, and effective. Few animals, having tangled with the jolt of an electric fence, are likely to try again. The gradual demise of the permanent fence in most of the cropland areas of Nebraska has changed the face of the landscape, opening up fields along roads. At the same time, the time-consuming and expensive farm chore of fence repairs has been reduced or eliminated.

In this specialized landscape of crops and livestock, one slice of disorder has persisted. Although the original vegetation of the state has been largely replaced by domestic plants, roadside vegetation in the state includes a wide array of native grasses, forbs, bushes, and trees. Flowering plants abound—prairie roses, goldenrod, sunflowers, coreopsis. So do weeds (milkweed, mullein, bindweed, and a variety of thistles), fruit-bearing plants (elderberry and chokecherry), and plants valued for their decorative features, such as bittersweet (Figure 7.19). Species of the cactus family are common in the western part of the state, and marijuana grows wild in the eastern and central counties (Figure 7.20). Altogether, Nebraska is home to more than seventeen hundred wild flowering plants.[9]

FIGURE 7.19. Elderberries.

FIGURE 7.20. Roadside marijuana attracts some out-of-state pickers.

RURAL COMMUNITIES

Rural areas are more than just collections of farms and fields. They are communities of individuals linked by proximity, common endeavors, and social institutions. In the nineteenth and early twentieth centuries exchange of labor was evident in moving livestock, making hay, and hand harvesting of corn. The informal network of neighbors also included the sharing of agricultural experience and ideas.

Sharing labor is less common today because so many of the shared activities have now been mechanized. Corn has been picked by machine on most farms for over forty years. Haying requires one farmer, rather than many workers with pitchforks or hay hooks. Cattle are relocated by truck. The informal network of agricultural experience survives, however. Most farmers receive an array of farm magazines, subscribe to marketing newsletters, have a county extension agent to consult, and perhaps even utilize a computer facility in determining the proper amount of water to apply to crops, but the most site-specific information a farmer can receive comes from neighbors. The exchange of ideas about proper rates of fertilization, preferred row width, probable yield, and the availability of rental land still takes place in the local tavern or cafe, along the road, or over coffee.

Rural Institutions

Rural communities also consist of more formal organizations, including churches and schools. Churches are particularly important in ethnic areas (Figure 7.21). Rural areas populated by Germans and Czechs are especially likely to maintain a local community church in the countryside (see Chapter 3).

Country schools performed community functions in every rural area of the state. The traditional one-room school not only educated farm children but also served as a polling place and community meeting hall. As schools have been closed or consolidated, the community functions they provided have been abandoned or transferred to nearby towns. In spite of consolidation pressures, a number of one-room schools still exist in Nebraska. Those that have been closed either stand empty or have been converted into residences or farm storage (Figure 7.22).

A few other landscape features give evidence of the rural neighborhood of the nineteenth and early twentieth centuries.

FIGURE 7.21. St. John's Lutheran Church near Auburn serves a surrounding community of German heritage. Note the cemetery, as well. (USDA, SCS)

FIGURE 7.22. Abandoned rural schools, mostly relics of an era of denser farm populations and limited mobility, dot the state. This one is in Cass County.

Rural cemeteries are found across the countryside, many of them still well maintained. Most are associated with a rural church, but some are secular and are governed by a local board of directors.

Other rural social institutions have survived into the late twentieth century. At county fairs, typically held in August, farmers gather to exhibit livestock (usually 4-H animals raised by farm children), look at tractors and implements, display crafts and foods, and discuss crop prospects. These agricultural activities are supplemented by carnivals, dances, and talent shows that attract many town residents as well. Evidence of the strength of rural communities can be seen in the food concessions operated by churches and in the neighborhood-based 4-H clubs. In western Nebraska rodeos offer local, regional, and national competitors the opportunity to display their skills and vie for prizes.

Villages and Their Communities

The countryside often housed many of the social institutions of rural areas, but small towns provided most of the economic functions. One- or two-block main streets provided congregating places for farmers—the grocery, the feed store, the hardware store, the bank, and, above all, the tavern. Perhaps at one end of Main Street were the elevators (or maybe just one), lined up along the railroad, which gave the town its purpose (see Chapter 2). Most townsites in the state exhibit a certain uniformity. The orthogonal town plan consists of a business street that crosses the railroad, often at a right angle (Figure 7.23). It was originally intended that businesses locate along this main street on both sides of the tracks, but most towns developed on one side while the other side languished. The T town plan envisioned development on only side of the railroad—along a business street leading away from the tracks (Figure 7.24). This is probably the predominant town form in Nebraska.[10] Many T towns today have a second business street along a highway paralleling the railroad. This

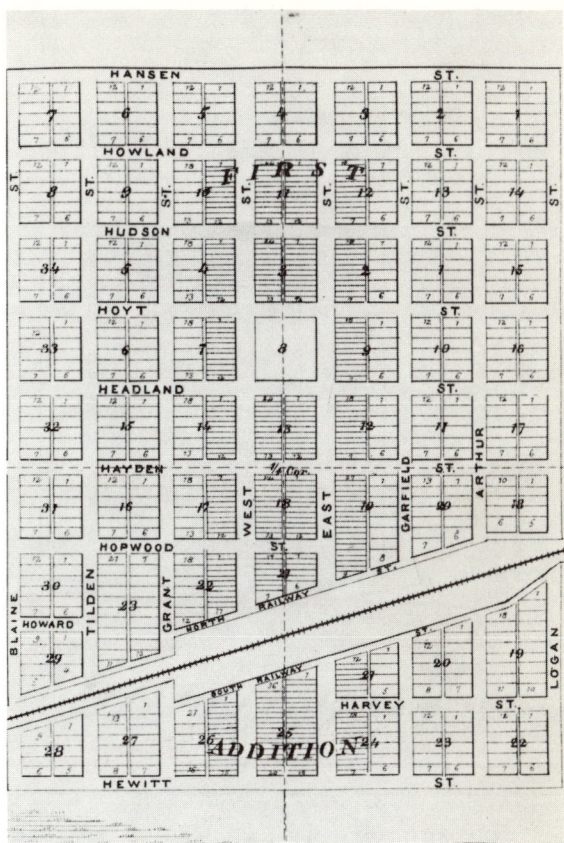

FIGURE 7.23. An orthogonal town plan with two parallel business streets. (NSHS)

street is typically lined with automobile-oriented businesses, whereas the cafe, grocery, hardware store, and bank are found along the platted business street.

Declining numbers of farms and improved mobility have cut into the business and social functions of most towns with fewer than five hundred people. These changes are clearly evident on the landscape in the form of closed businesses, abandoned schools, churches that share a priest or pastor with several other towns, and the general state of disrepair of the main street. That much modern American business activity has bypassed such places has certain advantages, however. In a town of four hundred one can still get away from the homogenized plastic restaurants of urban/

220 FARMS, FIELDS, AND COMMUNITIES

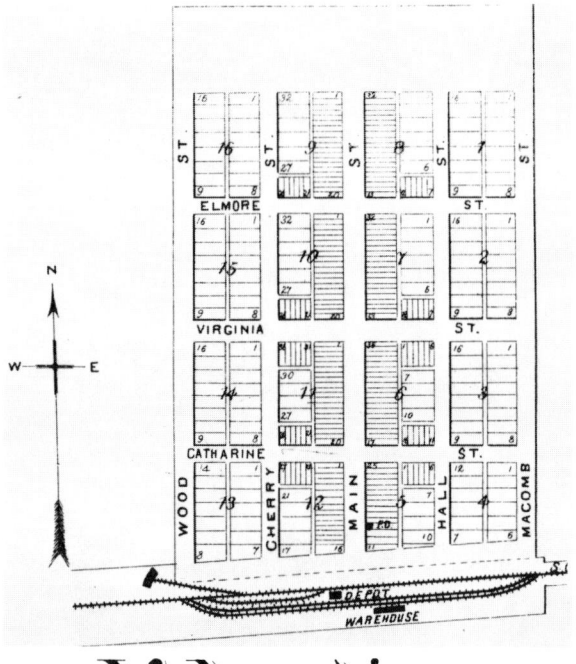

FIGURE 7.24. Valentine exhibited a typical T town plan in 1885. (NSHS)

interstate America and find large, juicy hamburgers, barbequed-rib dinners with mashed potatoes and gravy, homemade pie, shakes made with milk (!), and other fare that has not been preprocessed, frozen, and heated in a microwave oven.

HOW RURAL IS THE RURAL LANDSCAPE?

The past lives in Nebraska's rural landscape, from abandoned roads and farmhouses of an era of denser rural population to the architectural styles of the 1880s. Yet modern communications and transportation systems have brought pervasive changes to rural Nebraska. A landscape that once reflected permanence and rural values seems increasingly urban and temporary.

Mobile homes and metal silos have taken the places of Victorian frame houses and masonry silos. New farm houses are virtually indistinguishable from their suburban counterparts, and rural villages have sprouted their own subdivisions. These are national trends, diffused to Nebraska, that reflect changing preferences, tastes, and technology.

Central to these changes has been the redefinition of rural values. The farm as a way of life has slowly but steadily lost ground to the farm as a business.[11] Cash flow, equity, and interest rates are of more consequence now than are financial independence and use of local resources. Rural residents have come to resemble urbanites and suburbanites, and the rural landscape has acquired many urban features.

CHAPTER 8

THE COUNTRYSIDE AND THE CITY

At the turn of the century, rural America and urban America were two different worlds. Farmers populated rural neighborhoods; business and industry dominated the city. The rural community remained fairly isolated from urban influences and was centered around family-based, locally controlled institutions—schools, churches, cemeteries, and stores. Informal visiting was largely confined to the neighborhood. Work exchange took place within that neighborhood. A nearby village or town served as a trade center and as an outlet to the rest of the nation. Before 1920, "most people in the open country lived most of their lives within the confines of their rural community."[1]

Farmers shared similar values: a preference for financial independence, control over the processes and institutions that most directly affected them, and conservatism regarding social change. "Economically, socially, and politically the American farmer lived in a preindustrial age and embraced the values of that age."[2] Farming as a way of life was viewed as morally superior to life in the city. Urban America represented vice, poverty, and crowding. It also contained the economic power structure that impinged upon farm lives. From the city emanated the prices for farm commodities and for machinery and the credit needed for farm operations. Farmers were independent, yet they were constrained.[3]

By the late twentieth century, the nature of rural America has changed substantially. The role of the "outside world" now has pervasive influence on rural life. Farmers' livelihoods are linked to markets, futures, and grain harvests in the Soviet Union. Farming has become a business, and many rural values have changed accordingly.

Contact between farms and cities has increased: Improved transportation and communications links have broken down rural social and physical isolation. The distinctive traits that used to characterize rural people—speech, clothing, diet, entertainment, religion, politics, values—have faded as rural residents have come to resemble city dwellers.[4]

At the same time, the countryside, once solely the domain of farmers, has become more accessible to the general populace. Rural land is no longer simply farmland but is put to a number of other uses, many of them city oriented. As land has been converted to residential, transportation, recreational, and other uses, farmers have seen their influence on the countryside wane. Urban pressures infringe upon farm operations; this has prompted farmer dissatisfaction and hostility toward recent land-use developments. Ironically, the technological forces that brought farm and city together and that narrowed the differences between rural and urban places and people have resulted in rural-urban conflict.

URBANIZING THE FARMER

A number of specific factors—utilities, transportation systems, and public services—have brought the conveniences of urban living to most Nebraska farms. During the 1880s and 1890s many of the fixtures of modern life were introduced into cities in Nebraska, such as telephone systems, water and sewer systems, electricity, streetcar lines, and paved streets. Population numbers and affluence in a number of Nebraska communities made these improvements affordable. Rural areas, however, remained without electricity, indoor plumbing, or good-quality roads—rural income and rural densities were too low to justify the costs of modernization.

The Spread of Utilities

Gradually industrial America reached out to rural residents. The telephone began to break down the isolation of much of rural Nebraska early in the twentieth century. By 1940, 40 percent of Nebraska's farms had telephones. In 1950, the last year for which this information was collected, the figure was over 65 percent.[5]

In more densely populated rural areas, local power companies strung power lines from the towns into the countryside. Farmers not within reach of power lines often utilized home power plants—windmills generated electricity that was stored in batteries. About 25 percent of all farms had electricity in some form by 1940. Ten years later only 25 percent did *not* have electricity, and home power plants were a thing of the past (Table 8.1).[6] Electricity was first used to run washing machines, to power water pumps, and to provide lights. It also helped the farmer tune in the radio, and later the television, bringing urban and suburban America into living rooms of farm houses. By the 1970s farmers were acquiring mercury-vapor yard lights that illuminated the barnyard and driveway from dusk until dawn, dotting the country night with glowing circles of yellow.

The outhouse became a relic feature of the rural landscape. By 1970 only 7 percent of the rural households in the state did not have flush toilets, and nearly all had running water. In 1980, fewer than four thousand rural and small-town housing units lacked plumbing.[7] Most farmers still depend upon their own well and pump for water, but an increasing number have the option of connecting to a central water system; although the latter costs more, it may be more reliable and convenient. Water towers

TABLE 8.1

ELECTRICITY, AUTOMOBILES, AND ROADS

	Percent of Farms Reporting				
	Electricity	Automobile	Location on hard surface road	Location on gravel road	Location on dirt road
1920	9.7	75.6	NA	NA	NA
1925	NA	NA	.4	1.8	95.7
1930	16.5	91.8	.7	12.2	83.4
1940	28.8	88.8	5.4	31.9	60.3
1945	41.7	90.3	NA	NA	NA
1950	77.7	88.1	8.3	42.5	44.8
1954	94.6	91.9	NA	NA	NA

Source: U.S. Censuses of Agriculture

now sprout across the rural landscape in many parts of the state.

Transportation and Accessibility

If communications technology and the availability of utilities brought the urban world to the farm, transportation improvements allowed farmers access to the city. The turn-of-the-century farmer seldom went to town. One reason was that the amount of business to be transacted in town was substantially less than it is today. Furthermore, the trip was likely to take several hours in a horse-drawn wagon over nearly impassable roads. In 1925, 122,000 Nebraska farms were located on dirt or unimproved roads; fewer than 3,000 were on graveled or paved roads.[8]

Rural isolation began to break down with the growing influence of mail-order businesses and the introduction of Rural Free Delivery, both of which also threatened the economic viability of small villages and the cohesiveness of rural communities.[9]

Road improvements and the automobile made it easier for the farmer to get to town (Figure 8.1). At the same time, growing dependence upon commercially provided inputs to farming gave the farmer more reasons to go there. By 1950 more than half of Nebraska's farms were located on improved roads, and nearly everyone had an automobile.[10] Such accessibility reduced travel time to the nearest town from several hours to twenty minutes, except in the most sparsely populated parts of the Sandhills, where a one-hour drive is still common.

This mobility and the leisure time provided by mechanization of much farm work allowed farm families to participate in the social, economic, and cultural activities of the town. Farm men joined fraternal organizations; farm women, the ladies' auxiliaries. Farm children went to Little League, Girl Scouts, church youth organizations, dance lessons, and football practice and became nearly indistinguishable from children raised in town. Rural residents were "pulled into the orbit of city life."[11]

Farmers have become less distinctive in other ways, as well. Many depend upon off-farm income, particularly in times of depressed prices for agricultural commodities and during seasonal lulls in farm activities (see Chapter 5). Because of this

FIGURE 8.1. The automobile eliminated the isolation of rural residents. (USDA, SCS)

extra income and because thousands of marginal farmers have quit farming in the past several decades, average farm income has risen. Increased affluence has contributed to the greater availablity of utilities, improved mobility, and "modern" life styles in rural areas.

With increased use of purchased production inputs and a rising farm standard of living, the economic interdependence of town and country has become obvious to townspeople and farmers alike. Low farm prices concern the residents of towns, and the economic and social well-being of towns affects the services they can offer farmers. The growing business orientation of agriculture has weakened traditional rural social institutions and the agrarian values of individual autonomy, strong community spirit, and financial independence. In their place have grown values previously associated with the town and the city: efficiency, organization, standardization, growth, and progress.[12]

Schools and the Issue of Control

Not all farm residents accept increasing standardization and ties of farm to city with open arms. Changes in rural education since World War II have been met in some areas with outright hostility. From the nineteenth century through the 1940s, rural children were educated in local schools (Class I districts) that offered instruction in grades one through eight. This system allowed children to attend school close to home in an era when larger districts would have required excessive travel time. As rural mobility increased and rural population decreased, the Class I schools appeared to many as nineteenth-century anachronisms in a rural world of good roads and automobiles. But Nebraska, more than any other state, resisted school consolidation. In 1931 there were 7,255 school districts in the state. Twenty years later there were still 6,552 districts.[13]

In 1949 the state legislature passed a law to stimulate school consolidation. Strong support came from professional educators. Small towns favored consolidation as a means of reducing tax rates by bringing rural land into their districts, while upgrading facilities in order to retain accreditation.[14]

For rural areas there were two basic issues. One was that rural tax rates were usually somewhat lower—often considerably lower—than those of nearby towns. Farmers saw consolidation as an effort to shift an excessive tax burden onto them in a state where the greatest share of education expenses is still borne by local school districts.

The second issue was local autonomy. The rural school was the only significant remaining social institution that the local community continued to control. As one scholar has observed, "the issue of 'local control' . . . arose from an awareness of and hostility toward the process of cultural homogenization then taking place in American society."[15] To many rural residents, a school in town was not local enough and was not subject to local control.

By the 1970s, many rural school districts had consolidated with village or town districts (Figure 8.2). Continuing declines in

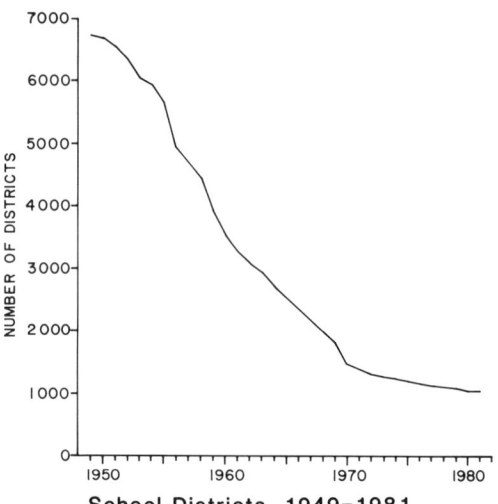

School Districts, 1949-1981

FIGURE 8.2. Based on data from Nebraska Department of Education.

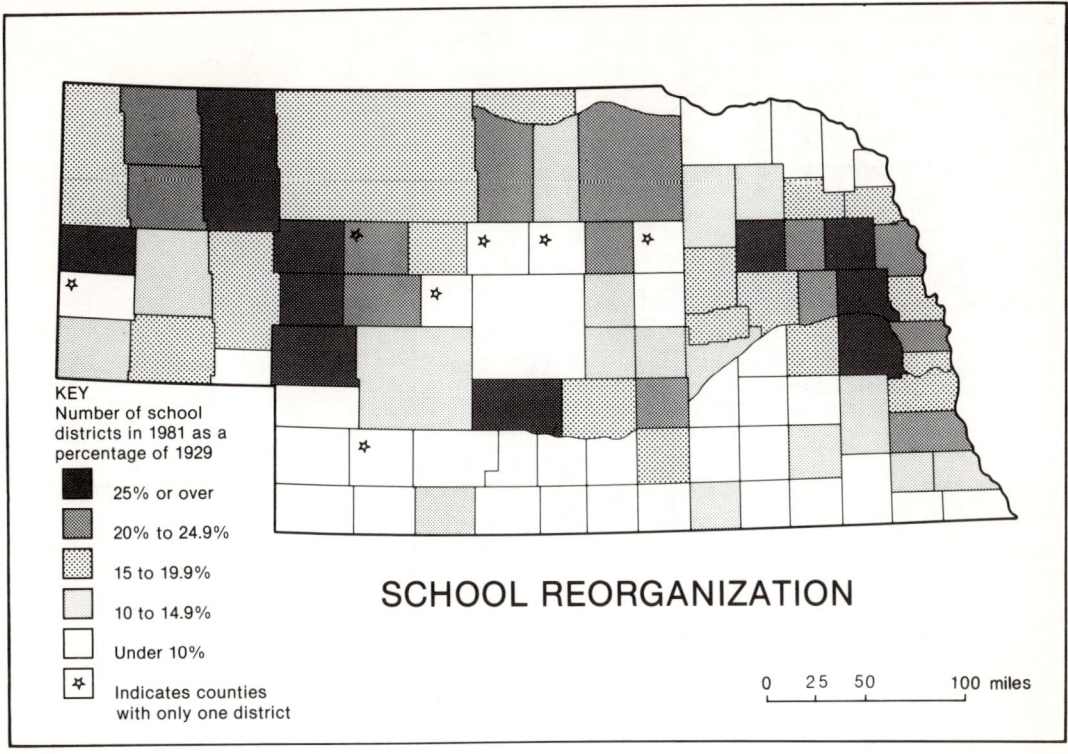

FIGURE 8.3.

rural population and school enrollment, combined with ease of access to towns and the greater range of educational activities and facilities such consolidated schools could offer, were of great importance in this transition. Nevertheless, a considerable number of one-room rural schools have survived.

Several counties still have more than twenty-five districts and in most northeastern counties 20 to 30 percent of the districts have survived during the past fifty years (Figure 8.3). Most complete consolidation has taken place in the Sandhills, where several counties now operate only one district. Most counties in southern Nebraska support fewer than ten districts (Figure 8.4).

To the extent that rural schools remain, rural neighborhoods of Nebraska continue to support an institution, the control of which remains primarily in local hands. However, as political power shifts toward urban areas, the likelihood of mandatory consolidation grows, and with it the almost complete loss of local autonomy for rural Nebraska.[16]

RURAL LAND, URBAN USES

By residence, if not by background, most Nebraskans live in cities. The growing numbers of urbanites, their affluence, and their mobility mean that the influence of urban Nebraska reaches far into rural areas. Land, however, is a finite commodity—about 48 percent of the state is cropland and 43 percent is grazing land. Only 6 percent of all land is not in farms.[17]

The growth in demand for recreation, energy, transportation, and waste disposal for Nebraska's largely urban populace has inevitably led to conflicts over the proper use of land and of the rural environment.[18] From the farmer's point of view, the conflict centers on consumption of farmland, in-

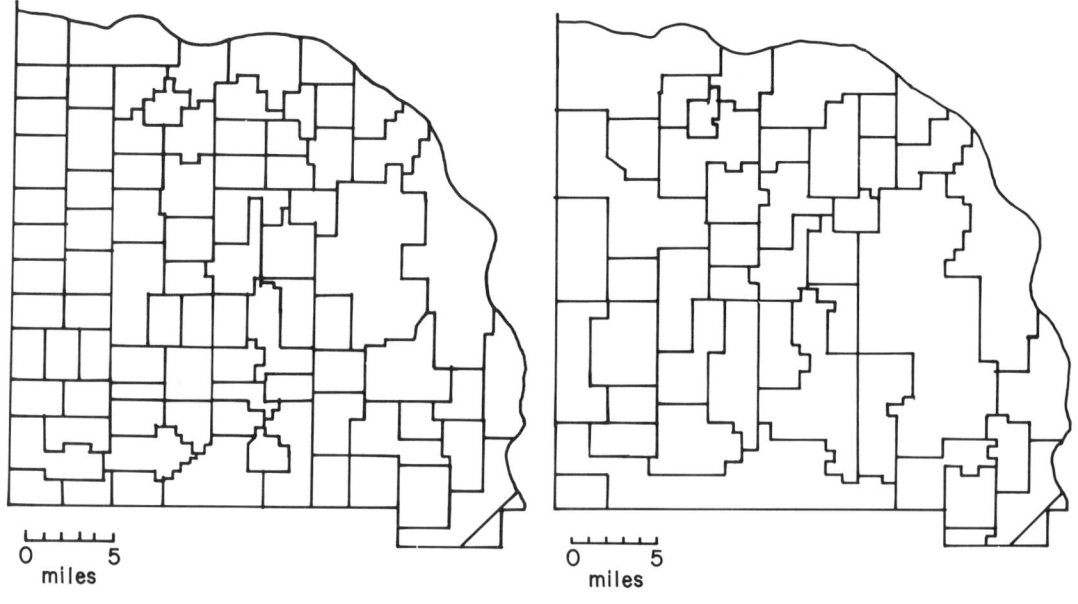
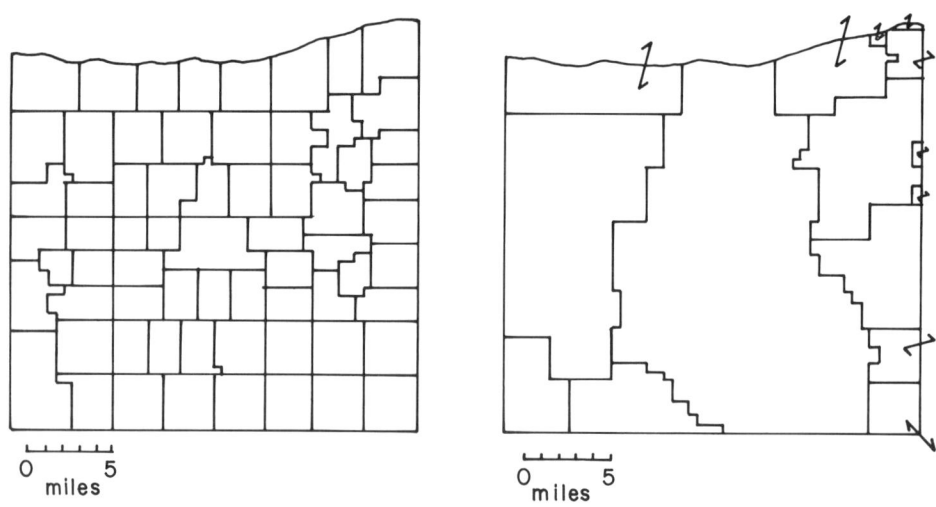

School District Reorganization in Two Counties

FIGURE 8.4.

Focus: The Rural School Controversy

The state should nurture its small, rural schools as the "real nest egg" in Nebraska's future, rather than attempting to dissolve them through mandatory redistricting, a legislative committee was told. . . . Several witnesses at a public hearing on school tax equity urged the Legislature's Education Committee to abandon a proposed school reorganization plan and find other ways to ease the property tax burden.

The hearing on Legislative Resolution 137 dealt with a study of alternatives to help provide tax equity for support of education while maintaining local control. But most who testified at the jammed public session viewed the measure as a threat to the state's small Class I school districts, which provide education only for elementary students. The study stemmed from Legislative Bill 210, which would shift part of the burden for school support from property taxes to sales and income taxes, and LB 319, which would mandate that Class I districts merge with larger districts.

Opponents argued that redistricting would be more costly, would erode local control and hamper the education and "personal attention" offered in Class I schools. Zeke Lowery of Burwell, saying he represented the Nebraska Stock Growers Association and citizens of several counties, told senators that LB 319 would discriminate against western Nebraska "and anybody who doesn't live in Omaha or Lincoln." Lowery argued for local control, saying parents and taxpayers in small districts kept closer watch on their children's education. He said Class I districts were not plagued by drugs, alcohol, and other problems that he said exist in large schools. "If we've got a problem, we look to the teachers, the school board members, and ourselves," Lowery said. "We can handle our own problems. Our small children don't have to ride a school bus for hours on a road that we wouldn't travel ourselves."

Merlin Wendt, a long-time member of a Class I school board in Cuming County, said the proposed legislation would "treat the symptom instead of the disease." Pat Cook of O'Neill, owner-operator of a cattle ranch that she said helps support three rural school districts, termed redistricting "usurpation of one of the fundamental freedoms of America. Mandatory redistricting would take our children away from their home district . . . and make them wards of another community for their education." She argued that property taxes were a local concern, saying the load could be lightened by doing away with "some of the frills."

Robert Mullendore of the Nebraska School Improvement Association termed mandatory redistricting an "intrusion into the rights of local people. We instead demand that you understand and accept the rural schools as a necessary way of life in Nebraska." He said Class I districts spend more per pupil than larger districts "and get more for our dollars in hard education. We leave out the wasted, wheel-spinning of top-heavy administrations, frivolous plants, inefficient transportation systems, and all the politicizing which plague our large neighbors." He urged the committee to consider a flat per-pupil grant from the state, regardless of location, the assessed value of a student's home district, or "any of the other catch-all crutches used to try to close us."

Sen. Howard Lamb of Anselmo said the "heart" of the redistricting controversy was concern that school mergers would mean exorbitant tax increases for owners of agricultural land, whose real estate holdings produce the lion's share of property taxes. Lamb said this example shows why the bill would be unfair: A farmer and a town resident have the same income. The farmer owns several hundred acres of high-priced land. The town resident owns only a house. The town resident lives in a school district with both elementary and secondary schools. His tax levy—the amount he pays according to the value of his house—is relatively high. The farmer lives in a school district with an elementary school only. The tax rate in that district is lower than in the town. But because the farmer owns a large amount of land, he pays the same dollar amount in school taxes as the town resident.

Lamb said it is not fair to require the farmer to pay more money for school taxes simply because the source of his income is land, and simply because schools in Nebraska depend heavily on property taxes.

Source: Omaha World Herald, Jan. 25, 1981 and Nov. 19, 1981. (Reprinted with permission of the Associated Press and the *Omaha World Herald.*)

terference with farm operations, and the quality of the rural environment.

Farmland Conversion

Water-based recreation in Nebraska takes place on reservoirs developed primarily for irrigation, flood control, or power generation. As abundant leisure time leads Nebraskans to seek more outdoor recreation opportunities, proposals have been made to build reservoirs primarily for recreation. This trend is generating opposition. Farmers east of Lincoln have protested that reservoirs for flood control and recreation planned for western Cass County will take farmland and cause law enforcement and traffic problems. As one farmer stated, "Cass County's going to be paying for Lincoln's recreation."[19] Supporters of such projects argue that more recreation opportunities should be provided near Nebraska's metropolitan areas, where the largest share of campers and boaters live. Expansion of recreation facilities for urban Nebraskans necessarily conflicts with farmers' desires to keep their resource base intact. Recreation facilities are generally viewed as undesirable by rural residents because of the traffic, noise, and litter they generate.[20]

Major water projects are usually met with some opposition because they withdraw land from agricultural production. The impact on state farm output may be minimal, but to affected farmers the difficulty of replacing land may be insurmountable. During the past five decades reservoirs on the Platte and in the Republican Valley have displaced farmers from thousands of acres.

Farmers have also forfeited farmland throughout the state to highway development. The wide right-of-way along Interstate 80, for example, has converted mostly fertile farmland to transportation use (Figure 8.5). Many former owners will never be able to acquire comparable land near their operations. Similar difficulties have accompanied highway relocations throughout the state. Land adjacent to interstate-highway interchanges has become attractive for commercial or industrial development. Clusters of urban activity, ranging from gas stations, motels, and restaurants to campgrounds and factories, are now found at most interchanges. Urban land use has come to the country.[21]

Impacts on Agricultural Activities

Use of rural land for nonfarm activities has also impinged upon farming operations and upon local control over rural communities.[22] Paralleling the nationwide growth in demand for electricity, Nebraskans have required increased capacity for generation and distribution of power. Most early generating facilities were concentrated in or near urban areas, but the large nuclear and coal-fired power plants built in the past decade require large expanses of land and abundant water and have been sited in the countryside (Figure 8.6).[23] Traffic on highways and rural roads, particularly during the construction stage, is viewed as a hazard for farmers. Some claim that radio-controlled warning sirens around nuclear facilities are annoying and disruptive and that they have stampeded cattle.

More widespread is concern about the high-voltage lines that radiate outward from large power plants to carry power across farm fields to distant locations. The poles are obstacles to field operations, and they preclude center-pivot irrigation where they cross fields. Some farmers worry that power companies will damage crops when they need to gain access to the lines.

Greatest opposition has been directed toward the 500,000-volt line proposed by the Nebraska Public Power District, which would link Nebraska with Manitoba for the seasonal exchange of power. The MANDAN line in Nebraska would directly affect about 250 landowners between Norfolk and Gavins Point dam. In addition to the objections regarding obstacles to farming and access, concern has been raised about the safety of the line and the possible harmful effects to livestock and people living and working near or under it.

Cities have come into more direct conflict

FIGURE 8.5. The Interstate 80 corridor has removed farmland from production. One mi (1.6 km) of right-of-way occupies about 40 acres (16 ha); an interchange like the one shown here takes up 60 acres (24 ha). Clusters of highway-oriented businesses and commercial corridors leading into towns and cities further alter the pattern of land use. (USDA, ASCS)

with the countryside in the search for sites to dispose of solid waste. The problem has been minor near small cities, but disposition of Omaha's waste has posed more serious difficulties. Local residents' concern with health, traffic, and pollution resulted in the closing of one landfill in Cass County, which had been used for Omaha's refuse. The county's comprehensive plan calls for a number of small landfills to handle trash and garbage from Cass County, but it does not provide for disposal of regional waste. The dilemma, from an urban viewpoint, is that a fragmented political landscape of independent towns and counties makes the solution of regional problems difficult. From the rural perspective, landfills are an undesirable facility with which they should not be saddled. They feel that Omaha should provide its own solution to a growing volume of waste, rather than exporting it.

Quality of the Rural Environment

Increased traffic, litter, and air pollution from power plants are some of the environmental costs that afflict rural Nebraska. In effect rural resources, particularly land, are used for essentially urban purposes, but

FIGURE 8.6. Land occupied by the Omaha Public Power District's generating station near Nebraska City. (USDA, ASCS)

the social, ecological, and aesthetic consequences of development are borne by the rural community.[24]

Rural hostility to urban encroachment is exacerbated by rural residents' distrust of outside influences and outsiders. Hunters, power-company employees, garbage trucks, pipelines, and even school buses symbolize the urban world. Their presence in the countryside is a reminder to farmers that the city wants part of rural Nebraska. Many perceive that urbanites, for their own benefit, wish to force upon rural areas inconvenience, ugliness, hazards, and expenses for which cities do not want responsibility.

However, local actions to control the undesirable effects of nonagricultural land uses have met considerable opposition. In spite of their concern over the quality of the rural environment and adverse impacts on farmland and farming activities, most farmers remain staunchly opposed to land-use controls, zoning, or planning. A strong belief in the sanctity of private property and the freedom of owners to do with their land as they please has overridden other considerations in most rural areas.[25]

MOVING TO THE COUNTRY

Conflicts over power lines and landfills are minor compared to the clash of interests that occurs when rural lands are converted to residential use. Prior to World War II, rural Nebraska was the domain of farmers who lived on or near the land they farmed. Rarely did people with jobs in cities, small towns, or even villages wish to live in the countryside. Rural areas were viewed as too isolated and inconvenient for anyone but farmers.[26]

The provision of better-quality roads not only gave farmers improved access to towns but also gave townspeople more access to the countryside. The advantages towns and cities held over rural areas in comfort and services diminished substantially with the availability of modern utilities and communications technology. Basic attitudes about the desirability of country living were being revised, as well.[27]

Rural Nonfarm Development

By the late 1960s large numbers of houses were being built outside towns, mostly as scattered individual purchases—"buckshot development"—rather than subdivision developments (Figure 8.7). Some rural population growth utilized existing housing, but most of it involved new construction:

New housing has a tendency to be strung out along rural roads—with an occasional stubby cul-de-sac or two cut into farm fields or woods in an effort at increasing density. The result is that a very small increase in residential land use can have a very large visual effect—producing a kind of semi-suburb that may stretch out in such a way as to affect the visual quality of wide areas of the landscape. Unlike the metropolitan pattern of subdivision the buckshot development pattern does not require a central city or even a major employment center to produce it; it just happens.[28]

Rural growth has taken place around nearly all Nebraska towns with more than a few

FIGURE 8.7. Buckshot development lines rural roads leading from Grand Island. Large lots take agricultural land and may interfere with farming operations. (USDA, ASCS)

TABLE 8.2

GROWTH OF SELECTED CITIES AND THEIR SUBURBS, 1970-1980

City	1980 Population	Percent Change, 1970-1980 City	Suburbs
Grand Island	33,180	2.5	71.6
Hastings	23,045	-2.3	11.6
Fremont	23,979	4.4	14.1
Kearney	21,158	10.3	68.7
Columbus	17,328	12.0	15.6
South Sioux City	9,339	17.9	98.4
York	7,723	13.9	10.0
Nebraska City	7,127	-4.2	20.5
Lexington	6,898	22.0	42.8
Plattsmouth	6,295	-1.2	40.4
Sidney	6,010	-6.1	59.5
Seward	5,713	7.9	27.8
Holdrege	5,624	-.2	51.9
Fairbury	4,885	-7.2	8.2
Crete	4,872	9.6	25.6
O'Neill	4,049	7.9	59.0
Broken Bow	3,979	6.6	21.5
Wahoo	3,555	-7.3	22.0
Auburn	3,482	-4.6	71.7
Valentine	2,829	6.3	75.8
David City	2,514	5.6	15.8
Neligh	1,893	7.3	29.5
Burwell	1,383	3.1	15.5

Source: U.S. Bureau of the Census, *1980 Census of Population and Housing, Advance Reports* (Washington: Government Printing Office, 1981).

thousand people and near numerous smaller places. Many a town or city with a stable population in the 1970s was bordered by rapidly growing rural precincts (Table 8.2).

Not far from Nebraska's metropolitan areas, large exurban housing developments have sprung up. The location of these clusters of housing is strongly influenced by the availability of amenities. The presence of wooded land, hilly terrain, bluffs with a view, lakes, or rivers attracted developers. In essence, these projects are new towns, except that they are entirely residential and depend upon nearby communities for shopping and services.

Such a development is Beaver Lake, about 25 mi (40 km) south of Omaha, in Cass County (Figure 8.8). Beaver Lake was begun in the early 1970s as a complete residential community. Construction of the lake required clearing many of the trees that lined Rock Creek and the steeper slopes of the valley, although trees above the water line were preserved to help attract buyers. A county road that wound along the valley floor had to be relocated on the hillside to the north. When the permanent population of Beaver Lake began to grow, public services were required. The town of Murray, 2 mi (3.2 km) away, though receiving increased tax receipts, found itself with more students than the school could handle. Con-

FIGURE 8.8. Beaver Lake, one of the larger lake developments in Nebraska, and the nearby town of Murray. (USDA, ASCS)

solidation with Nehawka, about 9 mi (14.5 km) to the southwest, permitted the construction of a new high school between the two towns, but required a substantial mill levy for the district. Traffic on county roads, particularly on weekends, increased markedly.

The Suburban Fringe

More significant in total area and overall impact on the rural landscape has been the growth occurring on the fringes of Omaha, Lincoln, and some smaller cities. After World War II urban growth in the United States was characterized by low-density suburban sprawl, rather than by the more compact, contiguous growth of earlier decades. More and more subdivisions were developed on scattered sites, bypassing tracts closer to the city. This process of "leapfrog" growth has had important consequences for agriculture and the rural landscape, as well as for the city (Figure 8.9).

Leapfrog development has been especially pronounced around Omaha (Figure 8.10). More than 100,000 people live in two hundred unincorporated subdivisions, linguistically landscaped with standardized names like Greenbriar, Oak Hills Estates, and Stony Brook, scattered across Sarpy and western Douglas County.[29] Suburban growth is also attached to small towns in the metropolitan area.

One of the most important considerations in the choice of leapfrog sites is access to the services and benefits of the city—schools, shopping, and employment. Most developments are within 15 mi (24 km) of a sizable shopping area and no more than 30 mi (48 km) from major employment opportunities. Furthermore, developers are attracted by the existence of utilities (electric or natural gas lines) and highways. Utilities are sometimes available in the predevelopment countryside; paved roads are common. Almost all land in Sarpy and western Douglas counties is within 2 mi (3.2 km) of pavement. This accessibility makes much of that area prime residential land. Site characteristics such as well-

FIGURE 8.9. Leapfrog development bypasses some tracts of farmland for other, more attractive parcels. Farmers' abilities to function effectively in this environment are reduced by increased traffic, restrictions on activities, and the threat of vandalism.

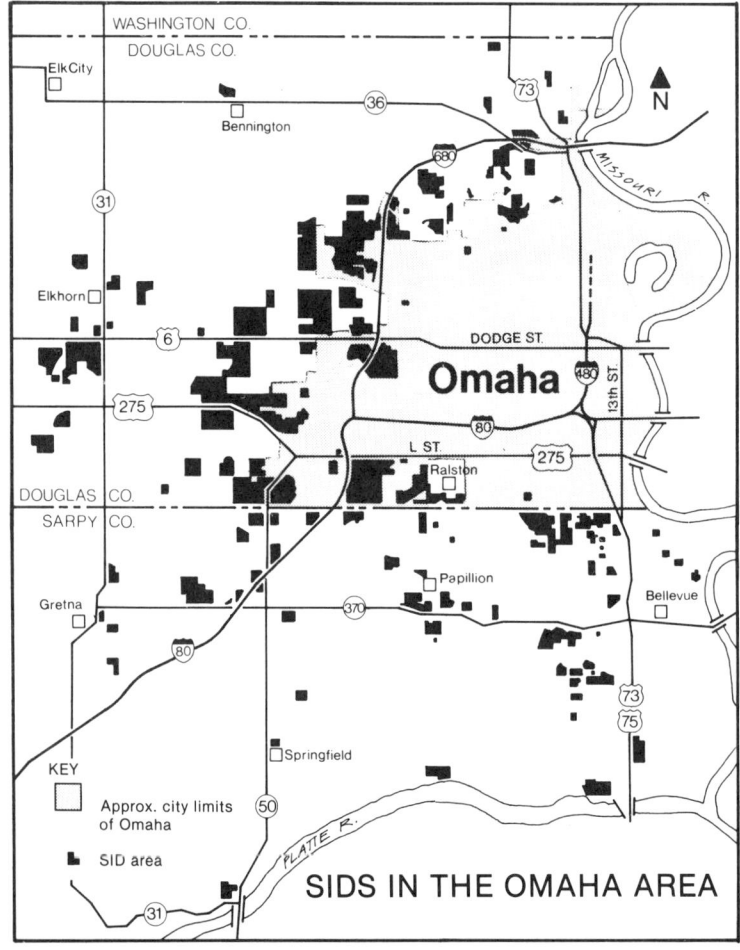

FIGURE 8.10. SIDs are unincorporated Sanitary and Improvement Districts. (*Omaha World Herald*)

drained soil, fairly level topography, and absence of noise pollution also influence developers' decisions.[30]

The presence of natural amenities makes some sites more desirable than others. Some Sarpy County developments are located along the Platte River, and the wooded bluffs along the Platte and north of Omaha near the Missouri River have attracted other developers (Figure 8.11). Amenities are typically reflected in the price of land, and they may partially compensate for the disadvantages of being a greater distance from the city.[31]

Finally, successful subdivisions attract others, and results in a clustered pattern. The selection of the site for the first development in a cluster depends on pioneer developers who correctly predict the directional thrust of suburban expansion.

> More venturesome developers attempt to read this thrust and to develop the cheaper land ahead of it. These "leapfroggers" assume or gamble that the leading edge will advance in their direction and thus will increase their site's access. . . . They may make the assumption, therefore, that the site is not at the moment in a prime location but that it will become so in time.[32]

Of course, by developing sites, developers help to fulfill their own prophecies about the direction in which the city will grow.

Other urbanites prefer to seek the good life in small-town Nebraska without giving up the employment, shopping, and social life of the city. Most villages and towns within easy commuting distance of Omaha or Lincoln are now bordered by suburban tract developments (Figure 8.12). Residents belong economically, and perhaps socially, to the city, but they reside in and utilize the services of the small town. Eagle, Palmyra, and Waverly (near Lincoln) and Springfield, Yutan, and Gretna (all near Omaha) vividly illustrate this trend (Table 8.3).

Impacts on Rural Areas

Urbanization of the countryside has had considerable impact on rural Nebraska. Land-use change is the most obvious effect. Land is converted from crop or livestock production to residential use, and roads are widened to handle increased traffic.[33] However, except for sites along major roads leading to town, farmland sold for individual residential plots appears to be that land least suitable for agriculture.[34] This is also often the case with larger develop-

FIGURE 8.11. Wooded sites are considered desirable locations for rural residential development.

FIGURE 8.12. Suburban tract development adjacent to the town of Springfield. (UNL, Cooperative Extension Service)

ments, particularly where they involve construction of a lake or include hilly, wooded terrain. Thus, the total amount of farmland converted to residential uses in Nebraska is but a small share of total farmland, except on the expanding edges of Omaha and Lincoln.

Farmers in the vicinity of buckshot urbanization and exurban developments have to deal with additional pressures on their operations. As urbanization moves into the countryside, land values rise because of the anticipation of further urban development.[35] Higher land values make farm expansion difficult, foster farm fragmentation, and result in higher property taxes. A dwindling number of farms is usually accompanied by a decline in the availability of agricultural services.[36]

Growing urbanization of the countryside eventually erodes farmers' political power and social and economic status. Complaints about standard farming practices may result in noise and odor regulations, restrictions on spraying, limitations on the use of roads for farm machinery, and other actions that

TABLE 8.3

POPULATION OF SELECTED TOWNS

ON THE URBAN FRINGE

Town	1960	1970	1980
Eagle	302	441	832
Gretna	745	1,557	1,609
Waverly	511	1,152	1,726
Yutan	335	507	631
Springfield	506	795	782
Palmyra	377	386	512

Source: U.S. Bureau of the Census, <u>1980 Census of Population</u> (Washington: Government Printing Office, 1981)

directly affect farming operations. Increased vandalism and a general upsetting of the existing rural order further weaken the position of farmers.[37]

The quality of the rural physical environment may be adversely affected by urban development. Many rural areas and small communities are ill equipped to provide adequate environmental services such as solid-waste disposal or pollution treatment. Water pollution from inadequate septic tanks is not uncommon.[38] Open space is lost through conversion of rural land to urban uses.

Urban growth in the countryside also affects the ability of small towns and villages to provide services desired by new residents. Pressure on local schools and roads may deplete already scarce funds and require increased taxes. Generally, owners of rural acreages and developments expect a higher level of services, such as libraries, roads, and fire protection, than is traditional in rural areas; this results in further strained relations with the farm population.[39]

The degree of impact depends on the nature of the development. The private, public, and social costs of small-town subdivisions are considerably less than the costs of leapfrog development. In 1976, the cost of building lots and house construction in the Gretna area was 69 percent higher in scattered developments than in compact developments adjacent to the town (Table 8.4). The larger lots in scattered developments cost nearly three times as much as those in compact developments, and school costs were nearly double. Street, police, and other government costs were higher in the developments adjacent to Gretna, but these are understated for scattered residential areas to the extent that their residents utilize Gretna's streets, playgrounds, and parks, which are supported only by Gretna taxpayers. Social and environmental costs were uniformly higher in the scattered pattern (Table 8.5), which also took more farmland out of production per housing unit.[40]

County zoning has been used to direct rural growth and minimize its undesirable effects. In 1975 the state legislature passed

TABLE 8.4

RESIDENTIAL DEVELOPMENT COSTS,

GRETNA, NEBRASKA

Category	Per Unit Costs in Constant 1975 Dollars		Difference	
	Compact Development Pattern	Scattered Development Pattern	Per Unit	Percent
Private Costs				
Building Lot	$ 4,657	$12,679	$ +8,022	+172.3
Construction	26,382	39,709	+13,327	+50.5
Subtotal	$31,039	$52,388	$+21,349	+68.8
Public Costs				
School	$ 1,443	$ 2,630	$ +1,187	+82.3
General Government	401	192	-209	-108.9
Street and Road	371	154	-217	-58.5
Police	62	41	-21	-51.2
Fire	2	11	+9	+450.0
Subtotal	$ 2,279	$ 3,028	$ +749	+32.9

Source: Paul S.T. Lee, "Cost of Compact vs. Scattered Land Use Development, A Case Study: Gretna, Nebraska," Review of Applied Urban Research 4, No. 9(September 1976):4. Used by permission of Center for Applied Urban Research, University of Nebraska-Omaha.

TABLE 8.5

SOCIAL AND ENVIRONMENTAL COSTS BY DEVELOPMENT

PATTERN, GRETNA, NEBRASKA

Category	Compact Development Pattern	Scattered Development Pattern
Crime	Lower	Higher
Natural Hazards	Less	Greater
Health and Sanitation	Better	Poor
Air, Water and Noise Pollution	Less	Higher
Wildlife Destruction	Less	Greater
Food Reduction	Less	Greater

Source: Paul S.T. Lee, "Cost of Compact vs. Scattered Land Use Development, A Case Study: Gretna, Nebraska," Review of Applied Urban Research 4, No. 9(September 1976):4. Used by permission of Center for Applied Urban Research, University of Nebraska-Omaha.

a bill requiring county-wide zoning in all counties containing a city of 5,000 to 100,000 people. Some communities, recognizing the high costs of providing services to scattered residential housing in farm areas, have adopted zoning ordinances. In an effort to slow conversion of land, some counties have established large minimum sizes for rural residential lots.[41]

Nebraska has also implemented a differential assessment scheme to attempt to protect agricultural land from urban encroachment. The state permits assessment of farmland at both its value for agricultural use and its true market value. Taxation takes place at the lower rate until the land is converted to nonagricultural uses, at which time deferred taxes on the difference between the two assessments become due.

Zoning and deferred taxation will not prevent continued proliferation of scattered housing. Large-lot zoning may actually result in greater rates of conversion of agricultural land. Tax incentives are helpful to individuals who intend to continue farming, but for those who are undecided or who intend to sell, the financial benefits of deferral "are slight when compared with the market value of developable land."[42] Both actions may, however, slow the rate of farmland conversion and help to direct urban expansion.

IRONIES OF RURAL-URBAN INTERACTION

Technological, economic, and social forces have blurred the distinctions between rural and urban Nebraskans. City and countryside differ little in income, availability of utilities, political preferences, or social activities. Yet the transportation and communications systems that gave farmers access to town and city now bring urban housing, lakes, boats and garbage trucks into the countryside. Ironically, the forces that dissolved rural-urban differences have generated rural-urban conflict. Access is a double-edged sword.

Urban Nebraskans, perhaps because of their rural backgrounds, have been attracted to the rural environment for its farms, fields, trees, streams, wildlife, and open space. They desire the best of both worlds with the disadvantages of neither—urban shopping and employment without urban densities, pollution, and crime; rural air and space without farm hours and drudgery.[43]

In their search they are joined by other urbanites with similar inclinations. In the process they not only disrupt the rural environment which they so avidly seek, but they bring with them some degree of the congestion, noise, and pressure on open space that they sought to escape. If they select a house in a prime rural residential area and the thrust of suburban expansion is in their direction, eventually they may be surrounded by the city.

Residential developments beyond the built-up limits of the city place pressures not only on farmers and rural communities but also on the city toward which they are oriented. The most pronounced impacts are generally associated with the largest urban complexes where dispersed development has diverted attention, funds, and growth from the heart of the city.

CHAPTER 9

URBAN NEBRASKA

Urban sprawl has had dramatic impacts on the form of cities in the late twentieth century. Yet the automobile, the factor most directly related to the contemporary physical expansion of Nebraska's cities, is only the latest in a series of technological and social forces that have shaped urban areas and the system of cities. For more than a century, changes in technology, economy, values, policy, and social structure have been reflected in the patterns of activities and land use in cities, in the urban landscape, and in the interrelationships among cities.

Local and national economic forces have influenced the uses to which urban land is put—commerce, industry, transportation, housing, and, on the outskirts, agriculture. Social forces such as race, ethnicity, and residential preferences have been reflected in the social geography of cities. The political process, including planning, has had a profound influence on urban growth and development, especially in recent years. The physical landscape has impeded urban growth in some directions, but has made expansion in other directions easier.

Perhaps most important, changing technology has influenced city growth and development. Construction technology has been an important factor in the appearance of the urban landscape; industrial technology has affected land-use needs, transportation demands, and the location of manufacturing; the physical expansion of cities and the spread of urban influence have been made possible by transportation technology. Patterns of streets and roads, retailing, industry, and housing are largely products of a succession of transportation systems.

Changing economic, social, political, and technological processes are reflected imperfectly in cities and urban systems. Features of earlier eras, formed under different conditions, persist. Networks of streets, railroads, and highways, for example, are modified slowly. Older buildings survive because of the investment they represent, because of their historic or aesthetic value, or at least because the cost of demolition is too high. In most Nebraska cities, nineteenth-century forces are clearly evident in contemporary landscapes and patterns.

Finally, cities are also products of the countryside. Most smaller cities have served as suppliers of rural areas—provisioning farmers and marketing farm products. Larger cities have generally been somewhat more diversified in function, but in economy, transportation, background, and outlook they remain closely tied to rural Nebraska.

CITIES OF THE PIONEER ERA: 1854–1880

In the western United States, cities were in the vanguard of the frontier (Figure 9.1).[1] In the earliest years of white settlement, few Nebraskans were concerned with the

FIGURE 9.1. Thirteenth and Farnam streets, Omaha, during the territorial period. The territorial capitol building is barely visible in the upper left. (NSHS)

development of an agricultural system, but most were interested in the profits to be made from investment in growing cities (see Chapter 2).

Cities of the territorial period performed specialized functions as transportation centers. Their prosperity depended upon their locations as outposts of a culture, rather than upon exploitation of local or regional resources.[2] Nebraska City and Omaha became the largest cities in 1860 because they were transshipment points—goods bound for the West had to be transferred from steamboats to wagons and, after 1865, to trains. A number of smaller towns—Plattsmouth, Brownville, St. Stephen, Wyoming—hoped to translate riverfront location into urban growth.

Even with freighting or the capital, early towns were small because they lacked a surrounding population sufficient to support large-scale retailing. Nebraska's peripheral location relative to the nation's population centers meant manufacturing was limited and could not be counted upon to sustain urban growth. Uncertainty surrounded the prospects of most of these early towns and cities. Investments were made with more hope than guarantee of a return. Consequently, the urban landscape of the territorial era exhibited an impermanent and haphazard appearance. Owners could hardly justify the high cost of good-quality buildings in a settlement that might not exist in a year or two. In Omaha and other cities the earliest construction "was designed for expedient development rather than design quality."[3] Even the first state capitol built in Lincoln was so poorly constructed that it had to be replaced in little over a decade.[4]

Few buildings from this earliest period remain in Nebraska. Shoddily erected commercial buildings were replaced by more substantial structures after the Civil War. Many early log cabins and board shacks that sufficed during the territorial speculative boom were likewise supplanted by more permanent residences. A few well-built houses were constructed in early settlements, but in Omaha subsequent expansion of the commercial district into surrounding residential neighborhoods resulted in the razing of many early homes. A number of residences from the territorial era still stand in Nebraska City and Brownville.

The Union Pacific Railroad gave Omaha access to the markets, goods, and population centers to the east and west. It quickly became the wholesale, retail, and transportation center of the state, a position it has held ever since. It easily survived removal of the capital to the prairie village of Lancaster (soon to be renamed Lincoln) in 1868. Other cities were substantially smaller than this primate city as early as 1870.[5]

As farms were established and grew in number, cities and towns began to serve central-place functions—that is, they developed as retail and service centers for surrounding rural populations. To be sure, many towns continued as transportation centers, particularly Omaha and such smaller places along the Union Pacific main line as North Platte and Sidney. Because a complex rail network did not develop until the 1880s, the urban system was still in its infancy and the rail links were not sufficient to have integrated the state's central places into a tightly knit hierarchy.

The railroad brought prosperity and growth to towns and cities, but nowhere to as great a degree as Omaha. It was still a frontier community in many ways, with muddy streets, taverns on every corner, numerous gambling halls, and dozens of bordellos, but the city also acquired a library, theaters, schools (both public and private), and numerous churches. By 1870, the growing city was developing distinctive spatial segregation of land uses. Immediately northeast of downtown were the Union Pacific yards. Rail lines ran along the east edge of downtown and turned southwest, following a valley that penetrated the bluffs. The growing working class was found in proximity to the rails both north and south of downtown. The elite class, in contrast, concentrated between 18th and 20th streets on the hill overlooking the heart of the city.[6] This early socioeconomic pattern has persisted to the present to a remarkable degree.

BOOM AND EXPANSION—OMAHA AND LINCOLN: 1880–1920

Omaha was vibrant and growing during the 1870s, with an 1880 population of thirty thousand. Even more rapid growth occurred during the next decade. The 1880s boom, which affected Lincoln, Kearney, Beatrice, Norfolk, Hastings, and other cities in addition to Omaha (Figure 9.2), was built upon industrial and agricultural development, as well as speculative optimism.[7]

One of the largest smelting companies in the world, located in Omaha, employed one thousand workers by 1892. Other important industries included lead works, iron works, brick manufacturing, food processing, distilling, and brewing.[8]

The most important manufacturing activity, however, was large-scale meat packing which began in the mid-1880s.[9] Omaha's rail access to eastern markets was certainly a major factor in its success as a meat-packing center, but the industry could not thrive until sufficient agricultural development had occurred in surrounding rural communities. Much of Nebraska and western Iowa, Omaha's hinterland, was still in a stage of transition from pioneer to commercial agriculture prior to 1880. During

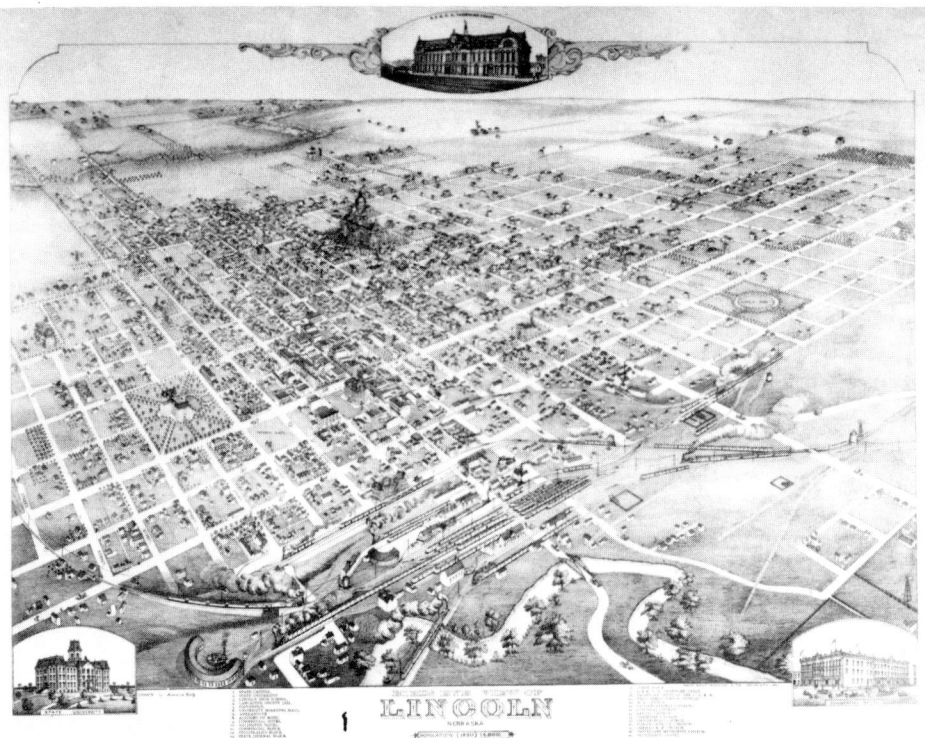

FIGURE 9.2. Bird's-eye view of Lincoln, 1880, looking southeast. The University of Nebraska is in the left center of the photograph; the capitol is in the upper center. The city was mostly confined to the area between 6th and 18th streets. (NSHS)

the 1880s expansion of the rail network provided nearly every community with access to modern transportation and made Omaha a logical point to which farmers would ship livestock.

Omaha's manufacturing activities—mostly basic, or income-generating, activities—brought money into the city and the state and fueled additional urban growth and commercial expansion. Every job in manufacturing, particularly in industries that exported their products, meant additional jobs in retailing and services. Workers in the packing houses patronized grocers, clothiers, carpenters, saloons, and coal dealers, all of which increased in number as the number of manufacturing jobs grew. Retail and service workers required goods and services in turn, leading to an upward spiral in nonbasic, or income-circulating, employment—a multiplier effect.[10] The city developed a thriving retail district to supply this growing urban market.

As rural counties filled up with farmers and as rail density increased, Nebraska's urban system blossomed during the 1870s and 1880s. Omaha secured its position at the top of the emerging urban hierarchy. The rail system connected the rural population to the commercial outlets of Omaha. The city became a wholesaling center for the state and for much of western Iowa, supplying dry goods, shoes and boots, agricultural implements, hardware, and groceries to merchants in the hinterland.[11] Some of the manufacturing activities of the city, such as brewing and distilling, also depended upon that expanding population.

Lincoln, second in size and influence, served a smaller local and regional market. Through its rail connections, it became an important wholesale center for Beatrice, Hastings, York, Crete, Fairbury, and other cities south and west of the capital. Omaha dominated most of the third-order central places—Nebraska City, Grand Island, Kearney, Fremont, and Plattsmouth—as well as emerging centers such as Norfolk, North Platte, and Columbus, which served smaller regional markets with specialized retail goods and services. Smaller places provided local populations with low-order goods—groceries, general merchandise, and some services.[12]

Urban Real Estate

Industrial expansion in the 1880s generated dramatic population growth (Table 9.1). Omaha doubled its population in the first five years of the decade and grew to over 100,000 by 1890. Lincoln doubled in size between 1885 and 1887. City promoters, officials, developers, and landowners, almost giddy from the boom psychology of the period, predicted even more growth in the years ahead.[13] Real estate speculation was rampant. In 1880, Omaha contained only five thousand residential dwellings. One thousand more were built in the next two years. In 1887, at the peak of the boom, more than two thousand houses were constructed.[14] Developers rushed to cash in on growth. Fashionable suburbs for the elite of Omaha and Lincoln were promoted. Subdivisions were platted

TABLE 9.1

POPULATION GROWTH IN NEBRASKA CITIES,

1880-1890

	1880	1885	% change 1880-1885	1890[a]	% change[a] 1880-1890
Omaha	30,518	61,835	102	140,452 (102,430)	360 (236)
Lincoln	13,003	20,004	53	55,154 (34,440)	324 (165)
Nebraska City	4,183	5,597	34	11,494 (7,550)	175 (80)
Plattsmouth	4,175	5,796	39	8,392 (5,910)	101 (42)
Fremont	3,013	4,014	33	6,747	124
Grand Island	2,963	5,040	70	7,536	154
Hastings	2,817	7,980	183	13,584 (6,000)	382 (113)
Beatrice	2,447	5,211	113	13,836 (8,460)	465 (246)
Columbus	2,131	2,573	21	3,134	47
York	1,259	2,085	66	3,405	170
Crete	1,870	2,258	21	2,310	24
Kearney	1,782	3,601	102	8,074	353
Falls City	1,583	2,070	31	2,102	33
Blair	1,317	2,132	62	2,069	57
Fairbury	1,251	1,423	14	2,630	110
Norfolk	547	1,949	256	3,038	455
North Platte	363	2,540	600	3,055	742
McCook	---	1,254	---	2,346	---
Holdrege	---	1,026	---	2,601	---

[a]Figures in parentheses are estimated populations for six cities shown to have had incorrect census counts for 1890. Edgar Z. Palmer, "The Correctness of the 1890 Census of Population for Nebraska Cities," Nebraska History 32(1951):259-67.

Source: U.S. Censuses of Population; 1885 Census of Nebraska.

> **Focus: Kountze Place—An Early Omaha Suburb**
>
> Banker Herman Kountze was one man who sought to cash in on the real estate boom in Omaha. On land he had owned since the 1860s he developed Kountze Place between Locust and Pratt, 16th to 24th. The cornfields of North Omaha slowly gave way to housing with one of the first dwellings built . . . in 1886. The following two years witnessed rapid growth in the new suburb with approximately thirty new homes each year. . . .
>
> The North Omaha neighborhood received a boost with the decision to hold the 1898 Trans-Mississippi Exposition on a portion of the development north of Pinkney Street. The great fair made Omahans aware of that part of the city and encouraged building nearby. Impact was not immediate in Kountze Place, but home construction began to increase in the suburb after 1903. . . . Kountze Park was laid out on the former Grand Court of the Exposition between Pinkney and Pratt, 19th to 21st. . . .
>
> As an upper middle class suburb in the 1880s, Kountze Place exhibited some of the most stylish architecture in the city. Many of the residents hired architects to design their homes and the result showed late Victorian, Queen Anne, and Colonial Revival styles. . . . All three members of one of the most prominent architectural firms in the city, Mendelssohn, Fisher, and Lawrie, chose to reside in Kountze Place. . . . The suburb had its share of prominent businessmen, too. . . . While Kountze Place developed primarily as a residential suburb, it also held a number of institutions, including the Presbyterian Theological Seminary and several churches. . . .
>
> Kountze Place retained its character until the 1940s when the longtime residents could no longer maintain the large homes. Many dwellings were divided into apartments during World War II and their former owners moved to newer homes. The Seminary closed during the war, and the churches declined as fewer neighborhood residents supported them. . . . The area also began to experience racial transition as Blacks were slowly able to push out of their restricted living area farther south. The North Presbyterian Church building provided an illustration of neighborhood change. The Presbytery gave the building, which formerly housed a white congregation, to a Black congregation and re-named it Calvin Memorial Presbyterian. . . .
>
> *Source:* Garneth O. Peterson, "Historical Framework," in *A Comprehensive Program for Historic Preservation in Omaha* (Omaha: Omaha City Planning Department, 1980), pp. 26–28, reprinted by permission.

as far from downtown Omaha as the town of Benson, well beyond the urbanized area of the period.[15]

Although the wealthy neighborhoods expanded, the greatest population growth was among the working classes. The prime determinant of the location of working-class neighborhoods continued to be the railroad. In Lincoln, these communities clustered along the rail lines running north and south from the west edge of downtown. In Omaha, workers were concentrated south of downtown and in South Omaha, a town laid out when the packing industry was developed. Earliest settlement in South Omaha was between 23rd Street and the railroads, south of H Street.[16]

Intracity Transportation

The physical expansion of Omaha and Lincoln would not have been possible without the development of a transportation system to move people with reasonable speed from one place to another. Street railways, initially powered by horses, were in place in Omaha as early as 1867 and were electrified in the late 1880s. By 1890, 90 mi (145 km) of streetcar lines connected South Omaha to Omaha and extended north and northwest from downtown as far as 40th and Cuming and 22nd and Ames (Figure 9.3). By 1912 electrified rails reached as far as Bellevue, Florence, the developing suburbs of Benson and Dundee, and Council Bluffs, Iowa. The growth of the city and the extension of street railways went hand in hand.[17] Lincoln's street railways encouraged early expansion to the south and later to the east (Figure 9.4).

Streetcars also facilitated the separation of workplace from residence and the increased specialization of land use. Workers

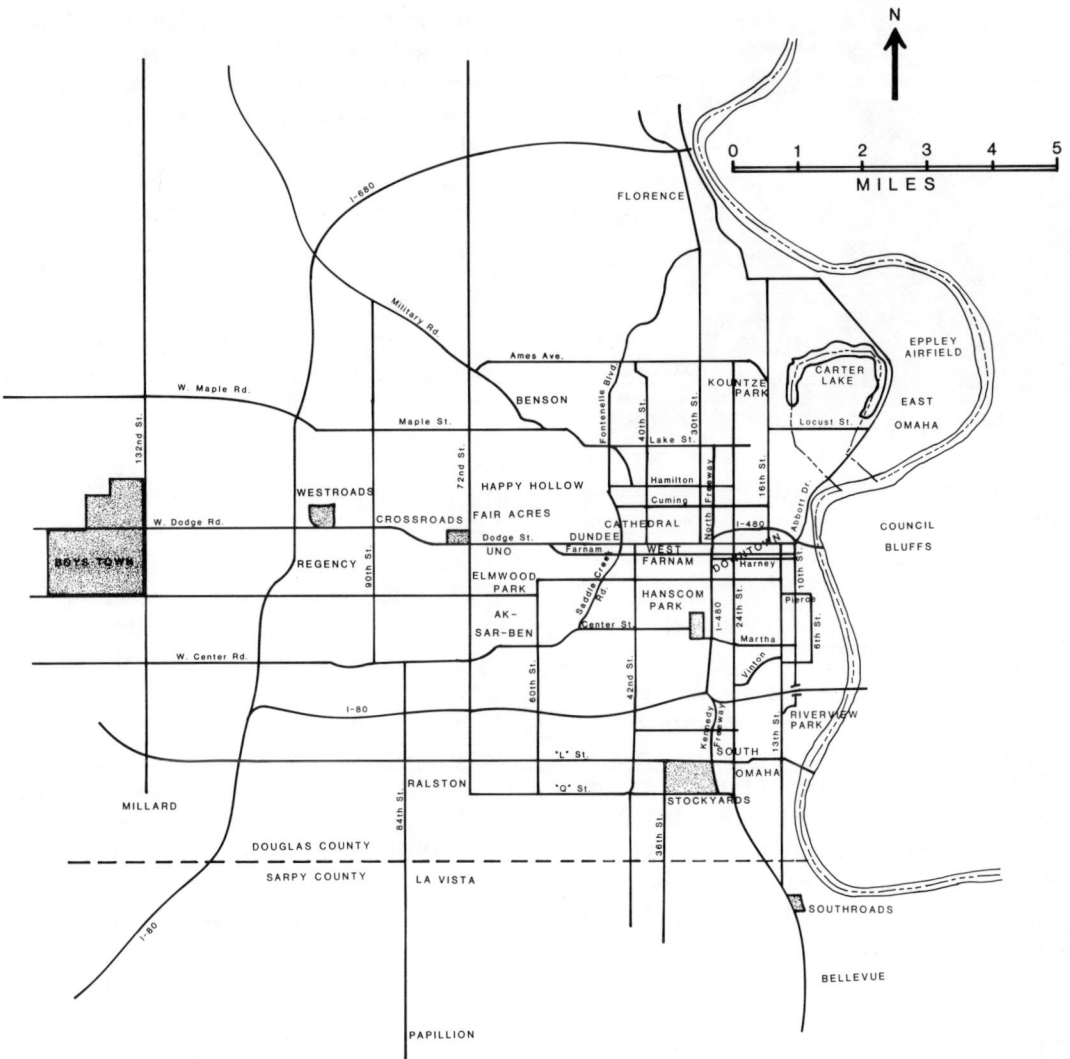

FIGURE 9.3. Omaha today.

no longer had to live in or near the city core, but could spread out into almost exclusively residential neighborhoods. The process of residential development became more specialized, as entire neighborhoods were laid out and planned from the ground up. Other parts of the city became specialized industrial or commercial districts. Mass transit also permitted greater scale in industrial and commercial operations.

Depression in the 1890s ended the real estate and transportation boom, but renewed prosperity after the turn of the century resulted in additional expansion. By 1920 Omaha contained 191,000 people, nearly double its size in 1900. Lincoln grew at a more moderate rate in this period, but by 1930 it housed 76,000 people, compared to 40,000 in 1900.

This phenomenal population growth was a product of migration from rural areas as well as from Europe. Workers, unskilled and semiskilled, flocked to the nation and the cities of Nebraska in the forty years from 1880 to 1920. Omaha's attraction was jobs in industries, packing plants, and railroads. Lincoln, with less industry, offered employment with the railroad.

FIGURE 9.4. A typical streetcar in Lincoln, 1908. (NSHS)

Ethnic Neighborhoods

Even before the period of rapid expansion, Omaha was a city of immigrants. Nearly a third of the city's residents in 1880 were foreign born (Table 9.2); immigrants and their children accounted for more than half the city's numbers. Germans, Irish, and Swedes were the most numerous foreigners in the frontier city and continued to live fairly close to the industrial sections of the city that provided employment. The Irish, for example, were concentrated near the Union Pacific shops. Germans clustered to the south of downtown, and Swedes were found mostly north of Dodge. A small, but growing, community of Czechs (Bohemians) was developing along south 13th and 14th streets (Figure 9.5).[18]

Urban expansion after 1880 drew more immigrants to Omaha and Lincoln. Lincoln, the capital city, was home to Germans and particularly to Russian Germans from the Volga region. The latter group concentrated along the rail lines north and south of town in the district still known as "Russian Bottoms." Omaha was ethnically more diverse. Toward the end of the century migrants from eastern and southern Europe became especially numerous and were more likely to cluster in one neighborhood than were the earlier groups. Italians established three settlements: Northern Italians were found north of downtown around 18th and Izard; Calabrese were concentrated near 24th and Poppleton; and Sicilians dominated an area just south and east of downtown near 6th and Pierce (Figure 9.6). Poles clustered near the Sheely Packing Company at 27th and Martha. Czechs continued to live on south 13th Street, but the development of the stockyards and the meatpacking industry drew many to South Omaha, east of the yards. In 1910 nearly one in eight residents of the city of South Omaha had been born in the Austro-Hungarian Empire—most of them were Czechs.[19]

Immediately south and southwest of the stockyards was a most diverse ethnic enclave. Here lived Lithuanians, Romanians, Serbs, Croatians, Hungarians, Slovenians, Greeks, and blacks. After World War I Mexican immigrants also entered this neighborhood.[20]

Blacks were located in Omaha as early as the 1860s, but their numbers grew rapidly after 1910, when they became concentrated on the near north side. The 24th and Lake area emerged as an important black business district during the teens. As late as 1930, however, the black community did not extend farther north than Maple Street and was located generally west of 20th. Jews also located on the north side, particularly north 24th Street, although another Jewish cluster was found on south 10th.[21]

Patterns in Streetcar Cities

Internally linked by electric streetcars, Omaha developed in an elongated fashion. Streetcar service spurred expansion to the south and north of downtown, but growth to the west occurred more slowly. By the eve of World War I, the city extended from Harrison Street on the Sarpy county line to the village of Florence—a north-south distance of 9 mi (15 km). Except in Benson, little development in Omaha took place west of 54th Street (only 4 mi—6.4 km—west of the Missouri River) until the 1920s.

Focus: The West Farnam and Cathedral Districts

The West Farnam area developed as an upper class suburb at the turn of the century. During its heyday from 1900 to 1920 the Gold Coast, as the West Farnam area was also called, housed the city's elite and was the site of dinners, dances, and weddings which set the standard for social activities in Omaha. The term "West Farnam" referred to not only a street, but a district including 32nd Avenue to 40th Street, Jones to Davenport. . . . Homes in the Cathedral neighborhood [immediately to the north] were generally not as elaborate as in West Farnam. . . . The district was settled after 1900 as the structure from which the neighborhood took its name began to rise.

Some of the earliest homes in the West Farnam area included those of Gurdon Wattles and Edward A. Cudahy on South 37th Street, F. B. Kirkendall's home at 3727 Jackson, and one built at 3716 Jones for the president of the Burlington Railroad. Other residents moved in after 1900 and the neighborhood began to exhibit the various period revival styles of architecture then in vogue. Some of the house types included English, Colonial, Georgian, Gothic, Tudor, and Romanesque. . . . Gottlieb Storz, the brewer, built a Jacobethan Revival stone house near 37th and Farnam in 1907. Storz's home, designed by Thomas Kimball and costing $16,000, featured classical moldings and columns, a Tiffany skylight, and fireplaces with a mosaic design. . . .

Although much of the Cathedral neighborhood was built as the new church went up, settlement began in the district as early as the 1880s, with the establishment of Sacred Heart Convent at 36th and Burt. The growth spurt of the 1880s brought more residents into the area since [a] . . . car line . . . provided ready access to downtown. The most expensive home . . . of the Cathedral District was George Joslyn's "castle" at 39th and Davenport. The $160,000 Scottish Baronial castle reflected the homes of Andrew Carnegie on the East Coast and in Scotland. . . .

By 1900 over twenty homes, mostly one and one-half to two stories, stood in the Cathedral neighborhood. A building boom in the first decade of the century brought thirty-one new home starts. Prices ranged from $1,900 to $30,000, although the average home cost about $5,800, easily affordable by middle and upper middle class families. . . .

Like the Gold Coast to the south, the Cathedral District's heyday lasted until the 1920s when yet another generation of sons and daughters would leave the drafty old mansions and move farther west to the new suburbs of Fairacres and Happy Hollow. The character of the neighborhood was altered as the number of professionals and proprietors of large business firms began to decrease and unskilled laborers moved into the duplexes and apartments which made up a majority of construction in the district by the 1920s. The exclusive homes on North 38th Street remained somewhat exempt from the neighborhood changes.

Although both the West Farnam and Cathedral neighborhoods changed after 1920, they continued to hold some of the character along North 38th Street and in parts of the Gold Coast. The conversion to more multi-family dwellings occurred only gradually in the decades after 1920 and thus the districts maintained a number of single-family homes. The two neighborhoods characterized the elegance of life for the upper classes in Omaha before the social changes brought on by World War I rendered them relics of an earlier age.

Source: Garneth O. Peterson, "Historic Framework," in *A Comprehensive Program for Historic Preservation in Omaha* (Omaha: Omaha City Planning Department, 1980), pp. 44–45, reprinted by permission.

TABLE 9.2

FOREIGN-BORN POPULATION OF OMAHA, 1870-1980

	Foreign-Born Population	Percent of total Population
1870	6,320	39.3
1880	9,930	32.5
1890	35,039	24.9
1900	23,552	23.0
1910	34,902	23.2
1920	35,381	18.6
1930	28,788	13.5
1940	22,311	10.0
1950	17,304	6.9
1960	14,383	4.7
1970	10,737	3.1
1980	10,164	3.2

Source: U.S. Censuses of Population

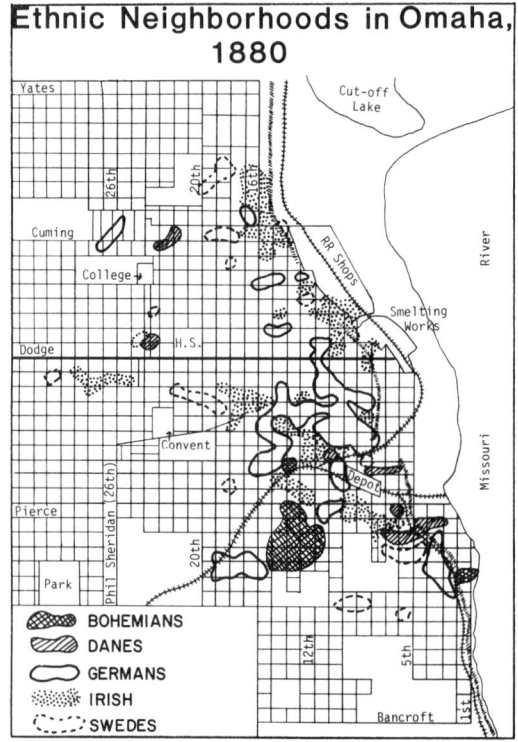

FIGURE 9.5. (Kathleen Louise Fimple)

FIGURE 9.6. Row housing was rare in Omaha. These houses are on south 6th Street.

> **Focus: Development of Omaha's Black Community**
>
> Blacks came to Nebraska as early as the 1860s and the 1870s and found jobs as ranch hands or on the construction gangs of the Union Pacific and the Burlington. The first "Great Exodus" of Blacks from the South occurred during the 1870s. Few possessed job skills, so most of the work open to them was in personal services, working as porters, waiters, and janitors. A few found jobs in the packing plants, smelter, or on the railroad, but these opportunities were limited since Blacks were competing with European immigrants for the available positions. The depression of the 1890s caused the Black population in the state to drop as many lost their jobs and left to try their luck elsewhere.
>
> The number of Blacks increased slowly from the turn of the century until World War I when the second great migration from the South began. Since many of their regular workers had gone to war after 1917, the packing plants paid the train fare for hundreds of southern Blacks to travel to Nebraska, while the railroads cooperated by granting the packers reduced rates for groups of twenty-five persons or more. This Exodus peaked in 1918 and brought in workers with job skills.
>
> Although the Black community in Omaha became most visible in the Teens and 1920s, it had existed . . . for several decades. Churches generally indicate the existence of a community and at least three of them served the Omaha Blacks before 1880: St. John's African Methodist Episcopal, organized 1865; African Baptist, organized 1874; and St. Philip the Deacon (Episcopal), organized 1878. St. John's built a structure on the corner of Webster and 18th Streets in 1867. Zion Church completed its new building at 23rd and Grant in the early 1890s. St. Philip the Deacon was at 19th and Cuming.
>
> Although 14th and Dodge provided a center for the Black community, they lived all over the city through the Teens. However, many of them tended to congregate on the Near North Side up to Lake Street around churches and businesses, or in South Omaha near the packinghouses. The great numbers of Blacks who arrived during the late Teens and early Twenties moved into Omaha's Near North Side, generally between 24th and 30th south of Lake Street. The . . . center of the community . . . gradually shifted to North 24th Street, which became the main business district for Blacks . . . in the 1920s.
>
> *Source:* Garneth O. Peterson, "Historical Framework," in *A Comprehensive Program for Historic Preservation in Omaha* (Omaha: Omaha City Planning Department, 1980), pp. 59–60, 70, reprinted by permission.

This city of 200,000, though compact by modern standards, was not crowded. Unlike larger eastern cities, where high residential population densities developed, Omaha's period of most rapid growth coincided with the mass-transit era. The burgeoning population did not have to be housed within walking distance of the downtown or the principal employment centers, but could be transported by the streetcar. As a consequence, Omaha (as well as Lincoln and the smaller cities in Nebraska) became a city of small, detached dwellings on rather large lots. Tenements were virtually unknown, and most residential structures housed no more than three families.[22]

Both Omaha and Lincoln took advantage of lower densities and developed extensive park systems. In Omaha, Hanscom Park and Riverview Park were in use by the end of the nineteenth century. Soon thereafter the city park board had acquired a number of additional parks and created a system of boulevards to link them.[23] Lincoln established parks both within the city and on the outskirts.

Although street railways made possible the decentralization of population in Omaha and Lincoln in the late nineteenth and early twentieth centuries, the circulation of goods within both cities was still tied to horses. The delivery of goods to and from cities relied almost exclusively on railroads. Wholesaling and industry were spatially constrained by their need for rail links to bring in raw materials and to ship out

FIGURE 9.7. Rail lines leading away from downtown Omaha spurred development of the industrial sector of the city. Nearby are working-class neighborhoods. (Union Pacific Railroad)

finished products. Until the internal combustion engine became widely used, these activities were confined to the older cores of Omaha and Lincoln and to the rail lines radiating outward from the cores. Similar constraints operated in those smaller cities with manufacturing and wholesaling activities.

The pattern of land use in both Lincoln and Omaha closely resembled the idealized structure of Hoyt's sectoral model of urban form.[24] In Omaha, manufacturing districts developed along the rail lines leading north and southwest of the city center (Figure 9.7). In Lincoln the same activities paralleled railroads northeast of downtown, where low-income neighborhoods also developed.

Omaha's wealthy moved west from their earliest clusters near the old territorial capitol. Lincoln's elite built south and later southeast of the Central Business District (CBD). Most middle-class expansion took place between the upper-income and lower-income sectors. These socioeconomic wedges, which emerged early in the history of both cities, have remained remarkably persistent to the present, except for some erosion of upper-class dominance near the CBD. In this sense, Omaha's Regency district is a sectoral successor to Capitol Hill, West Farnam, and Happy Hollow.

Commercial activity continued to cluster in the downtown area—the focus of streetcar lines—although some retailing also developed along south 13th, south 6th, and north and south 24th streets. These locations were accessible by streetcar and were among the more important ethnic neighborhoods in the city.[25]

AUTOMOBILES AND DECENTRALIZATION: 1920-1950

With the growing adoption of the automobile in the 1910s and 1920s, residential decentralization intensified. Omaha's population began to move west, and the city surrounded and incorporated the suburbs of Dundee and Benson. Lincoln expanded to the east and the towns of Belmont, College View, Havelock, and University Place became integrated into the city. High rates of auto ownership not only permitted families to live considerable distances from places of employment, but made possible larger lot sizes and a further reduction in residential density.

Low housing densities worked to the detriment of mass-transit systems. Streetcar systems were unable to fully serve the early automobile suburbs; these housed fewer potential riders, and their residents had access to personal transportation. This diffuse, low-density residential pattern continues to plague efforts to revitalize mass-transportation systems in Omaha and Lincoln.

Commercial and Industrial Patterns

As people moved their residences farther from the historic centers of the cities, commercial enterprises were drawn toward and into the new automobile suburbs. Major business centers developed in outlying districts and provided a wide range of mass-market consumer items. Strip commercial developments attracted automobile-related businesses, such as car dealers and service stations; those that required extensive floor space, such as furniture stores; or those that relied upon access to a highly mobile population. In Omaha, west Dodge Street, north 30th, L Street, and 72nd Street gradually usurped these functions from downtown and South Omaha. Lincoln businesses moved outward along O Street and eventually along 27th Street and north 48th. Even so, the downtowns remained the premier shopping areas in both cities and in smaller places until well after World War II. Here shoppers converged on specialty stores, clothing stores, and large department stores.[26]

In the same period industry also became more decentralized, but movement toward the suburbs was considerably slower than that of residential or commercial land use. A few industrial parks were developed on the periphery of both large and small cities, but dependence on rail transportation held many industries in the older industrial districts. Nevertheless, high land values in the center of cities, the congestion in such areas, and the growing importance of trucks for long-distance shipment of goods were significant centrifugal forces for manufacturing, and decentralization became more pronounced after World War II.[27]

Patterns in Small Cities

Land-use changes associated with the automobile in Omaha and Lincoln were replicated on a reduced scale in the smaller cities of the state. Most places with more than a few thousand people developed commercial strips, occupied by gas stations, auto dealers, and other functions oriented toward auto traffic. Most commerce, however, remained on Main Street. Until the 1960s, most smaller cities had thriving downtowns that included not only department stores, dime stores, banks, and hardware dealers but also groceries, restaurants, and other retail activities that had begun to decentralize in the larger cities. Churches and social organizations also clustered downtown, and government functions such as post offices and high schools were found in the downtown area.

This continued focus on the downtown reflected the relatively compact nature of smaller cities, few of which exhibited much peripheral residential growth before the late 1950s. It also was a product of the age of Nebraska's cities and towns. Most churches, schools, and businesses were established in the 1880s or around the turn of the century, an era when new construction was found almost entirely downtown. Agricultural depression in the 1920s, general economic depression in the 1930s, and war and recovery from it in the 1940s and early 1950s precluded new construction, and the older buildings continued to function satisfactorily.

When new construction became possible by the late 1950s, many institutions found they could only obtain sufficient land on the fringes of small cities. Almost universal automobile ownership made such locations acceptable, and downtown locations were gradually abandoned. Some businesses took the same outbound path, though the pace was slower. For most, the locational advantages of an established shopping district continued to outweigh the lure of greater expanses of land with better access and parking. Unlike Omaha and Lincoln, with their emerging shopping centers, most small cities could provide no similarly attractive alternative, and businesses stayed downtown.

THE SPRAWLING CITY: 1950–1980

By the middle of the 1950s, Lincoln, Omaha, and Nebraska's smaller cities were still fairly compact units. In Omaha, for example, suburban residential expansion had not yet pushed to the southwest of Ak-Sar-Ben. In Lincoln, open countryside predominated only 3 mi (4.8 km) east of downtown. Yet Omaha's population was over 250,000 and Lincoln had more than 100,000 people.

Residential Suburbanization

During the next decade and beyond, both cities grew rapidly in numbers and explosively in land area. Between 1950 and 1970, Omaha added 100,000 people, and Lincoln added 50,000. Omaha's suburban residential developments were scattered throughout Douglas and Sarpy counties—the contiguous built-up area stretched as far as Papillion on the southwest and past Boys Town on the west. Lincoln had fewer leapfrog developments in the countryside, but residential areas were located as far as 5 mi (8 km) east and south of downtown.

The causes of this growth are to be found in the cost and technology of transportation. During the postwar era, energy was abundant and inexpensive. Automobile use dominated urban transportation, whereas mass-transit use declined to a trickle. With widespread auto ownership came pressure for street and road improvement and construction. Development of the interstate highway system during the 1960s affected Omaha in particular. The city was not only connected by expressway with distant points in all directions, but was internally linked, as well. Suburbanites, especially on the southwest edge of the city, were able to abandon the slow, congested lanes of older streets in favor of the highspeed interstate corridor. Commuters could opt for even more distant residential locations, yet retain good access to the city. As a consequence, Omaha's growth was much more rapid to the southwest than in other directions.

It would be a serious mistake, however, to credit or blame only the interstate highway with urban expansion, at least in Nebraska. Many growing cities had no interstate highway at all, and some that lay along the interstate route exhibited expansion in all directions, not just along the high-speed highway. In fact Lincoln has grown rapidly *away* from the interstate highway, with only modest growth along or near the expressway. Other factors in expansion included the general availability and low cost of auto travel, the demand for larger lots and larger houses, and a preference for living close to a rural environment. In the expansion of the 1960s and 1970s, lot size increased markedly, overall urban population density dropped, and travel distances increased.

Lincoln continued to grow asymmetrically to the east and southeast. Land north and west of the city was less desirable because of frequent flooding of low-lying areas along Salt Creek and because of the predominance of industry and rail lines. The more popular residential areas have, for the most part, been on the hills overlooking the city from the southeast.

In Omaha, urban expansion during the

1960s and 1970s spread well beyond the city limits, particularly west and southwest of the city (Figure 9.8). Millard, which had fewer than four hundred residents in 1950, grew to over six thousand by 1970, the year before Omaha annexed it.

Older portions of Omaha began to lose population. Most areas east of 42nd Street declined during the 1960s. During the 1970s the area of loss moved to and beyond 72nd Street. Greatest population gains occurred in the most distant suburbs. By contrast, some neighborhoods in north Omaha lost more than half their populations during the decade (compare Figures 9.3 and 9.9 for location of census tracts). Outmigration was the rule in south Omaha, as well, but decreases were not as dramatic as north of Dodge Street.[28]

Changing Ethnic and Racial Patterns

Omaha neighborhoods showing the greatest outmigration and population decrease between 1970 and 1980 were predominantly black. Most black majority census tracts lost population during the 1970s, as blacks moved northwestward (compare Figues 9.3 and 9.10 for location of census tracts). In thirteen census tracts, black population increased and white population declined. These areas are labeled as "new entry" and "succession" in Figure 9.11. In two census tracts near downtown the white share of the population increased; this suggests displacement of blacks by whites.

As a result of rapid spatial expansion of the black community, racial segregation in Omaha appears to be decreasing. In

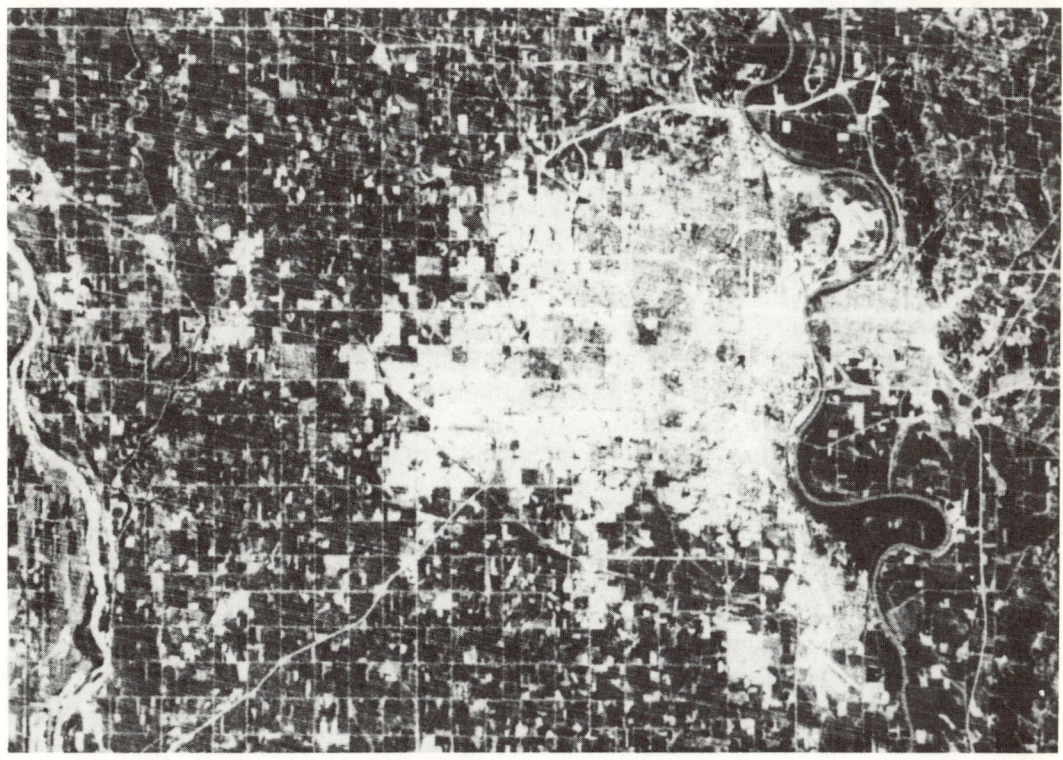

FIGURE 9.8. Satellite view of Omaha, with Council Bluffs, Iowa, across Missouri River, to east. Note the city's growth in the direction of Interstate 80 (the white line leading southwest). The city has also grown along transportation routes to the south (Bellevue is along the river, and Papillion is several miles to the west). A shortage of connections to the north has slowed suburban expansion in that direction. (Landsat photo)

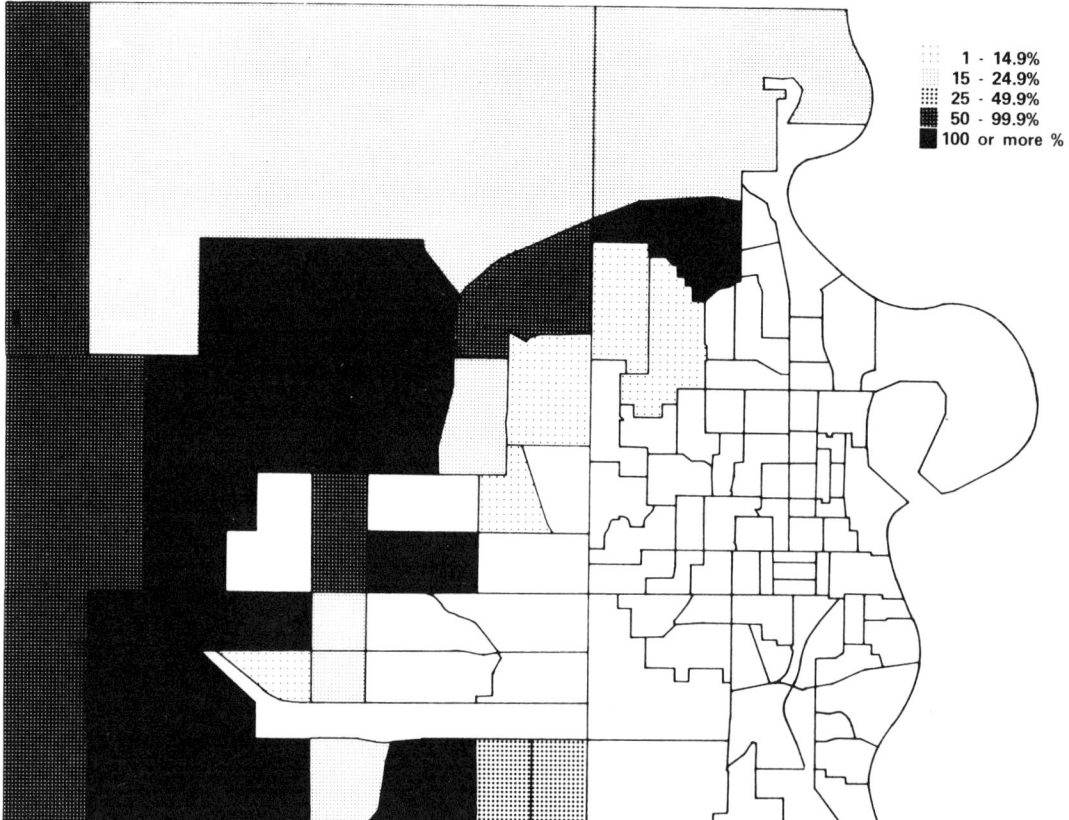

FIGURE 9.9. Percent population change in Douglas County by census tract, 1970–1980. (UNO) *A* (above) percent gain. *B* (facing page) percent loss.

1970, 19 percent of all blacks lived in census tracts that were 90 percent black, and only 25 percent lived in tracts where blacks were in the minority. By 1980, only 10 percent of all blacks lived in 90 percent black census tracts, and 47.5 percent lived in black minority tracts.[29]

Other population groups are more dispersed than blacks. The two thousand Indians in the Omaha area are widely distributed throughout the older parts of the city. The approximately eight thousand persons of Spanish origin have concentrated in south Omaha, but in no census tract do they constitute one-fourth of the population. Jews reside principally in a belt extending due west from downtown. In no area, however, do they constitute over 4 percent of total population.[30]

Except for blacks, ethnic and racial groups have been and remain interspersed with one another.[31] Even fairly segregated nationalities have never dominated large areas. For example, in 1912 the residents of 1108 and 1110 south Sixth Street, the heart of the Italian community, included the following surnames: Madigazzio, Piccolo, Pinis, Brtez, Kowski, Nelson, and Swope.[32] As immigrants became acculturated, ethnic residential patterns became less apparent. Only blacks became more segregated,[33] the process just now being reversed.

Omaha retains some persistent ethnic neighborhoods—identifiable by virtue of popular awareness and visible expressions of ethnic background. These ethnic icons help label neighborhoods as Czech, Jewish, or Italian, even though the population of

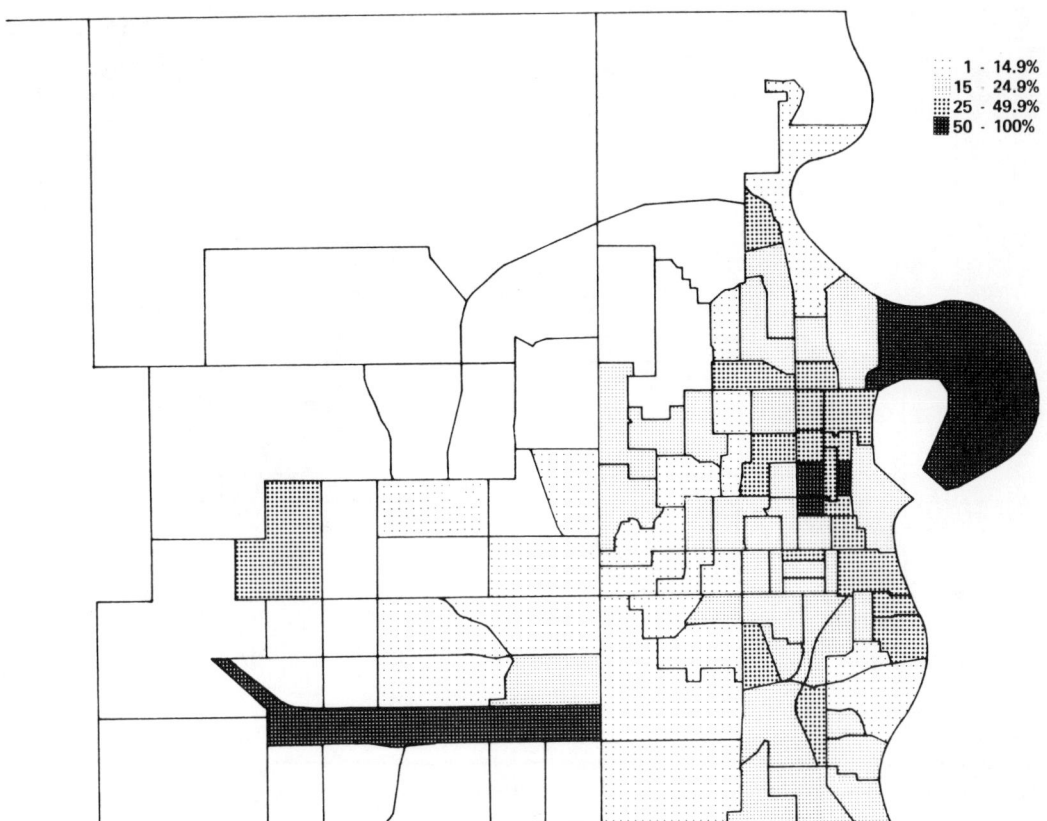

FIGURE 9.9 (continued).

the district might be quite diverse. On south 13th Street even the casual passerby can see the Bohemian Cafe, Vocelka's Bar, Masek's Bakery, the nearby Bohemian Brethren Presbyterian Church and the now abandoned St. Wenceslas Catholic Church. In the ethnically diverse area south of the stockyards one can identify St. Luke's Serbian Orthodox Church, the Lithuanian Bakery and Delicatessen, and Holy Cross Romanian Orthodox Church.[34]

Manufacturing Deconcentration

The outward growth of housing in Omaha and Lincoln, and the transportation system that made it possible, have had dramatic impacts on other forms of land use in Nebraska's urban areas. Both industries and commercial activities have become more decentralized in response to the relocation of workers and consumers, improved transportation systems in peripheral areas, and changing locational needs of manufacturing, retailing, and other activities.

Suburbanization of manufacturing has been especially pronounced in Omaha. Several centrifugal forces have contributed to this dispersion. As manufacturing has become more automated during the twentieth century, firms have sought larger expanses of land that permit all manufacturing functions to take place on one level. In older, inner-city locations land values are too high to permit such extensive use of land. Companies have come to rely more on trucks than trains for the transport of finished goods, so proximity to the railroad is no longer the attraction it once was, but access to high-speed highways has become much more important.[35] Consequently, industries have sought undeveloped land, both in the

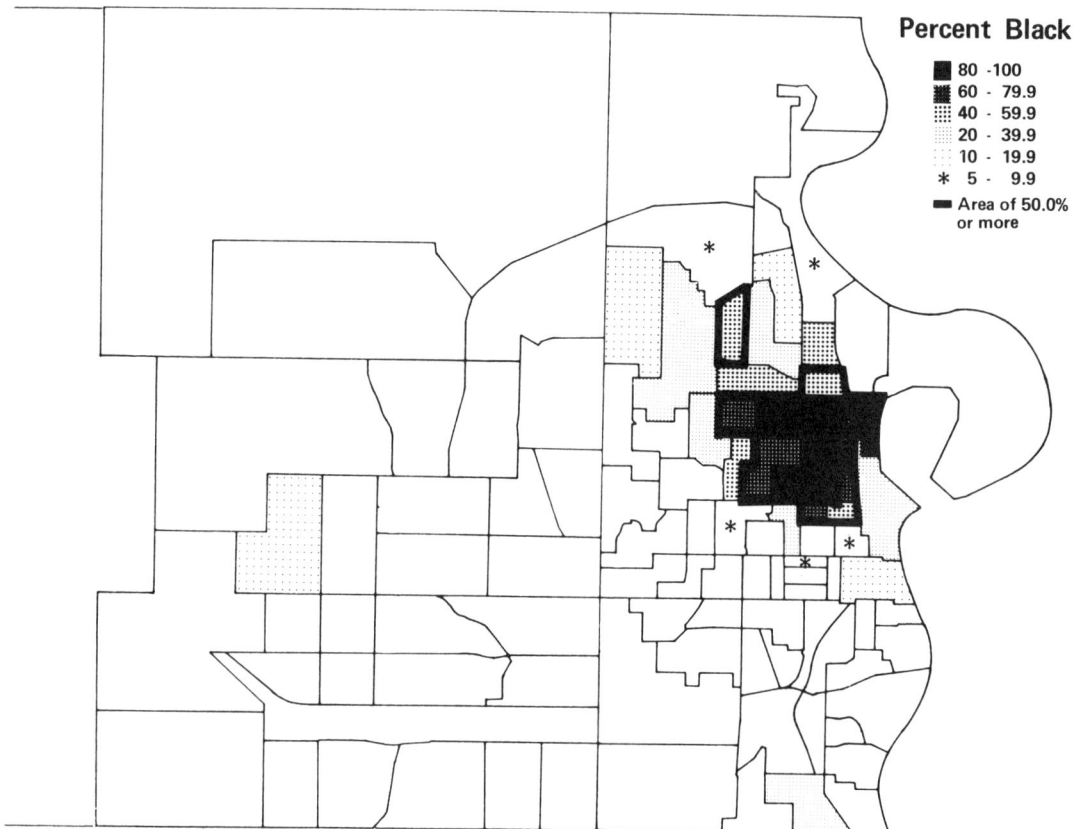

FIGURE 9.10. Black population of Douglas County by census tract, 1980. (UNO)

suburbs and in smaller cities and towns of the state (see Chapter 4).

The suburbanization of the work force is another powerful locational factor. Many larger manufacturers are now found on the suburban fringe or beyond. Western Electric located in Millard early in the postwar suburbanization boom. Valmont Industries, one of the larger employers in the metropolitan area, is in Valley, in the west end of Douglas County. Such fringe locations serve to further spur residential deconcentration, just as workers living in the suburbs attract manufacturing activities.

Probably the most dramatic expansion of industrial land use in Omaha occurred in the area between Interstate 80 and L Street, west of 72nd Street (Figure 9.12). This area has both good highway connections and railroad service. As industries have moved into this part of the city, its utility as a residential neighborhood has diminished.

Lincoln, traditionally less reliant on manufacturing, has experienced similar suburbanization of industry, particularly along the rail lines leading northeast from the city. Suburban residential development has proceeded in entirely different directions—to the southeast. Lincoln's smaller population and physical size permit relatively easy access to work from most residential areas. Furthermore, northeast Lincoln has contained sizable residential neighborhoods—and a labor force—for several decades.

Suburban locations for manufacturing are favored in many smaller cities, as well. Growing manufacturing centers such as Columbus, Grand Island, and Lexington

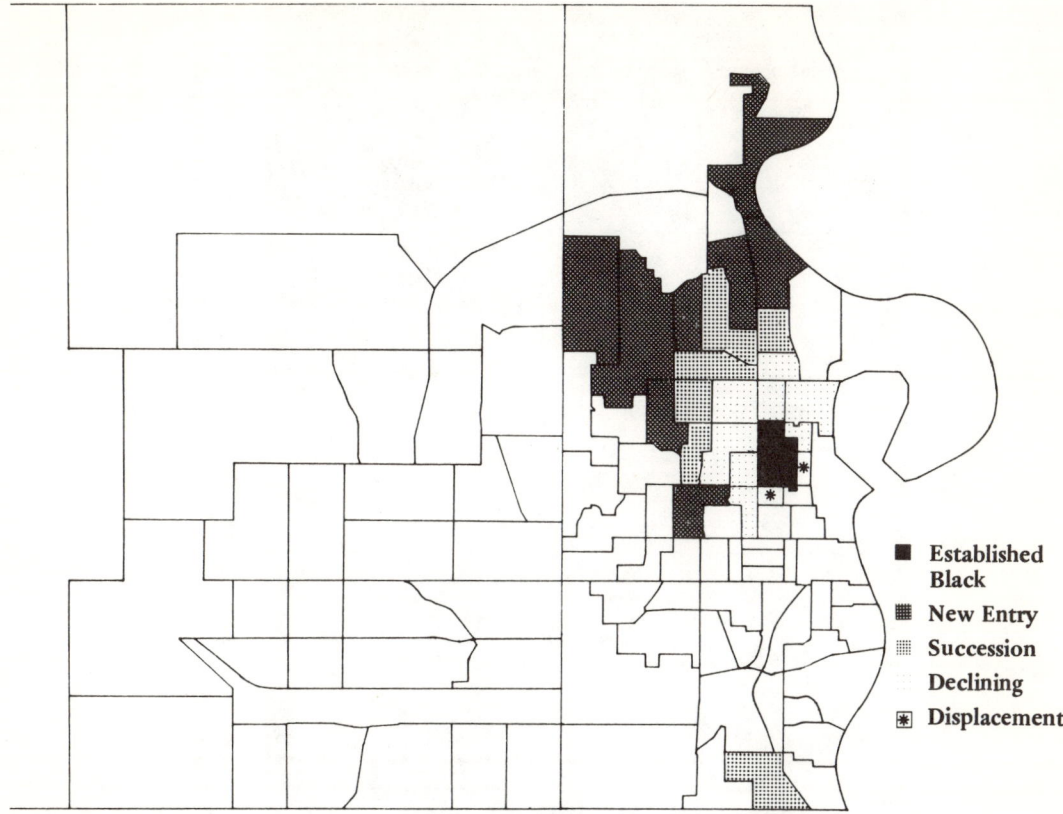

FIGURE 9.11. Racial change in Douglas County, 1970–1980 (east of 72nd St.). (UNO)

have been attractive to industry, in part because of the abundance of land near the city and adjacent to major highways.

Not all industrial activity now takes place in the suburbs, however. Much processing of agricultural commodities continues in older industrial zones because of reliance on rail transportation and because peripheral locations that offer no particular advantages would entail significant relocation costs. Grain mills and many food processors, for example, have not relocated to the extent that instruments or electronics firms have. For those latter operations, transportation and manufacturing technologies have increased their locational freedom.

Malls and Downtowns

Residential growth in the suburbs, which has led and been led by the deconcentration of manufacturing, has also proved a powerful inducement to the suburbanization of commercial activities. Retailing in Omaha and Lincoln has come to be dominated by planned suburban shopping centers.

Suburban residential expansion during the past two decades has coincided with rapidly growing demand for consumer items. Most suburban areas had few retail outlets available when housing was first developed. Malls moved into this void and capitalized on the improvements in highway transportation in the suburbs. As two-lane streets were converted into four- or six-lane highways in the suburbs, malls became more accessible than downtown to the growing, affluent population on the periphery (Figure 9.13). The success of shopping centers also hinged on technological changes in retailing that favored larger establishments, particularly in drugstores, supermarkets, and variety stores.[36]

FIGURE 9.12. Omaha's new industrial sector is served by railroads, highways, and expressways and occupies a 4-mi-long (6.4-km-long) strip. Immediately to the south and north are suburban residential developments. The more rectilinear pattern of streets just to the south of the industrial area is in Ralston, an older town now surrounded by newer residential construction. (USDA, ASCS)

FIGURE 9.13. Peripheral development of commercial activities in Columbus is indicated by strip retailing along two major thoroughfares in the city. Note the proliferation of new housing, particularly north and northwest of the city. The downtown area is near the center of the built-up area. (USDA, ASCS)

Although suburban shopping centers thrived on the expanding suburban residential market, suburbanization of retailing was not simply a response to a growing suburban population. In fact, the availability of a wide range of shopping facilities on the outskirts of cities made the suburbs more attractive as residential locations. Commerical and residential decentralization fed on one another, just as did suburban housing and industry.

The suburban commercial boom has had a devastating effect on many downtown areas in the United States, particularly in cities with 100,000 to 500,000 people. Omaha's CBD no longer is the dominant, or even a major, retail section in the metropolitan area. Many downtown retailers that opened suburban outlets in the malls closed their downtown stores during the 1970s. Between 1972 and 1977, the number of stores in downtown Omaha decreased from 288 to 188, and downtown retail sales fell from $82 million to $70 million. Meanwhile, retail sales in the whole city rose from $943 million to $1.36 billion, and both the Westroads and the Crossroads shopping malls in Omaha surpassed downtown sales totals.[37]

Lincoln's central business district has also suffered relative to suburban retailing, but not to the extent that has occurred in

TABLE 9.3

RETAILING IN OMAHA AND LINCOLN

	Lincoln		Omaha	
	1972	1977	1972	1977
Retail Sales ($Million)				
Metropolitan Area	408	688	1,237	1,943
City	394	638	943	1,357
Downtown	77	91	82	70
Largest Outlying				
Shopping District	48	113	63	103
Number of Stores				
Metropolitan Area	1,311	1,373	3,880	3,937
City	1,207	1,264	2,666	2,567
Downtown	197	181	288	188
Largest Outlying				
Shopping District	51	68	99	113

Source: U.S. Bureau of the Census, *1972 Census of Retail Trade* (Washington: Government Printing Office, 1975); *1977 Census of Retail Trade* (Washington: Government Printing Office, 1980).

Omaha (Table 9.3). Lincoln's downtown retail sales between 1972 and 1977 rose from $77 million to $91 million, making it the largest downtown retail center in the state. But total retail sales in the city jumped 60 percent to $638 million, and sales in the Gateway shopping center and surrounding area surpassed those of downtown, rising from $48 million to $113 million.[38]

Clearly, congestion and the shortage of parking in downtowns have reduced the number of shoppers and encouraged out-migration of retail firms. However, the distances many potential customers must travel to reach downtown and the availability of a variety of alternative shopping opportunities closer to the affluent suburban population have nearly destroyed downtown Omaha shopping. Lincoln has been less affected because of smaller size, less suburban competition, the concentration of state government employees in the downtown area, the presence of the university adjacent to downtown, and public policies supportive of downtown.

The Changing Face of Downtown

The exodus of retailers from Omaha's core did not mean the demise of downtown. Omaha saw a boom in office construction and jobs during the 1960s. By 1975, downtown Omaha had nearly 3.5 million sq ft (325,000 sq m) of private and corporate office space, approximately half the office space in the city. Additional office construction in the late 1970s and early 1980s has expanded that figure considerably (Figure 9.14). The downtown area is a major financial center. Numerous regional offices of federal agencies are located there, and city and county government offices have a new facility in the heart of downtown.[39]

Even as downtown Omaha's face changed, the suburbs became competitors in the provision of office space. Between 1965 and 1975, over 60 percent of the new office space constructed in Omaha was built in peripheral areas. Suburban offices sprang up in scattered locations and in three major clusters—west Dodge, 72nd and Center, and Regency. These three areas accounted for construction of over 1.1 million sq ft (102,000 sq m) of office space in that ten-year period. The older office cluster along Dodge between 30th and 50th showed the least growth during those years.[40]

Limited space in the downtown and East Dodge clusters and the lack of available raw land made the construction of new buildings difficult without complicated land packages and building demolition. Downtown construction has led to the destruction of historic landmarks and fostered greater historic preservation efforts. Suburban sites have few of these limitations. Furthermore, suburban land is cheaper and suburban offices are closer to their white-collar employees and to the executives and office managers who make relocation decisions. The disadvantages of locating away from the downtown office center have been minimized by improvements in telecommunications.[41] Access to the interstate highway and the appeal of a prestigious location (particularly in the case of Regency) have also attracted businesses to the three major suburban clusters.[42]

As a result of changes in the pattern of land use since World War II, Omaha and, to a lesser extent, Lincoln exhibit many of the features of the Multiple Nuclei Model developed by Harris and Ullman, which stresses urban decentralization.[43] The difficulties experienced by downtown Omaha and Lincoln have been felt in nearly all of Nebraska's smaller cities. In Norfolk and Nebraska City, Kearney and Alliance, the retail and service functions that once thrived downtown have been moving to the outskirts of town. Suburbanization of residences has not been a major centrifugal force, but improvements in transportation, availability of building lots, and changes in the ways of doing business are important factors in the relocation process. Competition to small city downtowns comes not from enclosed malls, but from sprawling discount stores and supermarkets with acres of parking. Such extensive land uses can seldom be accommodated on Main Street.

FIGURE 9.14. Downtown Omaha has become an important office center.

The principal highways of most cities with five thousand people are now lined with fast-food outlets, gas stations, motels, and other space-extensive businesses. Even professional services have moved to newer buildings on the outskirts of town. The downtown second-floor quarters once occupied by doctors, dentists, and lawyers either remain empty or have been converted into apartments. Although many downtowns remain vibrant and healthy, in others the exodus of restaurants, services, and shopping has left a void—one not likely to be filled by the construction of office buildings.

OMAHA AND LINCOLN: DIVERGENT PATHS OF DEVELOPMENT

Suburban growth and decline of the core characterize Omaha and Lincoln to a greater extent than smaller places in Nebraska. However, there are substantial differences between the two metropolitan areas in the suburbanization of residential and commerical land use.

Both cities have grown in population

TABLE 9.4

POPULATION CHANGE, CITIES AND SUBURBS

	City		Urbanized Area[a]	
	1980 Population	Percent Change, 1970-1980	1980 Population	Percent Change, 1970-1980
Omaha	314,255	-9.5	450,265[b]	5.5
Lincoln	171,932	15.0	173,550	13.1

[a] An Urbanized Area includes the population of the city, along with that of surrounding suburbs.

[b] Nebraska portion only.

Source: U.S. Bureau of the Census, <u>1980 Census of Population, Volume 1, Characteristics of the Population</u> (Washington: Government Printing Office, 1981).

and area during the postwar period, but Omaha's pattern of residential expansion has more closely paralleled national trends. Omaha's residential growth has been typified by leapfrog suburban developments. As these suburbs grew during the 1970s, the population of the city of Omaha declined by nearly 10 percent (Table 9.4).

Lincoln, by contrast, has few unincorporated Sanitary and Improvement Districts (Sids). Most residential expansion in the capital city has occurred adjacent to existing residential areas, with new developments being annexed immediately and almost automatically. Lincoln remains a more compact city, with little spillover into rural areas.

Omaha has experienced considerably more peripheral growth of retail activities, with nearly a dozen major suburban shopping developments competing for the city's business. Strip retail developments line most major city thoroughfares. Retail shopping in Lincoln has not shifted so dramatically away from the central business district, which only competes with one outlying center—Gateway. Other commercial districts in Lincoln serve primarily neighborhood needs, and strip developments seem to be less pronounced than in Omaha.

Omaha's greater physical size and population undoubtedly has contributed to the more rapid decline of its CBD. Omaha gives the sense of a large city—six-lane expressways carry rush-hour traffic to industries and office buildings from distant suburbs. Lincoln has more the "feel" of a small town—its numerous two-lane arterial streets are lined with residences rather than business establishments. Few residential neighborhoods in Lincoln are more than 6 mi (10 km) from the heart of downtown.

Whereas Omaha has witnessed the suburbanization of many employers, Lincoln's employment has remained concentrated near the city center. This is largely attributable to the dominant role of state government in Lincoln's economy. The university and state offices have helped to anchor the retail function of downtown Lincoln and to keep it strong, compared to downtowns in most cities of comparable size.

Renovating Downtown

Both cities have been active in downtown revitalization, but they have taken very different approaches. Omaha's downtown redevelopment plan, although it envisions downtown residential development and retail growth, has focused on drawing employers to the CBD. The heart of the plan is the Central Park Mall, a six-block-long open space emphasizing pedestrian use, outdoor entertainment attractions, and a waterway. It is hoped this facility and neighboring governmental buildings will attract business. Several major office buildings have already been constructed near the mall and others are planned.

Lincoln Center, on the other hand, is focused on attracting retailers to the CBD and on strengthening downtown's traditional commercial dominance of the city. Attention has been given to traffic circulation, the provision of parking, and pedestrian pathways linking major retail clusters and parking facilities.

Growth and City Policies

The two cities have implemented very different policies related to growth and its management. Metropolitan Omaha, encompassing three counties and a number of municipalities in two states, has found it difficult to direct urban growth. Much of Omaha's residential growth is now taking place in Sarpy County, over which the city has no jurisdiction.

Lincoln has not been so constrained. The city and Lancaster County have developed a comprehensive regional plan that encourages expansion to the north and west of downtown, while discouraging further growth to the east because it would have disruptive impacts on the downtown area. "Among these is the potential to severely weaken Lincoln Center as the Gateway area would become central to the area of urbanization. Additionally, the polarity between home and work would be severely aggrevated [sic], and the potential for additional travel demand in an east-west direction would be increased."[44] Furthermore, development to the east would require substantial expenditures for public infrastructure—roads and utilities. At the same time, the public investment in downtown Lincoln would be wasted. The downtown area "contains huge amounts of public and private investment in the form of buildings, utilities, and streets, and it continues to receive significant amounts of public and private capital. Therefore, to allow Lincoln Center to lose its dominant role would be to waste the millions of dollars of public and private investment made over time."[45]

The objective of the Lincoln-Lancaster plan is to encourage concentric residential growth, which will maintain the health of the downtown area, require less public investment, and encroach less on the high-quality agricultural land east of the city. Lincoln has managed to avoid the leap-frogging associated with Omaha and other cities through city ownership of utilities. City policy is to not extend utilities beyond the city limits and to strongly resist proposals for noncontiguous residential developments.

Lincoln has actively discouraged peripheral commercial development in order to maintain the attractiveness of the CBD and support concentric residential development. Entertainment, for example, is heavily oriented toward downtown, where numerous restaurants and nearly all theaters in the city are located. Downtown Omaha, by contrast, supports no movie theaters, and its relatively few restaurants oriented toward the evening trade are concentrated in the redeveloped Old Market area.

Lincoln has been further aided in its commitment to contiguous development by not being bisected by an expressway. Omaha's suburban expansion was significantly spurred by the interstate highway, which sliced through older residential neighborhoods and led directly to the center of the city (Figure 9.15). Additional expressways have been proposed to link downtown Omaha to areas north and west. The most controversial aspect of this transportation plan is the proposed North Freeway, which has been constructed as far as Lake Street. Land has been acquired to extend the freeway farther north, so that eventually it will link downtown with Interstate 680.[46] Supporters believe the road will enhance economic development of north and northwest Omaha and give residents of those areas better access to downtown. Suburban expansion, which has been more restrained to the north than to the southwest of the city, would probably also be stimulated. Critics of the plan suggest that the benefits would accrue primarily to suburbanites who

FIGURE 9.15. Interstate highways lead to Omaha from many directions, but have also led residents to more distant suburban housing. Note the North Freeway (upper left), about 2 mi (3.2 km) of which have been constructed. Expressways in central Omaha consume a considerable amount of land and have displaced housing. (USDA, ASCS)

would travel through the older areas of north Omaha, but that the costs would be born by disrupted north Omaha communities.[47]

By contrast, Lincoln has depended upon a system of less heavily traveled urban streets and highways. Only a few streets outside the center of the city are multilane. Plans for a proposed Northeast Radial Highway, which would have connected northeastern Lincoln to downtown, have been shelved, following defeat at the polls.

Lincoln and Omaha vividly illustrate urbanism and urban change in Nebraska. Lincoln—the seat of government functions and services, with a growing industrial component—retains much of the appearance of small-town America and, as such, is closer in form and function to the smaller cities of the state. Omaha, the industrial heart of the state, with its diverse ethnic population reminiscent of the manufacturing cities of the East and the Midwest, has paralleled national urban developments—suburban growth, retail abandonment of the CBD, and a high-speed transportation network that has fed peripheral growth and central-city decline. In each city may lie some indication of the urban future of Nebraska and the nation.

CHAPTER 10

CULTURE, ENVIRONMENT, AND THE FUTURE

Nebraska possesses a distinctive physical landscape, mix of resources, population distribution, urban pattern, agriculture, industrial base, rural landscape, and historical development. But the state is also part of a national culture and a world economic system—the uses of its resources are largely determined by national and world demand; its agricultural, industrial, and urban activities and technologies are derived from national trends; changes in population characteristics and distribution parallel those occurring on regional and national levels.

Although one can examine the state from the perspective either of its unique attributes or that of its representativeness of the larger system, an accurate depiction of the state requires both approaches. To ignore the larger influences upon the state's geography is to consider Nebraska as an isolated entity, which it surely is not. To stress only national and international patterns is to ignore Nebraska and the specific human and natural resources upon which its development has been based.

Both internal and external forces will shape Nebraska in the future. However, the social, economic, and political interdependence of the state with the rest of the nation and the world suggests that extralocal trends will be disproportionately influential. Among the major factors likely to affect future geographic patterns in the state in the future are the availability of energy, technological developments, public policy decisions, changing life-style preferences, and attitudes toward resource use.

The "rural renaissance" of the 1970s was fueled by inexpensive energy for transportation, public funding for highways, and changing attitudes toward rural and small town life. Migration into and out of communities and the state as a whole responded to economic, social, and attitudinal variables. The loss of population in some areas has been a product of the increasing economies of scale produced by technologically sophisticated agriculture. The future pattern will depend upon whether or not the rural population turnaround was a quirk or the harbinger of a long-term trend.

The growth of the urban fringe and decline at the center of cities are national trends also found in Nebraska. Decentralization of population, commerce, and industry in Omaha, Lincoln, and smaller cities is a response to national energy supply, public policy regarding transportation systems, the technology of manufacturing and retailing, and residential preferences.

Should those forces change at the national level, they would most certainly be reflected in Nebraska.

The decentralization of manufacturing and the increasing concentration of retailing in larger centers are among the more significant economic trends within the state. Both are products of the increased mobility provided by the automobile and improved highways. Rural industrialization in Nebraska has been made possible by the federal interstate highway system and inexpensive energy, as well as by the availability of productive workers in Nebraska's rural communities. The degree to which the Platte Valley–Interstate 80 corridor continues to prosper will depend on national forces affecting the location of manufacturing and the cost of transportation. The economic health of small communities away from that transportation corridor may well hinge on the continuing centralization tendencies operating in retailing and services in the United States.

Even agriculture, with its dependence on soil, climate, and water resources, is a product of national and international forces. Modern agriculture's dependence upon fossil fuels and technological innovation links Nebraskans to world resources and industrial activity. Increasing farm size, concentration of land ownership, and agricultural specialization are national trends shaped by national farm and food policy, agricultural technology, and the economics of agricultural production.

But not all the factors are external. The people of the state and its natural resources are not microcosms of the nation, carefully imitating every national trend. The decisions Nebraskans make individually and collectively can alter or modify national and international influences upon the state.

This is most clearly the case in the interface between culture and Nebraska's environment. Webb maintained that the flat, treeless, subhumid Great Plains offered such a contrast to the humid region from which settlers came that adaptation was essential for survival: "In the early nineteenth century they . . . came out on the Great Plains, an environment with which they had no experience. The result was a complete though temporary breakdown of the machinery and ways of pioneering."[1] Only when the drought of the 1890s demonstrated the inadequacy of humid-land techniques and crops did adaptation occur.

Yet many, perhaps even most, farmers continued to believe in the desirability of subduing an uncooperative environment, rather than bowing to it. The belief in environmental subjugation was expressed in support for rainmakers and for "rain follows the plow" theorists. When they were discredited, turn-of-the-century promoters hailed Nebraska as part of an irrigated Western Empire.[2] Alas, the variability of Nebraska's climate shifted in the other direction, bringing moist years, good crops, and diminished support for irrigation.

When drought struck again in the 1930s, "blowing soil came to symbolize dramatically the breakdown of an agricultural system that was the basis of the region's economy and social order."[3] Grassland unsuited to cultivation, which had been plowed up and planted to crops during the 1910s and 1920s, was returned to grass cover. Farmers planted shelterbelts and adopted strip-cropping and stubble mulching to reduce wind erosion. They endorsed fallow wheat production to conserve soil moisture. They became "defensive farmers" to cope with a risky environment.[4] Through adaptation, however incomplete, the agricultural system became accommodated to a subhumid climate.

Yet the central agricultural resources of the state continue to be threatened. Periodically, a "false philosophy of plenty, a myth of inexhaustibility"[5] places pressures on soil and water. Subduing the environment remains more attractive than accommodation to its realities—fertile, yet exhaustible, soil and abundant water in finite amounts.

The irrigation boom of the past thirty years has been based on an almost unimaginable wealth of groundwater. With adequate groundwater reserves, rain is not only superfluous, it can be almost inconvenient. The climate has become a substantially less powerful influence on the lives of many farmers and thereby on the state. Irrigation does not supplant the natural environment, however. As so many irrigators have discovered, abundant does not mean limitless. Even as new irrigated areas are opened up in the Sandhills, other areas face the threat of reversion to dryland agriculture within a few decades unless the mining of groundwater can be halted.

Soil erosion continues to threaten Nebraska's productive base. Since the 1930s millions of acres have been afforded protection by terracing, contour farming, windbreaks, strip-cropping, minimum tillage, and other conservation practices. Still, severe storms can remove more than 30 tn of soil per acre (67 t per ha) from inadequately protected land, and poor management of delicate Sandhills soils can produce wind erosion in excess of 90 tn per acre (202 t per ha) each year. Farmers, lured by the belief that massive doses of fertilizer can balance erosion losses and squeezed by high expenses and low prices, may defer expenditures for soil conservation. The conversion of agricultural land to other uses—notably transportation and housing—removes soil from production even more effectively than does erosion. Once converted, this is space not likely to revert to agriculture.

The threats to both groundwater and soil resources are embodied in the recent expansion of center-pivot irrigation in parts of the Sandhills. Here the resources of the state meet face to face with national trends in agricultural industrialization. Government policies encourage the development of inexpensive rangeland for irrigated agriculture. Cheap energy and sophisticated technology make it possible. Where sites are properly selected and managed, the net impact on resources, agriculture, and communities can be very positive.

During the 1920s "some farmers overlooked [soil] limitations and chose a cropping system for maximum return under best weather conditions, rather than for protection during unfavorable ones."[6] Some irrigation development of the 1970s resembles that pattern. Too often lands have been chosen for development solely on the basis of cost and water availability. Pivots have been placed indiscriminately. Where land is too steep, hills have been chopped off. Soil quality has been all but ignored in some situations. If water has to be mined, it has been.

Properly implemented, irrigation has proved a boon to thousands of Nebraska farmers. It has brought a higher level of earnings and sheltered farmers from some of the risks of farming in a subhumid climate. And these goals have been accomplished without severely depleting the renewable resources of soil or groundwater reserves. If they are consumed at a rate equal to or slower than that at which they are regenerated, they will last forever. Those who take their stewardship of natural resources seriously can make use of abundance and still retain it. They recognize the meaning of necessity of accommodating their enterprises to the reality of the environment. Those who would argue for the subjugation of the environment must accept the necessity, even the desirability, of mining soil and water resources. In the long run, mines extract resources. When mines are exhausted, they are abandoned.

If Nebraskans insist upon the sustainability of their resources, those resources will remain available for future use. Such a decision may not be easy, however. Nebraskans value independence and individual decision making. But resource decisions have both individual and collective consequences. Soil erosion on one farm can damage the productive capacity of neighboring land. Overpumping by one irrigator can deplete the resource of others.

Mechanisms for implementing collective action are available. Groundwater control areas can be established, placing limits on individual use of a common resource. Zoning can be used to slow the movement of urban residences into the countryside. Government funding is available to help with soil conservation. But collective implementation of controls restricts the right of individuals to determine the use of their land.

Property rights are not, however, unlimited. Some argue that property owners have certain obligations: "While private property is a social right that is respected and understood in our society, there is also a social mortgage on all private property requiring that in return for protection from encroachers the public holds the owner responsible for the wise use of the land."[7] Nebraskans must determine the balance that will be struck between individual rights and collective enforcement of that mortgage.

Nebraska's future will be as much a product of values as of energy, technology, resources, or policy, whether local, national, or global. The questions about Nebraska's future revolve around the interrelationships of this culture and this environment. Should the state's inhabitants seek accommodation with or subjugation of the subhumid environment? Should the state's resources be viewed as mines to be exploited or as fields to be harvested? Should agriculture stress short-term output or long-term permanence? These are values questions. Their answers depend upon the decisions made by the people of the state, as well as upon distant and uncontrollable forces.

NOTES

For references cited in the notes a shortened form is used. If the source given in a note is listed in the Selected Bibliography, only the author's name and a short title appear in the note. For those sources not listed in the Selected Bibliography, full publication data are given at the first occurrence in a note; thereafter the shortened form is used.

CHAPTER 1

1. Brown, *Historical Geography of the United States*.
2. Allen, *Passage Through the Garden;* James C. Olson, *History of Nebraska;* Herbert E. Bolton, *Coronado, Knight of Pueblos and Plains* (Albuquerque: University of New Mexico Press, 1964).
3. Elliot Coues, ed., *The Expeditions of Zebulon Montgomery Pike*, 3 vols. (New York: Francis P. Harper, 1895), vol. 2, p. 525.
4. In Reuben Gold Thwaites, ed., *Early Western Travels*, 32 vols. (Cleveland: Arthur H. Clark, 1905).
5. Edward E. Hale, *Kanzas and Nebraska* (Boston: Phillips, Sampson and Company, 1854).
6. Bayard Taylor, *Colorado: A Summer Trip* (New York: G. P. Putnam and Son, 1867).
7. Powell, *Report on the Lands of the Arid Region of the United States*. For an example of the attacks on Powell, see Charles Dana Wilber, *The Great Valleys and Prairies of Nebraska and the Northwest* (Omaha: Daily Republican Print, 1881).
8. William B. Hazen, "The Great Middle Region of the United States," *North American Review* 120 (1875):1-34.

9. Lawson and Stockton, "Desert Myth and Climatic Reality."
10. Merlin P. Lawson, "Toward a Geosophic Climate of the Great American Desert. The Plains Climate of the Forty-Niners," in Blouet and Lawson, *Images of the Plains*, pp. 101-113.
11. G. Malcolm Lewis, "Three Centuries of Desert Concepts in the Cis-Rocky Mountain West," *Journal of the West* 4 (1965):457-468; John L. Allen, "Geographical Knowledge and American Images of the Louisiana Territory," *Geographical Review* 62 (1972):13-39.
12. Waldo R. Wedel, "Some Early Euro-American Percepts of the Great Plains and Their Influence on Anthropological Thinking," in Blouet and Lawson, *Images of the Plains*, pp. 13-20; Merlin P. Lawson, "A Behavioristic Interpretation of Pike's Geographical Knowledge of the Interior of Louisiana," *Great Plains-Rocky Mountain Geographical Journal* 1 (1972):58-64.
13. Allen, *Passage Through the Garden;* William H. Goetzmann, *Exploration and Empire* (New York: Alfred A. Knopf, 1967).
14. Lawson, ed., *Climatic Atlas of Nebraska*.
15. Ibid.
16. Ibid.
17. Ibid.; John R. Borchert, "The Climate of the Central North American Grassland," *Annals of the Association of American Geographers* 40 (1950):1-39.
18. Again, these comments refer to "average" conditions in a state with a high degree of variability.
19. Lawson, *Climatic Atlas of Nebraska*.
20. Ibid.; Borchert, "Climate of the Central North American Grassland."
21. Lawson, Reiss, Phillips, and Livingston, *Nebraska Droughts*.

22. Bradley H. Baltensperger, "Plains Promoters and Plain Folk: Pre-Migration and Post-Settlement Images of the Central Great Plains" (Ph.D. dissertation, Clark University, 1974).

23. Warrick and Bowden, "The Changing Impacts of Droughts in the Great Plains."

24. Lawson, *Climatic Atlas of Nebraska;* John R. Borchert, "The Dust Bowl of the 1970s."

25. Lawson, *Climatic Atlas of Nebraska;* Ian Burton, Robert W. Kates, and Gilbert F. White, *The Environment as Hazard* (New York: Oxford University Press, 1978).

26. Lawson, *Climatic Atlas of Nebraska.*

27. Ibid.; Snowden D. Flora, *Hailstorms of the United States* (Norman: University of Oklahoma Press, 1956).

28. Lawson et al., *Nebraska Droughts.*

29. Keech and Bentall, *Dunes on the Plains;* H.T.U. Smith, "Dune Morphology and Chronology in Central and Western Nebraska," *Journal of Geology* 73 (1965):557-578.

30. Keech and Bentall, *Dunes on the Plains;* George E. Condra, *The Potash Industry of Nebraska* (Lincoln: Nebraska Bureau of Publicity, 1918).

31. A. L. Lugn, *The Origin and Sources of Loess in the Central Great Plains and Adjoining Areas of the Central Lowlands*, University of Nebraska Studies, n.s. no. 26 (Lincoln: University of Nebraska, 1962); H. E. Wright, Jr., "Vegetational History of the Central Great Plains," in *Pleistocene and Recent Environments of the Central Great Plains*, edited by Wakefield Dort, Jr., and J. Knox Jones, Jr. (Lawrence: University of Kansas Press, 1970), pp. 157-172.

32. Vincent H. Dreeszen, "The Stratigraphic Framework of Pleistocene Glacial and Periglacial Deposits in Nebraska," in Dort and Jones, *Pleistocene and Recent Environments;* E. C. Reed, V. H. Dreeszen, C. K. Bayne, and C. B. Schultz, "The Pleistocene in Nebraska and Northern Kansas," in *The Quaternary of the United States*, edited by H. E. Wright, Jr., and David G. Frey (Princeton: Princeton University Press, 1965), pp. 187-202.

33. Elder, *Soils of Nebraska.*

34. Aandhl, *Soils of the Great Plains.*

35. Williams and Murfield, eds., *Agricultural Atlas of Nebraska.*

36. Wright, "Vegetational History of the Central Great Plains"; James C. Malin, "The Grassland of North America: Its Occupance and the Challenge of Continuous Reappraisals," in *Man's Role in Changing the Face of the Earth*, edited by William L. Thomas, Jr. (Chicago: University of Chicago Press, 1956), pp. 350-366; Conrad Moore, "Man and Fire in the Central North American Grassland, 1585-1890: A Documentary History" (Ph.D. dissertation, University of California at Los Angeles, 1974); Robert B. Kaul, "Vegetation of Nebraska (Circa 1850)," map (Lincoln: University of Nebraska Conservation and Survey Division, 1975).

37. John E. Weaver, *The North American Prairie.*

38. Henry D. Foth and John W. Schafer, *Soil Geography and Land Use* (New York: Wiley and Sons, 1980).

39. Ibid.; R. P. Matelski, "Great Soil Groups of Nebraska," *Soil Science* 88 (1959):228-239; Aandahl, *Soils of the Great Plains.*

40. Williams and Murfield, eds., *Agricultural Atlas of Nebraska.* Other sources indicate inflow from other states is closer to 1 million acre-ft (1.2 billion cu m). *Report on the Framework Study.* See also Ray Bentall and F. Butler Shaffer, *Availability and Use of Water in Nebraska, 1975.*

41. *Report on the Platte River Basin, Nebraska Level B Study;* see also Bentall, *Nebraska's Platte River.*

42. Bentall, *Nebraska's Platte River.*

43. *Report on the Platte River Basin, Nebraska Level B Study*, pp. 46-54; Instream Flows Study Task Force, *Nebraska Policy Issue Study on Instream Flows*, pp. 30-32.

44. Bentall, *Nebraska's Platte River.* See also *Report on the Platte River Basin, Nebraska Level B Study.*

45. *Report on the Platte River Basin, Nebraska Level B Study.*

46. Ibid.

47. *Nebraska's Natural Resources, A Report of the STAR Committee on Natural Resources* (Lincoln: University of Nebraska Institute for Agriculture and Natural Resources, 1976).

48. Instream Flows Study Group Task Force, *Nebraska Policy Issue Study on Instream Flows.*

49. Ibid.

50. Ibid.; *State Comprehensive Outdoor Recreation Plan* (Lincoln: Nebraska Game and Parks Commission, 1979).

51. Instream Flows Study Group Task Force, *Nebraska Policy Issue Study on Instream Flows; State Comprehensive Outdoor Recreation Plan.*

52. Instream Flows Study Group Task Force, *Nebraska Policy Issue Study on Instream Flows.*

53. L. Carl Brandhorst, "The North Platte Oasis: Notes on the Geography and History of

an Irrigated District," *Agricultural History* 51 (1977):166-172.

54. J. Michael Jess and Stanley M. Christensen, "Surface Water Use in Nebraska's Platte River Valley" (Lincoln: Nebraska Department of Water Resources, 1980).

55. Reed, *Groundwater Atlas of Nebraska*.

56. Keech and Bentall, *Dunes on the Plains*, pp. 10-12; Williams and Murfield, *Agricultural Atlas of Nebraska*, pp. 6-9.

57. Reed, *Groundwater Atlas of Nebraska*.

58. *Nebraska's Natural Resources*.

59. Williams and Murfield, *Agricultural Atlas of Nebraska*.

60. Paul H. Gessaman, "Initial Perspectives on Nebraska's State Water Planning and Review Process" (Lincoln: University of Nebraska–Lincoln, Department of Agricultural Economics, 1981).

61. Johnson and Pederson, *Groundwater Levels in Nebraska, 1981*.

62. A. J. McClanahan, "Districts Mull Billing for Recharged Water," *Sunday World Herald* (Omaha), November 8, 1981, p. 13B.

63. Johnson and Pederson, *Groundwater Levels in Nebraska*.

64. Ibid.

65. Ibid.

66. Ray Bentall, "Inflow Decline Poses Problems," *Farm, Ranch and Home Quarterly* 27, no. 2 (1980):8-10; James Denney, "The Frenchman: Will Anything Save It?" Omaha *World-Herald*, June 29, 1980; Robert Richter, "A Reservoir Dies in the Frenchman Basin," *Prairie Sentinel* (Walthill, Nebr.) (August-September 1982), p. 10.

67. Eric G. Lappala, "Changes in the Water Supply in the Upper Republican Natural Resources District, Southwest Nebraska, from 1952-75," U.S. Geological Survey Open-File Report 76-498 (Lincoln, 1976).

68. Johnson and Pederson, *Groundwater Levels in Nebraska;* Denney, "The Frenchman."

69. Lappala, "Changes in the Water Supply."

70. Paul H. Gessman and J. David Aiken, "Instream Flows I: The Issue Described," G79-439 (Lincoln: University of Nebraska, Cooperative Extension Service, 1979). See also Gessaman and Aiken, "Instream Flows II: Physical and Legal Considerations," G79-440 (Lincoln: University of Nebraska, Cooperative Extension Service, 1979); and J. David Aiken, "Legal Aspects for Recognizing Instream Water Uses and Related Environmental Values in Nebraska," Staff Paper 1979-#14 (Lincoln: University of Nebraska–Lincoln, Department of Aricultural Economics, 1979).

71. J. David Aiken, "Interbasin Surface Transfers Stir Debate," *Farm, Ranch and Home Quarterly* 28, no. 1 (1981):6-7.

72. *Summary of the Nebraska Research for the Six-State High Plains Ogallala Aquifer Study*.

73. See, for example, a collection of articles in the *Sunday World Herald*, October 11, 1981, pp. 1A, 13A-14A.

74. Johnson and Fischer, "The Economics of the Proposed O'Neill Irrigation Project."

75. Ibid.

76. Gessaman, "Initial Perspectives," estimates that projected state government expenditures for 1980-1983 for the State Water Planning and Review Process will approach $4 million.

77. J. David Aiken and Paul H. Gessaman, "An Overview of Ground Water Rights, Part II: Legal Aspects of Ground Water Management," G79-442 (Lincoln: University of Nebraska Cooperative Extension Service, 1979).

78. *Summary of the Nebraska Research for the Six-State High Plains Ogallala Aquifer Study*.

79. *Platte River Basin, Nebraska Level B Study: Hydrology and Hydraulics Technical Paper* (Omaha: Missouri River Basin Commission, 1975), pp. 131-166; *Report on the Platte River Basin, Nebraska Level B Study*, pp. 65-73.

80. *Platte River Basin, Nebraska Level B Study, Hydrology and Hydraulics*, p. 142.

81. Instream Flows Study Group Task Force, *Nebraska Policy Issue Study on Instream Flows*, pp. 43-58.

82. Ibid., pp. 75-87.

83. Gessaman, "Initial Perspectives"; James Aucoin, *Water in Nebraska*.

CHAPTER 2

1. Alexander Spoehr, "Cultural Differences in the Interpretation of Natural Resources," in *Man's Role in Changing the Face of the Earth*, edited by William L. Thomas (Chicago: University of Chicago Press, 1956), pp. 93-102.

2. This account of the prehistoric population of the central plains is taken primarily from Wedel, *Prehistoric Man on the Great Plains*, although much of the information is conveniently summarized in Olson, *History of Nebraska*. For additional information see also Waldo R. Wedel, "The Great Plains," in *Prehistoric*

Man in the New World, edited by Jesse D. Jennings and Edward Norbeck (Chicago: University of Chicago Press, 1964), pp. 193–220; and David Mayer Gradwohl, *Prehistoric Villages in Eastern Nebraska*, Publications in Anthropology, no. 4 (Lincoln: Nebraska State Historical Society, 1969).

3. George E. Hyde, *The Pawnee Indians* (Norman: University of Oklahoma Press, 1974); Richard White, "The Cultural Landscape of the Pawnees," *Great Plains Quarterly* 2 (1982):31–40.

4. Olson, *History of Nebraska*.

5. Waldo R. Wedel, "The High Plains and Their Utilization by the Indian," *American Antiquity* 29 (1963):1–16.

6. John C. Ewers, "Intertribal Warfare as the Precursor of Indian-White Warfare on the Northern Great Plains," *Western Historical Quarterly* 6 (1975):397–410; H. B. Hassrick, *The Sioux: Life and Customs of a Warrior Society* (Norman: University of Oklahoma Press, 1964).

7. Quoted in Brown, *Historical Geography of the United States*, p. 378.

8. Wedel, "High Plains and Their Utilization"; Brown, *Historical Geography of the United States*.

9. Brown, *Historical Geography of the United States*, pp. 378–383.

10. Abraham P. Nasatir, *Before Lewis and Clark* (St. Louis: St. Louis Historical Documents Foundation, 1952). For information specific to Nebraska, see Olson, *History of Nebraska*.

11. Olson, *History of Nebraska*; Nasatir, *Before Lewis and Clark*.

12. The literature on Lewis and Clark is voluminous. Among the more important recent works is Allen, *Passage Through the Garden*. Several editions of the journals of Lewis and Clark are available, including Bernard DeVoto, ed., *The Journals of Lewis and Clark* (Boston: Houghton Mifflin, 1953); and the more comprehensive version, Reuben Gold Thwaites, ed., *The Original Journals of the Lewis and Clark Expedition*, 8 vols. (New York: Dodd, Mead and Co., 1904–1905). A new edition of the journals is now in preparation under the auspices of the University of Nebraska's Center for Great Plains Studies. Regarding Pike and Long, see Donald Jackson, ed., *The Journals of Zebulon Montgomery Pike with Letters and Related Documents*, 2 vols. (Norman: University of Oklahoma Press, 1966); Reuben Gold Thwaites, ed., *Early Western Travels*, 32 vols. (Cleveland: Arthur H. Clark, 1905); and Merlin P. Lawson, "A Behavioristic Interpretation of Pike's Geographical Knowledge of the Interior of Louisiana," *Great Plains-Rocky Mountain Geographical Journal* 1 (1972):58–64.

13. Wishart, *The Fur Trade of the American West, 1807–1840*; David J. Wishart, "Images of the Northern Great Plains from the Fur Trade," in Blouet and Lawson, *Images of the Plains*, pp. 45–55. See also David J. Wishart, "Cultures in Cooperation and Conflict: Indians in the Fur Trade on the Northern Great Plains, 1807–1840," *Journal of Historical Geography* 2 (1976): 311–328.

14. Olson, *History of Nebraska*.

15. Wishart, "Images of the Northern Great Plains"; Dale L. Morgan, *Jedediah Smith and the Opening of the West* (Lincoln: University of Nebraska Press, 1964).

16. Richard E. Jensen, "Bellevue: The First Twenty Years, 1822–1842," *Nebraska History* 56 (1975):339–374; Olson, *History of Nebraska*.

17. Roy F. Nichols, "The Kansas-Nebraska Act: A Century of Historiography," *Mississippi Valley Historical Review* 43 (1956):187–212.

18. Olson, *History of Nebraska*.

19. Ibid. See also Charles Howard Richardson, "Early Settlement of Eastern Nebraska Territory: A Geographical Study on the Original Land Survey" (Ph.D. dissertation, University of Nebraska, 1968).

20. Sheldon, *Land Systems and Land Policies in Nebraska*.

21. See Paul W. Gates, "Homesteading in the High Plains," *Agricultural History* 51 (1977):109–134; Sheldon, *Land Systems and Land Policies*; Homer Socolofsky, "Land Disposal in Nebraska, 1854–1906."

22. McIntosh, "Use and Abuse of the Timber Culture Act."

23. Quoted in Olson, *History of Nebraska*, p. 161.

24. Ibid.; Agnes Horton, "Nebraska's Agricultural College Land Grant," *Nebraska History* 30 (1949):50–76.

25. Overton, *Burlington West*. See also Steven J. Bellovich, "A Geographical Appraisal of Settlement Within the Union Pacific Land Grant in Eastern Nebraska, 1869–1890" (Ph.D. dissertation, University of Nebraska, 1974).

26. Olson, *History of Nebraska*. For interpretations of the role of speculation in western development, see Robert P. Swierenga, *Pioneers and Profits: Land Speculation on the Iowa Fron-*

tier (Ames: Iowa State University Press, 1968).

27. See several works by Roger L. Welsch: *Sod Walls: The Story of the Nebraska Sod House* (Broken Bow, Nebr.: n.p., 1968); "The Meaning of Folk Architecture: The Sod House Example," *Keystone Folklore* 21, no. 2 (1976–1977):34–49; "Nebraska Log Construction: Momentum in Tradition," *Nebraska History* 61 (1980):310–335; and "The Nebraska Soddy," *Nebraska History* 48 (1967):335–342. See also Everett Dick, *The Sod House Frontier* (Lincoln: Johnsen Publishing Co., 1954); and Edward E. Dale, "Wood and Water: Twin Problems of the Prairie Plains," *Nebraska History* 29 (1948):87–106.

28. Roger L. Welsch, "No Fuel Like an Old Fuel," *Natural History* 89, no. 11 (November 1980):76–81.

29. Dale, "Wood and Water."

30. Hewes, "Early Fencing on the Western Margin of the Prairie"; Rodney O. Davis, "Before Barbed Wire: Herd Law Agitations in Early Kansas and Nebraska," *Journal of the West* 6, no. 1 (January 1967):41–52.

31. Hewes, "Early Fencing"; Webb, *The Great Plains*.

32. Socolofsky, "Land Disposal in Nebraska, 1854–1906"; Allan G. Bogue, *From Prairie to Corn Belt* (Chicago: University of Chicago Press, 1963); Fite, *The Farmers' Frontier, 1865–1900*.

33. Fite, *The Farmers' Frontier*, p. 45. See also Homer Socolofsky, "Success and Failure in Nebraska Homesteading," *Agricultural History* 42 (1968):103–107.

34. A. R. Mortensen, "Mormons, Nebraska and the Way West," *Nebraska History* 46 (1965):259–272.

35. Merrill J. Mattes, *The Great Platte River Road: The Covered Wagon Main Line via Fort Kearny to Fort Laramie*, Nebraska State Historical Society Publications, vol. 25 (Lincoln: Nebraska State Historical Society, 1969); Unruh, *The Plains Across*; Olson, *History of Nebraska*.

36. Olson, *History of Nebraska*; Roger T. Grange, "Fort Robinson, Outpost on the Plains," *Nebraska History* 39 (1958):191–240.

37. William E. Lass, *From the Missouri to the Great Salt Lake*, Nebraska State Historical Society Publications, vol. 26 (Lincoln: Nebraska State Historical Society, 1972).

38. Raymond W. Settle and Mary L. Settle, *War Drums and Wagon Wheels: The Story of Russell, Majors and Waddell* (Lincoln: University of Nebraska Press, 1966).

39. Merrill J. Mattes and Paul C. Henderson, "The Pony Express: Across Nebraska from St. Joseph to Fort Laramie," *Nebraska History* 41 (1960):83–122.

40. Athearn, *Union Pacific Country*.

41. Samuel Bowles, *Across the Continent* (Springfield, Mass.: Samuel Bowles and Co., 1865), pp. 20–22.

42. Bowden, "The Great American Desert and the American Frontier, 1800–1882." See also Bradley H. Baltensperger, "Newspaper Images of the Central Great Plains in the Late Nineteenth Century," *Journal of the West* 19, no. 2 (April 1980):64–70.

43. Emmons, *Garden of the Grassland*; Baltensperger, "Plains Promoters and Plain Folk."

44. Nebraska State Superintendent of Immigration, *The State of Nebraska, Illustrated by a New and Authentic Map, . . .* (Lincoln: J. H. Noteware, State Superintendent of Immigration, 1873), p. 9.

45. Baltensperger, "Plains Promoters and Plain Folk."

46. Ibid.

47. B. M. Davenport, *Resources of Nebraska* (Nebraska City, Nebr.: Press Printing Office, 1869), p. 4.

48. Powell, *Report on the Lands of the Arid Region*.

49. Baltensperger, "Plains Promoters and Plain Folk."

50. Samuel Aughey, *Sketches of the Physical Geography and Geology of Nebraska* (Omaha: Daily Republican Book and Job Office, 1880); Wilber, *The Great Valleys and Prairies of Nebraska and the Northwest*. See also Walter Kollmorgen and Johanna Kollmorgen, "Landscape Meteorology in the Plains Area," *Annals of the Association of American Geographers* 63 (1973):424–441; and Henry Nash Smith, "Rain Follows the Plow: The Notion of Increased Rainfall for the Great Plains, 1844–1880," *Huntington Library Quarterly* 10 (1947):169–193.

51. Baltensperger, "Plains Promoters and Plain Folk." See also Baltensperger, "Newspaper Images of the Central Great Plains."

52. Emmons, *Garden in the Grassland*; Baltensperger, "Plains Promoters and Plain Folk"; Overton, *Burlington West*; Barry B. Combs, "The Union Pacific Railroad and the Early Settlement of Nebraska, 1868–1880," *Nebraska History* 50 (1969):1–26. See also Luebke, "Ethnic Group Settlement on the Great Plains."

53. See, for example, J. C. Miller, "Ghost Towns in Otoe County," *Nebraska History* 18

(1937):185–189; and G. H. Gilmour, "Ghost Towns in Cass County," *Nebraska History* 18 (1937):181–184.

54. Andreas, *History of the State of Nebraska*.

55. Hudson, "Towns of the Western Railroads," citation on p. 43.

56. Ibid. See also Hudson, "The Plains Country Town."

57. *The Seven Per Cent. Gold Loan of the Kansas Pacific Railway* (n.p., 1869).

58. The term *delocalization* was introduced by Pertti Pelto in *The Snowmobile Revolution*. It refers to the process by which resources for a given culture cease to be primarily locally derived, but instead become nonlocal as the group's ties to the "outside world" strengthen. Delocalization is associated with greater vulnerability to decisions and forces outside the control of the group.

59. Webb, *The Great Plains*, p. 8.

60. For the development of agriculture in Nebraska in the late nineteenth century, see Sweedlun, "A History of the Evolution of Agriculture in Nebraska, 1870–1930"; and Baltensperger, "Plains Promoters and Plain Folk."

61. Baltensperger, "Agricultural Adjustments to Great Plains Drought: The Republican Valley, 1870–1900."

62. Robert N. Manley, "In the Wake of the Grasshoppers: Public Relief in Nebraska, 1874–1875," *Nebraska History* 44 (1963): 255–275; Fite, *Farmers' Frontier*, pp. 55–74.

63. Bowden, "Desert Wheat Belt, Plains Corn Belt: Environmental Cognition and Behavior of Settlers in the Plains Margin, 1850–99"; Baltensperger, "Agricultural Adjustments."

64. *Nebraska State Journal* (Lincoln), August 6, 1886, p. 4.

65. Baltensperger, "Agricultural Adjustments."

66. Ibid.; Bowden, "Desert Wheat Belt."

67. Clark C. Spence, *The Rainmakers: American "Pluviculture" to World War II* (Lincoln: University of Nebraska Press, 1980).

68. Fite, *Farmers' Frontier*, pp. 127–131; Robert G. Dunbar, "Agricultural Adjustments in Eastern Colorado in the Eighteen-Nineties," *Agricultural History* 18 (1944):41–52; James C. Malin, "The Adaptation of the Agricultural System to Subhumid Environment," *Agricultural History* 10 (1936):118–141.

69. Brandhorst, "The North Platte Oasis"; Timothy J. Rickard, "The Great Plains as Part of an Irrigated Western Empire, 1890–1914," in Blouet and Lawson, *The Great Plains*, pp. 81–98; Baltensperger, "Agricultural Adjustments."

70. Baltensperger, "Agricultural Adjustments."

71. Ibid.; Baltensperger, "Plains Promoters and Plain Folk"; Mary W. H. Hargreaves, *Dry Farming in the Northern Great Plains, 1900–1925* (Cambridge: Harvard University Press, 1957).

72. Kollmorgen, "The Woodsman's Assaults on the Domain of the Cattleman."

73. Olson, *History of Nebraska*.

74. Gressley, *Bankers and Cattlemen*.

75. William D. Aeschbacher, "Development of Cattle Raising in the Sandhills," *Nebraska History* 28 (1947):41–64; Richards with Van Ackeren, *Bartlett Richards: Nebraska Sandhills Cattleman*.

76. C. Barron McIntosh points out that many Kinkaiders were not able to obtain claims on the better lands of the Sandhills because cattlemen already controlled the valleys. The Kinkaiders were left primarily upland dunes totally unsuitable for agriculture. See his "Forest Lieu Selections on the Sand Hills of Nebraska." See also C. Barron McIntosh, "Patterns from Land Alienation Maps," *Annals of the Association of American Geographers* 66 (1976):570–582; and Bowen, "Environmental Perception and Geographic Change in Southwest Sheridan County."

77. Marshall Bowen, "The Kinkaid Act and the Southern Sheridan County Sandhills of Nebraska," *Rocky Mountain Social Science Journal* 9 (1972):39–49.

78. Warrick and Bowden, "The Changing Impacts of Droughts in the Great Plains."

79. The twentieth-century reaction to drought problems differed from that in the nineteenth century, when state officials and newspaper editors preferred to blame "doomsayers" and the weak willed for problems. During the severe 1930s drought there was an appreciation of other forces that contributed to agricultural problems. An average of 21 percent of farm families across the plains states received some form of emergency relief during the 1930s, and outmigration and destitution were less pronounced. Ibid. See also Donald Worster, *Dust Bowl: The Southern Plains in the 1930s* (New York: Oxford University Press, 1979); and R. Douglas Hurt, *The Dust Bowl: An Agricultural and Social History* (Chicago: Nelson-Hall, 1981).

CHAPTER 3

1. U.S. Bureau of the Census, *1980 Census of Population,* vol. 1, *Characteristics of the Population* (Washington, D.C.: Government Printing Office, 1982); Roy W. Meyer, *History of the Santee Sioux* (Lincoln: University of Nebraska Press, 1967). See also Ethel Nurge, ed., *The Modern Sioux: Social Systems and Reservation Culture* (Lincoln: University of Nebraska Press, 1970).

2. Janet A. McDonnell, "Land Policy on the Omaha Reservation: Competency Commissions and Forced Fee Patents," *Nebraska History* 63 (1982):399–411.

3. See, for example, Bryan Higgins, "Urban Indians: Patterns and Transformations," *Journal of Cultural Geography* 2 (1982):110–118.

4. Mary Ann Jakl, "The Immigration and Population of Nebraska to 1870" (M.A. thesis, University of Nebraska, 1936).

5. Ibid.

6. See Zelinsky, *The Cultural Geography of the United States.*

7. Robert G. Athearn, *In Search of Canaan: Black Migration to Kansas, 1879–80* (Lawrence: University of Kansas Press, 1978); W. Sherman Savage, *Blacks in the West* (Westport, Conn.: Greenwood Press, 1976).

8. Beryl Decker, "The Lost Pioneers: Negro Homesteaders in Nebraska," *Negro Digest* 12, no. 7 (May 1963):63–66; Lillian Anthony-Welch, "Black People: The Nation-Building Vision," in *Broken Hoops and Plains People,* pp. 99–151; U.S. Bureau of the Census, *Thirteenth Census of the United States, 1910,* vol. 3 *Population* (Washington, D.C.: Government Printing Office, 1913).

9. U.S. Bureau of the Census, *1980 Census of Population.*

10. Among the important general works on the history of immigration to the United States are Maldwyn Allen Jones, *American Immigration* (Chicago: University of Chicago Press, 1960); and Marcus L. Hansen, *The Immigrant in American History* (Cambridge: Harvard University Press, 1940).

11. Luebke, "Ethnic Group Settlement on the Great Plains." See also *Broken Hoops and Plains People;* and Rife, *Germans and German-Russians in Nebraska: A Research Guide to Nebraska Ethnic Studies.*

12. See, for example, Robert C. Ostergren, "Prairie Bound: Migration Patterns to a Swedish Settlement on the Dakota Frontier," in Luebke, *Ethnicity on the Great Plains,* pp. 73–91.

13. Oscar Winther, "The English in Nebraska, 1857–1880," *Nebraska History* 48 (1967):209–224.

14. Henry W. Casper, *History of the Catholic Church in Nebraska,* 3 vols. (Milwaukee: Bruce Publishing Co., 1960–1966); James McShane and Nadine Murphy, "The Irish: The Heritage of Charles Stuart Parnell," in *Broken Hoops and Plains People,* pp. 369–395.

15. Casper, *History of the Catholic Church.*

16. U.S. Bureau of the Census, *Fifteenth Census of the United States: 1930,* vol. 3, *Population* (Washington, D.C.: Government Printing Office, 1932). The 1970 census was the last to ask questions on country of birth and of parents' birth.

17. Hildegard B. Johnson, "The Location of German Immigrants in the Middle West," *Annals of the Association of American Geographers* 41 (1951):1–41; Luebke, *Immigrants and Politics: The Germans of Nebraska, 1880–1900.* See also Heinz Kloss, *Atlas of Nineteenth and Early Twentieth Century German American Settlements* (Marburg, West Germany: N. G. Elwert, 1974).

18. Fred C. Koch, *The Volga Germans, in Russia and the Americas, from 1763 to the Present* (University Park: Pennsylvania State University Press, 1977); Timothy J. Kloberdanz, "Plainsmen of Three Continents: Volga German Adaptation to Steppe, Prairie, and Pampa," in Luebke, *Ethnicity on the Great Plains,* pp. 54–72.

19. Richard Sallet, *Russian-German Settlements in the United States,* trans. by La Vern Rippley and Armand Bauer (Fargo: North Dakota Institute for Regional Studies, 1974); James R. Griess, *The German-Russians: Those Who Came to Sutton* (Hastings, Nebr.: n.p., 1968).

20. U.S. Bureau of the Census, *1970 Census of Population* (Washington, D.C.: Government Printing Office, 1973).

21. Sandoz, *Old Jules;* Philip E. Vogel, "The Holland, Nebraska, Locality: A Comparative Study of Dutch and Non-Dutch Occupance" (M.A. thesis, University of Nebraska, 1956).

22. Paul A. Olson, "Scandinavians: The Search for Zion," in *Broken Hoops and Plains People,* pp. 237–289.

23. Donald K. Watkins, "Danes and Danish on the Great Plains: Some Sociolinguistic As-

pects," in *Languages in Conflict: Linguistic Acculturation on the Great Plains*, edited by Paul Schach (Lincoln: University of Nebraska Press, 1980), pp. 58–76.

24. U.S. Bureau of the Census, *1970 Census of Population*.

25. Rose Rosicky, *A History of the Czechs [Bohemians] in Nebraska* (Omaha: Czech Historical Club of Nebraska, 1929); Joseph G. Svoboda, "Czechs: The Love of Liberty," in *Broken Hoops and Plains People*, pp. 153–191.

26. Rosicky, *History of the Czechs;* Casper, *History of the Catholic Church.*

27. Rosicky, *History of the Czechs;* Robert I. Kutak, *The Story of a Bohemian-American Village* (New York: Arno Press and *New York Times*, 1970, originally published in 1933).

28. Rosicky, *History of the Czechs.*

29. Casper, *History of the Catholic Church;* Meroe J. Owens, "John Barzynski, Land Agent," *Nebraska History* 36 (1955):81–91.

30. U.S. Bureau of the Census, *1970 Census of Population.*

31. Betty Levitov, "Italians: La Famiglia," in *Broken Hoops and Plains People*, pp. 337–368.

32. Carol Gendler, "The Jews of Omaha: The First Sixty Years" (M.A. thesis, University of Nebraska at Omaha, 1968); Oliver B. Pollak, "The Jewish Peddlers o Omaha," *Nebraska History* 63 (1982):474–501.

33. Gendler, "Jews of Omaha"; Murray Frost, "A Demographic Analysis of the Omaha Jewish Community," *Review of Applied Urban Research* 5, no. 1 (January 1977):1–4.

34. Betty Levitov, "Jews: The Exodus People," in *Broken Hoops and Plains People*, pp. 291–336.

35. Ralph Grajeda, "Chicanos: The Mestizo Heritage," in *Broken Hoops and Plains People*, pp. 47–98. See also Carey McWilliams, *North from Mexico: The Spanish-Speaking People of the United States* (New York: Greenwood Press, 1968).

36. Domingo H. Cabacungan, "The Japanese: Buddha and Christ," in *Broken Hoops and Plains People*, pp. 407–416.

37. Zelinsky, *Cultural Geography of the United States.*

38. Frederick C. Luebke, "Legal Restrictions on Foreign Languages in the Great Plains States, 1917–1923," in *Languages in Conflict: Linguistic Acculturation on the Great Plains*, edited by Paul Schach (Lincoln: University of Nebraska Press, 1980), pp. 1–19.

39. Report of the Nebraska State Council of Defense, cited in Jack W. Rodgers, "The Foreign Language Issue in Nebraska, 1918–1923," *Nebraska History* 39 (1958):1–22.

40. Rodgers, "Foreign Language Issue"; Luebke, "Legal Restrictions on Foreign Languages."

41. Bradley H. Baltensperger, "Agricultural Change Among Great Plains Russian Germans," *Annals of the Association of American Geographers* 73 (1983):75–88; Bradley H. Baltensperger, "Agricultural Change Among Nebraska Immigrants, 1880–1900," in Luebke, *Ethnicity on the Great Plains*, pp. 170–189.

42. Roger L. Welsch, "Germans from Russia: A Place to Call Home," in *Broken Hoops and Plains People*, p. 231.

43. Evidence of increased ethnic awareness has been provided by surveys of ethnic identification. See J. Allen Williams, Jr., David R. Johnson, and Miguel A. Carranza, "Ethnic Assimilation and Pluralism in Nebraska," in Luebke, *Ethnicity on the Great Plains*, pp. 210–229.

44. The information on 1970–1980 changes is from the U.S. Bureau of the Census, *1980 Census of Population*, vol. 1, *Characteristics of the Population.*

45. Beale, "The Revival of Population Growth in Nonmetropolitan America"; David R. DiMartino, "Demographic Changes in Nebraska, 1970–80," *Review of Applied Urban Research* 9, no. 5 (1981):1–8.

46. For a summary, see Amos H. Hawley and Sara Mills Mazie, "An Overview," in Hawley and Mazie, *Nonmetropolitan America in Transition*, pp. 3–23.

47. John M. Wardwell, "The Reversal of Nonmetropolitan Migration Loss," in Dillman and Hobbs, *Rural Society in the U.S.*, pp. 23–33; Frank A. Clemente and Richard S. Krannich, "Energy," in Dillman and Hobbs, *Rural Society in the U.S.*, pp. 34–43; Fuguitt and Zuiches, "Residential Preferences and Population Distribution."

48. Fuguitt, "City and Village Population Trends in the Plains States."

49. Lonsdale, *Economic Atlas of Nebraska.*

50. Bureau of Vital Statistics, *Statistical Report, 1980* (Lincoln: Nebraska State Department of Health, 1981).

51. Ibid.

52. Donald E. Pursell, "Natural Population Decrease: Its Origins and Implications on the

Great Plains," in Lawson and Baker, *The Great Plains: Perspectives and Prospects*.

53. Bureau of Vital Statistics, *Statistical Report, 1980;* Herbert I. Sauer, "Geographic Differences in the Risk of Premature Death," *Business and Government Review* (May–June 1970):19–26.

54. U.S. Bureau of the Census, *1980 Census of Population*.

55. Ibid.

56. "Nebraska's Changing Age Structure," *Business in Nebraska* 61, no. 7 (October 1981).

57. See David L. Brown and Calvin L. Beale, "Diversity in Post-1970 Population Trends," in Hawley and Mazie, *Nonmetropolitan America in Transition*, pp. 27–71, on the relationship between outmigration of young adults and rising median age in much of the Great Plains. See also Lonsdale, *Economic Atlas of Nebraska*.

58. Lonsdale, *Economic Atlas of Nebraska*.

59. Ibid.

60. "Migration Trends and Patterns in Nebraska," *Business in Nebraska* 60, no. 32 (June 1981).

61. Gessaman, "Migration and Population Change in Nebraska: The Recent Experience and Speculations About the Future."

62. Clemente and Krannich, "Energy," pp. 36–37.

63. Hart, "The Middle West." See also Gastil, *Cultural Regions of the United States*.

64. At a 1981 show of irrigation equipment held in Grand Island, a particularly sophisticated lateral-move irrigation system fascinated farmers and the media alike. The device "walked" from one outlet of the buried water source to the next, clamped on automatically, and later unclamped as the sprinkler system moved through the field. Although the cost of the system was prohibitive for nearly all Nebraska farmers, its price was seldom discussed. The technical aspects of the device were of much greater moment.

65. Everett M. Rogers and Rabel J. Burdge, *Social Change in Rural Societies*, 2d ed. (New York: Appleton-Century-Crofts, 1972).

66. See Daniel Elazar, *American Federalism: A View from the States* (New York: Thomas Y. Crowell, 1972); and Gastil, *Cultural Regions of the United States*, for examinations of political traditions in the United States and how they relate to Nebraska.

67. A notable study of the relationship between nationality and electoral behavior is Luebke, *Immigrants and Politics*.

68. James R. Shortridge, "Patterns of Religion in the United States," *Geographical Review* 66 (1976):420–434; Wilbur Zelinsky, "An Approach to the Religious Geography of the United States; Patterns of Church Membership in 1952," *Annals of the Association of American Geographers* 51 (1961):139–193; Gaustad, *Historical Atlas of Religion in America*.

69. Gaustad, *Historical Atlas of Religion in America*.

70. For a related study in Missouri, see Edward Hassinger and John S. Holik, "Changes in the Number of Rural Churches in Missouri, 1952–1967," *Rural Sociology* 35 (1970):354–366.

71. Stoddard, "Changing Patterns of Some Rural Churches."

72. Gastil, *Cultural Regions of the United States*, summarizes research into national patterns of these and other indicators of regional cultures.

73. Ruth F. Hale, "A Map of Vernacular Regions in America" (Ph.D. dissertation, University of Minnesota, 1971).

CHAPTER 4

1. *Economic Development in Nebraska: A Planning Perspective;* estimates by Nebraska Department of Labor.

2. Charles L. Bare, "Nebraska Personal Income," *Business in Nebraska* 62, no. 5 (September 1982):1–3, 6; Lonsdale, *Economic Atlas of Nebraska;* U.S. Department of Agriculture, *Farm Income Statistics*, Statistical Bulletin 609 (Washington, D.C.: Economics, Statistics, and Cooperatives Service, 1978), p. 37.

3. Bare, "Nebraska Personal Income."

4. See Lonsdale, *Economic Atlas of Nebraska*.

5. *Survey of Current Business* (April 1981; April 1982); Donald E. Pursell, "Median Family Income, 1979," *Business in Nebraska* 62, no. 7 (October 1982).

6. Jerome A. Deichert, "Poverty of Nebraska Counties," *Business in Nebraska* 62, no. 11 (November 1982).

7. *Economic Development in Nebraska*.

8. Lonsdale, *Economic Atlas of Nebraska*.

9. Ibid.

10. Ibid.

11. *Nebraska Economic Projections 1975–2000*.

12. Lonsdale, *Economic Atlas of Nebraska*.

13. Ibid.; James R. Schmidt, "Crude Oil Production in Nebraska," *Business in Nebraska* 61, no. 2 (August 1981).

14. Olson, *History of Nebraska*.

15. Ibid.

16. Lonsdale, *Economic Atlas of Nebraska*; U.S. Bureau of the Census, *1977 Census of Manufactures* (Washington, D.C.: Government Printing Office, 1980).

17. A good summary of the factors involved in industrial growth in nonmetropolitan areas can be found in Lonsdale and Seyler, *Nonmetropolitan Industrialization*. See also Kale, "Industrial Development Trends in the Northern Plains States"; Gene Summers, Sharon Evans, Frank Clemente, E. M. Beck, and Jon Minkoff, *Industrial Invasion of Nonmetropolitan America* (New York: Praeger Publishers, 1976); and John L. Dietz, "Tractors to Capacitors: An Analysis of the Impact of New Manufacturing Plants on Small Agricultural Communities of the Northern Great Plains" (Ph.D. dissertation, Syracuse University, 1971).

18. Richard E. Lonsdale, John C. Kinworthy, and Thomas R. Doering, *Attitudes of Manufacturers in Small Cities and Towns of Nebraska* (Lincoln: Nebraska Department of Economic Development, 1976); *Labor Supplies for Nonmetropolitan Manufacturing Plants in Small Communities of the Central Great Plains* (Lincoln: Nebraska Department of Economic Development, 1979).

19. See Hawley and Mazie, *Nonmetropolitan America in Transition*.

20. Lonsdale, *Economic Atlas of Nebraska*.

21. Ibid.; *Directory of Nebraska Manufacturers*.

22. *Directory of Nebraska Manufacturers*. See also Lonsdale, *Economic Atlas of Nebraska*.

23. Lonsdale, *Economic Atlas of Nebraska*.

24. Ibid.; *Directory of Nebraska Manufacturers*.

25. *Directory of Nebraska Manufacturers*.

26. Ibid.

27. Lonsdale, *Economic Atlas of Nebraska*.

28. Ibid.

29. Ibid.

30. Ibid.

31. Dale G. Anderson, Floyd D. Gaibler, and Mary Berglund, *Economic Impact of Railroad Branch-Line Abandonments: Results of a South-central Nebraska Case Study*, Nebraska Agricultural Experiment Station Bulletin SB541 (Lincoln: University of Nebraska, 1976).

32. A number of studies of the impacts of branch-line abandonment are reviewed in Dale G. Anderson, "Economic Implications of Railroad Branchline Abandonments for Rural Shippers: An Evaluation of Recent Research Findings," Department of Agricultural Economics Staff Paper 1978-#7 (Lincoln: University of Nebraska–Lincoln, 1978).

33. Nebraska Public Service Commission, *Annual Report, 1978–80* (Lincoln: Nebraska Public Service Commission, 1980).

34. Ibid.

35. Chuck Hassebrook, "Alliance Struggles with Boom Town Expansion," *New Land Review* 3, no. 1 (Winter 1977):8, 10.

36. Lonsdale, *Economic Atlas of Nebraska*.

37. Data from the Nebraska Department of Roads.

38. Lonsdale, *Economic Atlas of Nebraska*.

39. The concepts of low- and high-order goods and threshold populations have been widely explored. A convenient summary is Berry, *The Geography of Market Centers and Retail Distribution*.

40. Amos H. Hawley and Sara Mills Mazie, "An Overview," in Hawley and Mazie, *Nonmetropolitan America in Transition*, p. 12.

41. Bremer, *Agricultural Change in an Urban Age*.

42. Albert J. Larson, "Change in Service Functions in Small Town Nebraska, 1963–1980," paper presented at the International Geographical Union Commission on Rural Development symposium, Fresno, Calif., April 1981.

43. Lamb, *Metropolitan Impacts on Rural America*.

44. Larson, "Change in Service Functions."

45. Ibid.

46. Michael K. Miller, "Health and Medical Care," in Dillman and Hobbs, *Rural Society in the U.S.*, pp. 216–223; Roger A. Rosenblatt, "Health and Health Services," in Hawley and Mazie, *Nonmetropolitan America in Transition*, pp. 614–642.

47. Mark David Menchik, "The Service Sector," in Hawley and Mazie, *Nonmetropolitan America in Transition*, pp. 231–254.

CHAPTER 5

1. Bremer, *Agricultural Change in an Urban Age*.

2. Eugene Mather, "Cattle Ranching in the Sand Hills of Nebraska" (Ph.D. dissertation, University of Wisconsin, 1951).

3. U.S. censuses of agriculture.

4. J. Patrick Madden, *Economies of Size in Farming: Theory, Analytic Procedures, and a Review of Selected Studies,* U.S.D.A. Agricultural Economics Report 107 (Washington, D.C.: Government Printing Office, 1976); Raup, "Societal Goals in Farm Size."

5. Bruce B. Johnson and Ronald J. Hanson, *Nebraska Farm Real Estate Market Developments, 1980-81,* Department of Agricultural Economics Report no. 118 (Lincoln: University of Nebraska–Lincoln, 1981).

6. Ibid.

7. Ibid.

8. Lonsdale, *Economic Atlas of Nebraska.*

9. R. J. Hanson and R.G.F. Spitze, "Dual Employment Increasingly Important to Small Farmer Income," Department of Agricultural Economics Staff Paper 1975-#5 (Lincoln: University of Nebraska–Lincoln, 1975); Bruce B. Johnson, Ronald J. Hanson, and Stuart L. Bartruff, *Off-Farm Income and Dual Employment Characteristics Among Eastern Nebraska Farm Families,* Department of Agricultural Economics Report no. 114 (Lincoln: University of Nebraska–Lincoln, 1980).

10. Hanson and Spitze, "Dual Employment," p. 9. See also C. Milton Coughenour and Ronald C. Wimberley, "Small and Part-Time Farmers," in Dillman and Hobbs, *Rural Society in the U.S.: Issues for the 1980s,* pp. 347-356.

11. Williams and Murfield, *Agricultural Atlas of Nebraska.*

12. *Nebraska Agricultural Statistics, Annual Report, 1980-1981.*

13. Leslie Sheffield, "The Cost of Center Pivot Irrigation Now," *Irrigation Age* (January 1975):12-15.

14. Hart, *The Look of the Land,* pp. 89-92.

15. Lynn Nejezchleb, "Structure and Efficiency of Nebraska Farms," *Business in Nebraska* 61, no. 14 (January 1981):1-6.

16. Jeffrey Pribbeno, Bruce Johnson, and Maurice Baker, *Farm Corporations in Nebraska,* Department of Agricultural Economics Report no. 78 (Lincoln: University of Nebraska–Lincoln, 1977).

17. Ibid.

18. *Wheels of Fortune.*

19. Ibid.

20. See Lynn Spivak, "Petersburg Residents Voice Opposition to Irrigation," *New Land Review* (Spring 1980):1, 3.

21. Vogeler, *The Myth of the Family Farm.*

22. Richard D. Rodefeld, "The Nature, Magnitude, and Consequences of Change in Farm Organizational, Occupational, and Class Structure," in *Change in Rural America: Causes, Consequences, and Alternatives,* edited by Richard D. Rodefeld, Jan Flora, Donald Voth, Isao Fujimoto, and Jim Converse (St. Louis: C. V. Mosby Co., 1978), pp. 121-128.

23. Ibid.

24. Rodefeld, "Trends in U.S. Farm Organizational Structure and Type."

25. Ibid.

26. William D. Heffernan, "Sociological Dimensions of Agriculture Structures in the United States," *Sociologia Ruralis* 12 (1972):481-499; Richard D. Rodefeld, "The Changing Organizational and Occupational Structure of Farming and the Implications for Farm Work Force Individuals, Families, and Communities" (Ph.D. dissertation, University of Wisconsin, 1974); and Olaf F. Larson, "Agriculture and the Community," in Hawley and Mazie, *Nonmetropolitan America in Transition,* pp. 148-193.

27. Rodefeld, "Nature, Magnitude, and Consequences of Change."

28. William D. Heffernan, "Structure of Agriculture and Quality of Life in Rural Communities," in Dillman and Hobbs, *Rural Society in the U.S.: Issues of the 1980s,* pp. 337-346, citing p. 341.

29. Schmedemann, "Issues of Ownership and Control of Agricultural Land in the Great Plains." Rodefeld, "Changing Organizational and Occupational Structure of Farming," has calculated that a complete changeover to industrial-type farms in Wisconsin would result in a 94 percent decrease in farm numbers, a 1,700 percent increase in farm size, and a 46 percent decrease in the farm labor force. Similar changes would presumably result from comparable structural changes in Nebraska agriculture.

30. Bruce B. Johnson, "Farmland Price Trends and Implications," *Business in Nebraska* 60, no. 30 (May 1981), p. 6; Johnson and Hanson, *Nebraska Farm Real Estate Market Developments.*

31. Everett G. Smith, Jr., "Fragmented Farms in the United States," *Annals of the Association of American Geographers* 65 (1975):58-70.

32. Sublett, *Farmers on the Road.*
33. Ibid.
34. Ibid.
35. Ibid.
36. Donald B. Deal, "Sidewalk Farming in the Specialized Wheat Region of Nebraska" (M.A. thesis, University of Nebraska, 1967).
37. Leslie Hewes, *The Suitcase Farming Frontier* (Lincoln: University of Nebraska Press, 1973); Deal, "Sidewalk Farming."
38. Hewes, *Suitcase Farming Frontier,* p. 183.
39. Williams and Murfield, *Agricultural Atlas of Nebraska.*
40. Ibid.
41. Ibid.
42. Ibid.
43. Marty Strange and Chuck Hassebrook, *Take Hogs, for Example* (Walthill, Nebr.: Center for Rural Affairs, 1981). See also several articles on hog confinement in *New Land Review* (Spring 1980):6–8.
44. Williams and Murfield, *Agricultural Atlas of Nebraska.*
45. U.S. Bureau of the Census, *1978 Census of Agriculture.*
46. Ibid.
47. *Nebraska Agricultural Statistics, Annual Report: 1973-1974; 1979-1980.*
48. *Nebraska Agricultural Statistics, Annual Report: 1979-1980.*
49. William F. Lagrone and Ronald D. Krenz, *Corn Production Practices in Selected States, 1978,* Department of Agricultural Economics Report no. 108 (Lincoln: University of Nebraska–Lincoln, 1980).
50. William F. Lagrone and Ronald D. Krenz, *Hard Red Winter Wheat Production Practices in Selected States, 1978,* Department of Agricultural Economics Report no. 110 (Lincoln: University of Nebraska–Lincoln, 1978).
51. D. E. Smika, "Summer Fallow for Dryland Winter Wheat in the Semiarid Great Plains," *Agronomy Journal* 62 (1970):15–17.
52. Thomas D. Isern, *Custom Combining on the Great Plains: A History* (Norman: University of Oklahoma Press, 1982).
53. Williams and Murfield, *Agricultural Atlas of Nebraska.*
54. Ibid.
55. Paarlberg, *Farm and Food Policy Issues of the 1980s;* and Jerry D. Stockdale, "Who Will Speak for Agriculture?" in Dillman and Hobbs, *Rural Society in the U.S.,* pp. 317–327.
56. Stockdale, "Who Will Speak for Agriculture?" p. 320.
57. Vogeler, *Myth of the Family Farm.*

CHAPTER 6

1. Alvin L. Bertrand, "Rural Social Organizational Implications of Technology and Industry," in Ford, *Rural U.S.A.,* pp. 75–88, citing p. 76. See also Earle D. Ross, "Retardation in Farm Technology Before the Power Age," *Agricultural History* 30 (1956):11–18.
2. U.S. censuses of agriculture, 1910, 1940; Wayne D. Rasmussen, "The Impact of Technological Change on Agriculture, 1862–1962," *Journal of Economic History* 22 (1962):578–599.
3. Shover, *First Majority—Last Minority.*
4. See Bremer, *Agricultural Change in an Urban Age.*
5. Ibid.
6. *Nebraska Agricultural Statistics, Annual Report: 1980-1981.*
7. Chuck Hassebrook, "Bigger Machinery—Bigger Farms—An Endless Spiral," *New Land Review* (Winter 1978):3.
8. Richard D. Rodefeld, *The Direct and Indirect Effects of Mechanizing U.S. Agriculture* (Montclair, N.J.: Allanheld, Osmun, and Co., 1981).
9. Bremer, *Agricultural Change in an Urban Age.*
10. Pimentel et al., "Food Production and the Energy Crisis." See also Perelman, "Farming with Petroleum"; and Vaclav Smil, Paul Nachman, and Thomas V. Long II, *Energy Analysis and Agriculture: An Application to U.S. Corn Production* (Boulder, Colo.: Westview Press, 1983).
11. *Nebraska Agricultural Statistics,* various annual issues. See also Wilhite, *Changing Fields.*
12. U.S. Bureau of the Census, *1978 Census of Agriculture* (Washington, D.C.: Government Printing Office, 1981).
13. Clifford M. Hardin, foreword to *Contours of Change, U.S.D.A. Yearbook of Agriculture, 1970* (Washington, D.C.: Government Printing Office, 1970), p. xxxiii.
14. Michael Perelman, "Efficiency in Agriculture: The Economics of Energy," in *Radical Agriculture,* edited by Richard Merrill (New York: Harper Colophon, 1976), pp. 64–86.
15. Buttel and Larson, "Farm Size, Structure, and Energy Intensity." See also Frederick H.

Buttel, William Lockeretz, Martin Strange, and Elinor Terhune, *Energy and Small Farms: A Review of Existing Literature and Suggestions Concerning Future Research*, Research Agenda for Small Farms Monograph 2 (Washington, D.C.: National Rural Center, 1980); and Luther Tweeten, "The Economics of Small Farms," *Science* 219 (1983):1037–1041.

16. Vogeler, *Myth of the Family Farm*; Perelman, "Efficiency in Agriculture."

17. William Lockeretz et al., "Field Crop Production on Organic Farms in the Midwest," *Journal of Soil and Water Conservation* 33 (1978):130–134; and Warren W. Sahs, "Organic and Inorganic Nitrogen Sources for Irrigated Corn" (unpublished paper, University of Nebraska–Lincoln).

18. John S. Steinhart and Carol E. Steinhart, *Energy: Sources, Uses, and Role in Human Affairs* (North Scituate, Mass.: Duxbury Press, 1974), p. 68.

19. Dan McCurry, "Tarnished Gold," *New Land Review* (Winter 1978):12.

20. *Wheels of Fortune;* McKnight, "Great Circles on the Great Plains."

21. "Center Pivot Irrigation Systems in Nebraska, 1981," map (Lincoln: University of Nebraska–Lincoln, Conservation and Survey Division, 1983).

22. *Nebraska Agricultural Statistics, Annual Report: 1980-1981.*

23. Stone, "Effects of Center Pivot Irrigation"; Stephen F. Hoesel, "The Impact of Center-Pivot Irrigation on the Sandhills of Nebraska" (M.A. thesis, University of Nebraska at Omaha, 1973).

24. Lamphear and Roesler, *Impact Analysis of Irrigated Agriculture on Nebraska's Economy, 1967–1970;* Philip E. Vogel, "A Geographic Study of Some of the Effects of Irrigation in the Nebraska Bostwick Irrigation Project" (Ph. D. dissertation, University of Nebraska, 1960).

25. *Wheels of Fortune.*

26. *Center for Rural Affairs Newsletter* (June 1982).

27. *Wheels of Fortune.*

28. Ibid.

29. Ibid; conversation with Marty Strange, codirector, Center for Rural Affairs.

30. Data from U.S. Soil Conservation Service.

31. Ibid.

32. *Prairie Sentinel* (April–May 1982):8–11.

33. Stone, "Effects of Center Pivot Irrigation"; Rodefeld, *Direct and Indirect Effects of Mechanizing U.S. Agriculture.*

34. William Lockeretz, "The Dust Bowl: Its Relevance to Contemporary Environmental Problems," in Lawson and Baker, *The Great Plains: Perspectives and Prospects,* pp. 11–31; Lockeretz, "Lessons of the Dust Bowl."

35. "Guidelines for Livestock Waste Management" (Lincoln: Nebraska Department of Environmental Control, 1977).

36. See several short articles in *New Land Review* (Spring 1981):12–18; Bryan Jones, "Suits and Countersuits Galore," *Prairie Sentinel* (December 1981–January 1982):6–7.

37. Mary E. Exner and Roy F. Spalding, *Groundwater Quality of the Central Platte Region, 1974,* Resource Atlas no. 2 (Lincoln: University of Nebraska–Lincoln, Conservation and Survey Division, 1976); Mary E. Exner and Roy F. Spalding, "Evolution of Contaminated Groundwater in Holt County, Nebraska," *Water Resources Research* 15 (1979):139–147; J. R. Gormly and R. F. Spalding, "Sources and Concentrations of Nitrate-Nitrogen in Ground Water of the Central Platte Region in Nebraska," *Ground Water* 17 (1979):291–301.

38. R. A. Engberg, "Nitrate and Orthophosphate in Several Nebraska Streams," *U.S. Geological Survey Professional Paper* 750-C, pp. C215–C222.

39. Buttel, "Rural Natural Resource Use and the Environment," in Dillman and Hobbs, *Rural Society in the U.S.: Issues for the 1980s,* pp. 359–372; Buttel and Larson, "Farm Size, Structure, and Energy Intensity"; and C.H.M. van Bavel, "Soil and Oil," *Science* 197 (1977):213.

40. Fischer, "Environment and Farm Size"; Wilson Clark, "U.S. Agriculture Is Growing Trouble as Well as Crops," *Smithsonian* 5 (1975):59–65.

41. Fite, "Great Plains Farming," p. 256.

42. Pelto, *The Snowmobile Revolution.* See Note 58, Chapter 2 for an explanation of *delocalization.*

43. Rodefeld, "Causes of Change in Farm Technology, Size, and Organizational Structure"; and Vogeler, *Myth of the Family Farm.*

44. Warrick and Bowden, "Changing Impacts of Droughts in the Great Plains."

45. Bruce B. Johnson, "Irrigation, Energy, and Conservation: Some Economic Issues," Department of Agricultural Economics Staff Paper 1979-#3 (Lincoln: University of Nebraska–Lincoln, 1979).

46. Raup, "Societal Goals in Farm Size."
47. Bremer, *Agricultural Change in an Urban Age.*

CHAPTER 7

1. Hart, *The Look of the Land*, p. 115.
2. Bremer, *Agricultural Change in an Urban Age.*
3. Hewes, "Early Fencing on the Western Margin of the Prairie."
4. Thomas R. Walsh, "The American Green of Charles Bessey," *Nebraska History* 53 (1972):35-37.
5. Curtis J. Sorenson and Glen A. Marotz, "Changes in Shelterbelt Mileage Statistics over Four Decades in Kansas," *Journal of Soil and Water Conservation* 32 (1977):276-281.
6. Stone, "Effects of Center Pivot Irrigation."
7. Ibid.
8. D. Paul Miller, "Jansen, Nebraska, A Story of Community Adjustment," *Nebraska History* 35 (1954):127-136.
9. Lommasson, *Nebraska Wild Flowers.*
10. Hudson, "Towns of the Western Railroads"; and Hudson, "The Plains Country Town."
11. Bremer, *Agricultural Change in an Urban Age.*

CHAPTER 8

1. Glenn V. Fuguitt, "The City and the Countryside," *Rural Sociology* 28 (1963): 246-261.
2. Danbom, *The Resisted Revolution.* p. 4.
3. Bremer, *Agricultural Change in an Urban Age.*
4. See Fern K. Willits, Robert C. Bealer, and Donald M. Crider, "Persistence of Rural/Urban Differences," in Dillman and Hobbs, *Rural Society in the U.S.*, pp. 69-76; and Olaf F. Larson, "Values and Beliefs of Rural People," in Ford, *Rural U.S.A.*, pp. 91-112.
5. U.S. Bureau of the Census, *U.S. Census of Agriculture: 1950* (Washington, D.C.: Government Printing Office, 1952).
6. Ibid.
7. U.S. Bureau of the Census, *1970 Census of Housing* (Washington, D.C.: Government Printing Office, 1973); U.S. Bureau of Census, *1980 Census of Housing* (Washington, D.C.: Government Printing Office, 1982).
8. U.S. Bureau of the Census, *U.S. Census of Agriculture: 1950.*
9. Fuller, *RFD: The Changing Face of Rural America;* Hudson, "The Plains Country Town."
10. U.S. Bureau of the Census, *U.S. Census of Agriculture: 1950.*
11. Berger, *The Devil Wagon in God's Country*, p. 209.
12. Bremer, *Agricultural Change in an Urban Age;* Danbom, *Resisted Revolution;* Fuguitt, "The City and the Countryside."
13. Data from Nebraska State Department of Education.
14. Bremer, *Agricultural Change in an Urban Age.*
15. Ibid., p. 185.
16. See Jonathan P. Sher and Rachel B. Tompkins, "Economy, Efficiency, and Equality: The Myths of Rural School and District Consolidation," in Sher, *Education in Rural America*, pp. 43-77.
17. Williams and Murfield, *Agricultural Atlas of Nebraska.*
18. Wilkening and Klessig, "The Rural Environment"; Marion Clawson, "Land Use Trends," in Hawley and Mazie, *Nonmetropolitan America in Transition*, pp. 645-667.
19. *Lincoln Journal,* January 17, 1979, p. 19.
20. Wilkening and Klessig, "Rural Environment."
21. Clawson, "Land Use Trends."
22. David Berry, "Effects of Urbanization on Agricultural Activities," *Growth and Change* 9, no. 3 (1978):2-7.
23. Wilkening and Klessig, "Rural Environment."
24. Frederick H. Buttel, "Rural Natural Resource Use and the Environment," in Dillman and Hobbs, *Rural Society in the U.S.*, pp. 359-372; Clemente and Krannich, "Energy."
25. Wilkening and Klessig, "Rural Environment."
26. Shover, *First Majority—Last Minority.*
27. Fuguitt and Zuiches, "Residential Preferences and Population Distribution."
28. Charles E. Little and W. Wendell Fletcher, "Buckshot Urbanization: The Land Impacts of Rural Population Growth," *American Land Forum Magazine* 2 (Fall 1981):10-35, quotation on p. 34.
29. Michael Kelly, "SID Root Brings 'Suburbia, Neb.,' " *Omaha World Herald*, October 28, 1981, pp. 29-30.

30. *Identification of Prime Residential Land in Rural Nebraska.*
31. Ibid.
32. Ibid., p. 21.
33. Wilkening and Klessig, "Rural Environment."
34. Michael Lundeen and Paul H. Gessaman, "Rural Zoning in Madison County," Department of Agricultural Economics Staff Paper 1980-#4 (Lincoln: University of Nebraska–Lincoln, 1980).
35. Robert Sinclair, "Von Thunen and Urban Sprawl," *Annals of the Association of American Geographers* 57 (1967):72–87.
36. Furuseth and Pierce, *Agricultural Land in an Urban Society.*
37. Ibid.; Berry, "Effects of Urbanization on Agricultural Activities."
38. Buttel, "Rural Natural Resource Use."
39. David L. Rogers, "Community Services," in Dillman and Hobbs, *Rural Society in the U.S.*, pp. 146–155; and Kenneth D. Rainey and Karen G. Rainey, "Rural Government and Local Public Services," in Ford, *Rural U.S.A.: Persistence and Change*, pp. 126–144.
40. Lee, "Cost of Compact vs. Scattered Land Use Development."
41. Lundeen and Gessaman, "Rural Zoning in Madison County."
42. Furuseth and Pierce, *Agricultural Land in an Urban Society*, p. 46.
43. Wilkening and Klessig, "Rural Environment."

CHAPTER 9

1. Richard C. Wade, *The Urban Frontier, The Rise of Western Cities, 1790–1830* (Cambridge: Harvard University Press, 1959).
2. See James E. Vance, Jr., *The Merchant's World: The Geography of Wholesaling* (Englewood Cliffs, N.J.: Prentice-Hall, 1970).
3. Omaha City Planning Department, *A Comprehensive Program for Historic Preservation in Omaha*, p. 75; Carol Gendler, "Territorial Omaha as a Staging and Freighting Center," *Nebraska History* 49 (1968):103–120; and Norman A. Graebner, "Nebraska's Missouri River Frontier," *Nebraska History* 42 (1961): 213–235.
4. Olson, *History of Nebraska.*
5. A primate city is one that is considerably larger than any other city in the urban system. Omaha's population in 1870 was over sixteen thousand. The second-largest place in the state, Nebraska City, had only six thousand. Lincoln, third in size, recorded only twenty-five hundred persons.
6. Omaha City Planning Department, *Comprehensive Program.*
7. Olson, *History of Nebraska.*
8. Omaha City Planning Department, *Comprehensive Program.*
9. Olson, *History of Nebraska.*
10. J. W. Alexander, "The Basic-Nonbasic Concept of Urban Economic Functions," *Economic Geography* 20 (1954):246–261.
11. Omaha City Planning Department, *Comprehensive Program.*
12. Berry, *Geography of Market Centers and Retail Distribution.*
13. Chudacoff, *Mobile Americans;* Olson, *History of Nebraska.* The 1890 census grossly overcounted the true population of several Nebraska cities. Palmer estimates Omaha to have actually contained 102,430 persons, rather than 140,452; see Edgar Z. Palmer, "The Correctness of the 1890 Census of Population for Nebraska Cities," *Nebraska History* 32 (1951):259–267.
14. Chudacoff, *Mobile Americans.*
15. Omaha City Planning Department, *Comprehensive Program.*
16. Fimple, "Midwestern Mosaic"; Omaha City Planning Department, *Comprehensive Program.*
17. Chudacoff, *Mobile Americans;* Thavenet, "History of Omaha Public Transportation." The interrelationships between street railways and suburban expansion in this period have been carefully examined in Warner, *Streetcar Suburbs.*
18. Fimple, "Midwestern Mosaic."
19. Omaha City Planning Department, *Comprehensive Program;* Works Progress Administration, *The Italians of Omaha* (Omaha: Independent Printing Co., 1941); U.S. Bureau of the Census, *Thirteenth Census of the United States, 1910* (Washington, D.C.: Government Printing Office, 1913).
20. Omaha City Planning Department, *Comprehensive Program;* McMorris, "The People Who Make Up Omaha"; John G. Bitzes, "The Anti-Greek Riot of 1909—South Omaha," *Nebraska History* 51 (1970):199–224.
21. Garneth O. Peterson, "Historical Framework," in Omaha City Planning Department,

Comprehensive Program; Gendler, "Jews of Omaha"; Omaha City Planning Department, *Comprehensive Program.*

22. Chudacoff, *Mobile Americans.*

23. Omaha City Planning Department, *Comprehensive Program.*

24. Homer Hoyt, *The Structure and Growth of Residential Neighborhoods* (Washington, D.C.: Federal Housing Administration, 1939).

25. Chudacoff, *Mobile Americans.*

26. Yeates and Garner, *North American City.*

27. E. M. Kitagawa and D. J. Bogue, *Suburbanization of Manufacturing Industry Within Standard Metropolitan Statistical Areas* (Oxford, Ohio: Scripps Foundation, 1955); Yeates and Garner, *North American City;* Allan R. Pred, "The Intrametropolitan Location of American Manufacturing," *Annals of the Association of American Geographers* 54 (1964):165–174.

28. "An Examination of Population Changes, 1970–80," *Review of Applied Urban Research* 8, no. 3 (March 1980):1–5; Paul S. T. Lee, "Intra-Urban Migration and Omaha's Westward Expansion," *Review of Applied Urban Research* 4, no. 3 (March 1976):1–4; DiMartino, "Omaha Area Demographic Change, 1970–80"; and John J. Zipay, *The Changing Population of the Omaha SMSA 1860–1967 with Estimates for 1970* (Omaha: University of Omaha, Omaha Urban Area Research Project, 1967).

29. Three indexes of black concentration decreased substantially during the 1970s, with the index of dissimilarity falling from 84.5 to 77.3: Frost, "Distribution of Omaha's Black Population." A value of 100 for the index of dissimilarity would mean a group is totally segregated—it constitutes the entire population of one area and is not found elsewhere. A value of zero would mean the group is completely dispersed in the total population. See Chudacoff, "New Look at Ethnic Neighborhoods."

30. DiMartino, "Omaha Area Demographic Change"; Murray Frost, "A Demographic Analysis of the Omaha Jewish Community," *Review of Applied Urban Research* 5, no. 1 (January 1977):1–4; Frost, "Distribution of Omaha's Black Population."

31. Chudacoff, "New Look at Ethnic Neighborhoods."

32. Ibid. Indexes of dissimilarity for Omaha were calculated for 1920 by country of birth: Czechoslovakia—59.4; Poland—55.8; Italy—53.1; Austria—45.7; Russia—44.3; Canada—16.4; England—16.4; Sweden—15.5; Denmark—12.2; Ireland—12.1; Germany—11.0.

33. Chudacoff, "New Look at Ethnic Neighborhoods," p. 91; Omaha City Planning Department, *Comprehensive Program.*

34. Chudacoff, "New Look at Ethnic Neighborhoods"; Charles R. Gildersleeve and Scott Samson, "Field Information on the Ethnic Iconography of Omaha" (unpublished field guide, n.d.).

35. Yeates and Garner, *North American City;* G. C. Cameron, "Intraurban Location and the New Plant," *Papers of the Regional Science Association* 31 (1973):125–143.

36. Yeates and Garner, *North American City;* Brian J. L. Berry and Y. S. Cohen, "Decentralization of Commerce and Industry: The Restructuring of Metropolitan America," in *The Urbanization of the Suburbs,* edited by L. M. Masotti and J. K. Hadden, Urban Affairs Annual Reviews, vol. 7 (Beverly Hills, Calif.: Sage Publications, 1973), pp. 431–456.

37. U.S. Bureau of the Census, *1972 Census of Retail Trade* (Washington, D.C.: Government Printing Office, 1973); U.S. Bureau of the Census, *1977 Census of Retail Trade* (Washington, D.C.: Government Printing Office, 1978); "Omaha's Central Business District," *Review of Applied Urban Research* 7, no. 4 (July 1976):1–6.

38. U.S. Bureau of the Census, *1977 Census of Retail Trade.*

39. "A Statistical Guide to Omaha's Central Business District" (Omaha: Greater Omaha Chamber of Commerce, 1981).

40. Ludwig, "The Changing Distribution of Omaha's Office Space"; Armin K. Ludwig, "Location Decision Making in Three Suburban Omaha Office Clusters," *Review of Applied Urban Research* 5, no. 8 (August 1977):1–4.

41. Ludwig, "Changing Distribution of Omaha's Office Space"; Murray Frost and Armin K. Ludwig, "Interstate Freeways Attract New Office Sites," *Review of Applied Urban Research* 7, no. 10 (October 1979):1–8.

42. Ludwig, "Location Decision Making."

43. Chauncy D. Harris and Edward L. Ullman, "The Nature of Cities," *Annals of the American Academy of Political and Social Science* 142 (1945):7–17.

44. *The Lincoln–Lancaster County Comprehensive Regional Plan,* p. 84.

45. Ibid., p. 10.

46. "Attitudes Toward the Construction of

an Urban Expressway: The North Omaha Case," *Review of Applied Urban Research* 2, no. 9 (September 1974):1–7.

47. Ibid.; "Relocation Impact of North Freeway Alternatives," *Review of Applied Urban Research* 2, no. 12 (December 1974):1–7.

CHAPTER 10

1. Webb, *The Great Plains,* p. 8.

2. Timothy J. Rickard, "The Great Plains as Part of an Irrigated Western Empire, 1890–1914," in Blouet and Luebke, *The Great Plains: Environment and Culture,* pp. 81–98.

3. Lockeretz, "Lessons of the Dust Bowl," p. 560.

4. Leslie Hewes, "Agricultural Risk in the Great Plains," in Blouet and Luebke, *The Great Plains: Environment and Culture,* pp. 157–185.

5. Hugh H. Bennett, *Soil Conservation* (New York: McGraw Hill, 1939).

6. Lockeretz, "Lessons of the Dust Bowl," p. 563.

7. Marty Strange, "Of Whooping Cranes and Family Farms: Another Look at the High Plains Study," *Journal of Soil and Water Conservation* 38 (1983), pp. 28–32, quoting p. 32. See also Paul H. Gessaman, "Rugged Individualism: Recurring Myth or Reemerging Giant," in Lawson and Baker, *The Great Plains: Perspectives and Prospects,* pp. 267–275.

ILLUSTRATION CREDITS

Illustrations not otherwise attributed are by the author.

Ash Grove Cement Co.: Fig. 4.5 (reproduced by permission).

Association of American Geographers: Fig. 2.19 (Bradley H. Baltensperger, "Agricultural Change Among Great Plains Russian Germans," *Annals of the Association of American Geographers* 73 [1983]:78) (reprinted by permission).

Burlington Northern Railroad: Fig. 4.14 (reproduced by permission).

Burlington Northern Railroad and Harr, Hedrich-Blessing: Fig. 4.16 (reproduced by permission).

Cartwright, Terry L.: Figs. 6.15 and 7.9 (reproduced by permission).

Center for Rural Affairs, Walthill, Nebraska: Fig. 5.15 (reproduced by permission).

Farm, Ranch, and Home Quarterly: Fig. 1.25 (Ray Bentall, "Inflow Decline Poses Problems," *Farm, Ranch, and Home Quarterly* 27, no. 2 [1980]:8–10) (reprinted by permission).

Fimple, Kathleen Louise: Fig. 9.5 ("Midwestern Mosaic: A Study of the Homogeneity of Ethnic Population in Omaha, Nebraska, 1880," M.S. thesis, South Dakota State University, 1978) (modified and reprinted by permission).

Johnston, Jeffrey P.: Fig. 1.18 (reproduced by permission).

Missouri River Basin Commission: Fig. 1.3 ("Flood Damage and Control" and "Hydrology and Hydraulics," technical papers in *Report on the Platte River Basin, Nebraska Level B Study,* 1976) (reprinted by permission).

NCLRS (Nebraska Crop and Livestock Reporting Service): Figs. 5.2, 5.20, 5.21, 5.22, 5.23, 5.24, 5.25, 5.26, 5.27, 5.28, 5.31, 5.32, 5.33, 5.34, 5.35, 5.36, and 5.37 based on materials from the agency.

Nebraska Department of Economic Development: Fig. 4.1 based on *Survey of Current Business* (April 1982):62 and *Nebraska Statistical Handbook, 1980–81,* 1981; Fig. 4.7 based on materials from the agency; Figs. 4.8 and 4.10 based on *Director of Nebraska Manufacturers,* 1982.

Nebraska Department of Health, Bureau of Vital Statistics: Fig. 3.19 (*Statistical Report of the Bureau of Vital Statistics,* 1981) (reprinted by permission); Figs. 3.20, 4.28, and 4.29 based on materials from the agency.

Nebraska Game and Parks Commission: Fig. 6.12 (photo by Jon Farrar; reproduced by permission).

Nebraska Legislative Council: Figs. 3.26 and 3.27 based on *Nebraska Blue Book, 1980–1981.*

Nebraska Natural Resources Commission: Fig. 1.29 (*Summary of the Nebraska Research for the Six-State High Plains Ogallala Aquifer Study,* 1981) (adapted by permission); Fig. 1.30 (September 1982 newsletter) (reprinted by permission).

Nebraska Public Power District: Fig. 4.18 (*Annual Report,* 1981) (adapted and reprinted with permission).

NSHS (Nebraska State Historical Society): Figs. 1.6, 2.2, 2.9, 2.10, 2.13, 2.14, 2.18, 6.1, 7.11, 7.17, 7.23, 7.24, 7.25, 9.1, 9.2, and 9.4 (reproduced by permission); Figs. 2.8, 2.20, and 3.3 (Solomon D. Butcher Collection) (reproduced by permission); Figs. 3.6 and 3.7 (photos by D. Murphy, courtesy Nebraska State

Historical Society); Fig. 7.1 (photo by J. Jeffries Spencer, courtesy Nebraska State Historical Society).

Nicholson, Kovac, Huntley, & Welsh and the Reinke Manufacturing Co.: Fig. 6.9 (reproduced by permission).

Omaha Public Power District: Fig. 4.19 (reproduced by permission).

Omaha World Herald: Fig. 8.10 (reproduced by permission).

Sandhills Cattle Association: Fig. 5.18 (photo by Margaret MacKichan; made available through and property of Sandhills Cattle Association).

Union Pacific Railroad: Figs. 4.13, 4.15, and 9.7 (reproduced by permission).

USDA, ASCS (U.S. Department of Agriculture, Agricultural Stabilization and Conservation Service): Figs. 1.10, 1.26, 3.14, 4.11, 5.3, 5.4, 6.13, 6.17, 8.5, 8.6, 8.7, 8.8, 9.12, 9.13, and 9.15.

USDA, SCS (U.S. Department of Agriculture, Soil Conservation Service): Figs. 4.27, 5.29, 6.7, 6.11, 6.14, 6.19, 7.13, 7.16, 7.21, and 8.1.

UNL (University of Nebraska–Lincoln), Bureau of Business Research: Fig. 3.22 (*Business in Nebraska* 61, no. 7 [1981]) (reprinted with permission); Fig. 3.25 based on Vernon Renshaw, *Nebraska Population Projections, 1975–2000,* Report no. 6, 1973: Fig. 4.2 based on materials from the agency; Fig. 4.17 based on Cliff M. Dobitz, "Electricity in Nebraska," *Business in Nebraska* 61, no. 22 [1982]; Fig. 4.24 based on Donald E. Pursell, "Nebraska Retail Sales," *Business in Nebraska* 61, no. 27 [1982].

UNL (University of Nebraska–Lincoln), Conservation and Survey Division, Institute of Agriculture and Natural Resources: Fig. 1.15 (Ray Bentall, "Nebraska's Platte River: A Graphic Analysis of Flows," *Nebraska Water Survey Paper* 53) (reprinted with permission); Fig. 6.20 (R. A. Engberg and R. F. Spaulding, *Groundwater Quality Atlas,* Resource Atlas no. 3, 1978) (reprinted with permission); Figs. 1.4, 1.19, 1.21, 1.22, 1.23, 1.24, 6.5, 6.6, and 6.10 (reprinted with permission); Figs. 1.8, 1.13, and 1.20 adapted from agency materials; Fig. 4.4 adapted from Mineral Resource Map, 1978; Fig. 1.14 based on agency materials.

UNL (University of Nebraska–Lincoln), Cooperative Extension Service, Institute of Agriculture and Natural Resources: Figs. 5.19, 5.30, 5.40, 6.16, 7.10, and 8.12 (photos by M. B. Stewart, Jr.: reproduced by permission).

UNL (University of Nebraska–Lincoln), Nebraska Water Resources Center: Figs. 5.39 and 6.4 (Donald A. Wilhite, *Changing Fields: Agricultural Land Use Changes in Nebraska, 1925–1974,* 1979) (reprinted by permission).

University of Nebraska Press: Fig. 2.4 (reprinted with permission); Fig. 3.5 (reprinted by permission); Figs. 5.1, 5.20, 5.21, 5.23, 5.27, 5.32, 5.34, and 5.37 (*Agricultural Atlas of Nebraska,* edited by James H. Williams and Doug Murfield, 1977, copyright University of Nebraska Press) (modified and reprinted by permission).

UNO (University of Nebraska–Omaha), Center for Applied Urban Research: Fig. 3.17 (*Review of Applied Urban Research* 9, no. 6 [June 1981]) (reprinted by permission): Figs. 9.9, 9.10, and 9.11 (David R. DiMartino, "Omaha Area Demographic Change 1970–80," *Review of Applied Urban Research* 9, no. 7 [July 1981]) (reprinted with permission).

SELECTED BIBLIOGRAPHY

Aandahl, Andrew R. *Soils of the Great Plains: Land Use, Crops, and Grasses.* Lincoln: University of Nebraska Press, 1982.

Allen, John L. *Passage Through the Garden. Lewis and Clark and the Image of the American Northwest.* Urbana: University of Illinois Press, 1975.

Andreas, A. T. *History of the State of Nebraska.* Chicago: The Western Historical Company, 1882.

Athearn, Robert G. *Union Pacific Country.* Chicago: Rand McNally & Company, 1971.

Aucoin, James. *Water in Nebraska.* Lincoln: University of Nebraska Press, 1984.

Baltensperger, Bradley H. "Agricultural Adjustments to Great Plains Drought: The Republican Valley, 1870–1900." In *The Great Plains: Environment and Culture,* edited by Brian W. Blouet and Frederick C. Luebke. Lincoln: University of Nebraska Press, 1979, pp. 43–59.

Beale, Calvin L. "The Revival of Population Growth in Nonmetropolitan America." Economic Research Service, U.S. Department of Agriculture, no. 605. Washington, D.C.: Government Printing Office, 1975.

Bentall, Ray. *Nebraska's Platte River: A Graphic Analysis of Flows.* Lincoln: University of Nebraska Conservation and Survey Division, Nebraska Water Survey Paper 53, 1982.

Bentall, Ray, and Shaffer, F. Butler. *Availability and Use of Water in Nebraska, 1975.* Lincoln: University of Nebraska Conservation and Survey Division, Nebraska Water Survey Paper 48, 1979.

Berger, Michael L. *The Devil Wagon in God's Country: The Automobile and Social Change in Rural America, 1893–1929.* Hamden, Conn.: Archon Books, 1979.

Berry, Brian J. L. *The Geography of Market Centers and Retail Distribution.* Englewood Cliffs, N.J.: Prentice-Hall, 1967.

Blouet, Brian W., and Lawson, Merlin P., eds. *Images of the Plains: The Role of Human Nature in Settlement.* Lincoln: University of Nebraska Press, 1975.

Blouet, Brian W., and Luebke, Frederick C., eds. *The Great Plains: Environment and Culture.* Lincoln: University of Nebraska Press, 1979.

Borchert, John R. "The Dust Bowl in the 1970s." *Annals of the Association of American Geographers* 61 (1971):1–22.

Bowden, Martyn J. "Desertification of the Great Plains: Will It Happen?" *Economic Geography* 53 (1977):397–406.

———. "Desert Wheat Belt, Plains Corn Belt: Environmental Cognition and Behavior of Settlers in the Plains Margin, 1850–99." In *Images of the Plains,* edited by Brian W. Blouet and Merlin P. Lawson. Lincoln: University of Nebraska Press, 1975, pp. 189–201.

———. "The Great American Desert and the American Frontier, 1800–1882: Popular Images of the Plains." In *Anonymous Americans: Explorations in Nineteenth Century Social History,* edited by Tamara K. Hareven. Englewood Cliffs, N.J.: Prentice-Hall, 1971, pp. 48–79.

Bowen, Marshall. "Environmental Perception and Geographic Change in Southwest Sheridan County." *Nebraska History* 51 (1970): 319–338.

Bremer, Richard G. *Agricultural Change in an Urban Age: The Loup Country of Nebraska, 1910–1970.* Lincoln: University of Nebraska Studies n.s. no. 51, 1976.

Broken Hoops and Plains People. Lincoln: Nebraska Curriculum Development Center, 1976.

Brown, Ralph Hall. *Historical Geography of the United States.* New York: Harcourt, Brace & World, 1948.

Burns, Nancy. "The Collapse of Small Towns on the Great Plains: A Bibliography." *Emporia State Research Studies* 31, no. 1 (1982):5-36.

Buttel, Frederick H. "Agriculture, Environment, and Social Change: Some Emergent Issues." In *The Rural Sociology of the Advanced Societies: Some Critical Perspectives,* edited by Frederick Buttel and Howard Newby. Montclair, N.J.: Allanheld, Osmun and Co., 1980, pp. 453-488.

Buttel, Frederick H., and Larson, Oscar W., III. "Farm Size, Structure, and Energy Intensity: An Ecological Analysis of U.S. Agriculture." *Rural Sociology* 44 (1979):471-488.

Cather, Willa. *My Antonia.* Boston: Houghton Mifflin, 1918.

Chudacoff, Howard P. *Mobile Americans: Residential and Social Mobility in Omaha, 1880-1920.* New York: Oxford University Press, 1972.

———. "A New Look at Ethnic Neighborhoods: Residential Dispersion and the Concept of Visibility in a Medium-Sized City." *Journal of American History* 60 (1973):76-93.

Danbom, David S. *The Resisted Revolution: Urban America and the Industrialization of Agriculture, 1900-1930.* Ames: Iowa State University Press, 1979.

Dick, Everett. *Conquering the Great American Desert: Nebraska.* Lincoln: Nebraska State Historical Society Publication no. 27, 1975.

Dillman, Don A., and Hobbs, Daryl J., eds. *Rural Society in the U.S.: Issues for the 1980s.* Boulder, Colo.: Westview Press, 1982.

DiMartino, David R. "Omaha Area Demographic Change, 1970-80." *Review of Applied Urban Research* 9, no. 6 (July 1981):1-13.

Directory of Nebraska Manufacturers. Lincoln: Nebraska Department of Economic Development, 1982.

Economic Development in Nebraska: A Planning Perspective. Lincoln: Nebraska Department of Economic Development, 1975.

Elder, John A. *Soils of Nebraska.* Lincoln: University of Nebraska Conservation and Survey Division, Resource Report no. 2, 1969.

Emmons, David M. *Garden in the Grasslands: Boomer Literature of the Central Great Plains.* Lincoln: University of Nebraska Press, 1971.

Engberg, R. A., and Spalding, R. F. *Groundwater Quality Atlas of Nebraska.* Lincoln: University of Nebraska Conservation and Survey Division, Resource Atlas no. 3, 1978.

Fimple, Kathleen Louise. "Midwestern Mosaic: A Study of the Homogeneity of Ethnic Population of Omaha, Nebraska, 1880." M.S. thesis, South Dakota State University, 1978.

Fischer, Loyd K. "Environment and Farm Size." Lincoln: University of Nebraska-Lincoln, Department of Agricultural Economics Staff Paper 1978-#9, 1978.

Fite, Gilbert C. *The Farmers' Frontier, 1865-1900.* New York: Holt, Rinehart and Winston, 1966.

———. "Great Plains Farming: A Century of Change and Adjustment." *Agricultural History* 51 (1977):244-256.

Ford, Thomas R., ed. *Rural U.S.A.: Persistence and Change.* Ames: Iowa State University Press, 1978.

Franzwa, Gregory M. *The Oregon Trail Revisited.* St. Louis: Patrice Press, 1972.

Frost, Murray. "Distribution of Omaha's Black Population." *Review of Applied Urban Research* 9, no. 6 (July 1981):14-16.

Fuguitt, Glenn V. "City and Village Population Trends in the Plains States." In *The Great Plains: Environment and Culture,* edited by Brian W. Blouet and Frederick C. Luebke. Lincoln: University of Nebraska Press, 1979, pp. 225-243.

Fuguitt, Glenn V., and Zuiches, James J. "Residential Preferences and Population Distribution." *Demography* 12 (1975):491-504.

Fuller, Wayne. *RFD: The Changing Face of Rural America.* Bloomington: Indiana University Press, 1964.

Furuseth, Owen J., and Pierce, John T. *Agricultural Land in an Urban Society.* Washington, D.C.: Association of American Geographers, Resource Publications in Geography, 1982.

Gastil, Raymond. *Cultural Regions of the United States.* Seattle: University of Washington Press, 1976.

Gaustad, Edwin S. *Historical Atlas of Religion in America.* New York: Harper & Row, 1976.

Gessaman, Paul H. "Migration and Population Change in Nebraska: The Recent Experience and Speculations About the Future." Lincoln: University of Nebraska Department of Agricultural Economics Staff Paper 1978-#3, 1978.

Goldschmidt, Walter. *As You Sow: Three Studies*

in the *Social Consequences of Agribusiness.* Montclair, N.J.: Allanheld, Osmun and Co., 1978.

Gregor, Howard F. *Industrialization of U.S. Agriculture: An Interpretive Atlas.* Boulder, Colo.: Westview Press, 1982.

Gressley, Gene M. *Bankers and Cattlemen.* New York: Alfred A. Knopf, 1966.

Hart, John Fraser. *The Look of the Land.* Englewood Cliffs, N.J.: Prentice-Hall, 1975.

———. "The Middle West." *Annals of the Association of American Geographers* 62 (1972):258-282.

Hawley, Amos H., and Mazie, Sara Mills, eds. *Nonmetropolitan America in Transition.* Chapel Hill: University of North Carolina Press, 1981.

Hewes, Leslie. "Early Fencing on the Western Margin of the Prairie." *Annals of the Association of American Geographers* 71 (1981): 499-526.

Higbee, Edward. *Farms and Farmers in an Urban Age.* New York: Twentieth Century Fund, 1963.

Historic Preservation in Nebraska. Lincoln: Nebraska State Historical Society, 1971.

Hudson, John C. "The Plains Country Town." In *The Great Plains: Environment and Culture,* edited by Brian W. Blouet and Frederick C. Luebke. Lincoln: University of Nebraska Press, 1979, pp. 99-118.

———. "Towns of the Western Railroads." *Great Plains Quarterly* 2 (1982):41-54.

Identification of Prime Residential Land in Rural Nebraska. Omaha: University of Nebraska at Omaha, Center for Applied Urban Research, 1978.

Instream Flows Study Task Force. *Nebraska Policy Issue Study on Instream Flows.* Lincoln: Nebraska Natural Resources Commission, 1981.

Johnson, Bruce B., and Fischer, Loyd K. "The Economics of the Proposed O'Neill Irrigation Project." Lincoln: University of Nebraska-Lincoln, Department of Agricultural Economics Staff Paper 1981-#4, 1981.

Johnson, Martin S., and Pederson, Darryll T. *Groundwater Levels in Nebraska, 1981.* Lincoln: University of Nebraska Conservation and Survey Division, Nebraska Water Survey Paper no. 52, 1982.

Jones, Bryan. *The Farming Game.* Lincoln: University of Nebraska Press, 1983.

Kale, Steven. "Industrial Development Trends in the Northern Plains States." In *The Great Plains: Perspectives and Prospects,* edited by Merlin P. Lawson and Maurice E. Baker. Lincoln: University of Nebraska Center for Great Plains Studies, 1981, pp. 205-219.

———. "Small-Town Population Change in the Central Great Plains: An Investigation of Recent Trends." *Rocky Mountain Social Science Journal* 12, no. 1 (1975):29-43.

Keech, C. F., and Bentall, Ray. *Dunes on the Plains: The Sand Hills Region of Nebraska.* Lincoln: University of Nebraska Conservation and Survey Division, Resource Report no. 4, 1978.

Kollmorgen, Walter M. "The Woodsman's Assaults on the Domain of the Cattleman." *Annals of the Association of American Geographers* 59 (1969):215-239.

Kraenzel, Carl F. *The Great Plains in Transition.* Norman: University of Oklahoma Press, 1955.

Kramer, Mark. *Three Farms: Making Milk, Meat, and Money from the American Soil.* Boston: Little, Brown & Co., 1980.

Lamb, Richard. *Metropolitan Impacts on Rural America.* Chicago: University of Chicago, Department of Geography Research Paper no. 162, 1975.

Lamphear, F. Charles, and Roesler, Theodore W. *Impact Analysis of Irrigated Agriculture on Nebraska's Economy, 1967-1970.* Lincoln: University of Nebraska, Bureau of Business Research, Nebraska Economics and Business Report no. 8, 1974.

Larson, Albert J. "The Hamlets of Nebraska." Ph.D. dissertation, University of Nebraska, 1969.

Larson, Albert J., and Soot, Siim. "The Use of Population Centers of Gravity in Historical Geographic Analysis: The Nebraska Case." *The Iowa Geographer* no. 23 (1973):23-34.

Lawson, Merlin P., ed. *Climatic Atlas of Nebraska.* Lincoln: University of Nebraska Press, 1977.

Lawson, Merlin P., and Baker, Maurice E., eds. *The Great Plains: Perspectives and Prospects.* Lincoln: University of Nebraska Center for Great Plains Studies, 1981.

Lawson, Merlin P.; Reiss, A.; Phillips, R.; and Livingston, K. *Nebraska Droughts: A Study of Their Past Chronological and Spatial Extent with Implications for the Future.* Lincoln: University of Nebraska-Lincoln, Department of Geography Occasional Paper no. 1, 1971.

Lawson, Merlin P., and Stockton, Charles W. "Desert Myth and Climatic Reality." *Annals*

of the Association of American Geographers 71 (1981):527–535.
Lee, Paul S. T. "The Cost of Compact vs. Scattered Land Use Development. A Case Study: Gretna, Nebraska." *Review of Applied Urban Research* 4, no. 9 (1976):2–6.
Lincoln–Lancaster County Comprehensive Regional Plan, rev. issue. Lincoln: City of Lincoln and Lancaster County, 1982.
Lockeretz, William. "The Lessons of the Dust Bowl." *American Scientist* 66 (1978):560–569.
Lommasson, Robert C. *Nebraska Wild Flowers.* Lincoln: University of Nebraska Press, 1973.
Lonsdale, Richard E., ed. *Economic Atlas of Nebraska.* Lincoln: University of Nebraska Press, 1977.
Lonsdale, Richard E., and Seyler, H. L., eds. *Nonmetropolitan Industrialization.* Washington, D.C.: V. H. Winston and Sons, 1979.
Ludwig, Armin K. "The Changing Distribution of Omaha's Office Space." *Review of Applied Urban Research* 4, no. 1 (January 1976):1–4.
Luebke, Frederick C. "Ethnic Group Settlement on the Great Plains." *Western Historical Quarterly* 8 (1977):405–430.
———. *Immigrants and Politics: The Germans of Nebraska, 1880–1900.* Lincoln: University of Nebraska Press, 1969.
Luebke, Frederick C., ed. *Ethnicity on the Great Plains.* Lincoln: University of Nebraska Press, 1980.
McIntosh, C. Barron. "Forest Lieu Selections in the Sand Hills of Nebraska." *Annals of the Association of American Geographers* 64 (1974):87–99.
———. "Use and Abuse of the Timber Culture Act." *Annals of the Association of American Geographers* 65 (1975):347–362.
McKnight, Tom L. "Great Circles on the Great Plains: The Changing Geometry of American Agriculture." *Erdkunde* 33 (1979):70–79.
McMorris, Robert. "The People Who Make Up Omaha." *Sunday World Herald* (Omaha), October 15, 1961–January 28, 1962.
Malin, James C. *The Grassland of North America: Prolegomena to its History with Addenda and Postscripts.* Gloucester, Mass.: Peter Smith, 1967.
Mather, Cotton E. "The American Great Plains." *Annals of the Association of American Geographers* 62 (1972):237–257.
Meinig, Donald W., ed. *The Interpretation of Ordinary Landscapes.* New York: Oxford University Press, 1979.
Nebraska Agricultural Statistics, Annual Report. Lincoln: Nebraska Crop and Livestock Reporting Service, published annually.
Nebraska Economic Projections 1975–2000. Lincoln: University of Nebraska Bureau of Business Research Report no. 7, 1974.
Nebraska's Agriculture, 1980–1985. A Summary. Lincoln: University of Nebraska–Lincoln, Institute of Agriculture and Natural Resources, STAR Report, 1976.
Nebraska's Economy and Other Related Growth Aspects. A Report of the STAR Committee on Economy and Growth. Lincoln: University of Nebraska–Lincoln, Institute of Agriculture and Natural Resources, 1976.
Okada, Yasuo. *Public Lands and Pioneer Farmers: Gage County, Nebraska, 1850–1900.* Tokyo: Keio University, 1971.
Olson, James C. *History of Nebraska,* 2d ed. Lincoln: University of Nebraska Press, 1966.
Omaha City Planning Department. *A Comprehensive Program for Historic Preservation in Omaha.* Omaha: Omaha City Planning Department, 1980.
Overton, Richard C. *Burlington West: A Colonization History of the Burlington Railroad.* Cambridge: Harvard University Press, 1941.
Paarlberg, Don. *Farm and Food Policy Issues of the 1980s.* Lincoln: University of Nebraska Press, 1980.
Paullin, Charles O. *Atlas of the Historical Geography of the United States.* Edited by John K. Wright. New York: American Geographical Society, 1932.
Pelto, Pertti. *The Snowmobile Revolution: Technology and Social Change in the Arctic.* Menlo Park, Calif.: Cummings Publishing Co., 1973.
Perelman, Michael. "Farming with Petroleum." *Environment* 14 (1972):8–13.
Pimentel, David et al. "Food Production and the Energy Crisis." *Science* 182 (1973): 443–449.
Powell, John Wesley. *Report on the Lands of the Arid Region of the United States, with a More Detailed Account of the Land of Utah.* Washington, D.C.: Government Printing Office, 1879.
Raup, Philip M. "Corporate Farming in the U.S." *Journal of Economic History* 33 (1973):274–290.
———. "Societal Goals in Farm Size." In *Size, Structure, and Future of Farms,* edited by Earl O. Heady and A. Gordon Ball. Ames:

Iowa State University Press, 1972, pp. 31–38.

Reed, E. C. *Groundwater Atlas of Nebraska.* Lincoln: University of Nebraska Conservation and Survey Division, 1966.

Renshaw, Vernon D. "The Nebraska Population and Economy, 1975." *Nebraska Economic and Business Reports* no. 11, July 1975.

―――. *Nebraska Population Projections, 1975–2000.* Lincoln: University of Nebraska, Bureau of Business Research Report no. 6, 1973.

Report on the Framework Study. Lincoln: Nebraska Natural Resources Commission, 1971.

Report on the Platte River Basin, Nebraska Level B Study. Omaha: Missouri River Basin Commission, 1976.

Richards, Bartlett, Jr., with Van Ackeren, Ruth. *Bartlett Richards: Nebraska Sandhills Cattleman.* Lincoln: Nebraska State Historical Society, 1980.

Rife, Janet Warkentin. *Germans and German-Russians in Nebraska: A Research Guide to Nebraska Ethnic Studies.* Lincoln: University of Nebraska Center for Great Plains Studies, 1980.

Rodefeld, Richard D. "The Causes of Change in Farm Technology, Size, and Organizational Structure." In *Change in Rural America: Causes, Consequences, and Alternatives,* edited by Richard D. Rodefeld, Jan Flora, Donald Voth, Isao Fujimoto, and Jim Converse. St. Louis: C. V. Mosby, 1978, pp. 217–237.

―――. "Trends in U.S. Farm Organizational Structure and Type." In *Change in Rural America: Causes, Consequences, and Alternatives,* edited by Richard D. Rodefeld, Jan Flora, Donald Voth, Isao Fujimoto, and Jim Converse. St. Louis: C. V. Mosby, 1978, pp. 158–177.

Rooney, John F.; Zelinsky, Wilbur; and Louder, Dean R., eds. *This Remarkable Continent: An Atlas of United States and Canadian Society and Cultures.* College Station, Tex.: Texas A&M Press, 1982.

Rugg, Dean S. *Spatial Foundations of Urbanism.* Dubuque, Iowa: Wm. C. Brown Co., 1972.

Rugg, Dean S., and Rundquist, Donald C. "Urbanization on the Great Plains: Trends and Prospects." In *The Great Plains: Perspectives and Prospects,* edited by Merlin P. Lawson and Maurice E. Baker. Lincoln: University of Nebraska Center for Great Plains Studies, 1981, pp. 221–246.

Saarinen, Thomas F. *Perception of the Drought Hazard on the Great Plains.* Chicago: University of Chicago, Department of Geography Research Paper no. 106, 1966.

Sandoz, Mari. *Old Jules.* Boston: Little, Brown & Co., 1935.

Schmedemann, Ivan W. "Issues of Ownership and Control of Agricultural Land in the Great Plains." In *The Great Plains: Perspectives and Prospects,* edited by Merlin P. Lawson and Maurice E. Baker. Lincoln: University of Nebraska Center for Great Plains Studies, 1981, pp. 193–202.

Sheldon, Addison E. *Land Systems and Land Policies in Nebraska.* Lincoln: Nebraska State Historical Society, 1936.

Sher, Jonathan P., ed. *Education in Rural America: A Reassessment of Conventional Wisdom.* Boulder, Colo.: Westview Press, 1977.

Shover, John L. *First Majority–Last Minority: The Transforming of Rural Life in America.* DeKalb: Northern Illinois University Press, 1976.

Socolofsky, Homer. "Land Disposal in Nebraska, 1854–1906; The Homestead Story." *Nebraska History* 48 (1967):225–248.

Stoddard, Robert H. "Changing Patterns of Some Rural Churches." *Rocky Mountain Social Science Journal* 7, no. 1 (1970):61–68.

Stone, Marvin D. "Effects of Center Pivot Irrigation on Land Use, Land Tenure, and Settlement Patterns on a Selected Great Plains Landscape, the Holt Table Portion of Holt County, Nebraska." Ph.D. dissertation, University of Kansas, 1977.

Studness, Charles M. "Development of the Great Plains Farming Frontier to 1953." Ph.D. dissertation, Columbia University, 1963.

Sublett, Michael D. *Farmers on the Road: Interfarm Migration and the Farming of Noncontiguous Land in Three Midwestern Townships, 1939–1969.* Chicago: University of Chicago, Department of Geography Research Paper no. 168, 1975.

Summary of the Nebraska Research for the Six-State High Plains Ogallala Aquifer Study. Lincoln: Nebraska Natural Resources Commission, 1981.

Supalla, Raymond J.; Lansford, Robert R.; and Gollehon, Noel R. "Is the Ogallala Going Dry?" *Journal of Soil and Water Conservation* 37 (1982):309–314.

Sweedlun, Verne S. "A History of the Evolution of Agriculture in Nebraska, 1870–1930." Ph.D.

dissertation, University of Nebraska, 1930.

Thavenet, Dennis. "A History of Omaha Public Transportation." M.A. thesis, University of Omaha, 1960.

Trewartha, Glenn T. "Some Regional Characteristics of American Farmsteads." *Annals of the Association of American Geographers* 38 (1948):196–225.

Unruh, John D. *The Plains Across: The Overland Emigrants and the Trans-Mississippi West, 1840–1860.* Urbana: University of Illinois Press, 1979.

Vogeler, Ingolf. *The Myth of the Family Farm: Agribusiness Dominance of U.S. Agriculture.* Boulder, Colo.: Westview Press, 1981.

Ward, David. *Cities and Immigrants.* New York: Oxford University Press, 1971.

Warner, Sam Bass. *Streetcar Suburbs.* Cambridge, Mass.: Harvard University Press, 1962.

Warrick, Richard A., and Bowden, Martyn J. "The Changing Impacts of Droughts in the Great Plains." In *The Great Plains: Perspectives and Prospects,* edited by Merlin P. Lawson and Maurice E. Baker. Lincoln: University of Nebraska Center for Great Plains Studies, 1981, pp. 111–137.

Weaver, John E. *Native Vegetation of Nebraska.* Lincoln: University of Nebraska Press, 1968.

———. *The North American Prairie.* Lincoln: Johnsen Publishing Co., 1954.

Webb, Walter Prescott. *The Great Plains.* Boston: Ginn and Co., 1931.

Wedel, Waldo. *Prehistoric Man on the Great Plains.* Norman: University of Oklahoma Press, 1961.

Wheels of Fortune. Walthill, Nebr.: Center for Rural Affairs, 1976.

Wilhite, Donald A. *Changing Fields: Agricultural Land Use Changes in Nebraska, 1925–1974.* Lincoln: University of Nebraska–Lincoln, Nebraska Water Resources Center, 1979.

Wilkening, Eugene A., and Klessig, Lowell. "The Rural Environment. Quality and Conflicts in Land Use." In *Rural U.S.A.: Persistence and Change,* edited by Thomas R. Ford. Ames: Iowa State University Press, 1978, pp. 19–34.

Williams, James H., and Murfield, Doug, eds. *Agricultural Atlas of Nebraska.* Lincoln: University of Nebraska Press, 1977.

Wishart, David J. *The Fur Trade of the American West, 1807–1840.* Lincoln: University of Nebraska Press, 1979.

Yeates, Maurice, and Garner, Barry. *The North American City,* 3d ed. New York: Harper & Row, 1980.

Zelinsky, Wilbur. *The Cultural Geography of the United States.* Englewood Cliffs, N.J.: Prentice-Hall, 1973.

EQUIVALENTS

The English/metric equivalents used in the text are:

1 in.	= 2.54 cm
1 ft	= 0.3048 m
1 mi	= 1.609 km
1 sq mi	= 2.59 sq km
1 acre	= 0.4047 ha
1 acre-ft	= 1233 cu m
1 cfs	= 0.028 cu m per second
1 gallon	= 3.785 l
1 gallon	= 0.00379 cu m
1 bu	= 35.238 l
1 lb	= 0.4536 kg
1 tn	= 0.907 t
°F	= 1.8°C + 32

INDEX

Adams County, 72, 76, 187(photo)
Agricultural-college scrip, 45
Agricultural regions, 137–141, 173, 174, 208
Agricultural specialization, 158, 160, 161, 170, 171(table), 180, 199, 208, 270
Agriculture
  adaptation to subhumid climate, 62–67
  assessment of land, 227, 238. *See also* Land values
  capital needs, 51, 144, 148, 161, 180, 190, 199
  commercialization of, 51, 62, 200, 224
  custom farming, 147, 165
  employment. *See* Employment, agriculture
  energy requirements, 180–183, 199, 200
  industrial, 153, 176, 181. *See also* Farms, corporations; Farms, industrial; Farms, mechanization
  investment in, 152, 153, 190
  minimum tillage, 193, 271
  nonresident investors, 152, 153, 190. *See also* Farms, corporations
  organic, 183
  pesticides, 181, 182
  pollution from, 196–199
  tax breaks, 145, 147, 161, 190
  technology, 199–201. *See also* Farms, machinery; Farms, mechanization; Irrigation, center-pivot
  See also Crops; Dry farming; Erosion; Farming, part-time; Farms; Farmsteads; Field patterns; Irrigation; Livestock; Panhandle, agriculture; Platte Valley, agriculture; Sandhills, agriculture
Ainsworth Project, 22
Air traffic. *See* Transportation
Alexandria, 62
Alfalfa, 138, 141, 172–174
  milling, 115(photo)

Alkali lakes, 11
Alliance, 85, 117, 120, 122, 263
American Fur Company, 44
Anselmo, 61(photo)
Antelope County, 139, 212(photo)
Antioch, 122
Arapahoe, 83
Arapahos, 40
Arbor Day, 209
Army Corps of Engineers, 22
Arthur, 85
Arthur County, 85, 134
Aughey, Samuel, 59
Automobiles, 223, 253–255

Bailey Yard, North Platte, 124
Banner County, 101, 110
Barbed wire, 51
Barns, 204, 205
Bassett, 151
Beans, dry edible, 141, 170, 171(table), 172, 173(map)
Beatrice, 62, 85, 117, 243, 245
Beaver Lake, 232
Bellevue, 44, 84, 132, 246, 255(photo)
Belmont, 253
Belvidere, 62
Benson, 246, 248, 253
Berlin, 83
Bessey, Charles, 210
Big Blue River, 16, 21(table), 25
Birth rate. *See* Population, birth rate
Bismarck Township, 84
Bison, 39, 40, 65
Blacks, 83
  early settlement, 71, 72
  in Omaha, 72, 248, 251, 255, 256, 258(map)
Blaine County, 105, 210

Blair, 107
Blizzards, 5, 8, 66
Boone County, 74, 76
Box Butte County, 77, 107, 202(photo)
Boyd County, 22, 25, 77, 97, 105, 138, 145
Boys Town, 130, 254
Brewster, 88(photo)
Broken Bow, 112, 116
Brown County, 22
Brownville, 125, 242, 243
Bruno, 84
Bryan, William Jennings, 99
Buckshot development, 231, 236
Buffalo County, 31, 134, 195(photo)
Burke Act, 46
Burlington and Missouri River Railroad, 48, 55, 59, 60, 77
Burlington Northern Railroad, 119, 120
Burt County, 76, 175(fig.), 177(photo), 191
Butler County, 75(map), 77, 100, 163, 206(photo)

Canoeing, 20, 21(photo)
Carleton, 62
Cass County, 38, 77, 108, 218(photo), 228, 229, 232
Cathedral district, 249
Catholics. *See* Roman Catholics
Cattle. *See* Livestock
Cattle drives, 65, 66
Cattle guards, 216
Cedar County, 76, 139(fig.), 174(photo)
Cemeteries, 219
Center-pivot irrigation. *See* Irrigation, center-pivot
Central Park Mall, 264
Chase County, 11, 25, 29(photo), 89, 139(fig.), 163
Chemical industry, 114
Cherry County, 13(photo), 66, 72, 79, 139(fig.), 142
Cheyenne County, 83, 100, 108, 110, 111(table), 139(fig.), 175(fig.)
Cheyennes, 40
Chimney Rock, 54(photo)
Churches, 217, 253
  ethnic congregations, 77(photo), 84
  rural, 102, 218(photo)
  See also Religion
Cities. *See* Suburban growth; Urban expansion; *individual cities*
Clay Center, 60
Clay County, 25, 60, 61(map), 76
Climate, 1-9

frost-free season, 3
precipitation, 3-5, 6(fig.), 7(fig.), 8(map)
subhumid, 1, 2, 63, 66, 67
temperature, 2, 3
variability, 9
See also Blizzards; Drought; Tornadoes
Colfax County, 77, 81, 113, 163
College View, 253
Columbus, 85, 112, 113, 116, 117, 245, 258, 261(photo)
Commutation. *See* Homestead commutation
Company of Explorers of the Upper Missouri, 41
Continentality. *See* Climate
Corn, 3, 63, 65, 137-139, 141, 163-165, 170, 180, 185, 188, 190
  hybrid, 185
Corn Belt, 59, 137, 138, 163, 173
Corn cribs, 206
Coronado, 1, 2, 39, 41
Corporate farms. *See* Farms, corporations
Council Bluffs, Iowa, 55, 246
County fairs, 219
Cozad, 116, 158
Crawford, 130
Crete, 60, 114, 245
Croatians, settlement in Omaha, 248
Crops, 162(table), 164(table), 170, 171(table), 172, 173. *See also* Alfalfa; Beans, dry edible; Corn; Sorghum; Soybeans; Sugar beets; Wheat
Culbertson, 64
Cuming County, 75(map), 76, 158
Custer County, 50(photo), 66, 72(photo), 139(fig.)
Czechs, settlement in Nebraska, 76-78, 81, 83, 84, 101, 102, 217, 248, 256

Dairying, 160
Dakota City, 83, 114
Dakota County, 87, 113
Dakotas, 40
Dams, 22, 24, 25, 30-33, 228
Dana College, 76
Danes, settlement in Nebraska, 76, 81, 84
Dannebrog, 84
Dannevirke, 84
Davenport, 62
David City, 129(photo)
Dawes County, 72, 85, 134
Dawes Severalty Act, 70
Dawson County, 19(photo), 138, 173, 175(fig.)
Death rate. *See* Population, death rate

Decentralization of industry. *See* Manufacturing, decentralization
Deferred taxation. *See* Agriculture, assessment of land
"Delocalization" (of resources), 62, 199
Democrats, 99–101
Department of Water Resources. *See* Nebraska Department of Water Resources
Deshler, 116
DeWitt, 116
Dismal River Culture, 39
Dixon County, 163
Dodge County, 77
Dorchester, 60
Douglas County, 72, 85, 87, 89, 95, 97, 106, 126, 191, 233, 254, 256(map), 257(map), 258(map), 259(map). *See also* Omaha
Downtown revitalization, 264
Downtowns, 252–254, 259, 261–265
Drought, 5, 64, 67, 200, 270
    1874, 63
    1890s, 5, 64
    1930s, 5
Dry edible beans. *See* Beans, dry edible
Dry farming, 65, 67
Dual employment. *See* Employment, off-farm
Dundee, 246, 253
Dundy County, 25, 151, 152(map), 153, 163, 191, 193(photo), 204
Dutch, settlement in Nebraska, 76

Eagle, 235
Edgar, 62
Education, in rural areas, 217, 218(photo), 224–227. *See also* School consolidation
Electricity, 222. *See also* Energy
Elkhorn River, 16, 17
Emigrant Trails, 53, 54
Employment
  agriculture, 103, 108
  government, 133, 134
  manufacturing, 114(table)
  off-farm, 147–148, 223
  See also Labor Force; Unemployment
Enders Reservoir, 25, 28(fig.), 30
Energy
  in agriculture. *See* Agriculture, energy requirements
  electricity generation, 125, 126(map), 222, 230(photo). *See also* Hydroelectric generation; Nuclear power plants
  home power plants, 222

See also Nuclear power plants; Oil; Windmills
English, settlement in Nebraska, 73, 74, 83
Environmental quality, 196, 199, 229, 230, 238
Eppley Airfield, 118(photo)
Erosion, 16, 191–196, 199, 271
  water, 191, 193, 195(photo)
  wind, 153, 191–194, 196, 270, 271. *See also* Strip Cropping
Ethnic festivals, 84
Ethnic groups. *See* Ethnic neighborhoods; Immigration; Lincoln, ethnic groups; Omaha, ethnic groups; *individual ethnic groups*
Ethnic neighborhoods, 59, 73, 75(map), 248, 250(map)
Exeter, 60
"Exodusters." *See* Blacks, early settlement

Fairbury, 245
Fairfield, 62
Fairmont, 60
Falls City, 107, 117
Farm consolidation. *See* Farms, size
Farm debt. *See* Agriculture, capital needs
Farm Holiday Movement, 100
Farming, part-time, 148. *See also* Employment, off-farm
Farmland conversion, 228, 235, 236, 238
Farm policy, 174, 176, 200
Farms
  corporations, 150–153, 199. *See also* Agriculture, industrial; Agriculture, non-resident investors
  family, 152, 153, 155
  fragmented, 155, 156, 236
  industrial, 153, 155
  larger-than-family-type, 153, 155
  machinery, 144, 148, 156, 178, 179
  managers, 150
  mechanization, 142, 177–183, 217
  numbers, 143(map), 144(fig.), 145
  size, 49, 142–144, 145(fig.), 154(fig.), 155, 178–180, 183, 270
  structure, 141–155
  tenant, 149–150
Farmsteads, 201, 208
  abandoned, 208
Farmyards, 207, 208
Farwell Project, 22, 24
Feedlots, 158(photo), 160, 196, 197(photo), 199
Feed processing plants, 114

Fencing, 50, 214, 216
  illegal, 66
  See also Hedgerows
Fertility rate. See Population, fertility rate
Fertilizer, 180–183, 185, 199
Fertilizer plants, 114, 132
Field patterns, 212–214
Fillmore County, 25, 77, 188
Flooding, 17, 18
Florence, 53, 246, 248
Food processing, 111, 113, 259
Foodways, 84
Fort Atkinson, 43
Fort Calhoun, 125
Fort Hartstuff, 54
Fort Kearny, 44
Fort Lisa, 43
Fort Niobrara, 54
Fort Robinson, 54, 72
Fort Robinson State Park, 130
Fort Sidney, 54
Foxley, William, 151, 213
Freighting, 54, 242
Fremont, 36, 55, 85, 87, 114, 117, 129, 245
Fremont, John C., 40
French, influence on Nebraska, 83
Frenchman Creek, 25, 30
Friedensau, 84
Frontier County, 140(photo)
"Functional usurpation" (of retail activities), 132
Fur trade, 43(map), 44

Gage County, 139(fig.), 170
Game and Parks Commission. See Nebraska Game and Parks Commission
Garden County, 11
"Garden of the West," 1
Garland, 83
Gateway shopping center, 264, 265
Gavins Point Dam, 228
Gering, 116
Germans, settlement in Nebraska, 73, 74, 76, 81, 83, 84, 101, 102, 217, 248
Germantown, 83
Glacial advance, 11
Glenville, 62
Gold Coast, in Omaha, 249
Gosper County, 22, 24
Government, 133–135, 265, 267
  employment. See Employment, government in small counties, 134
Grafton, 60
Grain bins, 205

Grain drying, 116, 206
Grand Island, 62, 79, 85, 87, 112–114, 116, 117, 126, 129, 158, 231(photo), 245, 258
Grant County, 145
Grasshoppers, 63
"Great American Desert," 1, 56
Greeks, settlement in Omaha, 248
Greeley County, 74, 93, 100, 105
Gretna, 235, 237
Gristmills, 110, 111(photo)
Groundwater, 22, 24(map), 25, 36, 271
  augmentation, 24
  contamination, 197–199
  depletion, 24(map), 25, 26–28(figs.), 30, 34(map), 271
  municipal use, 22, 34
  See also Irrigation
Groundwater control area, 33, 271

Haigler, 63
Hail, 9
Hall County, 31, 72, 73, 76, 139(fig.)
Hamilton County, 25, 163, 185, 188
Hamlets, 132. See also Towns, small
Happy Hollow, 252
Harvard, 60, 62
Hastings, 62, 85, 114, 116, 117, 129, 243, 245
Havelock, 253
Hay, 24, 140, 172, 173, 174(photo), 179(photo)
Hayes County, 93
Hazen, William B., 2
Hedgerows, 51, 52(photo), 210–213
Henderson, 76, 84, 112
High-order goods, 129
Highways, 88, 112, 122, 123, 228, 229, 254, 255(photo), 263, 266(photo). See also Roads; Transportation
Hitchcock County, 76, 108, 110
Hogs. See Livestock
Holdrege, 116, 117
Holland, 76
Holt County, 31, 74, 89, 139, 141(photo), 151, 152(map), 163, 188, 190, 196(photo), 199, 213
Homestead Act, 45, 47(fig.), 48, 49
Homestead commutation, 45, 48
Housing, 49, 50, 202–204, 220
Howard County, 22, 24, 76, 78
Hungarians, settlement in Omaha, 248
Hydroelectric generation, 19, 125

Immigrants, 73–81, 247, 248, 250(table). See also Lincoln, ethnic groups; Omaha, ethnic groups; individual ethnic groups

Imperial, 29(photo), 151
Income, per capita, 104–106
Indian lands, 44(map)
    white pressure on, 46
Indians. *See* Native Americans
Indian Territory, 69
Industrial agriculture. *See* Agriculture, industrial
Industrial parks, 253
Industry. *See* Manufacturing
Inland, 62
Instream use of water, 18–20, 30, 36
Instruments manufacturing, 116
Interstate highway. *See* Highways
Iowas, 39
Irish, settlement in Nebraska, 73, 248
Irrigation, 20(map), 24, 35(table), 36, 138, 165, 175, 184–192, 212, 270, 271
    center-pivot, 139–141, 148, 163, 172, 185, 187–191, 211, 213, 271
    groundwater, 33, 34. *See also* Groundwater; Groundwater control area
    manufacturing, 116
    nineteenth century, 22, 64, 65(table)
    surface water, 18, 22, 30, 31, 33, 34, 36
    See also Platte Valley, irrigation; Sandhills, irrigation
Italians, settlement in Nebraska, 78, 81, 248, 256

Jansen, 76, 214, 215(map)
Japanese, settlement in Nebraska, 80
Jefferson County, 76, 214, 215(map)
Jefferson, Thomas, 2
Jews, settlement in Nebraska, 79, 81, 83, 248, 256
Juniata, 62

Kearney, 79, 85, 116, 117, 129, 243, 263
Kearney County, 22, 24, 53, 66, 76, 226(map), 245
Kenesaw, 62
Keya Paha County, 22, 31
Kimball, 110
Kimball County, 11, 108, 110, 111(table)
Kingsley Dam, 22
Kinkaid Act, 66, 72, 79
Knox County, 70, 77, 106, 138
Kountze, Herman, 246
Kountze Place, 246

Labor force, 106–108, 112. *See also* Employment
Lake Maloney, 24

Lake McConaughy, 22, 24
Lakes. *See* Beaver Lake; Enders Reservoir; Lake Maloney; Lake McConaughy; Merritt Reservoir; Sherman Reservoir
Lancaster County, 72, 76, 85, 95, 97, 100, 101, 106, 134, 170, 175(fig.), 265. *See also* Lincoln
Land values, 145, 146(map), 147, 236, 253. *See also* Agriculture, assessment of land
Latvians, settlement in Lincoln, 78
Leapfrog development, 233, 234(photo), 235, 264, 265. *See also* Suburban growth
Lewis and Clark, 1, 2, 41, 43
Lexington, 112, 113, 116, 258
Limestone, 108
Lincoln, 36, 125, 133, 134, 228, 243, 247, 252, 263, 265
    early development, 62, 243–246, 248, 251
    ethnic groups, 70, 72, 76, 78, 79
    expansion, 233, 235, 236, 253
    growth policies, 265
    income, 105
    labor force, 106
    manufacturing, 112, 114, 116, 117, 258
    suburban development, 87, 254, 255, 263–265, 267
    trade and commerce, 126, 129, 244, 253, 259, 261
    transportation, 119, 120, 252(photo)
Lincoln County, 25, 100, 107, 151
Lincoln-Lancaster County comprehensive plan, 265
Lindsay, 116
Lithuanians, settlement in Omaha, 78, 248
Little Blue River, 16, 21(table)
Little Italy, 78
Livestock, 137–141
    cattle, 137–139, 141, 157–160
    hogs, 137, 159(table), 160, 161
    sheep, 141, 161
    See also Feedlots
Loess, 11
Logan County, 105
Log houses, 50, 202
Long, Stephen H., 1, 2
Louisville, 108, 109(photo)
Loup River, 16, 17, 34, 88, 212
Lowell, 62
Low-order goods, 126
Lutherans, 84, 101, 102

Machinery. *See* Farms, machinery; Manufacturing, machinery
Madison County, 73, 76

Malmo, 84
MANDAN, 228
Manufacturing, 110–117, 135, 259
  decentralization, 112, 253, 257, 269, 270
  employment. *See* Employment, manufacturing
  machinery, 116
  nineteenth century, 110, 111
  rural, 89, 112. *See also* Rural industrialization
  suburban, 113, 257, 258
  See also Lincoln, manufacturing; Omaha, manufacturing; Platte Valley, manufacturing
McCook, 110, 117
Meat packing, 111, 114, 243
Median age. *See* Population, age structure
Medical care, 132, 133
Mennonites, 76, 84, 214
Merrick County, 185
Merritt Reservoir, 22, 24
Metals, fabricated, 116
Methodists, 101, 102
Mexicans, settlement in Nebraska, 79–81, 83, 84, 248
Meyer v. Nebraska, 83
Midwesterners, 71, 98, 99, 102
Migration
  rural-to-urban, 85, 87, 88. *See also* Urbanization
  urban-to-rural, 98. *See also* Population, turnaround; "Rural renaissance"
Millard, 255, 258
Minden, 130
Minimum tillage. *See* Agriculture, minimum tillage
Mining, 108, 109(photo)
Missourias, 39, 44, 46
Missouri Fur Company, 43
Missouri River, 1, 16, 20, 30, 43
  transportation, 119. *See also* Navigation, Missouri River
Mobile homes, 204, 220
Moravian Brethren, 77
Mormons, 53
Morrill Act, 45, 81
Morrill County, 76
Morton, J. Sterling, 209
Multiple Nuclei Model, 263
Murray, 232

Nance County, 45, 46, 78
National Farms (company), 151
National Wild and Scenic Rivers System, 20

Native Americans, 37–41, 43–46, 69–71, 83. *See also* Arapahos; Cheyennes; Dakotas; Indian lands; Indian Territory; Iowas; Missourias; Omahas; Otos; Pawnees; Poncas
Natural Resources Districts, 33
Nature Conservancy, 33
Navigation, Missouri River, 19, 30
Nebraska City, 44, 53, 54, 55(photo), 107, 116, 117, 119, 125, 242, 243, 245, 263
Nebraska City–Fort Kearny cutoff, 54
Nebraska Culture, 38
Nebraska Department of Water Resources, 20, 33
Nebraska Game and Parks Commission, 20
Nebraska National Forest, 210
Nebraska Public Power District, 125
Nebraska Territory, 44
Nehawka, 83, 233
Neligh, 111(photo)
Nemaha County, 102(map), 134, 213(map)
Niobrara River, 20, 30, 31, 32(photo), 33
Nitrates, 197, 198(map), 199
Norden, 31
Norden Dam, 33
Norfolk, 85, 87, 88, 112, 113, 116, 117, 126, 129, 228, 243, 245, 263
Norris, George, 100
North Freeway, 265, 266(photo), 267
North Loup Project, 30
North Loup River, 31
North Omaha, 246, 265, 267
North Platte, 55, 64, 79, 85, 117, 120, 129, 137, 243, 245
Norwegians, settlement in Nebraska, 76
Nuckolls County, 76
Nuclear power plants, 127(photo), 228
Nursing homes, 133, 134(map)

O'Connor, 74, 84
Off-farm employment. *See* Employment, off-farm
Offutt Air Force Base, 133
Ogallala, 66, 112, 116, 133
Ogallala aquifer, 22, 33, 192
Oil, 108, 110
Old Market, Omaha, 265
Omaha, 36, 44, 54, 55, 100, 125, 133, 229, 235, 247(map), 250(photo), 255(photo)
  black population. *See* Blacks, in Omaha
  early development, 62, 242–252
  ethnic groups, 70, 78–80, 84, 247, 248, 250(map)
  expansion, 233, 235, 236, 253

income, 105
labor force, 106
manufacturing, 111–114, 116, 117, 243, 244, 257, 260(photo)
office buildings, 262, 263(photo)
population decline, 87
suburban development, 246, 254, 255, 263–265, 267
trade and commerce, 126, 129, 132, 244, 253, 259, 261–264
transportation, 119, 120, 243, 266(photo)
unemployment, 107
Omaha Public Power District, 125, 230(photo)
Omaha Reservation, 46
Omahas, 39, 43, 44, 69
O'Neill, 73, 84
O'Neill, "General" John, 74
O'Neill Unit, 31
Oneonta Culture, 39
Oregon Trail, 53
Organic farming. *See* Agriculture, organic
Otoe, 83
Otoe County, 76, 83, 139(fig.), 155(map), 197(photo), 210(map)
Oto Reserve, 46
Otos, 39, 43, 44, 46, 83
Oxbow Trail, 54

Palmyra, 235
Panhandle, 3, 9, 11, 15, 89, 93, 202
  agriculture, 140, 156, 165
"Paper towns," 59
Papillion, 85, 254, 255(photo)
Pawnee County, 76, 83, 95
Pawnees, 29, 40, 44–46
Perkins County, 11, 25, 88, 89, 141, 163
Phelps County, 22, 24, 75(map), 76
Pierce County, 76
Pike, Zebulon, 1, 2, 41
Pine Ridge, 11, 14(photo), 22, 210
Pine Ridge Agency, 41(photo)
Pioneer Village, 130
Place names, 83, 84
Plasi, 84
Platte County, 76, 113
Platte River, 16, 17, 18(fig.), 20, 30, 34, 235
Platte Valley, 199, 228, 270
  agriculture, 19(photo), 115(photo), 137, 138, 158, 163, 173
  income, 105
  irrigation, 163, 174, 185
  manufacturing, 89, 103, 113, 114
  population, 85

Plattsmouth, 44, 65, 107, 132, 242, 245
Plumbing, in rural areas, 222
Poles, settlement in Nebraska, 78, 81, 83, 84, 101, 102, 248
Political parties. *See* Democrats; Populists; Republicans
Polk, 181
Polka bands, 84
Polk County, 76
Ponca, 83
Poncas, 39, 41, 43, 45
Pony Express, 55
Population
  age structure, 95–97, 106
  birth rate, 93–95
  death rate, 94, 95
  density, 85
  fertility rate, 93, 94
  outmigration, 97
  rural, 135, 222
  turnaround, 88. *See also* Migration, urban-to-rural
  See also Blacks; Immigrants; Native Americans; Towns, small, population growth
Populists, 100
Posen, 84
Potash, 11, 122
Poultry, 161, 163
Poverty, 105, 106
Powell, John Wesley, 1, 59
Power lines, 228
Prague, 84
Prairie fires, 15
Precipitation. *See* Climate
Pre-Emption Law, 45, 47(fig.)
Prehistoric resources, 38
Presbyterians, 101, 102
Prudential Insurance Company, 151
Publishing, 117

Rail abandonment, 119
Railroads, 119–122, 246, 258
  colonization activities, 59, 81
  construction, 55, 56
  in economic development, 62, 243, 244
  and the frontier, 57(maps), 58(map)
  landholdings, 48
  promotion activities, 58, 59
  town development, 60, 62
  See also Burlington and Missouri River Railroad; Burlington Northern Railroad; Union Pacific Railroad; Unit-trains
"Rain follows the plow," 59, 270

Rainmakers, 64
Ranching, 65, 66, 139
Recreation, 19, 20, 131(map), 228
Red Willow County, 63, 108, 110
Regency, 252, 263
Religion, 77, 78, 101, 102. *See also* Churches; *individual denominations*
Republican River, 16, 20, 30, 138, 228
Republicans, 99–101
Resources, prehistoric, 38
Richardson County, 76, 108
Rivers. *See* Instream use of water; Surface water; *individual rivers*
Roads, 223, 230, 231, 233. *See also* Highways; Transportation
Rock County, 89
Rodeos, 219
Roman Catholics, 101, 102
Romanians, settlement in Omaha, 248
Roosevelt, Franklin, 100
Rubber and plastics products, 116
Rural communities, 217–219, 221
Rural Free Delivery, 223
Rural industrialization, 132, 270. *See also* Manufacturing, rural
Rural isolation, 221, 223, 230
"Rural renaissance," 98, 269
Rural-urban conflict, 222, 228–238
Rural values, 220, 221, 224
Rural water systems, 222
Russell, Majors, and Waddell (company), 54
Russian Germans, settlement in Nebraska, 61(map), 76, 83, 84, 248

Saline County, 77, 78(photo), 100, 113
Sand and gravel, 108
Sandhills, 9(photo), 11, 12(map), 22, 93, 210, 223, 225
  agriculture, 66, 142, 145, 149, 150, 172
  irrigation, 139, 152, 153, 174, 191, 192, 213, 214, 271
  landscape, 202, 207–209, 214
  population characteristics, 81, 85, 100
  ranching, 66, 142(photo), 158(photo)
Sandoz, Jules, 76
Sanitary and Improvement Districts (SIDs), 234(map), 264
Santee, 116
Santee Reservation, 70
Sarpy County, 72, 85, 87, 94, 95, 133, 233, 235, 254, 265
Saunders County, 77, 226(map)
Sawmills, 110, 111

Scandinavians, settlement in Nebraska, 76, 83, 101
School consolidation, 132, 217, 224, 225, 226(map), 227. *See also* Education
Schuyler, 137
Scottsbluff, 79, 85, 112, 117, 126, 129
Scotts Bluff County, 70, 76, 81, 100, 139(fig.), 141, 149, 150, 161, 170, 172
Scotts Bluff National Monument, 130
SCS. *See* United States Soil Conservation Service
Serbs, settlement in Omaha, 248
Settlement, 44, 45, 48–51, 56–59, 241
  colonization, 59, 73, 74
  prehistoric, 37, 38
Sheelytown, 78
Sheep. *See* Livestock
Shelby, 121(photo)
Shelterbelts, 196(photo), 210, 211, 212(map), 213, 270
Sheridan County, 11, 66, 70, 76, 85, 211(photo)
Sherman County, 22, 24, 78, 100
Sherman Reservoir, 22, 24
Shopping centers, 264–265
Sidewalk farmers, 156
Sidney, 55, 110, 243
SIDs. *See* Sanitary and Improvement Districts
Silage, 173
Silos, 206, 207(photo)
Sioux County, 83
Slovenians, settlement in Omaha, 248
Snake River, 22
Sod houses, 50, 202
Soil Conservation Service. *See* United States Soil Conservation Service
Soils, 11, 15, 16
  conservation, 193, 272
  erosion. *See* Erosion
  sandy, 15, 188, 192
Sokol, 78, 84
Solid waste disposal, 229
Sorghum, 137, 170, 173, 181
South Omaha, 72, 246, 248, 253
South Sioux City, 87
Soybeans, 137, 168–170
Spade Ranch, 66
Spanish-speaking population, 256
Speculation, 48. *See also* "Paper towns"
Springfield, 235, 236(photo)
St. Joseph and Grand Island Railroad, 60
St. Stephen, 44, 242
Stanton County, 76, 88, 113

State Council of Defense, 83
Streamflow, 35(table)
 compacts, 20, 21(table)
 variability, 17
 See also Instream use of water; Surface water
Street railways, 246–248, 251–253
Strip cropping, 168(photo), 196, 212, 270, 271. *See also* Erosion, wind
Stromsburg, 84
Subirrigation, 23(map), 24
Suburban growth, 87, 233–237, 239, 241, 254, 255, 261(photo). *See also* Leapfrog development; Lincoln, suburban development; Omaha, suburban development
Sugar beets, 141, 170, 171(table), 172(map)
Suitcase farmers, 156, 157
Summer fallow. *See* Wheat, summer fallow
Surface water, 16–22. *See also* Instream use of water; Lakes; Rivers
Sutherland, 125
Sutherland Reservoir, 24
Sutton, 60
Swedeburg, 84
Swedehome, 84
Swedes, settlement in Nebraska, 76, 81, 84
Swiss, settlement in Nebraska, 76

Tarnov, 78
Taxes, on farm land, 227. *See also* Agriculture, assessment of land
Telephones, 222
Tenant farming. *See* Farms, tenant
Terraces, 193, 195(photo), 196, 197(photo), 212
Thomas County, 210
Thurston County, 46, 69, 70, 105–107
Timber Culture Act, 45, 47(fig.), 48
Tornadoes, 8
Tourism, 129, 130, 131(map)
Towns, small, 237
 decline, 180, 219
 impact of farm enlargement on, 181
 outmigration, 95
 population growth, 87–89. *See also* Migration
 retailing, 130, 132, 133, 180
Townsites, 59, 60, 219
Tractors, 177, 178(table), 179
Trade and commerce. *See* Lincoln, trade and commerce; Omaha, trade and commerce
Trails. *See* Cattle drives; Emigrant Trails; Freighting

Transbasin diversion, 30, 36
Transportation, 117–125, 135, 223, 246–248, 251–254, 255(photo), 265–267
 air traffic, 118(photo), 119
 buses, 123
 rail. *See* Railroads
 river, 119
 trucks, 123, 253
 urban, 246, 251, 252, 265–267. *See also* Street Railways
 See also Automobiles; Highways; Roads
Transportation equipment, manufacturing, 116
Tri-County Project, 22, 24

Unemployment, 107
Union Pacific Railroad, 48, 55, 56, 59, 119
United States Bureau of Reclamation, 22, 30, 31, 33, 153
United States Soil Conservation Service, 153, 192
Unit-trains, 119
University Place, 253
Upper Republican Culture, 37
Urban expansion, 241. *See also* Suburban growth
Urban growth policies, 265
Urbanization, 85, 87. *See also* Migration
Utilities, 222, 231, 233

Valentine, 220(map)
Valley, 116, 258
Valley County, 77, 78
Valmont Industries, 116, 258
Veterinary supplies, 114
Vodicka, Vaclav, 77

Wages, 107
Wakefield, 77(photo)
Warsaw, 84
Washington County, 76, 191
Water resources, 16–24. *See also* Dams; Flooding; Groundwater; Instream use of water; Irrigation; Lakes; Rivers; Rural water systems; Streamflow; Surface water
Waverly, 235
Wayne County, 76, 134
Webster County, 63
Weeping Water, 108
Welsh, settlement in Nebraska, 74
West Farnam, 249, 252
Wheat, 63, 137, 138, 140–142, 156, 165–168, 173, 181, 196
 summer fallow, 67, 165, 167(map)

Wheeler County, 72, 151, 193(photo), 194(photo), 213
Wholesale activity, 126
Wilber, 85
Wildcat Hills, 11
Wildlife, 36
Windbreaks, 211(photo), 214(photo). *See also* Hedgerows; Shelterbelts
Wind erosion. *See* Erosion, wind
Windmills, 206, 207

Winnebago reservation, 70
Wyoming, Nebraska, 53, 242

York, 245
York County, 76, 163, 188
Yugoslavs, settlement in Omaha, 78
Yutan, 235

Zoning, 230, 237, 238, 271, 272
Zybach, Frank, 185, 186